T0202772

Lecture Notes in Computer Science 14080

Founding Editors

Gerhard Goos
Juris Hartmanis

Editorial Board Members

The series Lecture Notes in Computer Science (LNCS), including its subseries Lecture Notes in Artificial Intelligence (LNAI) and Lecture Notes in Bioinformatics (LNBI), has established itself as a medium for the publication of new developments in computer science and information technology research, teaching, and education.

LNCS enjoys close cooperation with the computer science R & D community, the series counts many renowned academics among its volume editors and paper authors, and collaborates with prestigious societies. Its mission is to serve this international community by providing an invaluable service, mainly focused on the publication of conference and workshop proceedings and postproceedings. LNCS commenced publication in 1973.

Jonathan P. Bowen · Qin Li · Qiwen Xu
Editors

Theories of Programming and Formal Methods

Essays Dedicated to Jifeng He
on the Occasion of His 80th Birthday

 Springer

Editors
Jonathan P. Bowen ⓘ
London South Bank University
London, UK

Qin Li ⓘ
East China Normal University
Shanghai, China

Qiwen Xu ⓘ
University of Macau
Macau, China

ISSN 0302-9743   ISSN 1611-3349 (electronic)
Lecture Notes in Computer Science
ISBN 978-3-031-40435-1   ISBN 978-3-031-40436-8 (eBook)
https://doi.org/10.1007/978-3-031-40436-8

Prof. Jifeng He speaking at the World AI Conference (WAIC)
held in Shanghai, China, September 2022.
(Photograph supplied by Kelly He.)

Preface

The 80th birthday Festschrift symposium for Prof. Jifeng He (Jifeng@80) was held during September 2023, at the Shanghai Science Hall in Shanghai, China. This historic venue, illustrated on the front cover of these proceedings, was built in the early 20th century within the French Concession area, previously as a school and for other purposes. In the 1950s, it became the Science Hall and the facility has since been extended with newer buildings for scientific meetings and related activities.

This Festschrift volume contains papers in the broad area of formal methods by colleagues of Jifeng He, many of whom have been coauthors of academic papers with him. This proceedings is a follow-on volume to that associated with Jifeng He's 70th birthday Festschrift symposium; see the Springer LNCS 8051 volume published in 2013.

Reviewing of papers was undertaken by a mix of authors and external international reviewers. Each paper had five reviews, with two or more reviews by a reviewer who was not an author in this volume. All papers received a positive overall reviewing score. It is an indication of Jifeng's international reputation that reviewers are based in all the main continents of the world, with countries represented including Austria, Australia, Brazil, China, Denmark, France, Germany, India, Ireland, New Zealand, South Africa, the United Kingdom, and the United States.

In the initial section of the volume, three papers present aspects of Jifeng He's contributions to computer science. The first paper provides a lifetime overview of Jifeng's research contributions. especially in the area of formal methods. The following two papers provide more information with respect to developments in UTP (Unifying Theories of Programming) and rCOS (refinement calculus of object systems), two approaches in which Jifeng provided foundational underpinning. In the next two sections, we include papers by colleagues and coauthors with Jifeng while he was at the University of Oxford and also on the European ProCoS project on Provably Correct Systems during this time. The following sections include colleagues of Jifeng from China and Europe. The final section includes a paper related to Jifeng's recent roadmap for UTP in the future.

June 2023

Jonathan P. Bowen
Qin Li
Qiwen Xu

Organization

Programme Chairs

Jonathan P. Bowen	London South Bank University, UK
Qin Li	East China Normal University, China
Qiwen Xu	University of Macau, Macao SAR, China

Local Organizers

Kelly He	Shanghai, China
Qin Li	East China Normal University, China
Ting Su	East China Normal University, China
Qiwen Xu	University of Macau, Macao SAR, China

Paper Reviewers

Bernhard K. Aichernig	TU Graz, Austria
Richard Banach	University of Manchester, UK
Jonathan P. Bowen	London South Bank University, UK
Michael Butler	University of Southampton, UK
Andrew Butterfield	Trinity College Dublin, Ireland
Ana Cavalcanti	University of York, UK
Jim Davies	University of Oxford, UK
John Derrick	Unversity of Sheffield, UK
Brijesh Dongol	University of Surrey, UK
Simon Foster	University of York, UK
Martin Fränzle	Carl von Ossietzky Universität Oldenburg, Germany
Shilpi Goel	Amazon Web Services, USA
Lindsay Groves	Victoria University of Wellington, New Zealand
Kim G. Larsen	Aalborg University, Denmark
Ian J. Hayes	The University of Queensland, Australia
Warren Hunt	The University of Texas at Austin, USA
Cliff B. Jones	Newcastle University, UK
Qin Li	East China Normal University, China
Zhiming Liu	Southwest University, China

Acknowledgements

Jonathan Bowen thanks Huibiao Zhu at East China Normal University for inviting him to join the editorial team. The editors would like to thank the presenters together with their coauthors for their contributions to this volume and the Festchscrift celebration itself, as well as the reviewers for significantly improving the final versions of the included papers. We are grateful for the support of Springer's Lecture Notes in Computer Science (LNCS) team for help in the publication of this volume.

Finally, thank you to Jifeng He for many years of collaboration and friendship with authors of papers in this Festschrift volume, as well as help in organizing the event. We wish him a very happy 80th birthday:

You are truly inspirational, and always have so much passion and energy in what you do. Even at the age of 80, you are still very actively involved in many different fronts; it just shows that age is only a number!

Contents

Jifeng He's Research Influence

Jifeng He at Oxford and Beyond: An Appreciation

Jonathan P. Bowen[1]([⊠])[iD] and Huibiao Zhu[2][iD]

[1] School of Engineering, London South Bank University,
Borough Road, London SE1 0AA, UK
jonathan.bowen@lsbu.ac.uk
[2] Software Engineering Institute, East China Normal University, Shanghai, China
hbzhu@sei.ecnu.edu.cn
http://www.jpbowen.com

Abstract. This paper provides an overview of Jifeng He's academic achievements while at Oxford University in the UK, and later in Macau and Shanghai, together with his legacy internationally. He was an important researcher on the European ESPRIT ProCoS projects and Working Group on "Provably Correct Systems". Subsequently and most notably, this led to collaboration with Tony Hoare on *Unifying Theories of Programming* (UTP), resulting in a jointly authored book and later conference series on the subject. Jifeng returned to his native China in 1998, first at the United Nations University in Macau and then at the East China Normal University in Shanghai from 2005 to 2019. In recent years, Jifeng has been the founder of an Artificial Intelligence (AI) research institute, focusing on the application of AI technology in large-scale industrial software systems. His scientific contributions have been recognized through his election to membership of the Chinese Academy of Sciences. This paper is structured in broadly chronological order, starting with a brief biography and then covering Jifeng He's academic contributions successively in Oxford, Macau, and Shanghai. The paper concludes with an overall appreciation of his major achievements.

Keywords: Formal methods · Provably Correct Systems · Unifying Theories of Programming

1 Introduction

This paper aims to provide a non-technical overview of Jifeng He's main academic achievements during his career, as well as a chronological account of his main affiliations. Subsection 1.1 provides a brief overall biography and Subsect. 1.2 describes some early practical contributions in China. Section 2 covers his research at the University of Oxford in the United Kingdom, especially in collaboration with Tony Hoare. He then moved to the United Nations University in Macau, as reported in Sect. 3. Latterly until his retirement, he was based at the

J. P. Bowen et al. (Eds.): *Theories of Programming and Formal Methods*, LNCS 14080, pp. 3–18, 2023.
https://doi.org/10.1007/978-3-031-40436-8_1

East China Normal University in Shanghai, as described in Sect. 4. The paper concludes with an overall appreciation of his achievements in Sect. 5. Overall, this paper provides a personal reflection of the authors in their collaboration with Jifeng over the years.

1.1 Brief Biography

Jifeng He was born in Shanghai China, in August 1943. He graduated in 1965 from the Department of Mathematics at Fudan University, located in Shanghai. Since 1965, he has held a position at East China Normal University (ECNU) in Shanghai, successively serving as a teaching assistant and then lecturer, and was promoted to full professor in 1986. In 1988, he was awarded the title of *National Young and Middle-aged Experts with Outstanding Contributions*. From 1980 to 1981, he was a visiting scholar at Stanford University and the University of San Francisco in California, United States. From 1983 to 1998, he worked as a senior researcher in the Programming Research Group (PRG) at the Oxford University Computing Laboratory (OUCL) in the United Kingdom, collaborating extensively with Tony Hoare [54], based in Oxford although retaining his position at ECNU. He was an important researcher on the European ProCoS project from 1989.

From 1998, Jifeng worked as a senior researcher at the International Institute of Software Technology of the United Nations University (UNU/IIST) in Macau. During 2002 to 2019, he was the Dean of the Software Engineering Institute at East China Normal University. In 2002, he joined the first group of lifelong professors of East China Normal University. He was elected in 2005 as an academician of the Chinese Academy of Sciences, the highest scientific recognition in China. He received an honorary doctorate from the University of York (UK) in 2009. In December 2015, he was awarded the French National Palm Education Knight Medal. From 2017, Jifeng started to consider the issues around trustworthiness in Artificial Intelligence (AI). In 2019, Jifeng was appointed as the Distinguished Professor at Tongji University located in Shanghai. Jifeng's research interests have included sound methods for the specification of computer systems, communications, applications, and standards, as well as techniques for designing and implementing those specifications in software and/or hardware with high reliability.

This paper provides a non-technical overview of Jifeng's academic achievements. More technical details related to some of his contributions are available elsewhere in this volume [59,63,71].

1.2 Practical Contributions

This paper is mainly about the theoretical contributions of Jifeng at Oxford, UNU/IIST, and ECNU. It should be noted that Jifeng also has made remarkable practical contributions. In 1982, Jifeng led a team to undertake one of the 38 major scientific and technological research projects of the State Council in China, the *Office Chinese Character Information Processing System*, whose core

Fig. 1. Jifeng He speaking at a BCS-FACS event in London, 2018. (See also Fig. 3.)

technology was the independent self-development of China's first *Chinese Character Relational Database System* (ECNIS), which provided a practical Chinese character information processing platform for China's "paperless" office. It was widely used in the field of office work by various domestic institutions at that time. The scientific research achievements won the first prize of the Shanghai Excellent Software Award in 1985 and the Outstanding Scientific and Technological Achievements Award of the National Education Commission in 1986.

2   University of Oxford

From 1983 to 1998, Jifeng worked as a senior researcher (a "Senior Research Officer") in the Programming Research Group (PRG) at the Oxford University Computing Laboratory (OUCL) in the UK. He mainly collaborated with the leader of the PRG, Tony Hoare, who invited him to come to Oxford during a visit to China. Although Jifeng retained his position at East China Normal University during this time, he spent most of his time working as a researcher in Oxford, mainly with Tony Hoare. From 1989, he was a significant contributor on the European ProCoS project concerning "Provably Correct Systems", instigated by Tony Hoare and others.

Before the ProCoS project, Jifeng collaborated with Tony Hoare on research concerning the "weakest prespecification", generalizing the concept of Edsger Dikstra's weakest precondition. This was first published as a PRG Technical Monograph in 1985 [44], then as two related journal papers in 1986 [45,46], and also as a shorter summary journal paper in 1987 [52]. Later they collaborated with Jeff Sanders on data refinement [27] and prespecification for such refinement [48]. Jifeng was also a coauthor of the highly cited 1987 *Laws of Programming* paper by Tony Hoare et al. [51], presenting a complete set of algebraic laws for Edsger Dijkstra's nondeterministic sequential programming language.

2.1   Provably Correct Systems ("ProCoS")

From 1989, Tony Hoare led the ProCoS "Basic Research Action" (ESPRIT BRA 3104) project on Provably Correct Systems with European partners in Denmark (under Dines Bjørner) and Germany (under Hans Langmaack and also Ernst-Rüdiger Olderog), as well as in the UK (initially with Cliff Jones and also Ursula Martin) [1]. This ran in parallel with the UK Information Engineering Directorate (IED) SAFEMOS project in "Totally Verified Systems" with the University of Cambridge (under Mike Gordon), SRI Cambridge (under Roger Hale), and INMOS (under David May and David Shepherd) [2,10]. Subsequently, the ProCoS II project [15] and the ProCoS-WG Working Group continued the work of ProCoS in the 1990s [16]. Jifeng He was a key researcher involved with ProCoS, especially working on program compilation aspects of the project, and collaborated on tutorials about the project [14]. Ultimately, this work led to his important ideas on Unifying Theories of Programming, as described later in Subsect. 2.2.

Verifiable Compiling Specification: The ProCoS project studied verifying computer-based systems from requirements through to programming and compilation. Initial research considered an algebraic approach to the verifiable compiling specification and prototyping of the ProCoS level 0 programming language, based on a subset of the Occam programming language [47], with prototyping using logic programming in Prolog by Jonathan Bowen [12], based on a shallow embedding approach [7]. Later, recursion was also considered [23]. This approach was further developed to cover the specification, verification, and prototyping of an optimized compiler [25]. Jifeng also collaborated with Tony Hoare and Augusto Sampaio on a normal-form approach to compiler design [50]. In 1994, Jifeng published a complete book on provably correct systems, covering the modelling of communication languages and the design of optimized compilers [21].

Real-time Systems: Later work on ProCoS by Jifeng He and others considered a time interval semantics and the implementation of a real-time programming language [24]. Further work covered hybrid parallel programming and the implementation of synchronised communication [20]. Jifeng collaborated with Roger Hale on the SAFEMOS project concerning a real-time programming language

[19]. He also undertook research with others, including Hussein Zedan, on real-time refinement [65], a predictive semantics for the refinement of real-time systems [64], and a specification-oriented semantics for real-time system refinement [66].

Hardware Compilation: Ian Page and Wayne Luk at Oxford introduced ideas of compiling an Occam-like programing language including parallelism directly into hardware for implementation as a netlist of gate-level components on a Field-Programmable Gate Array (FPGA) chip. These ideas were adopted on the ProCoS project, including by Jifeng. Initial ideas were published in a highly cited conference paper on a provably correct hardware implementation of the Occam programming language [28], led by Jifeng in collaboration with Ian Page and Jonathan Bowen. This work was also undertaken collaboratively as part of the SAFEMOS project by Jonathan Bowen et al. [11] and with Jianping Zheng, using a simulation approach for provably correct hardware compilation [39]. Further papers on the specification and verification of a hardware compilation scheme [8] and an algebraic approach to hardware compilation [9] appeared later.

2.2   Unifying Theories of Programming (UTP)

Starting during ProCoS, for example in considering the connection between algebraic and operational semantics [26], and continuing afterwards, Jifeng collaborated with Tony Hoare on their magnum opus *Unifying Theories of Programming* (UTP), published in 1998 [49]. An associated paper was presented at the *4th International Seminar on Relational Methods in Computer Science* (RelMiCS) [32]. UTP considers the challenge of connecting different forms of semantics. For example, it is possible to link algebraic, denotational, and operational semantics, including demonstrating their equivalence. In parallel, Jifeng also collaborated on highly cited work with Karen Seidel and Annabelle McIver on probabilistic models for the Guarded Command Language (GCL) [36], with Qiwen Xu and Willem-Paul de Roever on the rely-guarantee method for verifying shared variable concurrent programs [72], and with Tony Hoare on a trace model for pointers and objects [53].

The UTP book has spawned a community of researchers, including a regular UTP symposium. Jifeng [22] and Tony Hoare [62] were later both keynote presenters at the UTP 2016 Symposium in Reykjavik, Iceland [17]. It is interesting to consider papers connected to UTP, using the visual representation provided by the *Connected Papers* website (https://connectedpapers.com). It can be noted that Jim Woodcock is a major contributor of UTP papers, together with his collaborator Ana Cavalcanti, both at the University of York. They have developed *Circus*, an integration of the formal notations of Z, CSP, and Carroll Morgan's refinement calculus, underpinned by UTP, as described elsewhere in this volume [71].

3   United Nations University

In 1998, the year of publication of the *Unifying Theories of Programming* book with Tony Hoare [49], Jifeng took up a position with United Nations University International Institute of Software Technology (UNU/IIST) in Macau as a senior researcher. UNU/IIST was initially established under the leadership of Dines Bjørner, who headed the Danish partner on the ProCoS project, the Technical University of Denmark. In this section, we consider some important contributions of Jifeng during his time at UNU/IIST.

Verilog Hardware Description Language: Modern hardware design typically uses a Hardware Description Language (HDL) to express designs at various levels of abstraction. An HDL is a high-level programming language, with usual programming constructs such as assignments, conditionals, and iterations, together with appropriate extensions for real-time, concurrency and data structures suitable for modelling hardware. Verilog is an HDL that has been standardized and widely used in industry. Verilog programs can exhibit a rich variety of behaviours, including event-driven computation and shared-variable concurrency.

The semantics for Verilog is very important to help in ensuring the correctness of hardware design. With fellows and colleagues based at UNU/IIST, London South Bank University (LSBU), and ECNU, a series of research studies on Verilog semantics were undertaken. The operational semantics was explored by Jifeng in collaboration with Qiwen Xu, Huibiao Zhu, Jonathan Bowen, and others [13,37,40,57], including the animation of Verilog's operational semantics. Verilog's denotational semantics [77] has also been explored based on the operational semantics using Duration Calculus [73].

Later, the linking between the denotational semantics and operational semantics for Verilog has been successfully investigated under a discrete-time model, developed by Huibiao Zhu based on Jifeng's original ideas [74–76]. More recently, a mechanical approach using the Coq proof assistant tool has been applied in unifying the Verilog semantics by Feng Sheng et al. [67,68], against developing on Jifeng's theoretical research. The soundness and completeness of the operational semantics is verified based on the algebraic semantics via the mechanical approach in Coq. Similarly, the correctness of the algebraic laws has also been verified using a mechanical approach supported by Coq. This semantics research on Verilog semantics demonstrates the successful application of UTP in Verilog.

Advanced Features of Duration Calculus: Duration Calculus (DC) was originally proposed by Zhou Chaochen with Tony Hoare and Anders Ravn [73] as part of the ProCoS project to provide a precise formalism for requirements involving timing constraints. Several advanced features of Durational Calculus were later investigated by Jifeng in collaboration with Qiwen Xu [38], including initial and final values, stability, left and right neighbourhood values, and chopping points, aiming to integrate several variants of Duration Calculus. A link between the untimed refinement calculus and the timed one in this framework was studied, where the timed version preserves the laws of untimed programming.

rCOS: A refinement calculus of object systems (named rCOS) was studied [35,59,60], in collaboration with Zhiming Liu and Xiaoshan Li, defining an observation-oriented semantics for a relational object-based language with a rich variety of features including subtypes, visibility, inheritance, type casting, dynamic binding, and polymorphism. The logic of rCOS is a conservative extension of standard predicate logic. rCOS relates the notions of refinement and data refinement in imperative programming to refactorings and object-oriented design patterns for responsibility assignments. The investigation for rCOS shows the successful application of UTP in object orientation. Further more detailed information on rCOS is provided in another paper in this volume [59], including the formal use of the Unified Modeling Language (UML) [56].

4   East China Normal University

From 2002 to 2019, Jifeng He was the Dean of the Software Engineering Institute at East China Normal University in Shanghai. During this period, despite his additional administrative duties as Dean, he pioneered the theory and technology of model-based trustworthy software design. The related achievements have been widely adopted by key departments in China. Even as Dean, Jifeng continued to lead teams undertaking active research. Some notable contributions are outlined below.

Web Services: With the development of Internet technology, web services and web-based applications increasingly play an important role in information systems. Business Process Execution Language (BPEL) is used for specifying the behaviour of business processes. BPEL contains several interesting features, including scope-based compensation and fault handling. A model for BPEL-like languages and a transaction calculus have been proposed by Jifeng [29,41]. The denotational semantics and a set of algebraic laws were also investigated. In addition, the lining of semantics for web services was also explored by Huibiao Zhu, Jifeng, and others [78–80].

Unification of CSP and CCS: The Calculus of Communicating Systems (CCS) of Robin Milner [61] and Communicating Sequential Processes (CSP) of Tony Hoare [42] are two major examples of the process calculi family. A process may be defined by a transition system, which is the approach taken in setting up the framework of CCS. Meanwhile, traces are the foundation of the definition of CSP. The unification of CCS and CSP was studied by Jifeng in collaboration with Tony Hoare [30,31], and it has been proved that CSP is a retract of CCS. It is claimed that the technique of retraction is a common and useful form of unification.

HRML Language: A hybrid modelling language (HRML) [33] was proposed by Jifeng and Qin Li, with a set of novel combinators. The complex combinations of testing and reaction behaviours were conducted to model the physical world and its interaction with the control program. With the introduction of the new hybrid structures *when* and *until*, three types of guards were defined to model the condition under which the system controller switches to a new mode. A denotational semantics was studied for the HRML language using the UTP approach.

A New Roadmap for UTP: A new roadmap [34] was also proposed by Jifeng and Qin Li, for linking theories of programming, which is one of the new directions for the UTP approach. The new methodology takes an algebra of programs as its basis; it generates both denotational and operational representations from the algebraic refinement relation. A testing structure has been studied, representing the execution behaviours of programs. This new roadmap was successfully applied for the Guarded Command Language (GCL) and CSP. It is believed that this new roadmap can be applied to other types of programs with new modern features. A Coq proof assistant implementation of the program algebra in Jifeng's UTP roadmap is included in this volume [63].

5 Conclusion

The Scopus database (https://www.scopus.com) is widely recognized as an important indicator of scientific publication record, although with a limited set of approved journals and restricted access. This orders papers by citation count. The Scopus list of top-ten academic papers coauthored by Jifeng (omitting a survey paper) are listed in Table 1. Note that Scopus has two entries for [27] separately under its main title and subtitle (which have been combined into a single entry in Table reftopten), and does not include books. For example, the UTP book [49] is probably Jifeng's most influential work. So one should always treat such automatically generated publication statistics with caution.

In September 2013, Jifeng's 70th birthday was celebrated at East China Normal University with an international three-day Festschrift and an associated proceedings volume edited by Zhiming Liu, Jim Woodcock, and Huibiao Zhu [58], held in association with the International Conference on Theoretical Aspects of Computing (ICTAC). This included a paper on Jifeng's connections within the formal methods community [3]. During this event, a poster of Jifeng was on display in a public walkway in Shanghai (see Fig. 2). The following is a translation of the statement on the poster:

> He is the first [Chinese] academician in the field of computer science in Shanghai, has initiated an international school of software theory, and is acknowledged as a leader in Asian software theory. At the age of 70, he always cares about students, promotes the reform of undergraduate education and teaching, manages to organize awards and grants for students, teaches with a scientific attitude, and educates people with care.

It is interesting to try to imagine a similar public display for a computer scientist in the West.

Table 1. Jifeng He's top ten most cited academic papers on the Scopus database in 2023.

No.	Title	Authors	Year	Ref.
1.	Laws of programming	Tony Hoare, Ian Hayes, Jifeng He, Carroll Morgan, Bill Roscoe, Jeff Sanders, Ib Holm Sørensen, Michael Spivey, and Bernard Sufrin	1987	[51]
2.	Data refinement refined – Resume	Jifeng He, Tony Hoare, and Jeff Sanders	1986	[27]
3.	Probabilistic models for the Guarded Command Language	Jifeng He, Karen Seidel, and Annabelle McIver	1997	[36]
4.	The rely-guarantee method for verifying shared variable concurrent programs	Qiwen Xu, Willem-Paul de Roever, and Jifeng He	1997	[72]
5.	rCOS: A refinement calculus of object systems	Jifeng He, Xiaoshan Li, and Zhiming Liu	2006	[35]
6.	Prespecification in data refinement	Tony Hoare, Jifeng He, and Jeff Sanders	1987	[48]
7.	A formal semantics of UML sequence diagram	Xiaoshan Li, Zhiming Liu, and Jifeng He	2004	[56]
8.	The weakest prespecification	Tony Hoare and Jifeng He	1987	[52]
9.	Normal form approach to compiler design	Tony Hoare, Jifeng He, and Augusto Sampaio	1993	[50]
10.	A process algebraic framework for specification and validation of real-time systems	Adnan Sherif, Ana Cavalcanti, Jifeng He, and Augusto Sampaio	2010	[69]

In October 2018, Jifeng gave a presentation for the BCS-FACS (Formal Aspects of Computing Science) Specialist Group in London to celebrate the 20th anniversary of the publication of the book on UTP [49] (see Fig. 3), chaired by Jonathan Bowen (the chair of the FACS group itself). Tony Hoare, Jifeng's coauthor, provided introductory remarks and Jim Woodcock of the University of York, a leading UTP researcher, provided a summary at the end of the talk. This event also celebrated the 30th anniversary of the *Formal Aspects of Computing* journal and the 40th anniversary of FACS itself [5].

Jifeng has been a major contributor to research into formal methods during his career as a computer scientist. His collaboration with Tony Hoare, especially on the Unifying Theories of Programming, has been particularly fruitful. Tony Hoare is brilliant at initiating new ideas in computer science, but Jifeng's contributions to UTP are equal (if not greater) in stature, as noted by Jim Woodcock [70] (page 291). Jifeng's role has been very important in ensuring that the ideas are mathematically sound [6] and he added great insights to formulations using

Fig. 2. Poster of Jifeng He in Shanghai, 2013.

UTP, including for simplifying the algebraic semantics of CSP. Jifeng's collaboration with Tony Hoare on UTP has been crucial to its success. Tony Hoare has noted [43]:

> Jifeng has a long record of achievement and is enjoying the highest international regard. Jifeng has an extraordinary skill as an applied logician and was always glad to undertake the most difficult problems, and in a day or two came back with a proof or counter-example.

Commenting on their collaboration of ten year's UTP research and the resulting book, Tony Hoare adds [43]:

> I must emphasise that all the effective research was conducted by Jifeng, who formalized the definitions, postulated the axioms, and proved the theorems. I enjoyed discussing the goal of research with him, and I wrote much of the English prose. But all of the new results were due to him. Since leaving Oxford, Jifeng has successfully resolved all the main issues which were unable to put into the original book, and has developed further remarkable insights.

With this paper providing a summary of Jifeng's lifetime of achievements, and echoing Tony Hoare's sentiments, we thank Jifeng for furthering the foundations of computer science over his career.

Fig. 3. Jifeng He and Tony Hoare at the BCS-FACS event celebrating 20 years since the publication of their UTP book, held in London, 2018. (See also Fig. 1.)

Acknowledgements. Jonathan Bowen is grateful for financial support provided by Museophile Limited. The comments from the reviewers were very helpful in improving the final version of this paper. Influenced by [59], the number of references in this paper is also 80 to match Jifeng's birthday. Finally, both authors are extremely grateful for many years of collaboration with Jifeng, more fully referenced elsewhere [4], and wish him a very happy 80th birthday.

References

1. Bjørner, D., et al.: A ProCoS project description: ESPRIT BRA 3104. Bull. Eur. Assoc. Theor. Comput. Sci. **39**, 60–73 (1989). http://researchgate.net/publication/256643262

2. Bowen, J.P. (ed.): Towards Verified Systems, Real-Time Safety Critical Systems, vol. 2. Elsevier, Amsterdam (1994)

3. Bowen, J.P.: A relational approach to an algebraic community: from Paul Erdős to He Jifeng. In: Liu et al. [58], pp. 54–66. https://doi.org/10.1007/978-3-642-39698-4_4

4. Bowen, J.P.: A personal formal methods archive. ResearchGate (2019). https://doi.org/10.13140/RG.2.2.31943.65447

5. Bowen, J.P.: FACS events, 2018–2020. FACS FACTS **2020**(1), 7–21 (2020). https://www.bcs.org/media/5204/facs-dec19.pdf

6. Bowen, J.P.: Review on theories of programming: the life and works of tony Hoare. Form. Aspects Comput. **34**(3–4), 1–3 (2022). https://doi.org/10.1145/3560267

7. Bowen, J.P., Gordon, M.J.C.: A shallow embedding of Z in HOL. Inf. Softw. Technol. **37**(5–6), 269–276 (1995). https://doi.org/10.1016/0950-5849(95)99362-Q

8. Bowen, J.P., He, J.: An approach to the specification and verification of a hardware compilation scheme. J. Supercomput. **19**(1), 23–39 (2001). https://doi.org/10.1023/A:1011184310224

9. Bowen, J.P., He, J.: An algebraic approach to hardware compilation. In: Gabbar, H.A. (ed.) Modern Formal Methods and Applications, pp. 151–176. Springer, Dordrecht (2006). https://doi.org/10.1007/1-4020-4223-X_7

10. Bowen, J.P., He, J., Hale, R.W.S., Herbert, J.M.J.: Towards verified systems: the SAFEMOS project. In: Mitchell, C., Stavridou, V. (eds.) Mathematics of Dependable Systems, Institute of Mathematics and Its Applications Conference Series, vol. 55, pp. 23–48. Oxford University Press (1995). http://researchgate.net/publication/2525857

11. Bowen, J.P., He, J., Page, I.: Hardware compilation. In: Bowen [2], chap. 10, pp. 193–207. https://doi.org/10.1016/B978-0-444-89901-9.50019-7

12. Bowen, J.P., He, J., Pandya, P.K.: An approach to verifiable compiling specification and prototyping. In: Deransart, P., Maluszyński, J. (eds.) PLILP 1990. LNCS, vol. 456, pp. 45–59. Springer, Heidelberg (1990). https://doi.org/10.1007/BFb0024175

13. Bowen, J.P., He, J., Xu, Q.: An animatable operational semantics of the Verilog hardware description language. In: ICFEM 2000: Third IEEE International Conference on Formal Engineering Methods, pp. 199–207. IEEE (2000). https://doi.org/10.1109/ICFEM.2000.873820

14. Bowen, J.P., et al.: Provably correct systems – FTRTFT'94 tutorial. In: Third International School and Symposium, Formal Techniques in Real Time and Fault Tolerant Systems. No. [COORD JB 7/1] in ProCoS document, Christian-Albrechts-Universität, Lübeck, Germany, September 1994. http://researchgate.net/publication/2420842, School Material

15. Bowen, J.P., Hoare, C.A.R., Langmaack, H., Olderog, E.R., Ravn, A.P.: A ProCoS II project final report: ESPRIT basic research project 7071. Bull. Eur. Assoc. Theor. Comput. Sci. **59**, 76–99 (1996). http://researchgate.net/publication/2255515

16. Bowen, J.P., Hoare, C.A.R., Langmaack, H., Olderog, E.R., Ravn, A.P.: A ProCoS-WG working group final report: ESPRIT working group 8694. Bull. Eur. Assoc. Theor. Comput. Sci. **64**, 63–72 (1998). http://researchgate.net/publication/2527052

17. Bowen, J.P., Zhu, H. (eds.): UTP 2016. LNCS, vol. 10134. Springer, Cham (2017). https://doi.org/10.1007/978-3-319-52228-9

18. Bowen, J.P., Li, Q., Xu, Q. (eds.): Theories of Programming and Formal Methods: Essays Dedicated to Jifeng He on the Occasion of His 80th Birthday, LNCS, vol. 14080. Springer, Berlin, Heidelberg (2023). https://doi.org/10.1007/978-3-031-40436-8

19. Hale, R.W.S., He, J.: A real-time programming language. In: Bowen, J.P. (ed.) Towards Verified Systems, Real-Time Safety Critical Systems, vol. 2, chap. 6, pp. 115–130. Elsevier (1994)

20. He, J.: Hybrid parallel programming and implementation of synchronised communication. In: Borzyszkowski, A.M., Sokołowski, S. (eds.) MFCS 1993. LNCS, vol. 711, pp. 537–546. Springer, Heidelberg (1993). https://doi.org/10.1007/3-540-57182-5_45

21. He, J.: Provably Correct Systems: Modelling of Communication Languages and Design of Optimized Compilers. International Series in Software Engineering. McGraw-Hill, New York (1994)

22. He, J.: A new roadmap for linking theories of programming. In: Bowen and Zhu [17], pp. 26–43. https://doi.org/10.1007/978-3-319-52228-9_2

23. He, J., Bowen, J.P.: Compiling specification for ProCoS language PLR$_0$. ProCoS document [OU HJF 6], Oxford University Computing Laboratory (1991). http://researchgate.net/publication/319069362

24. He, J., Bowen, J.P.: Time interval semantics and implementation of a real-time programming language. In: Fourth Euromicro Workshop on Real-Time Systems, pp. 110–115. IEEE (1992). https://doi.org/10.1109/EMWRT.1992.637480

25. He, J., Bowen, J.P.: Specification, verification and prototyping of an optimized compiler. Form. Aspects Comput. **6**(6), 643–658 (1994). https://doi.org/10.1007/BF03259390

26. He, J., Hoare, C.A.R.: From algebra to operational semantics. Inf. Process. Lett. **45**, 75–80 (1993). https://doi.org/10.1016/0020-0190(93)90219-Y

27. He, J., Hoare, C.A.R., Sanders, J.W.: Data refinement refined resume. In: Robinet, B., Wilhelm, R. (eds.) ESOP 1986. LNCS, vol. 213, pp. 187–196. Springer, Heidelberg (1986). https://doi.org/10.1007/3-540-16442-1_14

28. He, J., Page, I., Bowen, J.P.: Towards a provably correct hardware implementation of Occam. In: Milne, G.J., Pierre, L. (eds.) CHARME 1993. LNCS, vol. 683, pp. 214–225. Springer, Heidelberg (1993). https://doi.org/10.1007/BFb0021726

29. He, J.: Transaction calculus. In: Butterfield, A. (ed.) UTP 2008. LNCS, vol. 5713, pp. 2–21. Springer, Heidelberg (2010). https://doi.org/10.1007/978-3-642-14521-6_2

30. He, J., Hoare, C.A.R.: CSP is a retract of CCS. In: Dunne, S., Stoddart, B. (eds.) UTP 2006. LNCS, vol. 4010, pp. 38–62. Springer, Heidelberg (2006). https://doi.org/10.1007/11768173_3

31. He, J., Hoare, C.A.R.: CSP is a retract of CCS. Theor. Comput. Sci. **411**(11–13), 1311–1337 (2010). https://doi.org/10.1016/j.tcs.2009.12.012

32. He, J., Hoare, C.A.R.: Unifying theories of programming. In: RelMiCS: 4th International Seminar on Relational Methods in Computer Science, pp. 97–99. Warsaw, Poland, September 1998

33. He, J., Li, Q.: A hybrid relational modelling language. In: Gibson-Robinson, T., Hopcroft, P., Lazić, R. (eds.) Concurrency, Security, and Puzzles. LNCS, vol. 10160, pp. 124–143. Springer, Cham (2017). https://doi.org/10.1007/978-3-319-51046-0_7

34. He, J., Li, Q.: A new roadmap for linking theories of programming and its applications on GCL and CSP. Sci. Comput. Program. **162**, 3–34 (2018). https://doi.org/10.1016/j.scico.2017.10.009

35. He, J., Li, X., Liu, Z.: rCOS: a refinement calculus of object systems. Theor. Comput. Sci. **365**(1–2), 109–142 (2006). https://doi.org/10.1016/j.tcs.2006.07.034

36. He, J., Seidel, K., McIver, A.: Probabilistic models for the guarded command language. Sci. Comput. Program. **28**, 171–192 (1997)

37. He, J., Xu, Q.: An operational semantics of a simulator algorithm. In: Arabnia, H.R. (ed.) Proceedings of the International Conference on Parallel and Distributed Processing Techniques and Applications, PDPTA 2000, 24–29 June 2000, Las Vegas, Nevada, USA. CSREA Press (2000)

38. He, J., Xu, Q.: Advanced features of Duration Calculus and their applications in sequential hybrid programs. Form. Aspects Comput. **15**(1), 84–99 (2003). https://doi.org/10.1007/s001650300001

39. He, J., Zheng, J.: Simulation approach to provably correct hardware compilation. In: Langmaack, H., de Roever, W.-P., Vytopil, J. (eds.) FTRTFT ProCoS 1994. LNCS, vol. 863, pp. 336–350. Springer, Heidelberg (1994). https://doi.org/10.1007/3-540-58468-4_172

40. He, J., Zhu, H.: Formalising VERILOG. In: Proceedings of the 2000 7th IEEE International Conference on Electronics, Circuits and Systems, ICECS 2000, Jounieh, Lebanon, 17–20 December 2000, pp. 412–415. IEEE (2000). https://doi.org/10.1109/ICECS.2000.911568

41. He, J., Zhu, H., Pu, G.: A model for BPEL-like languages. Front. Comput. Sci. China **1**(1), 9–19 (2007). https://doi.org/10.1007/s11704-007-0002-7

42. Hoare, C.A.R.: Communicating Sequential Processes. International Series in Computer Science, Prentice Hall, Hoboken (1985)

43. Hoare, C.A.R.: Recommendation letter (2002). Private communication via K. He (May 2023)

44. Hoare, C.A.R., He, J.: The weakest prespecification. Technical Monograph PRG-44, Oxford University Computing Laboratory, Programming Research Group, Oxford, UK, June 1985

45. Hoare, C.A.R., He, J.: The weakest prespecification: Part I. Fund. Inform. **9**(1), 51–84 (1986). https://doi.org/10.3233/FI-1986-9104

46. Hoare, C.A.R., He, J.: The weakest prespecification: Part II. Fund. Inform. **9**(2), 217–251 (1986). https://doi.org/10.3233/FI-1986-9205

47. Hoare, C.A.R., He, J., Bowen, J.P., Pandya, P.: An algebraic approach to verifiable compiling specification and prototyping of the ProCoS level 0 programming language. In: Directorate-General XIII of the Commission of the European Communities (ed.) ESPRIT '90 Conference, pp. 804–818. Kluwer Academic Publishers (1990). https://doi.org/10.1007/978-94-009-0705-8_65

48. Hoare, C.A.R., He, J., Sanders, J.W.: Prespecification in data refinement. Inf. Process. Lett. **25**(2), 71–76 (1987). https://doi.org/10.1016/0020-0190(87)90224-9

49. Hoare, C.A.R., He, J.: Unifying Theories of Programming. Series in Computer Science, Prentice Hall, Hoboken (1998)

50. Hoare, C.A.R., He, J., Sampaio, A.: Normal form approach to compiler design. Acta Informatica **30**(8), 701–739 (1993). https://doi.org/10.1007/BF01191809

51. Hoare, C.A.R., et al.: Laws of programming. Commun. ACM **30**(8), 672–686 (1987)

52. Hoare, C.A.R., He, J.: The weakest prespecification. Inf. Process. Lett. **24**, 127–132 (1987). https://doi.org/10.1016/0020-0190(87)90106-2

53. Hoare, C.A.R., He, J.: A trace model for pointers and objects. In: Guerraoui, Rachid (ed.) ECOOP 1999. LNCS, vol. 1628, pp. 1–18. Springer, Heidelberg (1999). https://doi.org/10.1007/3-540-48743-3_1

54. Jones, C.: List of Tony Hoare's publications. In: Jones and Misra [55], pp. 394–315. https://doi.org/10.1145/3477355.3477375, Appendix D

55. Jones, C.B., Misra, J. (eds.): Theories of Programming: The Life and Works of Tony Hoare, ACM Books, vol. 39. Association for Computing Machinery (2021). https://doi.org/10.1145/3477355

56. Li, X., Liu, Z., He, J.: A formal semantics of UML sequence diagram. In: Proceedings of the Australian Software Engineering Conference (ASWEC), pp. 168–177. IEEE (2004). https://doi.org/10.1109/ASWEC.2004.1290469

57. Li, Y., He, J.: Formalising Verilog: operational semantics and bisimulation. Technical report 217, UNU/IIST, P.O. Box 3058, Macau SAR, China, November 2000

58. Liu, Z., Woodcock, J.C.P., Zhu, H. (eds.): Theories of Programming and Formal Methods, LNCS, vol. 8051. Springer, Berlin, Heidelberg (2013). https://doi.org/10.1007/978-3-642-39698-4

59. Liu, Z.: Linking formal methods in software development – a reflection on the development of rCOS. In: Bowen et al. [18], this volume. https://doi.org/10.1007/978-3-031-40436-8_3

60. Liu, Z., He, J., Li, X.: rCOS: refinement of component and object systems. In: de Boer, F.S., Bonsangue, M.M., Graf, S., de Roever, W.-P. (eds.) FMCO 2004. LNCS, vol. 3657, pp. 183–221. Springer, Heidelberg (2005). https://doi.org/10.1007/11561163_9

61. Milner, R.: A Calculus of Communicating Systems. Springer, Heidelberg (1980). https://doi.org/10.1007/3-540-10235-3_11

62. Möller, B., Hoare, C.A.R., Müller, M.E., Struth, G.: A discrete geometric model of concurrent program execution. In: Bowen and Zhu [17], pp. 1–25. https://doi.org/10.1007/978-3-319-52228-9_1

63. Mu, R., Li, Q.: A Coq implementation of the program algebra in Jifeng He's new roadmap for linking theories of programming. In: Bowen et al. [18], this volume. https://doi.org/10.1007/978-3-031-40436-8_15

64. Scholefield, D., Zedan, H., He, J.: A predicative semantics for the refinement of real-time systems. In: Brookes, S., Main, M., Melton, A., Mislove, M., Schmidt, D. (eds.) MFPS 1993. LNCS, vol. 802, pp. 230–249. Springer, Heidelberg (1994). https://doi.org/10.1007/3-540-58027-1_11

65. Scholefield, D., Zedan, H., He, J.: Real-time refinement: semantics and application. In: Borzyszkowski, A.M., Sokołowski, S. (eds.) MFCS 1993. LNCS, vol. 711, pp. 693–702. Springer, Heidelberg (1993). https://doi.org/10.1007/3-540-57182-5_60

66. Scolefield, D., Zedan, H., He, J.: A specification-oriented semantics for the refinement of real-time systems. Theor. Comput. Sci. **131**, 219–241 (1994)

67. Sheng, F., Zhu, H., He, J., Yang, Z., Bowen, J.P.: Theoretical and practical aspects of linking operational and algebraic semantics for MDESL. ACM Trans. Softw. Eng. Methodol. **28**(3), 14:1–14:46 (2019). https://doi.org/10.1145/3295699

68. Sheng, F., Zhu, H., He, J., Yang, Z., Bowen, J.P.: Theoretical and practical approaches to the denotational semantics for MDESL based on UTP. Form. Aspects Comput. **32**(2–3), 275–314 (2020). https://doi.org/10.1007/s00165-020-00513-4

69. Sherif, A., Cavalcanti, A., He, J., Sampaio, A.: A process algebraic framework forspecification and validation of real-time systems. Form. Aspects Comput. **22**, 153–191 (2010). https://doi.org/10.1007/s00165-009-0119-6

70. Woodcock, J.: Hoare and He's unifying theories of programming. In: Jones and Misra [55], chap. 13, pp. 287–315. https://doi.org/10.1145/3477355.3477369

71. Woodcock, J., Cavalcanti, A., Foster, S., Oliveira, M., Sampaio, A., Zeyda, F.: UTP, *Circus*, and Isabelle. In: Bowen et al. [18], this volume. https://doi.org/10.1007/978-3-031-40436-8_2

72. Xu, Q., de Roever, W.P., He, J.: The rely-guarantee method for verifying shared variable concurrent programs. Form. Aspects Comput. **9**(2), 149–174 (1997). https://doi.org/10.1007/BF01211617

73. Zhou, C., Hoare, C.A.R., Ravn, A.P.: A calculus of durations. Inf. Process. Lett. **40**(5), 269–276 (1991)

74. Zhu, H., Bowen, J.P., He, J.: Deriving operational semantics from denotational semantics for Verilog. In: APSEC 2001: Eighth Asia-Pacific Software Engineering Conference, pp. 177–184. IEEE (2001). https://doi.org/10.1109/APSEC.2001.991475

75. Zhu, H., Bowen, J.P., He, J.: From operational semantics to denotational semantics for Verilog. In: Margaria, T., Melham, T. (eds.) CHARME 2001. LNCS, vol. 2144, pp. 449–464. Springer, Heidelberg (2001). https://doi.org/10.1007/3-540-44798-9_34

76. Zhu, H., Bowen, J.P., He, J.: Soundness, completeness and non-redundancy of operational semantics for Verilog based on denotational semantics. In: George, C., Miao, H. (eds.) ICFEM 2002. LNCS, vol. 2495, pp. 600–612. Springer, Heidelberg (2002). https://doi.org/10.1007/3-540-36103-0_61
77. Zhu, H., He, J.: A semantics of Verilog using duration calculus. In: Proceedings of the International Conference on Software: Theory and Practice, pp. 421–432 (August 2000)
78. Zhu, H., He, J., Li, J., Bowen, J.P.: Algebraic approach to linking the semantics of web services. In: Fifth IEEE International Conference on Software Engineering and Formal Methods (SEFM 2007), 10–14 September 2007, London, England, UK, pp. 315–328. IEEE Computer Society (2007). https://doi.org/10.1109/SEFM.2007.4
79. Zhu, H., He, J., Li, J., Bowen, J.P.: Algebraic approach to linking the semantics of web services. Innov. Syst. Softw. Eng. **7**(3), 209–224 (2011). https://doi.org/10.1007/s11334-011-0172-1
80. Zhu, H., He, J., Li, J., Pu, G., Bowen, J.P.: Linking denotational semantics with operational semantics for web services. Innov. Syst. Softw. Eng. **6**(4), 283–298 (2010). https://doi.org/10.1007/s11334-010-0134-z

UTP, *Circus*, and Isabelle

Jim Woodcock[1]([⊠]) [iD], Ana Cavalcanti[1] [iD], Simon Foster[1] [iD], Marcel Oliveira[3] [iD],
Augusto Sampaio[2] [iD], and Frank Zeyda[4] [iD]

[1] The University of York, York, UK
{jim.woodcock,ana.cavalcanti,simon.foster}@york.ac.uk
[2] Universidade Federal de Pernambuco, Recife, Brazil
acas@cin.ufpe.br
[3] Universidade Federal do Rio Grande do Norte, Natal, Brazil
marcel@dimap.ufrn.br
[4] Guadalajara, Mexico
https://www-users.york.ac.uk/~jw524/,
https://www-users.york.ac.uk/~alcc500/,
https://www-users.york.ac.uk/~sf786/, https://dimap.ufrn.br/~marcel/,
https://www.cin.ufpe.br/~acas/, https://www.linkedin.com/in/frank-zeyda/

Abstract. We dedicate this paper with great respect and friendship to
He Jifeng on the occasion of his 80th birthday. Our research group owes
much to him. The authors have over 150 publications on unifying theories
of programming (UTP), a research topic Jifeng created with Tony Hoare.
Our objective is to recount the history of *Circus* (a combination of Z,
CSP, Dijkstra's guarded command language, and Morgan's refinement
calculus) and the development of Isabelle/UTP. Our paper is in two
parts. (1) We first discuss the activities needed to model systems: we
need to formalise data models and their behaviours. We survey our work
on these two aspects in the context of *Circus*. (2) Secondly, we describe
our practical implementation of UTP in Isabelle/HOL. Mechanising UTP
theories is the basis of novel verification tools. We also discuss ongoing
and future work related to (1) and (2). Many colleagues have contributed
to these works, and we acknowledge their support.

Keywords: *Circus* · CSP · Isabelle/HOL · Isabelle/UTP · refinement
calculus · UTP · Unifying theories of programming · He Jifeng · Z

1 Dedication

Jim Woodcock met He Jifeng in Oxford in the early 1980s. Jim was working
for GEC Hirst Research Centre and regularly visited Oxford to teach courses
for industry. He collaborated with Jifeng in teaching Z, program refinement, and
CSP. This collaboration continued after Jifeng moved to the United Nations University in Macau, where Jim became a visiting professor. In 2013, with Zhiming

---

F. Zeyda—Independent Researcher.

J. P. Bowen et al. (Eds.): *Theories of Programming and Formal Methods*, LNCS 14080, pp. 19–51, 2023.
https://doi.org/10.1007/978-3-031-40436-8_2

Liu and Huibiao Zhu, Jim helped to celebrate Jifeng's 70th birthday, organising a collection of essays [64], an international training school on UTP [65], and a colloquium on theoretical computer science [63]. Jim's research groups at the Universities of Oxford, Kent, and York took their intellectual basis from the sound foundations of the Z notation, data refinement, CSP, functional programming, and unifying theories of programming. Jifeng made significant contributions in each of these areas. We were delighted when Jifeng accepted an Honorary Doctorate conferred by the University of York at a ceremony in Beijing on 17 April 2010. All authors are grateful for the inspiration, good taste, and mathematical excellence he provided and continues to provide, which greatly influences our work.

Thank you, Jifeng!

2   Introduction

We describe in this paper our work since 2000 inspired by He Jifeng and Tony Hoare and their unifying theories of programming (UTP). We watched the origins of UTP. Jim recalls enthusiastic but puzzling meetings over lunch in the common room in Oxford with Tony and Jifeng mysteriously discussing ok', $wait'$, and the tradeoff between different fixed points. Tony left Oxford in 1998 and Jifeng shortly afterwards. The UTP book [59] was launched at Tony's retirement symposium, where we gave a copy to every participant. Tony and Jim gave a short course on UTP at the symposium. This was the origin of Jim's long-standing course. We describe UTP and its development in [113].

UTP is particularly well suited as a basis for writing and reasoning about heterogeneous models, capturing various aspects of a system: data, reaction, time, architecture, and so on. In UTP, we found the theoretical basis for cyber-physical systems (CPS). In a CPS, computer-based algorithms control and monitor a physical device; potentially, humans interact with networked physical devices. A CPS senses and changes the physical world. Modelling a CPS requires heterogeneous notations: discrete programming models for control; continuous models for physical dynamics, including hydraulics, mechatronics, and others; protocols for human interaction; and continuous and probabilistic models for assumptions about an uncertain environment. The diversity of the heterogeneous semantics required for CPS requires a unifying theory of semantics: UTP.

This paper describes our work, past, present, and future, on *Circus*, a multi-paradigm modelling language. *Circus* is a concrete realisation of UTP.

In Sect. 3, we discuss our research work on *Circus*. It makes the choices for designing a language suitable for UTP semantics with parsers, type-checkers, static and dynamic analysers, model checkers, theorem provers, and code generators. In Sect. 4, we discuss our implementation of UTP and *Circus* in the Isabelle/UTP theorem prover. Additional exciting projects that use *Circus* but did not involve our research group are briefly described in Sect. 5. Section 6 describes ongoing and future directions for research on *Circus*, Isabelle/UTP and their applications, and Sect. 7 summarises our work.

3   *Circus*

Two activities needed to model a system are formalising its data model and behaviour. Model-oriented languages like Z [62,100,107,110] describe state-based aspects, and process algebras like CSP [58] describe behavioural patterns. We add a third dimension for system development: a refinement calculus [75]. Combining these three aspects motivates *Circus*, where a system process groups data and control constructs and the behaviours of all implementations are specified.

Dijkstra, Back, Morris, and Morgan used predicate transformers [31] as the basis of semantic models for imperative refinement calculi [7,75,76]. Hoare and Roscoe use different models as the basis of theories of refinement for CSP, the failures-divergences model [58,90,91]. Fischer surveyed some of the work that combines the two approaches [38]. Fischer and Smith [39,99] both provide a failures-divergences model for Object-Z classes to present the semantics for combinations of Object-Z and CSP. Although they consider data refinement for these combinations, they do not give refinement laws.

Woodcock et al. [119] use the failures model to give behavioural semantics to abstract data types. The semantics of *Circus* requires a model combining the notions of refinement for CSP and imperative programs. UTP [59] is a framework that makes this combination possible by unifying the programming discipline across many different computational paradigms.

The semantic setting provided by UTP is the theory of alphabetised relations. Interesting sub-theories are built by defining mappings corresponding to healthiness conditions capturing different aspects of the sub-theory. Hoare and He [59] first create a sub-theory of precondition-postcondition pairs within the relational calculus. This is the theory of designs (see [117] for a tutorial introduction to designs and Harwood et al. [56] for an introduction to Galois connections). Next, they build a theory of reactive processes that is disjoint from the theory of designs. Finally, they use reactive healthiness conditions to embed designs within the theory of reactive processes. The result is the theory of CSP processes (see [24] for a tutorial account of this embedding and connections between it and Roscoe's semantics based on the failures-divergences model).

In what follows, we survey the main contributions that led to the design, formalisation, extension, and application of *Circus*.

3.1   A Concurrent Language for Refinement [108,114]

We start by describing the origin of *Circus*. In 2000, Jim Woodcock visited Ana Cavalcanti in Brazil while on sabbatical from Oxford. They formed a reading group with Augusto Sampaio to study Hoare and He's textbook on UTP [59]. Chapter 8 describes a unifying theory for communication in process algebras. The book considers ACP, CCS, CSP, and the data-flow language SDL.

In the reading group, we were inspired particularly by Theorem 8.2.2 in the book (Closure of CSP Processes). It states two properties: (1) The UTP theory for CSP processes defines a complete lattice that is closed under sequential composition. (2) The lattice also contains $\mathbf{R}(x := e)$, where x is any list of stored program variables, e is a corresponding list of well-defined expressions, and $\mathbf{R}$

is the healthiness function for reactive processes (see [59, Theorem 8.0.2, p. 208] for the definition of the reactive healthiness conditions). The proof of the first conclusion follows from the following fact:

P is a CSP process **iff**

$$P = \mathbf{R}(\neg\, P[false, false/wait, ok'] \vdash P[false, true/wait, ok']) \qquad [\dagger]$$

The predicate $P[false, false/wait, ok']$ describes the divergences of the CSP process P. The process P has been properly started: $wait = true$ explicitly and $ok = true$ implicitly, since we are in the precondition: before the $\vdash$. We select divergence: $ok' = false$. The complement $\neg\, P[false, false/wait, ok']$ describes the situations where P does not diverge. In the postcondition, after $\vdash$, the predicate $P[false, true/wait, ok']$ describes the conditions under which P reaches a stable state: $wait = true$ and $ok' = true$. It describes the stable failures of P.

Two things snagged our attention here. First, the property marked [$\dagger$] states that every CSP process can be expressed as a reactive design. Every CSP process behaves as described by a reactive assumption-commitment pair. In our subsequent work on *Circus*, we used this property to give uniform, specification-oriented semantics to the operators of *Circus*, establishing a way of specifying *Circus* processes as contracts. Second, the reactive assignment reminded us that the UTP semantics for CSP is *state-rich*. The UTP semantics of CSP describes the representation of states that react to the same input differently depending on the current state value recorded in program variables.

So the reading group asked itself the question:

What if we used the Z notation to specify abstract data types to accompany CSP definitions of processes?

This question is the origin of the *Circus* notation.

We presented *Circus* for the first time at a workshop at Trinity College Dublin [114]. Our formulation of the language gave a calculational approach to writing programs that are similar to occam [60] and Handel-C [67]. Our paper [114] describes the language, the rationale for its design, and a case study in its use: a reactive ring buffer with a cached head, which became a famous case study for showing off the features of *Circus*. The ring acts as a bounded buffer in the formal sense that it has the following properties:

1. The ring is a FIFO queue.
2. If the ring has spare capacity, it cannot refuse an input.
3. If the ring is not empty, it cannot refuse to output.

Each cell in the buffer is modelled as an active process. To ensure no (perceived) refusal of output (3), we cache the head of the buffer. This avoids the delay required to fetch the head so that it is immediately available.

3.2   The Steam Boiler in *Circus* [115]

Another well-known case study is the steam-boiler problem, which has become a standard benchmark in modelling and verification. It was first proposed by

Bauer [12] and subsequently popularised by Jean-Raymond Abrial as the subject of a Dagstuhl workshop [2]. The workshop proceedings contain the problem description and 22 solutions. Abrial's solution is published separately [1].

The problem is to program the control system for a steam boiler. The control software exists within a physical environment with the following elements: (1) the steam boiler; (2) a sensor to detect the level of the water in the boiler; (3) a valve to evacuate the boiler; (4) a sensor to measure the quantity of steam being produced; (5) four pumps supplying the boiler with water; (6) four pump controllers; (7) an operator's desk; and (8) a message transmission system. Our solution to the problem consists of four processes operating in parallel. (1) The *Timer* ensures the cycle begins every five seconds. (2) The *Analyser* inputs messages from the physical units and analyses their content. (3) Once the analysis is complete, it offers an information service to the *Controller*, which decides on the actions to be taken. (4) It generates outputs for the *Reporter*, which offers a reporting service to the *Controller* by gathering its outputs and packaging them for dispatch to the physical units. It then signals the completion of the cycle.

Our solution structure was guided by the drive to efficiently use the FDR model checker [53]. We had to overcome two obstacles: the state explosion problem and the use of loose constants. The latter complicates model checking because loose constants must be given specific values that define a concrete finite model. An argument is then required to extrapolate these specific values to arbitrary ones (a small model theorem). The steam boiler depends on several of these constants. Any practical instantiation leads to a massive number of states.

Our solution separates the *Controller* and its finite-state machine from the *Analyser* and the rich state it constructs from input message history. The *Analyser* digests the incoming messages and makes this digest available to the *Controller* as abstract events. This makes the *Controller* amenable to fully automatic model checking using FDR. Significantly, the *Analyser*'s abstract events correspond to concepts in the requirements, so they help validate the *Analyser*'s behaviour. Extrapolation from the abstract behaviour of the *Controller* to the concrete realities of the requirements is provided by the *Analyser*. It is like a retrieve function from the concrete details of the state to an abstract interpretation of those details, in the sense of data refinement [110].

3.3   The Semantics of *Circus* [116]

The semantics of *Circus* provides a model for processes and their components. In [116], we use a Z specification to describe the semantics of *Circus* processes and of *Circus* actions, which have an imperative state, as relations. The process model is a Z specification, and the action model is a Z schema. We used Z as a concrete notation for UTP's relational calculus because we could parse and type-check it and prove various consistency results.

Circus includes support to define imperative assignments, conditionals, loops, and the reactive behaviour of communication, parallelism, and internal and external choice. All combinations of model-based formalisms and process algebras that had been published before we defined the semantics of *Circus* describe concurrent programs as communicating abstract datatypes. For example, this is the case with CSP_Z [38] and CSP ∥ B [95]. Communicating abstract datatype is a valuable but limited design pattern. We took a different approach and did not identify events with datatype operations. The result is a programming language suitable for developing concurrent programs in a more general style.

Our goals in designing the semantics of *Circus* were: (1) ease of use for those familiar with Z and CSP; (2) encapsulation of the process model; and (3) the possibility of reusing existing theories, techniques, and tools. We had to decide how best to formulate the semantics. Imperative refinement calculi like those of Back [7], Morgan [75], and Morris [76], are normally given predicate transformer semantics. Theories of refinement for CSP are based on the failures-divergences model [58,90]. A connection between weakest preconditions and CSP exists [74], and a sound and complete refinement theory has been developed based on it [120]. We use a fourth approach: UTP, where both state and communication aspects of concurrent systems are integrated with a state-based failures-divergences model described pointwise. This leads to a simple and elegant definition of refinement and a sound foundation for refinement calculi.

3.4   Refinement in *Circus* [26, 27, 94]

Having set out the semantics of *Circus*, our next step was to define its refinement relation [94]. Each *Circus* process has a state and accompanying actions that define both internal state transitions and changes in control flow during execution. We explained the meaning of refinement for processes and their actions and proposed a sound data refinement technique. Refinement laws for CSP and Z are directly relevant and applicable to *Circus*, but our focus was on new laws for processes that integrate state and control. We presented new results about the distribution of data refinement through CSP operators adopted in *Circus*.

We illustrated our ideas with the development of a distributed system of cooperating processes. We proposed a refinement approach whose typical starting point is a centralised specification of an application. The development process moves towards a distributed solution. The approach is supported by two families of laws (for algorithmic and data refinement) that allow the incremental splitting of *Circus* processes using parallelism. The overall approach is illustrated by a case study (the reactive buffer again) that, although simple, is interesting enough to demonstrate the proposed strategy in all its relevant details.

A *Circus* system describes a set of processes. Each process encapsulates a local state and has its reactive behaviour defined by actions in that state. In [26], we present refinement laws to support the development of these actions from more abstract descriptions. These laws form the basis of a systematic development strategy for *Circus* based on formal refinement, addressing all the language's constructs. It complements the work in [94] by proposing laws of actions, including the laws of CSP [58,91] and of ZRC [28], a refinement calculus for Z.

In addition, since *Circus* allows us to specify actions using a mixture of Z schemas and CSP constructs, we require new laws. For example, there are novel laws to introduce parallelism and external choice from Z schema expressions.

These laws are added to a comprehensive set of refinement laws of CSP to support program development in *Circus*. The work extends the forward simulation laws proposed for *Circus* [94] to address all the action operators of *Circus*. It illustrates how these laws can be proved from the semantics of *Circus*. Parts of the development of the distributed cached-head ring buffer from its centralised specification are used to illustrate the laws of actions and forward simulation.

In [27], we present a refinement strategy for *Circus*. The strategy unifies the theories of refinement for processes and their constituent actions and provides a coherent technique for stepwise refinement of concurrent and distributed programs involving rich data structures. This kind of development is carried out using *Circus*'s refinement calculus. We describe some of its laws for the simultaneous refinement of state and control behaviour, including splitting a process into parallel components. We illustrate the strategy and the laws using a case study that shows the complete development of a distributed program.

3.5 Predicate Transformers in the Semantics of *Circus* [29]

One of the main objectives of the *Circus* work is the definition of refinement methods for concurrent programs. The original semantic model for *Circus* is defined using UTP, expressed in Z. In [29], we present equivalent semantics based on predicate transformers. With this new model, we provide an adequate basis for formalising refinement and verification-condition generation rules.

This new framework makes it possible to include logical variables and angelic nondeterminism in *Circus*, neither of which are straightforward in the relational setting. The consistency of the relational and predicate transformer models gives us confidence in their accuracy. Only much later did we study angelic nondeterminism in a relational setting [25]. The work to define a UTP theory to study *Circus* processes and angelic nondeterminism was led by Pedro Ribeiro [85–87].

We present in [29] a new predicate transformer: the weakest reactive precondition. It characterises the weakest precondition that guarantees that a given condition holds in all later observable, not necessarily final, states of a reactive program. We define the weakest reactive precondition of a unifying theory relation that defines a reactive system. From this, we calculate the weakest reactive precondition semantics for *Circus*. This new semantic model is a convenient step towards the complete justification of our extension to an existing refinement calculus for Z [28] that includes all *Circus* constructs.

Roscoe and Hoare [92] present laws that completely characterise occam and that are cast in terms of the occam's denotational semantics [89], although no proof of equivalence was carried out. The laws presented in that work are equality-based algebraic semantics. Unlike our work, they are not intended to support the development of programs by refinement.

3.6 A *Circus* Semantics for Ravenscar Protected Objects [6]

Burns et al.'s Ravenscar profile [14] is a subset of the Ada 95 tasking model [10]. The Ravenscar profile does not allow Ada's rendezvous construct for task communication. Instead, tasks in Ravenscar communicate through shared variables, usually encapsulated inside protected objects. This makes protected objects fundamental building blocks in Ravenscar programs, providing a safe mechanism for accessing the shared data between various tasks.

The Ravenscar profile is intended to be certifiable and deterministic, to support schedulability analysis, and to meet tight memory constraints and performance requirements. With Atiya and King [6], we give semantics to protected objects using *Circus* and prove several of its essential properties: consistency, determinism, deadlock-freedom, livelock-freedom, totality, and non-stopping behaviour. This was the first time that these properties had been verified. Interestingly, all the proofs are conducted in Z, even those concerning reactive behaviour. A compliance notation for concurrent systems [5] provides a cost-effective technique for verifying Ravenscar programs based on this formal semantics.

Lundqvist et al. [68] provide an alternative formal model of Ravenscar's protected objects in UPPAAL [13]. Their model deals specifically with the timing of calls to protected objects. Model checking is used to verify the protected object model considering only a few tasks: three. No statement was made about the model's validity for more tasks. Our proofs are valid for any number of tasks.

3.7   Using *Circus* for Safety-Critical Applications [111]

In [111], we illustrate the use of *Circus* via the example of the steam boiler discussed in Sect. 3.2. We focus on an interesting semantic gap between synchronisation in CSP and, therefore, *Circus*, and in programs: a kind of abstract event. In CSP, an abstraction is sometimes used in which atomic synchronisations can be system-wide, between many processes, rather than being restricted to only two participants. In [111], we deal with a simple instance of this phenomenon of multi-synchronisation, which shows the power of *Circus*'s calculational approach to reasoning about reactive systems via refinement of abstract models.

We base our model of the steam boiler controller here on O'Halloran's description [78] that expresses its functional requirements as firing rules. These are in the form **if** a **then** b, where event a enables event b, subject to environmental constraints. The implicit inference engine defined by these firing rules is nonmonotonic, as it must forget previously inferred facts as the system evolves. The result is a valuable design pattern for synthesising reactive controllers.

A suitable language to implement this model as a controller for an actual steam boiler is occam [60], given its close relationship with CSP. We might likely choose Communicating Sequential Processes for Java (JCSP), a Java class library that implements CSP processes and process combinators [106]. We immediately, however, face the semantic gap mentioned above. CSP allows the synchronisation of events between many processes, but occam and JCSP restrict this, for efficiency reasons, to just two participants. In our paper [111], we apply *Circus*'s refinement calculus to bridge this semantic gap.

In this work, we consider a collection of parallel processes indexed over I, each repeatedly executing some individual transaction, represented by the event

$t.i$, with $i \in I$ and synchronising the transactions by alternating them with a globally shared event m. The *Circus* process models this:

$$(\|_m \, i : I \bullet (\mu X \bullet m \to t.i \to X)) \setminus \{m\}$$

Every process participates in the multi-way synchronisation on m, whereas only the i-th process participates in the independent event $t.i$. The event m is hidden from the environment, so crucially for this development, we know the identities of all of m's participants. If the membership were dynamic, then we would need to develop a protocol to manage its membership.

We use *Circus*'s refinement calculus to derive a protocol equivalent to this system of parallel processes, but where there is no multi-way synchronisation. Our first step is to convert the i-th process into an action system [8]. We then reintroduce parallelism to create a simple protocol that synchronises transactions. It is now at the code level of occam or JCSP.

A more interesting problem occurs when the multi-way synchronisation is part of an external choice, and our solution above is not applicable in such a situation. We have calculated efficient two-phase commit protocols to deal with these synchronisation patterns. Although these programs are much more complex than the one calculated in this paper, the same development strategy is used. The abstract program is reduced to a normal form, which contains no multi-way synchronisations since it is sequential. This normal form is then partitioned into new parallel processes that implement a protocol for synchronising individual transactions. This approach is later adopted in [50] in the context of an automated strategy for translation from *Circus* to JCSP.

3.8   Formal Development of Industrial-Scale Systems in *Circus* [81]

In [80], we present the use of the *Circus* refinement strategy to derive a concrete distributed fire-control system from an abstract centralised *Circus* specification. This real-world system is one of the most significant case studies on the *Circus* refinement strategy [27] and translation rules [81].

The fire-control system considers two building areas, each divided into two zones. Two extra zones are used for detection only. Fire detection happens in a zone, and a gas discharge may occur in the area that contains that zone. The system includes a display panel with lamps to indicate whether the system is on or off, system faults, whether a fire has been detected, whether the alarm has been silenced, and the need to replace actuators and gas discharges. The system can be in one of three modes: manual, automatic, or disabled.

In manual mode, an alarm sounds when a fire is detected, and the corresponding detection lamp is lit on the display. The alarm can be silenced, and the system returns to normal when the reset button is pressed. In manual mode, a gas discharge needs to be manually initiated. In automatic mode, fire detection is followed by the alarm being sounded; however, if a fire is detected in the second zone of the same area, the second stage alarm is sounded, and a countdown starts. When the countdown finishes, the gas is discharged, and the circuit fault lamp is illuminated in the display; the system mode is switched to disabled. In disabled mode, the system only indicates the need to replace the actuators, identify relevant faults, and reset. The system returns to its normal mode after the actuators are replaced, and the reset button is pressed.

The motivation for the fire-control system refinement is the distribution of the control for efficiency. In [80], we use the refinement strategy in [23] to develop a concrete distributed system using three refinement iterations: the first one splits the system into an internal controller and a controller for the areas. In the second iteration, the internal controller is subdivided into two further controllers, separating a controller just for the display. Finally, the third iteration splits the controller's areas into individual controllers for each area.

The result of refining a *Circus* specification is a *Circus* program written in a combination of CSP and guarded commands. We, therefore, need a link between *Circus* and a practical programming language to implement this program.

In [81], we present rules to translate *Circus* programs to Java programs that use JCSP (see [106] and the discussion in Sect. 3.7). These rules can be used as a complement to the *Circus* algebraic refinement technique or as a guideline for implementation. They link the results of refinement in the context of *Circus* and a practical programming language in current use. The rules can also be used as the basis for a tool that mechanises translation [11,50]. In [81], we demonstrate the application of the rules using the industrial fire-control system.

The main objective of that work was to provide a translation strategy for implementing *Circus* programs in a widely used language. Using the JCSP [105, 106] library and a rule-based approach ensures that the obtained programs can be traced back to the *Circus* model. The rules justify and generalise our development of the fire-control system. With this work, we provide empirical evidence of the expressive power of *Circus* and that the refinement strategy in [27] and the translation to Java apply to industrial systems.

3.9   A Denotational Semantics for *Circus* [82, 83]

Although usable for reasoning about *Circus* specifications, the semantics in [116] is not appropriate to prove properties of *Circus* itself. This is because it is a shallow embedding in which *Circus* constructs are defined as a Z specification. Yet another language is used as a metalanguage to define the semantics. The main drawback is that we can not use shallow embedding to prove the laws of *Circus*'s distinguishing development technique. In [82], we present an alternative: a definitive reference for the denotational semantics using UTP.

We redefined the *Circus* semantics. We mechanised it using ProofPower-Z [4], a commercial HOL-based theorem prover for Z. We implemented the UTP theories needed for the semantics of state-rich CSP (relations, designs, reactive processes, and the CSP healthiness conditions) [84]. Our semantics for *Circus* is then given using reactive designs. We proved over 90% of the 146 proposed refinement laws. These proofs range over the structure of the language and include all the data simulation laws. Their proofs can be found in [79].

We used a simple strategy to prove $P = Q$ or $P \sqsubseteq Q$. (1) Flatten P to a single reactive design $\mathbf{R}(pre_P \vdash post_P)$. (2) Flatten Q to a single reactive design $\mathbf{R}(pre_Q \vdash post_Q)$. (3) Use lemmas and theorems from the ProofPower UTP library and predicate calculus to transform the first reactive design into the second one (in case of refinement, an inverse implication is the required result). Flattening the programs involves definitions and theorems that transform program structures into a single reactive design. For instance, if P is the sequence P_1 ; P_2, the following lemma transforms it into a single reactive design.

Lemma 1.

$$\mathbf{R}(P_1 \vdash Q_1) \, ; \, \mathbf{R}(P_2 \vdash Q_2) \, = $$
$$\mathbf{R}(\, P_1 \wedge \neg \, ((okay' \wedge \neg \, wait' \wedge Q_1) \, ; \, \neg \, P_2)$$
$$\vdash$$
$$((wait' \wedge Q_1) \vee (okay' \wedge \neg \, wait' \wedge Q_1 \, ; \, Q_2)) \,)$$

for P_1 not mentioning dashed variables and P_1, Q_1, P_2, and Q_2 all $\mathbf{R2}$*-healthy.*

The result of our mechanisation is a definitive reference for the denotational semantics of *Circus* using UTP and reactive designs.

Finally, we note that *Circus* also has an operational semantics [51,118]. In [51], there are considerations on a formal link to the denotational semantics. Furthermore, as we have already explained, the algebraic laws have been proved from the denotational semantics, establishing the usual links suggested by UTP.

3.10   Time and Synchronicity in *Circus* [16,97]

*Circus*Time Action (CTA) is a timed version of *Circus*, explored by Sherif and others, including He Jifeng [96,97]. It introduces discrete-time slots of event sequences. CTA provides a two-tier view of history. The top-level records history as a sequence of time slots. The bottom-level records history as an event sequence within a given slot. This is reminiscent of super-dense time, an important tool for modelling simultaneity in discrete-event simulations. The slots model events separated in time, whilst each slot models simultaneous but ordered events.

We worked with Andrew Butterfield on a synchronous version of *Circus*. Our work in [16] takes inspiration from CTA and is compatible with the general structure of the *Circus* language. We develop a generic framework of UTP theories for describing systems whose behaviour is characterised by regular (top-level) time slots. The slotted-*Circus* framework is parametrised by how event histories are observable within a slot (the bottom level). We instantiate this bottom-level history in a variety of ways: as simple traces or multisets of events or as the more complex micro-slot structures used in our operational semantics for Handel-C (a high-level programming language that targets low-level hardware, most commonly used in the programming of FPGAs) [18].

One of the original motivations behind this work was to re-cast existing semantics for Handel-C into the UTP framework so that *Circus* can be used as a specification language. Using this time-slot model, the Handel-C denotational [17] and operational semantics are defined. Still, the slot structure has varying complexity, depending on which language constructs we wish to support. The slotted-*Circus* framework is a foundation for formulating the common parts of these models, making it easier to explore the key differences.

3.11   The Miracle of Reactive Programming [112]

UTP uses Tarski's relational calculus, with theories defined by complete lattices of predicates ordered under refinement. Roscoe's semantics for CSP uses a complete partial order (CPO) [90]. So UTP offers an exciting addition: the reactive miracle, the top of the lattice. In [112], we present two simple properties of reactive miracles: prefixing a miracle with an event and offering an external choice between a process and a miracle. Both processes have interesting properties: each violates an essential axiom of the standard failures-divergences model for CSP. Of course, that is why the reactive miracle is not in Roscoe's CPO.

All three UTP theories involved in modelling CSP processes are complete lattices rather than the CPOs of the standard models for CSP. As complete lattices, they each have a top element. The top of the design lattice is the familiar miracle from the refinement calculus: $w : [true, false]$ [75]. This design is always guaranteed to terminate if it is started (precondition $true$), and when it does terminate, it achieves the impossible (it makes $false$ $true$).

Morgan demonstrates a specific application of miracles [73]. He shows that a miracle can enable conditional data refinement even when the condition involves concrete variables. Some reasoning is then needed at the concrete level to eliminate the miracle, which can never be executed. Morgan illustrates another use for miracles: a naked guarded command can be given weakest precondition semantics. For guard G, command com, and postcondition α, the weakest precondition for the guarded command $\mathbf{wp}(G \rightarrow com, \alpha)$ is $G \Rightarrow \mathbf{wp}(com, \alpha)$. We note that a guarded command does not satisfy the Law of the Excluded Miracle [31]: $\mathbf{wp}(com, false) = false$; for example, $\mathbf{wp}(G \rightarrow com, false)$ is $G \Rightarrow \mathbf{wp}(com, false)$, which is different from $false$. In [74], Morgan uses this definition to give semantics to an action system [8] (see also [120]).

The tops of the reactive and the CSP lattices in UTP were unexplored when we wrote [112]. The reactive miracle is $\top = \mathbf{R1}(\mathbf{true} \vdash wait \wedge \amalg)$. This is reactive-healthy but infeasible (miraculous) if properly started. We proved the following result for an external choice between a prefixed process and a miracle:

$$a \rightarrow Skip \ \square \ \top \ = \ (\mathbf{true} \vdash (\amalg \lhd wait \rhd \neg \ wait' \wedge tr' = tr \ ^\frown \ \langle a \rangle \wedge v' = v))$$

This process terminates immediately, having performed the event a. There is no state in which the process is waiting for the environment to perform a: it happens *instantly*. This makes the event a urgent.

In [112], we explore some applications of miracles. We show how to make two events a and b simultaneous, but ordered: we prune away the state between a and b. Next, we show how to implement deadlines. For example, if b must occur within 10 time units, we can model this using a new deadline operator: we write b **deadline** $10 \; \hat{=} \; (b \rightarrow Skip) \; \triangleright_{10} \; \top$, where $\triangleright_{10}$ is the timeout operator. In this process, there are no states 10 time units from initiation in which b has not happened. This captures a very strong requirement: there is no alternative to meeting the deadline. Further applications of miracles are explored in [103, 104].

Reactive miracles have proved indispensable to provide a sound semantic basis for real-time extensions of *Circus*. A real-time variant of *Circus* has, for instance, been used to give an architectural infrastructure model [72] of Safety-Critical Java (JRS 302) [66]—a subset of Java tailored for the engineering of safety-critical real-time systems. Nelson already realised that, despite their unimplementability, miracles are useful in refinement-based systems development, much like complex numbers in solving differential equations. Our work rediscovers and reiterates this claim in the context of reactive programming in general, and *Circus* in particular, with UTP giving us the right framework and vocabulary to make this integration as smooth as possible.

4   Isabelle/UTP

We describe Isabelle/UTP[1], our practical implementation of UTP that can be used to mechanise UTP theories and turn them into verification tools. We cover the history of Isabelle/UTP and motivate the design decisions behind its development: in each section, we account for a major step in the Isabelle/UTP design as it evolved. Isabelle/UTP was born out of necessity to support UTP-based software engineering, and this continues to be our motivation to this day.

4.1   Beginnings

Isabelle/UTP [46] is a shallow embedding of the UTP in Isabelle. Its development began in 2012, during the COMPASS project[2]. Nevertheless, Isabelle/UTP is a natural development of previous UTP mechanisations, notably by Marcel Oliveira [84] and Abderrahmane Feliachi [32, 36] (with Burkhart Wolff).

COMPASS created a sophisticated toolset for modelling and verifying "systems of systems". We developed a modelling language, CML (COMPASS Modelling Language), with formal UTP semantics, a task led by Jim Woodcock. Thus, an applicable verification tool for UTP was needed. Simon Foster's task was to develop a theorem prover for UTP and CML based on Isabelle/HOL.

As envisioned, this tool needed to combine two important characteristics. On the one hand, it needed to provide the fidelity necessary to express refinement laws, including side conditions, which often imposed syntactic constraints. On the other hand, it needed to be suitable for scalable verification. Whilst these had been separately achieved in the mechanisation of Oliveira and Feliachi, they had not been achieved in either work. Oliveira's mechanisation [84], as a relatively

---

[1] Isabelle/UTP Website: http://isabelle-utp.york.ac.uk.
[2] Comprehensive Modelling for Advanced Systems of Systems, EU FP7 Project 287829.

deep embedding, had fidelity but lacked the automation necessary to make it scalable. Feliachi's mechanisation [32,36] had automation and scalability as a shallow embedding but could not express syntactic side conditions.

4.2   Laws and Side Conditions, and the Deep Model

We consider the well-known assignment commutativity law:

$$(x := e \,;\, y := f) = (y := f \,;\, x := e) \text{ provided } x \neq y, x \notin fv(f), y \notin fv(e)$$

To express this law, as written, we need to (1) compare different program variables and (2) check the variables mentioned in an expression. However, a function like fv, which determines the free variables of an expression, is *meta-logical* since it allows us to make arguments based on the syntactic structure of a term. It exists in Isabelle and most other provers but as a function in Isabelle/ML inaccessible from HOL. This is important because if fv were an Isabelle function, then equality would cease to be useful, as we could not, for instance, prove that $x \cdot 0 = 0$ (for $x \in \mathbb{R}$), since $fv(x \cdot 0) = \{x\} \neq \{\} = fv(0)$.

At the same time, formal methods are awash with laws that use such side conditions. Another example is the frame rule from separation logic:

$$\frac{\{P\}\,C\,\{Q\}}{\{P * R\}\,C\,\{Q * R\}} \; mod(C) \cap fv(R)$$

This likewise requires that we calculate the free variables in R and the set of variables that command C modifies. We seem to have hit a roadblock—we cannot have fv and similar syntax functions without breaking our logic.

However, Oliveira [84] discovered a neat solution. He created a function $UnrestVar : REL\_PRED \rightarrow \mathbb{P}\,NAME$, which calculates the set of names (i.e. variables) that a predicate does not depend on, i.e. those that are "unrestricted". Unlike fv, $UnrestVar$ is a *semantic* rather than a syntactic function. It does not compute the syntactically present names but those that have some bearing on the predicate's meaning. For example, $x \cdot 0$ does not depend on x since it always evaluates to 0. Thus, $UnrestVar(x \cdot 0) = NAME$, since this expression does not depend on any variable: it is semantically equivalent to 0.

It turns out that $UnrestVar$ is sufficient to express the side conditions of our assignment law and similar laws. This function has a much older pedigree: an analogue is found in Tarski's famous Cylindric Algebra [57], an algebraic basis for first-order logic with equality. In this setting, we can express $UnrestVar$ as the greatest set A of names such that $(\exists A.\,P) = P$. Quantifying the names in A does not change P because P does not depend on them.

Oliveira's solution avoids the need for fv. However, there is still a problem because $UnrestVar$ requires that we formalise names and, as later realised in the work of Zeyda [123], types. The problem is that names and types are also meta-logical. If we formalise them, we cut ourselves off from the proof assistant's representation of names and types, with a resulting loss of algorithms like α-renaming and type checking. We have to implement these ourselves.

So, when we first developed Isabelle/UTP, we followed Oliveira [84] and Zeyda [123] in building our representation of names, types, and a value universe [45]. We call this a "deep model", rather than a "deep embedding" because we do not formalise a syntax tree for predicates, just for the underlying value universe. In this approach, a predicate is denoted as a set of functions recording the possible values of the correct type that a variable can take. We must, therefore, formalise names, types, values, and the typing relation.

In HOL, types are bounded by a given cardinal, and so the value universe is technically limited to a strict subset of the possible types constructible in HOL. Thus, we needed to exhibit an explicit injection into our universe whenever we wanted to use a type in a UTP predicate or program. We did find a way of automating it somewhat, but this did not work well. Though we retained the fidelity of Oliveira's model, we could not match the automation of Feliachi. This became obvious even for small examples in CML. Our technique did not scale to allow model verification. This was all too painfully pointed out in Wolff's gracious and factual review of our UTP 2014 paper [45].

Nevertheless, whilst we could not support verification, our techniques substantially benefited from Isabelle's proof automation. Using automated theorem provers, through the *sledgehammer* interface, we proved many more theorems with much less effort than Oliveira with ProofPower-Z. However, we must credit Oliveira's achievement, for he went remarkably far in mechanising UTP, with some proof scripts running hundreds of lines. We learned valuable lessons, but a new foundation for Isabelle/UTP was needed.

4.3 Lenses

Burkhart pointed out that our value universe injections could be expressed more generically using lenses [40]. This was vital for the next version [49]. Lenses are simple algebraic structures: for a set S of states and V of values, a lens $x : V \Rightarrow S$ is a pair of functions $get : S \to V$ and $put : V \to S \to S$, which obey three intuitive algebraic laws, such as $get(put\,x\,s) = x$. Lenses are ubiquitous in the foundations of computer science; for example, Back and von Wright [7] use a similar algebraic structure to characterise variables.

We have described lenses in Isabelle/UTP at length [46]. We use them to model program variables and their mutations for a given state. Every variable x of type A in a given state space S is allocated a lens $x : V \Rightarrow S$. Lenses can also be used to characterise sets of variables using a combinator $x \oplus y$ that produces a lens of type $A \times B \Rightarrow S$ with a product view. Thus, we can also model a program's frame (or "footprint"), part of the state space that a program can modify. Crucially, lenses allow us to escape the need to formalise names and types. Each variable name is in the host logic, and its type is given by its view.

Lenses can be semantically compared in various ways, providing a means to express side conditions. We have the independence relation $x \bowtie y$, which means that x and y refer to different parts of the state, and it is algebraically characterised as the commutativity of the *put* functions. A preorder $a \preceq b$ states that a characterises a smaller region than b; for example, $x \preceq x \oplus y$. If we consider lenses a and b as "sets", then $\preceq$ is the subset relation, and $\oplus$ is the set union operator. Finally, we have an equivalence formed by the cycle of $\preceq$, that is $x \approx y = (x \preceq y \wedge y \preceq x)$, which allows us to characterise laws like $x \oplus y \approx y \oplus x$.

These relations do not compare lenses based on their (meta-logical) names but their semantics. The use of lenses, therefore, allows us to reuse all the host logic facilities for manipulating names. Moreover, this approach avoids the aliasing problem. Even if we have two variables with different names, they will not be independent if they point to the same store region.

UnrestVar also finds an elegant characterisation with lenses. First, we note that program expressions and assertions are modelled as functions as usual in a shallow embedding. An expression operating over store S with type V is a total function $S \rightarrow V$. An expression like $x + y > 5$ can be modelled, using lenses, as $\lambda s.\, get_x(s) + get_y(s) > 5$, though this translation was facilitated through a deep expression syntax. We can then ask whether such an expression semantically depends on a particular lens. If an expression's output value does not change when we change a variable, then clearly, there is no dependence on it. We therefore define $x \sharp e \Leftrightarrow (\forall v\, s.e(put_x\, v\, s) = e(s))$, our version of *UnrestVar*, which tells us that x is unrestricted in e. As shown below, this relation is precisely what we need to characterise the assignment commutativity law and other related laws:

$$(x := e\, ;\, y := f) = (y := f\, ;\, x := e) \text{ provided } x \bowtie y, x \sharp f, y \sharp e$$

In words, the assignments commute provided that (1) the variables are independent; (2) f does not depend on x; and (3) e does not depend on y. This law and other "laws of programming" are theorems of our definitions [46]. As we see later, we can also express a variant of the frame rule.

4.4   UTP and Designs

With a scalable foundation for Isabelle/UTP, we could tackle a significant challenge: mechanisation of the reactive-design hierarchy and the *Circus* language with its UTP semantics. During the development of our various versions of Isabelle/UTP, *Circus* served as a baseline, and we had several iterations of the mechanisation of the operators and healthiness conditions.

Upon our lens-based expression model, we developed UTP's relational calculus. A (potentially heterogeneous) relation in Isabelle/UTP is an expression $S_1 \times S_2 \rightarrow \mathbb{B}$. As in the Z notation, relations typically range over unprimed (x) and primed variables (x'). In Isabelle/UTP, this is achieved using lenses **fst** : $S_1 \Rightarrow S_1 \times S_2$ and **snd** : $S_2 \Rightarrow S_1 \times S_2$ that project the pre- and post-states. We distinguish lenses on the "flat state" (S) from those in the relational state ($S \times S$), a distinction implicit in languages like Z. We then proved the relational calculus laws found in the UTP book and related publications. This includes a detailed account of UTP theories, defined by a set of idempotent healthiness functions, and accompanying theorems, including Knaster-Tarski.

We tackled the design theory from here, allowing us to model relational programs that may exhibit divergence. Our mechanisation raised many questions about the encoding of the design turnstile notation ($P \vdash Q$). Should P and Q be permitted to refer to the ok variable? Should P be allowed to refer to only the pre-state or also the post-state? In Isabelle, we can use the type system to impose restrictions like this by construction. The answer to the first question became clear: ok is semantic machinery used only by $\vdash$, so a UTP theory should not touch it when defining concrete specifications.

The answer to the second question is a little less clear since, in the UTP theory of reactive designs, the precondition can refer to the post-state value of the trace tr to express constraints on permitted communications. As a result, Isabelle/UTP has two turnstile operators: $P \vdash_r Q$, with $P : S_1 \times S_2 \to \mathbb{B}$ and $p \vdash_n Q$, with $p : S_1 \to \mathbb{B}$. The latter is sometimes called a "normal design" [55], hence the n subscript. The benefit of using this second turnstile operator is that side conditions in many theorems can be avoided, thanks to the type system. This improves the efficiency of verification for normal designs.

4.5   UTP Theories

In more detail, a UTP theory consists of (1) a set of observational variables; (2) a set of healthiness conditions; and (3) a signature for constructing elements of the theory that satisfy the healthiness conditions. Like classes in object-oriented programming, UTP theories are extensible by adding more observational variables and healthiness conditions. These conditions can be seen as invariants.

Feliachi's encoding of UTP included an elegant approach to encoding alphabets using extensible records. Each UTP theory is allocated its record type, which gives the observational variables as fields. Since alphabets are types, using variables outside the alphabet equates to a type error. Successive extensions of the UTP theory add fields to the alphabet types. Thanks to Isabelle's polymorphism, functions defined and theorems proved in super-theories are then applicable in sub-theories. For example, a theorem proved in designs is applicable in reactive designs. Moreover, type inference can determine the hierarchy's most general alphabet of a relation. A downside is that multiple inheritance is unsupported because extensible records are implemented using type variables. Nevertheless, this limitation can be mitigated if the hierarchy is carefully constructed.

A side effect of lenses is that we could easily adapt and expand on this approach. We can express constraints on how relations use observational variables with lenses. For example, the alphabet of a design consists of ok, ok', and the program variables and their dashed counterparts. We model this with a parametric alphabet type: a record type α *des* enriched with lenses, where the type parameter α can extend the alphabet with the program variables. The healthiness functions then have types like $(\alpha \ des) \ hrel \to (\alpha \ des) \ hrel$ of functions over a homogeneous relation whose alphabet contains ok. (The actual type is more general because we also support heterogeneous relations.)

With this setup, we can mechanise one of the most complex UTP operators—alphabet extension, which allows us to add (and remove) variables from a relation's alphabet. Our encoding gives us a special lens: $more_L : \alpha \Rightarrow \alpha\ des$. It views the part of the alphabet that does not contain ok, which is the program-variable space or any extension of designs. With this lens, alphabet extension becomes a kind of type coercion, such as $\alpha\ hrel \rightarrow (\alpha\ des)\ hrel$, which lifts a relation into the theory of designs. This is how we implement the design turnstile variants $\vdash_r$ and $\vdash_n$. Alphabet coercions can become complex. Nevertheless, these coercions are invisible in resulting verification tools and improve user experience by making UTP-based programs and models correct by construction.

4.6   Reactive-Design Hierarchy

With a solid theory of designs in place, we proceeded to mechanise reactive designs. This was a significant task, and the reactive-design hierarchy is the most extensive library in Isabelle/UTP, running to about 14,000 lines of Isabelle code. We now give a summary of the main developments.

We mechanised the theory of reactive processes and several variants [42] motivated by the mechanisation and Andrew Butterfield's **R3h** [15] As required by the UTP framework, we proved that the healthiness functions are idempotent, monotonic, continuous, and critical closure results. One crucial design decision was to collect the program variables in a single alphabet variable st, which made separating the program space from semantic machinery (encoded via other alphabet variables such as ok, tr, ref, and so on) more accessible.

We also identified two useful subtheories. Reactive relations express possible behaviours using the alphabet variables tr and tr', recording observed traces, and st and st'. Reactive relations are typically used in postconditions. Reactive conditions have the additional restriction of not referring to st' and having the trace of events $tr' - tr$ prefix closed. Reactive conditions are used in preconditions.

We generalised reactive processes so that tr is drawn from a "trace algebra" [43,88], a form of a cancellative monoid. The original account has tr as a sequence of events, but sometimes other trace models are desirable, such as piecewise-continuous functions for hybrid systems. It turns out that none of the libraries of laws in [24,59] depend on tr being a sequence, and trace algebra is a sufficient basis. Having performed the generalisation, Isabelle/UTP reproved all the laws automatically, illustrating the practical benefits of proof automation. If we had done this on paper, it would have taken weeks instead of minutes.

We then created reactive designs by combining designs and reactive processes. After that, the subsequent significant development, from a verification standpoint, was the introduction of the reactive-contract notation $[P \vdash Q \mid R]$, which is a core constructor of the reactive-design theory [42]. It consists of a precondition P, a postcondition R, and a "pericondition" Q, a new concept suggested by Canham [19]. The precondition is a reactive condition that describes initial states and communicating behaviour that the contract is willing to accept. Violation of the precondition leads to divergence. The pericondition Q and postcondition R describe quiescent (or "intermediate") and terminating behaviours.

In the context of *Circus* and CSP, P corresponds to the complement of the divergences, Q to the set of failure traces, and R to the set of terminating traces. A significant result is that any reactive design can be expressed as a reactive contract.

There are at least two benefits to the use of reactive contracts. Firstly, it allows us to give uniform denotational semantics to all *Circus* operators. Secondly, it will enable us to automate refinement proofs about *Circus* models [44]. We have a refinement law that weakens the precondition and strengthens the peri- and postconditions. This is combined with a calculational proof strategy that allows us to compile any combination of reactive contracts using *Circus* operators into a single reactive contract, which can then be subjected to proof.

4.7 Optimisation and Modularisation

The development of the reactive-designs hierarchy and a *Circus* verification tool served to justify the overall design decisions of Isabelle/UTP. However, several components, notably the expression model, were suboptimal and hampered automation and usability. As we developed Isabelle/UTP, our knowledge of Isabelle/HOL grew, and we improved the design decisions.

Moreover, there was the question of how researchers outside of York could adopt Isabelle/UTP. The original development model was monolithic, with an ever-growing collection of Isabelle theories with many cross-dependencies. There could be little reuse of the components. Isabelle/UTP was a combination of design decisions you either accepted in full or did not.

For example, the library imposes a relational program model ($\mathbb{P}(S_1 \times S_2)$), although this is not universally popular. An alternative is a state transformer model, $S_1 \to \mathbb{P}(S_2)$, which though mathematically equivalent, has the advantage of forming a monad. In truth, several parts of Isabelle/UTP do not need to be wedded to this program model, notably the lens and expression library.

As a result, we set out on a campaign of optimisation and modularisation. The resulting components, defined as Isabelle libraries, are as follows.

Optics. This is where the theory of lenses is defined and contains several related algebraic structures, notably symmetric lenses and prisms. These give an abstract characterisation to channels analogously to lenses. The Optics library also contains user commands, such as **alphabet** and **chantype** to create alphabet and channel types. This library continues to be under active development.

Shallow Expressions. As explained in Sect. 4.3, the original monolithic theory contained an expression model that mimics a deep embedding by introducing constructors for expressions. The motivation was to allow reasoning with the same granularity as a deep embedding. For example, we could encode laws like $(P \wedge Q)[e/x] = (P[e/x] \wedge Q[e/x])$ and $(\exists x. P)[e/y] = (\exists x. P[e/y])$ *if* $x \bowtie y$. However, this was a substantial overhead since we had to use the simplifier to execute substitutions. It also turned out to be unnecessary since we can directly harness Isabelle's internal λ-calculus-based substitution mechanisms.

Thus, the Shallow-Expressions library, instead of having deep abstract syntax, lifts expressions containing lenses (for example, assertions) to pure HOL expressions; for instance, $x + y$ becomes $\lambda\, s.\, get_x(s) + get_y(s)$ using Isabelle's syntax translation mechanism to perform the conversion. Nevertheless, as explained in Sect. 4.3, we can still execute substitutions and evaluate unrestriction conditions, so we retain the benefits of Oliveira's deep model. We also get a natural representation of ghost variables: they are simply the logical variables provided by HOL, as distinguished from program variables. Finally, with the shallow expressions, Isabelle/HOL also gives us direct access to *sledgehammer* and other proof facilities for reasoning about expressions. This gives us the proof scalability we need and brings us on par with different shallow embeddings.

Z Toolkit. To support *Circus* and related languages, we need the types, operators, and laws of Z [100]. This includes types like partial functions, finite functions, and partial surjections. Whilst the Isabelle/HOL standard library contains some of these, we preferred to develop our own to have greater control over the design decisions. Our Z_Toolkit library also includes support for code generation so that we can make some specifications executable. Moreover, we have recently worked with Makarius Wenzel (Isabelle's primary developer) to add the complete Z symbols into the Isabelle Unicode font and symbol library.

UTP. The modularisation leaves the main UTP library as a modest development, formalising predicates, relations, theories, and associated laws. This development continues, and we plan to have each UTP theory in a separate library.

A result of the modularisation is that we have been able to integrate our technology into collaborations that do not use UTP (at least knowingly). A recent development is an Isabelle-based verification tool for hybrid systems [48], which implements an extended version of Platzer's differential dynamic logic. This tool extensively uses the Shallow-Expressions library to support techniques like differential induction and differential ghosts. A result that we are pleased with is the inclusion of a separation-logic-style frame rule:

$$\frac{\{P\}\, C\, \{Q\} \qquad C\, \mathbf{nmods}\, A \qquad -A \,\sharp\, R}{\{P \wedge R\}\, C\, \{Q \wedge R\}}$$

Here, $C\, \mathbf{nmods}\, A$ is a semantic operator, like unrestriction, requiring that C does not modify any variables in A. We also need the frame invariant R to use no variables inside A. This requires constructing a lens's complement using an algebraic structure called a "scene", which is ongoing work (see Sect. 6). This being the case, we can add R as an invariant for a command C. This shows one of the real benefits of the UTP: to link concepts (separation logic and hybrid systems) from apparently very different areas of computer science.

4.8   Interaction Trees

Recently, we have mechanised Interaction Trees (ITrees) in Isabelle/UTP [47, 122]. These are coinductive structures that allow symbolic encoding of deterministic labelled transition systems. They can therefore support encoding and reasoning about operational semantics using coinductive techniques. Crucially, ITrees are executable, which allows us to take abstract models and programs, generate code for them, and finally animate them. Though ITrees can be infinite, languages like Haskell, which supports lazy evaluation, can evaluate them. Thus, we can use ITrees to animate deterministic *Circus* processes, for example. This is very valuable in software development since engineers can obtain prototypes.

Our ITrees library is built on the Shallow-Expressions and Z_Toolkit libraries. Integration with the rest of UTP is underway, allowing us to translate relational specifications into executable programs. Though ITrees are intrinsically deterministic, we can model nondeterminism with special events, enabling various strategies for resolving nondeterminism. We have applied this library in the development of a tool called Z_Machines, which supports system modelling in the style of Z and B, with both animation and verification support [121].

5 Other Contributions

We now consider two projects using *Circus* that did not involve our research group: the Xenon project and another theorem prover for *Circus*.

Freitas and McDermott used *Circus* in the Xenon project at the Naval Research Laboratory in Washington DC, USA. Xenon is a higher-assurance secure-separation hypervisor that allows a host computer to support multiple separated virtual machines that share memory and processing resources. Xenon is based on re-engineering the well-known Xen open-source hypervisor [70]. Xenon used formal specifications written in Z, CSP, and *Circus* [52,69] in security assurance. Freitas and McDermott modelled the fundamental definition of security, the hypercall interface behaviour, and the internal modular design. Security is based on noninterference expressed as a determinism property [70,93].

The Xenon Project is an industrial-scale application of *Circus*. The specification is 4,500 lines long: a substantial piece of mathematics. Some attractive technical advantages in modelling security properties in *Circus* arise from the combination of state and traces. Usually, proofs of noninterference require an unwinding theorem relating traces and states (see Goguen and Meseguer [54]). This is addressed in the definition of the *Circus* language. Xenon shows how *Circus* provides a powerful and natural way to describe state-rich and trace-rich concurrent behaviour in a single model amenable to refinement calculation.

Felliachi and colleagues developed machine-checked, formal semantics based on a shallow embedding of *Circus* in the Isabelle theorem prover [36]. They derive proof rules from the semantics and implement tactics for refinement of *Circus* processes involving data and behavioural aspects. Their proof environment supports syntax and semantics very close to our presentation of *Circus* in [82,83]. The theories are available in Isabelle's Archive of Formal Proofs [37].

Feliachi et al. used their mechanisation of *Circus* to provide a principled testing environment for concurrent systems [35]. They describe integrating formal testing in a proof environment as *theorem-prover based testing*, which takes advantage of the precise semantics of a specific specification language implemented in the theorem prover. They present a machine-checked formalisation of a testing theory. They experiment with this theory by testing an industrial case study: a message monitoring module. The component under test is embedded in 5k lines of Java code. It binds together various devices, including pacemaker controllers, using sophisticated data structures and operations, providing the primary source of complexity when testing. More details about this case study can be found in Feliachi's thesis [34] and in a technical report [33].

6 Quo Vadis *Circus*?

Work on *Circus* and Isabelle/UTP is ongoing and highly active. This section discusses current research and applications, and future directions (Sect. 6.1). We also include a brief industrial roadmap (Sect. 6.2) of outstanding work for transitioning *Circus* to a practical systems engineering and development setting.

6.1 Research Directions

Concerning extensions of *Circus*, we single out the hybrid state-rich process algebra called *CyPhyCircus* [41,48,77]. In addition to processes with states (like in *Circus*), a *CyPhyCircus* process can include continuous visible state components. As expected, its foundation is UTP. It is used in the RoboStar framework [20], which provides domain-specific notations for modelling robotics control-software design and simulations, physical platforms, and scenarios. A distinctive feature of RoboStar is that all these notations have formal semantics that is automatically generated and integrated via their common UTP foundations.

   CyPhyCircus has been used as a formal framework to give the semantics of RoboSim [20], capturing diagrammatic behavioural models for the platform and scenarios, and RoboWorld [21], a controlled natural language (CNL) used to record assumptions about the environment. The semantics of RoboSim diagrams and RoboWorld documents is a hybrid model due to the platform and environment's continuous nature, including quantities of interest such as velocity and temperature. From the semantics, it is possible, for instance, to generate tests or check whether the environment assumptions are satisfied by a simulation.

   As future work, the main challenges for *CyPhyCircus* as a hybrid process algebra concern automated reasoning. Notably, for the mechanised reasoning to scale, we need theorem-proving facilities. In this respect, we can benefit from the UTP theories and all the encoding already developed in Isabelle/UTP. We are currently developing bespoke automated proof methods to support verification of RoboSim models based on our hybrid verification tool [48]. To further improve automation, the plan is also to support model checking via translating *CyPhyCircus* models to hybrid automata accepted by model checkers [3].

   Another exciting research direction is our work on probability. One of its applications is also in the RoboStar context. More specifically, a probabilistic denotational semantics is defined in [109] for the RoboStar design notation, called RoboChart [71]. We base our work on the weakest completion semantics, which is, once more, based on UTP. The work relates standard semantics for a nondeterministic language with a probabilistic semantic domain via a forgetful function (from the latter to the former) and its converse for the other way around. The embedding using the converse of the forgetful function is proved to preserve the program structure. Finally, the probabilistic choice operator is defined.

In future work, we need to develop techniques for managing uncertainty. Several promising directions include partially observable Markov decision processes [61], dynamic epistemic logic [9], and the epistemic mu-calculus [98]. We will pursue a unifying theory that includes these and other approaches.

Many machine learning methods approximate a function between inputs and outputs. Reasoning about these approximate functions requires probabilistic techniques and presents many challenges. An outline of a probabilistic domain theory for robotics that includes learning components has been proposed by Thrun et al. [102]. We propose to formalise this theory.

A mechanised theory of quantum programming will provide a common framework for classical and quantum specifications, quantum program development, and analysis of program time and space complexity. Applications include quantum cryptographic protocols, where we must use distributed quantum programming with quantum channels. Hehner has established an initial basis for quantum programming in the UTP style [101]. We propose to continue this work.

Regarding work on Isabelle/UTP, current efforts focus on optimisation and modularisation (Sect. 4.7). More specifically, the Optics library defining the lenses (Sect. 4.3) contains several related algebraic structures (that is, symmetric lenses and prisms) and provides commands such as **alphabet** to create alphabet types and **chantype** to create channel types. In future, we will create additional commands to ease the creation of formal artifacts to support software engineering, in particular constructs from RoboChart and RoboSim.

We will also enrich this library with an axiomatic value model [124] that provides a convenient way to directly inject HOL types into a single given universe type to model state spaces without the need to instantiate them. We are considering a sound axiomatisation of higher-order UTP ([59, Chap. 9]) as well.

Our work with Interaction Trees has complemented the UTP relational hierarchy with operational semantic models that can be directly verified and executed. We are exploring using the Isabelle code generator to provide verified simulations and controller implementations in Haskell. Our Z-Machines tool [121] is under active development as a usable method for creating and verifying formal models, and we have a growing library of accompanying examples from [110].

Finally, our work on the Isabelle-based verification tool for hybrid systems discussed in Sect. 4.7 is a neat example of using UTP to link concepts from different computer science areas, separation logic and hybrid systems. Our main activity here is in development of case studies to validate the tool, and improve proof automation and scalability. In future, we will extend it to include concurrency primitives to support verification of multi-robotic systems such as swarms.

6.2   Industrial Roadmap

This section describes a roadmap to scale *Circus* adoption in industry. This is, in particular, finding ways to integrate *Circus* into modern workflows for model-driven development and model-based software engineering, including the underlying continuous integration, development, and verification pipelines. Our overarching aim is to make it easier for tool developers to harness the power of *Circus* and Isabelle/UTP. Future efforts may include the definition of a meta-model that can be integrated into common IDEs, such as the Eclipse framework, and plug-ins that encapsulate various checking and verification tasks on *Circus* models by outsourcing them to Isabelle/UTP.

A challenge we will have to face is to ease the learning curve for software engineers to understand, modify, write, and maintain *Circus* models as part of a model-based engineering workflow. AI-powered solutions such as CoPilot [30] are becoming more prevalent in supporting developers in producing models and code, from identifying issues to suggesting solutions based on natural-language queries and requirements. At the same time, projectional editors and low-code techniques may enable developers to produce design models before attaining deep and expert knowledge of the low-level modelling notation per se.

Moreover, many tools and IDEs for formal development and verification are now equipped with mechanisms for giving continuous feedback to the user to flag possible issues in models and code as soon as changes are made, automatically keeping verification conditions and proofs in sync with their models. Similar technology can be developed for *Circus* to facilitate system-level architectural engineering and code verification via a contract language that ties in nicely with commonly used platforms and implementation languages and technology.

We thus envisage an ecosystem of *Circus* tools that allow us to:

(1) **instantiate** *Circus* models based on common modelling patterns that are geared to particular application domains;
(2) seamlessly **interface** from IDEs such as Eclipse or Visual Studio Code with Isabelle/UTP to engineer, validate and refactor *Circus* models;
(3) support manual, semi-automatic, and automatic refinement through a bespoke **refinement editor** that makes system engineering via *Circus* amenable to software architects and industrial software developers;
(4) **trace** *Circus* models and their artefacts *up the refinement chain*: to informal or semiformal specifications, domain engineering, and product-line engineering models; and *down the refinement chain* to architectures written in UML/SysML or AADL, for instance, code-level contracts, and test cases;
(5) use a repository of verified **refinement patterns** that can be easily instantiated for particular modelling patterns and used to create a skeleton for implementation activities, including associated code-level contracts;
(6) integrated *Circus* models into static and run-time **testing** and **verification** activities and popular testing frameworks.

Regarding (1), we have already elicited many such modelling patterns as part of research targeting the application of *Circus* to several complementary application domains, including hybrid and control systems, robotics, and safety-critical concurrent and real-time implementations in Java and Ada.

Concerning (2), provers such as Isabelle already provide an API and protocols to communicate with external tools asynchronously. Still, high-level interfaces must be created on top of those low-level protocols to efficiently deal with changes to *Circus* models, and analyse their impact on proofs.

The aim of (3) is to disentangle the application of *Circus* refinement laws from a heavyweight proof framework. Once *Circus* refinement laws are proved in Isabelle/UTP, we may use a more bespoke and efficient tool to apply them and carry out large-scale refinements that may take advantage of a versatile tactic language and user-friendly GUI. Code generation in Isabelle enables us to potentially derive such a (critical) tool rigorously from proven laws.

Traceability (4) is essential when using model and proof artefacts of a *Circus*-based development as certification evidence in assurance cases. We hence require means to place *Circus* into the context of large-scale developments that often use a variety of complementary notations for requirements, architecture, design and HW/SW implementations, with clear traceability links to *Circus* models.

For (5), every modelling pattern should provide at least one refinement pattern and a collection of proved laws. Lastly, for (6), tying in with our work with Gaudel on a testing theory for *Circus* [22], we can leverage *Circus* to automate test-case generation and other testing activities.

The richness of the *Circus* language, and its UTP foundations, inherently opens several opportunities for combined verification solutions.

7   Conclusions

This paper reviewed two decades of our research on the stateful process algebra *Circus*, its UTP foundations, and the Isabelle/UTP theorem prover. Many colleagues and students have helped us to contribute to this agenda. We have published over 150 papers on UTP. This paper reviews only a fraction, and we will take future opportunities to complete the review of all our work.

One point to reflect on is why we have chosen Isabelle to mechanise UTP. The answer is mainly pragmatic. We want to be able to support scalable verification, and that means we want the best possible automation we can. This should not be at the expense of guaranteed soundness or fidelity, which is why we chose a foundational prover with strong support for automation.

Overall, an extensive body of research has already been carried out to (a) provide a firm semantic foundation for the *Circus* family of languages, (b) mechanise it in theorem provers, and (c) show, by way of examples and case studies drawn from both academic literature and the industrial realm, how *Circus* can be used to tackle the refinement-based development of safety-critical systems. Some current and future research directions have been discussed in the previous section, as well as an industrial roadmap to embody the techniques and tools we have developed for *Circus* into practical development environments.

Circus continues to attract interest from academia and industry. Its design is centred on the UTP principles. Jifeng's joint work with Tony has been the seed and the beautiful semantic infrastructure of our long-term research on *Circus*. We are confident that we will have much more to report in years to come.

Acknowledgements. We gratefully acknowledge all our UTP-based research collaborators, co-authors, and students. Thanks to all of you. This work has recently been funded by the UK EPSRC Grants EP/M025756/1, EP/R025479/1, EP/V026801/2, EP/S001190/1, and by the Royal Academy of Engineering Grant No CiET1718/45. Over the years, many other funding sources have been available to us, as detailed in the cited papers. Thank you.

References

1. Abrial, J.-R.: Steam-boiler control specification problem. In: Abrial, J.-R., Börger, E., Langmaack, H. (eds.) Formal Methods for Industrial Applications. LNCS, vol. 1165, pp. 500–509. Springer, Heidelberg (1996). https://doi.org/10.1007/BFb0027252
2. Abrial, J.-R., Börger, E., Langmaack, H. (eds.): Formal Methods for Industrial Applications: Specifying and Programming the Steam Boiler Control. LNCS, vol. 1165. Springer, Heidelberg (1996). https://doi.org/10.1007/BFb0027227
3. Althoff, M.: An introduction to CORA 2015. In: Frehse, G., Althoff, M. (eds.) 1st and 2nd International Workshop on Applied Verification for Continuous and Hybrid Systems. EPiC Series in Computing, vol. 34, pp. 120–151. EasyChair (2015)
4. Arthan, R.: ProofPower. Lemma 1 Ltd. (2017). https://www.lemma-one.com/ProofPower/index/
5. Atiya, D.M., King, S.: A compliance notation for verifying concurrent systems. In: Proceedings of the 24th International Conference on Software Engineering, ICSE 2002, pp. 731–732. Association for Computing Machinery (2002). https://doi.org/10.1145/581339.581475
6. Atiya, D.-A., King, S., Woodcock, J.C.P.: A *Circus* semantics for Ravenscar protected objects. In: Araki, K., Gnesi, S., Mandrioli, D. (eds.) FME 2003. LNCS, vol. 2805, pp. 617–635. Springer, Heidelberg (2003). https://doi.org/10.1007/978-3-540-45236-2_34
7. Back, R.J.R., Wright, J.: Refinement Calculus: A Systematic Introduction. Graduate Texts in Computer Science, Springer, New York (1998). https://doi.org/10.1007/978-1-4612-1674-2
8. Back, R., Kurki-Suonio, R.: Decentralization of process nets with centralized control. Distrib. Comput. **3**(2), 73–87 (1989). https://doi.org/10.1007/BF01558665
9. Baltag, A., Moss, L.S., Solecki, S.: The logic of public announcements and common knowledge and private suspicions. In: Gilboa, I. (ed.) Proceedings of the 7th Conference on Theoretical Aspects of Rationality and Knowledge (TARK-1998), Evanston, IL, USA, 22–24 July 1998, pp. 43–56. Morgan Kaufmann (1998)
10. Barnes, J.: Programming in ADA 95, 2nd edn. Addison-Wesley (1998)
11. Barrocas, S.L.M., Oliveira, M.V.M.: JCircus 2.0: an extension of an automatic translator from Circus to Java. In: Welch, P.H., Barnes, F.R.M., Chalmers, K., Pedersen, J.B., Sampson, A.T. (eds.) 34th Communicating Process Architectures, CPA 2012, Organised Under the Auspices of WoTUG, Dundee, Scotland, UK, 26 August 2012, pp. 15–36. Open Channel Publishing Ltd. (2012)

12. Bauer, J.C.: Specification for a software program for a boiler water content monitor and control system. Technical report, Institute of Risk Research, University of Waterloo (1993)
13. Behrmann, G., et al.: UPPAAL 4.0. In: 3rd International Conference on the Quantitative Evaluation of Systems, pp. 125–126. IEEE Computer Society (2006)
14. Burns, A., Dobbing, B., Romanski, G.: The Ravenscar tasking profile for high integrity real-time programs. In: Asplund, L. (ed.) Ada-Europe 1998. LNCS, vol. 1411, pp. 263–275. Springer, Heidelberg (1998). https://doi.org/10.1007/BFb0055011
15. Butterfield, A., Gancarski, P., Woodcock, J.C.P.: State visibility and communication in unifying theories of programming. In: Chin, W.N., Qin, S. (eds.) 3rd IEEE International Symposium on Theoretical Aspects of Software Engineering, pp. 47–54. IEEE Computer Society (2009)
16. Butterfield, A., Sherif, A., Woodcock, J.: Slotted-Circus. In: Davies, J., Gibbons, J. (eds.) IFM 2007. LNCS, vol. 4591, pp. 75–97. Springer, Heidelberg (2007). https://doi.org/10.1007/978-3-540-73210-5_5
17. Butterfield, A., Woodcock, J.: Semantic domains for Handel-C. In: Flynn, S., et al. (eds.) Second Irish Conference on the Mathematical Foundations of Computer Science and Information Technology, MFCSIT 2002. Electronic Notes in Theoretical Computer Science, Galway, Ireland, 18–19 July 2002, vol. 74, pp. 1–20. Elsevier (2002). https://doi.org/10.1016/S1571-0661(04)80762-X
18. Butterfield, A., Woodcock, J.: prialt in Handel-C: an operational semantics. Int. J. Softw. Tools Technol. Transf. **7**(3), 248–267 (2005). https://doi.org/10.1007/s10009-004-0181-6
19. Canham, S., Woodcock, J.: Three approaches to timed external choice in UTP. In: Naumann, D. (ed.) UTP 2014. LNCS, vol. 8963, pp. 1–20. Springer, Cham (2015). https://doi.org/10.1007/978-3-319-14806-9_1
20. Cavalcanti, A., et al.: RoboStar technology: a roboticist's toolbox for combined proof, simulation, and testing. In: Cavalcanti, A., Dongol, B., Hierons, R., Timmis, J., Woodcock, J. (eds.) Software Engineering for Robotics, pp. 249–293. Springer, Cham (2021). https://doi.org/10.1007/978-3-030-66494-7_9
21. Cavalcanti, A., Baxter, J., Carvalho, G.: RoboWorld: where can my robot work? In: Calinescu, R., Păsăreanu, C.S. (eds.) SEFM 2021. LNCS, vol. 13085, pp. 3–22. Springer, Cham (2021). https://doi.org/10.1007/978-3-030-92124-8_1
22. Cavalcanti, A.L.C., Gaudel, M.C.: Testing for refinement in *Circus*. Acta Informatica **48**(2), 97–147 (2011). https://doi.org/10.1007/s00236-011-0133-z
23. Cavalcanti, A.L.C., Sampaio, A.C.A., Woodcock, J.C.P.: A refinement strategy for *Circus*. Formal Aspects Comput. **15**(2–3), 146–181 (2003). https://doi.org/10.1007/s00165-003-0006-5
24. Cavalcanti, A., Woodcock, J.: A tutorial introduction to CSP in *Unifying Theories of Programming*. In: Cavalcanti, A., Sampaio, A., Woodcock, J. (eds.) PSSE 2004. LNCS, vol. 3167, pp. 220–268. Springer, Heidelberg (2006). https://doi.org/10.1007/11889229_6
25. Cavalcanti, A.L.C., Woodcock, J.C.P., Dunne, S.: Angelic nondeterminism in the unifying theories of programming. Formal Aspects Comput. **18**(3), 288–307 (2006). https://doi.org/10.1007/s00165-006-0001-8
26. Cavalcanti, A., Sampaio, A., Woodcock, J.: Refinement of actions in Circus. In: Derrick, J., Boiten, E.A., Woodcock, J., von Wright, J. (eds.) BCS FACS Refinement Workshop 2002, Refine 2002, Satellite Event of FLoC 2002. Electronic Notes in Theoretical Computer Science, Copenhagen, Denmark, 20–21 July 2002, vol.

70, pp. 132–162. Elsevier (2002). https://doi.org/10.1016/S1571-0661(05)80489-X

27. Cavalcanti, A., Sampaio, A., Woodcock, J.: A refinement strategy for Circus. Formal Aspects Comput. **15**(2–3), 146–181 (2003). https://doi.org/10.1007/s00165-003-0006-5

28. Cavalcanti, A., Woodcock, J.: ZRC – a refinement calculus for Z. Formal Aspects Comput. **10**(3), 267–289 (1998). https://doi.org/10.1007/s001650050016

29. Cavalcanti, A., Woodcock, J.: Predicate transformers in the semantics of Circus. IEE Proc. Softw. **150**(2), 85–94 (2003). https://doi.org/10.1049/ip-sen:20030131

30. Copilot: Your AI pair programmer. GitHub. https://copilot.github.com. Accessed 18 June 2023

31. Dijkstra, E.W.: A Discipline of Programming. Prentice Hall (1976). https://www.worldcat.org/oclc/019584451

32. Feliachi, A., Gaudel, M.-C., Wolff, B.: Unifying theories in Isabelle/HOL. In: Qin, S. (ed.) UTP 2010. LNCS, vol. 6445, pp. 188–206. Springer, Heidelberg (2010). https://doi.org/10.1007/978-3-642-16690-7_9

33. Feliachi, A., Gaudel, M.C., Wolff, B.: Exhaustive testing in HOL-Testgen/CirTa – a case study. Technical report 1562, LRI, July 2013

34. Feliachi, A.: Semantics-based testing for Circus. (Test basé sur la sémantique pour Circus). Ph.D. thesis, University of Paris-Sud, Orsay, France (2012). https://theses.hal.science/tel-00821836

35. Feliachi, A., Gaudel, M.-C., Wenzel, M., Wolff, B.: The *Circus* testing theory revisited in Isabelle/HOL. In: Groves, L., Sun, J. (eds.) ICFEM 2013. LNCS, vol. 8144, pp. 131–147. Springer, Heidelberg (2013). https://doi.org/10.1007/978-3-642-41202-8_10

36. Feliachi, A., Gaudel, M.-C., Wolff, B.: Isabelle/*Circus*: a process specification and verification environment. In: Joshi, R., Müller, P., Podelski, A. (eds.) VSTTE 2012. LNCS, vol. 7152, pp. 243–260. Springer, Heidelberg (2012). https://doi.org/10.1007/978-3-642-27705-4_20

37. Feliachi, A., Wolff, B., Gaudel, M.: Isabelle/Circus. Arch. Formal Proofs 2012 (2012). https://www.isa-afp.org/entries/Circus.shtml

38. Fischer, C.: How to combine Z with a process algebra. In: Bowen, J.P., Fett, A., Hinchey, M.G. (eds.) ZUM 1998. LNCS, vol. 1493, pp. 5–23. Springer, Heidelberg (1998). https://doi.org/10.1007/978-3-540-49676-2_2

39. Fischer, C., Wehrheim, H.: Failure-divergence semantics as a formal basis for an object-oriented integrated formal method. Bull. EATCS **71**, 92–101 (2000)

40. Foster, J.: Bidirectional programming languages. Ph.D. thesis, University of Pennsylvania (2009)

41. Foster, S.: Hybrid relations in Isabelle/UTP. In: Ribeiro, P., Sampaio, A. (eds.) UTP 2019. LNCS, vol. 11885, pp. 130–153. Springer, Cham (2019). https://doi.org/10.1007/978-3-030-31038-7_7

42. Foster, S., Cavalcanti, A.L.C., Canham, S., Woodcock, J.C.P., Zeyda, F.: Unifying theories of reactive design contracts. Theor. Comput. Sci. **802**, 105–140 (2020). https://doi.org/10.1016/j.tcs.2019.09.017

43. Foster, S., Cavalcanti, A.L.C., Woodcock, J.C.P., Zeyda, F.: Unifying theories of time with generalised reactive processes. Inf. Process. Lett. **135**, 47–52 (2018). https://doi.org/10.1016/j.ipl.2018.02.017

44. Foster, S., Ye, K., Cavalcanti, A.L.C., Woodcock, J.C.P.: Automated verification of reactive and concurrent programs by calculation. J. Log. Algebraic Methods Program. **121**, 100681 (2021). https://doi.org/10.1016/j.jlamp.2021.100681

45. Foster, S., Zeyda, F., Woodcock, J.: Isabelle/UTP: a mechanised theory engineering framework. In: Naumann, D. (ed.) UTP 2014. LNCS, vol. 8963, pp. 21–41. Springer, Cham (2015). https://doi.org/10.1007/978-3-319-14806-9_2

46. Foster, S., Baxter, J., Cavalcanti, A., Woodcock, J., Zeyda, F.: Unifying semantic foundations for automated verification tools in Isabelle/UTP. Sci. Comput. Program. **197**, 102510 (2020). https://doi.org/10.1016/j.scico.2020.102510

47. Foster, S., Hur, C., Woodcock, J.: Formally verified simulations of state-rich processes using interaction trees in Isabelle/HOL. In: Haddad, S., Varacca, D. (eds.) 32nd International Conference on Concurrency Theory, CONCUR 2021. LIPIcs, 24–27 August 2021, Virtual Conference, vol. 203, pp. 20:1–20:18. Schloss Dagstuhl - Leibniz-Zentrum für Informatik (2021). https://doi.org/10.4230/LIPIcs.CONCUR.2021.20

48. Foster, S., Huerta y Munive, J.J., Gleirscher, M., Struth, G.: Hybrid systems verification with Isabelle/HOL: simpler syntax, better models, faster proofs. In: Huisman, M., Păsăreanu, C., Zhan, N. (eds.) FM 2021. LNCS, vol. 13047, pp. 367–386. Springer, Cham (2021). https://doi.org/10.1007/978-3-030-90870-6_20

49. Foster, S., Zeyda, F., Woodcock, J.: Unifying heterogeneous state-spaces with lenses. In: Sampaio, A., Wang, F. (eds.) ICTAC 2016. LNCS, vol. 9965, pp. 295–314. Springer, Cham (2016). https://doi.org/10.1007/978-3-319-46750-4_17

50. Freitas, A., Cavalcanti, A.: Automatic translation from *Circus* to Java. In: Misra, J., Nipkow, T., Sekerinski, E. (eds.) FM 2006. LNCS, vol. 4085, pp. 115–130. Springer, Heidelberg (2006). https://doi.org/10.1007/11813040_9

51. Freitas, L.J.S.: Model checking *Circus*. Ph.D. thesis, University of York, Department of Computer Science (2006)

52. Freitas, L., McDermott, J.P.: Formal methods for security in the Xenon hypervisor. Int. J. Softw. Tools Technol. Transf. **13**(5), 463–489 (2011). https://doi.org/10.1007/s10009-011-0195-9

53. Gibson-Robinson, T., Armstrong, P.J., Boulgakov, A., Roscoe, A.W.: FDR3: a parallel refinement checker for CSP. Int. J. Softw. Tools Technol. Transf. **18**(2), 149–167 (2016). https://doi.org/10.1007/s10009-015-0377-y

54. Goguen, J.A., Meseguer, J.: Unwinding and inference control. In: Proceedings of the 1984 IEEE Symposium on Security and Privacy, Oakland, California, USA, 29 April–2 May 1984, pp. 75–87. IEEE Computer Society (1984). https://doi.org/10.1109/SP.1984.10019

55. Guttman, W., Möller, B.: Normal design algebra. J. Log. Algebraic Program. **79**(2), 144–173 (2010)

56. Harwood, W., Cavalcanti, A., Woodcock, J.: A theory of pointers for the UTP. In: Fitzgerald, J.S., Haxthausen, A.E., Yenigun, H. (eds.) ICTAC 2008. LNCS, vol. 5160, pp. 141–155. Springer, Heidelberg (2008). https://doi.org/10.1007/978-3-540-85762-4_10

57. Henkin, L., Monk, J., Tarski, A.: Cylindric Algebras, Part I. North-Holland (1971)

58. Hoare, C.A.R.: Communicating Sequential Processes. International Series in Computer Science. Prentice Hall (1985)

59. Hoare, C.A.R., He, J.: Unifying Theories of Programming. Series in Computer Science. Prentice Hall (1998)

60. Jones, G., Goldsmith, M.: Programming in OCCAM 2. International Series in Computer Science. Prentice Hall (1985)

61. Kaelbling, L.P., Littman, M.L., Cassandra, A.R.: Planning and acting in partially observable stochastic domains. Artif. Intell. **101**(1–2), 99–134 (1998). https://doi.org/10.1016/S0004-3702(98)00023-X

62. King, S., Sørensen, l.H., Woodcock, J.: Z, Grammar and Concrete and Abstract Syntaxes. Technical Monograph PRG-68. Oxford University Computing Laboratory, Programming Research Group (1988)
63. Liu, Z., Woodcock, J., Zhu, H. (eds.): ICTAC 2013. LNCS, vol. 8049. Springer, Heidelberg (2013). https://doi.org/10.1007/978-3-642-39718-9
64. Liu, Z., Woodcock, J., Zhu, H. (eds.): Theories of Programming and Formal Methods: Essays Dedicated to Jifeng He on the Occasion of His 70th Birthday. LNCS, vol. 8051. Springer, Heidelberg (2013). https://doi.org/10.1007/978-3-642-39698-4
65. Liu, Z., Woodcock, J., Zhu, H. (eds.): Unifying Theories of Programming and Formal Engineering Methods. LNCS, vol. 8050. Springer, Heidelberg (2013). https://doi.org/10.1007/978-3-642-39721-9
66. Locke, D., et al.: Safety-Critical Java Technology Specification, Public Draft. Java Community Process (2011)
67. Celoxica Ltd.: DK3: Handel-C Language Reference Manual (2002)
68. Lundqvist, K., Asplund, L., Michell, S.: A formal model of the Ada Ravenscar tasking profile; protected objects. In: González Harbour, M., de la Puente, J.A. (eds.) Ada-Europe 1999. LNCS, vol. 1622, pp. 12–25. Springer, Heidelberg (1999). https://doi.org/10.1007/3-540-48753-0_2
69. McDermott, J.P., Freitas, L.: Using formal methods for security in the Xenon project. In: Sheldon, F.T., Prowell, S.J., Abercrombie, R.K., Krings, A.W. (eds.) Proceedings of the 6th Cyber Security and Information Intelligence Research Workshop, CSIIRW 2010, Oak Ridge, TN, USA, 21–23 April 2010, p. 67. ACM (2010). https://doi.org/10.1145/1852666.1852742
70. McDermott, J.P., Kirby, J., Montrose, B.E., Johnson, T., Kang, M.H.: Re-engineering Xen internals for higher-assurance security. Inf. Secur. Tech. Rep. 13(1), 17–24 (2008). https://doi.org/10.1016/j.istr.2008.01.001
71. Miyazawa, A., Ribeiro, P., Li, W., Cavalcanti, A.L.C., Timmis, J., Woodcock, J.C.P.: RoboChart: modelling and verification of the functional behaviour of robotic applications. Softw. Syst. Model. 18(5), 3097–3149 (2019). https://doi.org/10.1007/s10270-018-00710-z
72. Miyazawa, A., Cavalcanti, A., Wellings, A.J.: SCJ-Circus: specification and refinement of safety-critical Java programs. Sci. Comput. Program. 181, 140–176 (2019). https://doi.org/10.1016/j.scico.2019.01.002
73. Morgan, C.: Data refinement by miracles. Inf. Process. Lett. 26(5), 243–246 (1988). https://doi.org/10.1016/0020-0190(88)90147-0
74. Morgan, C.: Of wp and CSP. In: Feijen, W.H.J., van Gasteren, A.J.M., Gries, D., Misra, J. (eds.) Beauty Is Our Business. MCS, pp. 319–326. Springer, New York (1990). https://doi.org/10.1007/978-1-4612-4476-9_37
75. Morgan, C.: Programming from Specifications. International Series in Computer Science, 2nd edn. Prentice Hall (1994)
76. Morris, J.M.: A theoretical basis for stepwise refinement and the programming calculus. Sci. Comput. Program. 9(3), 287–306 (1987). https://doi.org/10.1016/0167-6423(87)90011-6
77. Foster, S., Huerta y Munive, J.J., Struth, G.: Differential Hoare logics and refinement calculi for hybrid systems with Isabelle/HOL. In: Fahrenberg, U., Jipsen, P., Winter, M. (eds.) RAMiCS 2020. LNCS, vol. 12062, pp. 169–186. Springer, Cham (2020). https://doi.org/10.1007/978-3-030-43520-2_11
78. O'Halloran, C.: Identifying critical requirements. Technical report, Systems Assurance Group, QinetiQ Malvern (2002)

79. Oliveira, M.V.M.: Formal derivation of state-rich reactive programs using Circus. Ph.D. thesis, University of York, UK (2005). https://ethos.bl.uk/OrderDetails. do?uin=uk.bl.ethos.428459

80. Oliveira, M.V.M., Cavalcanti, A.L.C., Woodcock, J.C.P.: Refining industrial scale systems in *Circus*. In: East, I., Martin, J., Welch, P., Duce, D., Green, M. (eds.) Communicating Process Architectures. Concurrent Systems Engineering Series, vol. 62, pp. 281–309. IOS Press (2004)

81. Oliveira, M.V.M., Cavalcanti, A.L.C., Woodcock, J.C.P.: Formal development of industrial-scale systems in Circus. Innov. Syst. Softw. Eng. **1**(2), 125–146 (2005). https://doi.org/10.1007/s11334-005-0014-0

82. Oliveira, M.V.M., Cavalcanti, A.L.C., Woodcock, J.C.P.: A denotational semantics for Circus. In: Aichernig, B.K., Boiten, E.A., Derrick, J., Groves, L. (eds.) Proceedings of the 11th Refinement Workshop, Refine@ICFEM 2006. Electronic Notes in Theoretical Computer Science, Macao, 31 October 2006, vol. 187, pp. 107–123. Elsevier (2006). https://doi.org/10.1016/j.entcs.2006.08.047

83. Oliveira, M.V.M., Cavalcanti, A.L.C., Woodcock, J.C.P.: A UTP semantics for Circus. Formal Aspects Comput. **21**(1–2), 3–32 (2009). https://doi.org/10.1007/ s00165-007-0052-5

84. Oliveira, M.V.M., Cavalcanti, A.L.C., Woodcock, J.C.P.: Unifying theories in ProofPower-Z. Formal Aspects Comput. **25**(1), 133–158 (2013). https://doi.org/ 10.1007/s00165-007-0044-5

85. Ribeiro, P., Cavalcanti, A.L.C.: Designs with angelic nondeterminism. In: 7th International Symposium on Theoretical Aspects of Software Engineering, pp. 71–78. IEEE (2013). https://doi.org/10.1109/TASE.2013.18

86. Ribeiro, P., Cavalcanti, A.: Angelicism in the theory of reactive processes. In: Naumann, D. (ed.) UTP 2014. LNCS, vol. 8963, pp. 42–61. Springer, Cham (2015). https://doi.org/10.1007/978-3-319-14806-9_3

87. Ribeiro, P., Cavalcanti, A.L.C.: Angelic processes for CSP via the UTP. Theor. Comput. Sci. **756**, 19–63 (2019). https://doi.org/10.1016/j.tcs.2018.10.008

88. Ribeiro, P.: A unary semigroup trace algebra. In: Fahrenberg, U., Jipsen, P., Winter, M. (eds.) RAMiCS 2020. LNCS, vol. 12062, pp. 270–285. Springer, Cham (2020). https://doi.org/10.1007/978-3-030-43520-2_17

89. Roscoe, A.W.: Denotational semantics for occam. In: Brookes, S.D., Roscoe, A.W., Winskel, G. (eds.) CONCURRENCY 1984. LNCS, vol. 197, pp. 306–329. Springer, Heidelberg (1985). https://doi.org/10.1007/3-540-15670-4_15

90. Roscoe, A.W.: The Theory and Practice of Concurrency. Series in Computer Science. Prentice Hall (1997)

91. Roscoe, A.W.: Understanding Concurrent Systems. Texts in Computer Science, Springer, London (2010). https://doi.org/10.1007/978-1-84882-258-0

92. Roscoe, A.W., Hoare, C.A.R.: The laws of OCCAM programming. Theor. Comput. Sci. **60**, 177–229 (1988). https://doi.org/10.1016/0304-3975(88)90049-7

93. Roscoe, A.W., Woodcock, J.C.P., Wulf, L.: Non-interference through determinism. In: Gollmann, D. (ed.) ESORICS 1994. LNCS, vol. 875, pp. 31–53. Springer, Heidelberg (1994). https://doi.org/10.1007/3-540-58618-0_55

94. Sampaio, A., Woodcock, J., Cavalcanti, A.: Refinement in *Circus*. In: Eriksson, L.-H., Lindsay, P.A. (eds.) FME 2002. LNCS, vol. 2391, pp. 451–470. Springer, Heidelberg (2002). https://doi.org/10.1007/3-540-45614-7_26

95. Schneider, S.A., Treharne, H.: CSP theorems for communicating B machines. Formal Aspects Comput. **17**(4), 390–422 (2005). https://doi.org/10.1007/s00165-005-0076-7

96. Sherif, A., Jifeng, H.: Towards a time model for *Circus*. In: George, C., Miao, H. (eds.) ICFEM 2002. LNCS, vol. 2495, pp. 613–624. Springer, Heidelberg (2002). https://doi.org/10.1007/3-540-36103-0_62

97. Sherif, A., Jifeng, H., Cavalcanti, A., Sampaio, A.: A framework for specification and validation of real-time systems using *Circus* actions. In: Liu, Z., Araki, K. (eds.) ICTAC 2004. LNCS, vol. 3407, pp. 478–493. Springer, Heidelberg (2005). https://doi.org/10.1007/978-3-540-31862-0_34

98. Shilov, N.V., Garanina, N.O.: Combining knowledge and fixpoints. Technical report preprint 98, A.P. Ershov Institute of Informatics Systems, Novosibirsk (2002). https://www.iis.nsk.su/files/preprints/098.pdf

99. Smith, G.: A semantic integration of object-Z and CSP for the specification of concurrent systems. In: Fitzgerald, J., Jones, C.B., Lucas, P. (eds.) FME 1997. LNCS, vol. 1313, pp. 62–81. Springer, Heidelberg (1997). https://doi.org/10.1007/3-540-63533-5_4

100. Spivey, J.M.: Z Notation – A Reference Manual. International Series in Computer Science, 2nd edn. Prentice Hall (1992)

101. Tafliovich, A., Hehner, E.C.R.: Quantum predicative programming. In: Uustalu, T. (ed.) MPC 2006. LNCS, vol. 4014, pp. 433–454. Springer, Heidelberg (2006). https://doi.org/10.1007/11783596_25

102. Thrun, S., Burgard, W., Fox, D.: Probabilistic Robotics. Intelligent Robotics and Autonomous Agents. MIT Press, Cambridge (2005)

103. Wei, K., Woodcock, J., Burns, A.: A timed model of Circus with the reactive design miracle. In: Fiadeiro, J.L., Gnesi, S., Maggiolo-Schettini, A. (eds.) 8th IEEE International Conference on Software Engineering and Formal Methods, SEFM 2010, Pisa, Italy, 13–18 September 2010, pp. 315–319. IEEE Computer Society (2010). https://doi.org/10.1109/SEFM.2010.40

104. Wei, K., Woodcock, J., Burns, A.: Timed Circus: timed CSP with the miracle. In: Perseil, I., Breitman, K.K., Sterritt, R. (eds.) 16th IEEE International Conference on Engineering of Complex Computer Systems, ICECCS 2011, Las Vegas, Nevada, USA, 27–29 April 2011, pp. 55–64. IEEE Computer Society (2011). https://doi.org/10.1109/ICECCS.2011.13

105. Welch, P.: Process oriented design for Java: concurrency for all. In: Sloot, P.M.A., Hoekstra, A.G., Tan, C.J.K., Dongarra, J.J. (eds.) ICCS 2002. LNCS, vol. 2330, pp. 687–687. Springer, Heidelberg (2002). https://doi.org/10.1007/3-540-46080-2_72

106. Welch, P.H., Aldous, J.R., Foster, J.: CSP networking for Java *(JCSP.net)*. In: Sloot, P.M.A., Hoekstra, A.G., Tan, C.J.K., Dongarra, J.J. (eds.) ICCS 2002. LNCS, vol. 2330, pp. 695–708. Springer, Heidelberg (2002). https://doi.org/10.1007/3-540-46080-2_74

107. Woodcock, J.C.P.: Properties of Z specifications. ACM SIGSOFT Softw. Eng. Notes **14**(5), 43–54 (1989). https://doi.org/10.1145/71633.71634

108. Woodcock, J.C.P., Cavalcanti, A.L.C.: Circus: a concurrent refinement language. Technical report, Oxford University Computing Laboratory (2001)

109. Woodcock, J., Cavalcanti, A., Foster, S., Mota, A., Ye, K.: Probabilistic semantics for RoboChart. In: Ribeiro, P., Sampaio, A. (eds.) UTP 2019. LNCS, vol. 11885, pp. 80–105. Springer, Cham (2019). https://doi.org/10.1007/978-3-030-31038-7_5

110. Woodcock, J.C.P., Davies, J.: Using Z - Specification, Refinement, and Proof. International Series in Computer Science. Prentice Hall (1996)

111. Woodcock, J.: Using Circus for safety-critical applications. In: Cavalcanti, A., Machado, P.D.L. (eds.) Proceedings of the 6th Brazilian Workshop on Formal Methods, WMF 2003. Electronic Notes in Theoretical Computer Science, Campina Grande, Brazil, 12–14 October 2003, vol. 95, pp. 3–22. Elsevier (2003). https://doi.org/10.1016/j.entcs.2004.04.003

112. Woodcock, J.: The miracle of reactive programming. In: Butterfield, A. (ed.) UTP 2008. LNCS, vol. 5713, pp. 202–217. Springer, Heidelberg (2010). https://doi.org/10.1007/978-3-642-14521-6_12

113. Woodcock, J.: Hoare and He's unifying theories of programming. In: Jones, C.B., Misra, J. (eds.) Theories of Programming: The Life and Works of Tony Hoare, pp. 285–316. ACM/Morgan & Claypool (2021). https://doi.org/10.1145/3477355.3477369

114. Woodcock, J., Cavalcanti, A.: A concurrent language for refinement. In: Butterfield, A., Strong, G., Pahl, C. (eds.) 5th Irish Workshop on Formal Methods, IWFM 2001, Dublin, Ireland, 16–17 July 2001. Workshops in Computing, BCS (2001). https://doi.org/10.14236/ewic/IWFM2001.7

115. Woodcock, J., Cavalcanti, A.: The steam boiler in a unified theory of Z and CSP. In: 8th Asia-Pacific Software Engineering Conference (APSEC 2001), Macau, China, 4–7 December 2001, pp. 291–298. IEEE Computer Society (2001). https://doi.org/10.1109/APSEC.2001.991490

116. Woodcock, J., Cavalcanti, A.: The semantics of *Circus*. In: Bert, D., Bowen, J.P., Henson, M.C., Robinson, K. (eds.) ZB 2002. LNCS, vol. 2272, pp. 184–203. Springer, Heidelberg (2002). https://doi.org/10.1007/3-540-45648-1_10

117. Woodcock, J., Cavalcanti, A.: A tutorial introduction to designs in unifying theories of programming. In: Boiten, E.A., Derrick, J., Smith, G. (eds.) IFM 2004. LNCS, vol. 2999, pp. 40–66. Springer, Heidelberg (2004). https://doi.org/10.1007/978-3-540-24756-2_4

118. Woodcock, J., Cavalcanti, A., Freitas, L.: Operational semantics for model checking Circus. In: Fitzgerald, J., Hayes, I.J., Tarlecki, A. (eds.) FM 2005. LNCS, vol. 3582, pp. 237–252. Springer, Heidelberg (2005). https://doi.org/10.1007/11526841_17

119. Woodcock, J., Davies, J., Bolton, C.: Abstract data types and processes. In: Roscoe, A.W., Davies, J., Woodcock, J. (eds.) Proceedings of the 1999 Oxford-Microsoft Symposium in Honour of Sir Tony Hoare. Millennial Perspectives in Computer Science, pp. 391–405. Palgrave (2000)

120. Woodcock, J.C.P., Morgan, C.: Refinement of state-based concurrent systems. In: Bjørner, D., Hoare, C.A.R., Langmaack, H. (eds.) VDM 1990. LNCS, vol. 428, pp. 340–351. Springer, Heidelberg (1990). https://doi.org/10.1007/3-540-52513-0_18

121. Yan, F., Foster, S., Habli, I.: Automated compositional verification for robotic state machines using Isabelle/HOL. In: 27th International Conference on Engineering of Complex Computer Systems (ICECCS). IEEE (2023)

122. Ye, K., Foster, S., Woodcock, J.: Formally verified animation for RoboChart using interaction trees. In: Riesco, A., Zhang, M. (eds.) ICFEM 2022. LNCS, vol. 13478, pp. 404–420. Springer, Cham (2022). https://doi.org/10.1007/978-3-031-17244-1_24

123. Zeyda, F., Cavalcanti, A.L.C.: *Circus* model for the SCJ framework. Technical report, University of York, Department of Computer Science, York, UK (2012)

124. Zeyda, F., Foster, S., Freitas, L.: An axiomatic value model for Isabelle/UTP. In: Bowen, J.P., Zhu, H. (eds.) UTP 2016. LNCS, vol. 10134, pp. 155–175. Springer, Cham (2017). https://doi.org/10.1007/978-3-319-52228-9_8

Linking Formal Methods in Software Development
A Reflection on the Development of rCOS

Zhiming Liu[✉]🆔

School of Computer and Information Science, Southwest University,
Chongqing, China
zhimingliu88@swu.edu.cn

Abstract. The method of *refinement of object-oriented and component-based systems* (rCOS) has been developed based on the Unifying Theories of Programming (UTP) of Tony Hoare and Jifeng He. It is influenced by the doctrine of institutions, espoused by Joseph Goguen and Rod Burstall, for linking specification languages and verification techniques to support model-driven development of software systems. The research on rCOS has produced a body of knowledge and techniques, including the formal use of the Unified Modelling Language (UML), a theory of semantics and refinement of object-oriented programs, a theory of semantics and refinement of the component-based architecture of software systems, and prototypes of model-driven tools. These have been published in a number of papers and embodied in several lecture notes taught at many classes and training schools. In this Festschrift paper, I reflect on the research in the development of rCOS by giving a summary of the results with discussions on the fundamental ideas, the way it has been developed, its current status, and where it may take us in the future.

Keywords: UTP · institutions · rCOS · architecture modelling · Human-Cyber-Physical Systems

1 Introduction

I worked with Professor Jifeng He from 2001 to 2005 at the United Nations University International Institute for Software Technology (UNU-IIST, Macao). Our close collaboration started before that in 1998 and continued afterwards until 2007. Through those years and thereafter, Professor He has been a friend and mentor of mine. My research has developed under his inspiration and influence. The main outcome of the collaboration is the rCOS method for model-driven development of object and component systems.

Supported by the Chinese National NSF grant (No. 62032019) and the Southwest University Research Development grant (No. SWU116007).

J. P. Bowen et al. (Eds.): *Theories of Programming and Formal Methods*, LNCS 14080, pp. 52–84, 2023.
https://doi.org/10.1007/978-3-031-40436-8_3

In this Festschrift paper, I give a reflection on the development of the rCOS method to pay tributes to Jifeng's original contributions. I do this by providing a summary of the philosophical ideas, theory, methods and techniques embodied in rCOS. I also discuss how these can be related to practical software development. To this end, I first give a brief introduction to the areas where the contributions in rCOS are relevant.

Software Engineering: Software engineering has been developed from the studies and practices of writing *closed sequential programs*, through producing *software products*, to designing and implementing *software systems* (as products too), as described in the talk of Fred Brooks at ICSE 2018 [5]. In this process of advances, together with the advances in hardware and network technologies, the complexity of software development has been increasing in multiple dimensions, along with the increase in the size of applications and the complexity of requirements. As Brooks described in his talk, programming was mainly an activity where someone wrote programs used by themselves, and thus only required ad hoc testing and debugging; producing programs as products requires more work in documentation, more thorough and systematic testing, and quality assurance; designing and producing software systems requires even more work on the understanding of *interfaces*, analysis, verification, debugging and maintenance.

Theories, techniques, and tools have been developed and are still being developed for software development to support the mastering of the increasing complexity and requirements, and they are core constituents of software engineering as a system engineering discipline. The ever-growing complexities of systems and applications, as well as the theories, techniques, and tools, are reflected in the development of the software industry, as Brian Randell, who is another software engineering pioneer, described in his talk at ICSE 2018 [62], though gaps still exist.

Modelling: Modelling is essentially important and effective in all scientific and engineering disciplines. Let us take the view from Lee [33] that *"modelling is the trinity of the model, the thing being modelled and the modelling paradigm"*. Here the *modelling paradigm* refers to the underlying theory, techniques and tools for *analysis, simulation* and *verification* of properties of and relations between models. The "thing", either logical or physical, is either an engineering product or a system which is either pre-existing or to be constructed. In the former case, the models of the things are built for scientific study and analysis of the things that have expected or conjectured properties and relations through verification, simulation, and experiments. In the latter case, the models, properties, and relations serve as the *requirements specification* for the engineering product or system, and the correctness of the product and models are verified through logical reasoning, model-checking testing, and simulation.

It is important to note that a "thing" to be modelled usually has a well-defined structure, such that the thing is a composition of some constituent "things", and the structure is often hierarchical. Therefore, models are also *hierarchical* and, therefore, the modelling paradigm needs to support operations for *model compositions*. This is especially true in modelling engineering systems. A modelling paradigm which supports hierarchical model compositions is known as *compositional modelling* and *components-based modelling*. However, the latter notional emphasis on compositions of *heterogeneous models* involving heterogeneous things requires the linking of different modelling (sub-)paradigms. The notion of *interface contracts* [22,40,65] plays an important role in heterogeneous component-based modelling.

A model is not the "thing" that the model represents. It is an abstraction of the thing instead, from a particular viewpoint of the modeller based on their interest in the problem that they are solving. Therefore, in general, a whole model of a thing is an integration of models representing the different viewpoints of different modellers and/or at different times. A paradigm supporting integration of models of different viewpoints is known as a *multi-view modelling paradigm*.

In an engineering process, models of different levels of abstraction are usually needed for, say, analysis and validation of requirements, verification of designs in different phases, and verification and testing of implementations. The modelling paradigm must support establishing the correct relation between models of different levels of abstraction. The relation is generally defined by the notion of *refinement*, meaning that all properties of a higher-level model are preserved by a lower-level model. Rules, techniques, and algorithms are required in a modelling paradigm to support manipulations of models for building models at one level from models at other levels. These manipulations are called *model transformations* in *model-driven development* [35,41,59]. Paradigms with features including multi-view, compositional, and component-based modelling, and model refinement and abstraction, are important in the provision of systematic support for the engineering principles of *separation of concerns*, *divide and conquer*, and *reuse*. The rCOS method has been developed to reflect these features.

Formal Methods: The term *formal methods* refers to, in computer science and engineering, mathematically rigorous techniques and tools for the specification, design, and verification of software and hardware systems [6,73]. A formal method is essentially a modelling paradigm as defined in the paragraph immediately above. However, a formal method directly employs *formal logic systems* consisting of a *formal language*, a *proof system* and a *formal semantics* of the languages, together with the *meta-theory* of the formal logic system [72]. The meta-theory includes *expressiveness, soundness, completeness* and *decidability* of the logic system. The reasons why a formal method particularly needs a formal language include that programming languages, which the method treats, are formal, and syntactic guided inductive techniques are effective and computer-aided tools are essential which only take formal languages as inputs. Modelling paradigms in traditional scientific and engineering disciplines directly use mathematical language. This avoids the need for a separate semantic theory. A formal language in general is defined by a (usually finite) set of symbols, called the *alphabet* or the *signature*, and a set of rules, called *syntactic rules*, for forming grammatically *correct sentences*, also called *well-formed formulas* or *statements*.

Another important feature of formal methods is their applications in the specification, design, and verification of software systems, hardware systems, and systems with both software and hardware. In the life cycle of such a system, a number of formal methods are needed. There are a large number of formal methods [72] addressing different design concerns that model various viewpoints at different levels of abstraction. The use of multiple formal methods gives rise to the challenge of ensuring that they are used consistently. In fact, there is even not yet a commonly agreed notion of such consistency. This challenge is tackled using two approaches. One is through *linking* different formal methods in an *institution* and formal methods from different institutions [18]. This approach is based on *category theory*. The pioneering work on this approach is the *theory of institutions* [18]. The other approach is *unifying* different semantic theories of the languages used in formal methods. The most influential and well-studied work is *Unifying Theories of Programming* (UTP) [27] by Tony Hoare and Jifeng He.

The *Unified Modeling Language* (UML) proposed a framework for defining a collection of modelling languages that can be used in project development. However, there is little work on the relations of semantic models of the UML notations. The rCOS method is based on UTP, influenced by the theory of institutions, and it started with addressing the problem of formal and consistent use of UML notations.

This paper presents a reflection on the rCOS method, with discussions about its origins, where it contributes, and its possible further development. Through the discussion, where and how different formal methods are linked are shown based on the problems they address and their uses in various cycles of systems development. The organisation of the paper is as follows. Section 2 gives a unified overview of formal methods; Sect. 3 reflects on the ideas and development of the rCOS methods, including the formal use of UML, the semantics and refinement of objective-oriented (OO) systems that are effective, and the modelling of component-based architecture; Sect. 4 outlines some ideas on extending rCOS to modelling human-cyber-physical systems (HCPS); and Sect. 5 gives some concluding remarks and acknowledgements.

2 A Unified Overview of Formal Methods

Modern theories of computation and programming are developed from the computational models of λ-*calculus*, *recursive functions*, and *Turing machines*. Each of them can be seen as an extension to the formal logic system of arithmetic. These have provided the foundation for the design and implementation of programming languages, the design of programs, and the analysis of programs through logical reasoning about and decision algorithms for checking properties (i.e., model checking) of their executions. All programming languages so far are defined with formal syntax, as in formal logic systems, but they are usually implemented based on informal semantics. For rigorous reasoning and verification of programs, their *formal semantics* must be defined.

2.1 Semantic Theories

There are mainly three kinds of semantics theories, *operational semantics*, *denotational semantics*, and *axiomatic semantics*.

Operational Semantics: An operational formal semantics of a programming language is defined as a deduction system that the *execution configurations* must follow, which is similar to the deductions in λ-*calculus*. Such an operational semantics is also called a *term-rewriting semantics* [80]. The deduction system of operational semantics can also be defined by abstract state machines, similar to Turing machines, called *abstract machines* [56]. More abstract and more structured, thus generally used operational semantics are defined as a model of abstract machines, called *labelled transition systems* [61].

Denotational Semantics: The operational semantics of a programming language is regarded to be too close to particular implementations of the language. In other words, operational semantics expresses too many details of the execution of a program, and thus it is difficult to be used for abstract requirements specification and verification. Semantic theorists believe that the semantics of a programming language should be independent of its implementation to allow more implementations.

The denotational semantics employs the approach to defining an *interpretation* of the formal language of a logic system in a mathematical structure, called the *domain* of the interpretation [51]. In this approach, the meanings of the syntactic elements of a language are defined by mapping them to objects, called the *denotations* of the syntactic elements, in the domain.

For example, the alphabet of a formal language of a logic system or a programming language usually includes symbols representing variables, constants, functions and relations. The atomic sentences or statements, operators on sentences, etc., are defined using these symbols by syntactic rules. The denotations of constant symbols are given as elements of the denotational domain; the denotations of variables are given as *assignment functions* from the set of variables to the elements (called *values*) in the domain; the denotation of a sentence is given as a relation among elements in the domain, and the denotations of the operators on sentences are defined as operations on relations, inductively following the syntactic rules. The basics of the semantics of logic systems can be found in any book on mathematical logic, and the fundamental theory for denotational semantics of programming languages is the *Scott-Strachey domain theory* [17,67]. In our recent book [51], a unified view is presented on mathematical logic and the logic of programs.

Axiomatic Semantics: Axiomatic semantics defines the meaning of programs as formulas of a formal logic system, which is an extension to an existing formal logic system, such as first-order arithmetic. The semantics of an atomic sentence is defined as an axiom (scheme), and the semantics of a language operator is defined by an inference rule so that the semantics of a composite sentence can be inferred from the semantics of the atomic sentences. The properties of programs can then be reasoned about in the logic system. The pioneering work on axiomatic semantics is *Floyd-Hoare logic* [15,25], while Hoare Logic is the most well-studied and used axiomatic semantics.

Relations Between the Different Semantic Theories: Applying the approach of the semantic theory of formal logic systems to the development of denotational semantics of programming languages directly puts specification and analysis of program properties into the framework of formal logic systems, theorem proving and verification (including testing and model checking).

The correctness of the denotational semantics is usually justified based on operational semantics through an abstraction mapping from the operational semantics of sentences to their denotation, e.g., functions and relations on program states. A formal logic system which defines the axiomatic semantics of a programming language can be interpreted in its denotational semantics and operational semantics. This, together with the justification of denotational semantics based on operational semantics indicates the relation between the three approaches of semantics.

It is not difficult to understand that the semantics $[\![P]\!]$ of a program P is the set consisting the predicate pairs (p, q) such that $\{p\}P\{q\}$ holds in Hoare logic, i.e.:

$$[\![P]\!] = \{[p, q] \mid \{p\}P\{q\} \text{ is a theorem of Hoare logic}\}$$

This is then a denotational semantic view of axiomatic semantics. With this view, a pair $[p_0, q_0]$ of predicate formulas can be used as a requirements specification for the development of a program P such that $\{p_0\}P\{q_0\}$ is a theorem of Hoare logic. According to the *consequence rule* of Hoare logic, any program in the following set is correct with respect to the specification $[p_0, q_0]$ (or $\{p_0\}P\{q_0\}$ in Hoare logic):

$$\mathcal{P}([p_0, q_0]) = \{P \mid \{p\}P\{q\} \text{ and } (p_0 \rightarrow p) \wedge (q \rightarrow q_0)$$
$$\text{are theorems of Hoare logic}\}$$

This is the foundation of *programming from specifications* presented in [58].

Hoare and He's UTP presents a comprehensive theory which allows a program of different paradigms to be defined uniformly by a pair of first-order formulas, called the *pre-* and *post-conditions*, as its semantics. Here, the programs can be of "any" kind, concurrent and real-time programs as well as sequential programs. Further on, it is shown in the work of rCOS that a theory of semantics and refinement of object-oriented programs [10,24,78] and a theory of contract-based semantics and refinement [7,10,22,23] of component programming [70] are also established in this way.

2.2   Linking Formal Methods for Their Consistent Use

Formal methods in the early years were used to adopt formal logic (including Hoare logic) as the specification languages, interpreted in semantic models of programs, for formulating properties of programs. Reasoning and algorithm-based verification are carried out in the corresponding logic systems. Along with the increasing complexity of systems and dimensions of requirements, large numbers of abstract specification and modelling languages have been developed, and so are theories of their semantics. These together with the techniques and tools for reasoning and verification constitute a large number of formal methods. Included in the *Formal methods* Wikipedia page (as of 31 March 2023), there are about 30 specification languages, together with more than a dozen model-checking tools, which all need specification languages. These do not include the many modelling languages, e.g., model-driven and component-based modelling languages, languages for modelling embedded systems, etc.

Different specification (or modelling) languages are proposed for describing abstractions of different concerns and from different viewpoints of software developers. We can roughly classify the different languages based on the aspects of concerns and viewpoints.

Event-Based Methods: The representatives of this kind include automata-based models (e.g., I/O automata) [55], CSP [26,63] and CCS [57], and those alike [4]. Operational semantics are defined for these languages, and different theories of denotational semantics also exist, such as the models of *traces*, *failures*, or *divergences* [63]. Based on these theories, techniques of algebraic reasoning through the relations of *simulation* [57] and *refinement* [63] are developed. Models described with these languages abstract the internal computation away and describe the behaviour of interactions and concurrency among different components.

Data State-Based Methods: One class of state-based formal methods is associated with operational semantics. Well-known methods of this kind include *action systems* [3], the *B-Method* [1,66], *Alloy* [28], and *TLA+* [30,31]. Another class of state-based specification languages have denotational semantics and axiomatic semantics in Hoare logic. Examples of these formal methods include *VDM* [29] and the *Z notation* [69].

Combination of Event-Based and State-Based Methods: Throughout the cycles of software development, formal methods for sequential programming and for concurrent and communicating programs are involved, and both event-based and state-based methods are needed. Especially in an event-based model, before the occurrence of an event is the *internal execution* of an *atomic action* which is implemented by a piece of the program. The functional correctness of these atomic actions is specified and verified at a refined level of abstraction. However, there are formal approaches that unify event-based and state-based modelling and verification: value-passing CCS and CSP (in which the combination is limited), the Occam programming language (developed based on CSP) [64], and Event-B [2], for example.

General Unification of Formal Methods: In addition to the need for consistent use of multiple formal methods in system development, new language abstractions are required for systems with more functional and performance requirements, such as spacial and timing requirements and energy constraints, and concurrency between discrete digital systems and continuous physical systems as well as intelligent system (both artificial and human) in the emerging human-cyber-physical system (HCPS) [52,76]. We believe that, instead of defining a new comprehensive specification language and its semantic models from scratch, a method is desirable for extending and linking existing languages and their semantic models.

The theory of institutions of Goguen and Burstall and the theory and UTP of Hoare and He provide the theoretical basis and insight for this purpose. The former provides a theory and a method for linking different specification languages, models of sentences written in the languages, theories and proofs consistently; and the latter is a framework for defining new semantic models from existing ones. We present a very brief introduction to these two theories just to show the basic idea with some formalities. The reason is that I have found that the philosophical ideas of these two theories are not widely understood, by young researchers in particular. The purpose is to show their differences and relations (intuitively) and to propose a research topic on the study of the relationship between the two approaches.

2.3   Institutions

The theory of institutions is based on category theory. A *category* $\mathbf{C}$ is formed of two sorts of elements $ob(\mathbf{C})$ and $hom(\mathbf{C})$ which are respectively called *objects* and *morphisms*, such that:

- each morphism $m \in hom(\mathbf{C})$ has a *source* $a \in ob(\mathbf{C})$ and a *target* $b \in ob(\mathbf{C})$, the morphism is denoted as $m : a \to b$ and m is called a morphism or an *arrow* from a to b and $hom(a, b)$ denotes the set of arrows from a to b;
- a binary operation $\cdot$ on $hom(\mathbf{C})$, called *composition*, such that $m_2 \cdot m_1$ is defined for $m_1 \in hom(a, b)$ and $m_2 \in hom(c, d)$ if and only if $b = c$, and $m_2 \cdot m_1 \in hom(a, d)$;
- the operation $\cdot$ has the following two properties:
  - it is associative that if $(m_1 \cdot m_2)$ and $(m_1 \cdot m_2) \cdot m_3$ are defined, so are $m_1 \cdot (m_2 \cdot m_3)$ and it equals to $(m_1 \cdot m_2) \cdot m_3$;
  - for each object $o \in ob(\mathbf{C})$, there is an *identity morphism* $1_o : o \to o$ such that for any morphism $m : a \to b$, $1_b \cdot m = m = m \cdot 1_a$

It is easy to see that for any category $\mathbf{C}$, there is an *opposite category* $\mathbf{C}^{op}$ such that $ob(\mathbf{C}^{op}) = ob(\mathbf{C})$, and $hom(\mathbf{C}^{op}) = \{m^r : b \to a \mid m : a \to b \in hom(\mathbf{C})\}$. Another simple and important example of category is the *category of sets*, denoted as $\mathbf{Set}$ such that the objects of $\mathbf{Set}$ are sets and the set of morphisms $hom(S_1, S_2)$ are the total functions from S_1 to S_2.

Another important concept in category theory is the notion of *functors*. A functor F from a category $\mathbf{C}_1$ to category $\mathbf{C}_2$ consists of two mappings (F_o, F_m) where $F_o : ob(\mathbf{C}_1) \to ob(\mathbf{C}_2)$ is a mapping from the objects of $\mathbf{C}_1$ to those of $\mathbf{C}_2$, and $F_m : hom(\mathbf{C}_1) \to hom(\mathbf{C}_2)$ is a mapping from the morphisms of $\mathbf{C}_1$ to those of $\mathbf{C}_2$ such that for each morphism $m : a \to b$ of $\mathbf{C}_1$, $F_h(m)$ is a morphism from $F_o(a)$ to $F_o(b)$.

A category is called a **small category** if every of its object is a set, not a "proper class". Taking all small categories as the objects and the functors between the small categories as the morphisms, it forms a category, called *the category of small categories*, and it is denoted by $\mathbf{Cat}$.

Now recall that a specification language is defined from a set Σ of symbols, called the *signature* of the language, a number of syntactic rules for generating a *set of sentences* (or *well-formed formulas*), and each sentence has a *set of models*. Now, these are put together to form an *institution*.

Definition 1. Institution *An* institution *consists of*

- *a category* **Sign** *of* **signatures***;*
- *a functor Sen* : **Sign** $\rightarrow$ **Set** *which gives, for each signature* Σ*, the set of* **sentences** *Sen*(Σ)*, and for each signature morphism* $\sigma : \Sigma \rightarrow \Sigma'$*, the* **sentence translation morphism** *(or mapping) Sen*(σ) : *Sen*(Σ) $\rightarrow$ *Sen*(Σ')*, where often Sen*$(\sigma)(\varphi)$ *is written as* $\sigma(\varphi)$*;*
- *a functor* **Mod** : **Sign** $\rightarrow$ **Cat**^{op}*, which gives, for each signature* Σ*, the* category of models **Mod**$_{ob}(\Sigma)$*, and for each signature morphism* $\sigma : \Sigma \rightarrow \Sigma'$*, the* **reduct functor Mod**$_{ob}(\Sigma')$ $\rightarrow$ **Mod**(Σ)*;*
- **the satisfaction relation** $\models_\Sigma \subseteq$ **Mod**$(\Sigma) \times$ *Sen*(Σ)*, where* $(M, \varphi) \in \models_\Sigma$ *is written as* $M \models_\Sigma \varphi$

such that for each signature morphism $\sigma : \Sigma \rightarrow \Sigma'$ *in* **Sign***, the following* **satisfaction condition** *holds for each* $\varphi \in$ *Sen*(Σ) *and each* $M' \in$ **Mod**(Σ')

$$M' \models_{\Sigma'} \sigma(\varphi) \; iff \; \textbf{Mod}_{ob}(\sigma)(M') \models_\Sigma \varphi$$

The whole theory and rigorous use of the theory involve advanced knowledge and techniques in mathematics, *co-algebra* in particular. However, the intuition is rather clear. The truth that the satisfaction relation is invariant under a change of notation in an institution provides insight into how different methods can be used consistently in system development. The change in specification notation is usually about *refinement* and *abstraction* in terms of models, or in algebraic terms, *enlargement* or *quotienting* of context.

2.4   Unifying Theories of Programming (UTP)

A semantic model of programming in a paradigm is defined based on considering what information needs to be observed in the execution of a program. UTP provides a unified framework for defining different theories and semantics of programs in different paradigms and for describing different properties. A theory **T** of programs in a paradigm is about the characterisation of the behaviour of the programs by a set of *alphabetised predicates*. We also denote the set of predicates of a theory **T** by **T**. A predicate in the theory contains free variables in a designated set of variables representing the *observables*, called the *alphabet* of the predicate, and the set **T** of predicates are constrained by a set of axioms called *healthiness conditions*. The theory also defines a set of operators on the set **T** and these operators form the *signature* of the theory. The linking among different theories is based on the theory of *complete lattices* and *Galois connections*. We now introduce its basic ideas.

Relational Calculus: In the book of UTP [27], a theory **R** of relations is first introduced. In this theory, the observables are represented by a given set X of variables, together with their decorated versions[1] $X' = \{x' \mid x \in X\}$, and $\alpha = X \cup X'$ is called the *alphabet* of the theory, representing the observables. A program (or a specification) in this theory is defined by a first-order logic formula P, called a *relation*, associated with a subset αP of α such that P only mentions variables in αP. The set αP is called the *alphabet* of the relation P. Thus, a relation is written in the form $(\alpha P, P)$, and $\alpha P = in\alpha P \cup out\alpha P$.

The sets αP, $in\alpha P$ and $out\alpha P$ are, respectively, called the *alphabet*, *input alphabet* and *output alphabet* of the relation. The input alphabet is undashed variables representing initial values and the output alphabet variables stand for the final values of the relation, respectively. We only consider the case when $out\alpha P = in\alpha' P = \{x' \mid x \in in\alpha P\}$, and in such a case P is called a *homogeneous relation*.

The predicate P is interpreted on the domain $\mathcal{D} = \{(s, s') \mid s, s' : X \rightarrow V\}$, and $(s, s') \models P$ if $P(X/s, X'/s')$ holds, where X/s and X/s' denote substitutions of every variable $x \in X$ and $x' \in X'$ by the values $s(x)$ and $s'(x)$ in the states s and s', respectively. For example, $x' = x + 1$ specifies the relation such that for each (s, s') in the relation, $s'(x') = s(x) + 1$. There is a special class of predicates which do not mention variables in the output and they are called *conditions*. Predicates appearing in programs are only conditions. We use lowercase letters p, q, r, etc., to represent these *program stated predicates*, and use b for Boolean expressions in particular.

Signature: In addition to the notation of *alphabets* and values, a theory is also characterised by a collection of *operations* to form *expressions* or *terms* and a collection of *operators* to *compose* relations. These operations and operators form the *signature*[2] of the theory, denoted by Σ. We assume the operations and first-order logic operators in the signature and introduce some operators used in programming languages, just to show the essential idea.

For an assumed alphabet $\beta = in\beta \cup in\beta'$, an *assignment* $x := e$ is defined to be the relation

$$x := e =_{df} (\beta, (x' = e \wedge \bigwedge \{y' = y \mid y \in in\ \beta \text{ and } y \text{ differs from } x\})$$

where the variables $\alpha(e)$ of e are in $in\beta$. Therefore, the final value of x is the value of expression e obtained from the initial values of variables in e.

To define the sequential composition, we adopt the convention to use a single variable v to represent the vector of undashed variables. Then:

$$P; Q =_{df} \exists v_0 . P[v_0/v'] \wedge Q[v_0/v], \quad \text{provided } out\alpha P = in\alpha' Q$$
$$in\alpha(P; Q) =_{df} in\alpha P$$
$$out\alpha(P; Q) =_{df} out\alpha Q$$

---

[1] More mathematically, the decoration $'$ is a bijective mapping from X to X'.

[2] On terminologies, variables, values, operations and operators are included in the alphabet of a formal logic system; and they are included in the signature in the theory of institutions.

In a similar way, we can define more operators used in programming languages. A *conditional choice* between a relation P and Q according to a Boolean condition b is represented by $P \lhd b \rhd Q$. It behaves like P if the initial value of b is true, or like Q if the initial value of b is false:

$$P \lhd b \rhd Q =_{df} (b \wedge P) \vee (\neg b \wedge Q), \quad \text{provided } \alpha(b) \subseteq \alpha P = \alpha Q$$
$$\alpha(P \lhd b \rhd Q) =_{df} \alpha P$$

Conditional choice is *deterministic*, and the *non-deterministic choice* between P and Q is denoted by $P \sqcap Q$ and defined by disjunction:

$$P \sqcap Q =_{df} P \vee Q, \quad \alpha(P \sqcap Q) =_{df} \alpha P$$

The program which has no effect is defined by the identity relation

$$\textbf{skip} =_{df} v' = v, \text{ where } v \text{ is the vector of the input alphabet}$$
$$\text{and } v' \text{ the output alphabet}$$
$$\alpha(\textbf{skip}) =_{df} v \cup v'$$

We use $\textbf{skip}_\beta$ to denote the design $(\beta, \textbf{skip})$. Another important program is the one which has totally uncontrollable or chaotic behaviour. We represent this program by $\perp$ and it is defined by $\perp_\beta =_{df} \textbf{true}$, where β is the alphabet of $\perp_\beta$. Symmetrically, the *miracle* program on an alphabet β is defined by $\top_\beta =_{df} \textbf{false}$.

With the above definition, we can prove algebraic equations between relations, called laws of program. In what follows, we list a few laws.

$$P \lhd b \rhd P = P, \qquad\qquad P \lhd b \rhd Q = Q \lhd \neg b \rhd P$$
$$P; (Q; R) = (P; Q); R, \qquad (P \lhd b \rhd Q) \lhd c \rhd R = P \lhd b \wedge c \rhd (Q \lhd c \rhd R)$$
$$P; \textbf{skip}_{\alpha P} = P = \textbf{skip}_{\alpha P}; P, \quad (P \lhd b \rhd Q); R = (P; R) \lhd b \rhd (Q; R)$$

We have not yet seen the definition of a loop program which is written in the form $b * P$ and behaves like "while b holds repeat P", where $\alpha(b) \subseteq \alpha P$. This definition depends on the *fixed point* of the function $(P; \textbf{X}) \lhd b \rhd \textbf{skip}$. The existence of the *least fixed point* and *greatest fixed point* of this function is ensured by the fact that the set of relations forms a *complete lattice* with the partial order $P \sqsubseteq Q =_{df} [Q \Rightarrow P]$, $\perp$ and $\top$ bottom and top elements, where $[Q \Rightarrow P]$ means that the universal closure of the implication $Q \Rightarrow P$ is valid. When $[Q \Rightarrow P]$ holds, Q is called a *refinement* of P. The loop program is defined by the least fixed point $b * P =_{df} \mu\textbf{X}.((P; \textbf{X}) \lhd b \rhd \textbf{skip})$.

A Theory of Program Design: We use **R** to represent the theory of relations discussed above. We can easily see that neither $\textbf{true}; P = \textbf{true}$ nor $P; \textbf{true} = \textbf{true}$ holds for an arbitrary relation P in **R**. However, they both should hold for an arbitrary program P in all practical programming paradigms. Now we briefly introduce a theory, denoted by **D**, in which the above two equations hold. To this end, we introduce to the alphabet X and X' two new observables represented by the Boolean variables ok and ok'. The variables ok and ok' are not program variables held in the store, but they represent the observations that the program has started well and the program terminated well, respectively.

Furthermore, instead of allowing any arbitrary predicates as in $\mathbf{R}$, the predicates in $\mathbf{D}$ are restricted to form $P \wedge ok \Rightarrow Q \wedge ok'$. We called such a predicate a *design* and write it as $P \vdash Q$, where P and Q do not contain ok and ok'. The definitions of some operators need to be modified as follows, where $D_1, D_2 \in \mathbf{D}$

$$\mathbf{skip} =_{df} \mathbf{true} \vdash \overline{v}' = \overline{v}$$
$$\perp =_{df} \mathbf{false} \vdash \mathbf{true}$$
$$\top =_{df} \neg ok$$
$$x := e =_{df} Defn(e) \vdash x' = e \wedge unchange(others)$$
$$D_1 \lhd b \rhd D_2 =_{df} (Defn(b) \Rightarrow (b \wedge D_1) \vee (\neg b \wedge D_2))$$

where $\overline{v}$ and $\overline{v}'$ respectively denote the vectors of input and output alphabets, predicate $Defn()$ denotes the argument expression is defined for the initial values, and $unchange(others)$ in the context means that no other input variables than x in the given alphabet are changed.

An important theorem shows that the set of designs is closed under all the operators defined in theory $\mathbf{D}$. More operators can be defined, these include the declaration and undeclaration of local variables using existential quantification: $\mathbf{var}\ x =_{df} \exists x$ and $\mathbf{end}\ x =_{df} \exists x'$. These are used in the semantic theory of rCOS OO programming language.

Healthiness Conditions: In predicate logic, we can prove that the left zero law $(\perp; P) = P$ and the *left unit law* $(\mathbf{skip}; D) = D$. The *right zero law* $(D; \perp) = \perp$ and *right unit law* $(D; \mathbf{skip}) = D$ do not generally hold for arbitrary $D \in \mathbf{D}$. However, they are general properties for sequential programs. To characterise programs for which these laws hold, UTP adopts the approach to extending a logic system by adding more axioms, which are called *healthiness conditions*. The following four healthiness conditions are given to restrict the predicates further:

H1 $R = (ok \Rightarrow R)$
H2 $[R[false/ok'] \Rightarrow \mathbf{true}/ok']$
H3 $R = R; \mathbf{skip}$
H4 $(R; \mathbf{true}) = \mathbf{true}$

For the intuitive meaning of these healthiness conditions, we refer the reader to the book of UTP.

In predicate logic, it can be proven that a general relation R with or without ok and ok' in the alphabet, **H1** and **H2** hold iff R is a design. However, **H3** and **H4** have to be imposed as axioms, although the right unit law **H3** holds for any design of the form $p \vdash Q$, where p is a state property which does not have dashed variables. Most properties of sequential programs can be proven from the specifications of this special form.

It is proven that $\mathbf{D}$ constrained with the four healthiness conditions forms a complete lattice with the order $\sqsubseteq$, $\perp$ and $\top$, and the operators are continuous. This implies that $b * P =_{df} \mu \mathbf{X}.(P; \mathbf{X}) \lhd b \rhd \mathbf{skip}$ is in $\mathbf{D}$.

Linking Theories: We now understand theory **R** and **D** can be used as theories of programming. Theory **D** is a sub-theory of $\mathbf{R}^{\{ok,ok'\}}$ which extends **R** by adding two the two observable and the four healthiness conditions, meaning that the set of formulas in the former is a subset of the formulas in the latter.

In either **R** or **D**, we can encode Hoare logic and Dijkstra's calculus predicate transformer. Given a predicate P in **R** or **D**, and two state properties p and q, we define the *Hoare triple*

$$\{p\}P\{q\} =_{df} [P \Rightarrow (p \Rightarrow q')]$$

where p' is the predicate that all variables in q are replaced by their dashed version. Then, the axioms and inference rule hold in **D** and **R**.

Given a predicate P of **R** or **D** and a state property r, we define the *weakest precondition* of P for the postcondition r as:

$$\mathbf{wp}(P,r) =_{df} \neg(P; \neg r)$$

Then, the rules in the **wp** calculus are valid in **D** and **R**.

The above definitions show that the *theories* of Hoare logic and **wp** calculus can be mapped into the theory **D** and **R** and used consistently. It is noticed that **D** is a theory of *total correctness* of imperative sequential programming in which assignments have no side effects. **R** can be used for *partial correctness* analysis, although the left and right zero laws, as well as the left and right unit laws, can be imposed as healthiness conditions.

The linking between theories is in general studied by functions between them with desirable properties. For this, it is generally assumed that the theories are complete lattices. For any given theories **S**, **T** and **U**, a *link function L* from T to S is a total function declared by $L : \mathbf{T} \rightarrow \mathbf{S}$. The *identity function* $\mathbf{1_T}$ maps every element of **T** to itself, and the *composition* $M \circ L : \mathbf{T} \rightarrow \mathbf{U}$ of linking functions $L : \mathbf{T} \rightarrow \mathbf{S}$ and $H : \mathbf{S} \rightarrow \mathbf{U}$ is defined as $(M \circ L)(X) = M(L(X))$, for all $X \in \mathbf{T}$.

If a theory **S** is a subset of a theory **T**, there is always a very simple link H from **S** to **T** such $H(X) = X$, for every $X \in \mathbf{S}$, thus $X \in \mathbf{T}$. It is more interesting to seek a link in the opposite direction, from the super-set theory to the subset theory $L : \mathbf{T} \rightarrow \mathbf{S}$ such that $\mathbf{S} = \{L(Y) \mid Y \in \mathbf{T}\}$.

More general links are between theories with different observables and signatures. Such links are defined as *Galois connections*. The characterisation of Galois connections indicates their significance for the consistent use of different theories.

Definition 2. Galois connection *Given complete lattices* **U** *and* **T**, *let* L *be a function from* **U** *to* **T** *and* R *a function from* **T** *to* **U**. *The pair* (L, R) *is a* **Galois connection** *if for all* $X \in \mathbf{U}$ *and* $Y \in \mathbf{T}$

$$Y \sqsubseteq L(X) \quad \text{iff} \quad R(Y) \sqsubseteq X$$

Thus, a Galois connection allows us to analyse the properties in one theory and reuse the results in another. *I can intuitively see that the theory of institutions and UTP are closely related, but I do not know any formal study on the relation.* We will see that the rCOS method reflects the key ideas of these two theories of unification, although it is formulated formally only within UTP. *However, rCOS supports consistent but still separated uses of different formal methods, i.e., their specification languages, semantic theories, techniques and tools, specially developed for different design concerns in system development.* Writing all specifications and analysing their properties in the uniform notation of designs $P \vdash Q$ through the whole development would be unrealistic.

3   A Reflection on rCOS

The work on rCOS has been developed for the needs of teaching formal methods to undergraduate and graduate students, as well as training UNU-IIST fellows. It started in 1988 when object-oriented design and the Unified Modeling Language (UML) were becoming popular. The research has been evolving along with the advances in techniques for component-based and service-oriented programming, the model-driven development methodologies in particular. This section presents a summary of the development of the research with a discussion about the principle ideas and pointers to the main publications. The discussion will focus on problems, ideas for solutions and the ways to develop the solutions. We refer the reader to the papers cited in the discussions for technical details and examples, both illustrative examples and running examples, and those examples in the paper [10] and the lecture notes [39] in particular.

3.1   Formal Use of UML

UML became known to the software engineering community in 1998 or so. It was in that year when the head of my department at the University of Leicester (UK) asked to take over the teaching of the course on software development. The focus of the course was object-oriented (OO) developments. It was quite a challenge to me because I, as a young researcher in formal theories, had little knowledge of software engineering, and even less of OO design. The keyword "Unified Modelling Language" caught my attention I decided to learn and use it as the modelling language in the course.

Although there was a lot of hype about UML, many people in the formal method community were quite critical of it at the beginning; some people even called it "Undefined Modelling Language" in private. The main criticisms were that the syntax of UML models was not well defined (possibly due to that people were not used to the meta-modelling defining framework), and there was no formal semantics (it still does not have a standard one).

I did feel these were real issues and the biggest challenge in my teaching was to teach the students how to use quite a few UML models consistently and systematically through the development phases, from requirements modelling, through design modelling, to coding. Without imposing necessary formal aspects, it would be hard to solve this challenge, at least for me. I then decided to start a small project on "Formal Use of UML in Software Development" and obtained a small grant from EPSRC[3] in 1999 to support research visits by Jifeng and Xiaoshan Li.[4] I also spent an 8-month sabbatical at UNU-IIST in 2001, then joined UNU-IIST as a full-time member of staff in 2002. The close collaboration of us three had started then.

The first result of the work is presented in the paper "Formal and use-case driven requirements analysis in UML" [36]. There, the functional requirements of the system to be developed are defined by a set of related *business processes*. Each business process is presented by a *use case* and the relations of the business processes are represented in a group of *use case diagrams*. The realisation of the business processes involves *objects* of *concepts* in the domain. The notation of mathematical graph theory is used to represent the concepts, the nodes, called *classes*, and the relations among the objects of classes, called *associations*, by edges between the classes. This is a formal representation of *UML class diagrams at the level of requirements*, which we call *conceptual class diagrams* (CCD). More precisely, the graph notation with only nodes and edges is not expressive enough, and logical constraints on properties of objects of classes and associations among classes are often required and imposed on a CCD. Consider a library system for example, the constraint that 'a **Copy** of a **Publication** which *is Held for* a **Reservation** must be a **Copy** of the **Publication** which *is reserved by* the **Reservation**' is not able to be depicted in a CCD. Therefore, a UML comment with such as natural English sentence is required, and it can be formally specified by a sentence in a first-order logic language, e.g.:

$$\forall c : \textbf{Copy}, r : \textit{Reservation}.$$
$$isHeldFor(c, r) \rightarrow \exists p : \textbf{Publication}.(isReservedBy(p, r) \wedge isCopyOf(c, p))$$

In the above formalisation, the bold words are names of class names, the italic words association names, and variables range over instances (objects) of the corresponding classes (types). *Object constraint language* (OCL), as part of UML, can be used for specifying such constraints. A CCD with such logical constraints is called a *conceptual class model* (CMM).

The classes of a CCD, are called *conceptual classes* and they model the relevant *domain concepts*, instead of software classes. Therefore, a class in a CCD, in general, only has attributes and associations with other classes, but it does not have methods. The methods of a class will be designed to represent the responsibilities of the objects of the class for the realisation of the functional requirements elucidated in the use cases. This means what responsibilities are assigned to an object, represented as methods of the object, can only be decided in the design stage when the global functionalities of the use case are to be decomposed and delegated to the objects.

[3] Thanks to Cliff Jones for his support. He was our referee who we were allowed to recommend in the application.
[4] Xiaoshan was a mutual friend and close collaborator of Jifeng and me at the University of Macao and, sadly, passed away too young a few years ago.

The semantics of a CCM is defined to be the set of allowable *object-diagrams* (OD) which satisfy the constraints specified by the CCD and additional logical constraints, to represent the *state space* of the system. For example, the class diagrams *SmallBank* in Fig. 1(a) and *BigBank* in Fig. 1(b) are conceptual models for a small bank system and a big bank system, respectively. The OD in Fig. 2(a) is a valid state of both *SmallBank* and *BigBank*, but the OD in Fig. 2(b) is a valid state of *SmallBank*, but it is not avalid state of *SmallBank*. It is easy to see that all valid states of *SmallBank* are valid states of *BigBank*.

(a) Small bank   (b) Big bank

Fig. 1. Conceptual class diagrams

Functional requirements are represented as a *use case*, and the interactions between the *actors* and a use case of the system are regarded as *atomic actions* and their executions carry out transitions from valid states to valid states of the conceptual model, and thus their semantics are defined by the notion of designs in UTP. In this way, the notations of CCDs, ODs, use cases, and use case diagrams representing the functional architecture of the system to develop are unified, and their consistency is formalised. For example, suppose the current state of *BigBank* is in Fig. 2(b) and Mrs Mary Smith request system to transfer (say, represented by a use case action *transfer()*) 2,000 GBP from her account *a*2 to account *a*3 of Mr Bob Smith (that they share, say). The post-state after the execution is the state in Fig. 3.

An extension to the above work is presented in the paper [45]. There, a Java-style specification language is defined in which classes, attributes, and sub-classes (inheritance) in a conceptual class diagram are specified. Constraints on the state space modelled by object diagrams are specified by first-order predicate logic or OCL. For each use case, a *use case handler class* is introduced to declare *use case operations* as methods and the bodies of the methods are specified in UTP designs. Each *actor* of a use case is declared a class (corresponding to a process) and its method invokes methods of use case handler classes. Consistency between a conceptual class model and a use case model is formally defined as that the classes, attributes and inheritance relations can *fully support the specification of the methods in the use case handler classes*. A *refinement relation* on CCM is defined such that a CCM **CM**$_1$ is a *refinement* of a CCM **CM** if **CM**$_1$ supports any use case that **CM** supports. This captures the *use-case driven incremental and iterative* development process, known as the *Rational Unified Process* (RUP) to reflect the principle that *OO program design is mainly about the design of class structure*. For example, CCM *BigBank* is a refinement of CCM *SmallBank*, but not the other way around. The *transfer()* use case action is not supported by *SmallBank*.

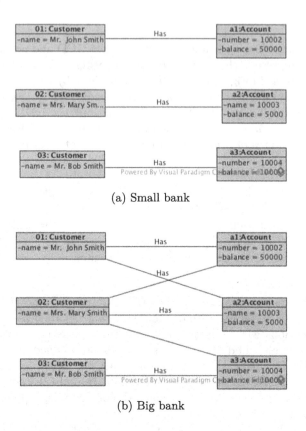

(a) Small bank

(b) Big bank

Fig. 2. Object diagrams

To provide a higher level of abstraction and to better support the separation of design concerns, abstract semantic models for use case sequence diagrams are defined by *labelled transition systems* in the paper [48]. The semantics of general UML sequence diagrams is formalised in the papers [37], and this is used for the refinement from use case sequence diagrams to the sequence diagram in the design stage. This is presented in a follow-up work [37]. Further work on consistency among the use of UML models based on the models in the above papers can be found in [8,38,44,46]. Through the research, we have come to the understanding that *it is reasonable for UML not to have standard semantics as different semantics should be defined for modelling different aspects of the system in different applications, and the meta-modelling technology has its advantage in developing tools for model transformations.*

There was a period of quite active concerns about the rigorous use of UML[5] and there is a volume of work on formalising models for UML by translating them to formal notations, such as CSP and B. However, there has been little work on

---

[5] There was even a "Rigorous UML Group", although its members were not necessarily from the formal method community.

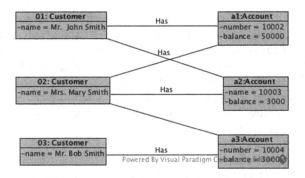

Fig. 3. Post-state of transfer operation

formal treatment of consistency and refinement of UML models. We are aware of the work in [14], which also noticed that UML lacks an explicit set of rules for ensuring that diagrams at different levels of abstraction are consistent. The authors defined such a set of rules, called diagram refinement, that is applicable to several kinds of UML diagrams (mostly for structural diagrams but also for use case diagrams). The work is based on the mathematical theory of graph homomorphisms.

3.2 Theory of Object-Oriented Semantics and Refinement

The work on formal and consistent use of UML discussed in the previous subsection can be classified into the so-called *lightweight formalism*. They alone do not address the complex issues of object-oriented programming languages, such as *side effects*, *polymorphism*, and *dynamic typing in method invocations*. Without well-studied semantics for object-oriented programs, it would have been difficult to address the refinement from requirements, through design, to implementation.

We thus proposed an abstract language for OO programming and called it the *rCOS OO language*, which is rather like the Java programming language. The semantic definition follows the ideas of UTP with the following features.

- To support type casting, dynamic type binding of method invocations and type safety analysis, variables are typed by *public*, *protected* and *private* and types of values of a variable can be of *primitive types* or *classes*. An object is defined recursively as a graph structure with nodes as objects and directed edges labelled by the names of the attributes in the source node, standing for the references from nodes to nodes (think of a UML object diagram). There is a unique root node of such a graph which represents the current object.
- At any time of its execution, the state of the program is an object graph, called a *state graph*, representing the object of the main program, i.e., the root is the object of the main class. The object nodes in a state graph contain the dynamic types of objects.

- The execution of a command of the program changes from such a state to another, by creating a new object and adding to the graph (e.g., to open a new account in the small bank system or the big bank system), changing the values of attributes of some objects in the graph (e.g., the *transfer()* action discussed earlier) or changing the edges of the graphs (e.g. make a customer to access an account in the big bank system). Therefore the semantics of the command (including method invocations) is defined as a relation between states in the UTP design.
- To support incremental program development, a class declaration is also defined as a design which modifies the changes in the static class structure of the program, which can be considered a textual formalisation of a UML class diagram. Class declaration is a development action done before program compilation.

Based on this semantic theory, *OO refinement* is defined at three levels. They are the *refinement of commands* including method invocations, *refinement of classes*, and *refinement of programs*. Class refinement also characterises *subtyping*. Refinement of programs including extension and modification of the class declarations of the program, as well as refinement of the main method and methods in the classes. This work is presented in the paper [24]. It was in this publication that the term "rCOS" was first used, standing for *Refinement Calculus of Object Systems*. The healthiness conditions **H1**–**H4** in Sect. 2.4 on the theory of program designs are inherited here, and based on them, algebraic laws of OO programs at the command level are also proven [68].

Further work on OO refinement is presented in [78] based on the semantic theory of OO programming. There, a set of refinement rules are given and shown to be *sound and relatively complete*. The first completeness theorem shows that without changing commands in the main method, any OO program can be transformed to a program in which there are only *inheritance relations* between classes without attributes which have types of classes (i.e., the edges in the corresponding UML class diagram are only inheritance associations). The second completeness states that any OO program can be refined to a non-OO program (an imperative procedural program) if equivalence transformation of the main method is also allowed.

It is worth emphasising that, in our theory, the General Responsibility Assignments Patterns (GRASP) for OO design [32] and refactoring rules proposed in [16] are shown to be refinement rules. These design patterns are very effective in OO design and maintenance, but to our best knowledge, there is little work on their study in a formal semantic theory. The GRASP approach is used to decompose a "grand functionality" of a class into "a number of functionalities" and assign these to *appropriate* classes.

The most effective pattern, which is thus most often used, is called the *Expert Pattern*. This assigns a responsibility to the information expert, i.e., the class which has information necessary to fulfil the responsibility. The refinement rule for Expert Pattern in rCOS is shown in Fig. 4. On the left of $\sqsubseteq$ in the figure, it specifies an operation with the functionality of *operation()* of class **C** which

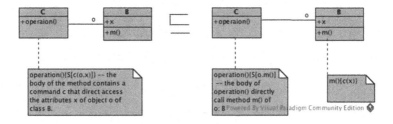

Fig. 4. Expert pattern as an OO refinement rule

information (data) x of class **B**. If the specified functionality can be realised (or refined) by a method $m()$ of **B**, the class model on the right $\sqsubseteq$ is in the figure is a refinement of the one on the right. Note that in rCOS bodies of methods are allowed to be specifications, instead of code.

The *High Cohesion Pattern* of GRASP is, for the purpose of better reuse and maintenance, aimed at avoiding having classes in a design with too many unrelated functionalities. It is represented as a refinement rule shown in Fig. 5. The refinement is in general for class decomposition of a complex class to a composition of micro and logically cohesive classes. The pattern is explained as follows:

- assume class **A** in Fig. 5a contains two sets of attributes x and y (including role names of associations with class **C**);
- class **C** are given responsibilities represented by methods m and n, and m only refers to attributes x;
- we can decompose (i.e., refinement) **A** into the model in Fig. 5b which consists of three classes **A**, **B** and **D** such that **B** maintains x only and it is assigned with the responsibility m;
- class **A** is responsible for coordinating the responsibilities of classes **B** and **D**. .

To decrease the overhead of object interactions and improve reuse and for easy maintenance, the *Low Coupling Pattern* is to have a model with fewer associations among classes. For example, the refined model in Fig. 5b can be further refined to the model in Fig. 6, which has lower coupling.

The refinement rules for GRASP can be used in the context of any larger class models that contain them. Furthermore, a class model $\mathcal{C}$ is a structural refinement of a class model $\mathcal{C}_1$, if $\mathcal{C}$ by be obtained by one of the following changes made to $\mathcal{C}_1$:

- adding a class,
- adding an attribute to a class,
- adding an association between two classes,
- increasing the multiplicity of a role of an association (that is equivalent to adding attributes at the level of program code),
- promoting an attribute of a subclass to its superclass,

72   Z. Liu

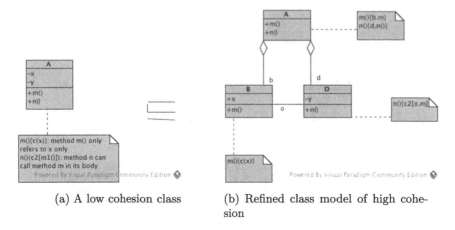

(a) A low cohesion class

(b) Refined class model of high cohesion

Fig. 5. Refinement for class decomposition

– promoting an association of a subclass to its superclass,
– adding a method to a class, and
– promoting a method of a subclass to its superclass.

We call these refinement rules *OO structural refinement rules*. The systematic
and rigorous study of OO structural refinement, together with the work on the
formal use of UML, provides the theoretical confidence towards my understanding and improved my teaching of software development with UML [39]. Now
we can see that the rCOS method provides a comprehensive use of UML with
a formal OO semantic basis on UTP. Furthermore, OO structural refinement,
such as the rules for the patterns of Expert, Low Coupling and High Cohesion
characterise the essential features of *microservice architectures* [74], which are
now popular in the software industry.

3.3 Component-Based Architecture Modelling

It was in the early 2000s when *component-based development* was causing the
attention of the software engineering community and *component-based diagrams*
were introduced into UML, although the term "component-based programming"
had come much earlier. I remember one day when Jifeng called me to his office
and said "we should extend our rCOS method to component-based programming". He showed me Szyperski's book [70] and said that he was reading it and
would spend a week or so to finish it. I must confess that I could not read such
a book that fast.

Naturally, our initial work on component-based modelling [23,43] extends
the rCOS model for OO programs and formulates the key notions about component software in Szyperski's book. *Interfaces* are defined to be first-class model
elements. An interface $\mathcal{I} = (M, A, O)$ consists of a list of class declarations M, a
list of field variables A with their types declared in M, and a list of operations

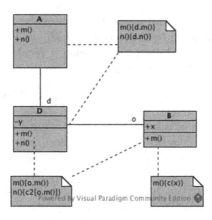

Fig. 6. A refinement of low coupling

O as methods specified in the rCOS OO language. The component specification is described by a *contract* that gives each operation a design. A *closed component* is an *implementation* of an interface in the rCOS OO language that has a *provided interface*. The implementation of an operation in the provided interface $\mathcal{I}$ can invoke services implemented in other components. The methods invoked by the operations in the provided interface form the *required interface* $\mathcal{R}$. Thus, an (open) component P is a parameterised program which takes a component implementing $\mathcal{R}$ as its input services. Therefore, the semantics of a component with a provided interface $\mathcal{I}$ and a required interface $\mathcal{R}$ is defined as a relation on the contracts of $\mathcal{I}$ and $\mathcal{R}$:

$$[\![P]\!] = \{(\mathcal{C}_{\mathcal{I}}, \mathcal{C}_{\mathcal{R}}) \mid (\mathcal{C}_{\mathcal{I}} \sqsubseteq P(\mathcal{C}_{\mathcal{R}})\}$$

where $P(\mathcal{C}_{\mathcal{R}})$ is the contract for the provided interface $\mathcal{I}$, calculated from the semantics of component program P with input services specified by the contract $\mathcal{C}_{\mathcal{R}}$. The relation $[\![P]\!]$ means that given any provided services which implement the required interface $\mathcal{R}$, the component with this input is a refinement of the contract $\mathcal{C}_{\mathcal{I}}$ of the provided interface $\mathcal{C}_{\mathcal{I}}$. The composition of interfaces, composition of components and refinements of components are defined.

In this model, the interactions between components are in general OO method invocations from a component to the components which provide it with the required services. To have distributed implementations of the components, middlewares, such as CORBA, are needed. However, the semantics of middleware are not formalised in this work. Further, a contract defined in the previous subsection specifies the static functionality of a component that does not require synchronisation when the operations are used. Such components are often used in the functional layer of a system. Processes and business rules are, however, accomplished by invoking particular sequences of operations. Also, synchronisations are needed when resources are shared. This means a synchronisation protocol using the functional operations must be imposed, often by composing a component in the functional layer and a component in the system layer.

To model synchronisation and interaction protocols, we define the notion of reactive design by introducing two fresh observables, $wait$ and $wait'$, for synchronisation. A design D on an alphabet α is called a *reactive design* if it satisfies the healthiness condition $\mathcal{W}(D) = D$, where:

$$\mathcal{W}(D) =_{df} = (true \vdash wait' \wedge ((\alpha' = \alpha) \wedge (ok = ok'))) \lhd wait \rhd D$$

For writing a specification of the *interface contract* for a *reactive component*, we introduce the notation of *guarded designs* of the form $g\&D$, where D is a design and g is a Boolean expression of the alphabet, called the *guard* of the design. The semantics of $g\&D$ is defined as $D \lhd g \rhd (true \vdash wait' \wedge ((\alpha' = \alpha) \wedge (ok = ok')))$, where α is the alphabet of the design D. We can prove that all guarded designs are reactive designs, and $\mathcal{W}^2(D) = \mathcal{W}(D)$ for all designs.

For the *implementation* of a reactive component, we use a language of *guarded methods* in which each guarded method is of the form $g\&m(in; out)$ and the body method $m(in; out)$ is written as a command c in the rCOS OO language. The semantics of $g\&m(in; out)$ is defined as the guarded design $g\&\mathcal{W}(D_c)$, where D_c is the semantics of c, defined in the subsection immediately above.

The work in [23] also shows the unification and their separation of uses of *designs for local functionality specification, traces for reactive behaviours, failures for deadlock* and *divergences for livelock*.

More concretely speaking, a (reactive) *contract* serves as a specification of an interface and now is defined as a tuple $\mathcal{C} = (\mathcal{I}, Init, \mathcal{S}, \mathcal{P})$ of an interface $\mathcal{I}$, an *initial condition* $Init$ specifying the allowable starting states, a *specification* $\mathcal{S}$ specifying each operation in $\mathcal{I}$ as a guarded design, and *protocol* $\mathcal{P}$ which is a set of sequences $\langle ?m_1(x_1), \ldots, ?m_k(x_k) \rangle$ of *invocations* to the interface operations acceptable by the interface. With the specification $\mathcal{S}$ of a contract, the *divergence set* $\mathcal{D}_\mathcal{C}$ and the *failure set* $\mathcal{F}_\mathcal{C}$ of a contract $\mathcal{C}$, as those defined for CSP processes in [63], are defined and the triple $(\mathcal{D}_\mathcal{C}, \mathcal{F}_\mathcal{C}, \mathcal{P})$ is called the model of *dynamic behaviour* for the contract. The *trace set* of a contract can be defined too.

A contract $\mathcal{C}_1$ is refined by a contract $\mathcal{C}_2$ if:

- the attributes of the two contracts are the same;
- the set O_1 of operations of $\mathcal{C}_1$ is a subset of the operations of $\mathcal{C}_2$, i.e. $\mathcal{C}_2$ provides no fewer services;
- $\mathcal{C}_2$ is not more likely to diverge, $\mathcal{D}_{\mathcal{C}_2} \subseteq \mathcal{D}_{\mathcal{C}_1}$;
- $\mathcal{C}_2$ is not more likely to block the client, $\mathcal{F}_{\mathcal{C}_2} \subseteq \mathcal{F}_{\mathcal{C}_1}$.

The refinement of one contract by another can be proven by *downward simulation* and *upward simulation* [19]. Another important point is that the specification $\mathcal{S}$ and the protocol $\mathcal{P}$ might not be *consistent* and the consistency can be checked. With the theory of contracts and refinements for components, the meaning of rCOS is extended to *Refinement of Component and Object Systems*.

In the keynote paper [22], special kinds of components, including *coordinators*, *connectors* and *controllers* are characterised, and the concepts in the semantic theory are related to notations used in software engineering. In the paper [7], the relation between specification $\mathcal{S}$ and the protocol $\mathcal{P}$ is further elaborated and introduced the notion of *processes* as a special kind of components. In this way, functional (or service) components are specified in the rCOS OO language without using guards, and interaction protocols are modelled as processes at the system level to control synchronisation. The behaviour of a process can then be specified by *traces, failures,* or *divergences* according to the properties to be analysed, and by input/out automata [55], *UML state diagrams* or especially by *interface automata* [12,13]. *This provides explicit support to multi-view modelling and separation of concerns to different modelling notations and underlying theories to be used consistently in component-based software development.*

3.4   rCOS Support for Model-Driven Development

To apply the rCOS method, we embed the modelling notations into software development processes and use them consistently according to the underlying theory of rCOS. To this end, we identify activities of the RUP process for model-driven development and associate them with modelling notations defined in rCOS.

In a top-down process, a requirements model of the use cases is identified and each use case is modelled as a component in the following steps:

1. their provided interfaces are the interactions with the actors and field attributes are modelled by conceptual class diagrams (which can be unified into a single one);
2. interaction protocols of use cases are modelled by sequence diagrams, and dynamic behaviour by state diagrams;
3. the functionalities of interface operations are specified by designs (pre- and post-conditions), focusing on what new objects are created, which attributes are modified, and the new links of objects that are formed; and
4. the requirements architecture is modelled by UML *component-based diagrams* reflecting the relations among use cases in the use case diagram.

A design process consists of the following modelling steps:

1. it takes each use case and designs each of its provided operations according to its pre- and post-conditions by using the OO refinement rules, the four patterns of GRASP in particular;
2. this decomposes the functionality of each use case operation into internal object interaction and computation, thus refining the use case sequence diagram into a *design sequence diagram* of the use case [10];
3. in the process of decomposition of the functionality of use-case operations to internal object interaction and computation, the requirements class model is refined into a *design class model* by adding methods and visibilities in classes according to responsibility assignments and directing of method invocations [10];
4. identify some of the objects in a design sequence diagram as the *component controller*, satisfying *six semantic invariant properties* (which can be checked by model checking) and then transform the design sequence diagram to a component-sequence diagram [34];

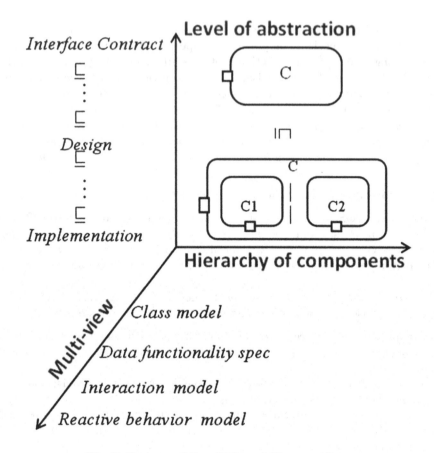

Fig. 7. Features of the rCOS modelling paradigm

5. a component diagram for each use case is generated (automatically) which is a decomposition of the use-case component in the requirements model to a composition of sub-components, and then the whole *component-based architecture model* at the requirements level is decomposed into a *component-based design architecture model* [34];
6. the coding from the design architecture model is not difficult and can be largely automatic [53].

The key features of the rCOS modelling paradigm, as shown in Fig. 7, are being *refinement-driven, hierarchically component-based,* and with *multi-view modelling in multiple notations with a unified semantics.* The component-based design process from a component-based requirements model is depicted in Fig. 8. The development process is applied to the CoCoMe benchmark problem [9] and the details are elaborated in [10]. The modelling and analysis framework of rCOS can also be applied for component integration in bottom-up development processes or a mixed top-down and bottom-up process, allowing the use and reuse

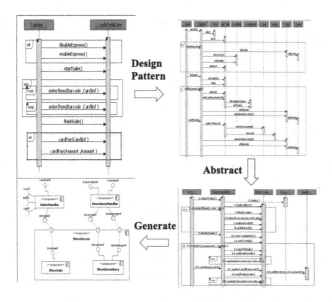

Fig. 8. Transformations from requirements model to design model

of existing models and implementations of components, as long as they have explicitly specified interfaces. Interface contracts in rCOS of component-based architecture support the characterisation of different security threats and for the design of protection and recovery from damages of security attacks [50]. The rCOS model of component-based architecture supports the design of fault-tolerant mechanisms so as restrict the propagation of *errors* caused by *faults* and *failures* [47] across interfaces of components [77].

The UML diagrams are translated to the rCOS notation by the rCOS Modeller. The tool for transformation from design sequence diagrams to component-sequence diagrams is presented in [34]. A tool for automatic prototyping from the requirements model is presented in [75]. The use of *low coupling* with *high cohesion* patterns supports the *microservice architecture* design [71,74].

4   Extension of rCOS to Model HCPS

The research on rCOS is not yet finished (I hope). We currently have a project on "Theory of Human-Cyber-Physical Computing and Software Defined Methodology". We are extending the rCOS component-based modelling notation to model system architectures of HCPS. We take the view of the architecture of an HCPS as comprising of *cyber systems*, a *communication network*, *physical processes*, *human processes*, and *interfaces*, where:

– the physical processes include, for example, mechanical, electrical and chemical processes;

- the cyber systems (information systems) are computing systems where:
  - some cyber systems (i.e., information systems) are responsible for data collection and processing, and
  - some cyber systems (controlling systems) are responsible for taking control decisions, based on the information provided by the information systems, to control physical processes;
- the human processes make control decisions based on the information provided by the information systems to physical processes;
- the interfaces are middleware systems between the physical systems, cyber systems and humans, including sensors and actuators, A/C and C/A converters, etc.;
- the sensors sense the physical processes, collect data about the behaviours of the physical processes and the data are transmitted to the information systems through the network;
- computer control decisions of the controlling systems and human control decisions are transmitted in the form of control commands through the network to corresponding actuators to carry out the control actions.

There is system software for the *coordination* and *orchestration* of the behaviours of the component systems and for *scheduling* the *physical, network, hardware, human,* and *software resources*. A particular need is components which are responsible for the switching of control between human and computer controllers.

The initial work is to extend the rCOS model of interfaces to *cyber-physical interfaces* (*CP-interfaces*) or *hybrid interfaces*. A CP-interface includes as its field variables both *signals* representing information on the states of physical processes, as well as program variables; and it includes both program operations and signals for interactions with the environment of the component. Also, a signal can be either discrete or continuous. A contract of a CP-interface then consists of a provided CP interface, a required CP interface, and a specification describing the functionality of the program operations and the behaviour (in differential or difference equations) of the signals in the interfaces.

With the above considerations, we propose a horizontally and vertically open and hierarchical component-based approach for a systems of systems model of HCPS architecture. This model supports top-down and bottom-up development and interface-based black-box system integration. It also supports continuous maintenance through sub-system upgrades and replacements of sub-systems. Furthermore, services and functions of an existing HCPS can be used as infrastructure to develop further sub-systems to be integrated into the system in a plug-and-play manner, and thus the architecture is ever evolving. The architecture style also supports component based design of security and fault-tolerance.

The dynamic behaviour of such a contract corresponds to two *hybrid input/output* automata [54], one for the provided CP interface and one for the required CP interface. It should be possible to specify them in Hybrid CSP [20] and analyse them in Hybrid Hoare logic [79] both developed with fundamental contributions from Jifeng. The initial ideas on the extension are presented in [40,42,52] and a proof of concept example is given in [60]. The *hybrid relation calculus* [21] proposed by Jifeng would also provide a theoretical foundation for further development of this work. Longer-term research is to link the method to that of the semantics of Simulink and SySML.

A significant challenge to modelling HCPS is that there is no computational model and theory for human interactions with cyber and physical systems. We are proposing a *human-cyber-physical automata* (HCPA). In this model, the human behaviour is represented by a neural network and the controller for control switching between human and machine is modelled as an oracle with a learning model too. It is important to note that we are not modelling general human intelligence, but the behaviour of a human in a given application when carrying out their tasks instead. The research on the full theory will involve tackling the difficulties in composing traditional computation models with AI models. An initial model of HCPA is defined with only one human process to control a physical process in collaboration with digital controllers. This model and a proof of concept case study are presented in the invited talk [76]. For the research problems in this project, we refer the reader to the editorial paper [52] and the lecture notes in [40]. The research will heavily involve the controllability and composability of AI systems, their composability with traditional computational systems, and the trustworthiness of these hybrid systems.

5   Conclusions and Acknowledgements

This paper has presented a summary of the development of the rCOS method, showing that Hoare and He's UTP is the theoretical root of rCOS. The summary focuses on a unified understanding of different formal theories with the belief that *uniformity in theory is for consistent use of formal methods to support the separation of design concerns in software systems development.*

Through the discussion, we show how the ideas, theoretical results and techniques in different publications on the rCOS method are linked and how they are related to well-studied formal methods.[6] The rCOS method helps to narrow the gap from the semantic theories to the engineering technologies and supports their consistent use in practice. The lecture notes in [39], although never officially published, have been used since 1998 and the teaching has been improved along with the development of the rCOS method. A plan and an architecture for the rCOS tool development were carefully proposed in [11,49], although it was not fully developed due to the lack of stable human resources. The current status of the tool is available at https://rise-swu.cn/rCOS.

Acknowledgements. There is a long list of names of collaborators who have contributed to the research on rCOS and I would like to thank them. In alphabetic order, the list includes Xin Chen, Zhenbang Chen, Ruzhen Dong, Dan Van Hung, Bin Lei, Dan Li, Xiaoshan Li , Jing Liu, Quan Long, Charles Morriset, Zongyan Qiu, Anders Ravn , Martin Schäf, Leila Silva, Volker Stolz, Shuling Wang, Ji Wang, Jing

---

[6] What a nice coincidence it is that there are 80 references in this paper to celebrate Jifeng's 80th birthday.

Yang, Lu Yang, Yilong Yang, Naijun Zhan, Miaomiao Zhang, Liang Zhao. They all spent time at UNU-IIST, at different periods, as fellows, PhD students, postdoctoral research fellows, or visitors. We all owe a big thanks to Jifeng for his guidance and/or influence over the years. We all congratulate him on his academic achievements, and wish him a very happy 80th birthday!

I would also like to thank Jonathan Bowen and Shmuel Tyszberowicz for their careful reading and comments on draft versions of this paper.

References

1. Abrial, J.R.: The B-Book: Assigning Programs to Meanings. Cambridge University Press, Cambridge (1996)
2. Abrial, J.R.: Modeling in Event-B: System and Software Engineering. Cambridge University Press, Cambridge (2010)
3. Back, R.J.R., von Wright, J.: Trace refinement of action systems. In: Jonsson, B., Parrow, J. (eds.) CONCUR 1994. LNCS, vol. 836, pp. 367–384. Springer, Heidelberg (1994). https://doi.org/10.1007/978-3-540-48654-1_28
4. Baeten, J.C.M., Bravetti, M.: A generic process algebra. In: Algebraic Process Calculi: The First Twenty Five Years and Beyond. BRICS Notes Series NS-05-3 (2005)
5. Brooks, F.P.: Learn the hard way - a history 1845–1980 of software engineering. In: Keynote at 40th International Conference on Software Engineering (ICSE 2018), Gothenburg, Sweden, 27 May–3 June 2018 (2018). https://www.icse2018.org
6. Butler, R.W.: What is formal methods? (2001). https://shemesh.larc.nasa.gov/fm/fm-what.html
7. Chen, X., He, J., Liu, Z., Zhan, N.: A model of component-based programming. In: Arbab, F., Sirjani, M. (eds.) FSEN 2007. LNCS, vol. 4767, pp. 191–206. Springer, Heidelberg (2007). https://doi.org/10.1007/978-3-540-75698-9_13
8. Chen, X., Liu, Z., Mencl, V.: Separation of concerns and consistent integration in requirements modelling. In: van Leeuwen, J., Italiano, G.F., van der Hoek, W., Meinel, C., Sack, H., Plášil, F. (eds.) SOFSEM 2007. LNCS, vol. 4362, pp. 819–831. Springer, Heidelberg (2007). https://doi.org/10.1007/978-3-540-69507-3_71
9. Chen, Z., Li, X., Liu, Z., Stolz, V., Yang, L.: Harnessing rCOS for tool support—the CoCoME experience. In: Jones, C.B., Liu, Z., Woodcock, J. (eds.) Formal Methods and Hybrid Real-Time Systems. LNCS, vol. 4700, pp. 83–114. Springer, Heidelberg (2007). https://doi.org/10.1007/978-3-540-75221-9_5
10. Chen, Z., Liu, Z., Ravn, A.P., Stolz, V., Zhan, N.: Refinement and verification in component-based model driven design. Sci. Comput. Program. **74**(4), 168–196 (2009)
11. Chen, Z., Liu, Z., Stolz, V., Yang, L., Ravn, A.P.: A refinement driven component-based design. In: 12th International Conference on Engineering of Complex Computer Systems (ICECCS 2007), pp. 277–289. IEEE Computer Society (2007)
12. De Alfaro, L., Henzinger, T.: Interface automata. ACM SIGSOFT Softw. Eng. Notes **26**(5), 109–120 (2001)
13. Dong, R., Zhan, N., Zhao, L.: An interface model of software components. In: Liu, Z., Woodcock, J., Zhu, H. (eds.) ICTAC 2013. LNCS, vol. 8049, pp. 159–176. Springer, Heidelberg (2013). https://doi.org/10.1007/978-3-642-39718-9_10
14. Faitelson, D., Tyszberowicz, S.S.: UML diagram refinement (focusing on class- and use case diagrams). In: Uchitel, S., Orso, A., Robillard, M.P. (eds.) Proceedings of

the 39th International Conference on Software Engineering, ICSE, Buenos Aires, Argentina, pp. 735–745. IEEE/ACM (2017). https://doi.org/10.1109/ICSE.2017. 73

15. Floyd, R.W.: Assigning meanings to programs. Proc. Am. Math. Soc. Symposia Appl. Math. **19**, 19–31 (1967)

16. Fowler, M.: Refactoring - Improving the Design of Existing Code. Addison-Wesley, Menlo Park (1999)

17. Gierz, G., Hofmann, K.H., Keimel, K., Lawson, J.D., Mislove, M., Scott, D.S.: Continuous Lattices and Domains, Encyclopedia of Mathematics and its Applications, vol. 93. Cambridge University Press (2003)

18. Goguen, J., Burstall, R.: Institutions: abstract model theory for specification and programming. J. ACM **39**(1), 95–146 (1992)

19. He, J.: Simulation and process refinement. Formal Aspect Comput. **1**(3) (1989)

20. He, J.: From CSP to hybrid systems. In: Roscoe, A.W. (ed.) A Classical Mind: Essays in Honour of C. A. R. Hoare, chap. 11, pp. 171–189. International Series in Computer Science, Prentice Hall, New York (1994)

21. He, J., Qin, L.: A hybrid relational modelling language. In: Gibson-Robinson, T., Hopcroft, P., Lazić, R. (eds.) Concurrency, Security, and Puzzles. LNCS, vol. 10160, pp. 124–143. Springer, Cham (2017). https://doi.org/10.1007/978-3-319-51046-0_7

22. Jifeng, H., Li, X., Liu, Z.: Component-based software engineering. In: Van Hung, D., Wirsing, M. (eds.) ICTAC 2005. LNCS, vol. 3722, pp. 70–95. Springer, Heidelberg (2005). https://doi.org/10.1007/11560647_5

23. He, J., Li, X., Liu, Z.: A theory of reactive components. Electron. Notes Theor. Comput. Sci. **160**, 173–195 (2006)

24. He, J., Liu, Z., Li, X.: rCOS: a refinement calculus of object systems. Theor. Comput. Sci. **365**(1–2), 109–142 (2006)

25. Hoare, C.A.R.: An axiomatic basis for computer programming. Commun. ACM **12**(10), 576–580 (1969)

26. Hoare, C.A.R.: Communicating sequential processes. Commun. ACM **21**(8), 666–677 (1978)

27. Hoare, C.A.R., He, J.: Unifying Theories of Programming. Series in Computer Science, Prentice Hall, London (1998)

28. Jackson, D.: Software Abstractions: Logic, Language, and Analysis. MIT Press, Cambridge (2006)

29. Jones, C.B.: Systematic Software Development using VDM. International Series in Computer Science, Prentice Hall, Englewood Cliffs (1990)

30. Lamport, L.: The temporal logic of actions. ACM Trans. Program. Lang. Syst. **16**(3), 872–923 (1994)

31. Lamport, L.: Specifying Systems: The TLA+ Language and Tools for Hardware and Software Engineers. Addison-Wesley, Boston (2002)

32. Larman, C.: Applying UML and Patterns: An Introduction to Object-Oriented Analysis and Design and the Unified Process, 2nd edn. Prentice Hall, Upper Saddle River (2001)

33. Lee, E.A.: The past, present and future of cyber-physical systems: a focus on models. Sensors **15**(3), 4837–4869 (2015)

34. Li, D., Li, X.S., Liu, Z.M., Stolz, V.: Automated transformations from UML behavior models to contracts. Sci. China Inf. Sci. **57**(12), 1–17 (2014). https://doi.org/ 10.1007/s11432-014-5159-8

35. Li, D., Li, X., Stolz, V.: QVT-based model transformation using XSLT. SIGSOFT Softw. Eng. Notes **36**, 1–8 (2011)

36. Li, X., Liu, Z., He, J.: Formal and use-case driven requirement analysis in UML. In: 25th International Computer Software and Applications Conference (COMPSAC 2001), Invigorating Software Development, Chicago, IL, USA, 8–12 October 2001, pp. 215–224 (2001)
37. Li, X., Liu, Z., He, J.: A formal semantics of UML sequence diagram. In: 15th Australian Software Engineering Conference (ASWEC 2004), Melbourne, Australia, 13–16 April 2004, pp. 168–177. IEEE Computer Society (2004)
38. Li, X., Liu, Z., He, J.: Consistency checking of UML requirements. In: 10th International Conference on Engineering of Complex Computer Systems, pp. 411–420. IEEE Computer Society (2005)
39. Liu, Z.: Software development with UML. Technical report. Technical Report 259, UNU-IIST: International Institute for Software Technology, the United Nations University, Macao (2002)
40. Liu, Z., Bowen, J.P., Liu, B., Tyszberowicz, S., Zhang, T.: Software abstractions and human-cyber-physical systems architecture modelling. In: Bowen, J.P., Liu, Z., Zhang, Z. (eds.) SETSS 2019. LNCS, vol. 12154, pp. 159–219. Springer, Cham (2020). https://doi.org/10.1007/978-3-030-55089-9_5
41. Liu, Z., Chen, X.: Model-driven design of object and component systems. In: Liu, Z., Zhang, Z. (eds.) SETSS 2014. LNCS, vol. 9506, pp. 152–255. Springer, Cham (2016). https://doi.org/10.1007/978-3-319-29628-9_4
42. Chen, X., Liu, Z.: Towards interface-driven design of evolving component-based architectures. In: Hinchey, M.G., Bowen, J.P., Olderog, E.-R. (eds.) Provably Correct Systems. NMSSE, pp. 121–148. Springer, Cham (2017). https://doi.org/10.1007/978-3-319-48628-4_6
43. Liu, Z., Jifeng, H., Li, X.: Contract oriented development of component software. In: Levy, J.-J., Mayr, E.W., Mitchell, J.C. (eds.) TCS 2004. IIFIP, vol. 155, pp. 349–366. Springer, Boston, MA (2004). https://doi.org/10.1007/1-4020-8141-3_28
44. Liu, Z., He, J., Li, X.: Towards a rigorous approach to UML-based development. In: Mota, A., Moura, A.V. (eds.) Proceedings of the Seventh Brazilian Symposium on Formal Methods, SBMF 2004. Electronic Notes in Theoretical Computer Science, Recife, Pernambuco, Brazil, 29 November–1 December 2004, vol. 130, pp. 57–77. Elsevier (2004)
45. Liu, Z., Jifeng, H., Li, X., Chen, Y.: A relational model for formal object-oriented requirement analysis in UML. In: Dong, J.S., Woodcock, J. (eds.) ICFEM 2003. LNCS, vol. 2885, pp. 641–664. Springer, Heidelberg (2003). https://doi.org/10.1007/978-3-540-39893-6_36
46. Liu, Z., He, J., Liu, J., Li, X.: Unifying views of UML. In: de Boer, F.S., Bonsangue, M.M. (eds.) Proceedings of the Workshop on the Compositional Verification of UML Models, CVUML 2003, Electronic Notes in Theoretical Computer Science, San Francisco, CA, USA, 21 October 2003, vol. 101, pp. 95–127. Elsevier (2003)
47. Liu, Z., Joseph, M.: Specification and verification of fault-tolerance, timing, and scheduling. ACM Trans. Program. Lang. Syst. **21**(1), 46–89 (1999)
48. Liu, Z., Li, X., He, J.: Using transition systems to unify UML models. In: George, C., Miao, H. (eds.) ICFEM 2002. LNCS, vol. 2495, pp. 535–547. Springer, Heidelberg (2002). https://doi.org/10.1007/3-540-36103-0_54
49. Liu, Z., Mencl, V., Ravn, A.P., Yang, L.: Harnessing theories for tool support. In: Proceedings of the Second International Symposium on Leveraging Applications of Formal Methods, Verification and Validation (ISoLA 2006), pp. 371–382. IEEE Computer Society (2006)

50. Liu, Z., Morisset, C., Stolz, V.: A component-based access control monitor. In: Margaria, T., Steffen, B. (eds.) ISoLA 2008. CCIS, vol. 17, pp. 339–353. Springer, Heidelberg (2008). https://doi.org/10.1007/978-3-540-88479-8_24
51. Liu, Z., Qiu, Z.: Introduction to Mathematical Logic - The Natural Foundation for Computer Science and System. China Science Publishing & Media Ltd. (2022). (in Chinese)
52. Liu, Z., Wang, J.: Human-cyber-physical systems: concepts, challenges, and research opportunities. Front. Inf. Technol. Electron. Eng. **21**(11), 1535–1553 (2020). https://doi.org/10.1631/FITEE.2000537
53. Long, Q., Liu, Z., Li, X., He, J.: Consistent code generation from UML models. In: Australian Software Engineering Conference, pp. 23–30. IEEE Computer Society (2005)
54. Lynch, N., Segala, R., Vaandrager, F.: Hybrid I/O automata. Inf. Comput. **185**, 105–157 (2003)
55. Lynch, N.A., Tuttle, M.R.: An introduction to input/output automata. CWI Q. **2**(3), 219–246 (1989)
56. McCarthy, J.: Recursive functions of symbolic expressions and their computation by machine. Part I. Commun. ACM **3**(4), 184–219 (1960)
57. Milner, R.: Communication and Concurrency. International Series in Computer Science, Prentice Hall, New York (1989)
58. Morgan, C.: Programming from Specifications. International Series in Computer Science, Prentice Hall, New York (1994/1998). https://www.cs.ox.ac.uk/publications/books/PfS/
59. Object Management Group: Meta Object Facility (MOF) 2.0 Query/View/Transformation Specification, Version 1.1 (2009)
60. Palomar, E., Chen, X., Liu, Z., Maharjan, S., Bowen, J.P.: Component-based modelling for scalable smart city systems interoperability: a case study on integrating energy demand response systems. Sensors **16**(11), 1810 (2016). https://doi.org/10.3390/s16111810
61. Plotkin, G.D.: The origins of structural operational semantics. J. Logic Algebraic Program. **60**(61), 3–15 (2004)
62. Randell, B.: Fifty years of software engineering or the view from Garmisch. In: Keynote at 40th International Conference on Software Engineering (ICSE 2018), Gothenburg, Sweden, 27 May–3 June 2018 (2018). https://www.icse2018.org
63. Roscoe, A.W.: Theory and Practice of Concurrency. International Series in Computer Science, Prentice Hall, Engelwood Cliffs (1997)
64. Roscoe, A.W., Hoare, C.A.R.: The laws of OCCAM programming. Theor. Comput. Sci. **60**(2), 177–229 (1988). https://doi.org/10.1016/0304-3975(88)90049-7
65. Sangiovanni-Vincentelli, A., Damm, W., Passerone, R.: Taming dr. frankenstein: contract-based design for cyber-physical systems. Eur. J. Control **18**(3), 217–238 (2012)
66. Schneider, S.: The B-Method: An Introduction. Cornerstones of Computing Series, Palgrave Macmillan, London (2001)
67. Scott, D., Strachey, C.: Toward a Mathematical Semantics for Computer Languages. No. PRG-6 (1971)
68. Silva, L., Sampaio, A., Liu, Z.: Laws of object-orientation with reference semantics. In: Cerone, A., Gruner, S. (eds.) Sixth IEEE International Conference on Software Engineering and Formal Methods, SEFM 2008, Cape Town, South Africa, 10–14 November 2008, pp. 217–226. IEEE Computer Society (2008). https://doi.org/10.1109/SEFM.2008.29

69. Spivey, J.M.: The Z Notation: A Reference Manual, 2nd edn. Prentice Hall, New York (1992)
70. Szyperski, C.: Component Software: Beyond Object-Oriented Programming, 2nd edn. Addison-Wesley Longman Publishing Co., Inc., Boston (2002)
71. Tyszberowicz, S., Heinrich, R., Liu, B., Liu, Z.: Identifying microservices using functional decomposition. In: Feng, X., Müller-Olm, M., Yang, Z. (eds.) SETTA 2018. LNCS, vol. 10998, pp. 50–65. Springer, Cham (2018). https://doi.org/10.1007/978-3-319-99933-3_4
72. Wang, J., Zhan, N., Feng, X., Liu, Z.: Overview of formal methods. J. Softw. **30**(1), 33–61 (2019). (in Chinese)
73. Wing, J.M.: A specifier's introduction to formal methods. Computer **23**(9), 8–22 (1990)
74. Xiong, J.L., Ren, Q.R., Tyszberowicz, S.S., Liu, Z., Liu, B.: MSA-lab: an integrated design platform for model-driven development of microservices. J. Softw. (2023). https://doi.org/10.13328/j.cnki.jos.006813. (in Chinese)
75. Yang, Y., Li, X., Ke, W., Liu, Z.: Automated prototype generation from formal requirements model. IEEE Trans. Reliab. **69**(2), 632–656 (2020)
76. Zhang, M., Liu, W., Tang, X., Du, B., Liu, Z.: Human-cyber-physical automata and their synthesis. In: Seidl, H., Liu, Z., Pasareanu, C.S. (eds.) ICTAC 2022. LNCS, vol. 13572, pp. 36–41. Springer, Cham (2022). https://doi.org/10.1007/978-3-031-17715-6_4
77. Zhang, M., Liu, Z., Morisset, C., Ravn, A.P.: Design and verification of fault-tolerant components. In: Butler, M., Jones, C., Romanovsky, A., Troubitsyna, E. (eds.) Methods, Models and Tools for Fault Tolerance. LNCS, vol. 5454, pp. 57–84. Springer, Heidelberg (2009). https://doi.org/10.1007/978-3-642-00867-2_4
78. Zhao, L., Liu, X., Liu, Z., Qiu, Z.: Graph transformations for object-oriented refinement. Formal Aspects Comput. **21**(1–2), 103–131 (2009)
79. Zou, L., Zhan, N., Wang, S., Fränzle, M., Qin, S.: Verifying simulink diagrams via a hybrid hoare logic prover. In: Ernst, R., Sokolsky, O. (eds.) Proceedings of the International Conference on Embedded Software, EMSOFT 2013, Montreal, QC, Canada, 29 September–4 October 2013, pp. 9:1–9:10. IEEE (2013). https://doi.org/10.1109/EMSOFT.2013.6658587
80. Şerbănuţă, T.F., Rosu, G., Meseguer, J.: A rewriting logic approach to operational semantics. Inf. Comput. **207**(2), 305–340 (2009)

Oxford Colleagues

Consciousness by Degree

Yifeng Chen[1(✉)] and J. W. Sanders[2]

[1] Peking University, Beijing, China
`cyf@pku.edu.cn`
[2] AIMS South Africa, Cape Town, Republic of South Africa
`jsanders@aims.ac.za`

Abstract. The authors have previously proposed that, with agents ranging from humans and other animals through cells to organisations and software, (e.g. AIs), a theory is possible which accounts in principle for agent consciousness. That theory has been previously developed from Booleans to numerical weights, hinting at degrees of awareness and consciousness.

In this paper, an agent's degree of awareness at any time is taken to reflect its freedom of choice amongst its possible behaviours. It is expressed as the number of actions which are enabled as a next behavioural step at that time and over which the agent has at least partial control. An agent is conscious of things which enable a fresh choice of action there, an enumeration of which provides its degree of consciousness. Those notions of degree are shown to provide a satisfactory account of realistic examples and to provide sensible elementary laws.

Valiant has shown that, in our terms, a living agent adapting daily to survive in its habitat as well its evolving in the very much longer term, can in both senses be expressed ecorithmically as learning. That approach is used here to consider the roles played by awareness and consciousness in the adaptation of an agent and a species.

1 Introduction

We assume that agents range from animals (humans and others both domesticated and wild) through cells to organisations and software (like AIs), and promote the view that different types of agent may exhibit different degrees of consciousness, quite possibly zero. The study of laws satisfied by agent consciousness is pertinent because of current popular and professional interest in the question of whether or not an AI, like a Large Language Model, can be conscious. Without some criteria, how are we to decide?

Agents exist in some context which we model as a system. We continue from our previous paper [6] to adopt the standard view that a model of any system is constrained by the interrelated criteria of breadth (or extent) and depth (or level of detail).

An agent's context is called its *habitat*, whose details depend on the domain and purpose of the model. Typically it includes other agents, features external

© The Author(s), under exclusive license to Springer Nature Switzerland AG 2023
J. P. Bowen et al. (Eds.): *Theories of Programming and Formal Methods*, LNCS 14080, pp. 87–109, 2023.
https://doi.org/10.1007/978-3-031-40436-8_4

and internal to the agent, and a 'catch-all' category called[1] the *backdrop*. The backdrop is deemed to be a default agent and the distinction between physical and backdrop features will be determined by emphasis of the model, taking account of the control of its dynamics. Examples of these ideas appear in the next section.

A system's dynamics includes the behaviour of its agents, one step at a time. Each step we call an *action*. An action may lie under the control of more than one agent including the backdrop. Indeed an agent is a system component characterised by having control (perhaps partial) of at least one action. A system is expressed as a data type, so that ongoing actions normally described by safety and liveness are expressed instead by their individual steps.

Any *scientific* approach to agent awareness and consciousness must be phrased in falsifiable terms. Thus we eschew an animal's 'state of mind' which is not falsifiable (at least with current neuroscience). Thus it is a matter of belief, not science, that a dog is happy when it wags its tail. An agent's actions we thus take to be observable only if they are falsifiable, which requires hypothesis testing if the actions occur probabilistically. Henceforth by 'observable' we mean falsifiably so.

Since Descartes and Locke, if not before, human consciousness has been thought of in terms of the means by which a person becomes aware of features in its habitat. A contemporary rendering is given by Bernard Baars's Global Workspace Theory, GWT, [1], which has inspired a dozen architectures purporting to account for consciousness of a feature at a time; see Sect. 7.

Our approach departs from those architectures in our insistence on falsifiability. The alternative taken has been the standard mathematical one: of offering laws satisfied by awareness and consciousness in the hope that eventually sufficiently many will accrue to characterise it. In case of shortfall there may still be sufficiently many laws to falsify consciousness of some agents. Also, in the absence of a *definition* it is still helpful to have *heuristics* for awareness and consciousness, which are strong enough to show consistency of the laws when there is any doubt.

In this paper we concentrate on the underlying model which is inspired by but simplifies those we have considered previously [5,6].

An agent is deemed heuristically to be *aware* of a feature (external or internal) at a given time which enables some action (in the sense of establishing its precondition) which is at least partially within the agent's control. The action need not occur, but it is a candidate for the agent's next behavioural step. In terms of a scheduling protocol $\mathcal{P}$ for the agent's next action, the agent is cognizant of the domain of $\mathcal{P}$, the actions from which it chooses, even though the protocol itself is unknown.

An agent is deemed heuristically to be *conscious* of something which causes a fresh choice of action, even though the protocol for making the choice still remains unknown.

---

[1] Called 'the environment' in our previous work [5,6].

The paper is structured as follows. Features are introduced with a light touch in Sect. 3 and used to express the awareness heuristically in both Boolean and numerical terms. The models are simple because of the restricted use made of features and of time. They are used to give corresponding new models of consciousness in Sect. 4.

To test the formalism, the case study of a simplified cell is presented in Sect. 5 and its degrees of awareness and consciousness computed. Adaptation of living agents, and the roles played by awareness, consciousness and the protocol $\mathcal{P}$, are considered in Sect. 6 using Valiant's concept of ecorithm. The paper ends with Related and further work, and a Conclusion.

But we start with an uncharacteristically anthropomorphic example which exemplifies the ideas mentioned above and motivates the heuristics used.

2 Cameo

It is an autumn afternoon. Two parents are feeding their 3-month-old daughter in response to her cries, whilst their 2-year-old son builds a tower with blocks in his bedroom and their pet Golden Retriever naps in its bed in a corner of the laundry beside its water bowl.

The parents are being guided by intuition with the upbringing of their son and so are now more experienced and relaxed with their daughter. They are alert to her needs and often anticipate them, burping her after feeding and checking her nappy if she seems discontented. Their son is becoming autonomous, beginning to assert himself and often able to play by himself, though at 2 still needs support and supervision. The dog (and the parents) have been well trained at the local *Canine Academy* and it is treated as one of the family. Suddenly it rouses to bark protectively after sensing a passing pedestrian outside, unheard by the parents.

Apparently having fed enough, the baby falls asleep. One parent goes to the kitchen to prepare dinner whilst the other takes the dog's lead off its peg in the hall. The dog rushes to the front door, tail wagging, in anticipation of its daily walk to the park. The son, hearing activity and knowing the schedule, emerges from his bedroom. As his parent puts the leash on the dog the son requests 'Me too' to join the trip to the park. Wanting to walk like his parent, he refuses to be seated in his stroller; for now anyway. The parents call farewell to each other and the walk begins.

On the way to the local park the dog, on the extensible leash, enthusiastically engages in its usual routine with every tree and lamp post whilst the boy, clasping his parent's hand, looks around curiously. The parent is idly contemplating some thoughts about work, when they come to a crossroad. Becoming instantly alert, the parent ensures that the dog is by their side, and begins to teach the boy the time-honoured algorithm involving looking each way before crossing the road. Suddenly a car approaches, much noisier and faster than usual. The dog watches it and growls, and the parent pauses to check their safety, then resumes the lesson, using the car to stress the danger of roads. The car fades into the distance and they cross.

At the park the dog, free of the leash, fruitlessly chases a bird searching for worms and insects in the grass. The boy roams free, and decides to collect acorns in a pile in his stroller. The parent keeps a watchful eye on both from a park bench whilst ruminating on what wine to open with dinner.

2.1 Discussion

The agents in the model underlying that Cameo include a family of four, their pet dog, a car driver, birds and perhaps worms and insects at the park, depending on the breadth of the model. For example He Jifeng does not happen to be included. The dog's external features include its bed, lead, trees and lamp posts along the way to the park; but the position of the planets is not included. Its internal features include its nature and nurture, with remembered locations and events; but biometrics are not included. Its backdrop includes the passage of the sun across the sky; again, its details depend on the depth and breadth of the model.

The dog's behaviour, by its nature (and species in particular) lives up to its epithet as man's best friend. As a result its actions often indicate surprising awareness of and attentiveness to the family's needs. Considering an agent to be aware of things which enable an action at least partially within its control, the dog is aware of food (which enables its eating), the family and other dogs (which alter its behaviour), its daily routine (which it anticipates), opportunities to play and for human attention.

The dog behaves differently at different times of the day, due to its awareness of the position of the sun overhead and ambient animal noises. The sun is an external feature lying beyond the control of any component of the system and so belongs to the backdrop.

A rock at the park undergoes dynamics, due to erosion by the elements. But since those lie beyond its control, the rock is not an agent.

By comparison, the nature and nurture of the parents means they coordinate closely with each other as guardians and providers. Other internal features include their aspirations and social expectations. They are aware of idle thoughts which enable their ability to relate them. But they are not aware, for instance, of current popular TV series. Their backdrop includes the domestic water supply and movement of the sun.

The baby is aware of far fewer features than the son who is aware of fewer than the parents. The baby is just becoming aware of the appearance and noise of the dog, which attracts her attention but enables no further action. The son is in addition keen to play with the dog as are the parents who also act to ensure its health and safety.

Counting the number of actions under each agent's control which are enabled by the dog, the baby has fewer than the son who has fewer than the parents.

The dog's awareness of its lead being taken from the peg enables a fresh action at that moment: its walk outside. On the walk to the park the parent is conscious only initially of taking steps, because care is required in descending the front doorsteps, and then in matching pace to that of the boy and the dog.

But then the footsteps becomes routine and the parent is no longer conscious of them. But they return immediately to consciousness if a fresh action becomes enabled; like recovering from tripping over a misaligned paving stone.

3 Features

We suppose that any system contains a set $\mathcal{F}$ of *features* (from our earlier work [5,6]) which are time dependent and influence agent and system behaviour. Features are compounded from a set *Basic* of (domain-dependent) features under Boolean combinators corresponding to 'non occurrence', 'joint occurrence', 'conditional occurrence', 'eventual conditional occurrence' and 'awareness', provided the result is observable as discussed in the Introduction.

Awareness is included as a feature because it plays an important role in an agent's choice of next behavioural step. For instance the dog's behaviour depends on its awareness of its lead being taken from the peg, and the parent's behaviour then depends on its awareness of the dog's awareness.

In the Cameo features include: 'the passing pedestrian'; 'the lead being taken from the peg' which leads to 'the daily walk', and so on. Features do not include 'radio waves' unless the system also includes an appropriate receiver, without which the waves are not observable.

Definition 1 (Features). *At any time the features of a system are either Basic, or defined in terms of the combinators:*

$$\mathcal{F} := Basic \mid \neg \mathcal{F} \mid \mathcal{F} \wedge \mathcal{F} \mid \mathcal{F} \Rightarrow \mathcal{F} \mid \mathcal{F} \Leftrightarrow \mathcal{F} \mid A_a \mathcal{F}$$

Since a combination belongs to $\mathcal{F}$ only if it is observable, even if f is a feature the inconsistent conjunction $f \wedge \neg f = false$ is not.

A feature's time dependence we treat modally, making the time variable explicit only when necessary. The notation A_a for agent a's awareness is chosen because we regard awareness as a modal operator and that notation resembles that used in epistemic and doxastic logic. We begin by giving the semantics behind the syntax A_a after which we deal with the logical combinators.

3.1 Awareness

The Cameo motivates a Boolean notion and a numerical one of agent awareness and consciousness.

An agent is deemed to be aware of something at time t which enables an action, at least partially within its control, then. The action is therefore a candidate for the agent's next action at t. The number of such actions is its degree of awareness at t.

To express that, a little notation is helpful.

(a) The set of actions which are at least partially within agent a's control at time t is called a's *ambit* and denoted $\mathcal{A}m(a,t)$ (from our earlier work [5,14]). For instance the dog's walk to the park lies in both its ambit and that of its owner. But the weather at the park belongs to the ambit of neither.

(b) For action α its precondition, pre α, holds at just those states s and inputs in from which α is defined and terminates. Writing α as a predicate in the four free variables s (state before), in (input), s' (state after) and out (output):

$$(\text{pre } \alpha)(s, in) \ := \ \exists \, s', out \cdot \alpha(s, in, s', out).$$

For instance the precondition for the dog to eat from its bowl is that it be by the bowl which contains acceptable food.

Time, as used in (a), is replaced (following tradition) by state in (b). The two are reconciled by replacing state in (b) by either time from $\mathbb{T}$ or in both cases by a trace of actions which have occurred, in order of occurrence.

Awareness of a feature f at time t, that f enables some action in a's ambit at t, makes sense only if $f(t)$ holds (which is why negation of features is essential). Simplifying the formalization:

$$\exists \alpha : \mathcal{A}m(a, t) \cdot f \wedge (f \Rightarrow \text{pre } \alpha)$$

leads to the definition:

$$A_a(f, t) \ := \ f(t) \wedge \exists \alpha : \mathcal{A}m(a, t) \cdot \text{pre } \alpha. \tag{1}$$

For instance the dog is aware of the passing pedestrian which enables its bark. Until then the humans are not aware of it, having more limited hearing. But then the parents' curiosity is aroused so the action of looking out the window is enabled by the dog's bark. An enabled action need not occur, so the parents may choose instead to continue what they are doing, perhaps because it is common for the dog to bark at pedestrians, or what they are doing is more important.

It is convenient to set:

$$\mathcal{S}(a, f, t) \ := \ \{\alpha : \mathcal{A}m(a, t) \mid f(t) \wedge \text{pre } \alpha\} \tag{2}$$

so that (1) becomes:

$$A_a(f, t) \ = \ \mathcal{S}(a, f, t) \neq \varnothing.$$

That leads to a definition of degree of awareness:

$$|A_a(f, t)| \ := \ \#\mathcal{S}(a, f, t). \tag{3}$$

That numerical measure is defined only for awareness $A_a(f, t)$ and not for features in general, as in our earlier work. The result is a simpler model requiring less commitment to unnecessary detail in examples.

3.2   Features Resumed

We can now return to the semantics of the Boolean combinators on features. Provided the result is observable, they are given pointwise on the time variable:

$$(\neg f)(t) := \neg f(t)$$
$$(f \wedge g)(t) := f(t) \wedge g(t)$$
$$(f \Rightarrow g)(t) := f(t) \Rightarrow g(t)$$
$$(f \twoheadrightarrow g)(t) := f(t) \Rightarrow \exists\, u \geq t \cdot g(u)$$
$$A_a(f, t) := \text{Definition (1).}$$

Evidently a compound scenario within a system can be described by a combination of features. For instance in the Cameo the lead being taken from its peg leads to the dog's walk and so on.

Simple laws of awareness involving those combinators appear in Fig. 1.

$$A_a(f, t) \Rightarrow f(t) \tag{4}$$

$$\begin{pmatrix} A_a(f, t) \\ A_a(g, t) \end{pmatrix} = A_a(f \wedge g, t) \tag{5}$$

$$\begin{pmatrix} A_a(f, t) \\ A_a(f \Rightarrow g, t) \end{pmatrix} \Rightarrow A_a(g, t) \tag{6}$$

$$A_a(f, t) \Rightarrow \nabla_a(f, t) \tag{7}$$

Fig. 1. Simple laws for awareness of agent a in the Boolean model, subject to the qualifications in Theorem 1. The dual modal operator is defined as usual, pointwise on t, by $\nabla_a(f) := \neg A_a(\neg f)$.

Theorem 1 (Laws for awareness). *The laws of Fig. 1 hold, Expressions (5) and (6) provided $\mathcal{A}m(a, t)$ is closed under the demonic choice of actions. Furthermore the implications are strict.*

Proof. Law (4) follows immediately since f is a conjunct in Definition 1 of $A_a(f, t)$. The converse clearly fails; for instance in the Cameo, the parents are not aware of the passing pedestrian when the dog is.

For Law (5) we reason that if f, g both hold at t they are consistent so $f \wedge g$ is also a feature and hence:

$$\begin{pmatrix} A_a(f, t) \\ A_a(g, t) \end{pmatrix}$$

$\equiv$ Definition (1) of awareness

$$\begin{pmatrix} \exists\, \alpha : \mathcal{A}m(a, t) \cdot f(t) \wedge \text{pre } \alpha \\ \exists\, \beta : \mathcal{A}m(a, t) \cdot g(t) \wedge \text{pre } \beta \end{pmatrix}$$

$\equiv$ logic

$$\exists\, \alpha, \beta : \mathcal{A}m(a, t) \cdot f(t) \wedge g(t) \wedge \text{pre } \alpha \wedge \text{pre } \beta$$

$$\equiv \qquad\qquad\qquad\qquad\qquad \text{pre } \alpha \wedge \text{pre } \beta = \text{pre } (\alpha \sqcap \beta)$$

$$\exists \alpha, \beta : \mathcal{A}m(a, t) \cdot f(t) \wedge g(t) \wedge \text{pre } (\alpha \sqcap \beta)$$

$$\equiv \qquad\qquad\qquad\qquad\qquad \gamma := \alpha \sqcap \beta; \Leftarrow \text{straightforward}$$

$$\exists \gamma : \mathcal{A}m(a, t) \cdot f(t) \wedge g(t) \wedge \text{pre } \gamma$$

$$\equiv \qquad\qquad\qquad\qquad\qquad\qquad\qquad\qquad \text{Definition 1 again}$$

$$A_a(f \wedge g, t).$$

The proof of Law (6) is similar using angelic choice $\alpha \sqcup \beta$ instead of demonic choice.

Law (7) requires simple propositional reasoning:

$$A_a(f, t)$$

$$\equiv \qquad\qquad\qquad\qquad\qquad\qquad\qquad\qquad\qquad\qquad \text{definition}$$

$$f(t) \wedge \exists \alpha : \mathcal{A}m(a, t) \cdot \text{pre } \alpha$$

$$\Rightarrow \qquad\qquad\qquad\qquad\qquad\qquad\qquad\qquad\qquad \text{logic, for any } X$$

$$f(t) \vee X$$

$$\equiv \qquad\qquad\qquad\qquad\qquad\qquad\qquad \text{logic, with } X := \neg \exists \beta \dots$$

$$\neg(\neg f(t) \wedge \exists \beta : \mathcal{A}m(a, t) \cdot \text{pre } \beta)$$

$$\equiv \qquad\qquad\qquad\qquad\qquad\qquad\qquad\qquad\qquad\qquad \text{definition}$$

$$\neg A_a(\neg f, t)$$

$$\equiv \qquad\qquad\qquad\qquad\qquad\qquad\qquad\qquad\qquad\qquad \text{definition}$$

$$\nabla_a(f, t).$$

Evidently the implication is strict. For example in the Cameo the dog may not be aware of the lack of water in its bowl because it is on the walk; so it is not aware of the presence of water.   □

A probabilistic choice between two actions is a special case of their demonic choice. By comparison the existence of the angelic combination of consistent actions is a strong assumption, leading to actions which backtrack and so on.

4   Consciousness

We now make the assumption that time is linear and discrete. If initialization is important to the model, the time domain $\mathbb{T}$ is often assumed to be an initial segment of $\mathbb{T} := \mathbb{N}$. In other words it is $\mathbb{N}$ or, if finite, the interval $[0, n]$ of integers. But if initialisation is unimportant and time infinite, a more convenient choice may be $\mathbb{T} := \mathbb{Z}$.

Either way we assume that each non-initial time $t : \mathbb{T}$ has a unique predecessor t^- and each non-final time has a unique successor t^+.

We regard an agent a as conscious of a feature f at time t if a is aware of f at t *via* a *fresh* action: one which was not enabled at t^-.

We define a modal operator C_a for consciousness by expanding A_a to incorporate freshness:

$$C_a(f,t) := \exists \alpha : Am(a,t) \cdot \begin{pmatrix} f(t) \\ (\text{pre } \alpha)(t) \\ \neg(\text{pre } \alpha)(t^-) \end{pmatrix}. \tag{8}$$

As always that existence does not mean the fresh action need be taken.

As with awareness, that Boolean notion extends to degrees by enumerating the fresh actions:

$$\mid C_a(f,t) \mid := \#\{\alpha : Am(a,t) \cdot \begin{pmatrix} f(t) \\ (\text{pre } \alpha)(t) \\ \neg(\text{pre } \alpha)(t^-) \end{pmatrix}\}. \tag{9}$$

And, as with the relationship between the Boolean and numerical models of awareness,

$$C_a(f,t) = \mid C_a(f,t) \mid > 0.$$

$$C_a(f,t) \Rightarrow A_a(f,t) \tag{10}$$

$$\begin{pmatrix} C_a(f,t) \\ C_a(g,t) \end{pmatrix} = C_a(f \wedge g, t) \tag{11}$$

$$\begin{pmatrix} C_a(f,t) \\ C_a(f \Rightarrow g, t) \end{pmatrix} \Rightarrow C_a(g,t) \tag{12}$$

$$C_a(f,t) \Rightarrow \nabla_a(f,t) \tag{13}$$

Fig. 2. Laws for consciousness corresponding to those of Fig. 1, subject to the qualifications of Theorem 2. The modal operator dual to C_a is defined by decorating the dual of A_a: $\nabla_a(f,t) := \neg C_a(\neg f, t)$.

Laws for consciousness that correspond to those of Fig. 1 are given in Fig. 2. Their correctness follows from both the content and method of Theorem 1.

Theorem 2 (Laws for consciousness). *The laws of Fig. 2 hold, (5) provided $Am(a,t)$ is closed under demonic choice and (6) provided it is closed under angelic choice of consistent actions. Furthermore the implications are strict.*

5   Case Study: A Cell

In this section we give an example of a system and an agent which is simple enough for its features to be identified more completely than in the Cameo and for the agent's awareness to be determined.

We choose to model an idealised typical cell and find it, not surprisingly, to be an agent which is aware but not conscious. No specialized biological knowledge[2] is assumed. We use the Z notation, mostly[3] as covered by Spivey [17].

The cell is distinguished from its environmental periplasm by a semipermeable membrane containing the cell's cytoplasm. For homeostasis, temperature and various concentrations like pH within the cell must remain within certain bounds. Temperature is determined by the environment but regulation of various concentrations in the cytoplasm is achieved by transpiration through the membrane, sometimes requiring energy from the cell. We abstract the various concentrations, but include as a fundamental feature $alive : \mathbb{B}$, whether or not the cell is alive. We suppose that for $t_0, t_1 : \mathbb{R}$ and temperature $temp$ in centigrade,

$$alive \Rightarrow t_0 \leq temp \leq t_1.$$

Transpiration is achieved by 'channels' which import nutrients (like sugars and amino acids) and which export the byproducts of metabolism (like sodium ions, or volatile compounds). A channel may be:

(a) *passive*, not requiring energy but working with the gradient by osmosis or diffusion or being 'facilitated'; or
(b) *active* requiring cell energy to work against a concentration gradient using one of several methods.

Energy is produced by the break down of ATP, *Adenosine Triphosphate*, with water to give ADP, *Adenosine Diphosphate*, and phosphorus; see Wikipedia, [20]: Adenosine triphosphate. ATP is produced and stored in the cell's mitochondria by the TCA (Citric Acid or Krebs Cycle); see the survey by Massimo Bonora *et al.*, [4]. We abstract that mechanism entirely, and instead consider just the amount of *energy* available in the cell; see Garrett Heinrich [9].

We begin by modelling a cell's active importing channel as follows.

5.1   Cell Importer

An *importer* is an active channel which imports certain kinds of molecule, of type $\mathbb{M}$ol, to the cell. It is formed from two *domains*, one atop the other, as shown in Fig. 3.

---

[2] A helpful reference for further relevant details is Wikipedia, [20], for instance: Cell membrane; Active transport; Facilitated diffusion; Ion channel.

[3] The definition of operation *Release* in two steps is nonstandard but hopefully clear.

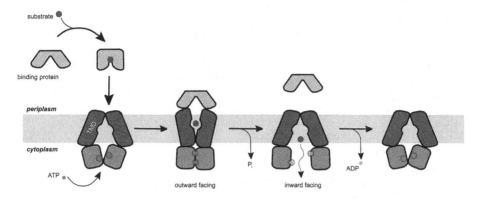

Fig. 3. Cross section of an importer through the cell membrane. Image from Wikipedia, [20]: ATP-binding cassette transporter (captured February 2023).

The domain contacting the periplasm, the *transmembrane domain*, has an outer gate, *tout*, to the periplasm and an inner gate, *tin*. Each is either closed or open, *tout*, *tin* : $\mathbb{B}$, with *false* representing closed. When the cell is live, if one of the gates is open the other is closed: $tin = \neg tout$.

Beneath is the *nucleotide-binding domain* whose outer gate *nout* contacts the cytoplasm and inner gate, *tin*, connects to the inner gate *nin*, so $tin = nin$. However now both gates of the nucleotide-binding domain may be closed, both may be open, or *nout* may be closed whilst *nin* is open. In summary $\neg(nout \wedge \neg nin)$, or $nout \Rightarrow nin$.

The two domains join in a cavity capable of holding a molecule of type $\mathbb{M}$ol (which depends on the kind of channel). Combining the four gate observables with the state of the cavity, the temperature and whether or not the cell is alive gives the importer's *State*. (Temperature is included to record the influence of the environment on the state of the cell).

Initially, both outer gates are closed, the inner gates are open and the cavity is empty. We describe initialisation as an operation which starts from an arbitrary state and terminates in an initial state, so we can use it later to reinitialise the state. As usual $\bot$ denotes the undefined state and $X_\bot$ denotes the type X augmented with $\bot$.

$\boxed{\begin{array}{l} \_State _____ \\ alive : \mathbb{B} \\ temp : \mathbb{R} \\ energy : \mathbb{R}^{\geq 0} \\ cavity : \mathrm{Mol}_\perp \\ tin, tout : \mathbb{B} \\ nin, nout : \mathbb{B} \\ \hline alive \Rightarrow \begin{pmatrix} t_0 \leq temp \leq t_1 \\ energy > 0 \\ tin = \neg tout \\ tin = nin \\ nout \Rightarrow nin \end{pmatrix} \end{array}}$

$\boxed{\begin{array}{l} \_Initialise _____ \\ \Delta State \\ \hline alive' \\ cavity' = \perp \\ \neg tout' \wedge \neg nout' \end{array}}$

The implication in the state invariant is not an equivalence because:

(a) the cell may die for other reasons; and
(b) if the cell dies after attaining unsafe levels, it remains dead even if they subsequently return to normal.

Importing a molecule to the cell *via* the importer channel is done in three stages: docking, *Dock*; followed by release, *Release*; then reinitialisation, *Initialise*:

$$Import := Dock \, \fatsemi \, Release \, \fatsemi \, Initialise.$$

Dock inputs a molecule m : Mol bound to a *binding protein* $bp(\ )$: Ptn from the periplasm, in the form $bp(m)$. Formally, that is defined by feature combination: $bp(m)(t) := (bp(\ )\&m)(t)$. *Dock* also inputs a quantum of energy, en_0, from the cell, as discussed above.

Dock requires both outer gates to be closed initially (from which it follows by the state invariant that both inner gates are open) and the *cavity* to be empty (its content equals $\perp$). Afterwards it ensures that *tout* is open, *nout* remains closed (so by the state invariant *tin* and *nin* are both closed), *nout* is closed, *bp* is empty, the cavity contains molecule m, and energy has been consumed.

$\boxed{\begin{array}{l} \_Dock _____ \\ \Delta State[cavity, tout, tin, nout, \\ \qquad\qquad nin, energy, alive] \\ bp(m)? : \mathrm{Ptn} \times \mathrm{Mol} \\ \hline alive \\ energy' = energy - en_0 \\ \neg tout \wedge tout' \\ \neg nout \wedge \neg nout' \\ cavity = \perp \\ cavity' = m? \end{array}}$

$\boxed{\begin{array}{l} \_\mathrm{pre}\ Dock _____ \\ State \\ bp(m)? : \mathrm{Ptn} \times \mathrm{Mol} \\ energy? : \mathbb{R}^+ \\ \hline alive \\ \neg tout \wedge \neg nout \\ cavity = \perp \\ C.energy \geq en_0 \end{array}}$

The precondition of *Dock* is that *tout* and *nout* are closed, the cavity is empty and the cell has sufficient energy.

Release assumes the conditions established by *Dock*. It outputs the empty binding protein, *bp( )*, closes *tout* and opens *tin*, *nin* and *nout* so that the molecule *m* in the cavity can enter the cytoplasm. We describe *Release* as two steps in sequence. In the first step, from *State* to *State'*, the upper outer gate closes whilst the lower outer gate remains closed, and *bp( )* is output. In the second step, from *State'* to *State''*, the upper outer gate remains closed whilst the other gates open and *m* is output to the cytoplasm.

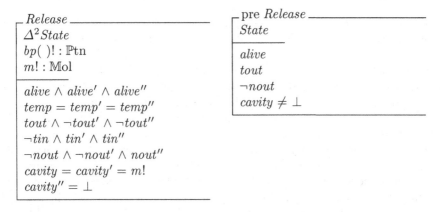

The precondition is that *tout* is open, *nout* is closed and the cavity is nonempty.

Finally the importer is reinitialised with operation *Initialise*, leaving it in a state satisfying pre *Dock* (except for the cell's energy level). Of course *Initialise* is total.

To be able to function against a concentration gradient, the system of gates must function like an airlock. We use that property to 'validate' the breadth and depth of our model of an importer; without some such validation we can have little confidence in the accuracy of our model.

Theorem 3 (Airlock). *The action Import at no time connects the periplasm and cytoplasm directly.*

Proof. Since *Import* is the sequential composition of three actions it suffices to show the claim for each, *Dock*, *Release* and *Initialise*. We show that at no time (not just at the end of each step) are all four gates open:

$$\neg(tout \land tin \land nin \land nout). \tag{14}$$

Initially both outer gates, *tout* and *nout*, are closed so (14) is established. We argue operationally, but in Hoare-logic style, that (14) is preserved during the animation of *Import*.

Dock keeps closed the lower gate *nout* whilst closing the inner gates *tin*, and *nin* and opening the upper outer gate *tout*. So (14) is maintained.

The first step of *Release* keeps closed the upper outer gate *tout* whilst the lower outer gate *nout* remains closed. The second step of *Release* keeps closed the upper outer gate *tout* whilst the lower three gates, *tin*, *nin* and *nout*, are opened. So (14) remains true.

Finally *Initialise* keeps closed the lower outer gate *nout* whilst the others, and *tout* in particular, are unchanged. We conclude that (14) is maintained throughout.   □

5.2   Cell Awareness

At any time our idealised cell may engage in the production of more ATP, or the import or export of molecules (including the ingredients or byproducts of the TCA cycle) on its channels like that described above with the four action steps of *Import*. Energy production also involves importing and exporting through the membrane of the mitochondria. The number of mitochondria depends on the metabolism requirements of the cell. In all, many actions are involved (characterising the breadth of study), each composed of many steps (depending on the depth of study).

We suppose for simplicity that the cell has 15 mitochondria, 20 importers, 20 exporters and 25 residual mechanisms. Each of those involves an action composed of steps in sequence, like *Import*. They are interdependent when resources are low, which for simplicity we overlook. The cell's degree of awareness of its internal activity f at t equals the number of actions in $Am(cell, t)$ which are enabled at t. Enumerating by the four kinds of mechanism, that might typically be:

$$A_{cell}(f, t) = 15 + 20 + 20 + 25$$
$$= 80.$$

However that awareness, although observable, does not enable any fresh action and so the cell is not conscious of f at t:

$$\neg C_{cell}(f, t)$$
$$\mid C_{cell}(f, t) \mid = 0.$$

6   Adaptation

We view a species, subject to evolution, as an agent in control of its DNA. The control is partial because of epigenetic influences; but that is sufficient for it to satisfy our definition of agenthood. On one hand such an agent adapts to its environment day-by-day and its species adapts by evolving generation-by-generation.

In this section we combine those forms of adaptation following Valiant's concept of ecorithm, to understand the roles played by awareness and consciousness in adaptation.

In interacting day-by-day with its habitat (including other agents), and buffeted by its backdrop, an agent adapts to survive. The result is a change in both the habitat and the agent's *nurture*. Evolving generation-by-generation the species improves its fitness to survive, subject to epigenetics and genetic mutations of its DNA. The result is a change in its *nature*.

Both forms of adaptation have been explained with the concept of an *ecorithm* by Leslie Valiant, [19] (who has been able to clarify and formalize Darwinian evolution in terms of machine learning). The 'fitness function' (or 'performance function' in Valiant's terms) evolves and maintains improvement towards a limit given by some mathematical, ideal function.

> *Making the assumption already implicit in Darwin's work-that different choices of action have various levels of benefit for the evolving entity-we can define the performance and the target in terms of the notion I call an ideal function. For any species (or other evolving entity), at any instant, in any specific environment, this ideal function will specify in every possible situation the most beneficial course of action.*
>
> Leslie Valiant, [19] p. 111.

We begin by formalising the life of a living agent in terms of its nature (DNA) and nurture (learning from its habitat). A machine-learning system learns how to classify a given datum on the basis of experience. The simple example of binary classification by means, used by Bernhard Schölkopf & Alexander Smola, [15]: Section 1.2, is specified in Fig. 6 of the Appendix as a data type. We now use those ideas to describe a living agent, culminating in Fig. 4.

6.1   Living Agent

The state of a living agent we take to consist of: whether or not it is alive, *live* : $\mathbb{B}$; its DNA, *dna* : *DNA*; its behaviour, or history of actions, *data* : seq *Action* from its ambit; the behaviour *habs* : seq *Action* of its habitat beyond its control; the behaviour *envs* : seq *Action* controlled by its backdrop, *e*; and its (unknown) choice protocol, $\mathcal{P}$, as above. We overlook the agent's identity.

Initially: the agent is alive with some DNA, dna_0; empty *data*, *habs* and *envs*; and some protocol $\mathcal{P}_0$.

It is no more straightforward to classify a living agent's interactions with its habitat than it is to provide details of $\mathcal{P}$.

> *Since the actions we take in one circumstance may influence what is the most beneficial action in another, it is the combination of all the action functions that is evaluated. The ideal one is that which produces most benefit in that snapshot of an environment.*
>
> Leslie Valiant, [19]; page 112.

Informed by *ML*, we describe the ways in which an agent's state can change. We include operations *Learn*, *Predict*, *FreeWill*, *Supervene*, *Vicinity*, *Beget* and

Die. Each requires the agent to be live. The operations *Learn* and *Predict* are as described by the general setting of the Appendix but using an unknown ideal function *FF* to update $\mathcal{P}$.

The details of *FreeWill* are concealed within the protocol $\mathcal{P}$. It is given as a separate operation because without it the classification of a living agent's interactions would seem incomplete. *Supervene* describes an action of the backdrop, either instantaneous by normal time scales like the eruption of Vesuvius, or incremental like an ice age. It may result in the agent's death, but anyway updates *envs*. *Vicinity* describes actions in the habitat which lie beyond the agent's control; it extends the trace *habs*. Like *Supervene*, its actions may well impact *a*'s behaviour.

Beget is the only operation to output an agent, the offspring *b*!. It is specified with partner a_0? and is asexual iff that equals the current agent. The function *Fme* describes how the offspring's DNA is formed from those of its parents, taking into account mutations and epigenetics. *Beget*'s precondition is that both the agent and its partner are alive.

After *Die* a living agent is no longer living (to state the obvious). Its control is difficult to specify because the operation may be internal to the agent, due to congenital malady or old age (Queen Elizabeth II), the result of actions of other agents (Julius Caesar) or of the environment (the population of Pompeii under erupting Vesuvius).

The specification of the type *Living agent* is naturally an extension of the type *ML*, which is the point of having considered it first. In spite of that we present it in Fig. 4 from scratch and for readability ignore various Z shortcuts.

In the spectrum of agents considered here, those which evolve are particularly important because they provide a way to understand the evolution of consciousness. It may be that there is an almost-Darwinian sense in which software evolves (did ChatGPT3.5 beget ChatGPT4?); certainly in the early years programming languages were classified by 'generation'. But for now we assume that evolution applies only to living agents.

6.2 Family Tree

Viewing a species as an agent we now extend the description of a single living agent to a species *via* its family tree, adapting ecologically. See Fig. 5.

The family tree consists of a sequence of finite sets of living agents, each an offspring of an agent in the previous generation. It also contains a fitness function (for simplicity we consider just one) which evolves by generation. In each generation all agents are live and share the same habitats and backdrops.

Initially the sequence is a singleton, the first generation consists of some nonempty set of agents and the fitness function is undefined, awaiting learning.

That concept of generation, represented by *g* in Fig. 5, requires comment. For the case of parthogenesis, asexual reproduction, it is well defined. Most human cultures have taboos against parent-child breeding, in which case *g* is also well defined. But otherwise, including for many animal species (see the interesting discussion of Victoria Pike *et al.*, [13], *g* needs to be defined as the length of the shortest path between the two sets of agents.

Fig. 4. The format of a living agent adapting day-to-day, in terms of machine-learning. Unknown procedures, like how the next action is the result of nature and nurture, or of free will, are abstracted in the next-step protocol $\mathcal{P}$ which is assumed to be updated in learning by FF. The agent's next action benefits from its nature and nurture by way of operation *Predict*.

Supervention by the backdrop may affect a whole generation as well as providing changes in the fitness function. It is total.

Each interaction of an agent with its habitat now consists of one of the operations *Learn*, *Predict*, *FreeWill*, *Vicinity*, *Beget* and *Die* from Fig. 4, the

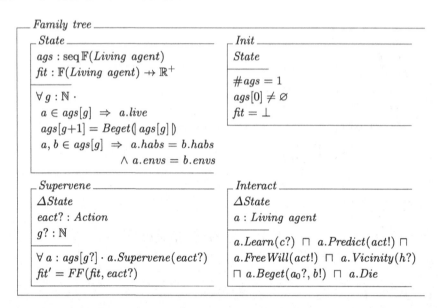

Fig. 5. The format for a family tree of living agents adapting and evolving in some habitat. Adaptation of a single agent to survive is as in Fig. 4, whilst evolution is described by supervention to change DNA between generations.

choice being made by its choice protocol. At this level we simply combine those actions nondeterministically.

6.3 Adaptation and Consciousness

What evolutionary advantage does consciousness confer?

Adapting day-to-day, a living agent is aware of features which enable some action for its protocol $\mathcal{P}$ to choose from. It is conscious of features which enable fresh actions and hence update the domain of $\mathcal{P}$. But whilst interacting and adapting, $\mathcal{P}$ changes incrementally as in machine learning.

Adapting in the long-term the species DNA is modified and as a result so is the protocol $\mathcal{P}$ (a change we allocate to FF). But now the change seems most unlikely to be incremental: arbitrary increments are likely. The only thing comparable in one generation would be a complete change of habitat, like animal migration or man walking on the moon.

Changes in $\mathcal{P}$ are thus either incremental, by generation, or possibly wild and unprecedented, in evolution. In terms of seeking a ground state in evolutionary phase space, presumably the goal of any species, that results in a well-known searching strategy which combines stepwise local search with jumps to avoid capture by local minima.

7   Related and Further Work

Russell and Whitehead and
Hegel and Kant,
Maybe I shall and maybe I shan't.
Maybe I shan't and maybe I shall.
Kant Russell Whitehead, Hegel et al.

Frederick Winsor, [21].

Our previous work (Chen & Sanders, [5,6]), used reflexivity to define consciousness as awareness of awareness and achieved reflexivity using the notion of 'feature' in an agent-based system. The model of feature strength was based on the observation that awareness and consciousness fade with time unless refreshed. A Boolean model was accompanied by a numerical one in which the strength of a feature was defined to be proportional to the inverse of the time since its occurrence.

When we came to use feature strength to give an account of examples, like those in the Cameo and the cell, we found that the assignment of weights to features, though elegant in theory, seemed too arbitrary in practice. Moreover, the justifying stability analysis seemed much too difficult.

In this paper we have considered an alternative, more restrictive, approach. It is still based on the number of possible behaviours under the control of the agent at any time and again supports agent consciousness by degree. But we have replaced consciousness as reflexive awareness with an approach which seems to work better on examples.

There is not much directly-related work, though of course the topic of consciousness is burgeoning. The Global Workspace Theory, GWT, of Bernard Baars [1] already mentioned has been very influential concerning human consciousness and its appreciation in terms of a means by which features are promoted to consciousness. Over the past two decades the idea of a global workspace has been refined by a dozen architectures, many explicitly computational like the Conscious Turing Machine [3] of Manuel & Lenore Blum.

Our work departs from the GWT architectural approach by insisting that agents be general and that as far possible concepts be falsifiable.

Stanislas Dehaene [7] has proposed that a human is conscious of any feature on which he or she can report. In our terms the form of the report may be predetermined (by the person's choice protocol) but its content is entirely feature dependent and so the report itself is fresh. That indicates consciousness in our terms, so our heuristic can be seen as generalising consciousness to arbitrary agents Dehaene's approach.

For further work, less related but nonetheless interesting and important, we refer to Section 6 of our earlier paper [5] which includes: Giulio Tononi's Information Integration Theory, IIT, [18]; Donald Hoffman's Computational Evolutionary Perception, CEP, [10]; Mark Solms & Karl Friston's use of the 'free-energy principle' in modelling homeostasis with the prospect of consciousness,

[16], Chapter 7; and the enticing evolutionary aspects of consciousness, briefly touched on here in Sect. 6.3: Simona Ginsburg & Eva Jablonska's [8].

We have not availed ourselves of Thomas Nagel's hugely influential view [12] that an agent is conscious iff *there is something it is like to be that agent*. Owen Holland [11] makes the point that Nagel's view is based on living agents and that for artificial agents it might instead be replaced by an approach founded in engineering, and he discusses the difference between physical and virtual AIs. Our approach, restricted to those cases, though different does not seem far away.

We have recently discovered the work of Yoshua Bengio, for instance [2], which also takes an entirely non-architectural approach to consciousness of AI (Large Language Models in particular) but at a lower level of abstraction. Nonetheless his priors have much in common with our features (when interpreted probabilistically) and may suggest a way forward with feature strength.

There is a desperate need for realistic case studies, particularly concerning the development of consciousness, which seems so far to lie in fiction.[4] Having identified a degree of consciousness, it would be interesting to consider the rate of change of consciousness during a living agent's lifetime.

This work has followed the classical view that time is linear and events, though they may be concurrent, are viewed in a sequential manner. For much of science that view is sufficient. It is fundamental to the global workspace metaphor and also provides the basis for the traces of concurrent computations. It may well be that a nonlinear time domain makes more sense in considering consciousness.

8   Conclusion

We conclude that agent awareness and consciousness may be explained by degree (without explicitly assigning strength to features) in a way which makes much sense in examples.

In the case study of a cell we have inferred that the cell is aware but not conscious, with a degree of awareness $| A_{cell}(f, t) | = 80$. Eighty? Eighty! **He Jifeng**, we offer salutations and congratulations on your 80th *Festschrift* and look forward to your 90th, and before then more of your hugely influential work from which we have benefitted directly and as part of the community.

A tiny step has been made towards a setting in which to study the ecological development and contribution of consciousness.

Acknowledgements. The authors acknowledge the support of Chinese grant 2021YFB0301100. They greatly appreciate the standard established by Jonathan Bowen, Xu Qiwen and Li Qin, under the auspices of Zhu Huibiao, in the difficult setting of a *Festschrift*. Jonathan in particular has gone far beyond the call of duty to ensure the event and publication a success.

They are grateful that the paper in this unfamiliar topic has benefitted considerably from five reviews with a range of backgrounds. We are extremely grateful to the referees for their patience and insights.

---

[4] *The Enigma of Kaspar Hauser*, Werner Herzog, originally *Jeder für sich und Gott gegen alle*, 1974.

Appendix: Machine Learning

A machine-learning system for binary classification of data in $\mathbb{R}^n$ may be specified as an abstract data type as follows, resulting in Fig. 6.

ML

$\mathbb{C} := \{C, \overline{C}\}$ partitions $\mathbb{D}$

State

$data : \mathrm{bag}(\mathbb{D})$

$m, \overline{m} : \mathbb{R}^n_\perp$

$m = mean(\lbag d : data \mid d \in C \rbag)$

$\overline{m} = mean(\lbag d : data \mid d \in \overline{C} \rbag)$

Init

State

$data = \lbag \rbag$

$m, \overline{m} = \perp$

Learn

$\Delta State$

$(d?, e?) : \mathbb{D} \times \mathbb{C}$

$e? = C \Leftrightarrow d? \in C$

$data' = data \uplus \lbag d? \rbag$

Assign

$\Delta State$

$d? : \mathbb{D}$

$c! : \mathbb{C}$

$(c! = C) \Leftrightarrow |d? - m| \leq |d? - \overline{m}|$

Fig. 6. A simple machine-learning system input, as described by Bernhard Schölkopf & Alexander Smola, [15]: Section 1.2. The system learns and assigns to an input datum 'the' class whose mean lies closer.

Assume a type $\mathbb{D}$ of data, already a subset of $\mathbb{R}^n$ for some $n > 0$, and a Boolean partition $\mathbb{D} = C \cup \overline{C}$ in which each datum is assigned to either C or its complement $\overline{C}$ (we use other notation for the mean), determined by its membership. We write $\mathbb{C}$ for the partition $\{C, \overline{C}\}$ and assume it remains constant.

The state of the machine-learning system consists of a bag, or multiset, *data*, of data seen so far, together with the means $m, \overline{m}$ of their assignments to $C, \overline{C}$ (respectively) so far. Initially the bag of data is empty, $data = \lbag \rbag$, with the means undefined $m, \overline{m} = \perp$.

Learning results from correctly-assigned input data. The training operator, *Learn*, takes a datum and its classification and adds the datum to *data* and updates the means. So *Learn* is total.

The assignment operator, *Assign*, assigns to an input datum the category to whose mean it is closer in $\mathbb{R}^n$. For a nonempty bag D of data we write its mean as $mean(D) := (\#D)^{-1} \sum D$, where $\sum$ denotes bag summation. *Assign* is non-deterministic if the input datum is equidistant from both means. Its precondition is that the means are well defined: *data* contains data from each class.

In general machine learning, assignment of a general class $\mathbb{C}$ to an unseen input $d?$ is done by a protocol $\mathcal{P}$ which has been learnt in the same way that $m, \overline{m}$ are learnt there (facilitating output of a class with mean closer to $d?$). In general the protocol is a relation:

$$\mathcal{P} : \text{bag}\,(\mathbb{D} \times \mathbb{C}) \times \mathbb{D} \;\leftrightarrow\; \mathbb{C}.$$

In the case of Fig. 6 with binary assignment it has the simple form:

$$\mathcal{P}(d?, m, \overline{m}, c!) :=$$
$$(c! = C) \Leftrightarrow |d? - m| \le |d? - \overline{m}|\,.$$

In general we assume $\mathcal{P}$ to be updated in learning by some function FF.

Some machine-learning systems first learn $\mathcal{P}$ and then use it to classifies input. Our description in Fig. 6 allows further learning at any stage, so the format more closely matches that of a living agent. For instance a young animal spends its early years learning whilst interacting with its habitat; a process which continues throughout its life.

References

1. Baars, B.J.: A Cognitive Theory of Consciousness. CUP, Cambridge (1998)
2. Bengio, Y.: The Consciousness Prior (2017). https://arxiv.org/abs/1709.08568
3. Blum, M., Blum, L.: A theoretical computer science perspective on consciousness (2020). https://arxiv.org/ftp/arxiv/papers/2011/2011.09850.pdf
4. Bonora, M., et al.: ATP synthesis and storage. Purinergic Signal **8**(3), 343–357 (2012)
5. Chen, Y., Sanders, J.W.: A modal approach to consciousness of agents. In: Margaria, T., Steffen, B. (eds.) ISoLA 2022. LNCS, vol. 13703, pp. 127–141. Springer, Cham (2022). https://doi.org/10.1007/978-3-031-19759-8_9
6. Chen, Y., Sanders, J.W.: A modal approach to conscious social agents. In: Steffen, B., Wirsing, M., Margaria, T. (eds.) Transactions on FoMaC. LNCS, Springer (2023, to appear)
7. Dehaene, S.: Consciousness and the Brain. Penguin, London (2014)
8. Ginsburg, S., Jablonka, E.: The Evolution of the Sensitive Soul: Learning and the Origins of Consciousness. MIT Press, Cambridge (2019)
9. Heinrich, G.: How to Measure the Energetic Status of Cells? Enzo Life Sciences, TechNotes (2022)
10. Hoffman, D.D., Singh, M.: Computational evolutionary perception. Perception **41**, 1073–1091 (2012)
11. Holland, O.: Forget the bat. J. Artif. Intell. Consciousness **7**(1), 83–93 (2020)
12. Nagel, T.: What is it like to be a bat? Philos. Rev. **83**(4), 435–450 (1974)
13. Pike, V.L., Cornwallis, C.K., Griffin, A.S.: Why don't all animals avoid inbreeding? Proc. R. Soc. B **288**, 20211045 (2021)
14. Sanders, J.W., Turilli, M.: Dynamics of control. UNU-IIST Report 353 (2007)

15. Schölkopf, B., Smola, A.J.: Learning with Kernels: Support Vector Machines, Regularization, Optimization, and Beyond. MIT Press, Cambridge (2002)
16. Solms, M.: The Hidden Spring: A Journey to the Source of Consciousness. W. W. Norton & Co., New York (2021)
17. Spivey, J.M.: The Z Notation: A Reference Manual, 2nd edn. Prentice Hall International Series in Computer Science (1992)
18. Tononi, G.: An information integration theory of consciousness. BMC Neurosci. **5**, 22, Article no. 42 (2004)
19. Valiant, L.: Probably Approximately Correct: Nature's Algorithms for Learning and Prospering in a Complex World. Basic Books, New York (2013)
20. Wikipedia: Cell membrane; Active transport; Cotransporter; Ion transporter; ATP; etc
21. Winsor, F.: The Space Child's Mother Goose. Purple Press House (1956). (2001 edition)

Specifying and Reasoning About Shared-Variable Concurrency

Ian J. Hayes[1]($^{(\boxtimes)}$) , Cliff B. Jones[2] , and Larissa A. Meinicke[1]

[1] School of Electrical Engineering and Computer Science,
The University of Queensland, Brisbane 4072, QLD, Australia
Ian.Hayes@uq.edu.au

[2] School of Computing, Newcastle University, 1, Science Square,
Newcastle upon Tyne NE4 5TG, UK

Abstract. Specifications are a necessary reference point for correctness arguments. Top-down descriptions of concurrent programs require a way of recording information about the environment in which the component will be required to function. It was shown in the 1980s that adding rely and guarantee conditions to pre and post conditions could support formal specification and reasoning about a class of concurrent systems. More recent research has both widened the class of specifications to include progress requirements and facilitated mechanisation of proofs. This paper describes the algebraic underpinnings that have made this possible. Particular attention is paid to notions of atomicity.

Keywords: shared-variable concurrency · rely-guarantee approach · refinement calculus · program algebra · atomic specification commands

1 Introduction

At the heart of an effective software development method is the ability to specify a program component independently from its implementation. From the point of view of deployment, such an independent specification should allow the use of a component to depend solely on its specification (and not on the details of a particular implementation of the component). Considering the task of its developers, the correctness of an implementation of a component should depend solely on its specification (and not the context(s) in which it is used). The techniques required to achieve this for sequential programs are both well established[1] and used in practical development environments.

When compared with sequential programs, reasoning about concurrent programs introduces the additional complexities of inherent nondeterminism and interference between threads that gives rise to an explosion of the number of possible execution paths between the interacting threads. While pre/postcondition pairs are sufficient to specify sequential components, concurrency introduces additional complexities:

---

[1] See for example the excellent review in [1].

© The Author(s), under exclusive license to Springer Nature Switzerland AG 2023
J. P. Bowen et al. (Eds.): *Theories of Programming and Formal Methods*, LNCS 14080, pp. 110–135, 2023.
https://doi.org/10.1007/978-3-031-40436-8_5

interference: a concurrent thread may modify variables accessed by a component at any point in its execution,

atomicity: programs might be written in high-level programming languages but evaluation of expressions and execution of (assignment) statements at the machine code level cannot be assumed to be atomic with respect to programming language concepts and

termination/progress: termination of operations may be affected by –or even rely on– interference from other threads, and operations may be required to wait for access to shared resources or locks.

Furthermore there are interactions between these issues: the granularity of atomicity affects the extent of the interference (e.g. a data structure controlled by a lock has a coarser granularity of atomicity); and handling progress properties requires an approach to interference that handles possibly non-terminating operations.

As for specifying sequential data structures/types, it is advantageous to make use of an abstract model of the (encapsulated) state of the data structure and make use of a data refinement that introduces a lower-level state for the implementation. For concurrent data structures the choice of representation can affect the manner in which the operations on the data structure may interfere with each other. Often the representation is chosen so that it distinguishes between data and control variables (e.g. locks), where the latter control access to the data structure and are usually of atomic types, whereas the former are typically not of atomic types and rely on the control variables being used to ensure mutual exclusion on the parts of the data being accessed by an operation.

The interference which is characteristic of shared-variable concurrency makes it difficult to achieve a compositional development method. Early concurrency research [3,4,51,52] provided approaches that were neither modular nor compositional – see [38] for more details on these early approaches.

This paper surveys an approach to the development of shared-variable concurrent programs. Specifically it looks back over 40 years of evolution of the rely-guarantee approach including recent research on showing how an algebraic reformulation of the basic idea can provide the key to effective mechanisation of concurrent program development. Section 2 examines the interaction of interference with program assertions, expression evaluation, and assignment commands. Section 3 focusses on abstracting interference by rely conditions and Sect. 4 brings in guarantee conditions to allow concurrent operations to be specified. Section 5 overviews an algebraic approach to specifying and refining concurrent programs. Section 6 looks at specifying atomic operations, which can be used to specify operations on shared data structures and to specify atomic machine operations, such as test-and-set. Section 7 examines termination of loops in the context of interference from parallel threads. Section 8 discusses the role of data abstraction and refinement in the context of concurrency. Section 9 examines operations that may have to wait for resources or locks; such operations may potentially wait forever.

Our overall goal is to provide a concurrent program refinement theory in Isabelle/HOL that supports the derivation and verification of concurrent programs, with all refinement laws used for deriving programs being proven valid within the theory. In particular, we avoid making assumptions about expression evaluation and assignment commands being atomic, and instead make use of laws that show they are effectively indivisible, given certain assumptions.

In this whole research arena, there are important conceptual distinctions and less critical differences in concrete syntax. It is important not to let the latter obfuscate the former and we have tried to tease apart these issues.

Connections with Prof. He Jifeng's Research

Jifeng's work with Tony Hoare on unifying theories of programming [31] has heavily influenced the approach taken to the trace semantics underlying our work, while the algebraic approach to programming derives from the earlier laws of programming [30]. His work on rely/guarantee concurrency [72] has also influenced our approach.

2   Atomicity

An operation executing within a thread is *atomic* if no parallel thread may observe an intermediate state of the operation and the operation cannot observe intermediate states of operations in parallel threads. Some programming language or machine architecture types can be considered atomic, i.e. for a read or write access of a variable of an atomic type, no concurrent thread can observe an intermediate state part way through an access. By contrast, for example, 64-bit integers on a 32-bit architecture do not form an atomic type. For the rest of this paper, we assume that scalar types (such as integers and booleans) are atomic; however, for structured types such as arrays and records, we make no atomicity assumptions about access of the whole structure but assume that access to their sub-components that are of atomic types is atomic. We do not assume that execution of programming language statements –nor evaluation of their conditions– is atomic.

2.1   Program Assertions

Assertions about the state of a program are essential for Floyd/Hoare-style reasoning about programs [21,29] but a program assertion may not be stable under interference from parallel components. An assertion, P, is a set of program states, and a relation, R, is a set of pairs of states, where a program state, σ, can be represented as a mapping from program variable names to their values, i.e. $\sigma\, x$, is the value of variable x in state σ.[2]

---

[2] The program state may also include a heap but no further discussion of heap store is included below.

Definition 1 (stable). *An assertion P on the program state space is* stable *under a relation R if and only if $\forall(\sigma, \sigma') \in R . (\sigma \in P \Rightarrow \sigma' \in P)$.*

In the examples we use characteristic predicates for assertions, so that $x > 0$ characterises the set of states $\{\sigma . \sigma x > 0\}$. Similarly, the predicate $x \leq x'$, in which x stands for the initial value of x and x' for the final value of x, characterises the relation $\{(\sigma, \sigma') . \sigma x \leq \sigma' x\}$. The assertion $l \geq r$ is not stable under interference that can decrease l or increase r, which is characterised by the predicate $l > l' \vee r < r'$ but $l \geq r$ is stable under interference that can neither decrease l nor increase r, that is, interference satisfying $l \leq l' \wedge r \geq r'$. Note that the interference under which an assertion and its negation are stable may be different. The definition of stable does not require that the program variables referenced within P are unmodified, for example, the assertion, *even i*, is stable under interference that increases i by 2.

2.2   Conditions

A program assertion, P, is used as a judgement about a single program state, σ; either σ is in P or it is not. On the other hand, conditions in if and while commands are evaluated in a context in which the program state may be modified (multiple times) by interference from the environment, and hence are evaluated over a sequence of potentially different states. Each reference to a variable within a condition may access its value in a different state, for example, the condition, $i = i$, may evaluate to false if its two accesses to i are in states with different values of i.

A common restriction [52] is that a condition contains at most one shared variable and at most one reference to that variable, thus ruling out a condition such as $i = i$. With this restriction, evaluating a condition over a sequence of states is equivalent to evaluating it in the single state in which the shared variable is accessed. If a condition satisfies this restriction, it is affected by interference in a similar manner to program assertions. For example, the condition, $i > 0$, in an if command may be true in the state in which i is accessed but it is not stable under the interference that may decrease i, and hence it may no longer be true when the start of the then branch of the if command is reached. However, if $i > 0$ evaluates to false, it will still be false when the start of the else branch is reached if the interference cannot increase i.

2.3   Expressions

As with conditions, evaluation of expressions can lead to anomalies, for example, for an integer variable i, the expression $i + i$ may evaluate to an odd value if i is modified between the two accesses to i, whereas $2 * i$ always evaluates to an even number because there is only a single access to i. Note that it is a valid refinement to replace $i + i$ by $2 * i$ but not vice versa.

We assume the syntax of an expression, e, consists of either a constant, k, a variable, v, a unary operator $\ominus$ applied to an expression, $\ominus e_1$, or a binary operator $\oplus$ applied to two expressions, $e_1 \oplus e_2$.[3] Evaluation of an expression in a (single) state σ, written e_σ, is defined in the usual manner. If an expression, e, evaluates to the same value before and after interference satisfying a relation R, we say that e is invariant under R.

Definition 2 (invariant-expression). *An expression, e, is* invariant *under a relation R if and only if $\forall (\sigma, \sigma') \in R \cdot e_\sigma = e_{\sigma'}$.*

For example, the expression, $i \bmod N$, is invariant under interference that increments i by the constant N, (i.e. under the relation $\{(\sigma, \sigma') \mid \sigma' i = \sigma i + N\}$), similarly, $i - i$, is invariant under any interference because evaluating $i - i$ in any single state gives 0. However, evaluating $i - i$ over a sequence of states (as for a programming language expression) under interference that may change i, may not give 0 because $i - i$ has two references to i that may be evaluated in different states to give different values. Expressions that only have a single reference can be reasoned about more easily.

Definition 3 (single-reference). *An expression, e, is* single reference *under a relation R, if and only if e is,*

- *either a constant, k, or an atomic variable, v,*
- *of the form, $\ominus e_1$, and e_1 is single reference under R, or*
- *of the form, $e_1 \oplus e_2$, in which both e_1 and e_2 are single reference under R, and either e_1 or e_2 is invariant under R.*

For example, for integer atomic variables i and j, the expression $(i \bmod 2) + j$, is single reference under interference, R, that may increment i by any multiple of 2 (including 0) and may modify j arbitrarily, because

- $i \bmod 2$, is single reference under R because
    - the atomic variable i is single reference under R, and
    - the constant 2 is both single reference and invariant under R,
- $i \bmod 2$ is invariant under R, and
- j is single reference under R.

That means the expression, $i \bmod 2$, evaluates to the same value, no matter in which state during its evaluation i is accessed, and hence any variance in the value of $(i \bmod 2) + j$, is due to the various values that j can take during the evaluation. If an expression is both single-reference and invariant under R, its evaluation over a sequence of states will return the same value as its evaluation in any of the states.

Other approaches to handling expressions [11,70] assume that the expression has only a single variable, v, that may be modified by the environment and that v is referenced only once. This is a strictly stronger requirement than Definition 3, for example, as shown above $(i \bmod 2) + j$ is single reference under interference that may increment i by a multiple of 2 and arbitrarily update j but it does not satisfy the stricter requirement that only one variable may be modified by interference because both i and j may be modified by the interference.

---

[3] Conditional "and" and "or" (&& and || in C, Java, etc.) are handled by conditional expressions, which we do not consider here.

2.4   Assignments

An assignment command, $x := e$, in a concurrent context may be subject to interference on variables referenced within e during its evaluation (as in Sect. 2.3) as well as interference that may modify x after it has been assigned. We assume accesses to x and variables within e are atomic.

Owicki [52], Xu et al. [72], Prensa Nieto [56], Stølen [65], Dingel [16], Schellhorn [58] and Sanan [57] treat a complete assignment as atomic, although they do allow interference before and after the assignment. Their reasoning makes use of preconditions and (single-state) postconditions that are stable under interference.

A common observation [7,52] is that, if an assignment only accesses at most a *single shared variable* (i.e. all other variables accessed are unchanged by interference) and there is only one access to that variable, the assignment can be thought of as being atomic—it can be viewed as happening atomically at the (single) point the shared variable is accessed. In an assignment, $x := e$, the single shared variable may be either x or some variable accessed within e (but not both). Hence these approaches commonly impose a syntactic restriction on programs that this property holds for all assignments. Any assignment for which the property does not hold needs to be broken down into a sequence of assignments that do satisfy the property, and which may require fresh local variables. This also introduces additional intermediate assertions and proof obligations.

The validity of the single shared variable approach cannot be proven in the above listed theories, due to their assumption that assignments are atomic. The approach we have taken does not assume assignments are atomic, which is in line with the fact that the (concurrent) semantics of programming language assignments is not atomic. That allows us to show, for example, that the above single shared variable approach is valid, but we can also generalise it to use the more general Definition 3 (single-reference), rather than single shared variable.

3   Interference and Rely Conditions

Pre and rely conditions should inform deployment decisions in that it should be established (preferably by proof) that the context in which an implementation will be deployed will satisfy these assumptions. However, considering the execution of an implementation, semantics must be given to situations where assertions (preconditions, intermediate assertions, loop invariants) of a component are violated by interference from concurrent threads in its environment. For example, consider the following assertion for a set of integers s and integer constant N.

$$s \subseteq \{0 .. N\} \tag{1}$$

The assertion states that all elements of the set s must be in the subrange 0 through N, inclusive. In the context of interference from the environment, the assertion may be invalidated by the environment adding an element outside

$\{0 .. N\}$ to s. However, if the interference only removes elements from s, (1) is *stable*, i.e. if it holds before the interference, it holds after. The interference can be represented by a *rely* condition, in this case the relation characterised by

$$s' \subseteq s \qquad (2)$$

in which s is the value of the set before the interference and s' is its value after. By Definition 1 (stable), (1) is stable under the rely condition (2) because

$$s' \subseteq s \vDash (s \subseteq \{0 .. N\} \Rightarrow s' \subseteq \{0 .. N\}).$$

In practice, there may be zero or more steps of interference from the environment, including steps that do not modify s. Such a sequence of environment steps satisfies the reflexive, transitive closure of R, R^*. For example, if each step satisfies $s' \subset s$, any sequence of zero or more steps satisfies $s' \subseteq s$, which is a reflexive and transitive relation. For this reason we consistently use relations that are both reflexive and transitive when abstracting interference as rely condition.

Lemma 1 (stable-many-steps). *If an assertion P is stable under a step of inference that satisfies R, it is stable under interference that satisfies R^*, that is, it is stable under zero or more steps of interference satisfying R.*

4   Rely/Guarantee Thinking

This paper focuses on shared-variable concurrency: reasoning about threads that experience and inflict interference on each other cannot be adequately specified with just pre and post conditions. The idea to add explicit rely and guarantee conditions should again be understood independently of concerns about a concrete syntax for recording specifications.

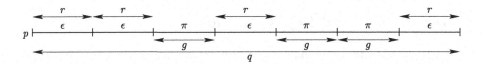

Fig. 1. Execution sequence of program (π) and environment (ϵ) steps, with precondition p, postcondition q, rely condition r and guarantee condition g. If the initial state satisfies p and all environment steps satisfy r, then all program steps must satisfy g and the postcondition q must be satisfied between the initial and final states.

The concept presented by Jones [34–36] can be understood by examining Fig. 1. His approach recovers the crucial property of compositionality by explicitly recording (and offering inference rules for reasoning about) interference. A rely condition r is a binary relation on program states that represents an assumption that any interference steps from the environment of the thread satisfy r between their before and after program states. To complement that, a thread also has a guarantee condition g, also a relation, that all its program steps must satisfy. A guarantee for a thread must imply the rely conditions of all the threads in its environment.

Consider the example of calculating the prime numbers up to some limit N using a parallel version of the sieve of Eratosthenes. It begins with a set s containing all natural numbers between 2 and N, and uses a set of parallel threads: the first removes all the multiples of 2, the second removes all the multiples of 3, and so on. A basic operation used by all the threads is removing a single element i from s under interference that cannot add elements to s but may remove elements, including i. The standard sequential pre/post specification of *remove*,

$$\text{pre } s \subseteq \{0 \mathinner{\ldotp\ldotp} N\} \wedge i \in \{0 \mathinner{\ldotp\ldotp} N\} \tag{3}$$
$$\text{post } s' = s - \{i\} \wedge i' = i \tag{4}$$

is inadequate: while the precondition is stable under interference satisfying the rely condition $s' \subseteq s \wedge i' = i$, the postcondition can be invalidated by interference that removes elements other than i from s. The alternative postcondition, $i \notin s'$, is stable under this interference but it is too weak on its own because it does not preclude the operation adding or removing elements other than i. This can be rectified by including a guarantee condition, $s - s' \subseteq \{i\} \wedge s' \subseteq s \wedge i' = i$, that must be satisfied by every program step made by the implementation of the operation. The specification of the concurrent *remove* operation becomes the following.

$$\text{pre } s \subseteq \{0 \mathinner{\ldotp\ldotp} N\} \wedge i \in \{0 \mathinner{\ldotp\ldotp} N\} \tag{5}$$
$$\text{rely } s' \subseteq s \wedge i' = i \tag{6}$$
$$\text{guar } s - s' \subseteq \{i\} \wedge s' \subseteq s \wedge i' = i \tag{7}$$
$$\text{post } i \notin s' \tag{8}$$

An important property of a postcondition is that it *tolerates* interference satisfying the rely condition, so that the postcondition will not be invalidated by such interference.

Definition 4 (tolerates). *A postcondition relation Q tolerates a rely condition R from precondition P, if*

$$\forall \sigma, \sigma' \mathpunct{.} \sigma \in P \wedge (\sigma, \sigma') \in (R^* \mathbin{\fatsemi} Q \mathbin{\fatsemi} R^*) \Rightarrow (\sigma, \sigma') \in Q \tag{9}$$

where $\fatsemi$ is relational composition.

Commonly R is reflexive and transitive, i.e. $R = R^*$. For the remove operation the rely condition $s' \subseteq s \wedge i' = i$ is both reflexive and transitive, so it is equal to its reflexive transitive closure, and hence its postcondition tolerates its rely condition from its precondition as follows.

$$s \subseteq \{0 \mathinner{\ldotp\ldotp} N\} \wedge i \in \{0 \mathinner{\ldotp\ldotp} N\} \wedge \atop (\exists s_1, i_1, s_2,, i_2 \mathpunct{.} (s_1 \subseteq s \wedge i_1 = i) \wedge i_1 \notin s_2 \wedge (s' \subseteq s_2 \wedge i' = i_2)) \vDash i \notin s'$$

A postcondition whose truth can be subverted by an interference step that satisfies the rely condition is problematic because the only valid refinement of a postcondition is to strengthen it (under the assumption of the precondition and $(R \vee G)^*$ as per the consequence rule 11 below). In the worst case there may be no feasible strengthening.

A postcondition tolerating interference R from a precondition P means that interference before and after the execution of its implementation preserves the postcondition. Interference during the execution is handled during the refinement of the specification.

4.1   Inference Rules

A Jones-style assertion represented in the form,

$$C \text{ sat } (P, R, G, Q) \tag{10}$$

is satisfied if every execution of the command C terminates and satisfies the relation Q end-to-end between its initial and final states provided the initial state satisfies P and every step of the environment of the thread satisfies R; in addition, every atomic program step of C satisfies the relation G between its before and after states provided all the environment steps up until that point have satisfied R and the initial state satisfied P.

There are various presentations in the literature of inference rules for such judgements. The earliest ones in [34] cope with inheriting the rely and guarantee conditions from the context by offering a consequence rule:

$$\text{consequence} \cfrac{\begin{array}{c}(P_2 \vDash P_1) \wedge (R_2 \vDash R_1) \wedge (G_1 \vDash G_2) \\ P_2 \wedge Q_1 \wedge (R_2 \vee G_1)^* \vDash Q_2 \\ C \text{ sat } (P_1, R_1, G_1, Q_1)\end{array}}{C \text{ sat } (P_2, R_2, G_2, Q_2)} \tag{11}$$

and an inference rule that checks that the rely and guarantee conditions are consistent between sibling threads (shown for clarity with only two threads):

$$\text{parallel} \cfrac{\begin{array}{c}(G_1 \vDash R_2) \wedge (G_2 \vDash R_1) \\ C_1 \text{ sat } (P_1, R_1, G_1, Q_1) \\ C_2 \text{ sat } (P_2, R_2, G_2, Q_2)\end{array}}{C_1 \parallel C_2 \text{ sat } (P_1 \wedge P_2, R_1 \wedge R_2, G_1 \vee G_2, Q_1 \wedge Q_2)} \tag{12}$$

Two points should be noted here:

- The parallel rule handles asymmetric threads; a simpler rule can be given where the threads have specifications that differ only in a parameter.
- The above rule shares with Hoare-like rules for sequential programming constructs the property that they can be read from hypotheses to conclusion to justify a step of decomposition; reading the rule from conclusion to hypotheses facilitates its use to justify top-down compositions.

The soundness of these rules for partial correctness has been shown with respect to an operational semantics of a programming language [11] which allows environment transitions satisfying the rely condition as well as program transitions [10].

The example used in the current paper is a parallel version of the Sieve of Eratosthenes for finding prime numbers. That example uses concurrent instances of threads that differ only by the value of a parameter; more interesting examples of the effectiveness of rely and guarantee conditions come from applications where the concurrent threads differ, which is the case with "Asynchronous Communication Mechanisms" (see [39]) or "On-the-fly Garbage collection" (see [41]).

5   Concurrent Refinement Algebra

The insights to be gained by studying the algebraic properties of programs in general –and concurrent constructs in particular– have been studied in [30,32]; this section provides an algebraic presentation of rely and guarantee conditions. This view also points the way to mechanisation of developments using the rely-guarantee approach.

For the satisfaction relation (10), the 4-tuple (p, r, g, q) can be viewed as a specification for the command c. Dingel's refinement calculus for rely/guarantee concurrency [16] viewed this 4-tuple as a specification command, in a manner similar to Morgan's specification command, $[p, q]$, for the sequential refinement calculus [46,47]. In the sequential refinement calculus it has been recognised that such a specification command can be split into an assertion command $\{p\}$ and a postcondition command $[q]$, so that $[p, q] = \{p\} ; [q]$. As a 4-tuple specification can become cumbersome, especially when some of the components are not relevant, the approach we have taken is to define four commands, pre p, rely r, guar g, and post q for the four components. The command pre p aborts if p does not hold initially, otherwise it allows any non-aborting behaviour. The command rely r aborts if its environment performs a step not satisfying r, otherwise it allows any non-aborting behaviour. The command guar g ensures all program steps satisfy the relation g between their initial and final states. The command post q ensures its initial and final states satisfy q end-to-end; it also terminates (see Sect. 7). The four commands can be combined to form a full specification equivalent to the 4-tuple using the weak conjunction operator $\Cap$, so that the satisfaction relation (10) can be written using the refinement relation $\succcurlyeq$, where for commands c and d, $c \succcurlyeq d$ means c is refined (or implemented) by d,[4]

$$\text{pre } p \Cap \text{rely } r \Cap \text{guar } g \Cap \text{post } q \succcurlyeq c \qquad (13)$$

---

[4] In our earlier papers we followed the sequential refinement calculus more closely and used, rely $r \Cap$ guar $g \Cap \{p\}$; post $q \succcurlyeq c$, but manipulating the sequential composition of the assertion $\{p\}$ is more complicated than using the conjoined form in (13) because $\Cap$ is an associative, commutative and idempotent operator. Given that $\{p\}$; post $q = $ pre $p \Cap$ post q, one can switch between the two as necessary. Note that $\{p\}$ terminates immediately if p holds initially, whereas pre p allows any non-aborting behaviour if p holds initially. Both abort if p does not hold initially.

where the weak conjunction of two commands, $c_1 \Cap c_2$, behaves as both c_1 and c_2 up to the point at which either c_1 or c_2 aborts at which point it aborts. For example, weak conjunction satisfies the following.

$$\text{Weak conjunction} \quad \frac{c_1 \text{ sat } (p_1, r_1, g_1, q_1) \quad c_2 \text{ sat } (p_2, r_2, g_2, q_2)}{(c_1 \Cap c_2) \text{ sat } (p_1 \cap p_2, r_1 \cap r_2, g_1 \cap g_2, q_1 \cap q_2)} \quad (14)$$

Weak conjunction is monotone in its arguments, i.e. if $c_1 \succcurlyeq d_1$ and $c_2 \succcurlyeq d_2$, then $c_1 \Cap c_2 \succcurlyeq d_1 \Cap d_2$. That allows one to provide a set of simpler refinement laws below that can be combined to give the equivalent of the consequence rule (11), in which the notation $p \lhd r$ stands for the relation r with its domain restricted to the set p.

$$\text{pre } p_1 \succcurlyeq \text{pre } p_2 \qquad \text{if } p_1 \subseteq p_2 \quad (15)$$
$$\text{rely } r_1 \succcurlyeq \text{rely } r_2 \qquad \text{if } r_1 \subseteq r_2 \quad (16)$$
$$\text{guar } g_1 \succcurlyeq \text{guar } g_2 \qquad \text{if } g_2 \subseteq g_1 \quad (17)$$
$$\text{pre } p \Cap \text{post } q_1 \succcurlyeq \text{pre } p \Cap \text{post } q_2 \qquad \text{if } p \lhd q_2 \subseteq q_1 \quad (18)$$
$$\text{rely } r \Cap \text{guar } g \Cap \text{post } q_1 \succcurlyeq \text{rely } r \Cap \text{guar } g \Cap \text{post } q_2 \quad \text{if } (r \cup g)^* \cap q_2 \subseteq q_1 \quad (19)$$

In addition, many refinement rules focus on refining a command c_1 to c_2 in the context of a rely r:

$$\text{rely } r \Cap c_1 \succcurlyeq \text{rely } r \Cap c_2, \quad (20)$$

where the precondition and guarantee are not relevant.

Some History. It is worth reviewing the path to our current approach. Our earlier approach to handling guarantee commands made use of a command, $(\text{Guar } g \,.\, c)$, that restricted the behaviour of the command c so that all program steps satisfy the guarantee relation g. Initially this command was defined directly in terms of an operational semantics [24]. However, in order to define its trace semantics, [25] introduced a *weak conjunction* operator[5] $\Cap$ and defined $(\text{Guar } g \,.\, c)$ via a weak conjunction of c with a construct that contained all possible non-aborting traces whose program steps satisfy g. We later realised that it was simpler to just define guar g as a command in its own right and write guar $g \Cap c$ in place of $(\text{Guar } g \,.\, c)$. That allowed us to discuss properties of guarantees, (e.g. strengthening and merging guarantees), in isolation, and avoided issues with nesting of guarantee and rely commands, thus leading to a simpler theory.

Our earlier approach also made use of a command, $(\text{Rely } r \,.\, c)$, that, if run in parallel with interference satisfying r, implemented c [25]. The effect of this rely command is to strengthen specification c to handle interference satisfying r. The theory using this earlier rely command was complicated because we needed to introduce a refinement relation, $\succcurlyeq_r$, parametrised by a rely condition r, further

---

[5] Called *strict conjunction* there because it is abort strict, i.e. $c \Cap \text{abort} = \text{abort}$.

parameterise the rely command with the rely condition, z, implicit within c, written $(\text{Rely } r \,.\, c_z)$, and introduce a predicate, $stops(c, r)$, characterising the set of states from which c terminates under interference satisfying r. Further complications were introduced when nesting guarantees within relies. This earlier approach used a *weak* specification command that only guaranteed to satisfy its postcondition for interference that satisfied the identity relation between states, whereas our newer approach uses a *strong* specification command that achieves its postcondition under any interference and is weakened by weakly conjoining it with the newer, rely r, command, in a similar way to a specification being weakened by adding a precondition. Note that in the new theory both the failure of a precondition and the failure of a rely condition are modelled by abort, that means the theory takes a consistent approach to handling assumptions.

In the newer approach, both guarantee and rely commands are defined in terms of other language primitives, and combined with other constructs using weak conjunction, an associative, commutative and idempotent operator. This results in a theory in which it is much easier to manipulate rely/guarantee specifications algebraically and completely avoids the issues with nesting of relies and guarantees with the earlier approach.

6 Specifying Atomic Operations

For a component of a concurrent program, one can distinguish whether a post-condition is to be met by a sequence of state transitions between the initial and final states of the component execution (as in [34]), or whether it needs to be met by what appears to other threads to be an atomic transition, albeit with the possibility of finite stuttering program steps (i.e. steps that do not change the observable program state) before and after (as used by Dingel in his refinement calculus [16]). We use the specification command $\langle q \rangle$ for a command that achieves the postcondition q atomically [28]. The command is allowed to perform a finite number of stuttering program steps before or after the atomic step establishing q and, of course, environment steps may be arbitrarily interleaved between its program steps. The stuttering steps represent program steps that do not modify the observable state (e.g. updates to hidden registers or branch instructions).

Low-level concurrent algorithms, such as those used to implement primitives like locks or message queues, often make use of machine instructions, such as compare-and-swap (CAS) and fetch-and-add (FAA), that are guaranteed to be atomic. Morgan [46,47] defined a specification command, $X\!:\![p, q]$, with X giving the set of variables that may be modified by the command. X is referred to as the *frame* of the command. Here we extend his framing notation to apply to any command, $X\!:\!c$, so that execution of c may only modify variables within X.[6] For example, a compare-and-swap (CAS) instruction (21) takes s and (typically local) *old*, *new* and *done* as parameters, it has a frame of s and *done*, and if s equals *old* it succeeds and updates s to *new* otherwise it fails and leaves s unchanged.

---

[6] The frame is a special form of guarantee that no variables outside X are modified.

The returned boolean value *done* indicates whether the CAS succeeded. An FAA instruction (22) has a frame of the variables x and y, it takes a value k and a variable x whose initial value is fetched and stored in the (local) variable y and then x is updated to $x + k$, all atomically.

$$done \leftarrow \mathsf{CAS}(\mathsf{ref}\ s, old, new) \mathrel{\widehat{=}} s, done : \langle (s = old \Rightarrow s' = new \wedge done') \wedge \quad (21)$$
$$(s \neq old \Rightarrow s' = s \wedge \neg done') \rangle$$

$$y \leftarrow \mathsf{FAA}(\mathsf{ref}\ x, k) \mathrel{\widehat{=}} x, y : \langle y' = x \wedge x' = x + k \rangle \quad (22)$$

While the instructions take place atomically, they may be preceded and followed by steps taken by their environment that may invalidate the relation.

The other situation in which atomic specifications are useful is for operations on concurrent data structures that are to be implemented using non-blocking algorithms (perhaps utilising atomic instructions such as CAS or FAA). The *remove* operation discussed earlier can also be specified using an atomic specification command.

$$\mathsf{pre}(s \subseteq \{0..N\} \wedge i \in \{0..N\}) \mathbin{\text{\small ⋔}} \mathsf{rely}(s' \subseteq s \wedge i' = i) \mathbin{\text{\small ⋔}} s : \langle s' = s - \{i\} \rangle \quad (23)$$

Note that the guarantee (7), $s - s' \subseteq \{i\} \wedge s' \subseteq s \wedge i' = i$, of the earlier specification is implicitly satisfied by the atomic specification: the postcondition ensures both $s - s' \subseteq \{i\}$ and $s' \subseteq s$ and the frame of s ensures $i' = i$.

As another example, a communication channel between two threads may be specified via a queue (qu) of messages sent by one thread but not yet received by the other. The operation to *receive* a message has a precondition that the queue is non-empty and the operation to *send* a message requires that the length of the queue is not at its upper bound N,

$$send(x) \mathrel{\widehat{=}} \mathsf{pre}(\#qu < N) \mathbin{\text{\small ⋔}} \mathsf{rely}(qu'\ \mathsf{suffixof}\ qu \wedge x' = x) \mathbin{\text{\small ⋔}} \quad (24)$$
$$qu : \langle qu' = qu \mathbin{\frown} [x] \rangle$$

$$x \leftarrow receive \mathrel{\widehat{=}} \mathsf{pre}(qu \neq []) \mathbin{\text{\small ⋔}} \mathsf{rely}(qu\ \mathsf{prefixof}\ qu' \wedge x' = x) \mathbin{\text{\small ⋔}} \quad (25)$$
$$qu, x : \langle qu = [x'] \mathbin{\frown} qu' \rangle$$

where qu is a sequence of elements, $\#s$ gives the number of items in the sequence s, the operator $\frown$ is sequence concatenation, $[x]$ is the singleton sequence containing x, and $[]$ is the empty sequence. This version of send/receive assumes a single sender and a single receiver: multiple senders or receivers would invalidate the rely conditions of send and receive, respectively.

7   Termination

If a thread, T, running concurrently with other threads is never scheduled to execute, the operation running in thread T will never terminate. For example, if the assignment $b := false$ in the parallel composition in (26) is never scheduled, the while loop (and hence the program) will never terminate [53].

$$b := true\ ;\ y := 0\ ;\ (b := false \parallel \mathsf{while}\ b\ \mathsf{do}\ y := y + 1) \quad (26)$$

If $b := false$ is scheduled and hence terminates, the whole program completes with the value of y being some (arbitrary) natural number. Hence a basic requirement for termination is that every thread is scheduled with minimal fairness [22].

Rather than building fairness into our primitive parallel operator, we make use of a command, fair, that rules out preemption by its environment forever (i.e. performing an infinite sequence of environment steps) [26]. When fair is conjoined with a command c, their combination, $c \cap$ fair, represents fair execution of c.

As fairness relates to scheduling threads, we do not build fairness into our encoding of primitive executable code commands, such as an assignment command, that is, such commands do not preclude the environment preempting them forever. Hence when showing "termination" of a command, we show that it takes a finite number of steps, unless it is preempted by its environment forever. We use the command, term, that performs a finite number of (program or environment) steps but may be preempted by its environment forever. If term is conjoined with fair, their combination, term $\cap$ fair, can perform only a finite number of steps. To show a command c terminates, we show term $\succcurlyeq c$, which implies term $\cap$ fair $\succcurlyeq c \cap$ fair, that is, fair execution of c performs only a finite number of steps. Although our primitive parallel operator ($\|$) does not impose fairness, one can define a fair parallel operator in terms of the primitive parallel and fair [26,27].

A more complex example is (27) in which we assume the decrement and increment of i are atomic. If the two threads alternately decrement and increment i, neither loop terminates but if i manages to get to 0 for the test in the left loop that loop will terminate and hence the other loop will terminate with i being 10 (and similarly if i gets to 10 for the test in the right loop).

$$i := 5 \, ; \, (\text{while} \, 0 < i \, \text{do} \, i := i - 1) \, \| \, (\text{while} \, i < 10 \, \text{do} \, i := i + 1) \qquad (27)$$

An important observation coming from this example is that one cannot abstract the interference imposed on the left loop by a *finite* number of increments of i because for any finite number, n, of increments of i, the left loop can iterate $n + 5$ times and terminate.

For partial correctness, one can use the following intuitive algebraic equivalence, similar to that used in Concurrent Kleene Algebra [33] and our earlier approach [23],

$$(\text{Rely} \, r \, . \, \text{post} \, q) \succcurlyeq_p d \iff \text{post} \, q \succcurlyeq_p (d \, \| \, \langle r \rangle^\star) \qquad (28)$$

where $\succcurlyeq_p$ represents partial correctness refinement, $\langle r \rangle^\star$ represents a finite number of iterations of an atomic program step that satisfies r between its before and after states. Hence $d \, \| \, \langle r \rangle^\star$ represents executing d with a finite number of interference steps satisfying r. If that is partially correct with respect to specification post q, d is partially correct with respect to the specification (Rely r . post q).

Unfortunately, this approach does not extend easily to handling total correctness because, as in the example program (27), the interference from the environment is not guaranteed to be finite. Note that replacing $\langle r \rangle^\star$ with $\langle r \rangle^\omega$, which allows either finite or infinite iteration, means that $d \, \| \, \langle r \rangle^\omega$ has infinite behaviour (because $\langle r \rangle^\omega$ does) and hence will not refine post q because post q requires termination.[7]

Interference may affect the stability of a loop's guard or its negation. For example, the following code is an implementation of the remove operation specified by the weak conjunction of (5), (6), (7) and (8), assuming access to s is atomic.

$$\text{while } i \in s \text{ do}(so := s; sn := so - \{i\}; done \leftarrow \text{CAS}(s, so, sn)) \qquad (29)$$

The condition $i \in s$ is not stable under interference that can remove elements (including i) from s and hence the body of the loop cannot assume $i \in s$ as its precondition (as it would for a loop in a sequential program). However, the negation of the condition, $i \notin s$, is stable under interference that may remove elements from s and not change i, and hence when the loop terminates it does stably establish $i \notin s$. Note that the flag $done$ from the CAS is not used because it may be a concurrent thread that removes i, rather than the CAS, possibly after the CAS but before the test of i in the loop guard.

For a while loop running within a thread, the conventional approach of using a loop variant to show termination may be invalidated if interference can increase the loop variant. However, if the interference never increases the variant, its use to show termination is still valid. For example, the while loop in the code of the remove operation (29) terminates under interference that can only remove elements from s; one can use the set s as the variant expression under the well-founded order of strict finite set inclusion $s \supset s'$ to show termination of the loop because either the CAS succeeds and establishes $i \notin s$ stably or the CAS fails because interference removes some element (possibly i) from s, thus decreasing the loop variant.

8   Data Abstraction and Interference

With sequential programs, employing abstract data types proves to be extremely effective in creating understandable specifications and design histories. Interestingly, most examples of developments using rely-guarantee conditions employ data abstraction and reification (see [37]). With concurrency, there can be the additional bonus that avoidance of data races can be thought out on abstract objects rather than on detailed representations.

The choice of data representation for the implementation can be crucial for reducing the contention/interference between threads. The interference on the abstraction can be completely different to that on its representation. For the sieve example an obvious choice of representation for the set s is as a bitmap. Because N is expected to be larger than the number of bits in a word (say, 64), an array of $\lceil (N+1)/64 \rceil$ words is required, each word representing 64 elements of the set. While interference will still occur when threads are accessing the

---

[7] To handle termination one may combine (28) with an extra condition to handle termination [25] but that approach becomes quite complicated.

same word in the array, threads accessing separate words will not interfere, in particular, it is not necessary to lock the complete data structure, and updates to the individual words can be done via a compare-and-swap (CAS) instruction, and hence do not require locks.

Simpson's algorithm for achieving an Asynchronous Communication Mechanism [62,63] allows one thread to read the most up to date value of a buffer, d, written by a second thread. Abstractly, the mechanism provides atomic *read* and *write* operations, where d may contain multiple words (i.e. access to d is not atomic (at the hardware level)).

$$r \leftarrow read \mathrel{\widehat{=}} \mathsf{rely}(r' = r) \mathbin{\text{\small ⋒}} r : \langle r' = d \rangle \tag{30}$$

$$write(v) \mathrel{\widehat{=}} \mathsf{rely}(v' = v) \mathbin{\text{\small ⋒}} d : \langle d' = v \rangle \tag{31}$$

To avoid locking, Simpson's algorithm uses a 2×2 matrix of buffers and carefully arranges their access so that if both threads are active, the slot used by the reading thread differs from that of the writing thread. The slots used are determined by a number of control bits, each of which can be atomically accessed, unlike the buffer itself. Such representations are common for non-blocking algorithms. In the development presented in [39], the number of slots and their arrangement is not determined in the first representation. Not only does this open up a space of alternative representations, it also pinpoints the issues of data races on the slots that are carefully avoided by Hugo Simpson's clever 2×2 organisation. Sorting out race freedom on the intermediate abstraction provides a clear understanding and record of the design.

The message queue from Sect. 6 can be represented by a cyclic buffer of $N+1$ elements (i.e. $buf \in \{0 .. N\} \to Value$) plus an index r of the next element to be read and an index w of the next element to be written. If $r = w$ the queue is empty and the queue is full if $(w + 1 = r) \mod (N + 1)$. Note that the queue only stores at most N elements but the size of the buffer is $N + 1$. The extra element allows empty and full queues to be distinguished. The coupling invariant between the queue and its representation can be defined as follows.

$$qu = extract(buf, r, w) \text{ where}$$

$$extract(buf, r, w) \mathrel{\widehat{=}} \text{if } r = w \text{ then } [\,] $$
$$\text{else } (buf\ r) \mathbin{\frown} extract(buf, (r + 1) \bmod (N + 1), w)$$

While access to the elements of buf is not assumed to be atomic, the index variables r and w are assumed to be atomic. The implementations of *send* (24) and *receive* (25) on the representation become the following.

$$send(x) \mathrel{\widehat{=}} buf[w] := x \,;\, w := (w + 1) \bmod (N + 1)$$

$$x \leftarrow receive \mathrel{\widehat{=}} x := buf[r]; r := (r + 1) \bmod (N + 1)$$

In *send*, the assignment to $buf[w]$ does not have to be atomic; it does not become part of the queue until w is updated. While the assignment command updating w is not assumed to be atomic, its store into w is atomic. Similarly, the assignment,

$x := buf[r]$, in *receive* does not have to be atomic because both r and $buf[r]$ are not modified by interference from the sending thread. The update of r removes the first element from the queue. Again the assignment command updating r is not assumed to be atomic but its store into r is atomic. Note that only the sending thread updates w and only the receiving thread updates r. This separation of the control variables that are written by each thread is similar to the way the control variables are used for Simpson's algorithm.

9 Progress

9.1 Waiting for Resources

Termination of an operation that is accessing a shared resource (or lock) requires cooperation from the other threads accessing the resource. Using a variant within a single thread is not applicable to showing that the waiting thread eventually gains control of the resource (or lock). In the simple case the thread with the resource may eventually signal it has finished using the resource and if no other threads are contending for the resource, the waiting thread can acquire the resource and continue, but if the resource is never released, the waiting thread will never make progress. Hence when specifying operations like acquiring a resource or lock, one needs to accommodate the possibility of the operation never terminating if the resource is never released by the thread holding it.

Precondition Versus Termination. For sequential programs, total correctness requires that if the precondition holds initially, the operation terminates. However, for concurrent programs, the precondition holding initially does not ensure an operation will terminate because it may need to wait for a resource and hence its termination is conditional on the behaviour of concurrent threads. For this reason, the identification of the set of initial states from which an operation is guaranteed to terminate with the precondition, as is standard for sequential programs, does not apply to concurrent programs. In fact, it is not in general possible to define a set of initial states that guarantee termination because termination may also be dependent on the interference from concurrent threads.

Deadlock. Waiting for a resource introduces the possibility of a set of threads deadlocking so that all threads are simultaneously waiting, e.g. if thread T_1 requests access to resource A and then resource B while thread T_2 requests access to resource B then resource A, the two threads may deadlock if thread T_1 gets A and then thread T_2 gets B because both threads are then waiting for access to the resource held by the other. As Dijkstra [15] recognised early on, one needs to consider how threads *cooperate* in order to reason about a set of parallel threads.

Starvation. In the more complex case where there is contention on a resource, although there may be no deadlock (i.e. some thread is making progress) it is possible for a thread to be starved if it always loses out to some other thread every time it tries to acquire the resource. To avoid this issue, access to a resource may be queued (e.g. using a ticket lock rather than a test-and-set lock) so that, provided every thread that acquires the resource eventually releases it, all threads will eventually get access to the resource.

9.2   Conditional Termination

The termination of operations that need to wait for resources is conditional on the behaviour of other threads. For example, the operation to acquire a test-and-set lock may repeatedly attempt to acquire the lock but it may repeatedly miss out because other threads are allocated the lock in preference to it. However, if there are no competing threads trying to acquire the lock, the acquire lock operation is guaranteed to succeed and terminate.

To express the conditional termination of an operation we use an extension of Pnueli's Linear Temporal Logic (LTL) [54]. Each LTL formula f is encoded as a command $\langle\!\langle f \rangle\!\rangle$, whose behaviours are exactly those that satisfy f. For the LTL formula that states that p holds in the initial state, we define an explicit $\iota\, p$ operator, but elide the "ι" within examples so that the notation better matches that of Pnueli.[8] To allow LTL formulae to distinguish program and environment steps, we introduce two new primitives: $\varPi\, r$, that must start with a program step satisfying the relation r, and $\mathcal{E}\, r$, that must start with an environment step satisfying the relation r.

LTL formula f	$\langle\!\langle f \rangle\!\rangle$	$\neg f$
$\iota\, p$	$\tau\, p \,;\, \alpha^\infty$	$\iota\, \overline{p}$
$\varPi\, r$	$\pi\, r \,;\, \alpha^\infty$	$\varPi\, \overline{r} \vee \mathcal{E}\ \text{univ}$
$\mathcal{E}\, r$	$\epsilon\, r \,;\, \alpha^\infty$	$\mathcal{E}\, \overline{r} \vee \varPi\ \text{univ}$
$\Diamond f$	$\alpha^* \,;\, \langle\!\langle f \rangle\!\rangle$	$\Box\, \neg f$
$\Box f$	$\nu x \,.\, (\langle\!\langle f \rangle\!\rangle \wedge (\alpha \,;\, x))$	$\Diamond\, \neg f$
$f_1 \wedge f_2$	$\langle\!\langle f_1 \rangle\!\rangle \wedge \langle\!\langle f_2 \rangle\!\rangle$	$\neg f_1 \vee \neg f_2$
$f_1 \vee f_2$	$\langle\!\langle f_1 \rangle\!\rangle \vee \langle\!\langle f_2 \rangle\!\rangle$	$\neg f_1 \wedge \neg f_2$

Fig. 2. Encoding LTL formulae as commands

The encodings of the LTL operators are defined in Figure 2,[9] where, $\tau\, p$, represents an instantaneous test that the current state is in the set of states p; α allows any single step, either program or environment and hence α^* allows any finite sequence of steps and α^∞ allows any infinite sequence of steps; and

---

[8] Note that p is a predicate on a single state, whereas $\iota\, p$ is an LTL predicate on a trace that holds if and only if p holds in the initial state of the trace. Formalisation in Isabelle/HOL requires an explicit operator, rather than using the type of p as done by Pnueli.

[9] The encoding used here is similar to that used in [12] for a trace semantics but here we encode *true* as α^∞ (rather than abort).

$\nu x \, . \, f(x)$ represents the greatest fixed point of the equation $x = f(x)$. Within temporal logic formulae $\wedge$ and $\vee$ are temporal logic operators, whereas in the encodings of commands they are lattice meet (strong conjunction) and join (non-deterministic choice) of commands, respectively.

The eventually operator, $\Diamond f$, can be thought of as being fair because f is established after a finite number of steps, and hence it disallows preemption by the environment forever. In line with our approach to handling termination, we also define an "unfair" eventually operator $\blacklozenge f$. Similarly, the always operator, $\Box f$, can be thought of as being unfair because it allows preemption by the environment forever, and hence we define a "fair" always operator $\blacksquare f$. The temporal logic formula fair_{LTL} requires that a program step is always eventually taken.[10] Its negation allows preemption by the environment forever.

$$\mathsf{fair}_{LTL} \,\widehat{=}\, \Box \Diamond (\Pi \text{ univ}) \tag{32}$$

$$\neg \mathsf{fair}_{LTL} = \Diamond \Box (\mathcal{E} \text{ univ}) \tag{33}$$

$$\blacklozenge f \,\widehat{=}\, \neg \mathsf{fair}_{LTL} \vee \Diamond f \tag{34}$$

$$\blacksquare f \,\widehat{=}\, \mathsf{fair}_{LTL} \wedge \Box f \tag{35}$$

The operators $\blacklozenge$ and $\blacksquare$ are deMorgan duals, that is, $\neg \blacklozenge f = \blacksquare \neg f$.

An operation for a thread with unique identifier, tid, to acquire a test-and-set lock can be specified to allow the operation to fail to terminate if the lock is always eventually not free or the operation is preempted forever. The non-terminating alternative behaviour is specified by $\langle\!\langle \Box \blacklozenge (lock \neq free) \rangle\!\rangle$, where $\blacklozenge$ is used rather than $\Diamond$ to allow preemption by the environment forever to lead to non-termination. The non-terminating behaviour does not change the program state and hence it has an empty frame, $\emptyset$.

$acquire(tid) \,\widehat{=}$
  $\mathsf{rely}(lock = tid \Rightarrow lock' = tid) \wedge (lock \neq tid \Rightarrow lock' \neq tid) \wedge tid' = tid \,\text{⋒}$
  $\{lock \neq tid\} \, ; (lock \! : \! \langle lock = free \wedge lock' = tid \rangle \vee \emptyset \! : \! \langle\!\langle \Box \blacklozenge (lock \neq free) \rangle\!\rangle)$ (36)

The condition under which it is guaranteed to terminate is that eventually the lock is always free, which can be expressed as the linear temporal logic formula $\Diamond \blacksquare (lock = free)$. Note that the operation may terminate even when this condition does not hold because it may successfully acquire the lock (the first alternative of the non-deterministic choice). The specification allows the environment to preempt it forever (because the atomic specification command allows that); fair execution of the operation would rule out that possibility.

A ticket lock has better termination properties than a test-and-set lock because it orders access to the lock. Each thread attempts to acquire a lock by initially taking a ticket (like in a bakery or delicatessen). The tickets are allocated in order of request. The ticket lock tracks the ticket number, $lock$, of the current holder of the lock and when that thread releases the lock, that number

---

[10] Here, fair_{LTL} equals command fair (from Sect. 7) conjoined with α^{∞} (our encoding of $true$ in these LTL formula).

is incremented so that the next thread in sequence acquires the lock. An acquire operation on a ticket lock is guaranteed to terminate provided every thread that acquires the lock, eventually releases it. The acquire operation consists of two phases: one to take a ticket and the other to wait until its ticket is the one currently being served, i.e. equal to *lock*. Taking a ticket can be specified as an atomic operation that sets the local variable tk to the current (global) counter value ct and increments ct, all atomically,

$$tk \leftarrow take\_ticket \;\widehat{=}\; tk, ct : \langle tk' = ct \wedge ct' = ct + 1 \rangle \tag{37}$$

which can be implemented by a fetch-and-add instruction (22), $tk \leftarrow \mathsf{FAA}(ct, 1)$. The second phase of acquire operation terminates when the current value of *lock* is the thread's ticket, tk, but it may fail to terminate if the lock never corresponds to the thread's ticket, i.e. $\Box(lock \neq tk)$.

$$
\begin{aligned}
&acquire\_lock(tk) \;\widehat{=}\; \\
&\quad \mathsf{rely}(lock \le lock' \le tk \wedge ct \le ct' \wedge tk' = tk) \; \Cap \\
&\quad \emptyset : ([lock' = tk] \vee \langle\!\langle \Box(lock \neq tk) \rangle\!\rangle)
\end{aligned} \tag{38}
$$

Another example is message channel send/receive operations with blocking when the buffer is full/empty, respectively. Note that the preconditions of the previous versions, (24) and (25), become wait conditions.

$$
\begin{aligned}
send(x) \;\widehat{=}\; &\mathsf{rely}(qu' \text{ suffixof } qu \wedge x' = x) \; \Cap \tag{39} \\
&(qu : \langle \#qu < N \wedge qu' = qu \frown [x] \rangle \vee \emptyset : \langle\!\langle \Box(\#qu = N) \rangle\!\rangle)
\end{aligned}
$$

$$
\begin{aligned}
x \leftarrow receive \;\widehat{=}\; &\mathsf{rely}(qu \text{ prefixof } qu' \wedge x' = x) \; \Cap \tag{40} \\
&(x, qu : \langle qu \neq [] \wedge qu = [x] \frown qu' \rangle \vee \emptyset : \langle\!\langle \Box(qu = []) \rangle\!\rangle)
\end{aligned}
$$

Related Work. To handle termination for a blocking await command of the form await *b* do *c*, that waits until condition *b* holds and atomically with the condition *b* succeeding executes *c*, Stølen [64,65] developed a rely/guarantee theory that augments Jones' quintuple with an additional wait condition, *w*, that characterised the set of states in which a thread can block.[11] The operation to acquire a test-and-set lock (36) is implemented by the command,

$$\mathsf{await}\ lock = free\ \mathsf{do}\ lock := tid.$$

Stølen developed a rule for showing parallel threads do not deadlock: if thread t_1 has a wait condition w_1 and postcondition q_1 and thread t_2 has a wait condition w_2 and postcondition q_2, if $\neg(w_1' \wedge w_2') \wedge \neg(w_1' \wedge q_2) \wedge \neg(w_2' \wedge q_1)$, deadlock is avoided, i.e. both t_1 and t_2 cannot be blocked at the same time, and if t_2 has terminated t_1 cannot be blocked, and if t_1 has terminated t_2 cannot be blocked. For the test-and-set lock example, one can use a wait conditions of $w_1 \;\widehat{=}\; lock \neq t_2$ and $w_2 \;\widehat{=}\; lock \neq t_1$ and noting $\neg(w_1' \wedge w_2') = (lock' = t_2 \vee lock' = t_1)$ meaning that one of the threads has acquired the lock.

---

[11] Xu Qiwen tackled the same issues in [71] in a similar way.

In the theory we have developed, we can define an await command with a body that is a postcondition relation q to be achieved atomically when b holds; it is guaranteed to terminate if the condition b eventually always holds, or to put it another way, infinite behaviour is allowed if it is always the case that eventually b is false.

$$\text{await } b \text{ do } q \mathrel{\widehat{=}} \langle b \lhd q \rangle \vee \emptyset \colon \langle\!\langle \square \blacklozenge \neg b \rangle\!\rangle \tag{41}$$

In later work, Stølen [66] gives two semantic interpretations —weak and strong fairness— of an await command. The weak fairness version corresponds to (41) and the strong fairness to the following.

$$\text{await}_{strong} \, b \text{ do } q \mathrel{\widehat{=}} \langle b \lhd q \rangle \vee \emptyset \colon \langle\!\langle (\blacklozenge \square \neg b) \rangle\!\rangle \tag{42}$$

Note the swap in the order of $\square \blacklozenge$ to $\blacklozenge \square$, meaning that the strong fairness await can only block forever if it is permanently disabled, whereas the weak fairness await can also block forever if b perpetually alternates between true and false.

10   Conclusions

10.1   Summary

The main role of this paper has been to evaluate approaches to specifying concurrent operations or programs in a rely/guarantee style. Because machines include instructions that behave atomically, it makes sense to include a form of specification that represents an atomic operation so that one can specify these instructions within the concurrency theory. Further, atomic specifications in conjunction with preconditions and rely conditions can be used to specify atomic operations on concurrent data structures [16].

The algebraic approaches of Hoare et al. [33], Armstrong et al. [2] and Hayes [18,23] make use of intuitive algebraic properties to handle rely conditions but suffer when it comes to handling termination, nontermination and nesting of constructs. Our initial theory that used a weak specification command forms part of a theory similar to the Concurrent Kleene Algebra of Hoare et al. [33] and the algebraic approaches of Armstrong et al. [2] and Hayes [23]. While this approach works well for handling partial correctness, when the approach is extended to handle total correctness, it becomes considerably more complex.

The combination of the strong specification command weakly conjoined with the (newer) rely command, rely r, that weakens the specification to only need achieve its postcondition in contexts where the environment satisfies the rely condition r, supports the specification of always terminating, conditionally terminating and non-terminating threads. That leads to a simpler, more expressive theory than our earlier approach that combined weak specification commands and the rely command, (Rely r . c), that strengthened the c to handle interference that satisfies r. Because the rely r and guar g commands in the newer theory are weakly conjoined, issues with nesting of older (Rely r . c) and (Guar g . c) commands are avoided.

The concurrent refinement algebra approach reported in this paper has been mechanised as a set of Isabelle/HOL theories. The early work on the general algebra is available within the Archive of Formal Proofs [18]. To support data refinement theories for handling localisation [45] and (coupling) invariants have been developed.

10.2 Related Work

There are many developments relating to rely-guarantee ideas that are not covered in the body of this paper; they include:

- local rely/guarantee reasoning is presented in [19];
- in [17] it is argued that deny and guarantee conditions are required to handle fork/join-like concurrency;
- explicit combinations of rely-guarantee thinking with concurrent separation logic (e.g. [50]) are presented in [20,68,69];
- more implicit combinations are used in [8,11,40];
- Barringer, Kuiper and Pnueli [5,6] show the relevance of rely-guarantee ideas to temporal logics;
- Moszkowski's Interval Temporal Logic (ITL) dates from [48,49]; a combination of ITL with rely-guarantee ideas (RGITL) is covered in [58–60,67] and progress aspects are discussed in [61];
- a notion of "Simulation" is developed in [44]; and
- progress and fairness issues are covered in [42,43].

Prenso Nieto [55,56] has developed Isabelle/HOL theories for rely/guarantee concurrency. Her approach assumes condition evaluation and assignment commands are atomic and allows a multiway parallel at the top level but no nested parallel.

A related topic is relaxed memory models used by machine architectures and compilers. For our work, we have assumed that the implementation can be augmented with appropriate fencing to ensure it respects the specification. Coughlin et al. [14] explicitly handle rely and guarantee conditions in the presence of weak memory models.

Acknowledgements. Thanks are due to Joakim von Wright for introducing us to program algebra, and Callum Bannister, Emily Bennett, Robert Colvin, Diego Machado Dias, Chelsea Edmonds, Julian Fell, Matthys Grobbelaar, Oliver Jeaffreson, Patrick Meiring, Tom Manderson, Joshua Morris, Dan Nathan, Katie Deakin-Sharpe, Kim Solin, Andrius Velykis, Kirsten Winter, and our anonymous reviewers for feedback on ideas presented in this paper and/or contributions to the supporting Isabelle/HOL theories. This work is supported by the Australian Research Council https://www.arc.gov.au under their Discovery Program Grant No. DP190102142 and a grant (RPG-2019-020) from the Leverhulme Trust.

References

1. Apt, K.R., Olderog, E.R.: Fifty years of Hoare's logic. Formal Aspects Comput. **31**(6), 751–807 (2019)
2. Armstrong, A., Gomes, V.B.F., Struth, G.: Algebras for program correctness in Isabelle/HOL. In: Höfner, P., Jipsen, P., Kahl, W., Müller, M.E. (eds.) RAMICS 2014. LNCS, vol. 8428, pp. 49–64. Springer, Cham (2014). https://doi.org/10.1007/978-3-319-06251-8_4
3. Ashcroft, E.A., Manna, Z.: Formalization of properties of parallel programs. In: Meltzer, B., Michie, D. (eds.) Machine Intelligence, vol. 6, pp. 17–41. Edinburgh University Press (1971)
4. Ashcroft, E.A.: Proving assertions about parallel programs. J. Comput. Syst. Sci. **10**(1), 110–135 (1975)
5. Barringer, H., Kuiper, R.: Hierarchical development of concurrent systems in a temporal logic framework. In: Brookes, S.D., Roscoe, A.W., Winskel, G. (eds.) CONCURRENCY 1984. LNCS, vol. 197, pp. 35–61. Springer, Heidelberg (1985). https://doi.org/10.1007/3-540-15670-4_2
6. Barringer, H., Kuiper, R., Pnueli, A.: Now you may compose temporal logic specifications. In: Proceedings of the Sixteenth Annual ACM Symposium on Theory of Computing, STOC 1984, pp. 51–63. Association for Computing Machinery, New York (1984). https://doi.org/10.1145/800057.808665
7. Bernstein, A.J.: Analysis of programs for parallel processing. IEEE Trans. Electron. Comput. **EC-15**(5), 757–763 (1966). https://doi.org/10.1109/PGEC.1966.264565
8. Bornat, R., Amjad, H.: Explanation of two non-blocking shared-variable communication algorithms. Formal Aspects Comput. **25**(6), 893–931 (2013). https://doi.org/10.1007/s00165-011-0213-4
9. Bornat, R., Amjad, H.: Inter-process buffers in separation logic with rely-guarantee. Formal Aspects Comput. **22**(6), 735–772 (2010)
10. Aczel, P.H.G.: On an inference rule for parallel composition (1983). Private communication to Cliff Jones http://homepages.cs.ncl.ac.uk/cliff.jones/publications/MSs/PHGA-traces.pdf
11. Coleman, J.W., Jones, C.B.: A structural proof of the soundness of rely/guarantee rules. J. Log. Comput. **17**(4), 807–841 (2007). https://doi.org/10.1093/logcom/exm030
12. Colvin, R.J., Hayes, I.J., Meinicke, L.A.: Designing a semantic model for a wide-spectrum language with concurrency. Formal Aspects Comput. **29**(5), 853–875 (2017). https://doi.org/10.1007/s00165-017-0416-4
13. Combi, C., Leucker, M., Wolter, F. (eds.): Eighteenth International Symposium on Temporal Representation and Reasoning, TIME 2011, Lübeck, Germany, 12–14 September 2011. IEEE (2011)
14. Coughlin, N., Winter, K., Smith, G.: Rely/guarantee reasoning for multicopy atomic weak memory models. In: Huisman, M., Păsăreanu, C., Zhan, N. (eds.) FM 2021. LNCS, vol. 13047, pp. 292–310. Springer, Cham (2021). https://doi.org/10.1007/978-3-030-90870-6_16
15. Dijkstra, E.: Cooperating sequential processes. In: Genuys, F. (ed.) Programming Languages, pp. 43–112. Academic Press (1968)
16. Dingel, J.: A refinement calculus for shared-variable parallel and distributed programming. Formal Aspects Comput. **14**(2), 123–197 (2002). https://doi.org/10.1007/s001650200032
17. Dodds, M., Feng, X., Parkinson, M., Vafeiadis, V.: Deny-guarantee reasoning. In: Castagna, G. (ed.) ESOP 2009. LNCS, vol. 5502, pp. 363–377. Springer, Heidelberg (2009). https://doi.org/10.1007/978-3-642-00590-9_26

18. Fell, J., Hayes, I.J., Velykis, A.: Concurrent refinement algebra and rely quotients. Archive of Formal Proofs (2016). http://isa-afp.org/entries/Concurrent_Ref_Alg. shtml. Formal proof development
19. Feng, X.: Local rely-guarantee reasoning. In: Proceedings of the 36th Annual ACM SIGPLAN-SIGACT Symposium on Principles of Programming Languages, POPL 2009, pp. 315–327. ACM, New York (2009). https://doi.org/10.1145/1480881. 1480922
20. Feng, X., Ferreira, R., Shao, Z.: On the relationship between concurrent separation logic and assume-guarantee reasoning. In: De Nicola, R. (ed.) ESOP 2007. LNCS, vol. 4421, pp. 173–188. Springer, Heidelberg (2007). https://doi.org/10.1007/978-3-540-71316-6_13
21. Floyd, R.W.: Assigning meanings to programs. In: Proceedings of Symposia in Applied Mathematics: Mathematics Aspects of Computer Science, vol. 19, pp. 19–32 (1967). https://doi.org/10.1090/psapm/019/0235771
22. van Glabbeek, R., Höfner, P.: Progress, justness, and fairness. ACM Comput. Surv. 52(4), 1–38 (2019). https://doi.org/10.1145/3329125
23. Hayes, I.J.: Generalised rely-guarantee concurrency: an algebraic foundation. Formal Aspects Comput. 28(6), 1057–1078 (2016). https://doi.org/10.1007/s00165-016-0384-0
24. Hayes, I.J., Jones, C.B., Colvin, R.J.: Refining rely-guarantee thinking. Technical report CS-TR-1334, Newcastle University (2012)
25. Hayes, I.J., Jones, C.B., Colvin, R.J.: Laws and semantics for rely-guarantee refinement. Technical report CS-TR-1425, Newcastle University (2014)
26. Hayes, I.J., Meinicke, L.A.: Encoding fairness in a synchronous concurrent program algebra. In: Havelund, K., Peleska, J., Roscoe, B., de Vink, E. (eds.) FM 2018. LNCS, vol. 10951, pp. 222–239. Springer, Cham (2018). https://doi.org/10.1007/978-3-319-95582-7_13
27. Hayes, I.J., Meinicke, L.A.: Encoding fairness in a synchronous concurrent program algebra: extended version with proofs (2018). arXiv:1805.01681 [cs.LO]
28. Hayes, I.J., Meinicke, L.A., Meiring, P.A.: Deriving laws for developing concurrent programs in a rely-guarantee style (2021). https://doi.org/10.48550/ARXIV.2103. 15292, https://arxiv.org/abs/2103.15292
29. Hoare, C.A.R.: An axiomatic basis for computer programming. Communications of the ACM 12(10), 576–580, 583 (1969). https://doi.org/10.1145/363235.363259
30. Hoare, C.A.R., et al.: Laws of programming. Commun. ACM 30(8), 672–686 (1987). Corrigenda: CACM 30(9):770
31. Hoare, C.A.R., He, J.: Unifying Theories of Programming. Series in Computer Science, Prentice Hall, London (1998)
32. Hoare, C.A.R., Möller, B., Struth, G., Wehrman, I.: Concurrent Kleene algebra. In: Bravetti, M., Zavattaro, G. (eds.) CONCUR 2009. LNCS, vol. 5710, pp. 399–414. Springer, Heidelberg (2009). https://doi.org/10.1007/978-3-642-04081-8_27
33. Hoare, C.A.R., Möller, B., Struth, G., Wehrman, I.: Concurrent Kleene algebra and its foundations. J. Log. Algebr. Program. 80(6), 266–296 (2011). https://doi. org/10.1016/j.jlap.2011.04.005
34. Jones, C.B.: Development methods for computer programs including a notion of interference. Ph.D. thesis, Oxford University (1981). Available as: Oxford University Computing Laboratory (now Computer Science) Technical Monograph PRG-25
35. Jones, C.B.: Specification and design of (parallel) programs. In: Proceedings of IFIP 1983, pp. 321–332. North-Holland (1983)

36. Jones, C.B.: Tentative steps toward a development method for interfering programs. ACM ToPLaS **5**(4), 596–619 (1983). https://doi.org/10.1145/69575.69577
37. Jones, C.B.: Splitting atoms safely. Theoret. Comput. Sci. **375**(1–3), 109–119 (2007). https://doi.org/10.1016/j.tcs.2006.12.029
38. Jones, C.B.: Three early formal approaches to the verification of concurrent programs. Mind. Mach. (2023). https://doi.org/10.1007/s11023-023-09621-5
39. Jones, C.B., Hayes, I.J.: Possible values: exploring a concept for concurrency. J. Log. Algebraic Methods Program. **85**(5, Part 2), 972–984 (2016). https://doi.org/10.1016/j.jlamp.2016.01.002
40. Jones, C.B., Yatapanage, N.: Reasoning about separation using abstraction and reification. In: Calinescu, R., Rumpe, B. (eds.) SEFM 2015. LNCS, vol. 9276, pp. 3–19. Springer, Cham (2015). https://doi.org/10.1007/978-3-319-22969-0_1
41. Jones, C.B., Yatapanage, N.: Investigating the limits of rely/guarantee relations based on a concurrent garbage collector example. Formal Aspects Comput. **31**(3), 353–374 (2019). https://doi.org/10.1007/s00165-019-00482-3
42. Liang, H., Feng, X.: A program logic for concurrent objects under fair scheduling. In: Proceedings of the 43rd Annual ACM SIGPLAN-SIGACT Symposium on Principles of Programming Languages, POPL 2016, pp. 385–399. ACM, New York (2016). https://doi.org/10.1145/2837614.2837635
43. Liang, H., Feng, X.: Progress of concurrent objects with partial methods. Proc. ACM Program. Lang. **2**(POPL), 20:1–20:31 (2018). https://doi.org/10.1145/3158108
44. Liang, H., Feng, X., Fu, M.: Rely-guarantee-based simulation for compositional verification of concurrent program transformations. ACM Trans. Program. Lang. Syst. **36**(1), 3:1–3:55 (2014)
45. Meinicke, L.A., Hayes, I.J.: Using cylindric algebra to support local variables in rely/guarantee concurrency. In: 2023 IEEE/ACM 11th International Conference on Formal Methods in Software Engineering (FormaliSE), 108–119 (2023). IEEE
46. Morgan, C.C.: The specification statement. ACM Trans. Prog. Lang. Syst. **10**(3), 403–419 (1988). https://doi.org/10.1145/44501.44503
47. Morgan, C.C.: Programming from Specifications, 2nd edn. Prentice Hall, London (1994)
48. Moszkowski, B.C.: Executing Temporal Logic Programs. Cambridge University Press, Cambridge (1986)
49. Moszkowski, B.: Executing temporal logic programs. In: Brookes, S.D., Roscoe, A.W., Winskel, G. (eds.) CONCURRENCY 1984. LNCS, vol. 197, pp. 111–130. Springer, Heidelberg (1985). https://doi.org/10.1007/3-540-15670-4_6
50. O'Hearn, P.W.: Resources, concurrency and local reasoning. Theoret. Comput. Sci. **375**(1–3), 271–307 (2007). https://doi.org/10.1016/j.tcs.2006.12.035
51. Owicki, S.: Axiomatic proof techniques for parallel programs. Ph.D. thesis, Department of Computer Science, Cornell University (1975)
52. Owicki, S.S., Gries, D.: An axiomatic proof technique for parallel programs I. Acta Inform. **6**(4), 319–340 (1976). https://doi.org/10.1007/BF00268134
53. Park, D.: On the semantics of fair parallelism. In: Bjøorner, D. (ed.) Abstract Software Specifications. LNCS, vol. 86, pp. 504–526. Springer, Heidelberg (1980). https://doi.org/10.1007/3-540-10007-5_47
54. Pnueli, A.: The temporal logic of programs. In: 18th Annual Symposium on Foundations of Computer Science, pp. 46–57. IEEE (1977)
55. Prensa Nieto, L.: Verification of parallel programs with the Owicki-Gries and rely-guarantee methods in Isabelle/HOL. Ph.D. thesis, Institut für Informatic der Technischen Universitaet München (2001)

56. Nieto, L.P.: The rely-guarantee method in Isabelle/HOL. In: Degano, P. (ed.) ESOP 2003. LNCS, vol. 2618, pp. 348–362. Springer, Heidelberg (2003). https://doi.org/10.1007/3-540-36575-3_24

57. Sanan, D., Zhao, Y., Lin, S.W., Yang, L.: $CSim^2$: compositional top-down verification of concurrent systems using rely-guarantee. ACM Trans. Program. Lang. Syst. **43**(1), 1–46 (2021)

58. Schellhorn, G., Tofan, B., Ernst, G., Pfähler, J., Reif, W.: RGITL: a temporal logic framework for compositional reasoning about interleaved programs. Ann. Math. Artif. Intell. **71**(1–3), 131–174 (2014). https://doi.org/10.1007/s10472-013-9389-z

59. Schellhorn, G., Tofan, B., Ernst, G., Reif, W.: Interleaved programs and rely-guarantee reasoning with ITL. In: Combi et al. [13], pp. 99–106 (2011). https://doi.org/10.1109/TIME.2011.12

60. Schellhorn, G.: Extending ITL with interleaved programs for interactive verification. In: Combi et al. [13] (2011). https://doi.org/10.1109/TIME.2011.31

61. Schellhorn, G., Travkin, O., Wehrheim, H.: Towards a thread-local proof technique for starvation freedom. In: Ábrahám, E., Huisman, M. (eds.) IFM 2016. LNCS, vol. 9681, pp. 193–209. Springer, Cham (2016). https://doi.org/10.1007/978-3-319-33693-0_13

62. Simpson, H.R.: Four-slot fully asynchronous communication mechanism. Comput. Digit. Tech. IEE Proc. E **137**(1), 17–30 (1990)

63. Simpson, H.R.: New algorithms for asynchronous communication. IEE Proc. Comput. Digit. Technol. **144**(4), 227–231 (1997)

64. Stølen, K.: Development of parallel programs on shared data-structures. Ph.D. thesis, Manchester University (1990). Available as UMCS-91-1-1 or revised version as https://breibakk.no/kst/PhD-thesis.htm

65. Stølen, K.: A method for the development of totally correct shared-state parallel programs. In: Baeten, J.C.M., Groote, J.F. (eds.) CONCUR 1991. LNCS, vol. 527, pp. 510–525. Springer, Heidelberg (1991). https://doi.org/10.1007/3-540-54430-5_110

66. Stølen, K.: Shared-state design modulo weak and strong process fairness. In: Diaz, M., Groz, R. (eds.) Formal Description Techniques, V, Proceedings of the IFIP TC6/WG6.1 Fifth International Conference on Formal Description Techniques for Distributed Systems and Communication Protocols, FORTE 1992, Perros-Guirec, France, 13–16 October 1992. IFIP Transactions, vol. C-10, pp. 479–498. North-Holland (1992)

67. Tofan, B., Schellhorn, G., Ernst, G., Pfähler, J., Reif, W.: Compositional verification of a lock-free stack with RGITL. In: Proceedings of International Workshop on Automated Verification of Critical Systems, Electronic Communications of EASST, vol. 66, pp. 1–15 (2013)

68. Vafeiadis, V.: Modular fine-grained concurrency verification. Ph.D. thesis, University of Cambridge (2007)

69. Vafeiadis, V., Parkinson, M.: A Marriage of rely/guarantee and separation logic. In: Caires, L., Vasconcelos, V.T. (eds.) CONCUR 2007. LNCS, vol. 4703, pp. 256–271. Springer, Heidelberg (2007). https://doi.org/10.1007/978-3-540-74407-8_18

70. Wickerson, J., Dodds, M., Parkinson, M.: Explicit stabilisation for modular rely-guarantee reasoning. In: Gordon, A.D. (ed.) ESOP 2010. LNCS, vol. 6012, pp. 610–629. Springer, Heidelberg (2010). https://doi.org/10.1007/978-3-642-11957-6_32

71. Xu, Q.: A theory of state-based parallel programming. Ph.D. thesis, Oxford University (1992)

72. Xu, Q., de Roever, W.P., He, J.: The rely-guarantee method for verifying concurrent programs. Formal Aspects Comput. **9**, 149–174 (1997)

The Consensus Machine: Formalising Consensus in the Presence of Malign Agents

A. W. Roscoe[1,2,3]($\boxtimes$) (iD), Pedro Antonino[1] (iD), and Jonathan Lawrence[1] (iD)

[1] The Blockhouse Technology Ltd., Oxford, UK
{pedro,jonathan}@tbtl.com
[2] Department of Computer Science, University of Oxford, Oxford, UK
awroscoe@gmail.com
[3] University College Oxford Blockchain Research Centre, Oxford, UK

Abstract. This paper is on the application of formal modelling in CSP and associated verification to decision making in decentralised systems. In particular we look at the problem of ensuring that decentralisation cannot allow two separate and apparently valid decisions to arise when exactly one is required. This is motivated by an approach to blockchain consensus where a primary choice mechanism may need to be supplemented by a back-up that comes into action if the primary one is seemingly blocked.

Keywords: Consensus · State machine · Blockchain · Process algebra · Formal methods

Dedication to He Jifeng on the occasion of his 80th birthday:

Jifeng and I worked together for many years at Oxford developing theories of verification and making them usable. Indeed we have gone on to use them successfully in many contexts, always rooted in algebra and abstraction. In this paper we show how these same two ideas can improve understanding in a relatively new domain—blockchain.
Bill Roscoe

1 Introduction

Consensus is a classical problem in the area of distributed, decentralised systems. It has regained the attention of the scientific community with the advent of blockchains. In these, consensus is used to ensure that participants in this distributed system agree what is the next block in this ever-extending chain of blocks; an initial *genesis block* is initially agreed amongst participants. This agreement on the next block in the chain is usually referred to as the *finality problem*, namely, how to determine the next (agreed-upon) *final* block. Here,

J. P. Bowen et al. (Eds.): *Theories of Programming and Formal Methods*, LNCS 14080, pp. 136–162, 2023.
https://doi.org/10.1007/978-3-031-40436-8_6

final means that it is immutable and will have that position in the blockchain for ever; it does not mean that it is the last block in the chain. A block in such a chain represents a sequence of transactions, each of which causes the state of the blockchain to evolve. So, in broad terms, blockchains are transaction-processing systems possessing an integrity-protected transaction history.

In this paper, we propose the concept of a *hierarchical consensus machine* as a means to solve the finality problem efficiently. In our formulation, this machine is composed of two consensus machines, say G and H, each of which is implemented by a distributed collection of agents, and it decides on a value that is agreed upon by (most of) its (well-behaved) agents. The number agreeing will have reached some pre-agreed threshold. While G is designed to be safe but not live, H is both safe and live. Broadly speaking, safety means that the machine decides on a single correct value, whereas liveness means that the machine eventually comes to a decision. Our definition of *correct* here is that it is the conclusion of one or more good agents who always follow the rules.

As part of our hierarchical machine, we also propose a handover protocol that transfers control from G to H whenever G is unable to come to a (timely) decision; this protocol ensures the liveness of the hierarchical machine as a whole. We create this concept by first introducing a didactic account of consensus machines using a *unitary consensus machine*. Furthermore, we propose a type of *stochastic reasoning* that is a useful mathematical tool to establish bounds on the number of participants in the agreement to achieve safety and liveness. In fact, the reason for having a machine G that is only safe as part of our hierarchical machine is that we can demonstrate with this type of stochastic reasoning that a much smaller number of participants are required to achieve safety alone as compared to machines that are both safe and live. The smaller number of participants should allow for a more efficient consensus protocol. We count on the incentive structures of blockchains and on the fact that ultimately H will reach a consensus to motivate malign agents to cooperate with good agents to reach a consensus via G. Malign agents' misbehaviour is the reason why G is not dependably live. Thus, persuading them to behave in a collaborative way should make G (efficiently) come to a decision more often. We formalise our notion of a hierarchical consensus machine using the CSP process algebra. The notions that we present here could be adapted to the general problem of consensus provided they are used in a similar context. In this paper we concentrate solely on this binary G/H case, but evidently this is open to extension.

As blockchains are being adopted by many industry sectors, finding efficient consensus protocols in this context has become a relevant research challenge. Our *hierarchical consensus machine* is a proposal in this direction that relies on an innovative type of stochastic reasoning and on a handover protocol. Taking advantage of incentive structures to motivate malign agents, who may deliberately seek to undermine this protocol, to behave appropriately is a peculiar aspect of consensus mechanisms in the area of blockchains. Our handover protocol is an important motivating factor for nudging malign agents in the right direction. It is conceived so that malign agents can delay a decision by our hierarchical consensus machine but they cannot prevent it from eventually coming to one.

It is also important in this regard that the protocol guarantees only a single decision, because without this the malign agents might manipulate it to induce a fork. A blockchain fork occurs when two contradicting histories—i.e. final blocks on the same height—are simultaneously accepted.

Conceptually this seems relatively clear. The problems come from getting it to work securely in the decentralised world of agents, some of whom are malign. We identify the following issues:

A. How to create a safe but not necessarily live consensus machine? This means identifying a set of *pickets* (i.e. block-producing agents) and coming up with a model of when there is sufficient evidence among these for both them to prove that a consensus has been achieved—and similarly agree that no consensus exists without such evidence.
B. Understanding the requirements for a consensus machine to be safe. This involves understanding how malign agents can overtly misbehave to try and undermine the consensus protocol.
C. Understanding the requirements for a consensus machine to be live. This involves understanding how malign agents can misbehave via non-participation.
D. How to create a safe and live consensus machine? We would expect the liveness to come from involving many more agents in the process—in comparison to obtaining safety alone—so that it is effectively impossible for there to be enough malign ones to block the machine's progress. We will find that the combinatorics of building a safe and live system are a natural—and naturally more demanding—extension of those for building a safe one.

This paper is organised as follows. In the next section, we introduce the necessary background to make the paper self-contained. We then introduce a didactic notion of a unitary consensus machine in Sect. 3, followed by the description of a stochastic model to reason about consensus decisions in Sect. 4. We present and formalise a notion of hierarchical consensus machines in Sect. 5, discuss related work in Sect. 6, and present our concluding remarks in Sect. 7.

2 Background

2.1 Blockchains

Blockchains were initially proposed as a decentralised way to implement digital currencies and prevent double spending, i.e. the possibility that the owner of some digital currency could spend it more than once [22]. However, they have evolved into generic decentralised auditing systems that do much more than just prevent double spending. For instance, with the advent of smart contracts—programs that are executed in the context of a blockchain—a developer can define by means of a program how transactions addressed to that smart contract are to be processed [4].

A blockchain is a *decentralised stateful transaction processing system*, sometimes referred to also as a *distributed ledger*. It receives transactions from its stakeholders, decides on which of those are valid, and performs alterations to its state that record the effects of these transactions. As a decentralised system, multiple agents collaborate to implement this behaviour. In this context, the term blockchain refers not just to the state comprising the transactions and blocks, but includes the entire system including the agents operating on the state.

A blockchain orders and stores valid transactions into *blocks* which are themselves ordered, giving rise, ultimately, to a *chain of blocks* representing the history of the blockchain. In practice, however, during its operation, a blockchain—or rather its agents—manipulate a *block tree*.

A block tree is a directed, finite and acyclic rooted tree defined by a pair (V, E) where V is a set of blocks and E is a set of backward links—the root (genesis block) is the only block without an outgoing link. The backward links are implemented by embedding the cryptographic hash of its predecessor block in the header of each block. A backward link exists from block B_2 to block B_1 *iff* $hash\_pointer(B_2) = hash(B_1)$, where $hash\_pointer()$ extracts the embedded backward link from a block, and $hash()$ is the cryptographic hash function used by the blockchain. This results in a unique path from every block back to the root (B_0), because (by the properties of the hash function) it is infeasible to construct a false predecessor block with the same hash.

However, because it is possible to construct many different valid successor blocks to any existing block, it is necessary for the blockchain's agents to have a mechanism to determine unambiguously which is the "true" successor to any given block. The motivation for this paper is to provide some machinery to assist the creation of accurate consensus mechanisms.

2.2   CSP and Its Semantics

Note: In this paper we use the machine-readable ascii version of CSP syntax (CSP_M) throughout, as opposed to the typeset blackboard syntax and symbols commonly used in books and papers.

CSP is based on instantaneous actions handshaken between a process and its environment, whether that environment consists of processes it is interacting with or, some notional external observer. It enables the modelling and analysis of patterns of interaction. The books [14, 27, 28] all provide thorough introductions to CSP. The main constructs that we will be using in this paper are set out below.

– The processes STOP, SKIP and DIV respectively do nothing, terminate immediately with the signal ✓ and diverge by repeating the internal action τ. RUN(A) and CHAOS(A) can each perform any sequence of events from A, but while RUN(A) always offers the environment every member of A, CHAOS(A) can nondeterministically choose to offer just those members of A it selects, including none at all.

- a -> P *prefixes* P with the single communication a which belongs to the set Σ of normal visible communications. Similarly [] x : A @ x -> P(x) (replicated external choice) offers a choice over A and then behaves accordingly.
- CSP has several *choice* operators. P [] Q and P |~| Q respectively offer the environment the first visible events of P and Q, and make an internal decision via τ actions whether to behave like P or Q.
  The asymmetric choice operator P [> Q offers the initial visible choices of P until it performs a τ action and opts to behave like Q. In the cases of P [] Q and P [> Q, the subsequent behaviour depends on what initial action occurs.
- P \ X (hiding) behaves like P except that all actions in X become (internal and invisible) τs.
- P [[R]] (renaming) behaves like P except that whenever P performs an action a, the *renamed* process must perform some b that is related to a under the relation R. R is specified using the CSP_M mapping syntax.
- P [| A |] Q is a *parallel* operator under which P and Q act independently except that they have to agree (i.e. synchronise or handshake) on all communications in A. A number of other parallel operators can be defined in terms of this, including P ||| Q = P [||] Q in which no synchronisation happens at all.

There are also other operators such as P ; Q (sequential composition), P /\ Q (interrupt) and P [| A |> Q (throwing an exception) for passing control from one process P to a second one. P /\ Q hands over control when Q performs a visible action, so that the handover if instigated by Q. In P [| A |> Q it is instigated by P performing an exception event a from the set A.

It is always asserted that the meaning, or semantics, of a CSP process is the pattern of externally visible communication it exhibits. As shown in [27,28], CSP has several styles of semantics, that can be shown to be appropriately consistent with one another. In this paper, we are concerned with *behavioural* semantics: CSP processes are identified with sets of observations that might be made from the outside. The best known behavioural models of CSP are based on the following types of observation: *Traces* are sequences of visible communications a process can perform. *Failures* are combinations (s, X) of a finite trace s and a set of actions that the process can refuse in a *stable* state reachable on s. A state is stable if it cannot perform τ. *Divergences* are traces after which the process can perform an infinite uninterrupted sequence of τ actions, in other words diverge. The models are then:

- T in which a process is identified with its set of finite traces;
- F in which it is modelled by its (stable) failures and finite traces;
- FD in which it is modelled by its sets of failures and divergences, both extended by all extensions of divergences: it is *divergence strict*.

2.3 FDR

FDR [10, 26–28] is a refinement checker between finite-state processes defined in CSP. First created in the early 1990's it has been regularly updated since. The latest version is FDR4.[1]

It uses CSP$_M$, the machine-readable version of CSP, which has been extended with a functional programming language related to Haskell. This enables the user to define complex networks and data operations succinctly, and to create functions that, given abstract representations of structures or systems, can automatically generate CSP networks to implement and check them. Perhaps the best-known example of this is the Security Protocol checker Casper [21] which, given an abstract representation of a cryptographic protocol and some security objectives for it, generates a CSP script which checks to see if the objectives are met. In a similar vein, compilers have been written from other notations to CSP such as Statecharts [13] and shared-variable programs (see Chapters 18 and 19 of [28]). A survey of the most important practical applications of FDR can be found in [2].

FDR is most often used to check refinements of the form `Spec [X= Impl`, where `Spec` is a process representing a specification in one of the standard CSP models `X`, usually traces, stable failures or failures-divergences. `Impl` is a CSP representation of the system being checked. To check whether a process `Impl` satisfies a particular property, `Spec` is constructed to represent the most general process (in the relevant model) exhibiting the required property.

FDR supports a number of techniques for attacking the state explosion problem, including hierarchical compression and symmetry reduction [11]. The algorithms underpinning FDR are set out in [10, 27–29].

3 The Unitary Consensus Machine

One of the main problems in designing a blockchain is devising how to select a unique successor for a given block; the initial (often termed *genesis*) block is pre-agreed between agents and assumed to exist, however there may be more than one plausible candidate for any subsequent block. This problem is often solved by a protocol that determines whether a block is *final* in blockchain terminology. Typically, the *finality* of a block is determined by a universally known, though potentially randomly selected, committee of agents, which we call *pickets*, that engage in a protocol by which they reach a *consensus* on the successor of a given block. We call such a system composed of interacting pickets that solves the problem of determining the finality of a block a *consensus machine*. Since blockchains are systems intended to cope with adversarial behaviour (coming from untrusted parties), these machines are designed to tolerate a certain proportion of malign agents. That is, the expected overall behaviour emerges from the interaction of pickets in spite of possible misbehaviour by malign agents

---

[1] Available at https://cocotec.io/fdr/.

amongst them. The notions described here can also be applied to the problem of reaching consensus for more general distributed systems.

We first illustrate how a *unitary consensus machine* works, i.e., how a single set of pickets can interact to reach consensus. Later, we build on this illustration to propose our *hierarchical consensus machine*. The informal description that we provide here illustrates the mechanism used by the hierarchical protocol we propose later.

Let P be a set of pickets, D be a set of possible decision values that the pickets are trying to reach consensus on, and $M \subseteq \mathcal{P}(P)$ the *decision sets* such that agreement by any set $m \in M$ commits the system to the agreed decision, where M is superset closed and contains P and $\mathcal{P}(S)$ gives the power set of S. Broadly speaking, the unitary consensus machine works as follows. For a given run of this machine P, M, and D are fixed and well-known. Each picket $p \in P$ locally decides on a single value $v_p \in D$ and broadcasts this chosen value. We assume that pickets have well-known public keys as part of agreed cryptographic signature schemes so they can create unforgeable digitally signed messages. The set $m_{o,v}$ denotes the set of pickets that have chosen value v according to the messages received by observer o. If $m_{o,v} \in M$, observer o knows that the machine has decided on value v. In this paper, we focus on a restricted scenario involving a single run of the machine, i.e., having pickets decide on a value a single time. There is no issue in extending this for a series of decisions where each is properly made before the next one starts.

We note that since the evidence for a decision will be an agreed and signed decision by sufficient agents for some $m \in M$, no-one can dispute a properly formed one. We require that whatever decision is made is agreed with by at least one benign agent that follows all the rules: this will be a property of M.

We require well-behaved consensus machines to additionally respect two properties:

- **Safety:** For observers o_1, o_2 and $v_1, v_2 \in D$, if $m_{o_1,v_1} \in M$ and $m_{o_2,v_2} \in M$, it must be the case that $v_1 = v_2$.
- **Liveness:** After observing the consensus machine run for stabilisation time t, an observer o is able to construct a set $m_{o,v}$ such that $m_{o,v} \in M$.

Intuitively speaking, the safety property forbids the machine from deciding on two distinct values (on the same run), whereas the liveness property ensures that the machine eventually decides on a value. Note that the liveness property implicitly accounts for enough pickets agreeing on a given value but also for their decision being conveyed in a timely manner.

We assume that malign agents can deviate from the expected picket behaviour arbitrarily. For instance, they could send as their chosen value v_1 to observer o_1 while sending a distinct value v_2 to observer o_2—this double choice is a common Byzantine behaviour expected of such malign agents.

The safety property depends on M considering the benign and malign agents in P. For instance, if sets $m_1, m_2 \in M$ are crafted so that there is no benign picket that is part of both m_1 and m_2, these two committees could decide on two distinct values on the same run. Thus, (i) any two sets in $m_1, m_2 \in M$ must have an overlapping benign picket to achieve the safety property. We can show (i) by contradiction. Let us assume that sets $m_{o_1,v_1} \in M$ and $m_{o_2,v_2} \in M$ with $v_1 \neq v_2$ were constructed. Then, by (i), $p' \in m_{o_1,v_1}$ and $p' \in m_{o_2,v_2}$, which implies that the benign picket p' choose two values v_1 and v_2, a contradiction.

To ensure liveness, one must assume or enforce that: (a) there is some *stabilisation time* by which point messages from benign pickets are delivered; and (b) a set $m \in M$ of benign pickets chooses the same value (in time for stabilisation); the stabilisation time is required to move away from impossibility results [9]. While (b) ensures a decision is made, (a) ensures that an observer can witness this decision. For our minimal unitary consensus machine presented in this section, we assume that such a set m exists as pickets are making their choice. In practice, however, if no set $m \in M$ could be constructed—when, for instance, pickets choose different values—the protocol would have a recovery mechanism by which pickets would choose another value to try and build such a m; the protocol would be constructed so that pickets converge into an agreed value after some time.

It is crucial to understand the dichotomy between safety and liveness in the setting we study: one can be more tolerant of malign pickets' involvement when crafting an M that is safe but not live as opposed to one that is safe and live; this observation follows from properties (i) and (b). There are decision sets M that abide by property (i) and yet cannot satisfy (b). For instance, we could have an M that abide by (i) but all its member include a malign picket. In these cases, the participation of benign nodes in the members of such an M ensure decisions are safe. However, the presence of malign pickets may cause a decision to never be reached as they can refuse to participate in the consensus protocol. This observation is one of the main principles guiding the design of our *hierarchical consensus machine*.

In the context of blockchains, a consensus machine is meant to determine the *true/canonical chain* by repeatedly picking successor blocks—and pruning the block tree in the process. These blocks, and the transactions that they contain, represent transitions in the state of the blockchain. They can account, for instance, for a transfer of digital currency or the execution of some code (i.e. via a smart contract). Thus, assuming that these transactions are deterministic, the consensus machine also determines the canonical sequence of states of the blockchain.

Blockchains are frequently set up with incentive and penalty structures that are designed to persuade the malign agents to follow the rules. We categorise malign behaviour as follows:

1. Overt malign behaviour. Making contributions to the central discussions and protocols of a chain or other decentralised system that will be seen and recognised as malign. Unless this wins votes or similar, it will quickly be recognised and the perpetrator punished.
2. Covert malign behaviour. Producing non-compliant structures that are kept hidden and only perhaps revealed later. For example developing a fork alongside the true chain.

3. Non-participation. Failing to make contributions that are expected of a good agent and thereby denying some correct action the majority it needs. The main issues with this is that it is harder to penalise because a good agent may encounter communication failures, a phenomenon that can also mean confusion about how an apparently non-participating agent should be interpreted. It is fairly standard to make gossiping assumptions about communications in blockchains to resolve such confusion.

The sorts of incentive structures implemented by blockchains are another important factor that guided the design of our hierarchical consensus machine. In particular, non-participation failures may cause the need to transfer control from one unitary consensus machine to another, in order to achieve overall liveness.

4   Stochastic Decisions

The security analysis of blockchains is usually predicated upon some assumed distribution of malign agents. So, we use probability to assemble sets of pickets and produce decision sets M. In this section, we discuss a central case of how this can support the picketing model. We assume that pickets are drawn from an agent population U where the probability that a randomly chosen agent is benign is p, and that they are selected independently and randomly from U so that the number of benign and malign pickets that make any decision set is governed by a binomial distribution, that is, $\binom{n}{k}p^k(1-p)^{n-k}$ gives the probability of having k benign agents when selecting n agents from U. Given this assumption, it is relatively easy to compute how likely it is that at most r out of n picket selections are benign: $F(p, n, r) = \sum_{i=0}^{r} \binom{n}{i}p^i(1-p)^{n-i}$.

Based on these s, we propose the idea of *stochastic impossibility*: an event so unlikely that in the whole history of a system it is very unlikely that one will happen, to the extent that it can be disregarded. This concept is parameterised by a *insignificance threshold* ϵ and an event that happens with probability $\xi \leq \epsilon$ is termed *stochastically impossible*. One might regard a one-in-a-million chance as small enough, but if many (say a million) choices are going to be made a year (approximately one every 30 s) it is clearly is not enough if a single one can corrupt a system. We believe that the $\epsilon = 10^{-18}$ is a reasonable starting point; in terms of the normal distribution, this value is close to 9σ ($\approx 10^{-19}$), where σ is the standard deviation, namely, the cumulative probability from $\mu + 9\sigma$ to infinity, where μ is the mean. This sort of σ-multiplier analysis is used in finance to model risk [7], and is justified as a consequence of the probabilistic laws of large numbers.

We can now understand how to create the decision thresholds M described earlier. Until now, we have informally referred to the groups of pickets selected to make our decisions as *sets*. However, because a given agent can validly be selected more than once (randomly *with replacement*) when assembling decision "sets", these groups are actually *multisets* (bags). This also explains why the binomial distribution is the appropriate model to use when computing the probability that at least a certain specified number of pickets in such a group are benign. In a population U of agents each with independent probability p of being benign, a randomly drawn sub-multiset of pickets $P \subseteq U$ is said to have (stochastically certainly) at least $k + 1$ benign agents if $F(p, k, |P|) < \epsilon$; this inequality means that having at most k benign agents is stochastically impossible. For fixed p, k, and ϵ, we can calculate the smallest $|P|$ so that at least $k + 1$ agents are benign; let us call this threshold value $td(p, k, \epsilon)$. Given that a multiset of pickets P where $|P| = td(p, k, \epsilon)$ has at least $k + 1$ benign agents, any sub-multiset $m \subseteq P$ such that (1) $|m| \geq |P| - (k + 1) + b$ includes at least b benign agents.

To achieve safety via (i), we need to have more than half of the $k + 1$ benign agents in any $m \in M$. So, by using $b = k/2 + 1$ in (1), we have that $|m| \geq |P| - k + \lceil k/2 \rceil$, where $k/2$ is integer division. Therefore, for $M = \{m \subseteq P \mid |m| \geq |P| - k + \lceil k/2 \rceil\}$, we have that property (i), and safety, is satisfied, modulo stochastic certainty.

To achieve liveness via (b), we need to have (2) $|m| \leq k + 1$, namely, at least a decision set that requires (modulo stochastic certainty) only the participation of benign agents for agreement. Thus, to have safety and liveness, one has to satisfy (1) and (2). The inequality (I) $|P| \leq \lfloor 3k/2 \rfloor + 1$ has to be satisfied in order to ensure both (1) and (2). This inequality gives the bounds that are usually referred to in consensus literature [8].

Table 1 illustrates some examples of calculation for the largest k such that $F(p, k, n = |P|) < \epsilon$, for some values of n (number of selected agents) and p (benignity probability) and where is fixed $\epsilon = 10^{-18}$. This calculation is analogous to the one presented. Red entries in the top left are where even seeing all agents agreeing does not prove this, as it is deemed possible that all the agents are malign, namely, for these values of p, n, and ϵ, there is no k such that $F(p, k, n) < \epsilon$. In purple areas, we have that k and n satisfy (I). We can achieve safety for all but the red cells in the upper left corner. However, safety and liveness can only be achieved for the purple cells in the right bottom corner. This pattern illustrates that achieving both safety and liveness requires larger sets of pickets and decision sets in comparison to achieving safety alone. For example, with $p = 0.95$ and $n = 50$, we have that $k = 25$. So, we have at least 26 benign agents amongst the 50 randomly and independently selected. Thus, to ensure safety, we can choose decision sets $m \subseteq P$ such that $|m| \geq 38$. Since (I) does not hold for $n = 50$ and $k = 25$, we cannot obtain safety and liveness. On the other hand, for $p = 0.95$ and $n = 100$, we have that $k = 66$, in which case (I) holds. For this case, we can have decision sets $m \subseteq P$ such that $|m| \geq 67$ to achieve liveness and safety. Smaller pickets and decision sets should also allow for more efficient agreement given that fewer agents need to actively take part in the protocol; this principle was one of the main drives in designing our hierarchical consensus machine.

Usually our systems do rely on decisions being made, and usually the systems are more efficient if they can persuade malign participants to contribute mostly as though they were good. Indeed for a consensus machine with a smaller set of pickets to deliver results, this is necessary. To achieve this they need three things: firstly strong incentives on agents not to misbehave and to participate

Table 1. Examples of k for different combinations of p and n, and fixed $\epsilon = 10^{-18}$. The p values were chosen with the consensus bounds of $> 2/3$ in mind.

p/n	20	30	40	50	60	80	100	200	400	600	1000
0.66	★	★	0	3	6	14	22	70	177	290	525
0.75	★	0	3	7	12	22	32	91	218	351	624
0.8	★	1	5	10	16	27	39	104	243	387	*682*
0.85	★	3	8	14	20	33	46	118	*269*	*425*	*742*
0.9	0	6	12	19	26	40	55	*134*	*298*	*466*	*807*
0.95	3	10	17	25	33	50	*66*	*153*	*331*	*512*	*878*

constructively, secondly a decision making mechanism that prevents the malign from inducing a bad decision, and thirdly a fallback mechanism that can force correct decisions (i.e. is both safe and live) when needed, all be it at the cost of lower efficiency. The last of these should convince opponents that they will not be able to permanently disrupt the system. The worst they can achieve is complication and delay. One cannot reasonably prevent the malign from covert mischief, but overtly saying the wrong thing or not doing what they are meant to will attract penalties and bans. The main motivation for the hierarchical consensus machine idea introduced next is providing the required fallback mechanism. It allows us to initiate a decision on the assumption that (most of) the malign agents participate normally in the knowledge that the carefully-picked (safe) decision sets will prevent a bad decision from being made; the (live) fallback allows a decision to be forced even when malign agents do not participate.

5 Formalising Hierarchical Consensus Machines in CSP

We have already described how a consensus machine proceeds when it consists of a single set of pickets synchronising in a rather abstract sense. We have also described how to pick decision sets so that one can achieve safety and liveness using a type of stochastic reasoning. In this section, we present a *hierarchical consensus machine*, let us call it *HM*, that is in itself a combination of two (sub-)consensus machines, let us call them, G and H. The machine G is safe and efficient, whereas H is less efficient but it is both safe and live; as explained in the previous section, the difference in efficiency comes from the size of picket and decision sets that are necessary to achieve these properties. In achieving safety without liveness, G can enter a situation very similar to the well-known phenomenon of deadlock, when malign agents refuse to take part and agree on a value. Deadlock is not normally an acceptable behaviour of a complete system, and certainly not in a blockchain. We propose a way to recover from such a deadlock in G by letting H take over. Specifically, we show how control of a decision-making procedure can be handed from one machine to the other. Despite G not being live, *HM* still is so thanks to H and the handover protocol we propose.

When passing decision making from G to H, the transition might come because the agents in G have the evidence that G will not be able to decide, or because malign agents in G fail to participate—in the latter case, G will not reach a decision but its agents are unable to determine that it will not. In both cases, we need to be careful that control will not be passed to H when some agents in G are already committed to a value, or at least that, in this case, H decides on the same committed value. So, our protocol does not prevent H and G both issuing decisions, but ensures that if they do, they are the same.

The more difficult of these cases is where the pickets in H take over on their own initiative. That is because if G's agents themselves decide to hand over, it will be because there is agreement to do so. Handing over to H means that G has not made the decision, and none of G's agents can validly believe it has, as that would be inconsistent with the agreement to hand over. When taking over from G, the H process does not have an immediate global effect on all the agents of G, so a decision may still be made later by G.

Our formulation is inspired by the large body of work on process algebra: understanding bodies of agents that run concurrently and interact by forms of synchronisation. There is an interesting analogy here with process algebra. CSP, particularly in later versions [27,28], has a number of ways in which one process can pass control to another. The throw operator P [| A |> Q runs like P until it throws an exception in the set A, which causes it to run like Q. On the other hand the interrupt operator P /\ Q has P run, but if Q performs any visible action it takes over.

We present and formalise in CSP two models for *HM*. The *abstract model* represents the behaviour of each machine G and H as a single CSP process. It abstractly depicts what is the expected emergent behaviour from their respective implementation each of which as an interactive distributed set of pickets. The main step of this abstraction is that the component consensus machines G and H are deemed to take an action only once there is agreement (in the sense we have already discussed) on the action. The *distributed model*, on the other hand, demonstrates precisely how the emergent behaviour of each machine can be realised in terms of such a set of pickets.

In other words the abstract model describes how we expect the protocol to work in every implementation, but the way in which the sequential processes it contains are implemented by decentralised collections implemented by G and H are not laid down. The distributed model illustrates one way of realising this.

The protocol we present here has much in common with mutual exclusion. We want to prevent something akin to a race condition. An obvious question is whether we could use a simple mutex between G and H and only allow one to make the decision. The answer is no: it is part of the make-up of G that it can deadlock at any time. If it were to seek the right to make the decision—via the shared mutex—but then deadlock, then *HM* would deadlock too; contrary to our specification.

5.1   Abstract Model

In the abstract model, each of G and H is modelled as a single CSP process, and they communicate via shared storage locations each of which is also represented as a CSP process and each machine has two locations it can write to. Intuitively speaking, machine G comes to a decision in a two-step process. It first *commits* to (i.e. pre-decides on) a value by writing it on its first location and then it *decides* on this value by writing to its second location. Before these writes it checks whether H has started by looking for a *started* signal written to H's first location. If at any point it detects that H has started, it stops by choice. After a timeout has elapsed, H starts. It initially checks whether G has come to a decision already. If so, it reaffirms that decision. Otherwise, it signals it has started its decision making process by writing a *started* signal value on its first storage location. If no value has been committed to by G at that point, H proceeds to make its own decision. Otherwise, again, it just echoes G's decision.

Machines G and H rely on storage locations to communicate and convey (pre-)decisions. The datatype values denotes the possible values stored in these locations: D1 and D2 are (pre-)decisions whereas quiet, start and null denote machine statuses. Locations are identified by elements in location. Locations 1 and 3 are controlled (i.e. written) by machine G whereas 2 and 4 are controlled by machine H. Channels read, write1 and write2 are used to manage locations whereas stepG, stepH, and timeoutstep denote internal actions of these machines. Finally, channel decision is used to communicate (pre-)decisions made by them.

```
datatype values = quiet | started | D1 | D2 | null

locations = {1..4}

channel read, write1: locations.values
channel stepG, stepH, timeoutstep

channel decision:{1,2}.{D1,D2}
```

The storage locations are defined by the following two processes. Writing to and reading from these locations are not atomic events. When a value y is written to location i (via write1.i?y) the storage goes into a non-deterministic state in which it allows for a read to retrieve the old value x. The event write2.i signals to this location that the value y has been properly written at which point reads deterministically return y. This non-determinism captures (i.e. abstracts) the asynchrony of the distributed system: the write begins when the decision is known somewhere and it ends when it is known at most of the network.

```
Store(i,x) = read.i!x -> Store(i,x)
    [] write1.i?y -> StoreND(i,x,y)

StoreND(i,x,y) = (read.i.x -> StoreND(i,x,y)
```

```
        |~| read.i.y -> StoreND(i,x,y))
[] write2.i -> Store(i,y)
```

We abstract away all activities of G and H except the steps they need to make to record the decision they make and the steps they need to record and coordinate it. For modelling purposes we assume here that G makes decision D1 and H makes D2 unless it is forced to follow G's decision because it cannot be sure G will not make a decision.

The machine G's behaviour is defined by the following CSP processes, with initial state given by G. As G0, it reads the status of machine H via location 2. If H has started already, it stops. Otherwise, if H is quiet, as process G1, it signals a pre-decision on value D1 by writing it to Location 1. If H is still quiet at that point, it consolidates this pre-decision with event write2.1. As process G2, it reads the status of H for the last time, before issuing a final decision on D1 as process G3. Note that the parallel combination of G0 and CHAOS in G captures G's incompleteness by allowing it to deadlock at any point.

```
G0 = (read.2.quiet -> stepG -> G1
  [] read.2.started -> STOP)

G1 = write1.1.D1 ->
     (read.2.quiet -> write2.1 -> stepG -> G2
     [] read.2.started -> STOP)

G2 = read.2.started -> STOP
     [] read.2.quiet -> stepG -> G3

G3 = decision.1.D1 -> write1.3.D1 -> write2.3 -> STOP

G = G0 [|Events|] CHAOS(Events)
```

The machine H's behaviour is defined by the following CSP processes, with initial state given by H. As H, it reads whether machine G has come to a decision by reading Location 3. If it detect a decision, it re-asserts this decision by writing D1 to Location 4. Otherwise, it interprets that a timeout has occurred and it moves on to make its own decision. As H1, it signals that it has started its decision making process by writing started to Location 2. As H2, it checks whether machine G has started at all. If it has, H re-asserts the pre-decision made by G—i.e., by writing D1 to Location 4. Otherwise, it proceed by making its own decision by writing D2 instead. Both of these decisions are captured by process H3.

```
H = read.3.null -> timeoutstep -> H1
    [] read.3.D1 -> write1.4.D1 -> write2.4 -> STOP

H1 = write1.2.started -> write2.2 -> stepH -> H2
```

```
H2 = read.1.null -> stepH -> H3(D2)
     [] read.1.D1 -> H3(D1)

H3(d) = decision.2.d -> write1.4.d -> write2.4 -> STOP
```

The hierarchical consensus machine behaviour is given by System. Note how machines *H* and *G* are interleaved in Machine and they rely on storage locations in Locations to interact as we discussed.

```
Locations = Store(1,null) ||| Store(2,quiet)
                 ||| Store(3,null) ||| Store(4,null)

Machines = G ||| H

System = Machines [|{|read,write1,write2|}|] Locations
```

We expect this abstract hierarchical consensus machine to be *safe and live*. By safe, we mean that if it comes to a decision, it decides on a single value, that is, each machine might even come to their own decision but their value must match. By live, we mean that System must not deadlock before a decision is made. We capture these two requirements by a refinement expression in CSP's stable failures model as follows.

```
Decisions = {write1.3.d, write1.4.d | d <- {D1,D2}}
Decision1 = {write1.3.d, write1.4.d | d <- {D1}}
Decision2 = {write1.3.d, write1.4.d | d <- {D2}}

DSystem = System \ diff(Events,Decisions)

Spec =(|~| x:Decision1 @ x -> CHAOS(Decision1))
        |~|
       (|~| x:Decision2 @ x -> CHAOS(Decision2))

assert Spec [F= DSystem
```

The refinement expression is built around decision events: all the decision events are members of Decisions, the decision events for value D1 are members of Decision1, and the events for value D2 are in Decision2. The specification process Spec allows a decision to be made on D1 and D2 initially. Once such a decision is made, only events deciding on that value are allowed be performed. Note that this process is not allowed to deadlock initially. Thus, the proposed refinement expression ensures that the behaviour of the system when projected onto decision events—given by DSystem—offers some decision event initially and stick to that decision value subsequently. We have used FDR to validate this refinement expression.

5.2   Distributed Model

The abstract model is useful from an analysis perspective: one can analyse the handover protocol itself while not needing to examine the implementation of each machine as a collection of interactive agents and the issues arising from such an implementation. Instead, issues with just the handover protocol itself can be identified and fixed. We can then argue either that a given approach to building the individual machines G and H will meet this model by construction, or test it by building a more detailed, distributed model in CSP for FDR.

In our model, each machine is a distributed system implementing a protocol that attempts to reach consensus in the presence of Byzantine agents. Intuitively speaking, our hierarchical machine works as follows. Machine G starts and tries to come to a decision on a unified value. After some appropriate amount of time—enough to allow G to come to a decision if agents can agree on a value—machine H starts. It checks whether machine G has *committed* to a value, i.e., it has pre-decided on it but might not have gathered enough evidence to properly decide on it. If so, machine H decides on that value. Otherwise, the agents in H are free to choose a value of their own. Like the abstract model, these machines communicate local decisions via storage locations.

Our more detailed CSP model is parameterised by some global functions. VALUES gives the universe of decision values, and NODES are the agent identifiers. For machine m, N(m) gives its number of agents, MNODES(m) are its agent identifiers, THRESHOLD(m) gives the level of agreement (i.e. how many agents) that is required for reaching consensus, G(m) gives the number of good agents, with GOOD(m) and BAD(m) identifying the good and malign agents in the machines, respectively. In the following, we describe in detail our CSP model.

```
datatype MACHINES = g | h

channel value : MACHINES.NODES.VALUES
channel prewrite, write : MACHINES.NODES.MACHINES.NODES.VALUES
channel setup_prewrite, setup_write : MACHINES.NODES.VALUES
channel decision : MACHINES.VALUES
channel decide : MACHINES.NODES.VALUES
channel timeout : MACHINES.NODES.MACHINES.NODES
channel end_round
```

We use event value.m.n.v to represent that the agent n in machine m has chosen as its decision value v, event setup_prewrite.m.n.v (setup_write.m.n.v) to signal that agent n in machine m has pre-decided (decided) on value v, and event pre-write.m.n.mm.nn.v (write.m.n.mm.nn.v) as a way to communicate to agent nn in machine mm that agent n in machine m has pre-decided (decided) on value v. The event decision.m.v is used to signal that machine m has decided on value v, whereas decide.m.n.v are convey that agent n in machine m has (locally) decided on value v. The event timeout.m.n.mm.nn denotes that agent nn in machine mm timed out when trying to read the decision from agent n in machine m. The event end_round is a modelling device used to signal that machine G has had enough time to come to a decision and that machine H is now taking over.

```
EmptyPreWriteLocation(n,m) =
    setup_prewrite.m.n?v -> FullPreWriteLocation(n,m,v)

FullPreWriteLocation(n,m,v) =
    prewrite.m.n?mm?a:MNODES(mm)!v -> FullPreWriteLocation(n,m,v)
```

The process EmptyPreWriteLocation(n,m) is a storage location that stores the pre-decision of agent n in machine m; each agent has such a location that it controls. It is a single-write multiple-reads one-place buffer.

```
EmptyWriteLocation(n,m) =
    setup_write.m.n?v -> FullWriteLocation(n,m,v)
    []
    timeout.m.n?mm?a:MNODES(mm) -> EmptyWriteLocation(n,m)

FullWriteLocation(n,m,v) =
    write.m.n?mm?a:MNODES(mm)!v -> FullWriteLocation(n,m,v)
    []
    decide.m.n.v -> FullWriteLocation(n,m,v)
```

The process EmptyWriteLocation is also a storage location that behaves similarly to the previous one. It stores decisions instead of pre-decisions. Moreover, it offers a timeout event if the location is empty—it allows agents reading from it to experience a timeout—and it uses the decide event to communicate the local decision of this agent.

```
GNode(n) =
    value.g.n?v -> setup_prewrite.g.n.v ->
        if v == 0 then PreWrite(n,g,{n},1,0,0)
        else if v == 1 then PreWrite(n,g,{n},0,1,0)
        else PreWrite(n,g,{n},0,0,1)
```

The control behaviour of agent n in machine G is given by process GNode(n). We design the agents so that they choose their local decision value independently (captured by event value) but they will come together, or not, to certify a unified decision. Once a value is chosen, it is written to the agent's pre-decision storage (via event setup_prewrite).

```
PreWrite(n,m,vs,c0,c1,c2) =
    (prewrite.m?a:diff(MNODES(m),vs)!m.n?v ->
        if v == 0 then PreWrite(n,m,union({a},vs),c0+1,c1,c2)
        else if v == 1 then PreWrite(n,m,union({a},vs),c0,c1+1,c2)
        else PreWrite(n,m,union({a},vs),c0,c1,c2+1))
    []
```

```
(timeout.m?a:diff(BAD(m),vs)!m.n ->
    PreWrite(n,m,union(vs,{a}),c0,c1,c2))
[]
(vs == MNODES(m) &
  if c0 >= THRESHOLD(m) then setup_write.m.n.0 -> EndOfRound
  else if c1 >= THRESHOLD(m) then setup_write.m.n.1 ->
  EndOfRound
  else if c2 >= THRESHOLD(m) then setup_write.m.n.2 ->
  EndOfRound
  else EndOfRound)


EndOfRound = end_round -> SKIP
```

The `PreWrite` process describes how an agent reads the pre-decisions of other agents in order to come to its own local decision. Once the agent has received a pre-decision or a timeout from all nodes, it goes on to either locally decide on a value or to conclude the decision making process without deciding on a value. If it has seen enough pre-decisions supporting value v—for instance, for $v == 0$, this is captured by condition `c0 >= THRESHOLD(m)`—the agent locally decides on v, writing this value to its decision storage location (via event `setup_write`). Note how the agent only accepts timeouts from malign agents; we assume that good agents deliver messages reliably and in a timely way. The process `EndOfRound` signals that machine's G time to come to a decision has elapsed, at which point, the agent terminates.

```
GGoodNode(n) = (GNode(n) [|{|setup_prewrite, setup_write|}|]
    (EmptyWriteLocation(n,g) ||| EmptyPreWriteLocation(n,g)))
```

A benign agent in machine G is a parallel process—given by process `GGoodNode`—that combines its storage locations and its control behaviour.

```
GoodAlpha(n,m) =
    Union({{| value.m.n, setup_prewrite.m.n, setup_write.m.n,
            decide.m.n, prewrite.m.n.mm.a, prewrite.mm.a.m.n,
            timeout.mm.a.m.n, timeout.m.n.mm.a, write.m.n.mm.a,
            write.mm.a.m.n, end_round | mm <- MACHINES,
            a <- MNODES(mm), (a != n or mm != m) |}})
```

`GoodAlpha(n,m)` gives the alphabet of the benign agent n in machine m.

```
HNode(n) =
    end_round ->
        Reader(n,{},0,0,0)

Reader(n,vs,c0,c1,c2) =
    (write.g?a:diff(MNODES(g),vs)!h.n?vv ->
        setup_prewrite.h.n.vv ->
```

```
            if vv == 0 then setup_write.h.n.0 -> EndOfRound
            else if vv == 1 then setup_write.h.n.1 -> EndOfRound
            else setup_write.h.n.2 -> EndOfRound)
    []
    (timeout.g?a:diff(MNODES(g),vs)!h!n ->
        Reader(n,union(vs,{a}),c0,c1,c2))
    []
    (vs == MNODES(g) &
        value.h.n?vv -> setup_prewrite.h.n.vv ->
            if vv == 0 then PreWrite(n,h,{n},1,0,0)
            else if vv == 1 then PreWrite(n,h,{n},0,1,0)
            else PreWrite(n,h,{n},0,0,1))
```

The control behaviour of a benign agent in machine H is given by process HNode(n). The initial **end_round** event and the requirements that we impose on the way in which agents synchronise on this event means that the agents of machine H only start after the agents of machine G have finished with their decision making interactions. This behaviour captures the assumption that agents have a reasonably synchronised clock and that they can come to a decision within a bounded time frame.

Once started, the agent's control behaviour in machine H is given by Reader. This process reads the local decisions made by agents in G. If one of them has decided on a given value—which means that machine G has committed to that value—we require that the agent in H decide on the same value. This behaviour ensures that if both machines come to a decision, they must agree on their decided value.

If no agent of G has decided on a value, the agents in H are free to choose their local decision values, and they move on to behave like process PreWrite to try and come to a unified decision as already mentioned.

```
HGoodNode(n) = (HNode(n) [|{|setup_prewrite, setup_write|}|]
    (EmptyWriteLocation(n,h) ||| EmptyPreWriteLocation(n,h)))
```

Similar to benign agents in G, a benign agent in H is a parallel combination of its control behaviour and storage locations as per process HGoodNode.

```
BadNode(n,m,c0,c1,c2) =
    timeout.m.n?mm?a:GOOD(mm) -> BadNode(n,m,c0,c1,c2)
    []
    (STOP
    |~|
    (prewrite.m.n.m?a:diff(MNODES(m),{n})?v ->
        BadNode(n,m,c0,c1,c2)
    []
    prewrite.m?a:diff(MNODES(m),c0)!m.n.0 ->
        BadNode(n,m,union(c0,{a}),c1,c2)
    []
```

```
prewrite.m?a:diff(MNODES(m),c1)!m.n.1 ->
  BadNode(n,m,c0,union(c1,{a}),c2)
[]
prewrite.m?a:diff(MNODES(m),c2)!m.n.2 ->
  BadNode(n,m,c0,c1,union(c2,{a}))
[]
card(c0) >= THRESHOLD(m) &
  (write.m.n?a.b!0 -> BadNode(n,m,c0,c1,c2)
  [] decide.m.n.0 -> BadNode(n,m,c0,c1,c2))
[]
card(c1) >= THRESHOLD(m) &
  (write.m.n?a.b!1 -> BadNode(n,m,c0,c1,c2)
  [] decide.m.n.1 -> BadNode(n,m,c0,c1,c2))
[]
card(c2) >= THRESHOLD(m) &
  (write.m.n?a.b!2 -> BadNode(n,m,c0,c1,c2)
  [] decide.m.n.2 -> BadNode(n,m,c0,c1,c2))))
```

The malign agent n in machine m is modelled by process BadNode(n,m). These agents can exhibit Byzantine behaviour but they are not allowed to behave completely arbitrarily: there are still some actions which these adversaries cannot perpetrate against benign agents. For instance, it can only offer event decide if it has gathered enough support for the corresponding decision—i.e., it cannot create a spurious local decision. This abstraction accounts for the following behaviour: a local decision by an agent must be associated with enough supporting evidence—in the form of pre-decisions—which are cryptographically signed by the agents generating that evidence. We assume malign agents cannot break cryptographic primitives and, thus, they cannot forge signatures by other agents. On the other hand, malign agents can pre-decide on more than one value, or even refuse to serve a request for a (pre-)decision.

```
BadAlpha(n,m) = {| prewrite.m.n.mm.a, prewrite.mm.a.m.n,
    write.m.n.mm.a, write.mm.a.m.n, decide.m.n, timeout.m.n.mm.a
    | mm <- MACHINES, a <- MNODES(mm), (a != n or mm != m) |}
```

The alphabet of malign agent n in machine m is given by BadAlpha(n,m).

```
AlphaBadNodes(m) = Union({BadAlpha(i,m) | i <- BAD(m)})
BadNodes(m) = || i : BAD(m) @
    [BadAlpha(i,m)] BadNode(i,m,{i},{i},{i})

AlphaGoodNodes(m) = Union({GoodAlpha(i,m) | i <- GOOD(m)})
GGoodNodes = || i : GOOD(g) @ [GoodAlpha(i,g)] GGoodNode(i)
GNodes = GGoodNodes [ AlphaGoodNodes(g)
    || AlphaBadNodes(g) ] BadNodes(g)
```

```
HGoodNodes = || i : GOOD(h) @ [GoodAlpha(i,h)] HGoodNode(i)
HNodes = HGoodNodes [ AlphaGoodNodes(h)
    || AlphaBadNodes(h) ] BadNodes(h)

Nodes = GNodes [union(AlphaGoodNodes(g),AlphaBadNodes(g))
            || union(AlphaGoodNodes(h),AlphaBadNodes(h))] HNodes
```

The processes GNodes and HNodes capture the behaviour of machines G and H, respectively, whereas Nodes captures how they interact to implement the handover protocol. In these processes, the appropriate agents run in parallel and they are required to synchronise on shared events.

```
Decider(m,c0,c1,c2) =
    decide.m?a:diff(MNODES(m),c0)!0 -> Decider(m,union({a},c0),c1,c2)
    []
    decide.m?a:diff(MNODES(m),c1)!1 -> Decider(m,c0,union({a},c1),c2)
    []
    decide.m?a:diff(MNODES(m),c2)!2 -> Decider(m,c0,c1,union({a},c2))
    []
    card(c0) >= THRESHOLD(m) & decision.m.0 -> Decider(m,c0,c1,c2)
    []
    card(c1) >= THRESHOLD(m) & decision.m.1 -> Decider(m,c0,c1,c2)
    []
    card(c2) >= THRESHOLD(m) & decision.m.2 -> Decider(m,c0,c1,c2)
```

The behaviour of agents described so far sets out how they make local decisions but they do not define how machine-level decisions are made. The Decider process is in charge of those. This centralised process collects local decisions made by the agents of a machine, offering a machine-level decision as soon as enough local decisions are gathered. This process is an abstraction that is useful for conciseness in specifying the behaviour of the machines but also for the sake of tractability. In a practical implementation of this protocol, each agent would implement the behaviour of the Decider process. Process System runs machines G and H with their respective Decider processes.

```
System = Nodes [|{|decide|}|]
    (Decider(g,{},{},{}) ||| Decider(h,{},{},{}))
```

We want to ensure that the system is safe – i.e. it must stick with one decision value once a decision is made—and live—i.e. it must offer a decision event before it is allowed to deadlock. Our discussion here is related to that on Sect. 4. In that section, we discussed how we can use a type of stochastic reasoning to choose the size of the set of pickets that is necessary to achieve a given number of good and malign agents, given some parameters for our stochastic model. In our CSP model, we talk about decision sets assuming that the pickets-set size and number of good and malign agents has been fixed, namely, the stochastic reasoning has already been used to find these numbers. So, we limit ourselves to discuss the size of decision sets that is necessary to achieve safety and liveness.

Safety is ensured by setting a threshold that requires the participation of more than half of the benign nodes, namely, for machine m, THRESHOLD(m) $\geq$ GOOD(m)/2 + BAD(m) + 1, where GOOD(m)/2 is truncated integer division—we require the number of agents in each machine to be at least 2. If this threshold is set, the machine cannot decide on two different values on the same run of the protocol. Assume that agents in G supported two values, say 0 and 1, then there must be THRESHOLD(g) many agents supporting either. That implies the existence of a benign agent that has supported two values, a possibility that our protocol does not allow; a contradiction. The same reasoning holds for H's independent decision. The requirement that H must decide on G's committed values, if one exists, ensures that if they both come to a decision, their value must match. As G can only commit to one value, by the same counting argument as before, H must decide on the same value as G.

Another assumption is required to ensure liveness. We expect H to come up with a decision if G fails to do so, but the agents in H may disagree on a decision value in the case they are left to independently select it. On a realistic implementation, agents will probably need to iterate if they fail to agree on a value within G or H until they eventually converge to a sufficiently agreed choice. How they achieve this is a separate topic but will likely involve coordinating input data and computing deterministically. For the sake of conciseness and tractability, we do not implement this process and we force enough benign agents in H to choose a common value (i.e. converge immediately), ensuring H comes to a decision. This immediate convergence is implemented by the Convergence process, which forces benign agents {0..CN} in machine H to choose the value CV—CN and CV are variables that parameterise our model. The *convergent system* is given by process CSystem. To achieve liveness, we need GOOD(m) $\geq$ THRESHOLD(m)— i.e., no malign agents are required to take part in the consensus—and that at least THRESHOLD(m)-many benign agents converge to the right value. From this inequality and the safety inequality before, one can derive the traditional lower bound on number of agents necessary for Byzantine agreement: $N = 3f + 1$ where N is the number of agents amongst whom f are malign.

```
AlphaConvergence = {| value.h.n | n <- {0..CN-1} |}

ConvergenceAux(0) = STOP
ConvergenceAux(i) = value.h.(i-1).CV -> ConvergenceAux(i-1)
Convergence = ConvergenceAux(CN)

CSystem = System [|AlphaConvergence|] Convergence
```

Similarly to what we did for the abstract model, we use the following refinement expression to capture these properties. The specification process Spec ensures that once a decision is made, only events deciding on that value are allowed be performed and that a decision event is offered initially—it can deadlock after a decision event is performed. Process DSystem captures a projection of CSystem's behaviour onto decision events. We have used FDR to validate some instances of our model where thresholds are set in a way to ensure safety and liveness as discussed. We have also tested instances with insufficient thresholds to demonstrate how the model breaks down under those.

```
Spec = |~| m : MACHINES, v : VALUES @
       decision.m.v -> CHAOS({decision.mm.v | mm <- MACHINES})

DSystem = CSystem \ diff(Events,{|decision|})

assert Spec [F= DSystem
```

Interestingly, the inequality required to achieve safety alone does not restrict the proportion of benign agents that take part in the protocol. If we have, for instance, a single benign agent in a machine, a threshold requiring unanimity for decisions would still ensure safety. On the other hand, when both the safety and liveness inequalities are required, $> 2/3$ of agents must be benign. Thus, as machine G only needs to be safe, it can rely on there being as few as a single benign agent, whereas machine H, which must be safe and live, is required to have $> 2/3$ benign agents. Based on our stochastic calculations, for a fixed probability of an agent being malign, the number of agents that need to be selected to get a sample including at least one benign agent should be, in general, much smaller than the number needed for a sample including $> 2/3$ benign agents. Therefore, the number of agents required to implement G should be, in general, much smaller than the agents required to implement H. This fact supports our claim that G should be faster at coming to a decision when compared to H, given the smaller number of agents that are required to interact.

In many cases the "pickets" making up the back-up machine H will be entire qualified population of block creators, rather than being randomly chosen. In this case the hierarchical machine will precisely be the optimistic mechanism G backed up by classic Byzantine agreement. Moreover, typically, the 4 locations used by our protocol will be implemented in a distributed way by the agents involved. The correctness will depend on the signature mechanisms the blockchain has in place and also forms of the gossiping assumptions described earlier.

6   Related Work

Many classical protocols [17,18,20,25] exist to solve the Byzantine agreement problem [24]. The emergence of blockchains renewed the research community's interest in this problem—and more generally on the problem of achieving consensus in distributed systems—leading to a number of new protocols [1,3,4,6,12,15,22,30,32].

The first consensus protocol proposed for blockchains was *Proof-of-Work* (PoW) in the context of Bitcoin [22]. Intuitively speaking, in this protocol, *miners* (i.e. block producer candidates) attempt to solve a cryptographic puzzle, and the first one who solves it is entitled to propose the next block to be added to the chain. Arguably, the main drawback of PoW protocols is how energy inefficient they can be [19,31]; the larger the network the more computing power is used to constantly solve these cryptographic puzzles. *Proof-of-Stake* (PoS) protocols have been proposed [1,5,12,15] as energy efficient alternatives to PoW ones. Hybrid PoW-PoS protocols have also been proposed [16].

In Proof-of-Stake protocols, agents signal their intention to participate in the block production process by *staking* a sum of cryptocurrency, i.e. the *stake*, they own. Staking means that this sum is locked (i.e. escrowed) for the duration of this process and it may be *slashed* as a means to punish malign behaviour. The frequency upon which agents are selected to participate in this process is proportional to the size of the stake. Note how in PoW computing power determines how often an agent is "selected" to produce a block as opposed to staked cryptocurrency in PoS. In PoS protocols, agents can be selected as a block producer but also as a member of a committee which is typically in charge of either electing block producers or *finalising blocks*, namely, determining whether a block is immutable and the only valid block at a given height. Before a block is deemed final, a number of candidate blocks at a given height might be "competing" to become final. Some PoS protocols rely on probabilistic mechanisms to determine the finality of a block—e.g. Algorand [12], Ouroboros [15]—whereas some others rely on deterministic mechanisms—e.g. Internet Consensus Computer [6], Casper FFG [5], Tendermint [3]. Our handover protocol is meant to be used as a part of a protocol to achieve deterministic finality, with our primary motivation being PoS. A PoS-based selection mechanism can be used to choose committees of agents—their sizes are based on our stochastic calculations—to implement machines G and H and to decide on the next *final* block using the handover protocol.

Despite being designed to be part of a fully-fledged blockchain consensus protocol, the handover protocol alone is closer in nature to mutual exclusion, though adapted for linking agreement protocols like Byzantine agreement [17, 20,23,32]. Abstractly speaking, these protocols have been designed around the use of the votes to form decisions and of a threshold/quorum to ensure safety. In fact, the PBFT (Practical Byzantine Fault Tolerance) protocol [20] specifically—and this voting mechanism more generally—has been a source of inspiration for many current blockchain protocols, including ours.

7   Conclusions

In this paper we have used formal tools to understand how consensus can arise in decentralised systems. Essentially we have set out a programmatic approach to laying down and analysing consensus: given a population of potential block creators and the potentially multiple perspectives of different users we need to establish a trust model that they are all happy with. We then have the job of having the blockchain select sufficient groups of pickets and decision criteria that all can be sure of any positive decisions they make.

On the assumption that we can incentivise most malign participants to participate apparently properly, this will give us all we need. But an essential part of such motivation is that the malign know that if they do not collaborate like this they will be defeated by a back up mechanism.

We have shown how to formalise both the primary and secondary mechanisms as Unitary Consensus Machines. While much of our treatment was inspired by process algebra, we were able to both design and verify the crucial protocol that links a hierarchy of decision making in CSP and FDR.

By allowing such hierarchical consensus decisions, we believe that we have tools for making blockchains more varied and flexible. We hope that our approach to creating the component machines which compose together to provide consensus can be automated.

It is only natural - to people steeped in such languages and tools - that CSP coupled with FDR is a good way to model complex interactions in decentralised consensus. We are pleased to have demonstrated the truth of this intuition. While the full systems representing consensus may be too involved to fit within the abstractions of such tools, it is comforting that like so many other areas of concurrent reasoning, we can find levels where they bring real benefit. We have modelled other aspects of blockchain using CSP and FDR.

We hope that others will be found, and that our tools for bringing clarity to the topic of consensus will find many interesting applications.

References

1. Bentov, I., Gabizon, A., Mizrahi, A.: Cryptocurrencies without proof of work. In: Clark, J., Meiklejohn, S., Ryan, P.Y.A., Wallach, D., Brenner, M., Rohloff, K. (eds.) FC 2016. LNCS, vol. 9604, pp. 142–157. Springer, Heidelberg (2016). https://doi.org/10.1007/978-3-662-53357-4_10
2. Brookes, S.D., Roscoe, A.W.: CSP: A Practical Process Algebra, 1 edn., pp. 187–222. Association for Computing Machinery, New York (2021)
3. Buchman, E., Kwon, J., Milosevic, Z.: The latest gossip on BFT consensus. CoRR abs/1807.04938 (2018). http://arxiv.org/abs/1807.04938
4. Buterin, V.: Ethereum: a next-generation smart contract and decentralized application Platform (2014). https://ethereum.org/whitepaper/
5. Buterin, V., Griffith, V.: Casper the friendly finality gadget. CoRR abs/1710.09437 (2017). http://arxiv.org/abs/1710.09437
6. Camenisch, J., Drijvers, M., Hanke, T., Pignolet, Y.A., Shoup, V., Williams, D.: Internet computer consensus. In: Proceedings of the 2022 ACM Symposium on Principles of Distributed Computing, PODC 2022, pp. 81–91. Association for Computing Machinery, New York (2022). https://doi.org/10.1145/3519270.3538430
7. Dowd, K., Cotter, J., Humphrey, C., Woods, M.: How unlucky is 25-sigma? J. Portfolio Manag. **34**, 76–80 (2008). https://doi.org/10.3905/jpm.2008.709984
8. Dwork, C., Lynch, N., Stockmeyer, L.: Consensus in the presence of partial synchrony. J. ACM (JACM) **35**(2), 288–323 (1988)
9. Fischer, M.J., Lynch, N.A., Paterson, M.S.: Impossibility of distributed consensus with one faulty process. J. ACM **32**(2), 374–382 (1985)

10. Gibson-Robinson, T., Armstrong, P., Boulgakov, A., Roscoe, A.W.: FDR3—a modern refinement checker for CSP. In: Ábrahám, E., Havelund, K. (eds.) TACAS 2014. LNCS, vol. 8413, pp. 187–201. Springer, Heidelberg (2014). https://doi.org/10.1007/978-3-642-54862-8_13
11. Gibson-Robinson, T., Lowe, G.: Symmetry reduction in CSP model checking. Int. J. Softw. Tools Technol. Transfer **21**(5), 567–605 (2019). https://doi.org/10.1007/s10009-019-00516-4
12. Gilad, Y., Hemo, R., Micali, S., Vlachos, G., Zeldovich, N.: Algorand: scaling byzantine agreements for cryptocurrencies. In: Proceedings of the 26th Symposium on Operating Systems Principles, SOSP 2017, pp. 51–68. Association for Computing Machinery, New York (2017). https://doi.org/10.1145/3132747.3132757
13. Harel, D.: Statecharts: a visual formalism for complex systems. Sci. Comput. Program. **8**(3), 231–274 (1987)
14. Hoare, C.A.R.: Communicating Sequential Processes. International Series in Computer Science. Prentice Hall (1985)
15. Kiayias, A., Russell, A., David, B., Oliynykov, R.: Ouroboros: a provably secure proof-of-stake blockchain protocol. In: Katz, J., Shacham, H. (eds.) CRYPTO 2017. LNCS, vol. 10401, pp. 357–388. Springer, Cham (2017). https://doi.org/10.1007/978-3-319-63688-7_12
16. King, S., Nadal, S.: Ppcoin: peer-to-peer crypto-currency with proof-of-stake. Self-published paper, 19 August 2012
17. Lamport, L.: The part-time parliament. ACM Trans. Comput. Syst. **16**(2), 133–169 (1998). https://doi.org/10.1145/279227.279229
18. Lamport, L., Shostak, R., Pease, M.: The Byzantine generals problem. ACM Trans. Program. Lang. Syst. **4**(3), 382–401 (1982). https://doi.org/10.1145/357172.357176
19. Li, X., Zhu, Q., Qi, N., Huang, J., Yuan, Y., Wang, F.Y.: Blockchain consensus algorithms: a survey. In: 2021 China Automation Congress (CAC), pp. 4053–4058 (2021). https://doi.org/10.1109/CAC53003.2021.9728000
20. Liskov, B.H., Wing, J.M.: A behavioral notion of subtyping. ACM Trans. Program. Lang. Syst. **16**(6), 1811–1841 (1994). https://doi.org/10.1145/197320.197383
21. Lowe, G.: Casper: a compiler for the analysis of security protocols. J. Comput. Secur. **6**(1–2), 53–84 (1998)
22. Nakamoto, S., et al.: Bitcoin: a peer-to-peer electronic cash system (2008)
23. Ongaro, D., Ousterhout, J.: In search of an understandable consensus algorithm. In: Proceedings of the 2014 USENIX Conference on USENIX Annual Technical Conference, USENIX ATC 2014, pp. 305–320. USENIX Association (2014)
24. Pease, M., Shostak, R., Lamport, L.: Reaching agreement in the presence of faults. J. ACM **27**(2), 228–234 (1980). https://doi.org/10.1145/322186.322188
25. Rabin, M.O.: Randomized byzantine generals. In: 24th Annual Symposium on Foundations of Computer Science (SFCS 1983), pp. 403–409 (1983). https://doi.org/10.1109/SFCS.1983.48
26. Roscoe, A.W.: Model-checking CSP. In: International Series in Computer Science. Prentice Hall (1994). http://www.cs.ox.ac.uk/people/bill.roscoe/publications/50.ps
27. Roscoe, A.W.: The Theory and Practice of Concurrency. Series in Computer Science. Prentice Hall (1998)
28. Roscoe, A.W.: Understanding Concurrent Systems. Springer, London (2010). https://doi.org/10.1007/978-1-84882-258-0

29. Roscoe, A.W., Gardiner, P.H.B., Goldsmith, M.H., Hulance, J.R., Jackson, D.M., Scattergood, J.B.: Hierarchical compression for model-checking CSP or how to check 10^{20} dining philosophers for deadlock. In: Brinksma, E., Cleaveland, W.R., Larsen, K.G., Margaria, T., Steffen, B. (eds.) TACAS 1995. LNCS, vol. 1019, pp. 133–152. Springer, Heidelberg (1995). https://doi.org/10.1007/3-540-60630-0_7
30. Wood, G.: Ethereum yellow paper. https://ethereum.github.io/yellowpaper/paper.pdf
31. Xiao, Y., Zhang, N., Lou, W., Hou, Y.T.: A survey of distributed consensus protocols for blockchain networks. IEEE Commun. Surv. Tutor. **22**(2), 1432–1465 (2020). https://doi.org/10.1109/COMST.2020.2969706
32. Yin, M., Malkhi, D., Reiter, M.K., Gueta, G.G., Abraham, I.: HotStuff: BFT consensus with linearity and responsiveness. In: Proceedings of the 2019 ACM Symposium on Principles of Distributed Computing, PODC 2019, pp. 347–356. Association for Computing Machinery, New York (2019). https://doi.org/10.1145/3293611.3331591

ProCoS Colleagues

Domain Modelling: A Foundation for Software Development

Dines Bjørner[✉]

The Technical University of Denmark, Fredsvej 11, 2840 Holte, Denmark
bjorner@gmail.com
https://www.imm.dtu.dk/~db

Abstract. Domain modelling, as per the approach of this paper, offers the possibility of describing software application domains in a precise and comprehensive manner – well before requirements capture can take place. We endow domain modelling with appropriate analysis and description calculi and a systematic method for constructing domain models. The present paper is a latest exposé of the *domain science & engineering* as published in earlier papers and a book. It reports on our most recent simplifications to the *domain analysis & description* approach.

The Triptych Dogma

In order to *specify* **software**,
we must understand its requirements.

In order to *prescribe* **requirements**,
we must understand the **domain**.

So we must **study, analyse** and **describe** domains.

1 Introduction

This paper introduces the possibility of a *new phase of software development*, one that precedes requirements engineering, as well as *a new way of looking at the world around us!*

Today's well-managed software development projects usually start with some form of *requirements "capture"*. Now the possibility arises to precede this phase of requirements engineering with an initial phase of domain engineering.

The present paper is an improvement over previously published accounts [13,16,17]: builds upon a simpler domain ontology (Fig. 1 on page 4); has fewer domain concepts (Sects. 3 and 5); and presents a more rational way of "deriving" behaviours from parts (Sect. 6). Taken together the presentation is thus made shorter and more precise.

The approach to the modelling of domains put forward in this paper has two major phases: modelling *external qualities* of the world as we see it, as it manifests itself to us, or otherwise, and modelling the *internal qualities*, as we

J. P. Bowen et al. (Eds.): *Theories of Programming and Formal Methods*, LNCS 14080, pp. 165–210, 2023.
https://doi.org/10.1007/978-3-031-40436-8_7

may not see it, but qualities that can be measured and/or spoken about. The modelling of external qualities has a few steps. The major step of modelling of external qualities is that of deciding upon the atomic-, Cartesian- and set-oriented parts. A minor step, following the major step, is that of identifying a notion of *endurant state*. The modelling of internal qualities has a few more steps. The modelling of *unique identifiers*; the modelling of *mereologies*; the modelling of *attributes*; and the modelling of *'intentional pull'*. It is this structuring into manageable stages and steps that reassures us, i.e., me, that the approach is sound.

1.1 What is a Domain ?

By a *domain* we shall understand a *rationally describable* segment of a *discrete dynamics* fragment of a *human assisted reality*, i.e., of the world: its *endurants*, i.e., *solid and fluid entities:* whether *natural* ["God-given"] or *artefactual* ["man-made"], their *parts* and *living species entities:* whether *atomic* or *compound* parts, respectively whether *plant* or *animal* living species, including *humans*— as well as its *perdurants:* the *behaviours* of *parts* and *living species*.

Clearly this *characterisation* does not possess the rigour that should be common in software development. Terms such as *rationally describable*, *discrete dynamics* and *human assisted reality* must be not just assumed, but must, below, be made more precise. Yet precision defies us: The domains we shall study, analyse and describe are not amenable to such precision. *The world is not formal.*

Thus the *domain analysis & description* methodology that we shall be concerned with is not directed at *continuous dynamics* systems such as we find them in for example aerospace applications. And we shall not, in this paper be concerned with the *human assistance* aspects. By *domain modelling* we mean the study, analysis and description of a domain.

If the domain already exists, then the modelling amounts to a faithful rendering of that domain but such that the resulting model, i.e., description, covers as wide a spectrum of domain instances as is deemed reasonable.[1]

We shall, in this paper, assume already existing domains. By *domain engineering* we mean the construction of domain models.[2]

1.2 Non-computable and Computable Specifications

When specifying[3] software we usually make use of a formal language – one whose semantics can be expressed mathematically. And the specification had better be *logically tractable*. Similarly for *prescribing requirements:* again a formal language can be deployed. And the requirement had better be *computable*. Typically, when

---

[1] Thus a railway domain model should desirably cover such instances as the railways of Denmark and Norway and Sweden, each one individually.

[2] The approach taken here can, however, also be used to devise new domains.

[3] By specifying software we mean specifying the design of the software. That design is derived from the software requirements.

we derive a *software specification*, $\mathcal{S}$, from a *requirements prescription*, $\mathcal{R}$, the *testing, model checking* and *proof* of some form of *correctness*, $\mathcal{D}, \mathcal{S} \models \mathcal{R}$, of the software design relies on not only on relations between the two documents: the $\mathcal{R}$ and $\mathcal{S}$, but also on the *domain description*, $\mathcal{D}$. But in *describing domains* we cannot assume computability. It is the task of *requirements engineering* to "derive" computable requirements from domain models. [17, *Chapter 9*] shows how. We refer to Sect. 8.2.3 on page 38 for summary comments.

1.3   Formal Method and Methodology

By a *method* we shall understand a set of *principles* for *selecting* and *applying* a number of *procedures, techniques* and *tools* for [effectively] *constructing* an *artefact*. By *methodology* we shall understand the *study* and *knowledge* of one or more *methods*. By a *formal method* we shall understand a *method* which *uses* one or more *formal specification languages* as per their intention: *specification* and *verification* (*formal tests, model checks* and *proofs of properties* of *domains descriptions,requirement prescriptions* and *software designs*). By a *formal specification language* we shall understand a language with a *formal syntax*, a *formal semantics* and a *proof system* with which to *describe & validate*[4] domains, prescribe & validate requirements and specify (design) & validate software.

Our domain analysis & description method has been developed, over the years, with this understanding of formal methods.

1.4   From Programming Languages to Domains

Domain stakeholders, those whose primary work is in and of the domain, name the entities of the domain and use these names, nouns and verbs, in communicating with other stakeholders. These utterings constitute a language, albeit an informal one. In a domain model we give *abstract syntax* to (roughly speaking) the *nouns*, Sects. 3 and 5, and *semantics* to (roughly speaking) the *verbs*, Sect. 6.

When, in comparison, we define the syntax and semantics of a programming language, that syntax and semantics covers all well-formed instances of programs in that language. Similarly, when, in consequence, we define the abstract syntax and semantics, i.e., a model, of a domain, that syntax and semantics covers all well-formed instances—we mean it, the model, to cover all well-formed instances of domains.

1.5   A Review

We present a latest exposé of the *domain science & engineering* of [13,16,17, *2015–2021*]. The first inklings of this *applied science* were first reported in [3, *1995–1997*], Volume III, Part IV, Chaps. 8–12, Pages 193–362 of [4, *2006*] cover several aspects of *domain engineering* – but not what we now consider the most important contribution to the field: namely that of the *analysis & description*

---

[4] test, check and verify.

calculi. First developments of the proposed *analysis and description calculi* were reported in [9,10, *Kyiv 2010*]. The recently published papers and book [13,16,17, *2015–2021*] illustrates the fact that the details of the *calculi* may change. The present paper reports on our most recent simplification to the *domain analysis & description* approach and the few extensions, RSL⁺, to the RSL specification language [32]. The domain modelling approach presented here has been honed over the last 30 years in numerous experiments. Some of these are reported in [15,18,19,22].

1.6   An Overview

1.6.1   A Domain Analysis and Description Ontology
Sections 3, 4, 5 and 6 represent the contribution of this paper. Figure 1 illustrates basic ideas of how we shall structure our *domain analysis & description.*

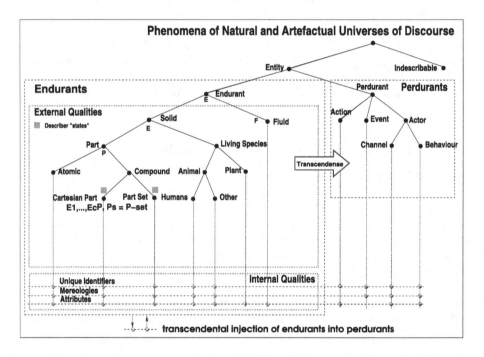

Fig. 1. An Analysis & Description Methodology Ontology

The *domain analyser cum describer*, i.e., the *domain modeller*, is confronted by a domain. How and where to start! Figure 1 is intended to be read top-down, left-to-right. So it suggests that the *domain modeller*, starts by looking "at the whole domain!". That is, at the ● right under the term Universes, between the r and the s!

1.6.2   Step-Wise Analysis and Description

Figure 1 then suggests, by the two lines emerging from that •, that the *domain modeller* poses the question, of the domain, is it (more or less) rationally describable, i.e., is_entity(ϕ), or not. If the *domain modeller* decides yes, it is so, then the analysis "moves" on to the Entity •. Now the question is, is the entity being observed, an endurant or a perdurant, (to be explained below), and so on. We now assume that the analysis proceeds along the left hand side dashed line ($\cdots\cdots$) box labeled 'Endurants'.

The so-called *external quality analysis* of endurants ends when reaching either of the Atomic, Cartesian or Part Set •s.[5] At this point the description proceeds to that of the *internal qualities* of endurants. From Fig. 1 You observe seven vertical [dashed] lines, emanating downwards from endurant bullets to cross three horizontal (bottom of the figure) lines. They "call" for the *domain modeller* to now analyse and describe the internal qualities of endurants: their *unique identification*, their *mereologies*, and their *attributes*.

Eventually the *domain modeller* has "traversed" the left hand side of Fig. 1. At this point a *transcendental deduction* takes place: The *domain modeller* now "morphs" *manifest* endurant parts into *behaviours*. The focal point here are the part behaviour signatures and definitions. Figure 1's right hand side hints at the issues to be covered and that the internal qualities are being a crucial element of behaviour definitions.

1.6.3   The Analysis and Description Prompts

Each • of Fig. 1 thus corresponds to an analysis or description prompt. There are two kinds of analysis prompts. Both are informal. The predicate analysis prompts and the function analysis prompts. There is two major kinds of description prompts. (α) external quality description prompts – with there being two such specific prompts: one for describing so-called *Cartesian* endurants (Sect. 3.3.1 on page 12), another for describing so-called *Part Set* endurants (Sect. 3.3.2 on page 12), and (β) internal quality description prompts with there being three such specific prompts: the *unique identifier* description prompt (Sect. 5.1.1 on page 16), the *mereology* description prompt (Sect. 5.2.1 on page 17), and the *attribute* description prompt (Sect. 5.3.2 on page 18). The predicate analysis prompts yield truth values. The function analysis prompts yield part endurants and the names of their type – which we shall call sorts. And the description prompts yield domain description texts – here in a slight extended version of the RAISE[6] [33] specification language RSL [32].[7,8]

---

[5] We shall, in this paper, not exemplify living species endurants.

[6] Rigorous Approach to Idustrial Software Engineering.

[7] RSL: RAISE Specification Language.

[8] Other formal specification languages are possible, f.ex.: VDM [23,24,30], Z [58], Alloy [42], or CafeOBJ [31].

1.7 RSL, RSL-text and RSL⁺

RSL is described in [32]. We use a subset of that RSL. Thus we shall not avail ourselves of the RSL module concepts of *object, class* and *scheme*. Basically, then, a specification expressed in RSL amounts to sequences of [alternating] *type, value* and *axiom* clauses – with, optionally, a single *channel* clause:

type	type	channel	type
...	...	...	...
value	value	type	value
...	...	...	...
axiom	axiom	value	axiom
...	...	...	...
		axiom	
...	...	...	...

RSL-text is an addition to RSL. In describing domains in RSL we shall be introducing *description prompts* which are informal functions which yield values of type RSL-text, that is, proper RSL texts. Quoting an RSL text: "text". shall denote an RSL-text.

RSL⁺ designate RSL-text plus, in this paper, one extension. That extension is that of the type and values of type names. If T denotes a type, i.e., a possibly infinite set of values, then ηT denotes a value, the name of type T, with ϕT denoting the type of type names.

The domain analysis & description method is informally explained in a mixture of English and RSL⁺. [12, *2014*] attempts a formalisation of an early version of RSL⁺.

1.8 A Computer Science Philosophy

We shall base our *domain analysis & description* approach on the philosophy of Kai Sørlander [53–57]. The issue here is: In *studying, analysing & describing* domains one is confronted with the basic [metaphysical] question[s]: *which are the absolutely necessary conditions for describing any world?*, that is: *what, if anything, is of such necessity, that it could under no circumstances be otherwise?*, or: *which are the necessary characteristics of any possible world?* In his work Sørlander rationally argues that space, time, Newton's laws, and a number of additional concepts are necessarily basic elements of any description of any domain.

1.9 Previous Work

We refer to Sect. 1.5 on page 3.

Axel van Lamsweerde [48, *2009*] and Michael A. Jackson [43, 44, *1995–2010*], as well as other *requirements engineering* researchers, do touch upon the issues of domains – such as that term is basically used here. But their *requirements analysis and prescription* do not "put it center stage", let alone mandate that the[ir] *requirements engineer* rely on an a priori established *domain description*. So they and others do not establish, as is the main focus of this contribution, calculi for the analysis & description of domains.

1.10   Structure of Paper

There are basically two parts to this paper. The main part consists of Sects. 2–3 and Sects. 5–6. They present a terse, comprehensive exposé of the *domain analysis & description* method of this paper. An appendix, the other part, Appendix 7, brings an example. For the domain modelling approach to be believable the example must open up for a realistic domain, one that is not "small".

• • •

We now explain *the domain description ontology* as a structured set of concepts for modelling domains, a set that shows their properties and the relations between them. *In simple terms, ontology seeks the classification and explanation of entities.*[9]

Figure 1 on page 4 is a graphical rendition of a *structured set of concepts for modelling domains.*

2   Universe of Discourse

Domain descriptions start with a terse sketch of the main facets of the domain followed by the naming of the domain.

---
1. **Universe of Discourse:** `calc_UoD`

Narration:
    Text
Formalisation:
    type UoD

---

1 ***Example***. *Universe of Discourse: We refer to Sect. 7.1 on page 25.*

3   External and Internal Qualities

Characterisation 1: External qualities: External qualities of endurants[10] of a domain are, in a simplifying sense, those properties of endurants that we can see, touch and which have spatial extent. They, so to speak, take form.

---

[9] *Google's English Dictionary* as provided by *Oxford Languages.*
[10] We refer to predicate prompt #2 below for a definition of *endurant*.

Characterisation 2: Internal qualities: Internal qualities of endurants of a domain are those which we may not be able to see or "feel" when touching an endurant, but they can, as we now 'mandate' them, be reasoned about. They have unique identifiers and mereologies,[11] And they have attributes that can be measured by some physical/chemical means, or be "spoken of" by intentional deduction.

3.1   Predicate Analysis of External Qualities of Endurants

Characterisation 3: Phenomenon: By a *phenomenon we shall understand a fact that is observed to exist or happen* ■ Examples of phenomena are: emotions of a human, the rivers, lakes, forests, mountains and valleys of mother nature; the railway tracks, their units, the locomotive of a railway system.

Domain Analysis Predicates: We shall define a number of domain analysis predicates. They are all referred to as prompts. Prompts are method tools. The domain modeller applies these to "real", i.e., actual world phenomena, that is, not to formal values. In the next 18 paragraphs we shall "reveal" a number of such predicates. First with a *reasonable definition (in slanted font)*, then with examples and some comments (in roman font).

Predicate Prompt 1: is_entity:*By an entity we shall understand something that can be observed, i.e., be seen or touched by humans, or that can be conceived as an abstraction of an entity; alternatively, a tangible or conceivable phenomenon is an entity* [49, *Vol. I, pg. 665*] ■ Some, but not necessarily all aspects of a river can be rationally described, hence can be still be considered entities. Similarly, many aspects of a road net can be rationally described, hence will be considered entities.

Predicate Prompt 2: *is_endurant: Endurants are those quantities of domains that we can observe (see and touch), in space, as "complete" entities at no matter which point in* time *– "material" entities that persists, endures* [49, *Vol. I, pg. 656*] ■ Street segments [links], street intersections [hubs], automobiles standing still in an automobile show room are endurants. Domain endurants, when eventually modelled in software, typically become data. Hence the careful analysis of domain endurants is a prerequisite for subsequent careful conception and analyses of data structures for software, including data bases.

Predicate Prompt 3: is_perdurant: *By a perdurant we shall understand an entity for which only a fragment exists if we look at or touch at any given snapshot in time. Were we to freeze time we would only see or touch a fragment of the perdurant* [49, *Vol. II, pg. 1552*] ■ Automobiles in action, container vessels sailing on the 7 seas and loading and unloading containers in harbours are examples of perdurants. Domain perdurants, when eventually modelled in software, typically become processes.

Endurants are either *solid* endurants, or are *fluid* endurants.

---

[11] We refer to Sects. 5.1 and 5.2.

Predicate Prompt 4: is_solid: *By a solid endurant we shall understand an endurant which is separate, individual or distinct in form or concept, or, rephrasing: a body or magnitude of three-dimensions, having length, breadth and thickness* [49, *Vol. II, pg. 2046*] ∎ Wells, pipes, valves, pumps, forks, joins, regulator, and sinks of a pipeline are solids.

Predicate Prompt 5: is_fluid: *By a fluid endurant we shall understand an endurant which is prolonged, without interruption, in an unbroken series or pattern; or, rephrasing: a substance (liquid, gas or plasma) having the property of flowing, consisting of particles that move among themselves* [49, *Vol. I, pg. 774*] ∎ Fluids are otherwise liquid, or gaseous, or plasmatic, or granular[12], or plant products[13], et cetera. Specific examples of fluids are: water, oil, gas, compressed air, etc. A container, which we consider a solid endurant, may be *conjoined* with another, a fluid, like a gas pipeline unit may "contain" gas.

We analyse endurants into either of two kinds: *parts* and *living species*. The distinction between *parts* and *living species* is motivated in Kai Sørlander's Philosophy [53–57].

Predicate Prompt 6: is_part: *By a part we shall understand a solid endurant existing in time and space and subject to laws of physics, including the causality principle and gravitational pull*[14] ∎

Natural and man-made parts are either atomic or compound.

Predicate Prompt 7: is_atomic: *By an atomic part we shall understand a part which the domain analyser considers to be indivisible in the sense of not meaningfully, for the purposes of the domain under consideration, that is, to not meaningfully consist of sub-parts* ∎ The wells, pumps, valves, pipes, forks, joins and sinks of a pipeline can be considered atomic.

Predicate Prompt 8: is_compound: Compound parts are those which are either *Cartesian-product-* or are *set-* oriented parts ∎

Predicate Prompt 9: is_Cartesian: Cartesian parts are those (compound parts) which consists of an "indefinite number" of two or more parts of distinctly named sorts ∎ Some clarification may be needed. (i) In mathematics, as in RSL [32], a value is a Cartesian ("record") value if it can be expressed, for example as $(a, b, ..., c)$, where $a, b, ..., c$ are mathematical (or, which is the same, RSL) values. Let the sort names of these be $A, B, ..., C$ – with these being required to be distinct. We wrote "indefinite number": the meaning being that the number is fixed, finite, but not specific. (ii) The requirement: 'distinctly named' is pragmatic. If the domain modeller thinks that two or more of the components of a Cartesian part [really] are of the same sort, then that person is most likely confused and must come up with suitably distinct sort names for these "same

---

[12] This is a purely pragmatic decision. "Of course" sand, gravel, soil, etc., are not fluids, but for our modelling purposes it is convenient to "compartmentalise" them as fluids!.

[13] i.e., chopped sugar cane, threshed, or otherwise. See footnote 12.

[14] This characterisation is the result of our study of relations between philosophy and computing science, notably influenced by Kai Sørlander's Philosphy.

sort" parts! (iii) Why did we not write "definite number" ? Well, at the time of first analysing a Cartesian part, the domain modeller may not have thought of all the consequences, i.e., analysed, the compound part. Additional sub-parts, of the Cartesian compound, may be "discovered", subsequently and can then, with the approach we are taking wrt. the modelling of these, be "freely" added subsequently! We refer to the road transport system example above. We there viewed (hubs, links and) automobiles as atomic parts. From another point of view we shall here understand automobiles as Cartesian parts: the engine train, the chassis, the car body, four doors (left front, left rear, right front, right rear), and the wheels. These may again be considered Cartesian parts.

Predicate Prompt 10: *is_part_set: Part sets are those which, in a given context, are deemed to meaningfully consist of an indefinite number* of sub-parts *of the same sort* ■ Examples of set parts are: the set of hubs of a road net hub aggregate, the set of links of a road net link aggregate, and the set of automobiles of an automobile aggregate – all of the road net transport that we are exemplifying.

Predicate Prompt 11: *is_living_species: By a living species we shall understand a solid endurant, subject to laws of physics, and additionally subject to causality of purpose. Living species must have some form they can develop to reach; a form they must be causally determined to maintain. This development and maintenancemust further engage in exchanges of matter with an environment* ■ It must be possible that living species occur in two forms: plants, respectively animals. Although we have not yet come across domains for which the need to model the living species of plants were needed. Hence:

Predicate Prompt 12: is_plant:*Plants are living species which are characterised by* development, form and exchange of matters with an environment ■

Predicate Prompt 13: is_animal:*Animals are living species which are additionally characterised by the* ability of purposeful movement ■

Predicate Prompt 14: *is_human: A* human *(a person) is an* animal, *with the additional properties of having* language, *being* conscious of having knowledge*(of its own situation), and* responsibility ■

Characterisation 4: Manifest Part: By a manifest part we shall understand a part which 'manifests' itself either in a physical, visible manner, "occupying" an AREA or a VOLUME and a POSITION in SPACE, or in a conceptual manner forms an organisation in Your mind! ■ As we have already revealed, endurant parts can be transcendentally deduced into perdurant behaviours – with manifest parts indeed being so.

Predicate Prompt 15: is_manifest:*is_manifest(e) holds if e is manifest* ■

Characterisation 5: *Structure: By a structure we shall understand an endurant concept that allows the domain modeller to rationally decompose a domain analysis and/or its description into manageable, logically relevant sections, but where these abstract endurants are not further reflected upon in the domain analysis and description* ■ Structures are therefore not transcendentally deduced into perdurant behaviours.

Predicate Prompt 16: is_structure:*is_structure (e) holds if e is a structure*
■

Examples of structures arise as the result of our analysis of parts. Thus a road net could be modelled as the composite of two structures: a set of hubs and a set of links (the stretches between two adjacent hubs, i.e., road intersections), cf. Items 6–7 on page 25.

Predicate Prompt 17: is_stationary:*An endurant part is stationary if it never changes position in space* ■

Predicate Prompt 18: *is_mobile: An endurant part is mobile if it may possibly change position in space* ■

We may need, occasionally, the distinction as now outlined:
Endurants are either *natural* endurants, or are *artefactual* endurants.

Predicate Prompt 19: *is_natural: By a natural endurant we shall understand one which has been created by nature.*

Predicate Prompt 20: *is_artefactual: By an artefactual endurant we shall understand one which has been created by humans.*

`Discrete Dynamic and Artefactual Domains:` In our initial characterisation of domains, Page 2, an emphasis was put on their *discrete dynamics and human assistedness.* The analysis and description calculi and, hence, our domain modelling, are therefore "geared" in that direction.

We are not offering to model time continuous domains. See Sect. 8.2.9 on page 39.

We summarise[15]:

---
2. Analysis Predicates
---

value	is_living_species: $E \rightarrow$ Bool	is_human: $E \rightarrow$ Bool
is_entity: $\Phi \rightarrow$ Bool	is_atomic: $E \rightarrow$ Bool	is_manifest: $E \rightarrow$ Bool
is_endurants: $E \rightarrow$ Bool	is_compound: $E \rightarrow$ Bool	is_structure: $E \rightarrow$ Bool
is_perdurant: $E \rightarrow$ Bool	is_animal: $E \rightarrow$ Bool	is_stationary: $E \rightarrow$ Bool
is_solid: $E \rightarrow$ Bool	is_plant: $E \rightarrow$ Bool	is_mobile: $E \rightarrow$ Bool
is_fluid: $E \rightarrow$ Bool	is_Cartesian: $E \rightarrow$ Bool	is_natural: $E \rightarrow$ Bool
is_part: $E \rightarrow$ Bool	is_part_set: $E \rightarrow$ Bool	is_artefactual: $E \rightarrow$ Bool

---

2 *Example. Analysis Predicates: In the example of Appendix 7–on page 25–37 we do not [explicitly] show the "application" of analysis predicates. They are tacitly assumed.*

3.2   Functional Analysis of External Qualities of Endurants

Given a compound endurant, that is, either a Cartesian or a part set, we analyse that compound, at the two ●'s of Fig. 1 on page 4, into its constituent endurants, respectively parts, and the name of the sort:

---
[15] Framed texts highlight *domain analysis & description* prompts.

---

3. determine_Cartesian_parts, determine_part_set

value

   determine_Cartesian_parts: E $\rightarrow$ (E1$\times\eta\,\Phi$)$\times$(E2$\times\eta\,\Phi$)$\times...\times$(Ec$\times\eta\,\Phi$)
   determine_Cartesian_parts(e) as (e1:ηE1,e2:ηE2,...,ec:ηEc)

   determine_part_set: E $\rightarrow$ P-set$\times\eta\,\Phi$
   determine_part_set(e) as ({p1,p2,...,ps}:ηP,)

The above calculation function signatures and characterisations illustrate two extensions to RSL [32]: ηP expresses the name of a sort P, and $\eta\,\Phi$ expresses the type of sort names.

Again we emphasize that these calculations are performed by the domain modeller. They are used in subsequent schemas for describing external qualities of endurants.

3.3 Descriptions of External Qualities of Endurants

Similarly, again at the two ∎'s of Fig. 1 on page 4, we are now ready to describe respectively Cartesian parts and part set parts.

3.3.1 Describing Cartesian Parts

---

4. descr_Cartesian

value

   descr_Cartesian: P $\rightarrow$ RSL-Text
   descr_Cartesian(p) $\equiv$
      "Narrative:
         [s] text on sorts
         [o] text on observers
         [a] text on axioms and/or proof obligations
      Formalisation:
         [s] type
               E1, E2, ..., Ec
         [o] value
               obs_E1: E$\rightarrow$E1, obs_E2: E$\rightarrow$E2, ..., obs_Ec: E$\rightarrow$Ec
         [a] axiom and/or proof obligation
               $\mathcal{A}/\mathcal{P}(...)$ "

---

3 *Example. Cartesians: We refer to Sect. 7.2.1 on page 25.*

3.3.2 Describing Part Sets

```
────────────────── 5. descr_part_set ──────────────────

value
    descr_part-set: P → RSL-Text
    descr_part_set(p) ≡
        " Narrative:
            [s] text on sorts
            [o] text on observers
            [a] text on axioms and/or proof obligations
        Formalisation:
            [s] type
                    P, Ps = P-set
            [o] value
                    obs_Ps: E→Ps
            [a] axiom and/or proof obligation
                    𝒜/𝒫(...) "
```

4 Example. *Part Sets: We refer to Sect. 7.2.2 on page 25.*

3.4 Endurant States

Characterisation 6: Endurant State: By an *endurant state* we shall understand any collection of endurant parts ■

```
────────────────── 6. obs_Σ ──────────────────

value
Σ = P-set
value
obs_Σ: E → Σ
obs_Σ(e) ≡
    if is_manifest(e)
    then
        is_atom(e) → {e},
        is_Cartesian(e) →
        let (p1:ηE1,p2:ηE2,...,pc:ηEc)=calc_cartesian_parts_and_sorts(e) in
        {p1,p2,...,pc}∪obs_Σ(p1)∪obs_Σ(p2)∪...∪obs_Σ(pc) end
        is_part-set(e) →
        let ({p1,p2,...,ps}:ηP)=calc_part_sets_parts_and_sort(e) in
        {p1,p2,...,ps}∪obs_Σ(p1)∪obs_Σ(p2)∪...∪obs_Σ(ps) end
    else {}
    end
```

5 Example. *Endurant State Examples: We refer to Sect. 7.2.3 on page 26.*

3.5   An Explication, I

The concept of *analysis predicates* and *part observer functions* is due to McCarthy [51, *Sect. 12–13*].

In [51] McCarthy introduces a notion of *abstract syntax*, Sect. 12, and *semantics*, Sect. 13. So far we have dealt, in our domain analysis, with syntax. There are three elements, according to McCarthy, to consider: the is_... predicates, the obs_... ["destructor"] functions, and, not shown, so far, in this paper, the mk_... constructor functions.

For compound abstract syntactic entities they are related as follows:

is_Cartesian(p) ≡
    let (p1:ηP1,p2:ηP2,...,pc:ηPc) = calc_Cartesian_parts_and_sorts(p) in
    p = mk_Cartesian(obs_P1(p),obs_P2(p),...,obs_Pc(p)) end

is_part_set(p) ≡
    let ({p1,p2,...,ps},ηP1) = calc_part_sets_parts_and_sort(p) in
    p = mk_part_set({p1,p2,...,ps}) end

The mk_... constructors were not introduced above. The reason is simple; a pragmatic decision: As the domain modeller proceeds in their work they may, when encountering Cartesian compounds, be free to leave some components (of the Cartesian) out, components that they may later introduce. So really, the first of the identities above ought be expressed as

is_Cartesian(p) ≡
    let (p1η:P1,p2:ηP2,...,pc:ηPc,...) = calc_Cartesian_parts_and_sorts(p) in
    p = mk_Cartesian(obs_P1(p),obs_P2(p),...,obs_Pc(p),...) end

We continue this explication in Sect. 5.5 on page 20.

4   Space and Time

The concepts of space and time can be *transcendentally deduced,* by rational reasoning, as has been shown in [53–57, *Kai Sørlander*], from the facts of *symmetry, asymmetry, transitivity* and *intransitivity* relations.

They are therefore facts of every possible universe.

4.1   Space

There is one given space. As a type we name it SPACE. We do not bother, here, about textual representation of spatial locations, but here is an example that would work in or near this globe we call our earth: Latitude 55.805600, Longitude 12.448160, Altitude 35 m[16].

---

[16] The author's house location!.

Also, in this paper, we do not present models of SPACE. But we do introduce such notions as (i) POINT: as SPACE being some dense and infinite collection of points; (ii) LOCATION: as the location in space of some point;

value   record_LOCATION: E → LOCATION

(iii) CURVE: as an infinite collection of points forming a mathematical curve – having a (finite or infinite) *length*; (iv) SURFACE: as an infinite collection of points forming a mathematical surface – having a (finite or infinite) *area*; and (v) VOLUME: as an infinite collection of points forming a mathematical volume – having a (finite or infinite) *volume*. We suggest it, as a domain science & engineering research topic, that somebody studies *a calculus or calculi of spatial modelling*.

4.2   Time

There is one given time. As a type we name it TIME. We do not bother, here, about textual representation of time, but here is an example: July 10, 2023: 15:19[17]. But we do introduce such crucial notions as *time interval* TI and operations on TIME and TI:

value
      −: TIME × TIME → TI
      +: TIME × TI → TIME
      ∗: Real × TI → TI

A crucial time-related operation is that of record_TIME. It applies to "nothing": record_TIME() and yields TIME.

value   record_TIME: Unit → TIME

5   Internal Qualities

We refer to the *Internal Qualities* characterisation on Page 8. We can justify the grouping of internal endurant qualities into three kinds: *unique identifiers*, cf. Sect. 5.1, *mereologies*, cf. Sect. 5.2, and *attributes*, cf. Sect. 5.3. To this we add the concept of *intentional pull*, cf. Sect. 5.4.

5.1   Unique Identification

On the basis of *philosophical reasoning*, within *metaphysics*, we [can] argue that parts are uniquely identifiable [53–57, *Kai Sørlander*]

---

[17] The time this text was last compiled!

5.1.1   Calculate Unique Identifiers

——————————— 7. **descr_unique_identifier** ———————

value
   descr_unique_identifier: P → RSL-Text
   descr_unique_identifier(p) ≡
      "Narrative:
         [s] text on unique identifier sort
         [o] text on unique identifier observer
         [a] text on axioms and/or proof obligations
      Formalisation:
         [s] type
               PI
         [o] value
               uid_P: P → PI
         [a] axiom and/or proof obligation
               $\mathcal{A}/\mathcal{P}(...)$ "

6 Example. *Unique Identifiers: We refer to Sect. 7.3.1 on page 26.*

5.1.2   Endurant Identifier States

Given the endurant state values, for the whole domain or for respective, manifest part sorts, one can define corresponding unique identifier values.

7 Example. *Unique Identifier State: We refer to Sect. 7.3.2 on page 27.*

5.1.3   Axioms

The number of manifest parts is the sames as the number of manifest part unique identifiers.

8 Example. *Unique Identifier Axiom: We refer to Sect. 7.3.3 on page 27.*

5.1.4   Endurant Retrieval

Given a unique identifier, π, of a manifest part, p, of an endurant state, σ, of a domain one can retrieve that part:

value
      $\sigma{:}\Sigma = \text{gen\_}\Sigma(\text{uod})$
      retr_P: $\Pi \rightarrow \Sigma \rightarrow P$
      retr_P$(\pi)(\sigma) \equiv$ let p:P • p $\in \sigma \wedge$ uid_P(p)$=\pi$ in p end

5.2   Mereology

Mereology is the study and knowledge of parts and part relations. It was first put forward, around 1916, by the Polish logician *Stanisław Leśniewski* [26,50].

Which are the relations that can be relevant to being an endurant ? There are basically two relations: (i) physical ones, and (ii) conceptual ones. (i) Physically two or more endurants may be topologically either adjacent to one another, like rails of a line, or within an endurant, like links and hubs of a road net, or an atomic part is conjoined to one or more fluids, or a fluid is conjoined to one or more parts. The latter two could also be considered conceptual "adjacencies". (ii) Conceptually some parts, like automobiles, "belong" to an embedding endurant, like to an automobile club, or are registered in the local department of vehicles, or are 'intended' to drive on roads.

5.2.1   Calculate Mereologies

----------------------------- 8. **descr_mereology** -----------------------------

```
value
    descr_mereology: P → RSL-Text
    descr_mereology(p) ≡
        "Narrative:
            [s] text on mereology type
            [o] text on  mereology observer
            [a] text on axioms and/or proof obligations
        Formalisation:
            [s] type
                    MT = 𝓜(p)
            [o] value
                    mereo_P: P → MT
            [a] axiom and/or proof obligation
                    𝒜/𝒫(...) "
```

$\mathcal{M}(\mathsf{p})$ is usually a type expression over unique identifiers of mereology-related parts.

9 Example. *Mereology: We refer to Sect. 7.4 on page 27.*

Given the definition of external qualities of a domain, and its unique identifier and mereology internal qualities one can analyse and describe many properties of that domain. The *routes* subsection (Page 28) of the mereology example, Example 9, illustrates one such property.

5.3   Attributes

Parts and fluids are typically recognised because of their spatial form and are otherwise characterised by their intangible, but measurable attributes. That is, whereas endurants, whether solid (as are parts) or fluids, are physical, tangible, in the sense of being spatial [or being abstractions, i.e., concepts, of spatial endurants], attributes are intangible: cannot normally be touched, or seen, but can be objectively measured. Thus, in our quest for describing domains where humans play an active rôle, we rule out subjective "attributes": feelings, sentiments, moods. Thus we shall abstain, in our domain science also from matters of psychology and aesthetics.

5.3.1   Functional Analysis of Attributes

Given a manifest part, p, that is, either an atom, or a Cartesian, or a part set, we calculate from that part, its constituent attributes values and types:

──────────────── 9. **determine_attributes** ────────────────

value
    determine_attributes: P → (a1×ηA1)×(a2×ηA2)×...×(aa×ηAa)

5.3.2   Describe Attributes

──────────────── 10. **descr_attributes** ────────────────

value
   descr_attributes: P → RSL-Text
      let ((,ηA1),(,ηA2),...,(,ηAa))=determine_attributes(p:P) in
   descr_attributes(p) ≡
     " Narrative:
        [s] text on attribute types
        [o] text on attribute observers
        [a] text on axioms and/or proof obligations
     Formalisation:
        [s] type
            A1 [=...], A2 [=...], ..., Aa [=...],
        [o] value
            attr_A1: P→A1, attr_A2: P→A2, ..., attr_Aa: P→Aa,
        [a] axiom and/or proof obligation
            $\mathcal{A}/\mathcal{P}$(...) "
     end

The domain modeller has thus determined/decided that A1, A2, ..., Aa are the "interesting" attributes of of parts of sort P. Attributes are often given a "concrete" form, hence the [= ...] where the ... is some type expression.

10 *Example. Attributes: We refer to Sect. 7.5 on page 29.*

5.3.3   Attribute Categories
Michael A. Jackson has proposed a structure of attributes [43].

Attribute Category 1: Static: By a static attribute we shall understand an attribute whose values are constants, i.e., cannot change.

Attribute Category 2: Dynamic: By a dynamic attribute we shall understand an attribute whose values are variable, i.e., can change. Dynamic attributes are either inert, reactive or active attributes.

Attribute Category 3: Inert: By an inert attribute we shall understand a dynamic attribute whose values only change as the result of external stimuli where these stimuli prescribe new values.

Attribute Category 4: Reactive: By a reactive attribute we shall understand a dynamic attribute whose values, if they vary, change in response to external stimuli, where these stimuli either come from outside the domain of interest or from other endurants.

Attribute Category 5: Active: By an active attribute we shall understand a dynamic attribute whose values change (also) of its own volition. Active attributes are either autonomous, or biddable or programmable attributes.

Attribute Category 6: Autonomous: By an autonomous attribute we shall understand a dynamic active attribute whose values change only "on their own volition". The values of an autonomous attributes are a "law onto themselves and their surroundings".

Attribute Category 7: Biddable: By a biddable attribute we shall understand a dynamic active attribute whose values are prescribed but may fail to be observed as such.

Attribute Category 8: Programmable: By a programmable attribute we shall understand a dynamic active attribute whose values can be prescribed.

We modify Jackson's categorisation. This is done in preparation for our exposé of behaviour signatures, cf. Sect. 6.4.1 on page 23. Figure 2 shows groupings of some of M. A. Jackson's basic categories.

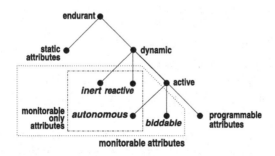

Fig. 2. An Attribute Ontology

Our motivation for modifying Jackson's attribute categories is as follows: when transcendentally deducing behaviours from parts we find that there are basically a need for distinguishing between only three major attribute categories the static, the monitorable, and the programmable attributes. Static attributes have their values passed "by value", as constants, programmable attributes have their values passed by "by reference", as variables who value can be changed, and monitorable attributes have their values passed by "by name" – as we shall see!

5.4 Intentional Pull

5.4.1 Characterisations
Intentionality as a philosophical concept is defined by the Stanford Encyclopedia of Philosophy[18] as *"the power of minds to be about, to represent, or to stand for, things, properties and states of affairs."*

Intent is then a usually clearly formulated or planned intention. An example of *intent* is that of roads made for automobiles and automobiles meant for roads.

Intentional Pull[19]: Two or more artefactual parts of different sorts, but with overlapping sets of intents may excert an intentional "pull" on one another. This intentional "pull" may take many forms. Let p_x: X and p_y:Y be two parts of different sorts (X,Y), and with common intent, ι. Manifestations of these, their common intent, must somehow be subject to constraints, and these must be expressed predicatively. When a composite artefact has an intentionality then its constituents have individual intentionalities that relate to these. The composite road transport system has intentionality of the roads serving the automobiles, and the automobiles have the intent of being served by the roads.

11 *Example. Intentional Pull: Road Transport: We refer to Sect.* 7.6 *on page 30.*

12 *Example. Intentional Pull: Double-entry Bookkeeping: Double-entry bookkeeping, also known as double-entry accounting, is a method of bookkeeping that relies on a two-sided accounting entry to maintain financial information. Every entry to an account requires a corresponding and opposite entry to a different account. The double-entry system has two equal and corresponding sides known as debit and credit. A transaction in double-entry bookkeeping always affects at least two accounts, always includes at least one debit and one credit, and always has total debits and total credits that are equal.[20].*

5.5 A Proof-Theoretic Explication, II

We remind You of Sect. 3.5 on page 14.

With the introduction of *analysis functions* and *observers* for *unique identifiers, mereology* and *attributes* we can now augment the is_..., uid_..., mereo_..., attr_A... observers introduced since Page 14.

---

[18] Jacob, P. (Aug 31, 2010). Intentionality. Stanford Encyclopedia of Philosophy (-seop.illc.uva.nl/entries/intentionality/ October 15, 2014, retrieved April 3, 2018.

[19] The term *intentional pull* is chosen so as to connote with the term *gravitational pull*.

[20] https://en.wikipedia.org/wiki/Double-entry_bookkeeping.

is_manifest(p:P) ≡
    let ((,ηA1),(,ηA2),(,ηAa)) = calc_attributes(p) in
    p = mk_P(uid_P(p),mereo_P(p),(attr_A1(p),attr_A2(p),...,attr_Aa(p))) end

6 Perdurants

A key point of our domain science & engineering approach is this: to **every manifest part** we transcendentally deduce a **unique behaviour.**

By **transcendental** *we shall understand the philosophical notion: the a priori or intuitive basis of knowledge, independent of experience.*

By a **transcendental deduction** *we shall understand the philosophical notion: a transcendental 'conversion' of one kind of knowledge into a seemingly different kind of knowledge.*

6.1 Channels

Part behaviours may interact. To express part behaviours and their interaction we use Hoare's CSP [38,39]. One may question this choice. In [7,11,14, *2009–2017*] we show *"that to every mereology there is a CSP expression"*. On that background we maintain that CSP is a reasonable choice—but invite the reader to suggest more appropriate mechanisms for handling behaviours and their communication.[21]

So, in general, we declare a RSL/CSP *channel*:

— 11. channel **declaration** —

channel { ch[{ui,uj}] | ui,uj:UI • {ui,uj}⊆*uis* } : M

Here ch is the name of the indexed array of channels and the indexes are, in general, any two element sets of unique part identifiers. That is: For every pair of part behaviours – identified but their unique part identifiers (ui,uj) – there is a channel, say ch[{ui,uj}].

M is the type of the messages communicate between behaviours of index ui,uj.

We shall develop, in Sect. 6.2.2, the specifics of the type, M, of channel messages.

6.2 Actors

By an *actor* we shall understand either an *action*, or an *event*, or a *behaviour*.

___

[21] Please bear in mind that the use, here, of CSP, is in the following context: the CSP clauses are not to be "interpreted" on a computer where this "computerisation" has to be "shared" with other computations; hence CSP *synchcronisation & communication* is "ideal" and reflects reality.

6.2.1   Actions

By an *action of a behaviour* we shall understand something which is local to a behaviour, and, which, when applied, potentially changes the states. Generally action clauses are expressed in RSL [32].

13 Example. *Road Transport Actions: We refer to Sect. 7.7.2 on page 33.*

6.2.2   Events

By an *event of a behaviour* we shall understand something that involves two behaviours, and, which, when applied, potentially changes the states of both behaviours. Event clauses are expressed using the CSP elements of RSL. That is, the CSP output "*!*" and input events "*?*":

    ch[{ui,uj}] ! expr
    let val = ch[{ui,uj}] ? ... end

14 Example. *Road Transport Events: We refer to Sect. 7.7.2 on page 33.*

6.3   State Access and Updates

We need define two functionals: one for changing the mereology of a part and another for changing the attribute value of a part. We therefore informally define the following functionals:

6.3.1   Update Mereologies

- part_update_mereology is a functional: it takes the following arguments: a part p of type P and a mereology value and yields a part of type P.
- The yielded result, p′, has the same unique identifier, as the argument part p,
- a new, the argument, mereology, as the argument part p,
- and the same attribute values for all attributes, as the argument part p.

value
    part_update_mereology: $P \rightarrow M \rightarrow P$
    part_update(p)(m) ≡
        let ((,ηA1),(,ηA2),...,(,ηAa)) = determine_attributes(p) in
        let p′:P • uid_P(p′)=uid_P(p)∧mereo_P(p′)=m∧
            ∀ ηA:$\eta\Phi$•ηA∈{ηA1,ηA2,...,ηAa}⇒attr_A(p′)=attr_A(p) in
        p′ end end

6.3.2 Update Attributes

– part_update_attribute is a functional: it takes the following arguments: a part p of type P and a pair of an attribute name and value, and yields a part p' of type P.
– The argument attribute name must be that of an attribute of the part.
– The yielded result p' has the same unique identifier and mereology as the argument part p,
– and the same attribute values for all attributes, as the argument part p, except for argument attribute (name) for which it now yields the argument attribute value.

value
    part_update_attribute: P → ΦA × A → P
    part_update_attribute(p)(ηA,a) ≡
        let ((,ηA1),(,ηA2),...,(,ηAa)) = determine_attributes(p) in
           assert: ηA∈{ηA1,,ηA2,...,,ηAa}
        let p':P • uid_P(p)=uid_P(p')∧mereo_P(p)=mereo_P(p')∧
          ∀ ηA:$\eta\Phi$•ηA∈{ηA1,,ηA2,...,,ηAa}\$\eta$A⇒attr_A(p')=attr_A(p) in
        p' end end

Examples of monitorable attributes are: an automobile's velocity and engine (cooler) temperature. Monitorable attributes usually change their values surreptitiously. That is, "behind the back", so-to-speak, of the part behaviour.

6.4 Behaviours

By a *behaviour* we shall understand a set of sequences of actions, events and behaviours.

6.4.1 Behaviour Signatures
We now come to a crucial point in our unrolling the *domain science & engineering method*. It is that of explaining the signature of behaviours, that is, the arguments ascribed to part behaviours. The general form of part *p* behaviour signatures is as follows.

────────────── 12. **Behaviour Signatures** ──────────────

value
p_behaviour: p:P→in,out {ch[{uid_P(p),ui}]|ui:UI•ui∈*uis*∧$\mathcal{M}ereo$(p)} Unit

Yes, that is it! The behaviour of a[ny] (manifest) part, p, is a function whose only argument is that part! The signature informs of the channels that p_behaviour may communicate with. The literal Unit informs that the behaviour may not yield any value, but, for example, go on "forever" having possibly effected a state change!

6.4.2   Behaviour Definitions

Behaviours, besides their signatures, are defined. That is, a *behaviour definition* *'body'* describes, in, for us, using RSL [32] with its embodiment of a variant of CSP [39], basically CSP clauses how it interacts with other behaviours, and, in basically RSL's functional specification (read: programming) clauses, how it otherwise "goes about its business"!

In fragment **I** the focus is on the possible [action] update of either biddable or programmable attributes.

---------------- 13. **Behaviour Definition, I** ----------------

p_behaviour(p) ≡
    let p′ = possible_update_of_biddable_and_programmable_attributes(p) in
    p_behaviour(p′) end

In fragment **II** the focus is on the possible [action] value access to any attributes.

---------------- 14. **Behaviour Definition, II** ----------------

p_behaviour(p) ≡ ... attr_A(p) ... p_behaviour(p)

In fragment **III** the focus is on the possible interaction with other behaviours, hence illustrates two events as seen from one behaviour.

---------------- 15. **Behaviour Definition, III** ----------------

p_behaviour(p) ≡
    ...
    let (val,ui) = $\mathcal{E}$(p) in ch[{uid_P(p),ui}] ! val end ;
    ...
    let uj = $\mathcal{I}$(p) in let (val′,uj) = ch[{uid_P(p),uj}] ? in
    ...
    p_behaviour(p) end end

---

15 *Example*. *Road Transport Behaviour Definitions: We refer to Sect. 7.7.4 on page 33.*

6.5   Domain Initialisation

By *domain initialisation* we mean the "start-up" of a behaviour for all manifest parts.

16 *Example*. *Road Transport Domain Initialisation: We refer to Sect. 7.8 on page 36.*

6.6 End of Domain Modelling Presentation

This concludes the four sections, Sects. 2, 3, 4 and 6, on domain modelling.

7 A Road Transport Domain Example

7.1 Naming and Sketch of Domain

We refer to Sect. 2 on page 7.
Narration:

1 The domain is referred to as RTD, the road transport domain.
2 The road transport domain comprises a set of automobiles and a road net of street intersections, called hubs, and [uninterrupted] street segments, called links. Automobiles drive in and out of hubs and links.

Formalisation:

type
1. RTD

7.2 Endurants: External Qualities

7.2.1 Cartesian Examples
We refer to Sect. 3.3.1 on page 12.

3 There is a road transport domain.

From road transport domains we can observe

4 a road net aggregate and
5 an automobile aggregate.

From the road net aggregate we can observe

6 an aggregate of hubs, i.e., street intersections, and
7 an aggregate of links, i.e., street segments (with no hubs).

type
3. RTD
4. RNA
5. AA
6. HA
7. LA

value
4. obs_RNA: RTD → RNA
5. obs_AA: RTD → AA
6. obs_HA: RNA → HA
7. obs_LA: RNA → LA

7.2.2 Part Sets
We refer to Sect. 3.3.2 on page 12.

8 There are hubs; from aggregate of hubs one can observe sets of hubs.
9 There are links; from aggregate of links one can observe sets of links.
10 There are automobiles; from aggregate of automobiles one can observe sets of automobiles.

type
8. H, Hs = H-set
9. L, Ls = L-set
10. A, As = A-set

value
8. obs_Hs: HA → Hs
9. obs_Ls: LA → Ls
10. obs_As: AA → As

7.2.3   Endurant States
We refer to Sect. 3.4 on page 13.

11 The singleton value *rtd* represents a road transport [domain] state.
12 The set value *hs* represents a state of all hubs of that road transport domain.
13 The set value *ls* represents a state of all links of that road transport domain.
14 The set value *as* represents a state of all automobiles of that road transport domain.

value
11. *rtd*:RTD,
12. *hs*:H-set = obs_Hs(obs_HA(obs_RNA(rtd))),
13. *ls*:L-set = obs_Ls(obs_LA(obs_RNA(rtd))),
14. *as*:A-set = obs_As(obs_AA(rtd))

7.3   Unique Identifiers

We refer to Sect. 7.3.1 on page 15.

7.3.1   Unique Identifiation
We shall only consider hubs, links and automobiles.

15 Hubs have unique identifiers.
16 Links have unique identifiers.
17 We define also a unique identifier observer for hubs and links.
18 Automobiles have unique identifiers.

type
15. HI
16. LI
18. AI
value
15. uid_H: H → HI
16. uid_L: L → LI
17. uid_HL: (H|L) → (HI|LI), uid_HL(hl) ≡ is_H(hl)→uid_H(hl), →uid_L(hl)
18. uid_A: A → AI

7.3.2 Unique Identifier State

19 The variable *his* contains all unique hub identifiers of the road transport domain 3 on page 25.
20 The variable *lis* contains all unique link identifiers of the road transport domain 3 on page 25.
21 The variable *ais* contains all unique automobile identifiers of the road transport domain 3 on page 25.

variable
14. $his = \{ \text{uid\_H(h)} \mid \text{h:H} \bullet \text{h} \in hs \}$.
19. $lis = \{ \text{uid\_L(l)} \mid \text{l:L} \bullet \text{l} \in ls \}$.
20. $ais = \{ \text{uid\_A(a)} \mid \text{a:A} \bullet \text{a} \in as \}$.

7.3.3 Unique Identifier Axiom

22 No two hubs, links and automobiles have the same unique identifier.
23 *ps* is the set of all hubs, links and automobiles.
24 *uis* is the set of all unique hub, link and automobile identifiers.

axiom
22. card hs = card his,
22. card ls = card lis,
22. card as = card ais,
22. card hs + card ls + card as = card his + card lis + card ais
value
23. $ps = hs \cup ls \cup as$
24. $uis = his \cup lis \cup ais$
axiom
22. card ps = card uis

7.4 Mereology

We refer to Sect. 7.4 on page 17.

25 The mereology of any hub is a pair: the possibly empty set of the unique identifiers of links leading into and/or out from the hub, and the set of the unique identifiers of automobiles that are allowed to drive in the hub.
26 The mereology of any link is a pair: the two element set of the unique identifiers of the two hubs that are connected by the link, and the set of the unique identifiers of automobiles that are allowed to drive on the link.
27 The mereology of any automobile is the set of the unique identifiers of hubs in and links on which the automobile may be driving.

type   value
25. H_Mer=LI-set×AI-set   25. mereo_H: H→H_Mer
26. L_Mer=HI-set×AI-set   26. mereo_L: L→L_Mer
27. A_Mer=(HI|LI)-set   27. mereo_A: A→A_Mer

28 Link and automobile identifiers of hub mereologies must be of the road trans-
    port domain.
29 Hub and automobile identifiers of hub mereologies must be of the road trans-
    port domain and there must be exactly two hub identifiers of those mereolo-
    gies.
30 Hub and links identifiers of automobile mereologies must be of the road
    transport domain.

axiom
28. ∀ (lis,ais):H_Mer•lis⊆lis∧ais⊆ais
29. ∀ (his,ais):L_Mer•his⊆his∧ais⊆ais∧card his=2
30. ∀ ris:A_Mer•ris⊆his∪lis

7.4.1   Routes

31 By a *route* (of a road net) we shall understand
    a an alternating sequence of one or more hub and link identifiers
32 such that
    a basis clause 0: the empty list is a route;
    b basis clause 1: a singleton list of a hub or a link identifier of the road net
       is a route;
    c inductive clause: the concatenation of a route, r, and the tail of a route
       r′ where the last element of r is identical to the first element of r′ is a
       route; and
    d extremal clause: and only such routes that can be formed using the above
       clauses are routes.

type
31. R′ = (HI|LI)*
31a. R = {| r:R′ | wf_R(r)(rtd) |}
value
31a. wf_R: R′ → RTD → Bool
31a. wf_R(r)(rtd) ≡
31a.   ∀ i,i+1:Nat • {i,i+1}⊆index(r) ⇒
31a.   let (ri,ri′) = (r[i],r[i+1]) in
31a.   is_LI(ri)∧is_HI(ri′)∧ ...
31a.   is_HI(ri)∧is_LI(ri′)∧ ...
31a.   end

32. routes: RTD×HI-set×LI-set → R-infset
32. routes(rtd,his,lis) ≡
32.   let rs = { ⟨⟩ }
32.   ∪ { ⟨hi⟩ | hi:HI • hi ∈ his }
32.   ∪ { ⟨li⟩ | li:LI • li ∈ lis }
32.   ∪ { r⌢tl r′ | {r,r′}⊆rs ∧ r[len r]=hd r′ } in
32c.   rs end
32.   pre: his={uid_H(h)|h:H•h ∈ obs_Hs(obs_AH(obs_RN(rtd)))} ∧
32.   lis={uid_L(l)|l:L•l ∈ obs_Ls(obs_AL(obs_RN(rtd)))}

7.5 Attributes

We refer to Sect. 7.5 on page 17.

7.5.1 Hubs, Links and Automobiles

Hub Attributes

33 Hubs have [traffic signal] states which are set of pairs, li,lj, of identifiers of the mereology links "signaling" that automobiles can connect from link li to link lj.

34 Hubs have [traffic signal] state spaces – designating the set of all possible hub states.

35 Hubs have a history; see Item 46 on page 31.

Link Attributes

36 Links have lengths.

37 Links have a history; see Item 47 on page 31.

Automobile Attributes

38 Automobiles have positions on the road net:
   a either *at a hub*,
   b or *on a link*, some fraction
   c down from an entry hub towards the exit hub.

39 Automobiles have a history; see Item 48 on page 31.

We postpone treatment of hub, link and automobile histories till Sect. 7.6.1.

type
33.   HΣ = (LI×LI)-set
34.   HΩ = HΣ-set
35.   H_Hist = ...

36. LEN
37. L_Hist = ...
38. A_Pos = At_Hub | On_Link
38a. At_Hub :: HI
38b. On_Link :: LI × HI × F × HI
38c. F = Real axiom ∀ f:F • 0<f<1
39. A_Hist = ...
value
33. attr_HΣ: H → HΣ
34. attr_HΩ: H → HΩ
35. attr_H_Hist: A → H_Hist
36. attr_LEN: L → LEN
37. attr_L_Hist: A → L_Hist
38. attr_APos: A → A_Pos
39. attr_A_Hist: A → A_Hist

We omit treatment of such automobile attributes as speed, acceleration, engine temperature, energy (gas, oil, electricity) level, mileage and trip counters, GPS (map) position, road surface temperature, gear position (reverse, neutral, forward (1, 2, 3, 4, 5), hand brake position, clutch position, accelerator pressure, brake pedal position, etc.

40 The link identifiers of a hub state must be of the mereology of that hub.
41 A hub state must be in the hub state space.
42 The automobile position must be on the road net.

axiom
40. ∀ h:H • h ∈ hs • let hσ = attr_HΣ(h), (lis,) = mereo_H(h) in
40.   ∀ (li,lj):(LI×LI) • (li,lj) ∈ hσ ⇒ {li,lj}⊆lis

41. ∀ h:H • h ∈ hs • attr_HΣ(h) ∈ attr_HΩ(h)

42. ∀ a:A • a ∈ as • let apos = attr_A_Pos(a) in
42.   cases apos of
42.   At_Hub(hi) → hi ∈ *his*,
42.   On_Link(li,fhi, ,thi) →
42.   let (his,ais) = mereo_L(retr_L(li,ls)) in
42.   {fhi,thi}⊆his ∧ uid_A(a) ∈ ais end
42.   end end

These were some well-formedness axioms. In Sect. 7.6.1 we shall treat well-formedness of hub, link and automobile histories.

7.5.2   Attribute Category Examples

Attribute categories are: HΣ (Item 33 on the preceding page) is a programmable attribute; HΩ (Item 34 on the previous page) is a static attribute; LEN (Item 36 on the preceding page) is a static attribute; A_Pos (Item 38 on the previous page) is a programmable attribute; GPS_Map is an inert attribute; Speed is a biddable attribute; Road_Surface_Temperature is an autonomous attribute; etcetera.

7.6   Intentional Pull

We refer to Sect. 7.6 on page 20.

7.6.1   Further Attributes

We start by formulating the hub, link and automobile history attribute definitions.

43 Hubs and links are entered and left by automobiles, i.e., marked by corresponding events.
44 Automobile enters and leaves hubs, i.e., marked by corresponding events.
45 Automobile enters and leaves links, i.e., marked by corresponding events.
46 Hub histories are time-stamped sequences of automobile enter/leave events – in decreasing order (most recent events are listed first),
47 Link histories are time-stamped sequences of automobile enter/leave events – in decreasing order (most recent events are listed first),
48 Automobile histories are time-stamped sequences of hub and link enter/leave events – in decreasing order (most recent events are listed first),
49 For convenience we "lump" hub and link histories into hub-link histories.

type
43. HL_OnOff = mkEnter(ai:AI) | mkLeave(ai:AI)
44. A_OnOff_H = mkEnterHub(s:HI) | mkLeaveHub(s:HI)
45. A_OnOff_L = mkEnterLink(s:LI) | mkLeaveLink(s:LI)
46. H_Hist = (s_t:TIME×s_oo:HL_OnOff)*
47. L_Hist = (s_t:TIME×s_oo:HL_OnOff)*
48. A_Hist = (s_t:TIME×s_oo:(OnOff_H|OnOff_L))*
49. HL_Hist = H_Hist | L_Hist
value
49. attr_HL_Hist: (H→H_Hist) | (L→L_Hist)

50 Automobile histories
    a alternate between being on hubs and being on links.
    b such that the *enter hub event time* is identical to the immediately "prior" *leave link event time*,
    c and such that these events are otherwise ordered in decreasing order of time.

axiom
50. ∀ a_hist:A_Hist •
50.   ∀ i:Nat • {i,i+1}⊆inds a_hist ⇒
50.   let (e1,e2)=(s_oo(a_hist[i]),s_oo(a_hist[i+1])),
50.   (t1,t2)=(s_t(a_hist[i]),s_t(a_hist[i+1])) in
50.   case (e1,e2)
50b.   (mkLeaveHub(hi),mkEnterLink(li)) → t1=t2,
50c.   (mkLeaveLink(li),mkEnterHub(hi)) → t1=t2,
50c.   (mkLeaveLink(li),mkEnterLink(li′)) → t1>t2,
50c.   (mkLeaveHub(hi),mkEnterHub(hi′)) → t1>t2,
50a.   → false
50.   end end

We leave the (narrative and formal) expression of the well-formedness of hub
and link histories to the reader! The above indicates that one has to be very
careful concerning well-formedness.

But we have not captured all of the constraints, i.e., well-formedness of the
history attributes. Next we secure full care!

7.6.2 An Intentional Pull

51 For all automobiles,
   a if their traffic history records that the automobile was entering [leaving]
     a hub (link) at a certain time,
   b then that hub's (link's) traffic history shall record that that automobile
     left [entered] that hub (link) at exactly that time;
52 and vice versa, for all hubs an links:
   a if the hub or link traffic history records that an automobile was leaving
     [entering] that hub, respectively link at a certain time,
   b then that automobile's traffic history shall record that that automobile
     entered [left] that hub, resp. link, at exactly that time.

axiom
51.   ∀ a:A • a ∈ as ⇒
51a.   let a_hist=attr_A_Hist(a), ai=uid_A(a) in
51a.   ∀ (t,on_off_hl) • (t,on_off_hl) ∈ elems a_hist ⇒
51a.   let hli • s(on_off_hl) in
51b.   let hl:(H|L)•hl ∈ hs∪ls • uid_HL(hl) = hli in
51b.   let hl_hist = attr_HL_Hist(hl) in
51b.   ∃! i:Nat•i∈ inds hl_hist •
51b.   on_off_hl=mkEnter(hli) → hl_hist[i]=(t,mkLeave(ai))
51b.   on_off_hl=mkLeave(hli) → hl_hist[i]=(t,mkEnter(ai))
51.   end end end end
52.   ≡

52a. $\forall$ hl:(H|L) • hl $\in$ $hs \cup ls$ $\Rightarrow$
52a.   let hl_hist=attr_HL_Hist(hl), hli=uid_HL(hl) in
52a. $\forall$ (t,on_off_ai) • (t,on_off_ai) $\in$ elems hl_hist $\Rightarrow$
52a.   let ai = ai(on_off_ai) in let a:A•a$\in$as • uis_A(a)=ai in
52a.   let a_hist = attr_A_Hist(a) in
52a. $\exists$! i:Nat•i$\in$ inds a_hist •
52a.   on_off_ai=mkEnter(ai) $\rightarrow$ on_off_ai[i]=(t,mkLeave(hli)),
52a.   on_off_ai=Leave(ai) $\rightarrow$ on_off_ai[i]=(t,Enter(hli))
52a.   end end end end

7.7   Perdurants

7.7.1   Channels

We refer to Sect. 7.7.1 on page 21.

    channel { ch[{ui,uj}] | ui,uj:(HI|LI|AI) • {ui,uj}$\subseteq his \cup lis \cup ais$ } : M

M will be defined in Sect. 7.7.2.2 on the facing page.

7.7.2   Domain Actions and Events   *7.7.2.1 Domain Actions*

We refer to Sect. 6.2.1 on page 22.

Automobile actions are here simplified to be those of

53 remaining (staying) in a hub (Item 64a on the following page) and
54 remaining (staying) on a link (Item 65a on the next page).

7.7.2.2 Domain Events

We refer to Sect. 6.2.2 on page 22.

Automobile events are here simplified to be those of

55 leaving a hub [in order to enter a link] (Item 66d on page 35 and Item 70 on page 36) and
56 entering a link [after having left a hub] (Item 66d on page 35 and Item 70 on page 36) and
57 leaving a link in order to enter a hub (Item 67c on page 35 and Item 75 on page 36).
58 entering a hub [after having left a link] (Item 67c on page 35 and Item 75 on page 36).

Thus contributions to M of Sect. 7.7.1 on the preceding page are:

type
55.   mkLeaveH(hi:HI,li:LI,ai:AI)
56.   mkEnterL(hi:HI,li:LI,ai:AI)
57.   mkLeaveL(li:LI,hi:HI,ai:AI)
58.   mkEnterH(li:LI,hi:HI,ai:AI)

7.7.3   Behaviour Signatures
We refer to Sect. 7.7.3 on page 23.

value

> hub: h:H → in,out { ch[{hi,ui}] | ui:(LI|AI)•ui∈lis∪ais } → Unit,
> link: l:L → in,out { ch[{li,ui}] | ui:(LI|AI)•ui∈lis∪ais } → Unit,
> auto: a:A → in,out { ch[{ai,ui}] | ui:(LI|HI)-set•ui∈lis∪his } → Unit.

7.7.4   Behaviour Definitions
We refer to Sect. 7.7.4 on page 24.

Automobile Behaviour

We omit consideration of the monitorable GPS_Map, Speed and Road_Surface_-Temperature attributes.

59 One interpretation of an automobile, auto,
60 focuses on its road position.
61 Either the automobile is at a hub,
62 or it is on a link.
63 There could be other focal points.

value
59. auto(a) ≡
60.   auto_pos(a)(attr_A_Pos(p),attr_A_His(a))
63.   ⌈⌉ ...

61. auto_pos(a)(At_Hub(hi),a_hist) ≡
61.   traversing_hub(a)(At_Hub(hi),a_hist)
61.   **pre:** attr_A_Pos(a)=At_Hub(hi) ∧ attr_A_Hist(a)=a_hist

62. auto_pos(a)(On_Link(li,fhi,f,thi),a_hist) ≡
62.   traversing_link(a)(On_Link(li,fhi,f,thi),a_hist)
62.   **pre:** attr_A_Pos(a)=On_Link(li,fhi,f,thi) ∧ attr_A_Hist(a)=a_hist

64 In traversing a hub an automobile
   a is either, internal non-deterministically, ⌈⌉, moving on inside the hub
   b or, internal non-deterministically, entering a link from the hub.

value
64. traversing_hub(a)(At_Hub(hi),a_hist) ≡
64a.   staying_at_H(a)(At_Hub(hi),a_hist)
64b.   ⌈⌉ entering_L(a)(At_Hub(hi),a_hist)
64.   **pre:** attr_A_Pos(a)=At_Hub(h) ∧ attr_A_Hist(a)=a_hist

64a. staying_at_H(a)(At_Hub(hi),a_hist) ≡ auto(a)

65 In traversing a link an automobile
 a is either, internal non-deterministically, $\sqcap$, moving on inside the link
 b – possibly advancing a bit, i.e., increasing its fraction position "down" the link,
 c or, internal non-deterministically, entering a hub from the link.

value
65. traversing_link(a)(On_Link(li,fhi,f,thi),a_hist) ≡
65a.   staying_on_L(a)(On_Link(li,fhi,f,thi),a_hist)
65c. $\sqcap$ entering_H(a)(On_Link(li,fhi,f,thi),a_hist)
65.   pre: attr_A_Pos(a)=On_Link(li,fhi,f,thi) ∧ attr_A_Hist(a)=a_hist

65a. staying_on_L(a)(On_Link(li,fhi,f,thi),a_hist) ≡
65b.   let f′:F • f≤f′<1 in assert: ∃ f′:F • f≤f′<1
65b.   let a′ = part_update(a)(ηA_Pos,On_Link(li,fhi,f′,thi))
65a.   auto(a′) end end
65a.   pre: attr_A_Pos(a)=On_Link(li,fhi,f,thi) ∧ attr_A_Hist(a)=a_hist

66 In entering a link
 a the automobile internal non-deterministically selects the link to be entered, and thus the next hub,
 b records the time,
 c updates its history and automobile position accordingly,
 d so informs the behaviour of the hub being left and the link being entered, while resuming being an automobile – with the updated history.

value
66. entering_L(a)(At_Hub(fhi),a_hist) ≡
66a.   let li:LI•li∈lis∧li∈mereo_H(retr_H(fhi)(σ)),
66a.   thi:HI•thi∈his∧thi∈mereo_L(retr_L(li)(σ))\{fhi},[22]
66b.   τ = record_TIME[23],
66b.   ai=uid_A(a) in
66a.   let a_pos = On_Link(fhi,li,0,thi) in
66c.   let a_hist′ = ⟨(a_pos,τ)⟩^a_hist in
66c.   let a′ = part_update(a)(ηA_Hist,a_hist′) in
66c.   let a″ = part_update(a′)(ηA_Pos,a_pos) in
66d.   (ch[{ai,fhi}] ! (mkLeaveH(fhi,li,ai),τ)
66d.   ‖ ch[{ai,li}] !(mkEnterL(li,fhi,ai),τ) ‖ auto(a″))
66.   end end end end end
66.   pre: attr_A_Pos(a)=At_Hub(fhi) ∧ attr_A_Hist(a)=a_hist

---

[22] For retr_··· see Sect. 5.1.4 on page 16.
[23] For record_TIME see Sect. 4.2 on page 15.

67 In entering a hub
    a the time is recorded,
    b the automobile history and position is updated,
    c and the behaviours of the link left link and hub entered are being so
      informed while the automobile resumes being an automobile – in the
      updated state.

value
67. entering_H(a)(On_Link(li,fhi,f,thi),a_hist) $\equiv$
67a.   let τ = record_TIME,
67a.   ai = uid_A(a),
67a.   a_pos = at_Hub(thi) in
67a.   let a_hist' = $\langle(a\_pos,\tau)\rangle$^a_hist in
67b.   let a' = part_update(a)(ηA_Hist,(τ,a_hist')) in
67b.   let a'' = part_update(a')(ηA_Pos,a_pos) in
67c.   (ch[ai,li] ! (mkLeaveL(li,thi,ai),τ) $\|$
67c.   ch[ai,thi] ! (mkEnterH(thi,li,ai),τ) $\|$ auto(a''))
67.   end end end end
67.   pre: attr_A_Pos(a)=On_Link(li,fhi,f,thi) $\wedge$ attr_A_Hist(a)=a_hist

Hub Behaviour

68 The hub behaviour
69 externally non-deterministically ($\lceil\rceil$) offers
70 to accept, non-deterministically, a *leave* message,
71 from any automobile in its mereology;
72 it prepares for proper insertion of this event into its traffic history
73 updating to an augmented traffic history, and, hence, hub state;
74 resuming to be the hub behaviour in the updated state;
75 or to accept, non-deterministically, an *enter* message,
76 again from any automobile in its mereology;
77 updating to an augmented traffic history, and, hence, hub state;
78 resuming to be the hub behaviour in the updated state.

value
68. hub(h) $\equiv$ let hi = uid_HI(h) in
70. $\lceil\rceil$ { let (mkLeaveH(hi',li,ai),τ) = ch[{hi,ai}] ? in assert: hi'=hi
73.   let h_hist' = $\langle(\tau,$mkEnter(ai))$\rangle$^attr_H_Hist(h) in
73.   let h' = part_update(ηH_Hist,h_hist') in
74.   hub(h')
71. | ai:AI • ai $\in$ ais end end end}
69. $\lceil\rceil$
75. $\lceil\rceil$ { let (mkEnterH(hi',li,ai),τ) = ch[{hi,ai}] ? in assert: hi'=hi
77.   let h_hist' = $\langle(\tau,$mkLeave(ai))$\rangle$^attr_H_Hist(h) in
77.   let h' = part_update(ηH_Hist,h_hist') in
78.   hub(h')
76. | ai:AI • ai $\in$ ais end end end } end

We leave the definition of link behaviours as an exercise!

7.8   Domain Initialisation

We refer to Sect. 7.8 on page 24.

We initialise a domain behaviour for all atomic endurants: hubs, links and automobiles.

79 The domain behaviour is the parallel composition of
80 the distributed parallel composition of all hub behaviours, with
81 the distributed parallel composition of all link behaviours, with
82 the distributed parallel composition of all automobile behaviours.

80. ‖ { hub(b) | h:H • h ∈ hs }
79. ‖
81. ‖ { link(l) | l:L • l ∈ ls }
79. ‖
82. ‖ { auto(a) | a:A • a ∈ as }

7.9   Verification

It remains to verify that the automobile, hub and link behaviours and the road transport domain initialisation satisfy the appropriate axioms and the intentional pull.

End of Example

8   Closing

8.1   The Current Calculi

The treatment of behaviours of Sect. 6.4.2 differs very much from that of Sects. 7.6 and 7.7 of [17]. The present one is very short, but results in a repeated use of the part_update functional. Our domain modelling approach allows a wide spectrum, in-between these behaviour signature and definition styles, for expressing behaviours. What remains fixed in the treatment of endurants: both of their external qualities, and of their internal qualities.

8.2   Some Issues

A number of issues need be addressed.

8.2.1   A New View of Software Development ?

Yes, we claim that this paper presents an additional view of software development! Aircraft designers and manufacturers employ professionally educated aeronautics engineers having state-of-the-art insight into aerodynamics. But, we claim, software companies do not, today, July 28, 2023, exhibit the same professionalism in their staffing. Software for health care (hospitals, etc.) are often developed by programmers with no previous professional insight into that area. Likewise for domains such as law, public administration, health care and tax administration. With sound methods for "deriving" requirements from domain models, cf. Sect. 8.2.7 on page 39, these software houses now have a possibility of becoming professional.

8.2.2   From Programming Language Semantics to Domain Models

Domain models give semantics to the nouns (endurants) and verbs (perdurants) spoken by domain workers. Just like the development of compilers for programming languages were based on formal models of their semantics, so we can now give semantics to the nouns and verbs spoken by domain workers, and, from these, using rigorous development methods, similar to those used for compiler development [25,28], develop trustworthy domain software.

8.2.3   Correctness: Verification, Checking, Testing

This paper has not dealt with the issue of correctness of domain models. A number of endurant and perdurant *Description* prompts have indicated that axioms and assertions[24] need be expressed. For domain assertions their correctness must, of course, be shown – using whichever (testing, model checking and proof) techniques are adequate. The axioms and assertions carry over into *Requirements* prescriptions and, from there, into software *Specifications*. Now the full-blown force of testing, model checking and proofs must be applied. As indicated in formula $\mathcal{D}, \mathcal{S} \models \mathcal{R}$, Sect. 1.2 on page 3, domain models now make proof obligations more clear.

8.2.4   No Recursive Domains!

Surprise, surprise! Yes, there are no recursively defined endurant sorts. Domains do not contain "recursive endurants".[25]

---

[24] i.e., proof obligations.

[25] Some readers may object, but we insist! If *trees* are brought forward, as an example of a recursively definable domain, then we argue: Yes, trees can be recursively defined. Trees can, as well, be defined as a variant of graphs, and you wouldn't claim, would you, that graphs are recursive? We shall consider the living species of trees (that is, plants), as atomic. In defining attribute types You may wish to model certain attributes as 'trees'. Then, by all means, You may do so recursively. But natural trees, having roots and branches cannot be recursively defined, since proper "subtrees" of trees would then have roots!

8.2.5 Domain Facets

There is more to domain engineering than this paper can cover. A main element of domain modelling is that of modelling also other than the *intrinsics* of domains – as so far covered. By a *domain facet* we shall understand *one amongst a finite set of generic ways of analysing a domain: a view of the domain, such that the different facets cover conceptually different views – and these views together cover the domain.*[26] [17, *Chapter 8*] covers methods for modelling additional facets – such as *support technology*, *rules & regulations*, *scripts* (or *contracts*), *license languages*, *management & organisation*, and *human behaviour*.

8.2.6 Algorithmics

Algorithms are the hall-mark and corner-stone of computing. So where is *"algorithmics"* [34, 36, *Harel*] in all this ? ! The straight answer is: algorithm concerns are not concerns of domain modelling!

Domain models focus on expressing properties. They do so using abstraction in general, and simple combinations of *proof theoretic* and *model theoretic* means such as defining abstract types, here called sorts, comprehension over sets, sequences and maps $\{f(i)|i:D\bullet\mathcal{P}(f,i)\}$, $\langle f(i)|i:D\bullet\mathcal{Q}(f,i)\rangle$, and $[\,f(i)\mapsto g(i)|i:D\bullet\mathcal{R}(f,g,i)\,]$. The predicates, $\mathcal{P}, \mathcal{Q}$ and $\mathcal{R}$ further raise the level of abstraction. It is in the efficient realization of these abstractions that algorithms play their part.

8.2.7 Requirements

In [17, *Chapter 9, 2021*] we show how to "derive", in a systematic manner, *requirements prescriptions* from *domain descriptions*. Requirements are for a *machine*[27] The *machine* is the *hardware* upon which the software to be developed is to be executed – as well as the [*auxiliary*] *software* "under which" that new software is performing (*operating system, database system, data communications software*, etc.). First requirements development proceeds in three stages: (i) a *domain requirements* stage in which requirements that can be expressed sõlely using terms from the domain are developed; (ii) an *interface requirements* stage in which requirements that can be express using terms from both the domain and the machine are developed; and (iii) a *domain requirements* stage in which requirements that can be expressed solely using terms from the machine are developed. [17] shows how *domain requirements* stage can be decomposed, sequentially, into *projection, initialisation, determination, extension* and *fitting* steps. For details on this and more we refer to [17].

8.2.8 Software Design

[4, *2005-2006*] shows how to further develop software from their requirements prescriptions.

---

[26] This characterisation clearly lacks sufficient formality. We refer to Sect. 8.2.16 below.
[27] – as suggested by Michael A. Jackson [43].

8.2.9 Continuity
As remarked in Sect. 3.1 on page 11 the calculi of this paper do not address the issue of modelling continuous dynamic phenomena. This is clearly a weakness. The Integrated Formal Methods conferences [45] initially set out to spur research aimed at amalgamating continuous and discrete specifications. Not much progress has been made, except: TLA$^+$ offers some form of hybrid systems [46]; Hybrid Event-B [2] likewise; and for Back's Action Systems there is a hybrid version [1].[28] We also refer to [59,60].

8.2.10 Modelling Concurrency
We have used Hoare's CSP [39] to model concurrency. There are other, in this case, graphical languages for modelling concurrency. We refer to Chaps. 12–15 of [5]. In these chapters I treat the modelling of four graphical specification languages: Petri Nets [52], Message Sequence Charts [40,41], State Charts [35] and Live Sequence Charts [29,37]. All of them are fascinating. Their graphics appeal to many of us – so I recommend to use them informally, aside, for the textual modelling shown in this paper. But they do not "merge" into formal, textual specification languages, like VDM-SL, RSL, Z, Alloy.

8.2.11 Modelling Temporality
Although time is modelled, as part of internal attribute properties, we have not shown the modelling of temporality of behaviours. In Chap. 15 of [5] I show how to merge Duration Calculus, DC [61] with RSL-Text. Another fascinating such formal specification language is *Leslie Lamport*'s TLA+: Temporal Logic of Actions [47].

8.2.12 Domain Specific Languages
A *domain specific language*, DSL, is a computer programming language specialised to a particular application domain. What we have shown here is not a DSL. Examples of DSLs could be programming languages for expressing calculations for railways or financial services or hospitals or other. [27, *Actulus*] reports on an actuarial programming language for life insurance and pensions. To give semantics for a specific DSL one invariably specifies a domain model. So that, then, is a rôle for domain modelling.

8.2.13 Three Rôles for Domain Models
There are three rôles for domain models: (i) to just simply study and understand a domain – irrespective of any ensuing software for that domain; (ii) to serve as a basis for the development of a DSL; and (iii) to serve as a basis for the development of [other] software for the domain.

---

[28] I acknowledge the mentioning of these three references to one of the reviewers of the resent paper.

8.2.14   How Comprehensive Should a Domain Model Be?

Clearly domain models for any reasonable domain can potentially be very large in terms of pages of description. So the question is: *how much of the "domain at large" should be included in a domain description ?*. We cannot, of course, give a general answer to that question. But we can say that the domain model must at least encompass those domain entities that will, or might, be referred to in a requirements prescription. That is, if it is found when developing a *domain requirements*[29] of a *requirements prescription*, that terms thought to be of the domain was not covered by the *domain description*, then, obviously, that description must be augmented.

We do expect there to be, eventually, available for general use, a few, domain models for selected domains.

For physics Newton and Leibniz[30] has given us a calculus with which to – more or less quickly – establish a model for some physical phenomenon. When control engineers then wish to set up some automatic control system for a phenomenon they first apply the Newton/Leibniz calculi to model the phenomenon, then, from that, somehow derive a *control model*. We advocate a similar approach, as already hinted at in our expressing the *Triptych Dogma* (Page 1).

The road transport domain modelled in Appendix 7 is one such domain. It has here been expressed in a way, devoid of any specific orientation. Based on the model of Appendix 7 we can envisage some such orientations as a *road pricing domain*, a *cadastral*[31] *map domain*, a *road development domain*, a *road maintenance domain*, etc.

8.2.15   Domain Laws

Physics has excelled in our understanding the world we live in by its *laws* and by the *calculi* it has spawned – calculi that enables us to *explain* what has happened and to *predict* what will or might happen. Domain modelling has already lead to some *domain laws* – such as illustrated by for example *intentional pulls*, cf. Sect. 5.4 on page 20 (approx. half a page) and Appendix 7.6 on page 30 (two pages). The study of *intentional pull* in domains has just started! Its counterpart in physics, *gravitational pull*, is "behind" many laws of physics.

8.2.16   A Domain Modelling Science?

A science of domain modelling systematically builds and organizes knowledge about the ways and means of modelling domains such that that knowledge can explain what these models express. As an example of there not yet being a sufficient scientific knowledge of domains we refer to our informal coverage of the concept of *domain facets*, cf. footnote 26 on page 38. A formal understanding of domains and what "facet"–distinguishes them, could help sharpen the

---

[29] Cf. Sect. 8.2.7 on the previous page.

[30] https://en.wikipedia.org/wiki/Leibniz%E2%80%93Newton_calculus_controversy.

[31] https://eng.gst.dk/danish-cadastre-office/cadastral-map.

characterisation of Sect. 8.2.5 on page 38. Such a formal understanding was first reported in [12, *2014*]. Of more specific nature we suggest, next, studies of some specific issues[32].

(i) An *"integrated"* form of use of *differential equations* with the present RSL^+, i.e., the extension of our approach to domain modelling to cover more specifically issues of continuity.

(ii) A *"further detailed"* understanding of the concept of *intentional pull*.

(iii) A study of a possible *Calculus of Perdurants*.

(iv) A study of examples of domain models with an emphasis on *human interaction*.

(v) Formal models of the analysis predicates and functions and the description functions, cf. [12].

Acknowledgment. A referee of this paper, many thanks to all five (!), suggested the following, slightly edited acknowledgment:

Laudatio: Prof. He Jifeng
– He Jifeng's work on a *Unifying Theory of Programming*, UTP – a monumental contribution – is seen as a domain model for programming languages covering a wide range of programming language paradigms.
– UTP is about unifying axiomatic, denotational and operational semantics all of which can be expressed in RSL. Hence, RSL could be used as a concrete language to define a *unifying theory of programming*.
– One could combine domain modelling and UTP in order to systematically develop and define formal *domain specific languages,* DSLs. It might result in a new unifying theory of DSLs.
I fully concur.

I gratefully acknowledge the opportunity given to me, to write this paper, during my PhD lectures, October–November 2022, at the TU Wien Informatics, Vienna, Austria, by Prof. Laura Kovacs. I also gratefully acknowledge comments by Klaus Havelund, Kazuhiro Ogata and Wolfgang Reisig. Finally, many thanks to Jonathan Bowen for his indefatigable work on getting this paper in proper form and this volume finished.

References

1. Back, R.J., Petre, L., Porres, I.: Generalizing action systems to hybrid systems. In: Formal Techniques in Real-Time and Fault-Tolerant Systems, pp. 202–213 (2000). https://doi.org/10.1007/3-540-45352-0_17, www.researchgate.net/publication/221654900_Generalizing_Action_Systems_to_Hybrid_Systems

2. Banach, R., Butler, M.: Modelling hybrid systems in event-B and hybrid event-B: a comparison of water tanks. In: Ogata, K., Lawford, M., Liu, S. (eds.) ICFEM 2016. LNCS, vol. 10009, pp. 90–105. Springer, Cham (2016). https://doi.org/10.1007/978-3-319-47846-3_7

3. Bjørner, D.: UNU/IIST reports on domain modelling. Research Report, UNU/IIST (1995–1997), UNUIIST:46: New Software Technology Development, UNUIIST:47:

---

[32] https://informatics.tuwien.ac.at/.

Software Support for Infrastructure Systems, UNUIIST:48: Software Systems Engineering - From Domain Analysis to Requirements Capture [- an Air Traffic Control Example], UNUIIST:58: Infrastructure Software Systems, UNUIIST:59: New Software Development, UNUIIST:60: Models of Enterprise Management: Strategy, Tactics & Operations - Case Study Applied to Airlines and Manufacturing, UNUIIST:61: Federated GIS+DIS-based Decision Support Systems for Sustainable Development - a Conceptual Architecture, UNUIIST:96: Models of Financial Services & Industries

4. Bjørner, D.: Software Engineering, Vol. 1: Abstraction and Modelling; Vol. 2: Specification of Systems and Languages; Vol. 3: Domains, Requirements and Software Design. Texts in Theoretical Computer Science, the EATCS Series. Springer, Heidelberg (2006)

5. Bjørner, D.: Software Engineering, Vol. 2: Specification of Systems and Languages. Texts in Theoretical Computer Science, the EATCS Series. Springer, Heidelberg (2006). Chapters 12–14 are primarily authored by Christian Krog Madsen. See [6, 8]

6. Bjørner, D.: Software Engineering, Vol. 2: Specification of Systems and Languages. Qinghua University Press (2008)

7. Bjørner, D.: On mereologies in computing science. In: Roscoe, A.W., Jones, C.B., Wood, K.R. (eds.) Reflections on the Work of C.A.R. Hoare, pp. 47–70. Springer, London (2010). https://doi.org/10.1007/978-1-84882-912-1_3, www.imm.dtu.dk/~dibj/bjorner-hoare75-p.pdf

8. Bjørner, D.: Chinese: Software Engineering, Vol. 2: Specification of Systems and Languages. Qinghua University Press (2010). Translated by Dr Liu Bo Chao et al

9. Bjørner, D.: Domain science & engineering - from computer science to the sciences of informatics, part I of II: the engineering part. Kibernetika sistemny analiz $2(4)$, 100–116 (2010)

10. Bjørner, D.: Domain science & engineering - from computer science to the sciences of informatics part II of II: the science part. Kibernetika sistemny analiz $2(3)$, 100–120 (2011)

11. Bjørner, D.: A rôle for mereology in domain science and engineering: to every mereology there corresponds a λ–expression. In: Calosi, C., Graziani, P. (eds.) Mereology and the Sciences. SL, vol. 371, pp. 323–357. Springer, Cham (2014). https://doi.org/10.1007/978-3-319-05356-1_12

12. Bjørner, D.: Domain analysis: endurants - an analysis & description process model. In: Iida, S., Meseguer, J., Ogata, K. (eds.) Specification, Algebra, and Software. LNCS, vol. 8373, pp. 1–34. Springer, Heidelberg (2014). https://doi.org/10.1007/978-3-642-54624-2_1, www.imm.dtu.dk/ dibj/2014/kanazawa/kanazawa-p.pdf

13. Bjørner, D.: Manifest domains: analysis & description. Formal Aspects Comput. $29(2)$, 175–225 (2017). www.imm.dtu.dk/ dibj/2015/faoc/faoc-bjorner.pdf. Accessed 26 July 2016

14. Bjørner,   D.:   To   every   manifest   domain   a   CSP   expression. J.   Log.   Algebraic   Methods   Program. $1(94)$,   91–108   (2018). www.imm.dtu.dk/ dibj/2016/mereo/mereo.pdf

15. Bjørner, D.: slAn assembly plant domain - analysis & description. Technical report, Technical University of Denmark, Fredsvej 11, DK-2840 Holte, Denmark (2019). www.imm.dtu.dk/ dibj/2021/assembly/assemblyline.pdf

16. Bjørner, D.: Domain analysis & description - principles, techniques and modelling languages. ACM Trans. Software Eng. Methodol. $28(2)$, 68p (2019). www.imm.dtu.dk/ dibj/2018/tosem/Bjorner-TOSEM.pdf

17. Bjørner, D.: Domain Science & Engineering - A Foundation for Software Development. EATCS Monographs in Theoretical Computer Science. Springer, Cham (2021). https://doi.org/10.1007/978-3-030-73484-8. A revised version of this book is [21]

18. Bjørner, D.: Rigorous Domain Descriptions. A compendium of draft domain description sketches carried out over the years 1995–2021 (2021). www.imm.dtu.dk/ dibj/2021/dd/dd.pdf

19. Bjørner, D.: Documents: a basis for government. In: United Natonans Inst., Festschrift for Tomas Janowski and Elsa Estevez, Guimaraes, Portugal (2022). www.imm.dtu.dk/ dibj/2022/janowski/docs.pdf

20. Bjørner, D.: Domain modelling - a primer (2023). A short version of [21]. xii+227 pages

21. Bjørner, D.: Domain science & engineering - a foundation for software development (2023). Revised edition of [17]. xii+346 pages

22. Bjørner, D.: Pipelines: a domain science & engineering description. In: FSEN 2023: Fundamentals of Software Engineering, 3–5 May 2023, Teheran, Iran (2023). www.imm.dtu.dk/~dibj/2023/tehran/tehran.pdf

23. Bjørner, D., Jones, C.B. (eds.): The Vienna Development Method: The Meta-Language. LNCS, vol. 61. Springer, Heidelberg (1978). https://doi.org/10.1007/3-540-08766-4

24. Bjørner, D., Jones, C.B. (eds.): Formal Specification and Software Development. Prentice-Hall, Hoboken (1982)

25. Bjørner, D., Nest, O.N. (eds.): Towards a Formal Description of Ada. LNCS, vol. 98. Springer, Heidelberg (1980). https://doi.org/10.1007/3-540-10283-3

26. Casati, R., Varzi, A.C.: Parts and Places: The Structures of Spatial Representation. MIT Press, Cambridge (1999)

27. Christiansen, D.R., Grue, K., Niss, H., Sestoft, P., Sigtryggsson, K.S.: Actulus modeling language - an actuarial programming language for life insurance and pensions. Technical report, edlund.dk/sites/default/files/Downloads/paper_actulus-modeling-language.pdf, Edlund A/S, Denmark, Bjerregårds Sidevej 4, DK-2500 Valby. (+45) 36 15 06 30. edlund@edlund.dk (2015). http://www.edlund.dk/en/insights/scientific-papers. This paper illustrates how the design of pension and life insurance products, and their administration, reserve calculations, and audit, can be based on a common formal notation. The notation is human-readable and machine-processable, and specialised to the actuarial domain, achieving great expressive power combined with ease of use and safety

28. Clemmensen, G.B., Oest, O.N.: Formal specification and development of an Ada compiler - a VDM case study. In: Proceedings of the 7th International Conference on Software Engineering, 26–29 March 1984, Orlando, Florida, pp. 430–440. IEEE (1984)

29. Damm, W., Harel, D.: LSCs: breathing life into message sequence charts. Formal Methods Syst. Design **19**, 45–80 (2001). Early version appeared as Weizmann Institute Technical report CS98-09, April 1998. An abridged version appeared in Proceedings of the 3rd IFIP International Conference on Formal Methods for Open Object-based Distributed Systems (FMOODS 1999), pp. pp. 293–312. Kluwer (1999)

30. Fitzgerald, J., Larsen, P.G.: Modelling Systems - Practical Tools and Techniques in Software Development. Cambridge University Press, Cambridge (1998). iSBN 0-521-62348-0

31. Futatsugi, K., Nakagawa, A., Tamai, T. (eds.): CAFE: An Industrial-Strength Algebraic Formal Method. Elsevier, Amsterdam (2000). Proceedings from an April 1998 Symposium, Numazu, Japan
32. George, C.W., et al.: The RAISE Specification Language. The BCS Practitioner Series, Prentice-Hall, Hemel Hampstead (1992)
33. George, C.W., Haxthausen, A.E., Hughes, S., Milne, R., Prehn, S., Pedersen, J.S.: The RAISE Development Method. The BCS Practitioner Series, Prentice-Hall, Hemel Hampstead (1995)
34. Harel, D.: Algorithmics –The Spirit of Computing. Addison-Wesley (1987)
35. Harel, D.: StateCharts: a visual formalism for complex systems. Sci. Comput. Program. **8**(3), 231–274 (1987)
36. Harel, D.: The Science of Computing – Exploring the Nature and Power of Algorithms. Addison-Wesley (1989)
37. Harel, D., Marelly, R.: Come, Let's Play - Scenario-Based Programming Using LSCs and the Play-Engine. Springer, Cham (2003). https://doi.org/10.1007/978-3-642-19029-2
38. Hoare, C.A.R.: Communicating sequential processes. Commun. ACM **21**(8), 666–677 (1978)
39. Hoare, C.A.R.: Communicating Sequential Processes. C.A.R. Hoare Series in Computer Science. Prentice-Hall International, Hoboken (1985). Published electronically: usingcsp.com/cspbook.pdf (2004)
40. ITU-T: CCITT Recommendation Z.120: Message Sequence Chart (MSC) (1992)
41. ITU-T: ITU-T Recommendation Z.120: Message Sequence Chart (MSC) (1999)
42. Jackson, D.: Software Abstractions: Logic, Language, and Analysis. The MIT Press, Cambridge (2006). iSBN 0-262-10114-9
43. Jackson, M.A.: Software Requirements & Specifications: A Lexicon of Practice, Principles and Prejudices. ACM Press, Addison-Wesley, Reading (1995)
44. Jackson, M.A.: Program verification and system dependability. In: Boca, P., Bowen, J. (eds.) Formal Methods: State of the Art and New Directions, pp. 43–78. Springer, London (2010). https://doi.org/10.1007/978-1-84882-736-3_2
45. Araki, K., et al. (eds.): IFM 1999–2013: Integrated Formal Methods. LNCS, vols. 1945, 2335, 2999, 3771, 4591, 5423, 6496, 7321, 7940, etc. Springer, Cham (1999–2019)
46. Lamport, L.: Hybrid Systems. In: Rischel, H., Ravn, A.P. (eds.) Workshop on Theory of Hybrid Systems. Lecture Notes in Computer Science, Springer (1992), https://lamport.azurewebsites.net/pubs/lamport-hybrid.pdf
47. Lamport, L.: Specifying Systems. Addison-Wesley, Boston (2002)
48. Lamsweerde, A.: Requirements Engineering: From System Goals to UML Models to Software Specifications. Wiley, Hoboken (2009)
49. Little, W., Fowler, H., Coulson, J., Onions, C.: The Shorter Oxford English Dictionary on Historical Principles. Clarendon Press, Oxford (1973, 1987). Two volumes
50. Luschei, E.: The Logical Systems of Leśniewksi. North Holland, Amsterdam, The Netherlands (1962)
51. McCarthy, J.: Towards a mathematical science of computation. In: Popplewell, C. (ed.) IFIP World Congress Proceedings, pp. 21–28 (1962)
52. Reisig, W.: Petrinetze: Modellierungstechnik, Analysemethoden, Fallstudien, 1st edn. Leitfäden der Informatik, Vieweg+Teubner (2010). 248 p.; ISBN 978-3-8348-1290-2
53. Sørlander, K.: Det Uomgængelige - Filosofiske Deduktioner [The Inevitable - Philosophical Deductions, with a foreword by Georg Henrik von Wright], 168 p. Munksgaard · Rosinante, Copenhagen (1994)

54. Sørlander, K.: Under Evighedens Synsvinkel [Under the viewpoint of eternity], 200 p. Munksgaard · Rosinante, Copenhagen (1997)
55. Sørlander, K.: Den Endegyldige Sandhed [The Final Truth], 187 p. Rosinante, Copenhagen (2002)
56. Sørlander, K.: Indføring i Filosofien [Introduction to The Philosophy], 233 p. Informations Forlag, Copenhagen (2016)
57. Sørlander, K.: Den rene fornufts struktur [The Structure of Pure Reason]. Ellekær, Slagelse (2022)
58. Woodcock, J.C.P., Davies, J.: Using Z: Specification, Proof and Refinement. Prentice Hall International Series in Computer Science (1996). http://www.comlab.ox.ac.uk/usingz.html
59. Xie, W., Xiang, S., Zhu, H.: A UTP approach for rTiMo. Formal Aspects Comput. **30**(6), 713–738 (2018). https://doi.org/10.1007/s00165-018-0467-1
60. Xie, W., Zhu, H., QiWen, X.: A process calculus BigrTiMo of mobile systems and its formal semantics. Formal Aspects Comput. **33**(2), 207–249 (2021)
61. Zhou, C.C., Hansen, M.R.: Duration Calculus: A Formal Approach to Real-time Systems. Monographs in Theoretical Computer Science. An EATCS Series, Springer, Cham (2004). https://doi.org/10.1007/978-3-662-06784-0

Concurrent Hyperproperties

Bernd Finkbeiner[1]([✉])[iD] and Ernst-Rüdiger Olderog[2]([✉])[iD]

[1] CISPA Helmholtz Center for Information Security, Saarbrücken, Germany
finkbeiner@cispa.de
[2] Carl von Ossietzky University of Oldenburg, Oldenburg, Germany
olderog@informatik.uni-oldenburg.de

Abstract. Trace properties, which are sets of execution traces, are often used to analyze systems, but their expressiveness is limited. Clarkson and Schneider defined *hyperproperties* as a generalization of trace properties to sets of sets of traces. Typical applications of hyperproperties are found in information flow security. We introduce an analogous definition of *concurrent* hyperproperties, by generalizing traces to *concurrent* traces, which we define as partially ordered multisets. We take Petri nets as the basic semantic model. Concurrent traces are formalized via causal nets. To check concurrent hyperproperties, we define *may* and *must testing* of sets of concurrent traces in the style of DeNicola and Hennessy, using the parallel composition of Petri nets. In our approach, we thus distinguish nondeterministic and concurrent behavior. We discuss examples where concurrent hyperproperties are needed.

Keywords: Hyperproperties · concurrent traces · Petri nets · may and must testing

1 Introduction

Among the most fundamental debates in the theory of concurrency is the distinction between *interleaving* semantics in the style of Milner [17] and Hoare [13], and *partial-order* (or *true concurrency*) semantics following the work of Petri [21], Mazurkiewicz [15], and Winskel [27]. In interleaving semantics, concurrency is reduced to its sequential nondeterministic simulation; in partial-order semantics, concurrency is modeled as causal independence.

In this paper, we revisit this classic debate in the modern setting of *hyperproperties*. Clarkson and Schneider defined hyperproperties as a generalization of trace properties, which are sets of traces, to *sets of* sets of traces [4]. Hyperproperties are a powerful class of linear-time properties that can express many notions related to information flow, symmetry, robustness, and causality. A typical example is *noninterference* [8], which is one of the most well-studied information-flow security policies. Noninterference requires that for all computations and for all sequences of actions of a high-security agent A, the resulting observations made by a low-security observer B are identical to B's observations that would result

© The Author(s) 2023
J. P. Bowen et al. (Eds.): *Theories of Programming and Formal Methods*, LNCS 14080, pp. 211–231, 2023.
https://doi.org/10.1007/978-3-031-40436-8_8

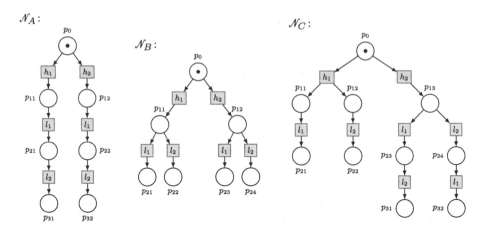

Fig. 1. Three example systems given as Petri nets.

without A's actions. While trace properties express properties of individual executions, hyperproperties express properties of sets of traces. This makes it possible to relate different executions, for example by requiring that certain observations are the same, without necessarily restricting the events on individual executions.

Since hyperproperties refer to traces, they are, at least in principle, immediately applicable to concurrent systems with interleaving semantics. However, the interleaving semantics leads to a fundamental problem, which we will illustrate with a sequence of example systems given as the Petri nets shown in Fig. 1. We employ the usual graphical representation of Petri nets: circles represent places and boxes represent transitions that are connected to places via directed arcs. In our setting, transitions are labeled by action symbols like h_1 and h_2. Black dots represent tokens, which represent the current points of activity. The simultaneous presence of several tokens models concurrent activities. The dynamic behavior of a Petri net is modeled by its token game that defines how tokens can move inside the net. A transition is enabled if all places connected to it with an ingoing arc carry a token. Firing the transition moves these tokens to the places connected to it with an outgoing arc. Branching from a place models nondeterministic choice, whereas branching from a transition models the start of a concurrent execution. As an example, consider the net $\mathcal{N}_C$ shown on the right in Fig. 1. From the initial place p_0, there is a nondeterministic choice between the transitions labeled with h_1 and h_2. Firing transition h_1 concurrently enables the transitions labeled with l_1 and l_2, whereas firing transition h_2 enables in place p_{13} the nondeterministic choice between the transitions l_1 and l_2. For more details on Petri nets we refer to Sect. 3.

For a start, consider the system $\mathcal{N}_A$ shown on the left in Fig. 1. We are interested in the secrecy property that the system's low-security behavior, as observable in the low-security events l_1 and l_2, is not affected by the high-security

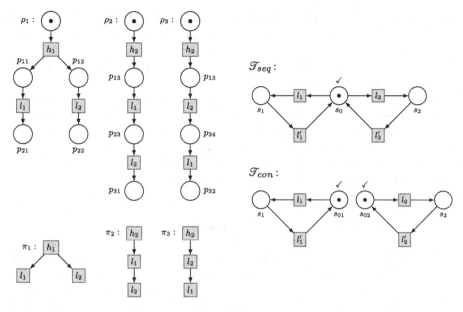

Fig. 2. *Left*: The three maximal runs ρ_1, ρ_2 and ρ_3 of $\mathcal{N}_C$ from Fig. 1, resulting by resolving every nondeterministic choice in $\mathcal{N}_C$, and their corresponding concurrent traces π_1, π_2 and π_3. *Right*: A sequential test $\mathcal{T}_{seq}$ for the concurrent hyperproperty that every pair of concurrent traces π and π' must agree on the occurrence *and* sequential ordering of the low-security events l_1 and l_2. In the test, the events l_1 and l_2 refer to π and l_1' and l_2' to π'. The place marked with the symbol ✓ notifies a successful test. Below is a concurrent test $\mathcal{T}_{con}$ for the weaker concurrent hyperproperty that every pair of concurrent traces π and π' must agree on the occurrence of the low-security events l_1 and l_2, but not on their sequential ordering. For instance, each each l_1 must be matched by l_1' before the next l_1 can occur, but l_2 may occur in between l_1 and l_1'.

events h_1 and h_2. Our system is secure. This is captured by the hyperproperty that *all* traces must agree on the occurrences and the ordering of l_1 and l_2, and indeed, the system has only two traces, $h_1 \cdot l_1 \cdot l_2$ and $h_2 \cdot l_1 \cdot l_2$, which, when projected to $\{l_1, l_2\}$, both result in the same sequence $l_1 \cdot l_2$ of low-security events.

Next, consider system $\mathcal{N}_B$ shown in the middle in Fig. 1. Informally, the system is still secure in the sense that an observer who sees only l_1 and l_2 cannot distinguish the situation where h_1 has occurred from the situation where h_2 has occurred. However, our previous hyperproperty is violated. The system has four traces: $h_1 \cdot l_1$, $h_1 \cdot l_2$, $h_2 \cdot l_1$, and $h_2 \cdot l_2$, which, when projected to $\{l_1, l_2\}$, result in two different traces, l_1 and l_2. This issue is due to the nondeterministic choice between l_1 and l_2, and can be addressed with possibilistic information-flow properties like *generalized noninterference* [16]. Generalized noninterference is weaker than normal noninterference: it requires that for every pair of traces π, π' *there exists* another trace π'', such that (1) π'' agrees with π on the low-security events $\{l_1, l_2\}$ and (2) π'' agrees with π' on the high-security events $\{h_1, h_2\}$.

Generalized noninterference is satisfied in $\mathcal{N}_B$. For example, for $\pi = h_1 \cdot l_1$ and $\pi' = h_2 \cdot l_2$, there exists $\pi'' = h_2 \cdot l_1$, which agrees with π on $\{l_1, l_2\}$ and with π' on $\{h_1, h_2\}$.

Finally, consider the *concurrent* system $\mathcal{N}_C$ shown on the right in Fig. 1. With the interpretation of concurrency as nondeterministic interleaving, the system has the four traces $h_1 \cdot l_1 \cdot l_2$, $h_1 \cdot l_2 \cdot l_1$, $h_2 \cdot l_1 \cdot l_2$, and $h_2 \cdot l_2 \cdot l_1$. Generalized noninterference is satisfied. However, the system is clearly not secure, because h_1 causes concurrent behavior, while h_2 causes sequential behavior. In a concurrent setting, this difference could be recognized by an attacker, who might, for example, synchronize with the system on a particular ordering, such as $l_1 \cdot l_2$. In a trace that begins with h_1, this will always work, while in traces that begin with h_2, the attacker might observe a deadlock when the system performs the order $l_2 \cdot l_1$.

In the security literature, this phenomenon has lead to the study of *branching-time* information-flow properties based on various notions of (bi-)simulation (cf. [3]). Often, however, such equivalences are too fine-grained, because they expose the point in time when an internal decision is made. Linear-time properties, and, hence, hyperproperties abstract from such implementation details. Can hyperproperties nevertheless recognize the difference between concurrent and sequential behavior?

In this paper, we propose *concurrent hyperproperties* as a positive answer to this question. Hyperproperties are based on the partial-order interpretation of concurrency. We stick to Clarkson and Schneider's definition of hyperproperties as sets of sets of traces, but generalize traces to *concurrent* traces, which we define as partially ordered multisets (pomsets). Figure 2 shows the three maximal runs ρ_1, ρ_2 and ρ_3 of system $\mathcal{N}_C$ and their corresponding concurrent traces. In a run, every nondeterministic choice has been resolved, but concurrent executions remain visible, like the concurrency of the transitions labeled with l_1 and l_2 in ρ_1. The concurrency of run ρ_1 is reflected in the partial order of the concurrent trace π_1. Note that $\mathcal{N}_C$ has four traces under the interleaving semantics (corresponding to the two nondeterministic choices and the two possible interleavings) but only three concurrent traces, because the concurrent execution is not resolved by nondeterminism. Since the concurrency is still present in the concurrent traces, a concurrent hyperproperty can distinguish nondeterminism from concurrency. Continuing our example, we can now specify secrecy in concurrent systems like $\mathcal{N}_C$ as the concurrent hyperproperty where every pair of concurrent traces agrees on the occurrence and ordering of the low-security events. Our example system clearly violates this requirement.

In the paper, we give a formal definition of concurrent hyperproperties and then provide an explicit mechanism for describing concurrent hyperproperties. We base this mechanism the concept of *testing processes* due to DeNicola and Hennessy [5,11]. There the interaction of a (nondeterministic) process and a user is explicitly formalized using a synchronous parallel composition. The user is formalized by a *test*, which is a process with some states marked as a *success*. It is defined when a process *may* pass a test and when it *must* pass a test. We transfer the concept of testing to concurrent traces. A concurrent hyperproperty is given as a test that has interactions with multiple concurrent runs. The test is successful for a given set of concurrent traces if it succeeds for all combinations of concurrent traces from the set.

For our example, such a test $\mathcal{T}_{seq}$ is shown on the right in Fig. 2. It can interact with any two of the runs ρ_1, ρ_2, ρ_3 corresponding to any two of the traces π_1, π_2, π_3 of $\mathcal{N}_C$. The interaction is via parallel composition that synchronizes on all transitions with the same label. To this end, the first run under test keeps the original labels l_1 and l_2, whereas the second run uses primed copies l_1' and l_2' of these labels. Thus $\mathcal{T}_{seq}$ allows for both possible orderings (l_1 then l_2, and l_2 then l_1) in the first trace and enforces that the second trace exhibits the same order. When $\mathcal{T}_{seq}$ is applied to the runs of the concurrent system $\mathcal{N}_C$ shown on the left of Fig. 2, it turns out that they may not pass this test, for instance, when ρ_1 and ρ_3', i.e., ρ_3 with primed labels, are tested for the sequence $l_1 \cdot l_1' \cdot l_2 \cdot l_2'$, this leads to a deadlock after l_1. This shows that the concurrent system $\mathcal{N}_C$ does not satisfy the concurrent hyperproperty. We will examine this in more detail in Sect. 5.

The test $\mathcal{T}_{con}$ checks a weaker concurrent hyperproperty, namely that each occurrence of l_1 is matched by an occurrence of l_1' before the next occurrence of l_1, and similarly for l_2 and l_2', but l_2 may occur in between l_1 and l_1'. When $\mathcal{T}_{con}$ is applied to any two of the runs ρ_1, ρ_2, ρ_3 shown on the left of Fig. 2, it turns out that they must pass this test. This shows that the concurrent system $\mathcal{N}_C$ satisfies this weaker concurrent hyperproperty. For more details see Sect. 5.

Our paper is organized as follows. In Sect. 2 we define the notion of concurrent hyperproperties and give examples of ascending sophistication. In Sect. 3 we recall the basic concepts from Petri nets that we take as our semantic model of concurrent systems. In particular, we define concurrent runs and the parallel composition of nets. In Sect. 4 we adapt the concept of testing developed by DeNicola and Hennessy to the setting of Petri nets. In Sect. 5 we discuss how various examples of concurrent hyperproperties can be tested. In Sect. 6 we briefly discuss the decidability of universal must testing and establish an undecidability result for universal may testing. In Sect. 7 we conclude the paper.

Dedication. We dedicate our paper to Jifeng He on the occasion of his 80th birthday. Jifeng has made many contributions to formalizing and relating different semantic models of computing, as exemplified in his book 'Unifying Theories of Programming' with Tony Hoare [12]. Out of this work grew also Jifeng's interest in testing [1,25,26], the concept that we employ for hyperproperties in this paper, although in an abstract setting of testing processes as introduced by DeNicola and Hennessy. The second author has very pleasant memories of the close cooperation with Jifeng within the EU Basic Research Action ProCoS (Provably Correct Systems) during the period 1989–1995 [10], and of various scientific meetings, in particular in Oxford, Oldenburg, and Shanghai.

2   Concurrent Hyperproperties

Clarkson and Schneider defined *hyperproperties* as a generalization of trace properties, which are sets of traces, to sets of sets of traces [4]. To give an analogous definition of *concurrent* hyperproperties, we generalize traces to *concurrent traces*, which we define as partially ordered multisets (pomsets).

Let Σ be a set of labels. A Σ-labeled partially ordered set is a triple $(X, <, \ell)$ where $<$ is an irreflexive partial order on a set X and $\ell : X \to \Sigma$ is a labeling function. Two such sets $(X, <, \ell)$ and $(X', <', \ell')$ are *isomorphic* if there exists a bijective mapping $f : X \to X'$ such that $f(x) < f(y) \Leftrightarrow x < y$ and $\ell'(f(x)) = \ell(x)$. A *partially ordered multiset (pomset)* over Σ is an isomorphy class of Σ-labeled partial ordered sets, denoted as $[(X, <, \ell)]$. A *totally ordered multiset (tomset)* is a pomset where $<$ is a total order [23].

We then refer to tomsets over Σ as *traces* and pomsets over Σ as *concurrent traces*. A *trace property* is a set of traces; a *hyperproperty* is a set of sets of traces. Analogously, a *concurrent trace property* is a set of concurrent traces, and a set of sets of concurrent traces is a *concurrent hyperproperty*. We denote with $\mathbb{T}(\Sigma)$ the set of all concurrent traces over Σ.

Example 1. A simple information flow policy for a concurrent system is to forbid any dependency of a low-security event labeled l (for *low*) on a high-security event labeled h (for *high*). Let $\Sigma = \{l, h\}$. The policy can be expressed as the concurrent trace property

$$T_1 = \{ \ [(X, <, \ell)] \in \mathbb{T}(\Sigma) \ \mid \ \forall x, y \in X . x < y \Rightarrow \ell(x) \neq h \vee \ell(y) \neq l \}.$$

Example 2. Consider the hyperproperty that every pair of concurrent traces agrees on the occurrence of the low-security events, independent on any other event. Let Σ_{low} be the set of low-security events. The requirement can then be formalized as the following concurrent hyperproperty H_1:

$$H_1 = \{ \ T \subseteq \mathbb{T}(\Sigma) \ \mid \forall [(X, <, \ell)], [(X', <', \ell')] \in T. \\ \exists \text{ bijection } f : X_{low} \to X'_{low} . \forall x \in X_{low} . \ell'(f(x)) = \ell(x) \ \}$$

where $X_{low} = \{x \in X \mid \ell(x) \in \Sigma_{low}\}$ and $X'_{low} = \{x \in X' \mid \ell'(x) \in \Sigma_{low}\}$.

In the introduction, we discussed the concurrent hyperproperty that every pair of concurrent traces agrees both on the occurrence and the ordering of the low-security events. This requirement can be formalized as the following concurrent hyperproperty H_2:

$$H_2 = \{ \ T \subseteq \mathbb{T}(\Sigma) \ \mid \forall [(X, <, \ell)], [(X', <', \ell')] \in T. \\ \exists \text{ bijection } f : X_{low} \to X'_{low} . \\ (\ \forall x \in X_{low} . \ell'(f(x)) = \ell(x) \\ \wedge \forall x, y \in X_{low} . f(x) <' f(y) \Leftrightarrow x < y) \ \}$$

Example 3. As a final example, we adapt the notion of generalized noninterference (GNI) [16] to concurrent traces. We identify the events as low-security and high-security: $\Sigma = \Sigma_{low} \cup \Sigma_{high}$. The policy then requires that for every pair of concurrent traces there exists a third concurrent trace that agrees with the first trace on the low-security events and with the second trace on the high-security events. Unlike the trace-based version discussed in the introduction, this version of GNI distinguishes nondeterminism from concurrency; in the example system $\mathcal{N}_C$ shown on the right in Fig. 1, GNI on traces is satisfied, but GNI on concurrent traces is violated. GNI on concurrent traces is expressed by the following concurrent hyperproperty H_3:

$$H_3 = \{ \ T \subseteq \mathbb{T}(\Sigma) \ \mid \forall [(X, <, \ell)], [(X', <', \ell')] \in T. \\ \exists [(X'', <'', \ell'')] \in T. \ F_{low} \wedge G_{high} \}$$

where

$$\begin{aligned} F_{low} &\equiv \exists \, \text{bijection} \ f : X_{low} \rightarrow X''_{low}. \\ &\quad (\ \forall x \in X_{low}. \ell''(f(x)) = \ell(x) \\ &\quad \wedge \forall x, y \in X_{low}. \, f(x) <'' f(y) \Leftrightarrow x < y), \\ G_{high} &\equiv \exists \, \text{bijection} \ g : X'_{high} \rightarrow X''_{high}. \\ &\quad (\ \forall x \in X'_{high}. \ell''(g(x)) = \ell'(x) \\ &\quad \wedge \forall x, y \in X'_{high}. \, g(x) <'' g(y) \Leftrightarrow x <' y), \\ X_{low} &= \{x \in X \mid \ell(x) \in \Sigma_{low}\}, \\ X''_{low} &= \{x \in X'' \mid \ell''(x) \in \Sigma_{low}\}, \\ X'_{high} &= \{x \in X' \mid \ell'(x) \in \Sigma_{high}\}, \\ X''_{high} &= \{x \in X'' \mid \ell''(x) \in \Sigma_{high}\}. \end{aligned}$$

3 Petri Nets

As a model for concurrent systems we take Petri nets because they distinguish the fundamental concepts of causal dependency, nondeterministic choice, and concurrency explicitly. We consider here safe Petri nets [24], with the transitions labeled by actions which serve as synchronization points in a parallel composition of such nets. We use the notation from [19], which is inspired by [9]. A *Petri net* or simply *net* is a structure $\mathcal{N} = (A, Pl, \longrightarrow, M_0)$, where

1. A is a finite communication alphabet with $\tau \notin A$,
2. Pl is a possibly infinite set of *places*,
3. $\longrightarrow \ \subseteq \mathscr{P}_{nf}(Pl) \times (A \cup \{\tau\}) \times \mathscr{P}_{nf}(Pl)$ is the *transition relation*,
4. $M_0 \in \mathscr{P}_{nf}(Pl)$ is the *initial marking*.

We let p, q, r range over Pl. The notation $\mathscr{P}_{nf}(Pl)$ stands for the set of all non-empty, finite subsets of Pl. An element $(I, u, O) \in \ \longrightarrow$ with $I, O \in \mathscr{P}_{nf}(Pl)$ and $u \in A \cup \{\tau\}$ is called a *transition (labeled with the action u)* and written as

$$I \xrightarrow{\ u\ } O.$$

For a transition $t = I \xrightarrow{\ u\ } O$ its *preset* or *input* is given by $pre(t) = I$, its *postset* or *output* by $post(t) = O$, and its *action* by $act(t) = u$. The letter τ is intended to model an *internal* action.

In the graphical representation of a net $\mathcal{N} = (A, Pl, \longrightarrow, M_0)$ we mention the alphabet A separately and display the components Pl, $\longrightarrow$ and M_0 as usual. Places $p \in Pl$ are represented as circles $\bigcirc$ with the name p outside and transitions

$$t = \{p_1, \dots, p_m\} \xrightarrow{\;u\;} \{q_1, \dots, q_n\}$$

as boxes $\boxed{u}$ carrying the label u inside and connected via directed arcs to the places in $pre(t)$ and $post(t)$:

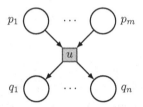

Since $pre(t)$ and $post(t)$ need not be disjoint, some of the outgoing arcs of $\boxed{u}$ may actually point back to places in $pre(t)$ and thus introduce *cycles*. Graphically, we employ then double-headed arrows between $\boxed{u}$ and the places in $pre(t) \cap post(t)$. The initial marking M_0 is represented by putting a token $\bullet$ into the circle of each $p \in M_0$.

Starting from the initial marking, the firing of transitions creates new markings $M \in \mathscr{P}_{nf}(Pl)$, which represent the global states of a Petri net. Formally, a transition t is *enabled* at a marking M if $pre(t) \subseteq M$. *Firing* such a transition t at M yields the successor marking $M' = (M - pre(t)) \cup post(t)$. We write then $M[t\rangle M'$. We assume here that $\cup$ is a disjoint union, which is satisfied if the net is *contact-free*, i.e., if for all $t \in \mathscr{T}$ and all reachable markings M

$$pre(t) \subseteq M \Rightarrow post(t) \subseteq (Pl - M) \cup pre(t).$$

The set of *reachable markings* of a net $\mathcal{N}$ is defined by

$$reach(\mathcal{N}) = \{M \mid \exists n \in \mathbb{N}. \exists t_1, \dots, t_n \in \mathscr{T}. \; M_0[t_1\rangle M_1[t_2\rangle \dots [t_n\rangle M_n = M\}.$$

For $n = 0$ inside this set, it is understood that $M_0 = M$ holds, so $M_0 \in reach(\mathcal{N})$. In the present setting, all reachable markings are non-empty, finite sets of places. Such Petri nets are called *safe* or *1-bounded* because every reachable marking contains at most one token per place. In general place/transition nets, the reachable markings can be multisets representing multiple tokens per place.

3.1   Causal Nets and Runs

Concurrent computations of a net can be described by *causal nets* [21,24]. Informally, a causal net is an acyclic net where all choices have been resolved. It can be seen as a net-theoretic way of defining a partial order among the occurrences of transitions in a net to represent their causal dependency.

We need more notation for a net $\mathcal{N} = (A, Pl, \longrightarrow, M_0)$. For a place $p \in Pl$ its *preset* is defined by $pre(p) = \{t \in \longrightarrow \mid p \in post(t)\}$ and its *postset* by $post(p) = \{t \in \longrightarrow \mid p \in pre(t)\}$. The *flow relation* $\mathcal{F}_{\mathcal{N}} \subseteq Pl \times Pl$ on the places of $\mathcal{N}$ is given by

$$p \; \mathcal{F}_{\mathcal{N}} \; q \quad \text{if} \quad \exists t \in \longrightarrow . \; p \in pre(t) \text{ and } q \in post(t).$$

$\mathcal{F}_{\mathcal{N}}$ is *well-founded* if there are no infinite backward chains

$$\cdots \; p_3 \; \mathcal{F}_{\mathcal{N}} \; p_2 \; \mathcal{F}_{\mathcal{N}} \; p_1.$$

A *causal net* is a net $\mathcal{N} = (A, Pl, \longrightarrow, M_0)$ such that

(1) all places are unbranched, i.e., $\forall p \in Pl . \; |pre(p)| \leq 1$ and $|post(p)| \leq 1$,
(2) the flow relation $\mathcal{F}_{\mathcal{N}}$ is well-founded, and
(3) the initial marking consists of all places without an ingoing arc, i.e.,

$$M_0 = \{p \in Pl \mid pre(p) = \emptyset\}.$$

By condition (1), there are no choices in $\mathcal{N}$. Condition (2) implies that the transitive closure of $\mathcal{F}_{\mathcal{N}}$ is irreflexive. Thus a causal net $\mathcal{N}$ is acyclic, so each transition occurs only once. Conditions (1)–(3) ensure that there are no superfluous places and transitions in causal nets: every transition can fire and every place is contained in some reachable marking. Also, every causal net is safe.

Following Petri's intuition, causal nets should describe the concurrent computations of a net. Thus we explain how causal nets relate to ordinary (safe) nets. To this end, we use the following notion of embedding.

Let $\mathcal{N}_1 = (A_1, Pl_1, \longrightarrow_1, M_{01})$ be a causal net and $\mathcal{N}_2 = (A_2, Pl_2, \longrightarrow_2, M_{02})$ be a safe net, where M_{01} and M_{02} denote the initial markings of $\mathcal{N}_1$ and $\mathcal{N}_2$, respectively. $\mathcal{N}_1$ is a *causal net of* $\mathcal{N}_2$ if $A_1 = A_2$ and there exists a mapping $f : Pl_1 \longrightarrow Pl_2$, which is extended elementwise to subsets $X \subseteq Pl_1$ by putting $f(X) = \{f(p) \in Pl_2 \mid p \in X\}$, such that the following holds:

1. $f(M_{01}) = M_{02}$,
2. $\forall M \in reach(\mathcal{N}_1) . \; f \downarrow M$, the restriction of f to $M \subseteq Pl_1$, is injective,
3. $\forall t \in \longrightarrow_1 . \; (f(pre(t)), act(t), f(post(t))) \in \longrightarrow_2$,

The mapping f is called an *embedding of* $\mathcal{N}_1$ *into* $\mathcal{N}_2$. Note that f distributes over the flow relation:

$$\forall p, q \in Pl_1 . \; (p \; \mathcal{F}_{\mathcal{N}_1} \; q \Rightarrow f(p) \; \mathcal{F}_{\mathcal{N}_2} \; f(q)).$$

In net theory, the pair $(\mathcal{N}_1, f)$ is called a *process* of $\mathcal{N}_2$ [2,21]. We call it a *(concurrent) run* of $\mathcal{N}_2$ and use the (possibly decorated) letter ρ for runs. A run $\rho = (\mathcal{N}_1, f)$ of $\mathcal{N}_2$ is called *maximal* if

$$\forall p \in Pl_1 . \; (\exists q \in Pl_2 . \; f(p) \; \mathcal{F}_{\mathcal{N}_2} \; q \Rightarrow \exists p' \in Pl_1 . \; p \; \mathcal{F}_{\mathcal{N}_1} \; p'),$$

so the run ρ cannot stop at a place p if there is an extension possible at the corresponding place $f(p)$ in $\mathcal{N}_2$.

3.2   Causal Nets Corresponding to Concurrent Traces

A causal net $\mathcal{N}$ *corresponds to* the concurrent trace (pomset) $[(X, <, \ell)]$, where

- $X = \longrightarrow$, the set of transitions of $\mathcal{N}$,
- $<$ is the transitive closure of the *immediate causal successor* relation $<_m$ between transitions: $t_1 <_m t_2$ holds for $t_1, t_2 \in \longrightarrow$ if $post(t_1) \cap pre(t_2) \neq \emptyset$,
- $\ell(t) = act(t)$ for every $t \in \longrightarrow$.

The irreflexive partial order $t_1 < t_2$ expresses that transition t_2 can occur only after transition t_1 has happened, so t_2 *causally depends* on t_1. If for transitions $t_1 \neq t_2$ neither $t_1 < t_2$ nor $t_2 < t_1$ holds, t_1 and t_2 are *causally independent* and can occur *concurrently*. Graphically, we represent these pomsets by showing each transition t labeled with $\ell(t) = u$ as a box $\boxed{u}$ and connecting these boxes with arcs representing the immediate causal successor relation $<_m$ (see Fig. 2).

Also, vice versa, if a concurrent trace $[(X, <, \ell)]$ is given, it is easy to construct a causal net $\mathcal{N}$ corresponding to the trace in the above sense. One just has to add the missing places to turn the trace into a causal net.

3.3   Parallel Composition

Petri nets with disjoint sets of places, but possibly overlapping communication alphabets can be composed in parallel. Thereby transitions with different actions are performed asynchronously, whereas transitions with the *same* action synchronize. For $\mathcal{N}_i = (A_i, Pl_i, \longrightarrow_i, M_{0i})$, $i = 1,2$, with $Pl_1 \cap Pl_2 = \emptyset$ their *parallel composition* is defined as follows:

$$\mathcal{N}_1 \parallel \mathcal{N}_2 = (A_1 \cup A_2, Pl_1 \cup Pl_2, \longrightarrow, M_{01} \cup M_{02}),$$

where

$$\begin{aligned}
\longrightarrow = \quad &\{ \ (I, u, O) \in \longrightarrow_1 \cup \longrightarrow_2 \mid u \notin A_1 \cap A_2 \ \} \quad \text{(asynchrony)} \\
\cup &\{ \ (I_1 \cup I_2, a, O_1 \cup O_2) \mid a \in A_1 \cap A_2 \text{ and} \qquad \text{(synchrony)} \\
&(I_1, a, O_1) \in \longrightarrow_1 \text{ and } (I_2, a, O_2) \in \longrightarrow_2 \ \}.
\end{aligned}$$

Note that actions labeled with the internal action τ never synchronize because τ does not appear in any communication alphabet A_i.

Up to bijective renaming of places, the parallel composition of nets is commutative and associative, i.e., for all nets $\mathcal{N}_1, \mathcal{N}_2, \mathcal{N}_3$:

$$\begin{aligned}
\mathcal{N}_1 \parallel \mathcal{N}_2 &= \mathcal{N}_2 \parallel \mathcal{N}_1, \\
\mathcal{N}_1 \parallel (\mathcal{N}_2 \parallel \mathcal{N}_3) &= (\mathcal{N}_1 \parallel \mathcal{N}_2) \parallel \mathcal{N}_3.
\end{aligned}$$

4   Testing

The idea of *testing* processes is due to De Nicola and Hennessy [5,11]. There the interaction of a (nondeterministic) process and a user is explicitly formalized using a synchronous parallel composition. The user is formalized by a *test*, which is a process with some states marked as a *success*. The authors distinguish between two options: a process may or must pass a test. A process P *may* pass a test T if in *some* maximal parallel computation with P, synchronizing on transitions with the same label, the test T reaches a *success* state. A process P *must* pass a test T if in *all* such computations the test T reaches a *success* state.

We transfer this notion of testing to Petri nets. A *test* is a Petri net, extended by a distinguished set $\checkmark \subseteq Pl$ of *successful* places: $\mathscr{T} = (A, Pl, \checkmark, \longrightarrow, M_0)$. In the graphical notation, we mark each place of this subset by the symbol $\checkmark$.

To perform a test $\mathscr{T}$ on a given Petri net $\mathscr{N}$, we consider the parallel composition $\mathscr{N} \| \mathscr{T}$. A run $\rho = (\mathscr{N}_R, f)$ of $\mathscr{N} \| \mathscr{T}$ is *deadlock free* if it is infinite, and it *terminates successfully* if it is finite and all places of $\mathscr{T}$ inside the parallel composition without causal successor are marked with $\checkmark$. A net $\mathscr{N}$ *may pass* a test $\mathscr{T}$ if there exists a maximal run of $\mathscr{N} \| \mathscr{T}$ which is deadlock free or terminates successfully. A net $\mathscr{N}$ *must pass* a test $\mathscr{T}$ if all maximal runs of $\mathscr{N} \| \mathscr{T}$ are deadlock free or terminate successfully.

To *check a hyperproperty* relating k concurrent traces on a system represented by a net $\mathscr{N}_0$, we investigate maximal runs $\rho_i = (\mathscr{N}_i, f_i)$ with $i = 1, \cdots, k$ of $\mathscr{N}_0$, where the causal nets $\mathscr{N}_i$ correspond to the concurrent traces of the hyperproperty, except that in $\mathscr{N}_i$ we relabel every action u of $\mathscr{N}_0$ into u_i. We will test the parallel composition $\mathscr{N}_1 \| \cdots \| \mathscr{N}_k$. The purpose of this relabeling is to have nets $\mathscr{N}_1, \ldots, \mathscr{N}_k$ that do not synchronize in this composition. To represent the hyperproperty, we suitably quantify existentially or universally over these k runs of $\mathscr{N}_0$ and thus arrive at the following possibilities of testing:

$$Q_1 \rho_1, \cdots, Q_k \rho_k. \ \mathscr{N}_1 \| \cdots \| \mathscr{N}_k \ m \text{ pass } \mathscr{T},$$

where $Q_i \in \{\exists, \forall\}$ and $m \in \{\text{may, must}\}$. $\mathscr{T}$ uses the subscripted labels of the form $u_1, \ldots, u_k$ to synchronize with the actions in $\mathscr{N}_1, \ldots, \mathscr{N}_k$.

We also use primed copies like u' and u'' instead of subscripts. For example, for $k = 2$, we use one causal net $\mathscr{N}$ having the original actions of $\mathscr{N}_0$ and one causal $\mathscr{N}'$ with every action u of $\mathscr{N}_0$ relabled into a primed copy u'. Then the above pattern specializes to

$$Q \rho. Q' \rho'. \ \mathscr{N} \| \mathscr{N}' \ m \text{ pass } \mathscr{T},$$

where $Q, Q' \in \{\exists, \forall\}$ and $m \in \{\text{may, must}\}$. Whereas $\mathscr{N}$ and $\mathscr{N}'$ have no common actions to synchronize on, the test $\mathscr{T}$ will synchronize with $\mathscr{N}$ and $\mathscr{N}'$ via common (unprimed and primed) actions, thereby checking the hyperproperty. Note that the explicit quantifiers refer to runs of the system $\mathscr{N}_0$ under test. Once these runs are fixed, may and must corresponds to existential and universal quantification over runs originating from the test.

5   Examples

We examine concurrent trace properties and concurrent hyperproperties for examples of concurrent systems. First consider the two Petri nets shown in

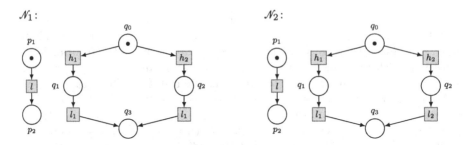

Fig. 3. *Left*: Petri net $\mathcal{N}_1$ consists of two concurrent subnets, one performs only the low-security action l and the other has a choice starting with different high-security actions h_1 and h_2, but then performing the *same* low-security action l_1, no matter whether h_1 or h_2 was chosen. *Right*: Petri net $\mathcal{N}_2$ looks identical to $\mathcal{N}_1$, but there is a subtle difference: the subnet on the right-hand side performs either l_1 or l_2 depending on the previous choice of h_1 or h_2, respectively.

Fig. 3. The net $\mathcal{N}_1$ consists of two concurrent subnets, one performs the low-security action l and the other has a choice starting with different high-security actions h_1 and h_2, but then both branches perform the same low-security action l_1. The net $\mathcal{N}_2$ has the same structure, except that the choice in the subnet on the right-hand side is now between performing action l_1 or action l_2 depending on the previous choice of the high-security actions h_1 or h_2, respectively. Note that due to the choices, each of the nets $\mathcal{N}_1$ and $\mathcal{N}_2$ have two maximal runs, one with actions h_1 and one with action h_2.

Let us check the trace property whether the low-security action l_1 can occur after l, independent of the high-security actions h_1 and h_2, To this end, we use the following test $\mathcal{T}$:

$$\mathcal{T}: \quad \boxed{\bullet} \rightarrow \boxed{l} \rightarrow \bigcirc \rightarrow \boxed{l_1} \rightarrow \checkmark$$
$$\qquad\quad s_0 \qquad\quad s_1 \qquad\quad s_2$$

This test is applied to each run of $\mathcal{N}_1$ and $\mathcal{N}_2$, respectively. We have

$$\forall \rho.\ \mathcal{N}_{1,\rho} \text{ must pass } \mathcal{T},$$

because $\mathcal{T}$ terminates successfully for each of the two maximal runs, independent of the choice of h_1 or h_2. Here $\mathcal{N}_{1,\rho}$ denotes the net of the run ρ of $\mathcal{N}_1$.

For $\mathcal{N}_2$ the test $\mathcal{T}$ is less successful. Let $\mathcal{N}_{2,h_1}$ and $\mathcal{N}_{2,h_2}$ be the nets for the two maximal runs of $\mathcal{N}_2$, depending on whether h_1 or h_2 is initially chosen. Then the parallel composition with $\mathcal{T}$ yields the results shown in Fig. 4. Note that synchronization is enforced on the common actions l and l_1, whereas h_1 and h_2 can occur asynchronously. In $\mathcal{N}_{2,h_1} \parallel \mathcal{T}$, the test terminates successfully, whereas $\mathcal{N}_{2,h_2} \parallel \mathcal{T}$ ends in a deadlock. Thus

$$\forall \rho.\ \mathcal{N}_{2,\rho} \text{ may pass } \mathcal{T},$$

but it is not the case that $\forall \rho.\ \mathcal{N}_{2,\rho}$ must pass $\mathcal{T}$. Here $\mathcal{N}_{2,\rho}$ denotes the net of the run ρ of $\mathcal{N}_2$.

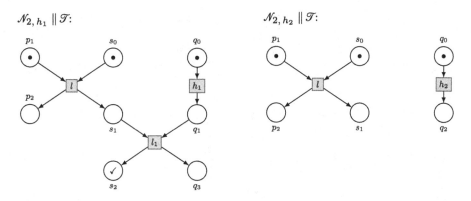

Fig. 4. Testing the two maximal runs of $\mathcal{N}_2$. In the middle, the places s_0, s_1, s_2 of test $\mathcal{T}$ in the parallel composition with these two runs are shown. *Left:* In $\mathcal{N}_{2,h_1} \parallel \mathcal{T}$, the test terminates successfully in s_2. *Right:* However, $\mathcal{N}_{2,h_2} \parallel \mathcal{T}$ ends in a deadlock, i.e., in places without ✓.

5.1   Testing the Concurrent Hyperproperties H_1 and H_2

Next we turn to Sect. 1 and consider the three runs shown in Fig. 2 stemming from system $\mathcal{N}_C$ in Fig. 1. First we check with the sequential test $\mathcal{T}_{seq}$ of Fig. 2 the concurrent hyperproperty whether every pair of concurrent traces π and π' agrees on the occurrence and ordering of the low-security events l_1 and l_2. This is property H_2 in Example 2. Figure 5 shows the outcomes of testing ρ_1 and ρ_3'. We conclude that $\rho_1 \parallel \rho_3'$ may pass $\mathcal{T}_{seq}$. More general, let $\mathcal{N}$ and $\mathcal{N}'$ be the nets of two runs ρ and ρ' corresponding to two traces π and π', respectively. If at least one of ρ and ρ' is instantiated with the concurrent run ρ_1, we have $\mathcal{N} \parallel \mathcal{N}'$ may pass $\mathcal{T}_{seq}$, otherwise $\mathcal{N} \parallel \mathcal{N}'$ may *not* pass $\mathcal{T}_{seq}$. Summarizing, we have

$$\exists \rho, \rho'. \mathcal{N} \parallel \mathcal{N}' \text{ may pass } \mathcal{T}_{seq}$$

and even

$$\forall \rho. \exists \rho'. \mathcal{N} \parallel \mathcal{N}' \text{ may pass } \mathcal{T}_{seq}$$

because we can instantiate ρ' with ρ_1, but *not* $\forall \rho, \rho'. \mathcal{N} \parallel \mathcal{N}'$ may pass $\mathcal{T}_{seq}$. However, no *must* property holds for two concurrent traces and the test $\mathcal{T}_{seq}$. This shows that the system $\mathcal{N}_C$ in Fig. 1 does not satisfy the concurrent hyperproperty H_2.

Now we check with concurrent test $\mathcal{T}_{con}$ of Fig. 2 the weaker concurrent hyperproperty whether every pair of concurrent traces π and π' agrees on the occurrence of the low-security events l_1 and l_2, i.e., each each l_1 must be matched by l_1', but l_2 may occur in between, and vice versa for l_2 and l_2' and a possibly intervening l_1. This is property H_1 in Example 2. Figure 6 shows the outcomes of testing ρ_1 and ρ_3. We conclude that $\rho_1 \parallel \rho_3$ must pass $\mathcal{T}_{seq}$. Indeed, we have

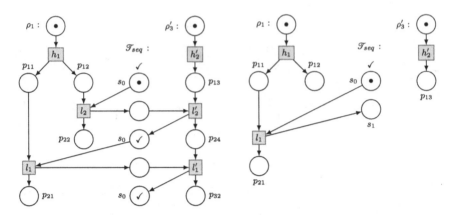

Fig. 5. Testing a concurrent hyperproperty with $\mathcal{T}_{seq}$. We consider the two maximal runs of the parallel composition $\rho_1 \parallel \mathcal{T}_{seq} \parallel \rho_3'$. *Left*: Here at first the alternative starting with l_2 of the test $\mathcal{T}_{seq}$ is chosen. This runs terminates successful. *Right*: Here at first the alternative starting with l_1 of $\mathcal{T}_{seq}$ is chosen. This runs ends in a deadlock because ρ_3 engages first in l_2.

$$\forall \rho, \rho'. \mathcal{N} \parallel \mathcal{N}' \text{ must pass } \mathcal{T}_{con}.$$

This shows that the system $\mathcal{N}_C$ in Fig. 1 satisfies the concurrent hyperproperty H_1.

5.2   Testing the Concurrent Properties T_1 and H_3

Consider the concurrent trace property T_1 of Example 1 for a net $\mathcal{N}$, where a low-security event l must not depend on a high-security event h. We check this by requiring that

$$\mathcal{N} \text{ must pass } \mathcal{T}_{hl}$$

for the following test $\mathcal{T}_{hl}$:

This test can terminate successfully after any (possibly empty) sequence of low-security events l. However, once a high-security event h occurs, the test terminates successfully only after any (possibly empty) sequence of further h events. Any low-security event l occurring after the first h will lead to a deadlock since the test does not offer any further synchronization on l.

Finally, we consider the concurrent hyperproperty H_3 of generalized noninterference of Example 3. As low-security events we take $l_1, l_2 \in \Sigma_{low}$ and as high-security events $h_1, h_2 \in \Sigma_{high}$. The property is checked by requiring that

$$\forall \rho, \rho'. \exists \rho''. \mathcal{N} \parallel \mathcal{N}' \parallel \mathcal{N}'' \text{ must pass } \mathcal{T}_{gni}$$

for the test $\mathcal{T}_{gni}$ shown in Fig. 7.

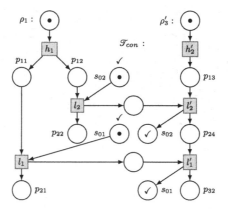

Fig. 6. Testing a concurrent hyperproperty with $\mathcal{T}_{con}$. We consider the unique maximal run of the parallel composition $\rho_1 \parallel \mathcal{T}_{con} \parallel \rho_3'$. This run terminates successfully because both concurrent components of the test end in a place marked with ✓.

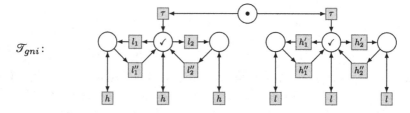

Fig. 7. Test $\mathcal{T}_{gni}$

In the two universally quantified runs ρ and ρ', this test uses labels l_1, l_2, h_1, h_2 in the net $\mathcal{N}$ of run ρ and copies l_1', l_2', h_1', h_2' in the net $\mathcal{N}'$ of ρ'. Likewise, in the existentially quantified run ρ'', the test uses labels $l_1'', l_2'', h_1'', h_2''$ in the net $\mathcal{N}''$ of ρ''.

Note that the test $\mathcal{T}_{gni}$ has an initial choice between the two internal τ actions, but the conjunction in H_3 is modeled by must testing, which requires that for each run ρ and ρ' both branches terminate with a success. In the left branch, the test is successful if it terminates when the low-security events l_1, l_2 are matched by corresponding events l_1'', l_2'', so that F_{low} holds. The three transitions labeled h are shorthands for the occurrence of any event $h_1, h_2, l_1', l_2', h_1', h_2', h_1'', h_2''$ that may intervene in this branch without any effect. In the right branch, the test is successful if it terminates when the high-security events h_1', h_2' are matched by corresponding events h_1'', h_2'', so that G_{high} holds. The three transitions labeled l are shorthands for the occurrence of any event $l_1, l_2, h_1, h_2, l_1', l_2', l_1'', l_2''$ that may intervene in this branch without any effect.

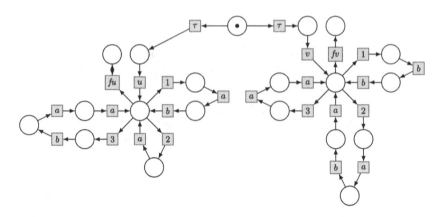

Fig. 8. Petri net $\mathcal{N}_I$ simulating the input I of the PCP

6 Decidability

Universal must testing of a net $\mathcal{N}_0$ of the form

$$(*) \qquad \forall \rho_1, \cdots, \forall \rho_k. \ \mathcal{N}_1 \parallel \cdots \parallel \mathcal{N}_k \ \text{ must pass } \mathcal{T},$$

can be decided because their falsification is a reachability problem. Indeed, the negation of $(*)$ means that there exist k runs of $\mathcal{N}_0$ that composed in parallel with $\mathcal{T}$ yield a finite net in which there exist places of $\mathcal{T}$ without causal successor that are not marked with ✓. Instead of referring to k runs of $\mathcal{N}_0$ we can equivalently refer to k copies $\mathcal{N}_{0,1}, \ldots, \mathcal{N}_{0,k}$ of $\mathcal{N}_0$, with suitably renamed action labels, and check the net $\mathcal{N} = \mathcal{N}_{0,1} \parallel \cdots \parallel \mathcal{N}_{0,k} \parallel \mathcal{T}$, with $\longrightarrow$ as its transition relation and $Pl_{\mathcal{T}}$ as the set of places inside $\mathcal{T}$, for the following property:

$$\exists M \in reach(\mathcal{N}). \ \exists p \in M \cap Pl_{\mathcal{T}}. \ p \notin \text{✓} \wedge \neg \exists t \in \longrightarrow. \ t \text{ is enabled at } M.$$

This is a reachability problem for Petri nets, which is decidable [14]. Since we consider safe Petri nets, this reachablity is PSPACE-complete [6].

By contrast, universal may testing quickly gets undecidable.

Theorem 1. *Universal may testing is undecidable for tests with two maximal runs.*

Proof. We reduce the *falsification* of the Post Correspondence Problem (PCP) [22] to universal may testing using a test with two maximal runs.   □

We present the proof idea for the PCP over the alphabet $\{a, b\}$. As an input, consider the set

$$I = ((u_1, v_1), (u_2, v_2), (u_3, v_3)),$$

of pairs of subwords, where

$$u_1 = ab, \ v_1 = bb, \ u_2 = a, \ v_2 = aba, \ u_3 = baa, \ v_3 = aa.$$

The PCP with this input is solvable by the correspondence $(2,3,1,3)$ because

$$u_2u_3u_1u_3 = a\,b\,a\,a\,a\,b\,b\,a\,a = v_2v_3v_1v_3.$$

The PCP input I is simulated by the Petri net $\mathcal{N}_I$ shown in Fig. 8. It consists of two branches that are selected by an initial choice between two internal actions. For distinguishing them in a test, the left branch starts with a transition labeled with u and the right branch with a transition labeled with v. Afterwards, their tokens reside in their center places from where they can nondeterministically choose which of the words u_i or v_i for $i \in \{1,2,3\}$ to perform next. For example, the left branch simulates the subword $u_1 = ab$ by the sequence of actions 1, a, and b, after which the token is again on the center place so that the next choice can be performed. After any finite number of choices each branch may stop its activity by performing the transition labeled with fu or fv, respectively.

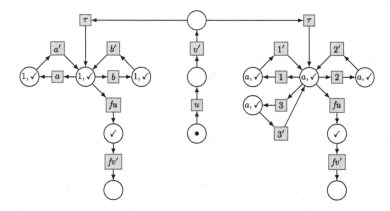

Fig. 9. Test $\mathcal{T}_{PCP}$ for checking whether two runs of $\mathcal{N}$ do *not* simulate a correspondence of the PCP. The left branch ends in the place without $\checkmark$ if the runs produce letter by letter the same word, the right branch ends in the place without $\checkmark$ if the runs have chosen the same sequence of indices.

In general, the PCP with input I simulated by a net $\mathcal{N}_I$ of the form above has *no* correspondence if and only if

$$\forall \rho, \rho' .\; \rho \,\|\, \rho' \text{ may pass } \mathcal{T}_{PCP}$$

for the test $\mathcal{T}_{PCP}$ shown in Fig. 9.

By contraposition, if the PCP has a correspondence, there exist maximal runs ρ and ρ' of $\mathcal{N}_I$ with nets $\mathcal{N}$ and $\mathcal{N}'$ such that the two maximal runs in $\mathcal{N} \parallel \mathcal{N}' \parallel \mathcal{T}_{PCP}$ stemming from the two branches in $\mathcal{T}_{PCP}$ are *not* sucessful, i.e., each branch ends in the unique place that is not marked by $\checkmark$.

The left branch of $\mathcal{T}_{PCP}$ ends in the place without $\checkmark$ if ρ and ρ' produce letter by letter the same word. Here the transitions labeled with unprimed symbols refer to ρ and transitions labeled with primed symbols refer to ρ'. The initial transitions labeled with u and v' ensure that the unprimed symbols refer to the left part of $\mathcal{N}_I$ simulating the u-part and that the primed symbols refer to (the primed version of) right part of $\mathcal{N}_I$ simulating the v-part of the proposed correspondence. Since the correspondence is finite, this branch of the test ends in the place without $\checkmark$ after performing fu and fv'.

The right branch of $\mathcal{T}_{PCP}$ ends in the place without $\checkmark$ if ρ and ρ' have chosen the same sequence of indices $1, 2, 3$ in producing the common word. Note that this branch checks the same runs ρ and ρ' than the left branch because ρ and ρ' are fixed initially.

There is one technical detail. Whereas the runs ρ and ρ' have no symbols in common because ρ uses only unprimed symbols and ρ' only primed versions of the symbols, the test $\mathcal{T}_{PCP}$ synchronizes in the parallel composition with $\mathcal{N} \parallel \mathcal{N}'$ on all its symbols except τ, i.e., on $a, b, a', b', u, v', fu, fv', 1, 2, 3, 1', 2', 3'$. To avoid unintended deadlocks we have to enable the left branch of $\mathcal{T}_{PCP}$ to be able to synchronize at every place marked with 1 with any transition lableled with $1, 2, 3, 1', 2'$ or $3'$, and vice versa, the right branch of $\mathcal{T}_{PCP}$ to be able to synchronize at every place marked with a with any transition lableled with a, b, a', b', u or v'. To enhance visibility, we dropped the loop transitions attached to these places allowing for these synchronizations.

For the example input I, Fig. 10 shows two maximal runs of $\mathcal{N}_I$, one with the original symbols and one with primed symbols, that simulate the correspondence (2,3,1,3) and cause the test $\mathcal{T}_{PCP}$ to end for each branch in the place that is not marked $\checkmark$.

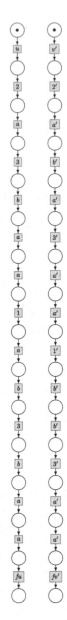

Fig. 10. Maximal runs of $\mathcal{N}$ simulating the correspondence $(2, 3, 1, 3)$.

7 Conclusion

We introduced the notion of *concurrent hyperproperties* as sets of sets of concurrent traces. This extends classical hyperproperties, which are sets of sets of traces. For analyzing concurrent hyperproperties, we used Petri nets as the underlying semantic model of concurrency. The analysis was performed by adapting *may and must testing* originally developed by DeNicola and Hennessy to our setting. Several examples illuminated the details of our approach.

As future work we envisage the introduction of suitable logics for specifying concurrent hyperproperties, extending HyperLTL for hyperproperties on traces (see [7] for an overview). A starting point could be event structure logic [18,20].

Acknowledgement. This work was supported by the European Research Council (ERC) Grant HYPER (No. 101055412).

References

1. Aichernig, B.K., He, J.: Refinement and test case generation in UTP. In: Aichernig, B.K., Boiten, E.A., Derrick, J., Groves, L. (eds.) Proceedings of the 11th Refinement Workshop, Refine@ICFEM 2006, Macao. Electronic Notes in Theoretical Computer Science, vol. 187, pp. 125–143. Elsevier (2006). https://doi.org/10.1016/j.entcs.2006.08.048
2. Best, E., Fernández, C.: Nonsequential Processes. Springer, Berlin (1988). https://doi.org/10.1007/978-3-642-73483-0
3. Busi, N., Gorrieri, R.: Structural non-interference in elementary and trace nets. Math. Struct. Comput. Sci. **19**(6), 1065–1090 (2009). https://doi.org/10.1017/S0960129509990120
4. Clarkson, M.R., Schneider, F.B.: Hyperproperties. J. Comput. Secur. **18**(6), 1157–1210 (2010). https://doi.org/10.3233/JCS-2009-0393
5. DeNicola, R., Hennessy, M.: Testing equivalences for processes. TCS **34**, 83–134 (1984). https://doi.org/10.1016/0304-3975(84)90113-0
6. Esparza, J., Nielsen, M.: Decidability issues for Petri nets - a survey. Bull. EATCS **52**, 244–262 (1994)
7. Finkbeiner, B.: Temporal hyperproperties. Bull. EATCS 123 (2017). http://eatcs.org/beatcs/index.php/beatcs/article/view/514
8. Goguen, J.A., Meseguer, J.: Security policies and security models. In: Proceedings of the IEEE Symposium on Security and Privacy, pp. 11–20. IEEE Computer Society (1982). https://doi.org/10.1109/SP.1982.10014
9. Goltz, U.: On representing CCS programs by finite petri nets. In: Chytil, M.P., Koubek, V., Janiga, L. (eds.) MFCS 1988. LNCS, vol. 324, pp. 339–350. Springer, Heidelberg (1988). https://doi.org/10.1007/BFb0017157
10. He, J., et al.: Provably correct systems. In: Langmaack, H., de Roever, W.-P., Vytopil, J. (eds.) FTRTFT 1994. LNCS, vol. 863, pp. 288–335. Springer, Heidelberg (1994). https://doi.org/10.1007/3-540-58468-4_171
11. Hennessy, M.: Algebraic Theory of Processes. MIT Press, Cambridge (1988)
12. Hoare, C.A.R., He, J.: Unifying Theories of Programming. Prentice Hall, Hoboken (1998)

13. Hoare, C.: A model for communicating sequential processes. In: McKeag, R., Mac-Naughten, A. (eds.) On the Construction of Programs, pp. 229–254. Cambridge University Press (1980)
14. Mayr, E.W.: An algorithm for the general Petri net reachability problem. SIAM J. Comput. **13**(3), 441–460 (1984). https://doi.org/10.1137/0213029
15. Mazurkiewicz, A.: Concurrent program schemes and their interpretations. DAIMI Rep. Ser. **6**(78) (1977). https://doi.org/10.7146/dpb.v6i78.7691
16. McCullough, D.: Noninterference and the composability of security properties. In: Proceedings of the IEEE Symposium on Security and Privacy, pp. 177–186. IEEE Computer Society (1988). https://doi.org/10.1109/SECPRI.1988.8110
17. Milner, R.: A Calculus of Communicating Systems, LNCS, vol. 92. Springer, Berlin (1980). https://doi.org/10.1007/3-540-10235-3, http://link.springer.com/10.1007/3-540-10235-3
18. Mukund, M., Thiagarajan, P.S.: A logical characterization of well branching event structures. Theor. Comput. Sci. **96**(1), 35–72 (1992). https://doi.org/10.1016/0304-3975(92)90181-E
19. Olderog, E.R.: Nets, Terms and Formulas: Three Views of Concurrent Processes and Their Relationship. Cambridge University Press, Cambridge (1991). https://doi.org/10.1017/CBO9780511526589
20. Penczek, W.: Branching time and partial order in temporal logics. In: Bolc, L., Szalas, A. (eds.) Time and Logics: A Computational Approach, pp. 203–257. UCL Press Ltd. (1995)
21. Petri, C.: Non-sequential processes. Technical Report. Internal Report GMD-ISF-77-5, Gesellschaft Math. Datenverarb., St. Augustin (1977)
22. Post, E.L.: A variant of a recursively unsolvable problem. Bull. Am. Math. Soc. **54**(4), 264–268 (1946). https://doi.org/10.1007/978-3-642-19835-9
23. Pratt, V.R.: The pomset model of parallel processes: unifying the temporal and the spatial. In: Brookes, S.D., Roscoe, A.W., Winskel, G. (eds.) CONCURRENCY 1984. LNCS, vol. 197, pp. 180–196. Springer, Heidelberg (1985). https://doi.org/10.1007/3-540-15670-4
24. Reisig, W.: Petri Nets - An Introduction. Springer, Heidelberg (1985). https://doi.org/10.1007/978-3-642-69968-9
25. Su, T., Fu, Z., Pu, G., He, J., Su, Z.: Combining symbolic execution and model checking for data flow testing. In: Bertolino, A., Canfora, G., Elbaum, S.G. (eds.) 37th IEEE/ACM International Conference on Software Engineering, ICSE 2015, vol. 1, pp. 654–665. IEEE Computer Society (2015). https://doi.org/10.1109/ICSE.2015.81
26. Su, T., et al.: A survey on data-flow testing. ACM Comput. Surv. **50**(1), 5:1–5:35 (2017). https://doi.org/10.1145/3020266
27. Winskel, G.: Event structures: Lecture notes for the Advanced Course on Petri Nets. Technical Report UCAM-CL-TR-95, University of Cambridge, Computer Laboratory (1986). https://www.cl.cam.ac.uk/techreports/UCAM-CL-TR-95.pdf

Chinese Colleagues

Characterizations of Parallel Real-Time Workloads

Xu Jiang[1(✉)], Jinghao Sun[2], and Wang Yi[1,3]

[1] Northeastern University, Shenyang, China
jiangxu@cse.neu.edu.cn
[2] Dalian University of Technology, Dalian, China
[3] Uppsala University, Uppsala, Sweden

Abstract. The work function, originally proposed by Bonifaci et al. [4], plays an important role in timing analysis of sporadic DAG parallel tasks. Later, Baruah [1] and Li et al. [10] provide different characterizations for Bonifaci's notion of work function. The consistency and correctness of these characterizations and Bonifaci's original result is so far a pending question. In this paper, we revisit the notion of work function based analysis techniques to answer the above pending question. We show that Baruah's characterization is equivalent to Bonifaci's original formulation, while Li's characterization is strictly stronger.

1 Introduction

Multi-cores are becoming mainstream platforms for real-time embedded systems to meet the rapidly increasing performance requirements and low power consumption [12,20,23]. To fully utilize the capacity of multi-cores, not only inter-task parallelism, but also intra-task parallelism need to be explored in the design and analysis of modern real-time systems, where individual tasks are parallel programs and can potentially utilize more than one core at the same time during their executions. This enables tasks with higher execution demands and tighter deadlines, such as those used in autonomous vehicles [8], video surveillance, computer vision, radar tracking and real-time hybrid testing [6]. Nowadays parallel programming languages (and software), such as Cilk family [3], OpenMP [14] and Intel's Thread Building Blocks [17], commonly support parallel task sets with intra-task parallelism (in addition to inter-task parallelism).

The origins of this work can be traced back to 1986 when Wang, one of the authors, first met Jifeng at the Marktoberdorf Summer School on Theoretical Computer Science. The encounter marked the beginning of their professional collaboration and personal friendship, which has lasted for nearly four decades. During the school, Wang, a Ph.D. student at the time, got to know Jifeng's work with Antony Hoare of algebraic theory on programming, which has deeply influenced on Wang's subsequent research in process algebras, formal verification, and real-time computing. As one of the leading teams in the country in the field of embedded and real-time systems, the authors wish to take this opportunity to thank Jifeng for his unwavering support, inspiration, and friendship. Happy Birthday, Jifeng!.

© The Author(s), under exclusive license to Springer Nature Switzerland AG 2023
J. P. Bowen et al. (Eds.): *Theories of Programming and Formal Methods*, LNCS 14080, pp. 235–256, 2023.
https://doi.org/10.1007/978-3-031-40436-8_9

A common way to model parallel real-time software systems is using recurrent directed acyclic graph (DAG) models. This motivates many recent work in the area of real-time scheduling for recurrent DAG task models [1,2,4,5,7,9–11,13, 15,16,18,19,21]. Real-time scheduling algorithms for DAG tasks can be classified into three paradigms: 1) decomposition-based scheduling [7,15,16,18]; 2) global scheduling (without decomposition) [1,4,9,13,21]; and 3) federated scheduling [2,10], which is the trade-off between decomposition-based scheduling and global scheduling. In this paper, we focus on the global EDF scheduling algorithm, which gives the maximum flexibility, e.g., it does not decompose DAG tasks, nor restrict a DAG task to dedicated cores. It schedules vertices in the DAG until either all cores are busy or no more vertices are ready.

Although the global EDF algorithm keeps the best flexibility, its schedulability analysis is a challenging problem. In the literature, a large part of the theoretical work on schedulability analysis of recurrent DAG tasks under global EDF uses a kernel notation, called the *work function*. Intuitively, for any given recurrent DAG task set $\mathcal{T}$, the positive integer t and α, and assuming that $\mathcal{T}$ is executed on infinite number of α-speed cores, the work function $work(\mathcal{T}, t, \alpha)$ defines the maximum workload released from $\mathcal{T}$ that must be executed during an interval of duration equal to t. (See in Sect. 4 for more details).

By applying the work-function-based methodology, researchers mainly derive the following three classical theoretical results.

– Bonifaci et al. [4] first propose the notation of the work function, which is originally used to derive the *speedup bound* of the DAG tasks. The speedup bound is a comparative metric with respect to some other (optimal) scheduler. A scheduling algorithm A provides a speedup bound of α if it can successfully schedule any task set $\mathcal{T}$ on m cores of speed α as long as the compared scheduler can schedule $\mathcal{T}$ on m cores of speed 1. The speedup bound shows how close the performance of a scheduler is to the compared one, but it cannot be directly used as a schedulability test.
– Li et al. [10] reformulate Bonifaci's main result, and derive a *capacity augmentation bound* of the DAG tasks. The capacity augmentation bound is an absolute metric that can be directly used for schedulability test. A scheduling algorithm A has a capacity augmentation bound of α if it can schedule any task set $\mathcal{T}$ (on m cores of speed 1) satisfying the following two conditions:
  • the total utilization of $\mathcal{T}$ is at most m/α, and
  • the worst-case critical path length of each task is at most $1/\alpha$ of its deadline.

Capacity augmentation bounds are stronger than speedup bounds in the sense that if a scheduler has a capacity augmentation bound of α, it is also guaranteed to have a resource augmentation bound of α. Based on the capacity augmentation bound, Li et al. [10] propose a simple linear-time schedulability test for scheduling recurrent DAG tasks under global EDF. Most importantly, Li et al. [10] prove that their capacity augmentation bound is the tightest one for the DAG task under global EDF algorithm.

– Baruah [1] also reformulates Bonifaci's main result, and proposes a pseudo-polynomial time schedulability analysis method for the DAG tasks under global EDF algorithm.

Our key observation is that although Li et al. [10] and Baruah [1] both state that they reformulate the same theorem of [4], their reformulations are totally different. Only one of them should be equivalent to the original theorem of [4]. In this paper, we devote to clarify which reformulation is the equivalent theorem to the original one of [4]. Through a deep insight into Bonifaci's main theorem, we find that Baruah's theorem is an equivalent state of Bonifaci's theorem in [4], and Li's theorem overwhelms Bonifaci's theorem, indicating that Li's theorem cannot be directly derived from Bonifaci's theorem. The correctness of Li's work needs a careful analysis. To this end, we reveal interesting properties of the work function, and try to provide a rigorous proof for Li's theorem. We extend Bonifaci's techniques to discuss the correctness of Li's theorem, but we only prove that Li's theorem is conditionally correct.

The rest of this paper is organized as follows. Section 2 discusses related work. In Sect. 3 we formally define the sporadic DAG task model and the global EDF algorithm. In Sect. 4 we revisit the notation of work function. In Sect. 5 we give a brief overview of the main theorem in [4], and revisit the existing reformulations of Bonifaci's theorem, and moreover, we discuss whether they are equivalent to the main theorem in [4]. The last section gives the conclusion.

2 Related Work

Bonifaci et al. [4] first introduce the notation of work function, and by using the work function based methodology, they propose the speedup bounds $2 - \frac{1}{m}$ and $3 - \frac{1}{m}$ for the DAG tasks under global EDF and global DM algorithms respectively. Baruah [1] reformulates the main theorem of [4], and improves the global schedulability analysis of [4]. Li et al. [9] analyze the global schedulability of DAG tasks via a methodology that is different from Bonifaci's work function method, and they propose the capacity augmentation bound of $4 - \frac{1}{m}$ for the implicit deadline DAG tasks under global EDF. Moreover, Li et al. [9] also prove that the capacity augmentation bound for the implicit deadline DAG tasks under global EDF is at least $\frac{3+\sqrt{5}}{2} \approx 2.618$. Sun et al. [21] propose the first constant capacity augmentation bound for the constraint deadline DAG tasks under global EDF, and for the implicit deadline DAG tasks, they exhibit the capacity augmentation bound of $3.82 - \frac{1}{m}$, which is better than the one proposed in [9]. The work function based methodology significantly promotes the theoretical work on capacity augmentation bound. Li et al. [10] reformulate the main theorem of [4], and propose the tightest capacity augmentation bound of DAG tasks under global EDF, i.e., they prove that the upper bound of the capacity augmentation bound achieves $\frac{2+\sqrt{5}}{2}$.

We observe that Li et al. [10] and Baruach [1] reformulate the same theorem of [4], and however, their reformulations are totally different. There must be one of them is not equivalent to the original theorem of [4]. If Li's theorem is not equivalent to Bonifaci's theorem, and, even worse, their theorem is not correct, then the capacity augmentation bound of $3.82 - \frac{1}{m}$ proposed by Sun et al. [21] should be the best known capacity augmentation bound for DAG tasks under global EDF.

3   System Model

This section presents a sporadic DAG task model for recurrent parallel tasks, and formally defines the runtime model by considering the global EDF scheduling algorithm.

3.1   Task Model

This section presents a model for recurrent DAG tasks. We consider a set of n independent sporadic DAG tasks: $\mathcal{T} = \{\tau_1, \tau_2, \cdots, \tau_n\}$. Each task τ_i is specified as a 3-tuple (G_i, D_i, T_i), where G_i is a directed acyclic graph (DAG), and D_i and T_i are positive integers, called the *deadline* and the *period* respectively.

The task τ_i repeatedly releases dag-jobs, and each dag-job of τ_i has a DAG-structure specified as $G_i = (V_i, E_i)$, where V_i is a set of vertices, and E_i is a set of directed edges between these vertices. Each vertex $v_i^x \in V_i$ denotes a sequential operation, and is characterized by a worst-case execution time (WCET) $c(v_i^x)$. The edges represent dependencies between the vertices: if $(v_i^x, v_i^y) \in E_i$ then vertex v_i^x must complete execution before vertex v_i^y can begin execution. A vertex v_i^x is the *predecessor* of the vertex v_i^y if there is an edge from v_i^x to (a predecessor of) v_i^y, and in this case, the vertex v_i^y is called the *successor* of v_i^x. A vertex v_i^x is called the *source* vertex of G_i if it has no predecessor. A vertex v_i^x is called the *sink* vertex of G_i if it has no successor. Multiple source vertices and sink vertices are allowed in the DAG G_i, and the DAG G_i are not required to be fully connected. Figure 1 shows two example tasks τ_1 and τ_2, each of which consists of 7 vertices in the DAG structure.

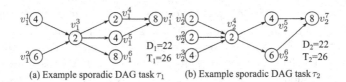

(a) Example sporadic DAG task τ_1 (b) Example sporadic DAG task τ_2

Fig. 1. An example task set consisting of two DAG tasks. Vertices are labeled with WECTs.

A release of a dag-job of τ_i at time-instant t means that all $|V_i|$ vertices $v_i^x \in V_i$ are released at time-instant t. The *period* T_i denotes the minimum duration of time that must elapse between the release of successive dag-jobs of

τ_i. Once a dag-job of τ_i is released at time-instant t, then all $|V_i|$ vertices that were released at time-instant t must complete execution by time-instant $t + D_i$. Recall that D_i is the *deadline* of τ_i.

We now introduce some useful notations related to a DAG task.

– **Volume.** The sum of the worst-case execution time of all vertices in G_i (the graph structure of τ_i's dag-job) is the volume vol_i of τ_i, i.e.,

$$vol_i = \sum_{v_i^x \in V_i} c(v_i^x) \tag{1}$$

For example, the volume of τ_1 in Fig. 1 is $vol_1 = 34$.

– **Length.** The length of the longest path in G_i (the graph structure of τ_i's dag-job) is the length len_i of τ_i, i.e.,

$$len_i = \max_{\pi \in G_i} \sum_{v_i^x \in \pi} c(v_i^x) \tag{2}$$

where π is the path of G_i. For example, the length of τ_1 is $len_1 = 6+2+4+8 = 20$.

– **Utilization.** For any task τ_i, we define its utilization u_i as follows.

$$u_i = \frac{vol_i}{T_i} \tag{3}$$

For example, the task τ_1 in Fig. 1 has an utilization as $u_1 = \frac{17}{13}$. Moreover, the total utilization of the task system $\mathcal{T}$ is denoted as follows.

$$U_{\Sigma} = \sum_{\tau_i \in \mathcal{T}} u_i \tag{4}$$

In the literatures, these parameters above are used in schedulability analysis, e.g., capacity augmentation bounds, see in Sect. 3.3 for more details.

3.2 Global EDF Algorithm

We consider a platform $\mathcal{P}$ that consists of m identical processing cores $p_1, p_2, \cdots, p_m$, and each of them has a speed $\alpha \geq 1$. We schedule the task set $\mathcal{T}$ on m cores of $\mathcal{P}$. More specifically, at any time instant t, if a core is executing a vertex of some task, then it is called the *busy* core, and otherwise, it is called the idle core. A vertex is *ready* for execution if all its predecessors are finished. A schedule is to assign ready vertices to idle cores until all the released vertices are finished.

In this paper, we schedule tasks by using global EDF (GEDF) algorithm. Under GEDF, at each time instant the scheduler selects the highest-priority ready vertices (at most m) for execution. Vertices of the same task share the same priority (ties are broken arbitrarily) and a vertex of a task with an earlier absolute deadline has a higher priority than a vertex of a task with a later absolute deadline. In particular, vertex-level preemption and migration are both permitted in GEDF. Without loss of generality, we assume the scheduling of the task set $\mathcal{T}$ starts at time 0 (i.e., the first dag-job of the task set is released at time 0).

3.3   Schedulability

A task set $\mathcal{T}$ is schedulable on m α-speed cores if a valid schedule exits on m α-speed cores such that all dag-jobs released by $\mathcal{T}$ meet their deadlines. In particular, when scheduled on m unit-speed cores, a schedulable task set must satisfy the following conditions.

Theorem 1 (Necessary Conditions for schedulability [9]). *A task set $\mathcal{T}$ is not schedulable (by any scheduler on m unit-speed cores) unless the following conditions hold.*

- *The length of each task τ_i is less than its deadline D_i, i.e.,*

$$len_i \leq D_i, \quad \forall \tau_i \in \mathcal{T} \tag{5}$$

- *The total utilization U_Σ is smaller than the number of cores, i.e.,*

$$\sum_{\tau_i \in \mathcal{T}} u_i \leq m \tag{6}$$

Clearly, if (5) is violated for some task, then its deadline is doomed to be violated in the worst case, even if it is executed exclusively on sufficiently many cores. If (6) is violated, then in the long term the worst-case workload of the system exceeds the processing capacity provided by the platform, and thus the backlog will increase infinitely which leads to deadline misses. We assume that *all task sets discussed in the reminder of this paper satisfy (5) and (6).*

Given a scheduling algorithm A, a task set $\mathcal{T}$ is A-schedulable on m α-speed cores if A meets all deadlines when scheduling any collection of dag-jobs that may be generated by the task set $\mathcal{T}$ on m α-speed cores. To verify whether a task set is A-schedulable is highly intractable (e.g., NP-hard in the strong sense [22]) even when there is a single DAG task. In the following we introduce two approximation metrics for A-schedulability analysis.

Definition 1 (Speedup Bound). *A scheduling algorithm A has a speedup bound α if any task set $\mathcal{T}$ that is schedulable on m unit-speed cores is A-schedulable on m α-speed cores.*

From Definition 1, we know that for any scheduling algorithm A with a speedup bound α, if a task set $\mathcal{T}$ is not A-schedulable on m α-speed cores, then all scheduling algorithms fail to schedule $\mathcal{T}$ on m unit-speed cores. Moreover, there are some task sets $\mathcal{T}$ such that they are not schedulable on m unit-speed cores, but they are A-schedulable on m α-speed cores. In this sense, the speedup bound α is a metric for approximately quantifying the quality of scheduling algorithms.

Definition 2 (Capacity Augmentation Bound). *A scheduling algorithm A has a capacity augmentation bound α if it can always schedule DAG task set $\mathcal{T}$ on m α-speed cores as long as $\mathcal{T}$ satisfies the above necessary conditions in (5) and (6).*

From Definition 2, for any scheduling algorithm A that has a capacity augmentation bound α, we can derive the sufficient conditions for A-schedulability analysis, i.e., a task set T is A-schedulable on m unit-speed cores if the following conditions both hold.

$$len_i \leq \frac{D_i}{\alpha}, \quad \forall \tau_i \in T$$
$$\sum_{\tau_i \in T} u_i \leq \frac{m}{\alpha}$$

A scheduling algorithm with a smaller speedup bound (as well as a smaller capacity augmentation bound) α is preferable. In particular, when the capacity augmentation bound $\alpha = 1$, the scheduling algorithm is optimal.

In the literature, researchers use the notation of the *work function* to derive the speedup bound and the capacity augmentation bound. In the next section, we introduce such an important notation.

4 Work Function

Bonifaci et al. [4] first introduce the notation of the *work function* and use it to originally characterize the amount of workload that could be generated by a sporadic DAG task when scheduled on unit-speed cores. Li et al. [10] and Baruah [1] further extend the notation of the work function to the scenarios with cores of speed α (larger than 1). In this section, we describe the work function defined in [1,10], which is in a manner consisting with the terminology introduced in Sect. 3.

We first define an ideal scheduling algorithm A_∞ as follows.

Definition 3 (Ideal Scheduling Algorithm A_∞). *The algorithm A_∞ schedules a task set T on infinite number of cores, and it allocates a core to each vertex v_i^x released by the tasks in T at the time-instant the vertex v_i^x is ready to execute, and executes the vertex v_i^x upon the allocated core until v_i^x completes its execution.*

We denote by J the collection of dag-jobs that may be released by the tasks in T, written as $J \vdash T$, and we say J is *feasible* if there is a valid schedule of J such that all dag-jobs of J meet their deadlines. We let $S_\infty(J, \alpha)$ be the schedule of J under the ideal algorithm A_∞ on the cores of speed α. We observe that the schedule $S_\infty(J, \alpha)$ executes each vertex as soon as it becomes ready to execute, thereby leaving as little work to be done later as possible.

Figure 2 shows the schedule of task set in Fig. 1 under A_∞ on unit-speed cores, where tasks τ_1 and τ_2 both successively release their dag-jobs with the period $T_1 = T_2 = 26$.

For any task τ_i of T, we denote by J_i the collection of the dag-jobs that may be released by τ_i, written as $J_i \vdash \tau_i$, and which is also contained in the schedule $S_\infty(J, \alpha)$, i.e., $J_i \subseteq J$. For any interval I, we denote by $work(J_i, I, \alpha)$ the amount

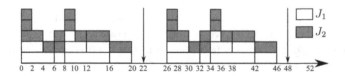

Fig. 2. An example schedule of task set in Fig. 1 under A_∞.

of execution occurring within the interval I in the schedule $S_\infty(J, \alpha)$ of dag-jobs in J_i *with deadlines that fall within* I. For example, in Fig. 2, $work(J_1, I, 1) = 4$ for the interval $I = [16, 22]$.

For any positive integer t, let $work(J_i, t, \alpha)$ be the maximum value that $work(J_i, I, \alpha)$ can take, over any interval I of duration equal to t, i.e.,

$$work(J_i, t, \alpha) = \max_{|I|=t} work(J_i, I, \alpha), \quad \forall \tau_i \in \mathcal{T} \tag{7}$$

Finally, we define the *work function* $work(\tau_i, t, \alpha)$ of the task τ_i as the maximum value of $work(J_i, t, \alpha)$, over all collection J_i of dag-jobs that may be released by the sporadic DAG task τ_i, i.e.,

$$work(\tau_i, t, \alpha) = \max_{J_i \vdash \tau_i} work(J_i, t, \alpha), \quad \forall \tau_i \in \mathcal{T} \tag{8}$$

We further extend the notation of the work function from individual tasks to task sets as follows. For any task set $\mathcal{T}$, the work function $work(\mathcal{T}, t, \alpha)$ of $\mathcal{T}$ is defined as the summation of the work functions of all tasks τ_i of $\mathcal{T}$, i.e.,

$$work(\mathcal{T}, t, \alpha) = \sum_{\tau_i \in \mathcal{T}} work(\tau_i, t, \alpha) \tag{9}$$

Figure 3 exhibits the work functions of schedule in Fig. 2.

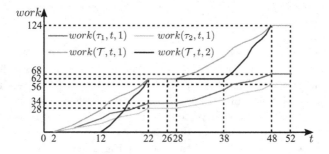

Fig. 3. The work functions of the schedule in Fig. 2.

In the following, we reveal some insights into the work function, which play the important role to support our observations in Sect. 5.1.

4.1   Monotonicity of the Work Function

We discuss whether the work function is a monotonic function with the time t and the speed α.

Lemma 1. *For any task τ_i, any speed $\alpha \geq 1$ and any time $t_1, t_2 \geq 0$, the following inequality holds.*

$$work(\tau_i, t_1, \alpha) \leq work(\tau_i, t_2, \alpha), \qquad if \ t_1 < t_2 \tag{10}$$

Proof. Suppose not, and we have

$$work(\tau_i, t_1, \alpha) > work(\tau_i, t_2, \alpha) \tag{11}$$

We let J_i be a collection of dag-jobs released by τ_i, and let $I_1 = [a, b]$ be an interval of duration equal to t_1, where a is the left boundary of I_1 and b is the right boundary of I_1. Without loss of generality, we assume that

$$work(\tau_i, t_1, \alpha) = work(J_i, I_1, \alpha) \tag{12}$$

We enlarge the interval I_1 into a larger interval I_2 by letting the left boundary of I_2 be $a - \Delta$ (where $\Delta = t_2 - t_1 > 0$), i.e., $I_2 = [a - \Delta, b]$. Since $I_1 \subset I_2$ and the larger interval I_2 may involve more work of J_i that must be done during this interval, we know that

$$work(J_i, I_1, \alpha) \leq work(J_i, I_2, \alpha) \tag{13}$$

By combining (11), (12) and (13), we have

$$work(J_i, I_2, \alpha) > work(\tau_i, t_2, \alpha)$$

and by (7) and (8), we know that $work(J_i, I_2, \alpha) \leq work(\tau_i, t_2, \alpha)$. This leads to a contradiction. □

From Lemma 1, it is easy to derive the following corollary.

Corollary 1. *For any task set $\mathcal{T}$, any speed $\alpha \geq 1$ and any time $t_1, t_2 > 0$, the following inequality holds.*

$$work(\mathcal{T}, t_1, \alpha) \leq work(\mathcal{T}, t_2, \alpha), \quad if \ t_1 < t_2 \tag{14}$$

Proof. It is directly proved by (9) and according to Lemma 1. □

Corollary 1 shows that the work function $work(\mathcal{T}, t, \alpha)$ is a non-decreasing function with time t. For example, the work functions in Fig. 3 all keep the non-decreasing properties.

Lemma 2. *For any task τ_i, any time $t \geq 0$ and any speeds $\alpha_1, \alpha_2 \geq 1$, the following inequality holds.*

$$work(\tau_i, t, \alpha_1) \geq work(\tau_i, t, \alpha_2), \qquad if \ \alpha_1 < \alpha_2 \tag{15}$$

Proof. For any collection J_i of the dag-jobs released by τ_i, and for any interval $I = [a, b]$ of duration equal to t, where a is the left boundary of I, we know that the ideal algorithm A_∞ on the cores of speed α_2 executes more work of J_i during the interval $[0, a]$, and therefore it leaves less work of J_i that to be done during I. Consequently, we have,

$$work(J_i, I, \alpha_1) \geq work(J_i, I, \alpha_2), \quad \forall J_i \vdash \tau_i, \ \alpha_1 < \alpha_2 \tag{16}$$

and by (7), we have

$$work(J_i, t, \alpha_1) \geq work(J_i, I, \alpha_2), \quad \forall J_i \vdash \tau_i, \ \alpha_1 < \alpha_2$$

and by (8), we have

$$work(\tau_i, t, \alpha_1) \geq work(\tau_i, t, \alpha_2)$$

This completes the proof.   □

Lemma 2 shows that the work function $work(\tau_i, t, \alpha)$ is a decreasing function of speed α. In the following corollary, we extend Lemma 2 from an individual task to the task set.

Corollary 2. *For any task set* T, *any time* $t \geq 0$ *and any speeds* $\alpha_1, \alpha_2 \geq 1$, *the following inequality holds.*

$$work(T, t, \alpha_1) \geq work(T, t, \alpha_2), \quad if \ \alpha_1 < \alpha_2 \tag{17}$$

Proof. It is directly proved by (9) and according to Lemma 2.   □

For example, in Fig. 3, the curve of work function $work(T, t, 2)$ is always below the curve of work function $work(T, t, 1)$.

4.2   Critical Points of the Work Function

In this section, we introduce some critical points of the work function $work(T, t, \alpha)$. We first define two types of *critical time points* of the work function as follows.

Definition 4 (Left Critical Time Point). *The left critical time point of the work function* $work(T, t, \alpha)$ *is the time-instant* t^* *that satisfies the following conditions.*

- $\forall t < t^*$, $work(T, t, \alpha) < work(T, t^*, \alpha)$, *and*
- $\forall \epsilon > 0$, $work(T, t^*, \alpha) = work(T, t^* + \epsilon, \alpha)$.

For example, in Fig. 3, $t = 22$ and $t = 48$ are both left critical time points of $work(T, t, 1)$.

Definition 5 (Right Critical Time Point). *The right critical time point of the work function* $work(T, t, \alpha)$ *is the time-instant* t^+ *that satisfies the following conditions.*

- $\forall t > t^+$, $work(\mathcal{T}, t, \alpha) > work(\mathcal{T}, t^+, \alpha)$, and
- $\forall \epsilon > 0$, $work(\mathcal{T}, t^+, \alpha) = work(\mathcal{T}, t^+ - \epsilon, \alpha)$.

For example, in Fig. 3, $t = 28$ is the right critical time point of $work(\mathcal{T}, t, 1)$, and $t = 38$ is the right critical point of $work(\mathcal{T}, t, 2)$.

Definition 6 (Flat Interval). *For any successive critical time points t^* and t^+, where t^* is the left critical time point, and t^+ is the right critical time point, the interval $F = [t^*, t^+]$ is called the flat interval.*

Clearly, for any flat interval $I = [t^*, t^+]$, and for any time-instant $t \in I$, we know that

$$work(\mathcal{T}, t^*, \alpha) = work(\mathcal{T}, t, \alpha) = work(\mathcal{T}, t^+, \alpha) \qquad (18)$$

For example, in Fig. 3, the interval $I = [22, 38]$ is the flat interval of $work(\mathcal{T}, t, 2)$.

Definition 7 (Slope Interval). *For any successive critical time points t^+ and t^*, where t^+ is the right critical time point, and t^* is the left critical time point, the interval $S = [t^+, t^*]$ is called the slope interval.*

For example, in Fig. 3, the interval $S = [38, 48]$ is the slope interval of $work(\mathcal{T}, t, 2)$.

Definition 8 (Non-Convex Slope Interval). *A slope interval S of the work function $work(\mathcal{T}, t, \alpha)$ is non-convex if the following inequality holds for any $t_1, t_2 \in S$, and any $\lambda \in (0, 1)$,*

$$\lambda work(\mathcal{T}, t_1, \alpha) + (1 - \lambda) work(\mathcal{T}, t_2, \alpha) \geq work(\mathcal{T}, \lambda t_1 + (1 - \lambda) t_2, \alpha).$$

Moreover, a work function is non-convex if it contains no convex slope interval.

Definition 9 (Encounter Point). *The encounter point of the work function $work(\mathcal{T}, t, \alpha)$ is the time point t^* such that for any speeds $\alpha_1, \alpha_2 \geq 1$,*

$$work(\mathcal{T}, t^*, \alpha_1) = work(\mathcal{T}, t^*, \alpha_2) \qquad (19)$$

For example, $t^* = 22$ and $t^* = 48$ are both the encounter points of $work(\mathcal{T}, t, \alpha)$.

In the following, we show how to identify an encounter point. Before going into details, we first give the following lemma.

Lemma 3. *For any time $t \geq 0$, if there is a collection J_i of dag-jobs released by the task τ_i and an interval $I = [a, b]$ of duration equal to t such that*

$$work(\tau_i, t, \alpha) = work(J_i, I, \alpha),$$

then the right boundary b of I must equal to $r_i + D_i$, where r_i is the release time of a dag-job of J_i.

Proof. Suppose not. There is an interval $I' = [a + \delta, b + \delta]$ of duration equal to t (where $\delta < T_i$), such that $work(J_i, I', \alpha) > work(J_i, I, \alpha)$. As illustrated in Fig. 4, although there may be a dag-job of τ_i released between the interval $[b, b+\delta]$, the work function $work(J_i, I', \alpha)$ does not involve the workload of such dag-job since its deadline does not fall in the interval I'. Therefore, $work(J_i, I', t)$ will not bring more workload than $work(J_i, I, t)$. More precisely, let $W[a, a+\delta]$ be the work done by A_∞ within the interval $[a, a+\delta]$, and we know that $W[a, a+\delta] \geq 0$. Moreover, since $work(J_i, I', \alpha) = work(J_i, I, \alpha) - W[a, a + \delta]$ (See in Fig. 4), we have: $work(J_i, I', \alpha) \leq work(J_i, I, \alpha)$. This contradicts the assumption. □

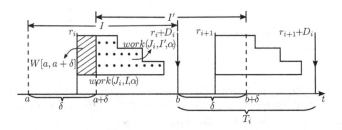

Fig. 4. Illustration for the proof of Lemma 3.

Lemma 4 reveals a sufficient condition for the encounter points of the work function $work(\tau_i, t, \alpha)$.

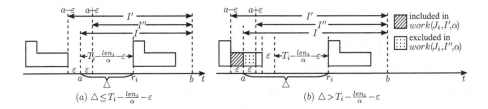

Fig. 5. Illustration for the proof of Lemma 5.

Lemma 4. *For any task τ_i, any speed $\alpha \geq 1$ and any time $t = kT_i + D_i$, $work(\tau_i, t, \alpha) = (k + 1)vol_i$.*

Proof. There must exist a collection J_i of dag-jobs released by the task τ_i and an interval $I = [a, b]$ of the duration equal to t, such that $work(J_i, I, \alpha) = work(\tau_i, t, \alpha)$. Since the length of the interval I equals to $KT_i + D_i$ and according to Lemma 3, the left boundary a of I equals to the release time r_i of a dag-job of J_i, and the right boundary b of I equals to the deadline $r_i + kT_i + D_i$ of the other dag-job of J_i. It indicates that $work(J_i, I, \alpha) = (k + 1)vol_i$, and therefore, $work(\tau_i, t, \alpha) = (k + 1)vol_i$. □

From Lemma 4, we directly derive the following corollary.

Corollary 3. *The time-instant t^* is an encounter point of the work function $work(\mathcal{T}, t, \alpha)$ for any $\alpha \geq 1$, if it satisfies $T_i | (t^* - D_i)$, $\forall \tau_i \in \mathcal{T}$.*

Proof. This is proved by Lemma 4 and according to Definition 9.

Lemma 5. *For any task τ_i, any speed $\alpha > 1$, and any time $t = kT_i + D_i + \Delta$ (where $\Delta < D_i$), the following conditions contradict with each other.*

$$work(\tau_i, t, \alpha) = work(\tau_i, t + \epsilon, \alpha), \quad \forall \epsilon > 0 \tag{20}$$
$$work(\tau_i, t, \alpha) > work(\tau_i, t - \epsilon, \alpha), \quad \forall \epsilon > 0 \tag{21}$$

Proof. There must exist a collection J_i of dag-jobs released by the task τ_i and an interval $I = [a, b]$ of duration equal to t such that $work(\tau_i, t, \alpha) = work(J_i, I, \alpha)$. According to Lemma 3, the right boundary b of I equals to $r_i + kT_i + D_i$, and the left boundary a of I equals to $r_i - \Delta$, where r_i is the release time of a dag-job of J_i, as illustrated in Fig. 5. There are two possible cases.

- If $\Delta \leq T_i - \frac{len_i}{\alpha} - \epsilon$ (See in Fig. 5(a)), we know that the work done by A_∞ within the interval $[a - \epsilon, a]$ equals to 0. Moreover, since $\Delta > 0$, we know that the work done by A_∞ within the interval $[a, a + \epsilon]$ equals to 0. Therefore, $work(J_i, I, \alpha) = work(J_i, I', \alpha)$ and $work(J_i, I, \alpha) = work(J_i, I'', \alpha)$, where $I' = [a - \epsilon, b]$ is the interval of duration equal to $t + \epsilon$, and $I'' = [a + \epsilon, b]$ is the interval of duration equal to $t - \epsilon$. According to Lemma 3, we have $work(\tau_i, t + \epsilon, \alpha) = work(\tau_i, t, \alpha)$ and $work(\tau_i, t - \epsilon, \alpha) = work(\tau_i, t, \alpha)$.
- If $\Delta > T_i - \frac{len_i}{\alpha} - \epsilon$ (See in Fig. 5(b)), we know that the work done by A_∞ within the interval $[a - \epsilon, a]$ must be larger than 0. Moreover, since $\Delta < D_i$, we know that the work done by A_∞ within the interval $[a, a + \epsilon]$ must be larger than 0. Therefore, $work(J_i, I, \alpha) < work(J_i, I', \alpha)$ and $work(J_i, I, \alpha) > work(J_i, I'', \alpha)$, where $I' = [a - \epsilon, b]$ is the interval of duration equal to $t + \epsilon$, and $I'' = [a + \epsilon, b]$ is the interval of duration equal to $t - \epsilon$. According to Lemma 3, we have $work(\tau_i, t + \epsilon, \alpha) > work(\tau_i, t, \alpha)$ and $work(\tau_i, t - \epsilon, \alpha) < work(\tau_i, t, \alpha)$.

In sum, we know that the conditions of Lemma 5 contradict with each other.

The following lemma ties the encounter point and the critical time point together, which plays a very important role to derive the main result in Sect. 5.1.

Lemma 6. *Any left critical time point t^* of the work function $work(\mathcal{T}, t, \alpha)$ must be an encounter point of $work(\mathcal{T}, t, \alpha)$.*

Proof. According to Corollary 3, for some time t^*, if $\forall \tau_i \in \mathcal{T}, T_i | (t^* - D_i)$, then t^* is an encounter point. Therefore, it is sufficient to prove this lemma by showing that the left critical time point t^* satisfies $T_i | (t^* - D_i)$, $\forall \tau_i \in \mathcal{T}$.

Suppose that there is a task τ_i such that $t^* = kT_i + D_i + \Delta$ with a positive integer $\Delta < D_i$, we aim to show that t^* is not a left critical time point. According to Lemma 5, we know that for any $\epsilon > 0$, there are two possible cases.

- If $work(\tau_i, t, \alpha) = work(\tau_i, t + \epsilon, \alpha)$ and $work(\tau_i, t, \alpha) \leq work(\tau_i, t - \epsilon, \alpha)$, then we know that $work(\mathcal{T}, t, \alpha) = work(\mathcal{T}, t + \epsilon, \alpha)$, and $work(\mathcal{T}, t, \alpha) \leq work(\mathcal{T}, t - \epsilon, \alpha)$, indicating that the first condition of Definition 4 does not hold.
- If $work(\tau_i, t, \alpha) \neq work(\tau_i, t + \epsilon, \alpha)$ and $work(\tau_i, t, \alpha) > work(\tau_i, t - \epsilon, \alpha)$, then we know that $work(\mathcal{T}, t, \alpha) \neq work(\mathcal{T}, t + \epsilon, \alpha)$, and $work(\mathcal{T}, t, \alpha) > work(\mathcal{T}, t - \epsilon, \alpha)$, indicating that the second condition of Definition 4 does not hold.

In sum, we know that t^* is not a left critical time point. □

5   A Review of the Main Result of [4]

Bonifaci et al. [4] first use the work function to derive a sufficient condition for the schedulability test. We now describe their main result in a manner consistent with the terminology introduced in above sections.

Theorem 2 (Lem. 3 of [4]). *Consider a collection J of dag-jobs released by the tasks in $\mathcal{T}$, and let $\alpha \geq 1$. Then at least one of the following holds:*

i all dag-jobs in J are completed within their deadline under global EDF on m cores of speed α, or
ii J is not feasible under A_∞ on unit-speed cores, or
iii there is an interval I such that any feasible schedule for J must finish more than $(\alpha m - m + 1)|I|$ units of work within I.

Proof Sketch of Theorem 2

It is sufficient to prove this theorem by assuming that both (i) and (ii) do not hold, and showing that (iii) satisfies. More specifically, J can be successfully scheduled by A_∞ on unit-speed cores, but fails to be scheduled by global EDF on m cores of speed α. In the following, the key point is to construct an interval I such that any feasible schedule of J must execute more than $(\alpha m - m + 1)|I|$ units of work within I.

Among all feasible schedule of J, we focus on the schedule $S_\infty(J, 1)$ (Recall that $S_\infty(J, 1)$ is obtained by scheduling J under A_∞ on unit-speed cores, and according to the assumption that A_∞ successfully schedules J, $S_\infty(J, 1)$ is feasible). For any feasible schedule, Bonifaci et al. [4] give the following observation.

Observation 1 *For any feasible schedule $S_f(J, 1)$ under scheduling algorithm A_f on m unit-speed cores, and for any interval I, the work of $S_f(J, 1)$ that must be done (by A_f) within I is larger than the work of $S_\infty(J, 1)$ that must be done (by A_∞) within I.*

Proof For any interval $I = [a, b]$, we denote by I' the interval before I, i.e., $I' = [0, a)$. We know that the following statement holds.

(∗) The work done by A_f (on m unit-speed cores) within I' is no more than the work done by A_∞ (on infinite number of unit-speed cores) within I'.

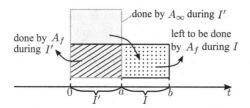

Fig. 6. Illustration for the proof of Observation 1.

By (*), we know that A_f leaves more work that must be done within I than the one that must be done by A_∞ within I, as illustrated in Fig. 6. This completes the proof.

Here we should note that the above observation cannot be extended to the feasible schedule $S_f(J, \alpha)$ such that J is scheduled by A_f on α-speed cores. This is because the key statement (*) cannot be satisfied on α-speed cores as shown in Example 1.

Example 1. Figure 7(a) gives a task τ_1, and we schedule it by A_∞ on unit-speed cores as shown in Fig. 7(b), and schedule it by the global EDF on 2 cores of speed 4 as shown in Fig. 7(c). Clearly, during the interval $[0, 2]$, all workload of a dag-job released by τ_1 is finished by A_f on 2 cores of speed 4, but only half of them is done by A_∞ on unit-speed cores, i.e., the workload done by A_∞ (on unit-speed cores) is less than the workload done by the global EDF (on 2 cores of speed 4).

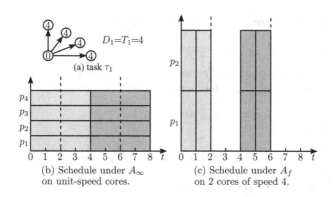

Fig. 7. The task τ_1 and its schedules discussed in Example 1.

Recall that $work(J, I, 1)$ denotes the work of J that must be done by A_∞ (on infinite number of unit-speed cores) within I, and denote by $work_f(J, I, 1)$

the work of J that must be done by A_f (on m unit-speed cores) within I, and according to Observation 1, we know that for any interval I,

$$work(J, I, 1) \leq work_f(J, I, 1) \tag{22}$$

Bonifaci et al. [4] construct an interval I^*, and prove that the work (denoted as $W_{edf}(J, I^*, \alpha)$) done by EDF on m α-speed cores within I^* is smaller than the work of J that must be done by A_∞ (on infinite number of unit-speed cores) within I^*, i.e.,

$$W_{edf}(J, I^*, \alpha) \leq work(J, I^*, 1)$$

and by (22), we know that

$$W_{edf}(J, I^*, \alpha) \leq work_f(J, I^*, 1)$$

and moreover, Bonifaci et al. [4] also show that

$$W_{edf}(J, I^*, \alpha) \geq (\alpha m - m + 1)|I^*|$$

and thus, we have

$$work_f(J, I^*, 1) \geq (\alpha m - m + 1)|I^*|$$

This completes the proof of Theorem 2.

It should be emphasized that Observation 1 is very important in the proof, which indicates that the feasible schedule mentioned in (iii) of Theorem 2 must be restricted on the unit-speed cores by default, even though it is not explicitly stated in the original theorem.

5.1   Existing Reformulations of Theorem 2

Baruah [1] and Li et al. [10] respectively reformulate Theorem 2 as follows.

Theorem 3 (Thm. 1 of [1]). *Sporadic DAG task set $\mathcal{T}$ is global EDF schedulable on m α-speed cores if the following conditions both hold.*

i For any task $\tau_i \in \mathcal{T}$, $len_i \leq D_i$, and
ii For any time $t \geq 0$,

$$work(\mathcal{T}, t, 1) \leq (\alpha m - m + 1) \times t \tag{23}$$

Theorem 4 (Lem. 8 of [10]). *Sporadic DAG task set $\mathcal{T}$ is global EDF schedulable on m α-speed cores if*

$$work(\mathcal{T}, t, \alpha) \leq (\alpha m - m + 1) \times t, \quad \forall t \geq 0 \tag{24}$$

Clearly, Theorem 3 and Theorem 4 are totally different, and only one of them is equivalent to Theorem 2. The following lemmas reveal which one is the equivalent reformulation.

Lemma 7. *Theorem 3 is equivalent to Theorem 2.*

Proof. On the one hand, (i) of Theorem 3 equivalently indicates that any collection J released by the tasks in $\mathcal{T}$ is feasible under A_∞ on unit-speed cores, i.e., $S_\infty(J,1)$ is feasible. Therefore, (ii) of Theorem 2 does not hold.

On the other hand, (ii) of Theorem 3 equivalently indicates that there is a feasible schedule of J, e.g. $S_\infty(J,1)$ under A_∞, such that the work of J that must be done by A_∞ within any interval I is no more than $(\alpha m - m + 1)|I|$, i.e., (iii) of Theorem 2 does not hold.

According to Theorem 2, (i) of Theorem 2 must hold, i.e., $\mathcal{T}$ is global EDF schedulable on m α-speed cores.

From Lemma 7, we know that Theorem 3 is correct. Moreover, Theorem 4 seems correct due to the following reasons.

- The task set $\mathcal{T}$ is assumed to be schedulable under A_∞ on unit-speed cores by default in [10], i.e., (ii) of Theorem 2 does not hold. Moreover, it obviously indicates that $\mathcal{T}$ is A_∞-schedulable on α-speed cores.
- (24) ensures that for any collection J released by the tasks of $\mathcal{T}$ the feasible schedule $S_\infty(J,\alpha)$ under A_∞ on α-speed cores satisfies the following condition: the work of J that must be done by A_∞ on α-speed cores within any interval I is no more than $(\alpha m - m + 1)|I|$, i.e., (iii) of Theorem 2 "does not" hold.

According to Theorem 2, $\mathcal{T}$ is global EDF schedulable on m α-speed cores. This seems complete the proof of Theorem 4.

However, the proof above may be incorrect. The reason is as follows. From Observation 1 and Example 1, we know that the feasible schedule mentioned in (iii) of Theorem 2 is assumed to be on unit-speed cores by default. Although the schedule $S_\infty(J,\alpha)$ used in Theorem 4 is feasible, it is not applied on unit-speed cores. Therefore, it is not sufficient to use Theorem 2 (nor Theorem 3) to prove Theorem 4. Actually, Theorem 4 overwhelms Theorem 3 as shown in the following lemma.

Lemma 8. *Theorem 4 overwhelms Theorem 3.*

Proof. From Corollary 2, we know that $\forall t \geq 0$ and $\alpha > 1$, $work(\mathcal{T},t,\alpha) \leq work(\mathcal{T},t,1)$. Therefore, if (23) holds, then (24) must hold. It indicates that Theorem 4 overwhelms Theorem 3, and according to Lemma 7, we complete the proof.

The following example reveals that Theorem 4 strictly overwhelms Theorem 3, i.e., there is a work function that satisfies (24), but does not satisfy (23).

Example 2. We consider the task τ_1 in Fig. 8(a), and schedule it by A_∞ as shown in Fig. 8(b) and (c).

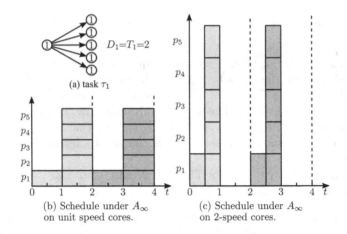

(a) task τ_1

(b) Schedule under A_∞ on unit speed cores.

(c) Schedule under A_∞ on 2-speed cores.

Fig. 8. An example task set and its schedule under A_∞.

The work function of τ_1 is given as follows.

$$work(\tau_1, t, \alpha) = \begin{cases} 0 & 0 < t \leq 2 - \frac{2}{\alpha} \\ 5\alpha t - 10\alpha + 10 & 2 - \frac{2}{\alpha} < t \leq 2 - \frac{1}{\alpha} \\ \alpha t - 2\alpha + 6 & 2 - \frac{1}{\alpha} < t \leq 2 \\ 6\lfloor \frac{t}{2} \rfloor + work(\tau_1, t - 2\lfloor \frac{t}{2} \rfloor, \alpha) & t > 2 \end{cases}$$

By letting $m = 3$ and $\alpha \geq 2$, we first show the violation of (23), i.e., there is a time point t such that $work(\tau_1, t, 1) > (\alpha m - m + 1)t = (3\alpha - 2)t$. Such a time point must exist, because $work(\tau_1, 0, 1) = 0$ and for any $t \in [0, 2 - \frac{1}{\alpha}]$, the gradient of $work(\tau_1, t, 1)$ equals 5α, which is larger than $3\alpha - 2$. As illustrated by Fig. 9, the blue curve represents the work function $work(\tau_1, t, 1)$, and during the interval $t \in (0, 1]$, we know that $work(\tau_1, t, 1) \geq (\alpha m - m + 1)t$.

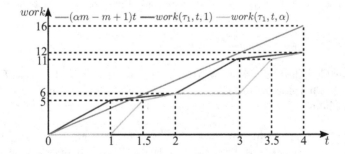

Fig. 9. The work function curves with $m = 3$ and $\alpha = 2$.

In the following, we show that (24) holds, i.e., $\forall t$, $work(\tau_1, t, \alpha) \leq (\alpha m - m + 1)t$ when $m = 3$ and $\alpha \geq 2$. As we know that the period of work function $work(\tau_1, t, \alpha)$ equals 2, we discuss the value of $\Delta = (\alpha m - m + 1)t - work(\tau_1, t, \alpha)$

(with $m = 3$ and $\alpha \geq 2$) in each period $t \in [2k, 2k+2]$ ($k = 0, 1, \cdots$). We further divide each period into three disjoint intervals as follows.

- When $t \in [2k, 2k + 2 - \frac{2}{\alpha})$, and since $\alpha \geq 2$, we have

$$\Delta \geq 6\alpha k - 10k \geq 0$$

- When $t \in [2k + 2 - \frac{2}{\alpha}, 2k + 2 - \frac{1}{\alpha})$, and since $\alpha \geq 2$, we have

$$\Delta \geq (6\alpha - 10)(k+1) + \frac{4}{\alpha} \geq 0$$

- When $t \in [2k + 2 - \frac{1}{\alpha}, 2k + 2]$, and since $\alpha \geq 2$, we have

$$\Delta \geq (6\alpha - 10)k + (6\alpha - 12) + \frac{2}{\alpha} \geq 0$$

In sum, we know that (24) holds for any time point t, as illustrated in Fig. 9, where the green curve representing the work function $work(\tau_1, t, \alpha)$ is always below the red curve representing $(\alpha m - m + 1)t$.

The following lemma shows a sufficient condition which ensures that if (24) holds, then (23) holds.

Lemma 9. *For any non-convex work function* $work(\mathcal{T}, t, \alpha)$*, (24) implies (23).*

Proof. Suppose not. There is a non-convex work function $work(\mathcal{T}, t, \alpha)$ that satisfies (24) holds, but violates (23), i.e., there is a time t such that

$$work(\mathcal{T}, t, 1) > (\alpha m - m + 1)t \qquad (25)$$

According to Lemma 1, the work function $work(\mathcal{T}, t, 1)$ is an increasing function, and thus, there must be a time $t < t^*$ such that

$$work(\mathcal{T}, t^*, 1) = (\alpha m - m + 1)t^* \qquad (26)$$

We consider two cases.

Case 1: t^* is in a flat interval $I = (a, b]$. From Definition 6, we know that

$$work(\mathcal{T}, a, 1) = work(\mathcal{T}, t^*, 1)$$

and by (27), we have

$$work(\mathcal{T}, a, 1) = (\alpha m - m + 1)t^*$$

and since $(\alpha m - m + 1)a < (\alpha m - m + 1)t^*$ (with $a < t^*$), we know that

$$work(\mathcal{T}, a, 1) > (\alpha m - m + 1)a \qquad (27)$$

From Definition 4, we know that a is a left critical time point, and according to Lemma 6, a must be an encounter point. From Definition 9, we know that

$$work(\mathcal{T}, a, 1) = work(\mathcal{T}, a, \alpha)$$

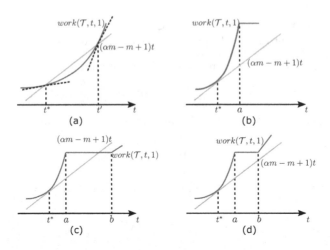

Fig. 10. Illustration for the proof of Lemma 9.

and by (27), we have

$$work(\mathcal{T}, a, \alpha) > (\alpha m - m + 1)a$$

It indicates that (24) does not hold for Case 1.

Case 2: t^* is in a slope interval I, and without loss of generality, we assume that the gradient of the work function $work(\mathcal{T}, t, 1)$ at t^* is no less than $\alpha m - m + 1$. Suppose not. The gradient of the work function $work(\mathcal{T}, t, 1)$ at t^* is no more than $\alpha m - m + 1$. According to the assumption (25) and since the slope interval I is non-convex, we know that there must be a time t' such that $work(\mathcal{T}, t', 1) = (\alpha m - m + 1)t'$, and where the gradient of the work function $work(\mathcal{T}, t, 1)$ at t' is larger than $\alpha m - m + 1$ as illustrated in Fig. 10(a).

In the following, we consider two cases.

- If there is no flat interval follows the slope interval I. Since the gradient of the work function $work(\mathcal{T}, t, 1)$ at t^* is no less than $\alpha m - m + 1$, and the slope interval I is non-convex, we know that for any $t > t^*$,

$$work(\mathcal{T}, t, 1) > (\alpha m - m + 1)t \tag{28}$$

Let a be the nearest encounter point after t^*, and according to Lemma 6 and Definition 9, $work(\mathcal{T}, a, 1) = work(\mathcal{T}, a, \alpha)$. By (28), we have the following inequality as shown in Fig. 10(b).

$$work(\mathcal{T}, a, \alpha) > (\alpha m - m + 1)a$$

- Otherwise, denote by $I' = [a, b]$ be the flat interval that follows the slope interval I. There are three cases.
  - $work(\mathcal{T}, a, 1) < (\alpha m - m + 1)a$. In this case, since the slope interval I is non-convex, and the gradient of the work function $work(\mathcal{T}, t, 1)$ at t^* is larger than $\alpha m - m + 1$, for any time $t \in (t^*, a]$, $work(\mathcal{T}, t, 1) > (\alpha m - m + 1)t$. This leads to a contradiction.

- $work(\mathcal{T}, a, 1) > (\alpha m - m + 1)a$ and $work(\mathcal{T}, b, 1) < (\alpha m - m + 1)b$ as illustrated in Fig. 10(c). In this cases, we know that there must be a time $t \in I$ such that $work(\mathcal{T}, t, 1) = (\alpha m - m + 1)t$, and we have discussed this in Case 1.
- $work(\mathcal{T}, b, 1) > (\alpha m - m + 1)b$ as illustrated in Fig. 10(d). In this case, according to Definition 6, we know that $work(\mathcal{T}, a, 1) = work(\mathcal{T}, b, 1)$, and thus, $work(\mathcal{T}, a, 1) > (\alpha m - m + 1)a$. According to Lemma 6, we have $work(\mathcal{T}, a, 1) = work(\mathcal{T}, a, \alpha)$. Therefore, we know that $work(\mathcal{T}, a, \alpha) > (\alpha m - m + 1)a$.

In sum, (24) does not hold for Case 2. This completes the proof.

6 Conclusion

Since Bonifaci first proposed the work function in [4], the work function plays a very important role in schedulability analysis of the sporadic DAG tasks. Especially, Li et al. [10] derive the best capacity augmentation bound for global EDF algorithm by using the work function methodology. This paper revisits the work function methodology, and shows that Lem. 8 of [10] which is said to be a reformulation of Lem. 3 of [4] is not equivalently reformulated from Lem. 3 of [4], and we prove that Lem.8 of [10] strictly overwhelms Lem. 3 of [4]. Thus, the main result of [10] should be carefully discussed.

References

1. Baruah, S.: Improved multiprocessor global schedulability analysis of sporadic DAG task systems. In: 26th Euromicro Conference on Real-Time Systems, pp. 97–105. IEEE (2014)
2. Baruah, S.: The federated scheduling of systems of conditional sporadic DAG tasks. In: International Conference on Embedded Software (EMSOFT), pp. 1–10. IEEE (2015)
3. Blumofe, R.D., Joerg, C.F., Kuszmaul, B.C., Leiserson, C.E., Randall, K.H., Zhou, Y.: Cilk: an efficient multithreaded runtime system. ACM SigPlan Notices 30(8), 207–216 (1995)
4. Bonifaci, V., Marchetti-Spaccamela, A., Stiller, S., Wiese, A.: Feasibility analysis in the sporadic DAG task model. In: 2013 25th Euromicro Conference on Real-Time Systems, pp. 225–233. IEEE (2013)
5. Ferry, D., Li, J., Mahadevan, M., Agrawal, K., Gill, C., Lu, C.: A real-time scheduling service for parallel tasks. In: 2013 IEEE 19th Real-Time and Embedded Technology and Applications Symposium (RTAS), pp. 261–272. IEEE (2013)
6. Huang, H.M., Tidwell, T., Gill, C., Lu, C., Gao, X., Dyke, S.: Cyber-physical systems for real-time hybrid structural testing: a case study. In: Proceedings of the 1st ACM/IEEE International Conference on Cyber-Physical Systems, pp. 69–78 (2010)
7. Jiang, X., Long, X., Guan, N., Wan, H.: On the decomposition-based global EDF scheduling of parallel real-time tasks. In: 2016 IEEE Real-Time Systems Symposium (RTSS), pp. 237–246. IEEE (2016)

8. Kim, J., Kim, H., Lakshmanan, K., Rajkumar, R.: Parallel scheduling for cyber-physical systems: analysis and case study on a self-driving car. In: Proceedings of the ACM/IEEE 4th International Conference on Cyber-Physical Systems, pp. 31–40 (2013)
9. Li, J., Agrawal, K., Lu, C., Gill, C.: Analysis of global EDF for parallel tasks. In: 25th Euromicro Conference on Real-Time Systems, pp. 3–13. IEEE (2013)
10. Li, J., Chen, J.J., Agrawal, K., Lu, C., Gill, C., Saifullah, A.: Analysis of federated and global scheduling for parallel real-time tasks. In: 26th Euromicro Conference on Real-Time Systems, pp. 85–96. IEEE (2014)
11. Li, J., Luo, Z., Ferry, D., Agrawal, K., Gill, C., Lu, C.: Global EDF scheduling for parallel real-time tasks. Real-Time Syst. **51**, 395–439 (2015)
12. Marongiu, A., Capotondi, A., Tagliavini, G., Benini, L.: Improving the programmability of STHORM-based heterogeneous systems with offload-enabled OpenMP. In: Proceedings of the First International Workshop on Many-core Embedded Systems, pp. 1–8 (2013)
13. Melani, A., Bertogna, M., Bonifaci, V., Marchetti-Spaccamela, A., Buttazzo, G.C.: Response-time analysis of conditional DAG tasks in multiprocessor systems. In: 27th Euromicro Conference on Real-Time Systems, pp. 211–221. IEEE (2015)
14. OpenMP Forum: OpenMP Application Program Interface, Version 3.0. OpenMP Architecture Review Board, May 2008. https://www.openmp.org/wp-content/uploads/spec30.pdf
15. Qamhieh, M., Fauberteau, F., George, L., Midonnet, S.: Global EDF scheduling of directed acyclic graphs on multiprocessor systems. In: Proceedings of the 21st International conference on Real-Time Networks and Systems, pp. 287–296 (2013)
16. Qamhieh, M., George, L., Midonnet, S.: A stretching algorithm for parallel real-time DAG tasks on multiprocessor systems. In: Proceedings of the 22nd International Conference on Real-Time Networks and Systems, pp. 13–22 (2014)
17. Reinders, J.: Intel Threading Building Blocks: Outfitting C++ for Multi-core Processor Parallelism. O'Reilly Media, Sebastopol (2007)
18. Saifullah, A., Ferry, D., Li, J., Agrawal, K., Lu, C., Gill, C.D.: Parallel real-time scheduling of DAGs. IEEE Trans. Parallel Distrib. Syst. **25**(12), 3242–3252 (2014)
19. Saifullah, A., Li, J., Agrawal, K., Lu, C., Gill, C.: Multi-core real-time scheduling for generalized parallel task models. Real-Time Syst. **49**, 404–435 (2013)
20. Stotzer, E., et al.: OpenMP on the low-power TI keystone II ARM/DSP system-on-chip. In: Rendell, A.P., Chapman, B.M., Müller, M.S. (eds.) IWOMP 2013. LNCS, vol. 8122, pp. 114–127. Springer, Heidelberg (2013). https://doi.org/10.1007/978-3-642-40698-0_9
21. Sun, J., et al.: A capacity augmentation bound for real-time constrained-deadline parallel tasks under GEDF. IEEE Trans. Comput. Aided Des. Integr. Circuits Syst. **37**(11), 2200–2211 (2018)
22. Ullman, J.D.: NP-complete scheduling problems. J. Comput. Syst. Sci. **10**(3), 384–393 (1975)
23. Wang, C., Chandrasekaran, S., Chapman, B., Holt, J.: libEOMP: a portable OpenMP runtime library based on MCA APIs for embedded systems. In: Proceedings of the 2013 International Workshop on Programming Models and Applications for Multicores and Manycores, pp. 83–92 (2013)

Towards Efficient Data-Flow Test Data Generation

Ting Su$^{1(\boxtimes)}$, Chengyu Zhang^2, Yichen Yan^1, Lingling Fan^3, Yang Liu^4,
Zhoulai Fu^5, and Zhendong Su^2

^{1} East China Normal University, Shanghai, China
tsu@sei.ecnu.edu.cn
^{2} ETH Zurich, Zürich, Switzerland
chengyu.zhang@inf.ethz.ch , zhendong.su@inf.ethz.ch
^{3} Nankai University, Tianjin, China
linglingfan@nankai.edu.cn
^{4} Nanyang Technological University, Singapore, Singapore
yangliu@ntu.edu.sg
^{5} State University of New York, Incheon, Korea
zhoulai.fu@sunykorea.ac.kr

Abstract. Data-flow testing (DFT) aims to detect potential data interaction anomalies by focusing on the points at which variables receive
values and the points at which these values are used. Such test objectives are referred as *def-use pairs*. However, the complexity of DFT still
overwhelms the testers in practice. To tackle this problem, we introduce a hybrid testing framework for data-flow based test generation: (1)
The core of our framework is symbolic execution (SE), enhanced by a
novel guided path exploration strategy to improve testing performance;
and (2) we systematically cast DFT as reachability checking in software
model checking (SMC) to complement SE, yielding practical DFT that
combines the two techniques' strengths. We implemented our framework
for C programs on top of the state-of-the-art symbolic execution engine
KLEE and instantiated with three different software model checkers. Our
evaluation on the 28,354 def-use pairs collected from 33 open-source and
industrial program subjects shows that (1) our SE-based approach can
improve DFT performance by 15–48% in terms of testing time, compared
with existing search strategies; and (2) our combined approach can further reduce testing time by 20.1–93.6%, and improve data-flow coverage
by 27.8–45.2% by eliminating infeasible test objectives. This combined
approach also enables the cross-checking of each component for reliable
and robust testing results.

Keywords: Data-flow Testing · Symbolic Execution · Model Checking

1 Introduction

It is widely recognized that white-box testing, usually applied at unit testing
level, is one of the most important activities to ensure software quality [4]. In

---

This paper was completed on Jifeng He's 80th birthday, May 2023.

this process, the testers design inputs to exercise program paths in the code, and validate the outputs with specifications [50]. Code coverage criteria are popular metrics to guide such test selection. For example, control-flow based criteria (*e.g.*, statement, branch coverage) require to cover the specified program elements, *e.g.*, statements, branches and conditions, at least once [100]. In contrast, data-flow based criteria [27,46,76] focus on the flow of data, and aim to detect potential data interaction anomalies. It validates the correctness of variable definitions by observing the values at the corresponding uses.

However, several challenges exist in generating data-flow based test cases: (1) *Few data-flow coverage tools exist.* To our knowledge, ATAC [52,53] is the only publicly available tool, developed two decades ago, to measure data-flow coverage for C programs. However, there are plenty of tools for control-flow criteria [96]. (2) *The complexity of identifying data flow-based test data overwhelms testers.* Test objectives *w.r.t.* data-flow testing are much more than those of control-flow criteria; more effort is required to satisfy a def-use pair than just covering a statement or branch, since the test case needs to reach a variable definition first and then the corresponding use. (3) *Infeasible test objectives* (*i.e.*, the paths from the variable definition to the use are infeasible) and *variable aliases* make data-flow testing more difficult.

To aid data-flow testing, many testing techniques have been proposed in the past few decades. For example, search-based approach [29,39,41,89] uses genetic algorithms to guide test generation to cover the target def-use pairs. It generates an initial population of test cases, and iteratively applies mutation and crossover operations on them to optimize the designated fitness function. Random testing [41,42] generates random test inputs or random paths to cover def-use pairs. Some work uses the idea of collateral coverage [62,77], *i.e.*, the relation between data-flow criteria and the other criteria (*e.g.*, branch coverage), to infer data-flow based test cases. However, these approaches are either *inefficient* (*e.g.*, random testing may generate a large number of redundant test cases) or *imprecise* (*e.g.*, genetic algorithms and collateral coverage-based approach may not be able to identify infeasible test objectives).

The preceding situations underline the importance of an automated, effective data-flow testing technique, which can efficiently generate test cases for target def-use pairs and detect infeasible ones therein. To this end, we introduce *a combined approach* to automatically generate data-flow based test data, which synergistically combines two techniques: dynamic symbolic execution and counterexample-guided abstraction refinement-based model checking. It takes as input the program under test, and (1) *outputs test cases for feasible test objectives*, and (2) *eliminates infeasible test objectives—without any false positives*.

Dynamic symbolic execution [20] is a widely-accepted and effective approach for automatic test case generation. It intertwines classic symbolic execution [26,58] and concrete execution, and explores as many program paths as possible to generate test cases by solving path constraints. As for counterexample-guided abstraction refinement-based (CEGAR) model checking [5,22,49], given the program source code and a temporal safety specification, it either statically proves that the program satisfies the specification, or returns a counterexample path to demonstrate its violation. This technique has been used to automatically verify safety properties of device drives [5,13,14], as well as test generation *w.r.t.* statement or branch coverage [12] from counterexample paths.

Although symbolic execution has been applied to enforce various coverage criteria (*e.g.*, statement, branch, logical, boundary value and mutation testing) [55,60,73,85,99], little effort exists to adapt symbolic execution to data-flow testing. To counter the path explosion problem, we designed a *cut-point guided path exploration strategy* to cover target def-use pairs as quickly as possible. The key intuition is to find a set of critical program locations that must be traversed through in order to cover the pair. By following these points during the exploration, we can narrow the path search space. In addition, with the help of path-based exploration, we can also more easily and precisely detect definitions due to variable aliasing. Moreover, we introduce a simple, powerful encoding of data flow testing using CEGAR-based model checking to complement our SE-based approach: (1) We show how to encode any data-flow test objective in the program under test and systematically evaluate the technique's practicality; and (2) we describe a combined approach that combines the relative strengths of the SE and CEGAR-based approaches. An interesting by-product of this combination is to let the two independent approaches cross-check each other's results for correctness and consistency.

In all, this paper makes the following contributions:

- We design a symbolic execution-based testing framework, and enhance it with an efficient guided path search strategy, to quickly achieve data-flow testing.
- We describe a simple, effective reduction of data-flow testing into reachability checking in software model checking to complement our SE-based approach.
- We implement the SE-based data-flow testing approach, and conduct empirical evaluation on both benchmark and industrial C programs. Our results show that the SE-based approach is both efficient and effective.
- We also demonstrate that the CEGAR-based approach can effectively complement the SE-based approach by reducing testing time and identifying infeasible test objectives. In addition, these two approaches can cross-check each other to validate the correctness and effectiveness of both techniques.

The initial idea of this hybrid data-flow testing approach was described in [84], and in this paper we have improved this idea in several aspects: (1) We optimized our original cut-point guided search with several exploration strategies (*e.g.*, backtrack), and made substantial efforts to implement our approach on the state-of-the-art symbolic execution engine KLEE [18] (previously implemented on our own concolic testing tool CAUT [84,85], which was capable of evaluating only 6 subjects), and further compared our approach with various existing testing strategies on KLEE. Due to the differences in the design and architecture between KLEE and CAUT, the implementation is not straightforward. But this effort brings several benefits: first, it provides a uniform and fair platform to investigate the effectiveness of our testing strategy with many existing state-of-the-art ones; second, it provides a robust platform to enable extensive evaluation of real-world subjects and better integration with model checkers; third, this extension of KLEE could benefit industrial practitioners and also academic researchers to apply or investigate data-flow testing. (2) We implemented and extended the model checking-based approach on two different techniques, *i.e.*, Counter-Example Guided Abstraction Refinement (CEGAR) [5,21,49] and Bounded Model Checking (BMC) [25], and comprehensively compared their effectiveness and performance for data-flow testing; (3) We rigorously setup a benchmark repository for data-flow testing, and extensively evaluated on 30 real-world programs with various data-flow usage scenarios, including seven non-trivial subjects from previous DFT research work [32,35,39,48,54,66,67], seven subjects from SIR [82], 16 subjects from SV-COMP [33] so as to gain a overall understanding of our hybrid testing framework. (4) We cross-checked each component to provide reliable testing results, investigated the reasons of inconsistent cases, and gave detailed discussions.

The paper is organized as follows. Section 2 surveys the related work in data-flow testing. Section 3 gives more background and Sect. 4 gives an overview of our testing framework with an illustrative example. Section 5 details our approach. Section 6 explains the design and implementation. Section 7 presents the evaluation results. Section 8 concludes the paper.

2   Related Work

This section discusses the closely related work: (1) data-flow based test generation, (2) directed symbolic execution, and (3) infeasible test objective detection.

2.1   Data-Flow Based Test Generation

Data-flow testing has been investigated in the past four decades [34–36,54,93]. Existing work can be categorized into five main categories according to the testing techniques. We only discuss typical literature work here. Readers can refer to a recent survey [86] for details.

The most widely used approach to is *search-based testing*, which utilizes meta-heuristic search techniques to identify test inputs for target def-use pairs. Girgis [41] first uses Genetic Algorithms (GA) for Fortran programs, and Ghiduk *et al.* [39] use GA for C++ programs. Later, Vivanti *et al.* [89] and Denaro *et al.* [29] apply GA to Java programs by the tool EvoSuite. Some optimization-based search algorithms [38,69,80,81] are also used, but they have only evaluated on small programs without available tools. *Random testing* is a baseline approach for data-flow testing [3,29,39,41,42]. Some researchers use *collateral coverage-based testing* [45], which exploits the observation that the test case that satisfies one target test objective can also "accidentally" cover the others. Malevris *et al.* [62] use branch coverage to achieve data-flow coverage. Merlo *et al.* [68] exploit the coverage implication between data-flow coverage and statement coverage to achieve intra-procedural data-flow testing. Other efforts include [65,66,77,78]. Some researchers use *traditional symbolic execution*. For example, Girgis [40] develops a simple symbolic execution system for DFT, which statically generates program paths *w.r.t.* a certain control-flow criterion (*e.g.*, branch coverage), and then selects those executable ones that can cover the def-use pairs of interest. Buy *et al.* [17] adopts three techniques, *i.e.*, data-flow analysis, symbolic execution and automated deduction to perform data-flow testing. However, they have provided little evidence of practice. Hong *et al.* [51] adopt *classic CTL-based model checking* to generate data-flow test data. Specifically, the program is modeled as a Kripke structure and the requirements of data-flow coverage are characterized as a set of CTL property formulas. However, this approach requires manual intervention, and its scalability is also unclear.

Despite the plenty of work on data-flow based testing, they are either inefficient or imprecise. Our work is the first one to leverage symbolic execution and software model checking techniques to achieve DFT efficiently and precisely.

2.2   Directed Symbolic Execution

Much research [31,61,64,95,97] has been done to guide path search toward a specified program location via symbolic execution. Do *et al.* [31] leverage data dependency analysis to guide the search to reach a particular program location, while we use dominator analysis. Ma *et al.* [61] suggest a call chain backward search heuristic to find a feasible path, backward from the target program location to the entry. However, it is difficult to adapt this approach on data-flow testing, because it requires that a function can be decomposed into logical parts when the target locations (*e.g.* the *def* and the *use*) are located in the same function. But decomposing a function itself is a nontrivial task. Zamfir *et al.* [97] narrow the path search space by following a *limited* set of critical edges and a statically-necessary combination of intermediate goals. On the other hand, our approach finds a set of cut points from the program entry to the target locations, which makes path exploration more efficient. Xie *et al.* [95] integrate fitness-guided path search strategy with other heuristics to reach a program point. The proposed strategy is only efficient for those problems amenable to its fitness functions. Marinescu *et al.* [64] use a shortest distance-based guided search method (like the adapted SDGS heuristic in our evaluation) with other heuristics to quickly reach the line of interest in patch testing. In contrast, we combine several search heuristics to guide the path exploration to traverse two specified program locations (*i.e.*, the *def* and *use*) for data flow testing.

2.3   Detecting Infeasible Test Objectives

As for detecting infeasible test objectives, early work uses constraint-based technique [44,71]. Offutt and Pan *et al.* [71] extract a set of path constraints that encode the test objectives from the program under test. Infeasible test objectives can be identified if the constraints do not have solutions. Recent work by Beckman *et al.* [10], Baluda *et al.* [6–8], Bardin *et al.* [9] use weakeast precondition to identify infeasible statements and branches. For example, Baluda *et al.* use model refinement with weakest precondition to exclude infeasible branches;

Bardin *et al.* applies weakest precondition with abstract interpretation to eliminate infeasible objectives. Marcozzi *et al.* [63] also use weakest precondition to identify polluting test objectives (including infeasible, duplicate and subsumed) for condition, MC/DC and weak mutation coverage. In contrast, our testing framework mainly use the CEGAR-based model checking technique to identify infeasible def-use pairs for data-flow testing. One close work is from Daca *et al.* [28], who combine concolic testing (CREST) and model checking (CPAchecker) to find a test suite *w.r.t.* branch coverage. Our work has some distinct differences with theirs. First, they target at branch coverage, while we enforce data-flow testing. Second, they directly modify the existing generic path search strategies of CREST, and backtrack the search if the explored direction has been proved as infeasible by CPAchecker. As a result, the performance of their approach (*i.e.*, avoid unnecessary path explorations) may vary across different search strategies due to the paths are selected in different orders. In contrast, we implement a designated search strategy to guide symbolic execution, and realize the reduction approach directly on model checkers. Although our approach is simple, it can treat model checkers as black-box tools without any modification and seamlessly integrate with KLEE. Model checking techniques have recently been adapted to aid software testing [15,37].

3   Problem Definition, Preliminaries and Challenges

3.1   Problem Definition

Definition 1 (Program Paths). *Two kinds of program paths, i.e., control flow paths and execution paths are distinguished during data-flow testing. Control flow paths are the paths from the control flow graph of the program under test, which abstract the flow of control. Execution paths are driven by concrete program inputs, which represent dynamic program executions. Both of them can be represented as a sequence of control points (denoted by line numbers), e.g., $l_1, \ldots, l_i, \ldots, l_n$.*

Definition 2 (Def-use Pair). *The test objective of data-flow testing is referred as a def-use pair, denoted by $du(l_d, l_u, v)$. Such a pair appears when there exists a control flow path that starts from the variable definition statement l_d (or the def statement in short), and then reaches the variable use statement l_u (or the use statement in short), but no statements on the subpaths from l_d to l_u redefine the variable v.*

In particular, two kinds of def-use pairs are distinguished. For a def-use pair (l_d, l_u, v), if the variable v is used in a computation statement at l_u, the pair is a *computation-use* (*c-use* for short), denoted by $dcu(l_d, l_u, v)$. If v is used in a conditional statement (*e.g.*, an `if` or `while` statement) at l_u, the pair is a *predicate use* (*p-use* for short). At this time, two def-use pairs appear and can be denoted by $dpu(l_d, (l_u, l_t), v)$ and $dpu(l_d, (l_u, l_f), v)$, where (l_u, l_t) and (l_u, l_f) represents the *true* and the *false* edge of the conditional statement, respectively.

Definition 3 (Data-flow Testing). *Given a def-use pair $du(l_d, l_u, v)$ in program P under test, the goal of data-flow testing[1] is to find an input t that induces an execution path p that covers the variable definition statement at l_d, and then covers variable use statement at l_u, but without covering any redefinition statements w.r.t v, i.e., the subpath from l_d to l_u is a def-clear path. The requirement to cover all def-use pairs at least once is called all def-use coverage criterion[2] in data-flow testing.*

In particular, for a c-use pair, t should cover l_d and l_u; for a p-use pair, t should cover l_d and its true or false branch, i.e., (l_u, l_t) and (l_u, l_f), respectively.

3.2   Symbolic Execution

Our data-flow testing approach is mainly built on the symbolic execution technique. The idea of symbolic execution (SE) was initially described in [26,58]. Recent significant advances in the constraint solving techniques have made SE possible for testing real-world program by systematically exploring program paths [20]. Specifically, two variants of modern SE techniques exist, *i.e.*, *concolic testing* (implemented by DART [43], CUTE [79], CREST [16], CAUT [85], *etc*) and *execution-generated testing* (implemented by EXE [19] and KLEE [18]), which mix concrete and symbolic execution together to improve scalability. In essence, SE uses *symbolic values* in place of *concrete values* to represent input variables, and represent other program variables by the *symbolic expressions* in terms of symbolic inputs. Typically, SE maintains a *symbolic state* σ, which maps variables to (1) the symbolic expressions over program variables, and (2) a symbolic path constraint pc (a quantifier-free first order formula in terms of input variables), which characterizes the set of input values that can execute a specific program execution path p. Additionally, σ maintains a program counter that refers to the current instruction for execution. At the beginning, σ is initialized as an empty map and pc as *true*. During execution, SE updates σ when an assignment statement is executed; and forks σ when a conditional statement (*e.g.*, **if**(e) s_1 **else** s_2) is executed. Specifically, SE will create a new state σ' from the original state σ, and updates the path constrain of σ' as $pc \wedge \neg(e)$, while updates that of σ as $pc \wedge (e)$. σ and σ', respectively, represent the two program states that fork at the *true* and *false* branch of the conditional statement. By querying the satisfiability of updated path constraints, SE decides which one to continue the exploration. When an *exit* or certain runtime error is encountered, SE will terminate on that statement and the concrete input values will be generated by solving the corresponding path constraint.

---

[1] In this paper, we focus on the problem of *classic data-flow testing* [39,89], *i.e.*, finding an input for a given def-use pair at one time. We do not consider the case where some pairs can be accidentally covered when targeting one pair, since this has already been investigated in collateral coverage-based approach [65,66].

[2] We follow the all def-use coverage defined by Rapps and Weyuker [75,76], since almost all of the literature that followed uses or extends this definition, as revealed by a recent survey [86].

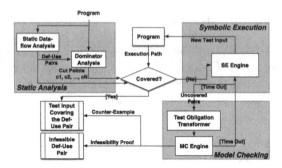

Fig. 1. Workflow of the combined approach for data-flow testing, which combines symbolic execution and software model checking (the CEGAR-based model checking in particular).

Challenges. Although SE is an effective test case generation technique for traditional coverage criteria, it faces two challenges in our context:

1. The SE-based approach by nature faces the notorious path-explosion problem. Despite the existence of many generic search strategies, it is challenging, in reasonable time, to find an execution path from the whole path space to cover a given pair.
2. The test objectives from data-flow testing include *feasible* and *infeasible* pairs. A pair is *feasible* if there exists an execution path which can pass through it. Otherwise it is *infeasible*. Without prior knowledge about whether a target pair is feasible or not, the SE-based approach may spend a large amount of time, in vain, to cover an infeasible def-use pair.

Section 4 will give an overview of our approach, and illustrate how our combined approach tackles these two challenges via an example in Fig. 2.

4   Approach Overview

Figure 1 shows the workflow of our combined approach for data-flow testing. It takes as input the program source code, and follows the three steps below to achieve automated, efficient DFT. (1) The *static analysis* module uses data-flow analysis to identify def-use pairs, and adopts dominator analysis to analyze the sequence of cut points for each pair (see Sect. 5.1). (2) For each pair, the *symbolic execution* module adopts the cut point-guided search strategy to efficiently find an execution path that could cover it within a specified time bound (see Sect. 5.2). (3) For the remaining uncovered (possibly infeasible) pairs, the *software model checking* module encodes the test obligation of each def-use pair into the program under test, and enforces reachability checking (also within a time bound) on each of them. The model checker can eliminate infeasible ones with proofs and may also identify feasible ones (see Sect. 5.3). If the testing resource permits, the framework can iterate between (2) and (3) by lifting the time bound

Table 1. Running steps of the enhanced symbolic execution approach for data-flow testing.

Steps	Pending Path	Priority Queue	Selected Path	Path Constraint (pc)
1	**1:** l_{4T}, **2:** l_{4F}	$(l_4,2)^1$, $(l_4,2)^2$	**1**	$y > 0$
2	**2:** l_{4F}, **3:** l_{4T},l_{9T}, **4:** l_{4T},l_{9F}	$(l_9,1)^4$, $(l_4,2)^2$, $(l_9,4)^3$	**4**	$y > 0 \wedge y == 0$
3	**2:** l_{4F}, **3:** l_{4T},l_{9T}	$(l_4,2)^2$, $(l_9,4)^3$	**3**	$y > 0 \wedge y \neq 0$
4	**2:** l_{4F}, **5:** l_{4T},l_{9T},l_{9T}, **6:** l_{4T},l_{9T},l_{9F}	$(l_4,2)^2$, $(l_9,1)^5$, $(l_9,1)^6$	prune **5,6**, select **2**	$y \leq 0$
5	**7:** l_{4F},l_{9T}, **8:** l_{4F},l_{9F}	$(l_9,4)^7$, $(l_9,1)^8$	**8**	$y < 0 \wedge y \neq 0$
6	**7:** l_{4F},l_{9T}, **9:** l_{4F},l_{9F},l_{13T}, **10:** l_{4F},l_{9F},l_{13F}	$(l_{13},1)^9$, $(l_9,4)^7$, $(l_{13},\infty)^{10}$	**9**	$y \leq 0 \wedge y \neq 0$
7	**7:** l_{4F},l_{9T}, **10:** l_{4F},l_{9F},l_{13F} **11:** $l_{4F},l_{9F},l_{13T},l_{14T}$, **12:** $l_{4F},l_{9F},l_{13T},l_{14F}$	$(l_{13},1)^{12}$, $(l_9,4)^7$, $(l_{13},\infty)^{10}$, $(l_{14},\infty)^{11}$	**12**	$y == 0 \wedge x \neq 0$

to continue test those remaining uncovered pairs. By this way, our framework outputs test cases for feasible test objectives, and weeds out infeasible ones by proofs—without any false positives.

4.1 Illustrative Example

Figure 2 shows an example program *power*, which accepts two integers x and y, and outputs the result of x^y. The right sub-figure shows the control flow graph of *power*.

Step 1: Static Analysis. For the variable *res* (it stores the computation result of x^y), the static analysis procedure can find two typical def-use pairs with their cut points:

$$du_1 = (l_8, l_{17}, res) \tag{1}$$
$$du_2 = (l_8, l_{18}, res) \tag{2}$$

Below, we illustrate how our combined approach can efficiently achieve DFT on these two def-use pairs—SE can efficiently cover the feasible pair du_1, and CEGAR can effectively conclude the infeasibility of du_2.

Step 2: SE-Based Data-Flow Testing. When SE is used to cover du_1, assume under the classic depth-first search (DFS) strategy [16,18,43,79,85,88] the *true* branches of the new execution states (ESs) are always first selected, we can get an execution path p after unfolding the while loops n times.

$$p = l_4, l_5, l_8, \underbrace{l_9, l_{10}, l_{11},\ l_9, l_{10}, l_{11}, \ldots}_{\text{repeated } n \text{ times}}, l_9, l_{13}, l_{14}, l_{15} \tag{3}$$

Here p already covers the definition statement (at l_8) *w.r.t.* the variable *res*. In order to cover the use statement (at l_{17}), SE will exhaustively execute program paths by exploring the remaining unexecuted branch directions. However, the *path (state) explosion problem*—hundreds of branch directions exist (including

```
1  double power(int x,int y
        ){
2      int exp;
3      double res;
4      if (y>0)
5          exp = y;
6      else
7          exp = -y;
8      res=1;
9      while (exp!=0){
10         res *= x;
11         exp -= 1;
12     }
13     if (y<=0)
14         if(x==0)
15         abort;
16         else
17             return 1.0/res;
18     return res;
19 }
```

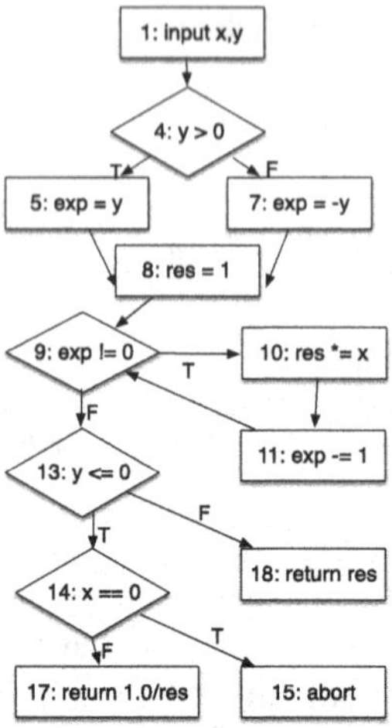

Fig. 2. An example: *power*.

those branches from the new explored paths)—will drastically slow down data-flow testing.

To mitigate this problem, the key idea of our approach is to reduce unnecessary path exploration and provide more guidance during execution. To achieve this, we designed a novel *cut-point guided search algorithm* (CPGS) to enhance SE, which leverages several key elements to prioritize the selection of ESs. First, we introduce *a guided search algorithm*, which leverages two metrics: (i) *cut points*, a sequence of control points that must be traversed through for any paths that could cover the target pair. For example, the cut points of du_1 are $\{l_4, l_8, l_9, l_{13}, l_{14}, l_{17}\}$. These critical points are used as intermediate goals during the search to narrow down the exploration space of SE. (ii) *instruction distance*, the distance between an ES and a target search goal in terms of number of program instructions on the control flow graph. Intuitively, an ES with closer (instruction) distance toward the goal can reach it more quickly. For example, when SE reaches l_9, it can fork two execution states, *i.e.*, following the *true* and the *false* branches. If our target goal is to reach l_{13}, the *false* branch will be prioritized since it has 1-instruction distance toward l_{13}, while the opposite branch has 3-instruction distance. Second, CPGS is enhanced by *a backtrack strategy* based on the number of executed instructions, which reduces the likelihood of trapping in tight loops. Third, we also introduce *a redefinition path pruning technique*, which detects and removes redundant ESs.

Table 1 shows the steps taken by our cut-point guided search algorithm to cover du_1. At the beginning, SE forks two ESs for the if statement at l_4, which produces two *pending paths*[3], *i.e.*, l_{4T} and l_{4F}[4]. In detail, we maintain a tuple $(c, d)^{i}$ that records the two aforementioned metrics for each pending path **i** in a priority queue, where c is the deepest covered cut point, and d is the shortest distance between the corresponding ES and the next target cut point. In each step, we choose the pending path **i** with the optimal value (c, d). For example, in Step **1**, Path **1** and Path **2** have the same values $(l_4, 2)$, and thus we randomly select one path, *e.g.*, Path **1**.

Later, in Step **2**, Path **1** produces two new pending paths, Path **3** and Path **4**. We choose Path **4** since it has the best value: it has sequentially covered the cut points $\{l_4, l_8, l_9\}$, and it is closer to the next cut point l_{13} than Path **3** on the control flow graph, so it is more likely to reach l_{13} more quickly. However, its *pc* is unsatisfiable. As a result, we give up exploring this pending path, and choose Path **3** (because it covers more cut points than Path **1**) in the next Step **3**, which induces Path **5** and Path **6**. At this time, our algorithm detects the variable *res* is redefined at l_{10} on Path **5** and Path **6**, according to the definition of DFT, it is useless to explore these two paths. So, Path **5** and Path **6** are pruned. This *redefinition path pruning* technique can rule out these invalid paths to speed up DFT. Note despite only two pending paths are removed in this case, a number of potential paths have actually been prevented from execution (see the example path in (3)), which can largely improve the performance of our search algorithm.

We choose the only remaining Path **2** to continue the exploration, which produces Path **7** and Path **8** in Step **5**. Again, we choose Path **8** to explore, which induces Path **9** and **10** in Step **6**. Here, for Path **10**, since it cannot reach the next target point l_{14}, its distance is set as ∞. As last, Path **9** is selected, and our algorithm finds Path **12** which covers du_1, and by solving its path constraint $y == 0 \wedge x \neq 0$, we can get one test input, *e.g.*, $t = (x \mapsto 1, y \mapsto 0)$, to satisfy the pair. The above process is enforced by the cut-point guided search, which only takes 7 steps to cover du_1. As we will demonstrate in Sect. 7, the cut point-guided search strategy is more effective for data-flow testing than the existing state-of-the-art search algorithms.

Step 3: CEGAR-Based Data-Flow Testing. In data-flow testing, classic data-flow analysis techniques [23,47,72] statically identify def-use pairs by analyzing data-flow relations. However, due to its conservativeness and limitations, infeasible pairs may be included, which greatly affects the effectiveness of SE for DFT. For example, the pair du_2 is identified as a def-use pair since there exists a def-clear control-flow path (*i.e.*, l_8, l_9, l_{13}, l_{18}) that can start from the variable definition (*i.e.*, l_8) and reach the use (*i.e.*, l_{18}). However, du_2 is infeasible (*i.e.*, no test inputs can satisfy it): If we want to cover its use statement at l_{18}, we cannot take the true branch of l_{13}, so $y > 0$ should hold. However, if $y > 0$, the variable *exp* will be assigned a positive value at l_5 by taking the true branch of l_4, and the redefinition statement at l_{10} *w.r.t.* the variable *res* will be executed.

---

[3] An pending path indicates a not fully-explored path (corresponding to an unterminated state).

[4] We use the line number followed by T or F to denote the *true* or *false* branch of the `if` statement at the corresponding line.

```
 1 │ double power(int x, int y){
 2 │     bool cover_flag = false;
 3 │     int exp;
 4 │     double res;
 5 │     ...
 6 │     res=1;
 7 │     cover_flag = true;
 8 │     while (exp!=0){
 9 │         res *= x;
10 │         cover_flag = false;
11 │         exp -= 1;
12 │     }
13 │     ...
14 │     if(cover_flag) check_point();
15 │     return res;
16 │ }
```

Fig. 3. The transformed function *power* with the test requirement encoded in high-lighted statements.

As a result, such a path that covers the pair and avoids the redefinition at the same time does not exist, and du_2 is an infeasible pair. It is rather difficult for SE to conclude the feasibility unless it checks all program paths, which however is almost impossible due to infinite paths in real-world programs.

To counter the problem, our key idea is to reduce the data-flow testing problem into the path reachability checking problem in software model checking. We encode the test obligation of a target def-use pair into the program under test, and leverage the power of model checkers to check its feasibility. For example, in order to check the feasibility of du_2, we instrument the test requirement into the program as shown in Fig. 3. We first introduce a boolean variable *cover_flag* at l_2, and initialize it as false, which represents the coverage status of this pair. After the definition statement, the variable *cover_flag* is set as true (at l_7); *cover_flag* is set as false immediately after all the redefinition statements (at l_{10}). We check whether the property *cover_flag==true* holds (at l_{14}) just before the use statement. If the check point is reachable, the pair is feasible and a test case will be generated. Otherwise, the pair is infeasible, and will be excluded in the coverage computation. As we can see, this model checking based approach is flexible and can be fully automated.

Combined SE-CEGAR Based Data-Flow Testing. In data-flow testing, the set of test objectives include feasible and infeasible pairs. As we can see from the above two examples, SE, as a dynamic path-based exploration approach, can efficiently cover feasible pairs; while CEGAR, as a static software model checking approach, can effectively detect infeasible pairs (may also cover some feasible pairs).

The figure below shows the relation of these two approaches for data-flow testing. The white part represents the set of feasible pairs, and the gray part the set of infeasible ones. The SE-based approach is able to cover feasible pairs efficiently, but in general, due to the path explosion problem, it cannot detect infeasible pairs (this may waste a lot of testing time). The CEGAR-based approach is able to identify infeasible pairs efficiently (but may take more time to cover feasible ones). As a result, it is beneficial to combine these two techniques to complement each other with their strengths. Section 7 will demonstrate our observations, and validate that the combined approach can indeed achieve more efficient data-flow testing by reducing testing time as well as improving coverage.

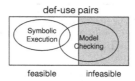

5   Our Approach

This section explains the details of our approach. Our approach includes three steps: (1) static analysis, (2) symbolic execution based data flow testing and (3) software model checking based data flow testing.

5.1   Static Analysis

To improve the performance of SE-based data-flow testing, we use dominator analysis to analyze a set of *cut points* to effectively guide path exploration. In the following, we give some definitions.

Definition 4 (Dominator). *In a control-flow graph, a node m dominates a node n if all paths from the program entry to n must go through m, which is denoted as $m \gg n$. When $m \neq n$, we say m strictly dominates n. If m is the unique node that strictly dominates n and does not strictly dominate other nodes that strictly dominate n, m is an immediate dominator of n, denoted as $m \gg^I n$.*

Definition 5 (Cut Point). *Given a def-use pair $du(l_d, l_u, v)$, its cut points are a sequence of critical control points $c_1, \ldots, c_i, \ldots, c_n$ that must be passed through in succession by any control flow paths that cover this pair. The latter control point is the immediate dominator of the former one, i.e., $c_1 \gg^I \ldots c_i \gg^I l_d \gg^I \ldots c_n \gg^I l_u$. Each control point in this sequence is called a cut point.*

Note the *def* and the *use* statement (*i.e.*, l_d and l_u) of the pair itself also serve as the cut points. These cut points are used as the intermediate goals during path search to narrow down the search space. For illustration, consider the figure below: Let $du(l_d, l_u, v)$ be the target def-use pair, its cut points are $\{l_1, l_3, l_d, l_6, l_u\}$. Here the control point l_2 is not a cut point, since the path

$l_1, l_3, l_d, l_4, l_6, l_u$ can be constructed to cover the pair. For the similar reason, the control points l_4 and l_5 are not its cut points.

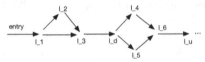

In practice, we use standard iterative data-flow analysis [47,72] to identify def-use pairs from the program under test. We give the implementation details in Sect. 6.

Algorithm 1: SE-based Data-flow Testing

Input: $du(l_d, l_u, x)$: a given def-use pair
Input: $C = \{c_1, c_2, \ldots, c_n\}$: the cut points of du
Output: input t that satisfies du or nil if none is found within the given time bound

1 let W be a worklist of execution states
2 let ES_0 be the initial execution state
3 $W \leftarrow W \cup \{ES_0\}$
   // the core process of symbolic execution
4 **repeat**
5   ExecutionState $ES \leftarrow$ selectState(W)
6   **while** $ES.instructionType\,!=FORK$ or $EXIT$ **do**
7   ES.executeInstruction()
8   **if** $ES.instructionType=EXIT$ **then** $W \leftarrow W \setminus \{ES\}$
9   **if** $ES.instructionType = FORK$ **then**
10   **Instruction** Fr $= ES$.currentInstruction;
11   **ExecutionState** $ES' \leftarrow$ **new** executionState(ES)
12   ES.newNode $\leftarrow$ Fr(T)
13   ES'.newNode $\leftarrow$ Fr(F)
14         $W \leftarrow W \cup \{ES'\}$
15   **PendingPath** $p \leftarrow ES$.path
16   **if** p *covers* du **then return** $t \leftarrow$ getTestCase(ES)
   // the redefinition path pruning heuristic
17   **if** *variable x (in du) is redefined by p* **then**
18         $W \leftarrow W \setminus \{ES, ES'\}$
19 **until** $W.size()=0$ or timeout()
   // the core algorithm of execution state selection
20 **Procedure** selectState(**reference** worklist W)
21 let ES' be the next selected execution state
   // j is the index of a cut point, w is the state weight
22 $j \leftarrow 0$, $w \leftarrow \infty$
23 **foreach** *ExecutionState* $ES \in W$ **do**
24   **PendingPath** $pp \leftarrow ES$.path
   // $c_1, \ldots, c_i$ are sequentially-covered, while c_{i+1} not yet
25     $i \leftarrow$ index of the cut point c_i on pp
26   **StateWeight** $sw \leftarrow$ distance$(es, c_{i+1})^{-2} +$ instructionsSinceCovNew$(es)^{-2}$
27   **if** $i > j \lor (i == j \land sw > w)$ **then**
28         $ES' \leftarrow ES$, $j \leftarrow i$, $w \leftarrow sw$
29 $W \leftarrow W \setminus \{ES'\}$
30 **return** ES'

5.2   SE-Based Approach for Data-Flow Testing

This section explains the symbolic execution-based approach for data-flow testing. Algorithm 1 gives the details. This algorithm takes as input a target def-use pair du and its cut points C, and either outputs the test case t that satisfies du, or nil if it fails to find a path that can cover du.

It first selects one execution state ES from the worklist W which stores all the execution states during symbolic execution. It then executes the current program instruction referenced by ES, and update ES according to the instruction type (Lines 6–14, $cf.$ Sect. 3.2). Basically, one instruction can be one of three types: $sequential\ instruction$ ($e.g.$, assignment statements), $forking\ instruction$ ($e.g.$, if statements, denoted as $FORK$), and $exit\ instruction$ ($e.g.$, program exits or runtime errors, denoted as $EXIT$). When it encounters sequential instructions, ES is updated accordingly by function $executeInstruction$ (Lines 6–7). Specifically, function $executeInstruction$ will internally (1) execute the current instruction, and (2) update ES (including the symbolic state, the reference to next instruction and the corresponding instruction type). When it encounters $FORK$ instructions, one new execution state ES' will be created. The two states ES and ES' will explore both sides of the fork, respectively, and the corresponding subpaths of ES and ES' will be updated to $ES.path+Fr(T)$ and $ES.path+Fr(F)$, respectively (Lines 9–14). Here, Fr denotes the forking point, and T and F represent the $true$ and $false$ directions, respectively. If the target pair du is covered by the pending path p of ES, a test input t will be generated (Line 16). If the variable x of du is redefined on p between the def and use statement, a redefinition path pruning heuristic will remove those invalid states (Lines 17–18, more details will be explained later). The algorithm will continue until either the worklist W is empty or the given testing time is exhausted (at Line 19).

The algorithm core is the state selection procedure, $i.e.$, $selectState$ (detailed at Lines 20–30), which integrates several heuristics to improve the overall effectiveness. Figure 4 conceptually shows the benefits of their combination (the red path is a valid path that covers the pair), which can efficiently steer exploration towards the target pair, and reduce as many unnecessary path explorations as possible: (1) the cut point guided search guides the state exploration towards the target pair more quickly; (2) the backtrack strategy counts the number of executed instructions to prevent the search from being trapped in tight loops, and switches to alternative search directions; and (3) the redefinition path pruning technique effectively prunes redundant search space. In detail, we use Formula 4 to assign the weights to all states, and achieve the heuristics (1) and (2).

$$state\_weight(es) = (c_{max}, \frac{1}{d^2} + \frac{1}{i^2}) \tag{4}$$

where, ES is an execution state, c_{max} is the deepest covered cut point, d is the instruction distance toward the next uncovered cut point, and i is the number of executed instructions since the last new instruction have been covered. Below, we explain the details of each heuristic.

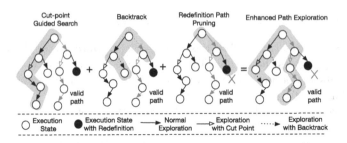

Fig. 4. Enhanced path exploration in symbolic execution: combine cut-point guided search, backtrack strategy and redefinition path pruning. Each subfigure denotes the execution tree generated by symbolic execution.

Cut Point Guided Search. The cut-point guided search strategy (at Lines 23–28) aims to search for the ES whose pending path has covered the deepest cut point, and tries to reach the next goal, *i.e.*, the next uncovered cut point, as quickly as possible. For an ES, its pending path is a subpath that starts from the program entry and reaches up to the program location of it. If this path has sequentially covered the cut point $c_1, c_2, \ldots, c_i$ but not c_{i+1}, c_i is the deepest covered cut point, and c_{i+1} is the next goal to reach. The strategy always prefers to select the ES that has covered the deepest cut point (at Lines 26–28, indicated by the condition $i > j$). The intuition is that the deeper cut point an ES can reach, the closer the ES toward the pair is.

When more than one ES covers the deepest cut point (indicated by the condition $i == j$ at Line 27), the ES that has the shortest distance toward next goal will be preferred (at Lines 26–28). The intuition is that the closer the distance is, the more quickly the ES can reach the goal. We use *dist(es, c_{i+1})* to present the distance between the location of *es* and the next uncovered cut point c_{i+1}. The distance is approximated as the number of instructions along the shortest control-flow path between the program locations of *es* and c_{i+1}.

Backtrack Strategy. To avoid the execution falling into the tight loops, we assign an ES with lower priority if the ES is not likely to cover new instructions. In particular, for each ES, the function *instrsSinceCovNew*, corresponding to i in Formula (4), counts the number of executed instructions since the last new instruction is covered (at Line 26). The ES, which has a larger value of *instrsSinceCovNew*, is assumed that it has lower possibility to cover new instructions. Intuitively, this heuristic prefers the ES which is able to cover more new instructions, if a ES does not cover new instructions for a long time, the strategy will backtrack to another ES via lowering the weight of the current ES.

Redefinition Path Pruning. A redefinition path pruning technique checks whether the selected ES has redefined the variable x in *du*. If the ES is invalid (*i.e.*, its pending path has redefined x), it will be discarded and *selectState* will choose another one (at Lines 17–18). The reason is that, according to the

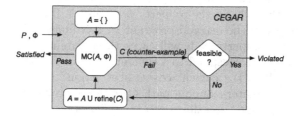

Fig. 5. Paradigm of CEGAR-based Model Checking

definition of DFT (*cf.* Definition 3), it is impossible to find def-clear paths by executing those invalid ESs.

Further, by utilizing the path-sensitive information from SE, we can detect variable redefinitions, especially caused by variable aliases, more precisely. Variable aliases appear when two or more variable names refer to the same memory location. So we designed a lightweight variable redefinition detection algorithm in our framework. Our approach operates upon a simplified three-address form of the original code[5], so we mainly focus on the following statement forms where variable aliases and variable redefinitions may appear:

- Alias inducing statements: (1) $p:=q$ ($*p$ is an alias to $*q$), (2) $p:=\&x$ ($*p$ is an alias to x)
- Variable definition statements: (3) $*p:=y$ ($*p$ is defined by y), (4) $v:=y$ (v is defined by y)

Here, p and q are pointer variables, x and y non-pointer variables, and ":=" the assignment operator.

Initially, a set A is maintained, which denotes the variable alias set *w.r.t.* the variable x of *du*. At the beginning, it only contains x itself. During path exploration, if the executed statement is (1) or (2), and $*q$ or $x \in A$, $*p$ will be added into A since $*p$ becomes an alias of x. If the executed statement is (1), and $*q \notin A$ but $x \in A$, $*p$ will be excluded from A since it becomes an alias of another variable instead of x. If the executed statement is (3) or (4), and $*p \in A$ or $x \in A$, the variable is redefined by another variable y.

5.3 CEGAR-Based Approach for Data-Flow Testing

Counter-example guided abstract refinement (CEGAR) is a well-known software model checking technique that statically proves program correctness *w.r.t.* properties (or specifications) of interest [56]. Figure 5 shows the basic paradigm of CEGAR, which typically follows an *abstract-check-refine* paradigm. Given the program P (*i.e.*, the actual implementation) and a safety property ϕ of interest, CEGAR first *abstracts* P into a model A (typically represented as a finite

---

[5] We use CIL as the C parser to transform the source code into an equivalent simplified form using the –dosimplify option, where one statement contains at most one operator.

automaton), and then *checks* the property ϕ against A. If the abstract model A is error-free, then so is the original program P. If it finds a path on the model A that violates the property ϕ, it will check the feasibility of this path: is it a genuine path that can correspond to a concrete path in the original program P, or due to the result of the current coarse abstraction? If the path is feasible, CEGAR returns a counter-example path C to demonstrate the violation of ϕ. Otherwise, CEGAR will utilize this path C to *refine* A by adding new predicates, and continue the checking until it either finds a genuine path that violates ϕ or proves that ϕ is always satisfied in P. Or since this model checking problem itself is undecidable, CEGAR does not terminate and cannot conclude the correctness of ϕ.

To exploit the power of CEGAR, our approach reduces the problem of data flow testing to the problem of model checking. The CEGAR-based approach can operate in two phases [12] to generate tests, *i.e.*, *model checking* and *tests from counter-examples*. (1) It first uses model checking to check whether the specified program location l is reachable such that the predicate of interest q (*i.e.*, the safety property) can be satisfied at that point. (2) If l is reachable, CEGAR will return a counter-example path p that establishes q at l, and generate a test case from the corresponding path constraint of p. Otherwise, if l is not reachable, CEGAR will conclude no test inputs can reach l.

The key idea is to encode the test obligation of a target def-use pair into the program under test. We instrument the original program P to P', and reduce the test generation for P to path reachability checking on P'. In particular, we follow three steps: (1) We introduce a variable *cover_flag* into P, which denotes the cover status of the target pair, and initialize it as *false*. (2) The variable *cover_flag* is set as *true* immediately after the *def* statement, and set as *false* immediately after all redefinition statements. (3) Before the *use* statement, we set the target predicate as *cover_flag==true*. As a result, if the use statement is reachable when the target predicate holds, we can obtain a counter-example (*i.e.*, a test case) and conclude the pair is feasible. Otherwise, if unreachable, we can safely conclude that the pair is infeasible (or since the problem itself is undecidable, the algorithm does not terminate, and gives *unknown*).

Generability of the SMC-Based Approach. This reduction approach is flexible to implement on any CEGAR-based model checkers. It is also applicable for other software model checking techniques, *e.g.*, Bounded Model Checking (BMC). Given a program, BMC unrolls the control flow graph for a fixed number of k steps, and checks whether the property p at a specified program location l is violated or not. Different from the modern (dynamic) symbolic execution techniques, BMC executes on pure symbolic inputs without using any concrete input values, and usually aims to systematically checking reachability within given bounds. Different from CEGAR, BMC searches on all program computations without abstraction and typically backtracks the search when a given (loop or search depth) bound is reached. Although BMC in general cannot prove infeasibility as certain, in Sect. 7 we will show the BMC-based approach can still serve as a heuristic-criterion to identify hard-to-cover (probably infeasible) pairs and particularly effective for specific types of programs. In fact, the infeasible pairs concluded by BMC can be regarded as valid modulo the given checking bounds.

6   Framework Design and Implementation

We realized our hybrid data-flow testing framework for C programs. In our original work [84], we implemented the SE-based approach on our own concolic testing based tool CAUT [85,91], while in this article we built the enhanced SE-based approach on KLEE [18], a robust execution-generated testing based symbolic execution engine, to fully exhibit its feasibility. As for the SMC-based approach, we instantiated it with two different types of software model checking techniques, i.e., CEGAR and BMC. In all, our framework combines the SE-based and SMC-based approaches together to achieve efficient DFT.

In the static analysis phase, we identify def-use pairs, cut points, and related static program information (e.g., variable definitions and aliases) by using CIL [70] (C Intermediate Language), which is an infrastructure for C program analysis and transformation. We first build the control-flow graph (CFG) for each function in the program under test, and then construct the inter-procedural CFG (ICFG) for the whole program. We perform standard iterative data-flow analysis techniques [47,72], i.e., reaching definition analysis, to compute def-use pairs. For each variable use, we compute which definitions on the same variable can reach the use through a def-clear path on the control-flow graph. A def-use pair is created as a test objective for each use with its corresponding definition. We treat each formal parameter variable as defined at the beginning of its function and each argument parameter variable as used at its function call site (e.g., library calls). For global variables, we treat them as initially defined at the beginning the entry function (e.g., the main function), and defined/used at any function where they are defined/used.

In the current implementation, we focus on the def-use pairs with local variables (intra-procedural pairs) and global variables (inter-procedural pairs). Following prior work on data-flow testing [89], we currently do not consider the def-use pairs induced by pointer aliases. Thus, we may miss some def-use pairs, but we believe that this is an independent issue (not the focus of this work) and does not affect the effectiveness of our testing approach. More sophisticated data-flow analysis techniques (e.g., dynamic data-flow analysis [30]) or tools (e.g., Frama-C [59]) can be used to mitigate this problem.

Specifically, to improve the efficiency of state selection algorithm (cf. Algorithm 1) in KLEE, we use the priority queue to sort execution states according to their weights. The algorithmic complexity is $\mathcal{O}(n \log n)$ (n is the number of execution states), which is much faster than using a list or array. The software model checkers are used as black-box to enforce data-flow testing. The benefit of this design choice is that we can flexibly integrate any model checker without any modification or adaption. CIL transforms the program under test into a simplified code version, and encodes the test requirements of def-use pairs into the program under test. Both SE-based and SMC-based tools takes as input the same CIL-simplified code. Function stubs are used to simulate C library functions such as string, memory and file operations to improve the ability of symbolic reasoning. To compute the data-flow coverage during testing, we implement the classic *last definition* technique [52] in KLEE. We maintain a table of def-use pairs, and insert probes at each basic block to monitor the program execution. The runtime routine records each variable that has been defined and the block where it was defined. When a block that uses this defined variable is executed, the last definition of this variable is located, we check whether the pair is covered. Our implementations are publicly available at [87].

7 Evaluation

This section aims to evaluate whether our combined testing approach can achieve efficient data-flow testing. In particular, we intend to investigate (1) whether the core SE-based approach can quickly cover def-use pairs; (2) whether the SMC-based reduction approach is feasible and practical; and (3) whether the combined approach can be more effective for data-flow testing.

7.1 Research Questions

- **RQ1:** In the data-flow testing *w.r.t.* all def-use coverage, what is the performance difference between different existing search strategies (*e.g.*, DFS, RSS, RSS-MD2U, SDGS) and CPGS (our cut point guided path search strategy) in terms of testing time and number of covered pairs for the SE-based approach?
- **RQ2:** How is the practicability of the CEGAR-based reduction approach as well as the BMC-based approach in terms of testing time and number of identified feasible and infeasible pairs?
- **RQ3:** How efficient is the combined approach, which complements the SE-based approach with the SMC-based approach, in terms of testing time and coverage level, compared with the SE-based approach or the SMC-based approach alone?

7.2 Evaluation Setup

Testing Environment. All evaluations were run on a 64bit Ubuntu 14.04 physical machine with 24 processors (2.60 GHz Intel Xeon(R) E5-2670 CPU) and 94 GB RAM.

Framework Implementations. The SE-based approach of our hybrid testing framework was implemented on KLEE (v1.1.0), and the SMC-based approach was implemented on two different software model checking techniques, CEGAR and BMC. In particular, we chose three different software model checkers[6], *i.e.*, BLAST [13] (CEGAR-based, v2.7.3), CPAchecker [14] (CEGAR-based, v.1.7)

---

[6] We use the latest versions of these model checkers at the time of writing.

and CBMC [24] (BMC-based, v5.7). We chose different model checkers, since we intend to gain more overall understandings of the practicality of this reduction approach. Note that the CEGAR-based approach can give definite answers of the feasibility, while the BMC-based approach is used as a heuristic-criterion to identify hard-to-cover (probably infeasible) pairs.

Program Subjects. Despite data-flow testing has been continuously investigated in the past four decades, the standard benchmarks for evaluating data-flow testing techniques are still missing. To this end, we took substantial efforts and dedicatedly constructed a repository of benchmark subjects by following these steps. *First*, we collected the subjects from prior work on data-flow testing. We conducted a thorough investigation on all prior work (99 papers [83] in total) related to data-flow testing, and searched for the adopted subjects. After excluding the subjects whose source codes are not available or not written in C language, we got 26 unique subjects [32,35,39,42,54,57,66–69,75,76,80,81,84,92,94]. We then manually inspected these programs and excluded 19 subjects which are too simple, we finally got 7 subjects. These 7 subjects include mathematical computations and classic algorithms. *Second*, we included 7 Siemens subjects from SIR [82], which are widely used in the experiments of program analysis and software testing [48,54,90]. These subjects involve numeral computations, string manipulations and complex data structures (*e.g.*, pointers, structs, and lists). *Third*, we further enriched the repository with the subjects from the SV-COMP benchmarks [33], which are originally used for the competition on software verification. The SV-COMP benchmarks are categorized in different groups by their features (*e.g.*, concurrency, bit vectors, floats) for evaluating software model checkers. In order to reduce potential evaluation biases in our scenario, we carefully inspected all the benchmarks and finally decided to select subjects from the "Integers and Control Flow" category based on these considerations: (1) the subjects in this category are real-world (medium-sized or large-sized) OS device drivers (*cf.* [11], Sect. 4), while many subjects in other categories are hand-crafted, small-sized programs; (2) the subjects in this category have complicated function call chains or control-flow structures, which are more appropriate for our evaluation; (3) the subjects do not contain specific features that may not be supported by KLEE (*e.g.*, concurrency, floating point numbers). We finally selected 16 subjects in total from the *ntdrivers* and *ssh* groups therein (we excluded other subjects with similar control-flow structures by diffing the code). The selected subjects have rather complex control-flows. For example, the average cyclomatic complexity of functions in the ssh group exceeds 88.5[7] (computed by *Cyclo* [1]) *Fourth*, we also included three core program modules from the industrial projects from our research partners. The first one is an engine management system (*osek_ control*) running on an automobile operating system conforming to the OSEK/VDX standard. The second one is a satellite gesture control program (*space_ control*). The third one is a control program (*subway_ control*) from a subway signal. All these three industrial pro-

---

[7] Cyclomatic complexity is a software metric that indicates the complexity of a program. The standard software development guidelines recommend the cyclomatic complexity of a module should not exceeded 10.

Table 2. Subjects of the constructed data-flow testing benchmark repository

Subject	#ELOC	#DU	Description
factorization	43	47	compute factorization
power	11	11	compute the power x^y
find	66	99	permute an array's elements
triangle	32	46	classify an triangle type
strmat	67	32	string pattern matching
strmat2	88	38	string pattern matching
textfmt	142	73	text string formatting
tcas	195	86	collision avoidance system
replace	567	387	pattern matching and substitution
totinfo	374	279	compute statistics given input data
printtokens	498	240	lexical analyzer
printtokens2	417	192	lexical analyzer
schedule	322	118	process priority scheduler
schedule2	314	107	process priority scheduler
kbfiltr	557	176	ntdrivers group
kbfiltr2	954	362	ntdrivers group
diskperf	1,052	443	ntdrivers group
floppy	1,091	331	ntdrivers group
floppy2	1,511	606	ntdrivers group
cdaudio	2,101	773	ntdrivers group
s3_clnt	540	1,677	ssh group
s3_clnt_termination	555	1,595	ssh group
s3_srvr_1a	198	574	ssh group
s3_srvr_1b	127	139	ssh group
s3_srvr_2	608	2,130	ssh group
s3_srvr_7	624	2,260	ssh group
s3_srvr_8	631	2,322	ssh group
s3_srvr_10	628	2,200	ssh group
s3_srvr_12	696	3,125	ssh group
s3_srvr_13	642	2,325	ssh group
osek_control	4,589	927	one module of engine management system
space_control	5,782	1,739	one module of satellite gesture control software
subway_control	5,612	2,895	one module of subway signal control software

grams were used in our previous research work [74,85,98], and have complicated data-flow interactions. *Finally,* to ensure each tool (where our framework is built upon) can correctly reason these subjects, we carefully read the documentation of each tool to understand their limitations, manually checked each program and added necessary function stubs (*e.g.,* to simulate such C library functions as string, memory, and file operations) but without affecting their original program logic and structures. This is important to reduce validation threats, and also provides a more fair comparison basis. In total, we got 33 subjects with different characteristics, including mathematical computation, classic algorithms, utility programs, device drivers and industrial control programs. These subjects allow us to evaluate diverse data-flow scenarios. Table 2 shows the detailed statistics of these subjects, which includes the executable lines of code (computed by *cloc* [2]), the number of def-use pairs (including intra- and inter-procedural pairs), and the brief functional description.

Search Strategies for Comparison.   To our knowledge, there exists no specific guided search strategies on KLEE to compare with our strategy. Thus, we compare our cut-point guided search strategy with several existing search strategies. In particular, we chose two generic search strategies (*i.e.*, depth-first and random search), one popular (statement) coverage-optimized search strategy. In addition, we implemented one search strategy for directed testing on KLEE, which is proposed by prior work [61,64,97]. We detail them as follows.

- *Depth First-Search (DFS)*: always select the latest execution state from all states to explore, and has little overhead in state selection.
- *Random State Search (RSS)*: randomly select an execution state from all states to explore, and able to explore the program space more uniformly and less likely to be trapped in tight loops than other strategies like DFS.
- *Coverage-Optimized Search (COS)*: compute the weights of the states by some heuristics, *e.g.*, the minimal distance to uncovered instructions (*md2u*) and whether the state recently covered new code (*covnew*), and randomly select states *w.r.t.* these weights. These heuristics are usually interleaved with other search strategies in a round-robin fashion to improve their overall effectiveness. For example, *RSS-COS:md2u* (*RSS-MD2U* for short) is a popular strategy used by KLEE, which interleaves *RSS* with *md2u*.
- *Shortest Distance Guided Search (SDGS)*: always select the execution state that has the shortest (instruction) distance toward a target instruction in order to cover the target as quickly as possible. This strategy has been widely applied in single target testing [61,64,97]. In the context of data-flow testing, we implemented this strategy in KLEE by setting the *def* as the first goal and then the *use* as the second goal after the *def* is covered.

7.3   Case Studies

We conducted three case studies to answer the research questions. Note that in this paper we focus on the classic data-flow testing [39,89], *i.e.*, targeting one def-use pair at one run. In ***Study 1***, we answer ***RQ1*** by comparing the performance of different search strategies that were implemented on KLEE. In detail, we use two metrics: (1) *number of covered pairs*, *i.e.*, how many def-use pairs can be covered; and (2) *testing time*, *i.e.*, how long does it take to cover the pair(s) of interest. The *testing time* is measured by the median value and the semi-interquartile range (SIQR)[8] of the times consumed on those covered (*feasible*) pairs[9].

In the evaluation, the maximum allowed search time on each pair is set as 5 min. Under this setting, we observed all search strategies can thoroughly test

---

[8] SIQR = (Q3-Q1)/2, which measures the variability of testing time, where Q1 is the lower quartile, and Q3 is the upper quartile.

[9] In theory, the symbolic execution-based approach cannot identify infeasible pairs unless it enumerates all possible paths, which however is impossible in practice. Therefore, we only consider the testing times of covered (feasible) pairs for performance evaluation.

each subject (*i.e.*, reach their highest coverage rates). To mitigate the algorithm randomness, we repeat the testing process 30 times for each program/strategy and aggregate their average values as the final results for all measurements.

In *Study 2*, we answer *RQ2* by evaluating the practicability of the SMC-based reduction approach on two different model checking techniques, CEGAR and BMC. Specifically, we implemented the reduction approach on three different model checkers, BLAST, CPAchecker and CBMC. We use the following default command options and configurations according to their user manuals and the suggestions from the tool developers, respectively:

BLAST: `ocamltune blast -enable-recursion -cref -lattice -noprofile`
         `-nosserr -quiet`
CPAchecker: `cpachecker -config config/predicateAnalysis.properties`
         `-skipRecursion`
CBMC: `cbmc --slice-formula --unwind nr1 --depth nr2`

We have not tried to particularly tune the optimal configurations of these tools for different subjects under test, since we aim to investigate the practicability of our reduction approach in general. Specifically, BLAST and CPAchecker are configured based on predicate abstraction. For BLAST, we use an internal script `ocamltune` to improve memory utilization for large programs; for CPAchecker, we use its default predicate abstraction configuration predicateAnalysis.properties. We use the option -enable-recursion of BLAST and -skipRecursion of CPAchecker to set recursion functions as *skip*. Due to CBMC is a bounded model checker, it may answer *infeasible* for actual *feasible* pairs if the given checking bound is too small. Thus, we set the appropriate values for the –unwind and –depth options, respectively, for the number of times loops to be unwound and the number of program steps to be processed. Specially, we determine the parameter values of –unwind and –depth options by a binary search algorithm to ensure that CBMC can identify as many pairs as possible within the given time bound. This avoids wasting testing budget on unnecessary path explorations, and also achieves a more fair evaluation basis. Therefore, each subject may be given different parameter values (the concrete parameter values of all subjects are available at [87]).

Specifically, we use two metrics: (1) *number of feasible, infeasible, and unknown pairs*; and (2) *testing (checking) time of feasible and infeasible pairs* (denoted in medians). The maximum testing time on each def-use pair is constrained as 5 min (*i.e.*, 300 s, the same setting in RQ1). For each def-use pair, we also run 30 times to mitigate algorithm randomness.

In *Study 3*, we answer *RQ3* by combining the SE-based and SMC-based approaches. We interleave these two approaches as follows: the SE-based approach (configured with the cut point-guided path search strategy and the same settings in *RQ1*) is first used to cover as many pairs as possible; then, for the remaining uncovered pairs, the SMC-based approach (configured with the same settings in *RQ2*) is used to identify infeasible pairs (may also cover some feasible pairs). We continue the above iteration of the combined approach until the maximum allowed time bound (5 min for each pair) is used up. Specifically, we

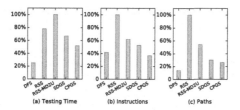

Fig. 6. Performance of each search strategy in terms of total testing time, number of executed program instructions, and number of explored program paths (normalized in percentage) on all 33 subjects.

increase the time bound by 3 times at each iteration, *i.e.*, 10 s, 30 s, 90 s and 300 s.

Specifically, we use two metrics: (1) *coverage rate*; and (2) *total testing time*, *i.e.*, the total time required to enforce data-flow testing on all def-use pairs of one subject. The coverage rate C is computed by Formula 5, where $nTestObj$ is the total number of pairs, and $nFeasible$ and $nInfeasible$ are the number of identified feasible and infeasible ones, respectively.

$$C = \frac{nFeasible}{nTestObj - nInfeasible} \times 100\% \tag{5}$$

In all case studies, the testing time was measured in CPU time via the *time* command in Linux. In particular, the testing time did not include IO operations for logging the testing results. We tested 31,634 ELOC with 28,354 pairs in total. It took us nearly one and half months to run the experiments and analyze the results.

7.4   Study 1

Table 3 shows the detailed performance statistics of different search strategies. The column *Subject* represents the subject under test, DFS, RSS, RSS-MD2U, SDGS, CPGS, respectively, represent the search strategies. For each subject/strategy, it shows the number of covered def-use pairs (denoted by N), the median value of testing times (denoted by M) and the semi-interquartile range of testing times (denoted by $SIQR$) on all covered pairs. In particular, for each subject, we underscore the strategy with lowest median value. The last row gives the total number of covered pairs. From Table 3, we can observe (1) Given enough testing time for all strategies (*i.e.*, 5 min for each pair), CPGS covers 4215, 2152, 1320 and 1563 more pairs, respectively, than DFS, RSS, RSS-MD2U and SDGS. It means CPGS achieves 40%, 21.3%, 12.1%, 14.6% higher data-flow coverage than these strategies, respectively. (2) By comparing the median values of CPGS with those of other strategies, CPGS achieves more efficient data-flow testing in 14/33, 23/33, 32/33, 26/33 subjects than DFS, RSS, RSS-MD2U and SDGS,

Table 3. Performance statistics of different search strategies for data-flow testing (the testing time is measured in seconds).

Subject	DFS		RSS		RSS-MD2U		SDGS		CPGS	
	N	M (SIQR)	N	M (SIQR)	N	M (SIQR)	N	M (SIQR)	N	M (SIQR)
factorization	22	0.07 (0.01)	22	0.07 (0.01)	22	0.08 (0.02)	22	0.05 (0.01)	22	0.06 (0.01)
power	6	0.14 (0.00)	9	0.12 (0.01)	9	0.05 (0.01)	5	0.04 (0.00)	9	0.04 (0.00)
find	77	0.89(0.64)	49	0.19 (0.54)	52	0.26 (0.31)	51	0.63 (3.35)	56	0.22 (0.12)
triangle	22	0.24 (0.06)	22	0.24 (0.03)	22	0.26 (0.05)	22	0.25 (0.09)	22	0.13 (0.01)
strmat	26	2.84 (1.41)	30	0.10 (0.02)	30	0.13 (0.03)	30	0.12 (0.16)	30	0.10 (0.02)
strmat2	28	2.85 (1.40)	32	0.09 (0.01)	32	0.11 (0.02)	32	0.11 (0.03)	32	0.09 (0.02)
textfmt	37	0.16 (0.08)	33	0.05 (0.01)	33	0.11 (0.04)	34	0.06 (0.01)	34	0.06 (0.01)
tcas	55	0.13 (0.03)	55	0.21 (0.07)	55	0.67 (0.43)	55	0.16 (0.06)	55	0.14 (0.06)
replace	69	0.77 (0.14)	308	1.96 (15.23)	312	30.31 (21.97)	295	4.67 (5.46)	309	1.15 (3.58)
totinfo	13	0.52 (0.07)	24	0.42 (0.13)	24	0.64 (0.08)	24	0.42 (0.06)	26	0.52 (0.05)
printtokens	48	0.96 (0.62)	115	34.69 (24.16)	106	33.68 (22.59)	107	16.40 (25.53)	115	12.23 (20.21)
printtokens2	124	0.47 (0.32)	148	0.80 (3.72)	149	20.67 (18.42)	149	0.83 (3.48)	154	0.51 (1.43)
schedule	15	0.16 (0.03)	83	0.23 (3.98)	86	0.76 (5.05)	77	0.22 (1.67)	86	0.22 (1.84)
schedule2	14	0.15 (0.02)	78	0.20 (0.12)	78	0.48 (1.11)	77	0.21 (0.10)	77	0.21 (0.08)
cdaudio	562	3.13 (0.41)	562	3.27 (0.48)	562	15.54 (7.11)	562	3.77 (2.52)	562	3.08 (0.51)
diskperf	285	0.89 (0.19)	302	0.97 (0.21)	302	1.97 (4.80)	299	0.95 (0.23)	302	0.92 (0.18)
floppy	249	0.62 (0.11)	249	0.67 (0.11)	249	2.11 (1.76)	249	0.72 (0.14)	249	0.66 (0.13)
floppy2	510	2.22 (0.37)	510	2.14 (0.42)	510	6.44 (3.44)	510	3.62 (1.66)	510	2.03 (0.39)
kbfiltr	116	0.26 (0.05)	116	0.28 (0.05)	116	0.49 (0.41)	116	0.31 (0.04)	116	0.27 (0.05)
kbfiltr2	266	0.97 (0.15)	266	0.94 (0.18)	266	4.18 (3.51)	266	2.11 (1.08)	266	0.90 (0.20)
s3_srvr_1a	113	0.72 (0.17)	171	0.75 (0.19)	171	0.76 (0.19)	165	0.65 (0.17)	171	0.58 (0.18)
s3_srvr_1b	30	0.08 (0.02)	43	0.08 (0.02)	43	0.07 (0.02)	43	0.07 (0.02)	45	0.08 (0.02)
s3_clnt	647	9.64 (2.01)	648	11.93 (2.64)	647	22.91 (8.19)	633	12.45 (2.45)	648	10.32 (1.88)
s3_clnt_termination	333	9.20 (1.64)	332	8.81 (1.87)	332	12.14 (1.29)	332	9.56 (1.74)	414	6.54 (1.03)
s3_srvr_2	414	14.35 (2.67)	695	24.23 (17.42)	695	31.86 (15.44)	681	19.93 (8.00)	695	16.45 (3.76)
s3_srvr_7	420	16.29 (3.44)	710	27.82 (20.06)	710	34.99 (17.11)	686	26.93 (12.46)	815	19.47 (5.41)
s3_srvr_8	416	16.77 (3.10)	704	23.61 (14.03)	698	36.15 (16.39)	690	23.45 (7.21)	798	17.04 (4.23)
s3_srvr_10	431	15.26 (2.40)	683	21.34 (5.19)	683	30.21 (7.03)	664	20.73 (5.85)	683	18.37 (3.90)
s3_srvr_12	433	25.76 (3.84)	395	39.51 (21.68)	539	64.25 (38.99)	486	39.50 (18.04)	724	25.88 (10.08)
s3_srvr_13	437	15.69 (2.07)	489	25.25 (18.07)	558	33.78 (21.20)	572	23.98 (11.49)	744	15.77 (6.12)
osek_control	398	7.69 (2.47)	426	15.77 (14.68)	549	23.32 (17.39)	538	14.17 (6.17)	639	6.15 (3.23)
space_control	582	15.90 (7.76)	812	33.49 (20.61)	990	48.77 (23.08)	961	28.86 (15.78)	1,178	6.32 (7.09)
subway_control	827	13.44 (7.69)	967	42.76 (28.65)	1,290	68.61 (31.73)	1,244	38.11 (21.46)	1,654	10.72 (6.72)
Total	8,025	–	10,088	–	10,920	–	10,677	–	12,240	–

respectively. Note that the median value of DFS is low because it only covers many easily reachable pairs, which also explains why it achieves lowest coverage.

Figure 6 shows the performance of these search strategies on all 33 subjects in terms of total testing time, the number of executed program instructions, and the number of explored program paths (due to the data difference, we normalized them in percentage). Note these three metrics are all computed on the covered pairs. Apart from DFS (since it achieves rather low data-flow coverage), we can see CPGS outperforms all the other testing strategies. In detail, CPGS reduces testing time by 15–48%, the number of executed instructions by 16–63%, and the number of explored paths by 28–74%. The reason is that CPGS narrows down the search space by following the cut points and prunes unnecessary paths.

Answer to RQ1: *In summary, our cut-point guided search (CPGS) strategy performs the best for data-flow testing. It improves 12–40% data-flow coverage, and at the same time reduces the total testing time by 15–48% and the number of explored paths by 28–74%. Therefore, the SE-based approach, enhanced with the cut point guided search strategy, is efficient for data-flow testing.*

Table 4. Performance statistics of the SMC-based reduction approach $CEGAR_{BLAST}$, $CEGAR_{CPAchecker}$ and BMC_{CBMC} for data-flow testing (the testing time is measured in seconds), where * denotes the numbers in the corresponding columns are only valid modulo the given checking bound for BMC_{CBMC}.

Subject	$CEGAR_{BLAST}$					$CEGAR_{CPAchecker}$					BMC_{CBMC}				
	F	I	U	M_F	M_I	F	I	U	M_F	M_I	F	I*	U*	M_F	M_I*
factorization	35	4	8	0.04	0.20	26	4	17	3.26	3.04	41	6	0	0.34	0.28
power	9	2	0	0.03	0.49	9	2	0	3.10	2.97	9	2	0	0.13	0.12
find	85	12	2	6.44	3.22	74	14	11	4.37	3.60	77	22	0	0.29	0.29
triangle	22	24	0	0.04	0.69	22	24	0	3.09	2.83	22	24	0	0.11	0.11
strmat	30	2	0	1.81	1.39	30	2	0	4.67	2.98	30	2	0	0.15	0.15
strmat2	32	6	0	5.08	1.46	32	6	0	4.91	3.79	32	6	0	0.15	0.15
textfmt	47	18	8	10.08	13.90	53	20	0	12.69	5.50	53	20	0	3.84	3.95
tcas	55	31	0	1.35	1.31	55	31	0	4.08	3.43	55	31	0	0.13	0.13
replace	275	73	39	6.17	13.60	211	48	128	11.21	10.84	339	48	0	101.47	93.20
totinfo	–	–	279	–	–	76	24	179	14.80	11.50	69	209	1	54.36	7.68
printtokens	165	57	18	6.15	13.67	178	58	4	8.94	6.22	169	71	0	15.94	9.26
printtokens2	188	4	0	13.35	7.25	188	4	0	13.21	6.48	187	5	0	28.29	28.89
schedule	37	0	81	0.05	–	92	22	4	7.82	11.13	85	33	0	33.04	31.15
schedule2	33	0	74	0.04	–	42	0	65	7.32	–	35	55	17	189.03	205.14
cdaudio	544	179	50	0.41	0.81	–	190	583	–	6.36	566	207	0	1.50	1.58
diskperf	270	117	56	0.16	0.41	265	119	59	5.08	5.18	304	139	0	0.89	0.85
floppy	240	69	22	0.18	0.43	244	65	22	4.75	5.23	250	81	0	0.72	0.71
floppy2	497	82	27	0.33	0.59	501	79	26	5.28	5.68	511	95	0	1.51	1.35
kbfiltr	107	49	20	0.09	0.10	107	51	18	3.85	3.61	116	60	0	0.32	0.32
kbfiltr2	249	74	39	0.15	0.20	249	76	37	4.14	4.28	264	98	0	0.56	0.54
s3_srvr_1a	123	295	156	2.69	1.37	123	295	156	4.94	4.13	170	404	0	0.69	0.69
s3_srvr_1b	43	96	0	0.36	0.80	43	96	0	3.31	3.26	43	96	0	0.16	0.16
s3_clnt	625	969	83	14.62	4.86	661	1012	4	9.72	5.12	665	1012	0	39.62	41.52
s3_clnt_termination	540	964	91	15.16	4.35	582	1012	1	10.11	5.42	583	1012	0	22.57	24.02
s3_srvr_2	418	1034	678	3.50	5.21	698	1344	88	11.00	5.25	704	1420	6	102.85	128.09
s3_srvr_7	393	1073	794	3.34	4.78	712	1458	90	11.09	5.43	721	1538	1	100.42	124.45
s3_srvr_8	425	1183	714	3.98	5.07	701	1529	92	10.70	5.58	706	1604	12	107.31	137.57
s3_srvr_10	414	1060	726	5.00	32.16	678	1432	90	8.40	4.45	683	1517	0	125.92	111.44
s3_srvr_12	388	1611	1126	4.13	7.00	759	2231	135	9.86	6.19	758	2345	22	125.43	144.04
s3_srvr_13	431	1111	783	4.43	5.61	745	1500	80	10.04	4.55	737	1569	19	111.75	137.98
osek_control	607	150	170	9.43	8.09	645	199	87	7.72	6.54	623	277	27	52.76	65.12
space_control	1012	457	270	13.34	14.72	1156	495	88	9.85	10.57	1137	579	23	67.23	75.94
subway_control	1543	842	510	21.52	25.73	1793	1013	89	21.18	14.12	1787	1069	27	93.91	121.67
Total	9882	11648	6824	–	–	11750	14455	2153	–	–	12531	15656	155	–	–

7.5   Study 2

Table 4 gives the detailed performance statistics of the SMC-based reduction approach for data-flow testing, where "–" means the corresponding data does not apply or not available[10]. For each implementation instance, it shows the number of feasible (denoted by F), infeasible (denoted by I) and unknown (denoted by U) pairs, and the median of testing times on feasible and infeasible pairs (denoted by M_F and M_I, respectively). The last row gives the total number of feasible, infeasible, and unknown pairs. Note that BLAST and CPAchecker implement CEGAR-based model checking approach, thereby they can give the *feasible* or *infeasible* conclusion (or *unknown* due to undecidability of the problem) without any false positives. As for CBMC, it implements the bounded model checking technique, and in general cannot eliminate infeasible pairs as certain. Thus, the numbers of infeasible pairs identified by CBMC are only valid modulo the given checking bound. From the results, we can see CPAchecker and CBMC are more effective than BLAST in terms of feasible pairs as well as infeasible pairs. In detail, BLAST, CPAchecker and CBMC, respectively, cover 9882, 11750, 12531 feasible pairs, and identify 11648, 14455 and 15656 infeasible ones.

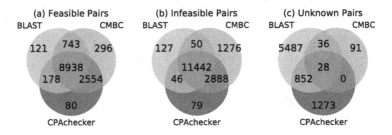

Fig. 7. Venn diagrams of (a) feasible, (b) infeasible and (c) unknown pairs concluded by the three model checkers BLAST, CPAchecker and CBMC for all subjects.

Figure 7 shows the venn diagrams of feasible, infeasible and unknown pairs concluded by the three model checkers BLAST, CPAchecker and CBMC. We can get several important observations: (1) The number of feasible and infeasible pairs identified by all the three model checkers accounts for the majority, occupying 69.2% and 71.9% pairs, respectively. It indicates both the CEGAR-based and BMC-based approaches are practical and can give consistent answers in most cases. (2) Although the infeasible pairs identified by the BMC-based approach are only valid modulo the given checking bound, we can see CBMC in fact correctly concludes a large portion of infeasible pairs. Compared with the infeasiblity results of CPAchecker, 91.8% (14,380/15,656) infeasible pairs identified by CBMC are indeed infeasible given appropriate checking bounds. Thus, the BMC-based approach can still serve as a heuristic-criterion to identify hard-to-cover (probably infeasible) pairs, and better prioritize testing efforts.

---

[10] BLAST hangs on *totinfo*, and CPAchecker crashes on parts of pairs from *cdaudio*.

(3) CPAchecker and CBMC have the largest number of overlapped pairs than the other combinations. They identify 94.7% feasible and 90.3% infeasible pairs, respectively. It indicates these two tools are more effective.

Answer to RQ2: *In summary, the SMC-based reduction approach is practical for data-flow testing. Both the CEGAR-based and BMC-based approaches can give consistent conclusions on the majority of def-use pairs. Specifically, the CEGAR-based approach can give answers for feasibility as certain, while the BMC-based approach can serve as a heuristic-criterion to identify hard-to-cover (probably infeasible) pairs when given appropriate checking bounds.*

7.6   Study 3

To investigate the effectiveness of our combined approach, we complement the SE-based approach with the SMC-based approach to do data-flow testing. Specifically, we realize this combined approach by interleaving these two approaches (the setting is specified in Sect. 7.3). Figure 8 shows the data-flow coverage achieved by KLEE, BLAST, CPAchecker, CBMC alone and their combinations (*e.g.*, the combination of KLEE and CPAchecker, denoted as KLEE+CPAchecker for short) on the 33 subjects within the same testing budget. We can see the combined approach can greatly improve data-flow coverage. In detail, KLEE only achieves 54.3% data-flow coverage on average for the 33 subjects, while KLEE+BLAST, KLEE+CPAchecker, and KLEE+CBMC, respectively, achieve 82.1%, 90.8%, and 99.5% coverage. Compared with KLEE, the combined approach instances, KLEE+BLAST, KLEE+CPAchecker, and KLEE+CBMC, respectively, improve the coverage by 27.8%, 36.5% and 45.2% on average. On the other hand, KLEE+BLAST improves coverage by 10% against BLAST alone, and KLEE+CPAchecker improves coverage by 7% against CPAchecker alone, respectively.

Figure 9 further shows the total testing time consumed by KLEE, BLAST, CPAchecker, CBMC and their combinations when achieving their peak coverage in Fig. 8. We can see that the combined approach can almost consistently reduce the total testing time on each subject. Specifically, compared with KLEE, the combined approach instances, KLEE+BLAST, KLEE+CPAchecker, and KLEE+CBMC, respectively, achieve faster data-flow testing in 30/33, 29/33, and 28/33 subjects, and reduce the total testing time by 78.8%, 93.6% and 20.1% on average in those subjects. Among the three instances of combined approach, KLEE+CPAchecker achieves the best performance, which reduces testing time by 93.6% for all the 33 subjects, and at the same time improves data-flow coverage by 36.5%. On the other hand, the combined approach instances, KLEE+BLAST and KLEE+CPAchecker, also reduce the total testing time of BLAST and CPAchecker by 23.8% and 19.9%, respectively.

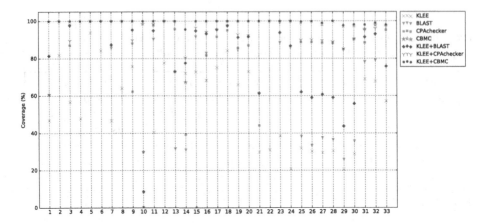

Fig. 8. Data-flow coverage achieved by KLEE, BLAST, CPAchecker, CBMC and their combinations (*i.e.*, KLEE+BLAST, KLEE+CPAchecker, KLEE+CBMC) within the same time budget. Each number on the X axis denotes the set of 33 subjects in our study. Note that the results of CBMC and KLEE+CBMC are only valid modulo the given checking bounds.

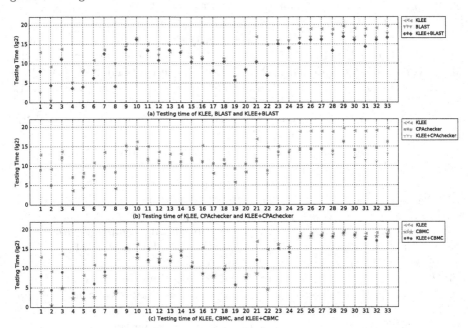

Fig. 9. Consumed time for data-flow testing by KLEE, BLAST, CPAchecker, CBMC and their combinations (*i.e.*, KLEE+BLAST, KLEE+CPAchecker, KLEE+CBMC) for reaching their respective highest coverage. Each point on the X axis denotes the set of 33 subjects in our study. Note that the Y axis uses a logarithmic scale.

Answer to RQ3: *In summary, the combined approach, which combines symbolic execution and software model checking, achieves more efficient data-flow testing. The model checking approach can weed out infeasible pairs that the symbolic execution approach cannot infer by 71.9%–97.2%. Compared with the SE-based approach alone, the combined approach can improve data-flow coverage by 27.8–45.2%. In particular, the instance KLEE+CPAchecker performs best, which reduces total testing time by 93.6% for all 33 subjects, and at the same time improves data-flow coverage by 36.5%. Compared with the CEGAR-based or BMC-based approach alone, the combined approach can also reduce testing time by 19.9–23.8%, and improve data-flow coverage by 7–10%.*

8 Conclusion

This paper introduces an efficient, combined data-flow testing approach. We designed a cut point guided search strategy to make symbolic execution practical; and devised a simple encoding of data-flow testing via software model checking. The two approaches offer complementary strengths: symbolic execution is more effective at covering feasible def-use pairs, while software model checking is more effective at rejecting infeasible pairs. Specifically, the CEGAR-based approach is used to eliminate infeasible pairs as certain, while the BMC-based approach can be used as a heuristic-criterion to identify hard-to-cover (probably infeasible) pairs when given appropriate checking bounds.

Acknowledgements. This work is in honor of Jifeng He's contribution to computer science, especially establishing the Unifying Theories of Programming (UTP). This work applies formal methods to support software testing, which was influenced by the work of Jifeng He. Ting Su, the lead author of this work, sincerely appreciate the academic guidance from his PhD supervisor Jifeng He.

References

1. Cyclo. http://www.gentoogeek.org/cyclo.html
2. ALDanial: cloc. GitHub (2018)
3. Alexander, R.T., Offutt, J., Stefik, A.: Testing coupling relationships in object-oriented programs. Softw. Test. Verif. Reliab. **20**(4), 291–327 (2010)
4. Ammann, P., Offutt, J.: Introduction to Software Testing, 1st edn. Cambridge University Press, New York (2008)
5. Ball, T., Rajamani, S.K.: The SLAM project: debugging system software via static analysis. In: Conference Record of POPL 2002: The 29th SIGPLAN-SIGACT Symposium on Principles of Programming Languages, Portland, OR, USA, 16–18 January 2002, pp. 1–3 (2002)
6. Baluda, M., Braione, P., Denaro, G., Pezzè, M.: Structural coverage of feasible code. In: The 5th Workshop on Automation of Software Test, AST 2010, 3–4 May 2010, Cape Town, South Africa, pp. 59–66 (2010)

7. Baluda, M., Braione, P., Denaro, G., Pezzè, M.: Enhancing structural software coverage by incrementally computing branch executability. Software Qual. J. **19**(4), 725–751 (2011)
8. Baluda, M., Denaro, G., Pezzè, M.: Bidirectional symbolic analysis for effective branch testing. IEEE Trans. Software Eng. **42**(5), 403–426 (2016)
9. Bardin, S., et al.: Sound and quasi-complete detection of infeasible test requirements. In: 8th IEEE International Conference on Software Testing, Verification and Validation, ICST 2015, Graz, Austria, 13–17 April 2015, pp. 1–10 (2015)
10. Beckman, N.E., Nori, A.V., Rajamani, S.K., Simmons, R.J., Tetali, S., Thakur, A.V.: Proofs from tests. IEEE Trans. Software Eng. **36**(4), 495–508 (2010)
11. Beyer, D.: Competition on software verification – (SV-COMP). In: Flanagan, C., König, B. (eds.) TACAS 2012. LNCS, vol. 7214, pp. 504–524. Springer, Heidelberg (2012). https://doi.org/10.1007/978-3-642-28756-5_38
12. Beyer, D., Chlipala, A.J., Henzinger, T.A., Jhala, R., Majumdar, R.: Generating tests from counterexamples. In: Proceedings of the 26th International Conference on Software Engineering, ICSE 2004, pp. 326–335. IEEE Computer Society, Washington, DC (2004)
13. Beyer, D., Henzinger, T.A., Jhala, R., Majumdar, R.: The software model checker BLAST: applications to software engineering. Int. J. Softw. Tools Technol. Transf. **9**(5), 505–525 (2007)
14. Beyer, D., Keremoglu, M.E.: CPACHECKER: a tool for configurable software verification. In: Gopalakrishnan, G., Qadeer, S. (eds.) CAV 2011. LNCS, vol. 6806, pp. 184–190. Springer, Heidelberg (2011). https://doi.org/10.1007/978-3-642-22110-1_16
15. Beyer, D., Lemberger, T.: Software verification: testing vs. model checking - a comparative evaluation of the state of the art. In: Strichman, O., Tzoref-Brill, R. (eds.) HVC 2017. LNCS, vol. 10629, pp. 99–114. Springer, Cham (2017). https://doi.org/10.1007/978-3-319-70389-3_7
16. Burnim, J., Sen, K.: Heuristics for scalable dynamic test generation. In: 23rd IEEE/ACM International Conference on Automated Software Engineering (ASE 2008), 15–19 September 2008, L'Aquila, Italy, pp. 443–446 (2008)
17. Buy, U.A., Orso, A., Pezzè, M.: Automated testing of classes. In: ISSTA, pp. 39–48 (2000)
18. Cadar, C., Dunbar, D., Engler, D.R.: KLEE: unassisted and automatic generation of high-coverage tests for complex systems programs. In: USENIX Symposium on Operating Systems Design and Implementation, pp. 209–224 (2008)
19. Cadar, C., Ganesh, V., Pawlowski, P.M., Dill, D.L., Engler, D.R.: EXE: automatically generating inputs of death. In: Proceedings of the 13th ACM Conference on Computer and Communications Security, CCS 2006, Alexandria, VA, USA, 30 October–3 November 2006, pp. 322–335 (2006)
20. Cadar, C., Sen, K.: Symbolic execution for software testing: three decades later. Commun. ACM **56**(2), 82–90 (2013)
21. Chaki, S., Clarke, E.M., Groce, A., Jha, S., Veith, H.: Modular verification of software components in C. In: Proceedings of the 25th International Conference on Software Engineering, 3–10 May 2003, Portland, Oregon, USA, pp. 385–395 (2003)
22. Chaki, S., Clarke, E.M., Groce, A., Jha, S., Veith, H.: Modular verification of software components in C. IEEE Trans. Software Eng. **30**(6), 388–402 (2004)
23. Chatterjee, B., Ryder, B.G.: Data-flow-based testing of object-oriented libraries. Technical report DCS-TR-382, Rutgers University (1999)

24. Clarke, E., Kroening, D., Lerda, F.: A tool for checking ANSI-C programs. In: Jensen, K., Podelski, A. (eds.) TACAS 2004. LNCS, vol. 2988, pp. 168–176. Springer, Heidelberg (2004). https://doi.org/10.1007/978-3-540-24730-2_15

25. Clarke, E.M., Kroening, D., Lerda, F.: A tool for checking ANSI-C programs. In: Proceedings of the Tools and Algorithms for the Construction and Analysis of Systems, 10th International Conference, TACAS 2004, Held as Part of the Joint European Conferences on Theory and Practice of Software, ETAPS 2004, Barcelona, Spain, 29 March–2 April 2004, pp. 168–176 (2004)

26. Clarke, L.A.: A program testing system. In: Proceedings of the 1976 Annual Conference, Houston, Texas, USA, 20–22 October 1976, pp. 488–491 (1976)

27. Clarke, L.A., Podgurski, A., Richardson, D.J., Zeil, S.J.: A formal evaluation of data flow path selection criteria. IEEE Trans. Software Eng. **15**(11), 1318–1332 (1989)

28. Daca, P., Gupta, A., Henzinger, T.A.: Abstraction-driven Concolic testing. In: Jobstmann, B., Leino, K.R.M. (eds.) VMCAI 2016. LNCS, vol. 9583, pp. 328–347. Springer, Heidelberg (2016). https://doi.org/10.1007/978-3-662-49122-5_16

29. Denaro, G., Margara, A., Pezzè, M., Vivanti, M.: Dynamic data flow testing of object oriented systems. In: 37th IEEE/ACM International Conference on Software Engineering, ICSE 2015, Florence, Italy, 16–24 May 2015, vol. 1, pp. 947–958 (2015)

30. Denaro, G., Pezzè, M., Vivanti, M.: On the right objectives of data flow testing. In: IEEE Seventh International Conference on Software Testing, Verification and Validation, ICST 2014, 31 March–4 April 2014, Cleveland, Ohio, USA, pp. 71–80 (2014)

31. Do, T., Fong, A.C.M., Pears, R.: Precise guidance to dynamic test generation. In: Proceedings of the 7th International Conference on Evaluation of Novel Approaches to Software Engineering (ENASE), pp. 5–12 (2012)

32. Eler, M.M., Endo, A.T., Durelli, V., Procópio-PR, C.: Covering user-defined dataflow test requirements using symbolic execution. In: Proceedings of the Thirteenth Brazilian Symposium On Software Quality (SBQS), pp. 16–30 (2014)

33. ETAPS: Competition on software verification (SV-COMP). ETAPS European Joint Conference on Theory & Practice of Software - TACAS 2017 (2017). https://sv-comp.sosy-lab.org/2017/

34. Foreman, L.M., Zweben, S.H.: A study of the effectiveness of control and data flow testing strategies. J. Syst. Softw. **21**(3), 215–228 (1993)

35. Frankl, P.G., Weiss, S.N.: An experimental comparison of the effectiveness of branch testing and data flow testing. IEEE Trans. Softw. Eng. **19**(8), 774–787 (1993)

36. Frankl, P.G., Iakounenko, O.: Further empirical studies of test effectiveness. In: SIGSOFT 1998, Proceedings of the ACM SIGSOFT International Symposium on Foundations of Software Engineering, Lake Buena Vista, Florida, USA, 3–5 November 1998, pp. 153–162 (1998)

37. Fraser, G., Wotawa, F., Ammann, P.: Testing with model checkers: a survey. Softw. Test. Verification Reliab. **19**(3), 215–261 (2009)

38. Ghiduk, A.S.: A new software data-flow testing approach via ant colony algorithms. Univ. J. Comput. Sci. Eng. Technol. **1**(1), 64–72 (2010)

39. Ghiduk, A.S., Harrold, M.J., Girgis, M.R.: Using genetic algorithms to aid test-data generation for data-flow coverage. In: APSEC, pp. 41–48 (2007)

40. Girgis, M.R.: Using symbolic execution and data flow criteria to aid test data selection. Softw. Test. Verif. Reliab. **3**(2), 101–112 (1993)

41. Girgis, M.R.: Automatic test data generation for data flow testing using a genetic algorithm. J. UCS **11**(6), 898–915 (2005)
42. Girgis, M.R., Ghiduk, A.S., Abd-elkawy, E.H.: Automatic generation of data flow test paths using a genetic algorithm. Int. J. Comput. Appl. **89**(12), 29–36 (2014)
43. Godefroid, P., Klarlund, N., Sen, K.: DART: directed automated random testing. In: Proceedings of the 2005 ACM SIGPLAN Conference on Programming Language Design and Implementation, pp. 213–223. ACM, New York (2005)
44. Goldberg, A., Wang, T., Zimmerman, D.: Applications of feasible path analysis to program testing. In: Proceedings of the 1994 International Symposium on Software Testing and Analysis, ISSTA 1994, Seattle, WA, USA, 17–19 August 1994, pp. 80–94 (1994)
45. Harman, M., Kim, S.G., Lakhotia, K., McMinn, P., Yoo, S.: Optimizing for the number of tests generated in search based test data generation with an application to the oracle cost problem. In: Third International Conference on Software Testing, Verification and Validation, ICST 2010, Paris, France, 7–9 April 2010, Workshops Proceedings, pp. 182–191 (2010)
46. Harrold, M.J., Rothermel, G.: Performing data flow testing on classes. In: SIGSOFT FSE, pp. 154–163 (1994)
47. Harrold, M.J., Soffa, M.L.: Efficient computation of interprocedural definition-use chains. ACM Trans. Program. Lang. Syst. **16**(2), 175–204 (1994)
48. Hassan, M.M., Andrews, J.H.: Comparing multi-point stride coverage and dataflow coverage. In: 35th International Conference on Software Engineering, ICSE 2013, San Francisco, CA, USA, 18–26 May 2013, pp. 172–181 (2013)
49. Henzinger, T.A., Jhala, R., Majumdar, R., Sutre, G.: Lazy abstraction. In: Conference Record of POPL 2002: The 29th SIGPLAN-SIGACT Symposium on Principles of Programming Languages, Portland, OR, USA, 16–18 January 2002, pp. 58–70 (2002)
50. Hierons, R.M., et al.: Using formal specifications to support testing. ACM Comput. Surv. **41**(2), 1–76 (2009)
51. Hong, H.S., Cha, S.D., Lee, I., Sokolsky, O., Ural, H.: Data flow testing as model checking. In: Proceedings of the 25th International Conference on Software Engineering, 3–10 May 2003, Portland, Oregon, USA, pp. 232–243 (2003)
52. Horgan, J.R., London, S.: ATAC: a data flow coverage testing tool for C. In: Proceedings of Symposium on Assessment of Quality Software Development Tools, pp. 2–10 (1992)
53. Horgan, J.R., London, S.: Data flow coverage and the C language. In: Proceedings of the Symposium on Testing, Analysis, and Verification, pp. 87–97. TAV4, ACM, New York (1991)
54. Hutchins, M., Foster, H., Goradia, T., Ostrand, T.J.: Experiments of the effectiveness of dataflow- and controlflow-based test adequacy criteria. In: ICSE, pp. 191–200 (1994)
55. Jamrozik, K., Fraser, G., Tillmann, N., de Halleux, J.: Augmented dynamic symbolic execution. In: IEEE/ACM International Conference on Automated Software Engineering, pp. 254–257 (2012)
56. Jhala, R., Majumdar, R.: Software model checking. ACM Comput. Surv. (CSUR) **41**(4), 21 (2009)
57. Khamis, A., Bahgat, R., Abdelaziz, R.: Automatic test data generation using data flow information. Dogus Univ. J. **2**, 140–153 (2011)
58. King, J.C.: Symbolic execution and program testing. Commun. ACM **19**(7), 385–394 (1976)

59. Kirchner, F., Kosmatov, N., Prevosto, V., Signoles, J., Yakobowski, B.: Frama-C: a software analysis perspective. Formal Asp. Comput. **27**(3), 573–609 (2015). https://doi.org/10.1007/s00165-014-0326-7
60. Lakhotia, K., McMinn, P., Harman, M.: Automated test data generation for coverage: haven't we solved this problem yet? In: Proceedings of the 2009 Testing: Academic and Industrial Conference - Practice and Research Techniques, pp. 95–104. IEEE Computer Society, Washington (2009)
61. Ma, K.-K., Yit Phang, K., Foster, J.S., Hicks, M.: Directed symbolic execution. In: Yahav, E. (ed.) SAS 2011. LNCS, vol. 6887, pp. 95–111. Springer, Heidelberg (2011). https://doi.org/10.1007/978-3-642-23702-7_11
62. Malevris, N., Yates, D.: The collateral coverage of data flow criteria when branch testing. Inf. Softw. Technol. **48**(8), 676–686 (2006)
63. Marcozzi, M., Bardin, S., Kosmatov, N., Papadakis, M., Prevosto, V., Correnson, L.: Time to clean your test objectives. In: 40th International Conference on Software Engineering, 27 May–3 June 2018, Gothenburg, Sweden (2018)
64. Marinescu, P.D., Cadar, C.: KATCH: high-coverage testing of software patches. In: Joint Meeting of the European Software Engineering Conference and the ACM SIGSOFT Symposium on the Foundations of Software Engineering, ESEC/FSE 2013, Saint Petersburg, Russian Federation, 18–26 August 2013, pp. 235–245 (2013)
65. Marré, M., Bertolino, A.: Unconstrained duas and their use in achieving all-uses coverage. In: Proceedings of the 1996 ACM SIGSOFT International Symposium on Software Testing and Analysis, pp. 147–157. ISSTA 199. ACM, New York (1996)
66. Marré, M., Bertolino, A.: Using spanning sets for coverage testing. IEEE Trans. Softw. Eng. **29**(11), 974–984 (2003)
67. Mathur, A.P., Wong, W.E.: An empirical comparison of data flow and mutation-based test adequacy criteria. Softw. Test. Verif. Reliab. 4(1), 9–31 (1994)
68. Merlo, E., Antoniol, G.: A static measure of a subset of intra-procedural data flow testing coverage based on node coverage. In: CASCON, p. 7 (1999)
69. Nayak, N., Mohapatra, D.P.: Automatic test data generation for data flow testing using particle swarm optimization. In: IC3 (2), pp. 1–12 (2010)
70. Necula, G.C., McPeak, S., Rahul, S.P., Weimer, W.: CIL: intermediate language and tools for analysis and transformation of C programs. In: Horspool, R.N. (ed.) CC 2002. LNCS, vol. 2304, pp. 213–228. Springer, Heidelberg (2002). https://doi.org/10.1007/3-540-45937-5_16
71. Offutt, A.J., Pan, J.: Automatically detecting equivalent mutants and infeasible paths. Softw. Test. Verif. Reliab. **7**(3), 165–192 (1997)
72. Pande, H.D., Landi, W.A., Ryder, B.G.: Interprocedural def-use associations for C systems with single level pointers. IEEE Trans. Softw. Eng. **20**(5), 385–403 (1994)
73. Pandita, R., Xie, T., Tillmann, N., de Halleux, J.: Guided test generation for coverage criteria. In: Proceedings of the 2010 IEEE International Conference on Software Maintenance, pp. 1–10. IEEE Computer Society, Washington (2010)
74. Peng, Y., Huang, Y., Su, T., Guo, J.: Modeling and verification of AUTOSAR OS and EMS application. In: Seventh International Symposium on Theoretical Aspects of Software Engineering, TASE 2013, 1–3 July 2013, Birmingham, UK, pp. 37–44 (2013)
75. Rapps, S., Weyuker, E.J.: Data flow analysis techniques for test data selection. In: Proceedings of the 6th International Conference on Software Engineering, ICSE 1982, pp. 272–278. IEEE Computer Society Press, Los Alamitos (1982)

76. Rapps, S., Weyuker, E.J.: Selecting software test data using data flow information. IEEE Trans. Software Eng. **11**(4), 367–375 (1985)
77. Santelices, R., Harrold, M.J.: Efficiently monitoring data-flow test coverage. In: Proceedings of the twenty-second IEEE/ACM International Conference on Automated Software Engineering, ASE 2007, pp. 343–352. ACM, New York (2007)
78. Santelices, R.A., Sinha, S., Harrold, M.J.: Subsumption of program entities for efficient coverage and monitoring. In: Third International Workshop on Software Quality Assurance, SOQUA 2006, Portland, Oregon, USA, 6 November 2006, pp. 2–5 (2006)
79. Sen, K., Marinov, D., Agha, G.: CUTE: a concolic unit testing engine for C. In: Proceedings of the 10th European Software Engineering Conference Held Jointly with 13th ACM SIGSOFT International Symposium on Foundations of software engineering, pp. 263–272. ACM, New York (2005)
80. Singla, S., Kumar, D., Rai, H.M., Singla, P.: A hybrid PSO approach to automate test data generation for data flow coverage with dominance concepts. J. Adv. Sci. Technol. **37**, 15–26 (2011)
81. Singla, S., Singla, P., Rai, H.M.: An automatic test data generation for data flow coverage using soft computing approach. IJRRCS **2**(2), 265–270 (2011)
82. SIR Project: Software-artifact infrastructure repository. NC State University. http://sir.unl.edu/php/previewfiles.php. Accessed July 2016
83. Su, T.: A bibliography of papers and tools on data flow testing. GitHub (2017). https://tingsu.github.io/files/dftbib.html
84. Su, T., Fu, Z., Pu, G., He, J., Su, Z.: Combining symbolic execution and model checking for data flow testing. In: 37th IEEE/ACM International Conference on Software Engineering, ICSE 2015, Florence, Italy, 16–24 May 2015, vol. 1, pp. 654–665 (2015)
85. Su, T., et al.: Automated coverage-driven test data generation using dynamic symbolic execution. In: Eighth International Conference on Software Security and Reliability, SERE 2014, San Francisco, California, USA, 30 June–2 July 2014, pp. 98–107 (2014)
86. Su, T., et al.: A survey on data-flow testing. ACM Comput. Surv. **50**(1), 5:1–5:35 (2017)
87. Su, T., Zhang, C., Yan, Y., Su, Z.: Towards efficient data-flow test data generation. GitHub (2019). https://tingsu.github.io/files/hybrid_dft.html
88. Tillmann, N., de Halleux, J.: Pex–white box test generation for .NET. In: Beckert, B., Hähnle, R. (eds.) TAP 2008. LNCS, vol. 4966, pp. 134–153. Springer, Heidelberg (2008). https://doi.org/10.1007/978-3-540-79124-9_10
89. Vivanti, M., Mis, A., Gorla, A., Fraser, G.: Search-based data-flow test generation. In: IEEE 24th International Symposium on Software Reliability Engineering, ISSRE 2013, Pasadena, CA, USA, 4–7 November 2013, pp. 370–379 (2013)
90. Wang, H., Liu, T., Guan, X., Shen, C., Zheng, Q., Yang, Z.: Dependence guided symbolic execution. IEEE Trans. Software Eng. **43**(3), 252–271 (2017)
91. Wang, Z., Yu, X., Sun, T., Pu, G., Ding, Z., Hu, J.: Test data generation for derived types in C program. In: TASE 2009, Third IEEE International Symposium on Theoretical Aspects of Software Engineering, 29–31 July 2009, Tianjin, China, pp. 155–162 (2009)
92. Weyuker, E.J.: The complexity of data flow criteria for test data selection. Inf. Process. Lett. **19**(2), 103–109 (1984)
93. Weyuker, E.J.: More experience with data flow testing. IEEE Trans. Software Eng. **19**(9), 912–919 (1993)

94. Wong, W.E., Mathur, A.P.: Fault detection effectiveness of mutation and data flow testing. Software Qual. J. **4**(1), 69–83 (1995)

95. Xie, T., Tillmann, N., de Halleux, J., Schulte, W.: Fitness-guided path exploration in dynamic symbolic execution. In: Proceedings of the 2009 IEEE/IFIP International Conference on Dependable Systems and Networks (DSN), pp. 359–368 (2009)

96. Yang, Q., Li, J.J., Weiss, D.M.: A survey of coverage-based testing tools. Comput. J. **52**(5), 589–597 (2009)

97. Zamfir, C., Candea, G.: Execution synthesis: a technique for automated software debugging. In: European Conference on Computer Systems, Proceedings of the 5th European Conference on Computer Systems, EuroSys 2010, Paris, France, 13–16 April 2010, pp. 321–334 (2010)

98. Zhang, C., et al.: SmartUnit: empirical evaluations for automated unit testing of embedded software in industry. In: 40th IEEE/ACM International Conference on Software Engineering, Software Engineering in Practice Track, ICSE 2018, 27 May–3 June 2018, Gothenburg, Sweden (2018)

99. Zhang, L., Xie, T., Zhang, L., Tillmann, N., de Halleux, J., Mei, H.: Test generation via dynamic symbolic execution for mutation testing. In: 26th IEEE International Conference on Software Maintenance (ICSM 2010), 12–18 September 2010, Timisoara, Romania, pp. 1–10 (2010)

100. Zhu, H., Hall, P.A.V., May, J.H.R.: Software unit test coverage and adequacy. ACM Comput. Surv. **29**(4), 366–427 (1997)

European Colleagues

Assume-Guarantee Reasoning for Additive Hybrid Behaviour

Pieter J. L. Cuijpers[1,2] , Jonas Hansen[3](✉) , and Kim G. Larsen[3]

[1] Technische Universiteit Eindhoven, Eindhoven, The Netherlands
p.j.l.cuijpers@tue.nl
[2] Radboud Universiteit, Nijmegen, The Netherlands
[3] Aalborg University, Aalborg, Denmark
{jonash,kgl}@cs.aau.dk

Abstract. Hybrid Automata describe dynamical systems where continuous behaviour interacts with discrete events. Resource Timed Automata (RTA), a subset of Hybrid Automata, adopt an additive composition scheme, in which discrete behaviour of components is executed concurrently, time is synchronized, and the evolution of continuous variables is arithmetically added up. Additive composition facilitates modelling and analysis of cumulative properties of continuous variables, such as conservation laws, typically manifested as the balancing of real-valued variables. In this paper, we present and exemplify an assume-guarantee framework aimed at additive compositional reasoning in the setting of hybrid systems. Crucially, we introduce a notion of refinement on so-called Resource Hybrid Automata (RHA), and show that it is a pre-congruence for additive composition. Furthermore - crucial for our assume-guarantee framework – we show that RHAs are closed under conjunction and admit a so-called quotient constructions (a dual operator to parallel composition). Finally, we demonstrate how the Statistical Model Checking (SMC) engine of the tool UPPAAL may be used to efficiently falsify refinements.

Keywords: Assume-Guarantee Reasoning · Hybrid Specification Theory · Resource Hybrid Automata · Additive Composition

1 Introduction

Hybrid Automata (HA) [22] are an extension of Timed Automata (TA) [2] combining timed discrete events with the continuous evolution of real-valued variables. Resource-, Priced-, Energy- and Weighted- Timed Automata [3,8,16,29,31] all define strict subsets of HA in which continuous dynamics cannot affect the timed discrete semantics of a system. These formalisms differ in their mechanics for dealing with composition. Of particular note are Resource Timed Automata (RTA) which adopt a so-called additive composition scheme aimed at simplifying the analysis of conservation laws e.g. resource balancing.

© The Author(s), under exclusive license to Springer Nature Switzerland AG 2023
J. P. Bowen et al. (Eds.): *Theories of Programming and Formal Methods*, LNCS 14080, pp. 297–322, 2023.
https://doi.org/10.1007/978-3-031-40436-8_11

In this paper we consider component-wise reasoning for additive composition over hybrid variables, henceforth referred to as resources, and study the hybrid extension of RTA, namely Resource Hybrid Automata (RHA).

Additive composition as studied in [16] extends the usual concurrent execution of discrete behaviour in synchronized time with a notion of resource accumulation both in terms of evolution and flow. This particular composition scheme, has, to the best of our knowledge, not received much attention in previous literature on hybrid systems. We argue that conservation laws follow naturally from additive composition and show that accumulation of shared resources across components directly corresponds to the problem of balancing said resources. We consider how behavioural requirements of a composite system can be expressed as a number of local and concise requirements on open additive parallel components. This kind of compositional reasoning is known as specification theory.

A *specification theory* interprets specifications as abstract under-specified descriptions of behaviour, which can generally be thought of as requirements to implementations. Formally, this is captured by a *satisfaction relation* between implementations and specifications, inducing for each specification S the set $[S]$ of the implementations satisfying it. Crucial to a specification theory is a notion of *refinement* between specifications. Refining a specification should result in a new specification which is stricter in terms of its implementation space. Now, a specification theory should also allow for both logical and structural *composition* of specifications.

In order to support step-wise refinement and compositional reasoning, it is vital that the notion of refinement is a pre-order over specifications (we write $S \sqsubseteq T$ to say that specification S refines T) and it must be a pre-congruence with respect to a composition of interest (we write $S \parallel T$ for a composition of two specifications). A fully expressive specification theory should ideally contain a *quotient* operator, a dual operator to the composition of specifications. If T is an overall specification of a composite system $P_1 \parallel P_2$ and S is a component specification for P_1, then the quotient specification $T\backslash\backslash S$ is the weakest requirement to the component P_2 in order for the composite system to satisfy T.

Mathematically, we have $S \parallel (T\backslash\backslash S) \sqsubseteq T$ for the quotient $T\backslash\backslash S$ of specifications S and T, and for every specification Q with $S \parallel Q \sqsubseteq T$ we have $Q \sqsubseteq T\backslash\backslash S$. In the setting of sequential, imperative programs Dijkstra's celebrated notions of *weakest precondition* and *strongest postcondition* effectively provide quotient constructs for sequential composition with respect to pre-and-post-condition specification pairs. Here He Jifeng has made seminal work with C.A.R. Hoare [24,26].

For concurrent systems, there have historically been two schools of specification theories: *Process Algebra* [6,23,34] and *Temporal Logic* [36]. In Process Algebra, specifications are process expressions with a variety of proposals for refinement orderings: e.g. trace-inclusion, bisimulation equivalence, ready-simulation, simulation, and failure-trace inclusion as reported in the linear-branching time spectrum [15]. In the late 80-ties, He Jifeng played a central role in improving the failure semantics for CSP [17,18]. In later work He Jifeng has proposed refinements for more complex settings including real-time [37], service- and object-oriented systems [19,21]. Moreover, Process Algebra has strong support for structural composition of specification, but lack general support for logical composition. In Temporal Logic, specifications are logical formula and refinement is simply logical implication. Temporal Logic has by nature full support for logical composition of specifications, but lack in general support for structural composition. What we seek is a specification oriented theory that unifies logical and process algebra frameworks, a theme that Hoare and He have developed in the unified theory of programming [20,25].

Also, in the late 80-ties, the notion of Modal Transition Systems [7,30,32,33] was introduced by Larsen and Thomsen as a means to provide a specification theory supporting both logical and structural composition. This theory of Modal Transition Systems has later been extended to the setting of timed as well as probabilistic systems [9,10,14]. The contributions of this paper may be seen as an extension of Modal Transition Systems to resource-aware concurrent systems. A particularly useful type of specification theories are those based on the notion of *contract*, first developed and promoted in the community of software engineering. So-called "design-by-contract", popularized by Bertrand Meyer, has roots in the classical work by Owicki-Gries [35] extending Floyd-Hoare logic (for sequential imperative programs) to the setting of concurrently executing programs, where interference on shared variables may occur. In the concurrent setting, contract specifications come as *Assume-Guarantee* (or Rely-Guarantee) pairs, where the Assumption states conditions on the effect on the shared variables by the system's environment, and the Guarantee are obligations of the systems operation on the shared variables. Early contributions were made by Jones [27], Abadi, Lamport and Wolper [28]. Later, He Jifeng together with Qiwen Xu and Willem-Paul de Roever gave a sound and complete proof system for rely-guarantee assertions [38] providing a compositional reformulation of the non-compositional Owicki-Gries method. More recently the notion of *interface automata* was introduced by Alfaro and Henzinger [1] and since then a number of frameworks has been proposed that can be seen as instances of contracts theories, with [5] providing a recent "meta-theory" of contracts and its application to software and systems.

Returning to general specification theories, we note that the quotient operator defines how a component helps to achieve a target behaviour T *for the system as a whole*, given an assumption S on its environment. In fact, it is shown in [4,12] how a contract framework can be built in a generic way on top of any specification theory which supports refinement, composition and quotienting of specifications. The resulting contract framework lifts refinement to the level of contracts and proposes a notion of contract composition on the basis of dominating contracts. In particular, it has been shown in [12] that one can weaken a guarantee G of an assume-guarantee contract, under assumption A: the weakened guarantee, denoted $G \gg A$, is simply $(A \parallel G) \backslash\backslash A$ and provides a combined specification equivalent to the original (A, G) pair. In this paper, we develop a complete specification theory aimed at the additive hybrid setting.

We characterize compositional reasoning within this domain and introduce a notion of refinement. We define appropriate products for the crucial operations logical and structural composition, together with its dual, namely the quotient product. Using this theory we show how assume-guarantee reasoning aimed at hybrid additivity is possible over specifications described by RHAs. In addition, we show that simulation based methods can be used to refute the existence of certain refinements.

Section 2 introduces our modelling language. Section 3 characterizes compositional reasoning and formally defines an additive hybrid specification theory. Section 4 formally introduces the assume-guarantee aspect and exemplifies it. Section 5 discusses practical computation methods for ascertaining refinement. Section 6 concludes our findings and discuss potential future research directions.

2   Resource Hybrid Automata

We first define our modelling language, followed by the characterization of an additive hybrid specification theory. We introduce Resource Hybrid Automata (RHA), which fundamentally define Linear Hybrid Automata [22] subject to additive composition as adopted by Resource Timed Automata (RTA) [16].

By $\mathcal{V} = \mathcal{V}^G \uplus \mathcal{V}^L$ we denote a partitioned set of real-valued global and local variables, which we think of as (non-)shared resources. We write $\sigma : \mathcal{V} \to \mathbb{R}$ or alternatively $\sigma \in \mathbb{R}^{\mathcal{V}}$ for a valuation of such variables. These are split into $\sigma_L : \mathcal{V}^L \to \mathbb{R}$ and $\sigma_G : \mathcal{V}^G \to \mathbb{R}$ in the obvious way. Furthermore, we define the following arithmetic over $\mathbb{R}^{\mathcal{V}}$: Let $\sigma, \sigma' \in \mathbb{R}^{\mathcal{V}}$ and $v \in \mathcal{V}$ then $(\sigma + \sigma')(v) = \sigma(v) + \sigma'(v)$ and dually for its inverse $-$. Additionally, let $v \in \mathcal{V}$ then $\mathbf{0}(v) = 0$. Thus valuations define the abelian group $(\mathbb{R}^{\mathcal{V}}, +, \mathbf{0})$.

Resources are subject to discrete updates and can be tested in constraints. To allow reasoning about resource additivity we require both our update- and constraint-algebra to be closed under negation, conjunction, addition $\oplus$ and quotient $\oslash$. Furthermore, we require that constraints are closed under side-effects $\triangleright$ which, for the sake of intuition and brevity, we characterize as updates.

Much like we can think of a conjunction of two updates/constraints as the join of their respective influence, i.e. what they have in common, an addition $\oplus$ is what they can do together, i.e. their arithmetic accumulated influence. A quotient $\oslash$ is the dual of addition. Here the question is what makes it possible to fulfil our goal (left operand) if we add it to something that already exists (right operand). We will see later how these operations naturally provide mechanisms for resource additivity.

Definition 1 (Resource Update). *We characterize the set of updates $\mathcal{U}(\mathcal{V})$ over $\mathcal{V}$ by the following abstract syntax:*

$$u ::== TT \mid \neg u \mid \epsilon \mid R \mid u \wedge u \mid u \oplus u \mid u \oslash u$$

where $R \subseteq \mathcal{V}$. Let $u_1, u_2 \in \mathcal{U}(\mathcal{V})$ be updates, then the evaluation of valuations $\sigma, \sigma' \in \mathbb{R}^{\mathcal{V}}$ in u denoted $(\sigma, \sigma') \models u$ is defined inductively on the structure of u:

- $(\sigma, \sigma') \models TT$:
- $(\sigma, \sigma') \models \neg u \Leftrightarrow (\sigma, \sigma') \not\models u$:
- $(\sigma, \sigma') \models \epsilon \Leftrightarrow \sigma = \sigma'$:
- $(\sigma, \sigma') \models R \Leftrightarrow \sigma'(v) = \begin{cases} 0, & v \in R, \\ \sigma(v), & v \notin R \end{cases}$:
- $(\sigma, \sigma') \models u \wedge u' \Leftrightarrow (\sigma, \sigma') \models u \wedge (\sigma, \sigma') \models u'$:
- $(\sigma, \sigma') \models u \oplus u' \Leftrightarrow \exists \varsigma, \varsigma' \in \mathbb{R}^{\mathcal{V}} : (\sigma, \varsigma) \models u \wedge (\sigma, \varsigma') \models u' \wedge \sigma' = \varsigma + \varsigma' - \sigma$:
- $(\sigma, \sigma') \models u \oslash u' \Leftrightarrow \forall \varsigma \in \mathbb{R}^{\mathcal{V}} : (\sigma, \varsigma) \models u' \Rightarrow (\sigma, \sigma' + \varsigma - \sigma) \models u$.

Definition 2 (Resource Constraint). *We characterize the set of constraints* $\mathcal{C}(\mathcal{V})$ *over* $\mathcal{V}$ *by the following abstract syntax:*

$$c ::== TT \mid \neg c \mid \sum_{i=1}^{n} v_i \cdot r_i \bowtie r \mid u \triangleright c \mid c \wedge c \mid c \oplus c \mid c \oslash c$$

where $r, r_i \in \mathbb{Q}$, $v_i \in \mathcal{V}$, $u \in \mathcal{U}(\mathcal{V})$ *and* $\bowtie \in \{\leq, \geq, ==, <, >\}$. *Let* u *be an update,* c' *be a constraint, then the evaluation of valuation* $\sigma \in \mathbb{R}^{\mathcal{V}}$ *in* c *denoted* $\sigma \models c$ *is defined inductively on the structure of* c:

- $\sigma \models TT$:
- $\sigma \models \neg c \Leftrightarrow \sigma \not\models c$:
- $\sigma \models \sum_{i=1}^{n} v_i \cdot r_i \bowtie r \Leftrightarrow \sum_{i=1}^{n} \sigma(v_i) \cdot r_i \bowtie r$:
- $\sigma \models u \triangleright c \Leftrightarrow \exists \sigma' \in \mathbb{R}^{\mathcal{V}} : (\sigma, \sigma') \models u \wedge \sigma' \models c$:
- $\sigma \models c \wedge c' \Leftrightarrow \sigma \models c \wedge \sigma \models c'$:
- $\sigma \models c \oplus c' \Leftrightarrow \exists \varsigma, \varsigma' \in \mathbb{R}^{\mathcal{V}} : \varsigma \models c \wedge \varsigma' \models c' \wedge \sigma = \varsigma + \varsigma'$:
- $\sigma \models c \oslash c' \Leftrightarrow \forall \sigma' \in \mathbb{R}^{\mathcal{V}} : \sigma' \models c' \Rightarrow \sigma + \sigma' \models c$.

As such, updates can reset sets of resources to zero and constraints define systems of linear inequalities over resources.

Definition 3 (Resource Hybrid Automata). *We define a resource hybrid automaton (RHA) as a tuple:*

$$H = \langle L, l_0, \mathcal{V}, E, \text{inv}, \text{rate} \rangle$$

where L *is a finite set of modes,* $l_0 \in L$ *is the initial mode,* $\mathcal{V} = \mathcal{V}_L \uplus \mathcal{V}_G$ *is a finite partitioned set of local and global variables,* $E \subseteq L \times \mathcal{C}(\mathcal{V}) \times \mathcal{U}(\mathcal{V}) \times L$ *is a finite set of edges,* $\text{inv} : L \to \mathcal{C}(\mathcal{V})$ *assigns an invariant constraint on resources to each mode and* $\text{rate} : L \to \mathcal{C}(\mathcal{V})$ *assigns a constraint to the first derivative of resources to each mode.*

An example RHA can be seen in Fig. 2.

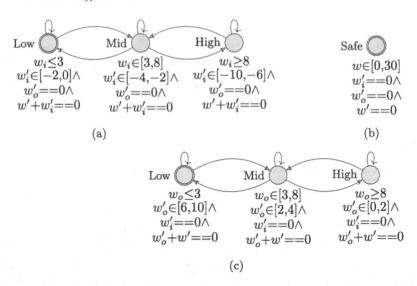

Fig. 1. (a) An RHA specification modelling a water intake valve. Depending on reservoir capacity (captured by global resource w_i), the water flow allowed by the valve is either in the interval $[-2,0]$, $[-4,-2]$ or $[-10,-6]$. (b) An RHA specification modelling a water output valve. Depending on reservoir capacity (captured by global resource w_o), the water flow allowed by the valve is either in the interval $[6,10]$, $[2,4]$ or $[0,2]$. (c) An RHA specification modelling the safe capacity of the pump's private water tank (captured by global resource w).

Let's consider a physical system, a water pump controller, governing two flow valves. One valve is connected to an input reservoir (characterized by resource w_i), which captures how the environment can make water available to the pump. Another valve is connected to an output reservoir (characterized by resource w_o), which captures how the pump can make water available to the environment. Both are connected to an internal water tank (characterised by resource w). Our system simply keeps track of capacity by regulating water flow from/to the environment using an internal tank for temporary storage. Figure 1 shows three RHAs, each modelling a component of our water pump controller.

Syntactically, RHA's are hybrid automata defined over additive oriented update and constraint algebra. Semantically their hybrid dynamics are interpreted as timed semantics. Specifically, the semantics of an RHA H denoted $[\![H]\!]$ is defined by a Resource Timed Transition System.

Definition 4 (Resource Timed Transition System). *We define a resource timed transition system (RTS) as a tuple $S = \langle X, \chi_L, \rightarrow \rangle$ where $X = X_L \times X_G$ is a set of pairs of local and global states, $\chi_L \in X_L$ is the initial local state, and $\rightarrow \subseteq X \times (\{\tau\} \cup \mathbb{R}_{\geq 0}) \times X$ is a timed transition relation, where discrete transitions are denoted by τ. We write $(x_L, x_G) \xrightarrow{\gamma} (x'_L, x'_G)$ whenever $((x_L, x_G), \gamma, (x'_L, x'_G)) \in \rightarrow$. Similarly, we write $(x_L, x_G) \not\rightarrow$ whenever $\forall x' \in X : ((x_L, x_G), \gamma, x') \notin \rightarrow$. Furthermore, we require that states form an abelian group*

$(X, +, \mathbf{0})$. For convenience we refer to the inverse of $+$ as $-$. We call a local state $x_L \in X_L$ reachable if there exists a sequence $x^i \xrightarrow{\gamma} x^{i+1}$ with $0 \leq i \leq n$ of transitions such that $x_L^0 = \chi_L$ and $x_L^n = x_L$.

Definition 5 (RHA Semantics). Let $H = \langle L, l_0, \mathcal{V}, E, \mathrm{inv}, \mathrm{rate} \rangle$ be an RHA. We define its semantics as an RTS $[\![H]\!] = \langle X, \chi_L, \rightarrow \rangle$ in which the local states are defined as products of a mode and the valuation of local variables $X_L = L \times \mathbb{R}^{\mathcal{V}_L}$, the global states are defined as valuations of global variables $X_G = \mathbb{R}^{\mathcal{V}_G}$, the initial local state is given by $\chi_L = (l_0, \mathbf{0})$, and $\rightarrow$ is the smallest relation satisfying:

- If $(l, c, u, l') \in E$, $\sigma \in \mathbb{R}^{\mathcal{V}}$, $\sigma \models \mathrm{inv}(l)$, $\sigma \models c$, $(\sigma, \sigma') \models u$ and $\sigma' \models \mathrm{inv}(l')$, then $((l, \sigma_L), \sigma_G) \xrightarrow{\tau} ((l', \sigma'_L), \sigma'_G)$:
- If $l \in L$, $\delta \in \mathbb{R}_{\geq 0}$, and $\phi : [0, \delta] \rightarrow \mathbb{R}^{\mathcal{V}}$ is a right-differentiable function with piece-wise constant derivative, such that for all $t \in [0, \delta]$ we have $\phi(t) \models \mathrm{inv}(l)$ and for $t \in [0, \delta)$ we have $\frac{d}{dt}\phi(t) \models \mathrm{rate}(l)$, then $((l, \phi_L(0)), \phi_G(0)) \xrightarrow{\delta} ((l, \phi_L(\delta)), \phi_G(\delta))$.

Discrete transitions in the automata defines τ transitions in its semantics, which we generally think of as internal.

Note that restricting flow behaviour to right-differential piece-wise constant solutions is a standard way to avoid problems with finite-set refutability when considering hybrid dynamics over a timed semantics [11]. Furthermore, any RTS generated by an RHA are time-reflexive and time-additive.

Theorem 1. Let H be an RHA. The following holds for $[\![H]\!] = \langle X, \chi_L, \rightarrow \rangle$: For all $x, x' \in X$, $\delta, \delta' \in \mathbb{R}_{\geq 0}$ we have: $[\![H]\!]$ is **time reflexive** $x \xrightarrow{0} x$, and $[\![H]\!]$ is **time additive** $x \xrightarrow{\delta + \delta'} x' \Rightarrow \exists x'' \in X : x \xrightarrow{\delta} x'' \wedge x'' \xrightarrow{\delta'} x'$.

3   Compositional Reasoning

With RHA and its semantic interpretation RTS we have a formal characterization of hybrid behaviour. We now turn our attention to component-wise abstraction and realization in terms of behavioural requirements. We start by motivating component-wise design and refinement with additivity using a simple example.

Our goal is to design a light controller, the kind that might be used to control the alternating blinking pattern of a warning light on top of an antenna or maybe a control console. There are a few rules we need to follow: the controller must provide an alternating light pattern, i.e. it must facilitate blinking mechanics for our light determined by some intervals, the light itself is limited in how much power it can consume depending on its brightness level, and it must interact with the electrical grid indirectly through a single battery. As such we are designing an open component, since we are only concerned with saturation. How the battery charges is handled by a different controller.

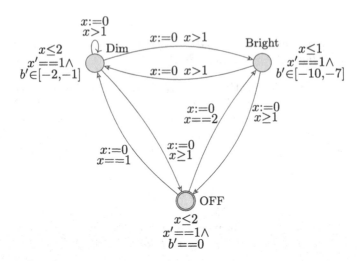

Fig. 2. An RHA, modelling a warning light controller. It has three modes; Dim, Bright and the initial mode OFF, each describes a distinct brightness. It is defined over two resources x (local) and b (global). The former characterizes a clock with constant rate 1 in all modes and is used to model timing behaviour. The latter describes a battery. It is used to model the light controllers interaction with its environment. Each mode (or rather each brightness level) define distinct battery saturation rates. Observe that when we interpret the model as blueprint for timed discrete requirements, infinitely many distinct blinking- and saturation-patterns are possible.

A system architect has provided us with a blueprint defined as an RHA that formally captures the rules we just discussed, which is depicted in Fig. 2. Of course, the light controller is only a single component of a larger system, which we collectively think of as the environment. Now, from the environment's perspective, the blueprint captures exactly what is assumed about our controller. On top of that, potential conservation rules in terms of energy for our battery is handled by the environment as well. Looking at Fig. 2 we immediately see the benefit of additive reasoning, since no consideration for how resource b i.e. our battery interacts with other components is necessary, it is simply assumed that the collective interaction over b across all components is handled in an additive manner.

Figure 2 defines abstract requirements. We now desire to create a concrete controller that behaves according to these requirements. Because it needs to be concretely realizable a few precautions needs to be considered; The controller must be specific in its battery saturations, it is not allowed to stop time, and any discrete behaviour whenever enabled must occur. To that end we introduce the model depicted in Fig. 3.

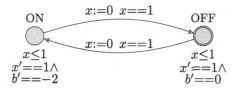

Fig. 3. An RHA, modelling a concrete realization of the light controller depicted in Fig. 2. It consists of two modes On and the initial mode OFF. Like Fig. 2, it is defined over the two resources x and b. Observe that this concrete light controller simply defines an altering pattern in which the light is turned off for 1 time unit, after which it is turned on for 1 time unit, during which it consumes exactly 2 units of power per time unit.

Now the question is, can we substitute our abstract model of Fig. 2 with the concrete model of Fig. 3 whenever we consider the light controller in other components of our system. To do so, we must ascertain whether the abstract controller can mimic any an all timed-discrete behaviour allowed by the concrete controller in all environments (in terms of the capacity of b and how it is charged). If this is indeed the case, then we do not have to consider the cumbersome abstract model whenever we desire to reason about our light controller, the simple concrete model is sufficient. This property is called refinement.

Adopting the usual terminology from specification theory we refer to RTS's as specifications. In this paper, we consider specifications that model the reaction of a system to changes in its environment. This means that a refinement of one specification into another should preserve those reactions, given a particular environment. (Note that in other works, other interpretations of transition systems lead to different notions of refinement. E.g. in [5], changes in the environment are explicitly modeled as input transitions of the RTS's, leading to a two-way type of simulation refinement).

Definition 6 (Refinement). *For $i \in \{1, 2\}$, let $S^i = \langle \mathrm{X}^i, \chi_L^i, \rightarrow_i \rangle$ be a specification. We assume that their global states are shared $\mathrm{X}_G^1 = \mathrm{X}_G^2$. We say that S^1 refines S^2, denoted $S^1 \sqsubseteq S^2$ iff there exists a binary relation $R \subseteq \mathrm{X}_L^1 \times \mathrm{X}_L^2$ defined over the local states such that $\chi_L^1 R \chi_L^2$ and for all $x^1 \in \mathrm{X}^1$ and $x^2 \in \mathrm{X}^2$ with $x_G^1 = x_G^2$ we find:*

- *If $x_L^1 R x_L^2$ and $x^1 \xrightarrow{\tau}_1 y^1$, then there exists $y^2 \in \mathrm{X}^2$ such that $x^2 \xrightarrow{\tau}_2 y^2$ with $y_L^1 R y_L^2$ and $y_G^1 = y_G^2$.*
- *If $x_L^1 R x_L^2$ and $x^1 \xrightarrow{\delta}_1 y^1$ for some $\delta \in \mathbb{R}_{\geq 0}$, then there exists $y^2 \in \mathrm{X}^2$ such that $x^2 \xrightarrow{\delta} y^2$ with $y_L^1 R y_L^2$ and $y_G^1 = y_G^2$.*

Crucially, refinements between specifications form a pre-order.

Theorem 2. *The refinement relation $\sqsubseteq$ is a pre-order over the set of all specifications.*

In specification theory, specifications for which there is a concrete realization in practice are called implementations. These implementations may occur at any place in the pre-order, as it is often possible to further refine behaviour of an already existing implementation, hence creating a refinement of that implementation. Without fixing the implementation mechanisms, we cannot determine which specifications are realizable precisely. However, we can rule out any specifications that are self-contradictory, block the progress of time, or contain unresolved non-deterministic choices. A specification that has these properties, such as Fig. 3, we call an implementation in this paper.

Definition 7 (Implementation). *Let $S = \langle X, \chi_L, \rightarrow \rangle$ be a specification, we say that S is an implementation if furthermore the following holds:*

- **Independent progression:** *For every reachable state $x \in X$ there exists $\gamma \in \{\tau\} \cup \mathbb{R}_{\geq 0}$ and $x' \in X$ such that $x \xrightarrow{\gamma} x'$;*
- **Discrete-determinism:** *For every reachable state $x, x', x'' \in X$, with $x \xrightarrow{\tau} x'$ and $x \xrightarrow{\tau} x''$, we find $x = x''$;*
- **Time-determinism:** *For every reachable state $x, x', x'' \in X$ and every $\delta \in \mathbb{R}_{\geq 0}$ with $x \xrightarrow{\delta} x'$ and $x \xrightarrow{\delta} x''$ we find $x' = x''$;*
- **Urgency:** *For every reachable state $x \in X$, if there exists $x' \in X$ with $x \xrightarrow{\tau} x'$, then there does not exists an $x'' \in X$ and $\delta \in \mathbb{R}_{\geq 0}$ with $\delta > 0$ and $x \xrightarrow{\delta} x''$.*

The syntactic notion of implementations naturally follows.

Definition 8 (Implementation RHA). *Let H be an RHA. We say that H is an implementation RHA whenever $\llbracket H \rrbracket$ is an implementation.*

The concrete light controller of Fig. 3 defines an implementation, another example is shown in Fig. 4.

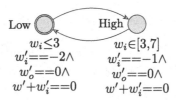

Fig. 4. An implementation RHA implementing the intake valve specification of Fig. 1a. Much like Fig. 3, the intake valve implementation is in a sense a restriction of behaviour.

An implementation is said to satisfy a specification if it only admits discrete/continuous behaviour allowed by the specification. The general notion of satisfaction is formally captured by refinement.

Definition 9 (Specification Satisfaction). *Let S be a specification and I an implementation. If I ⊑ S we say that I satisfies S. By [S] = {I | I ⊑ S} we denote the set of all implementations that satisfy S.*

This gives us a natural way of thinking about specification equivalence.

Definition 10 (Specification Equivalence). *We say that specifications S and S′ are equivalent, denoted S ≈ S′ iff [S] = [S′].*

It is not difficult to see that we could define specifications that could never be satisfied, e.g. if they contain contradictions. In practice, only those admitting implementations are of interest. This notion is usually referred to as consistency, and we characterize it using implementation spaces.

Definition 11 (Consistency). *We say that a specification S is consistent iff [S] ≠ ∅.*

Compositional reasoning in terms of component-wise refinement and abstraction crucially relies on a well defined notion of refinement within which substitutability is guaranteed. This means that whenever we have a composition of two specifications, by replacing one of the constituents with a refining component, it results in a refinement of the original composition. We now define two such compositions that pertain substitutability over refinement, namely logical- and structural-composition.

$b \in [0, 1]$ $b' == 1$

(a)   (b)

Fig. 5. (a) A Specification, modelling the battery capacity of the light controller, whose timing behaviour is defined by the specification depicted in Fig. 2. It consists of a single mode, the initial mode, and is defined over the global resource b. It invariantly requires that the battery capacity never exceeds 1 unit of energy and is never saturated beyond depletion. Note that any and all discrete transitions are allowed, captured by the self loop. (b) A Specification, modelling a power supply. It consists of a single mode, the initial mode, and is defined over the global resource b. It does not admit any discrete behaviour, however it defines a constant charging of 1 unit of power per time unit.

Before we dive into the formal definitions, we first motivate their existence and usefulness. Going back to our light controller specification of Fig. 2, together with a possible implementation thereof, shown in Fig. 3. Our goal is to introduce mechanisms for reasoning about compositions of specifications. Consider the specification modelled in Fig. 5a, which captures battery capacity requirements. We would like to capture the notion of joint refinement, in the sense that Fig. 3 should both refine the timing behaviour of Fig. 2 and the capacity restrictions imposed by Fig. 5a. One can think of the specifications as two distinct aspects of the same component. Their joined requirements is exactly captured by their logical composition.

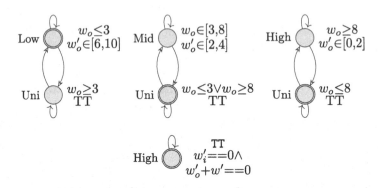

Fig. 6. Four RHA specifications whose logical composition refines the output valve specification of Fig. 1c, each modelling distinct responsibilities. All of them define a so-called universal mode Uni admitting an arbitrary flow of resource w_o up until some bound for which it must make a transition or define a flow that shift w_o away from said bound. In other words, each component do not care about w_o until its top mode invariant holds. Even though the output valve specification of Fig. 1c is relatively small, these three components are even smaller and arguably more intuitive.

Logical composition defines the joined behaviour of its constituents. As such an implementation satisfies the composition of two specifications if and only if both of these specifications are satisfied by said implementation.

Definition 12 (Logical Product). *Let $S^j = \langle X^j, \chi_L^j, \to_j \rangle$ for $j \in \{1,2\}$ be a specification, where $X_G^1 = X_G^2$. We define the logical product of S^1 and S^2, denoted $S^1 \wedge S^2$ as a new specification: $S^1 \wedge S^2 = \langle X, \chi_L, \to \rangle$, where $X_L = X_L^1 \times X_L^2$, $X_G = X_G^1$, $\chi_L = (\chi_L^1, \chi_L^2)$ and $\to$ is the smallest relation satisfying:*

$$\frac{(x_L^1, x_G) \xrightarrow{\gamma}_1 (y_L^1, y_G) \quad (x_L^2, x_G) \xrightarrow{\gamma}_2 (y_L^2, y_G)}{((x_L^1, x_L^2), x_G) \xrightarrow{\gamma} ((y_L^1, y_L^2), y_G)} \gamma \in \{\tau\} \cup \mathbb{R}_{\geq 0}$$

The logical product admits a transition if and only if its constituents both admits it. On the syntactic level we can compute the logical composition by the following RHA construction.

Definition 13 (Logical Composition). *Let $H^j = \langle L^j, l_0^j, \mathcal{V}, E^j, \mathrm{inv}^j, \mathrm{rate}^j \rangle$ for $j \in \{1,2\}$ be an RHA, where $\mathcal{V}_G^1 = \mathcal{V}_G^2$ and $\mathcal{V}_L^1 \cap \mathcal{V}_L^2 = \emptyset$. We define the logical composition of H^1 and H^2, denoted $H^1 \wedge H^2$ as a new RHA: $H^1 \wedge H^2 = \langle L, l_0, \mathcal{V}, E, \mathrm{inv}, \mathrm{rate} \rangle$, where $L = L^1 \times L^2$, $l_0 = (l_0^1, l_0^2)$, $\mathcal{V}_L = \mathcal{V}_L^1 \uplus \mathcal{V}_L^2$, $\mathcal{V}_G = \mathcal{V}_G^1$, $\mathrm{inv}\left((l^1, l^2)\right) = \mathrm{inv}^1(l^1) \wedge \mathrm{inv}^2(l^2)$, $\mathrm{rate}\left((l^1, l^2)\right) = \mathrm{rate}^1(l^1) \wedge \mathrm{rate}^2(l^2)$ and E is defined by the following rule:*

– If $(l^1, c^1, u^1, k^1) \in E^1$ and $(l^2, c^2, u^2, k^2) \in E^2$, then
$((l^1, l^2), c^1 \wedge c^2, u^1 \wedge u^2, (k^1, k^2)) \in E$

Figure 6 shows an example of the of type reasoning possible using logical composition.

As expected, the logical composition and product coincide.

Theorem 3. *Let H and H' be RHA then: $[\![H]\!] \wedge [\![H']\!] \approx [\![H \wedge H']\!]$.*

Referring back to the light controller, clearly, no positive battery requirements can ever be fulfilled by any implementation of Fig. 2, because only saturation is admitted. We are missing a power supply, something that charges our battery. Consider the specification of a power supply depicted in Fig. 5b. The question is whether the joined requirements of capacity and timed behaviour put in parallel with the power supply is captured by our implementation put in parallel with the power supply. As such the flow of resource b becomes the sum of the saturation provided by the controller and the charge induced by the power supply. This interaction is exactly captured by structural composition.

The structural composition defines the time synchronized and resource additive product behaviour of its constituents. As such given two implementations, each satisfying a distinct constituent, their parallel execution results in an implementation of their composition.

Definition 14 (Structural product). *Let $S^j = \langle X^j, \chi_L^j, \rightarrow_j \rangle$ for $j \in \{1, 2\}$ be a specification, where $X_G^1 = X_G^2$. We define the structural product of S^1 and S^2, denoted $S^1 \parallel S^2$ as a new specification: $S^1 \parallel S^2 = \langle X, \chi_L, \rightarrow \rangle$, where $X_L = X_L^1 \times X_L^2$, $X_G = X_G^1$, $\chi_L = (\chi_L^1, \chi_L^2)$ and $\rightarrow$ is the smallest relation satisfying:*

$$\frac{(x_L^1, x_G) \xrightarrow{\gamma}_1 (y_L^1, y_G^1) \quad (x_L^2, x_G) \xrightarrow{\gamma}_2 (y_L^2, y_G^2)}{((x_L^1, x_L^2), x_G) \xrightarrow{\gamma} ((y_L^1, y_L^2), y_G^1 + y_G^2 - x_G)} \gamma \in \{\tau\} \cup \mathbb{R}_{\geq 0}$$

$$\frac{(x_L^1, x_G) \xrightarrow{\tau}_1 (y_L^1, y_G) \quad (x_L^2, x_G) \xrightarrow{\tau}_2}{((x_L^1, x_L^2), x_G) \xrightarrow{\tau} ((y_L^1, x_L^2), y_G)}$$

$$\frac{(x_L^2, x_G) \xrightarrow{\tau}_2 (y_L^2, y_G) \quad (x_L^1, x_G) \xrightarrow{\tau}_1}{((x_L^1, x_L^2), x_G) \xrightarrow{\tau} ((x_L^1, y_L^2), y_G)}$$

As noted earlier, refinement indeed defines a precongruence over specifications in terms of the structural product.

Theorem 4. *If S, S'' and T are specifications such that $S \sqsubseteq S'$, then $S \parallel T$ exists iff $S' \parallel T$ exists, and given existence of these we find $S \parallel T \sqsubseteq S' \parallel T$.*

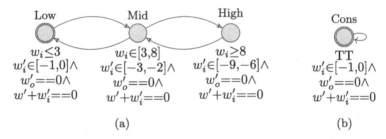

(a)   (b)

Fig. 7. (a) An RHA modelling modelling an intake valve. It is similar to the one depicted in Fig. 1a, however, it does not allow internal discrete behaviour in its operational modes, i.e. whenever a transition is made it must change mode. Additionally, it defines slightly different flow rates in Low, Mid and High. (b) Another RHA modelling an intake valve. This one is simple as all it does regardless of capacity is to continuously consume between -1 and 0 water per time unit while allowing any discrete behaviour. The structural composition of these two, however, do in fact refine the intake valve specification depicted in Fig. 1a. Note how resource additivity makes it possible to intuitively "add up" flows in a component-wise manner.

The structural product admits a transition if an only if either of its constituents allow a discrete transition or if both admit the same delay. Resource additivity is captured by our treatment of the global state-space in the target state, i.e. changes are added up. On the syntactic level we can compute the structural composition by the following RHA construction.

Definition 15 (Structural Composition).
Let $H^j = \langle L^j, l_0^j, \mathcal{V}^j, E^j, \mathrm{inv}^j, \mathrm{rate}^j \rangle$ for $j \in \{1,2\}$ be an RHA, where $\mathcal{V}_G^1 = \mathcal{V}_G^2$ and $\mathcal{V}_L^1 \cap \mathcal{V}_L^2 = \emptyset$. We define the structural composition of H^1 and H^2, denoted $H^1 \parallel H^2$ as a new RHA: $H^1 \parallel H^2 = \langle L, l_0, \mathcal{V}_L \uplus \mathcal{V}_G, E, \mathrm{inv}, \mathrm{rate} \rangle$, where $L = L^1 \times L^2$, $l_0 = (l_0^1, l_0^1)$, $\mathcal{V}_L = \mathcal{V}_L^1 \uplus \mathcal{V}_L^2$, $\mathcal{V}_G = \mathcal{V}_G^1$, $\mathrm{inv}\big((l^1, l^2)\big) = \mathrm{inv}^1(l^1) \wedge \mathrm{inv}^2(l^2)$, $\mathrm{rate}\big((l^1, l^2)\big) = \mathrm{rate}^1(l^1) \oplus \mathrm{rate}^2(l^2)$, and E is defined by the following rules:

- *If $(l^1, c^1, u^1, k^1) \in E^1$ and $(l^2, c^2, u^2, k^2) \in E^2$, then $\big((l^1, l^2), c^1 \wedge c^2, u^1 \oplus u^2, (k^1, k^2)\big) \in E$;*
- *If $(l^1, c, u, k) \in E^1$ and $\forall k^2 \in L^2 : (l^2, c^2, u^2, k^2) \notin E^2$, then $\big((l^1, l^2), c, u, (k, l^2)\big) \in E$;*
- *If $(l^2, c, u, k) \in E^2$ and $\forall k^1 \in L^1 : (l^1, c^1, u^1, k^1) \notin E^1$, then $\big((l^1, l^2), c, u, (l^1, k)\big) \in E$.*

Figure 7 shows an example of the type of reasoning possible using structural composition.

Note that RHAs are closed under additive structural composition as defined by Definition 15, this is generally not the case for Linear Hybrid Automata (LHA) under synchronized composition [22]. As expected, the structural composition and product coincide.

Theorem 5. *Let H and H' be RHA then: $\llbracket H \rrbracket \parallel \llbracket H' \rrbracket \approx \llbracket H \parallel H' \rrbracket$.*

Both logical and structural composition provide concise ways for capturing divided responsibilities of open components. A large specification can therefore be reasoned about in a component-wise manner using an intuitive notion of additivity over globally available resources.

The quotient composition of two specifications T, referred to as the 'target' and S, referred to as the 'existing component' results in a new specification X which for any implementation I where $S \parallel I \sqsubseteq T$ we have $I \sqsubseteq X$. In other words, the quotient defines the most permissive specification that characterizes the missing behaviour of the existing component in order to refine the target. In order to capture the quotient we make use of two new state types: $\bot$, which characterizes deadlock states and $\top$ which characterizes universal states. Deadlock states allow no behaviour, while universal states allow arbitrary behaviour.

Definition 16 (Quotient product). *Let* $S^j = \langle X^j, \chi_L^j, \to^j \rangle$ *for* $j \in \{1,2\}$ *be a specification, where* $X_G^1 = X_G^2$. *We define the quotient product of* S^1 *and* S^2, *denoted* $S^2 \backslash\backslash S^1$ *as a new specification:* $S^2 \backslash\backslash S^1 = \langle X, \chi_L, \to \rangle$ *where:* $X_L = (X_L^1 \times X_L^2) \uplus \{\bot, \top\}$, $X_G = X_G^1$, $\chi_L = (\chi_L^1, \chi_L^2)$, *and* $\to$ *is the smallest relation satisfying:*

$$\frac{(x_L^1, x_G) \xrightarrow{\gamma}_1 (y_L^1, y_G^1) \quad (x_L^2, x_G) \xrightarrow{\gamma}_2 (y_L^2, y_G^2)}{((x_L^1, x_L^2), x_G) \xrightarrow{\gamma} ((y_L^1, y_L^2), y_G^2 + x_G - y_G^1)} \gamma \in \{\tau\} \cup \mathbb{R}_{\geq 0}$$

$$\frac{(x_L^2, x_G) \xrightarrow{\tau}_2 (y_L^2, y_G^2) \quad (x_L^1, x_G) \not\xrightarrow{\tau}_1}{((x_L^1, x_L^2), x_G) \xrightarrow{\tau} ((x_L^1, y_L^2), y_G^2)}$$

$$\frac{(x_L^1, x_G) \not\xrightarrow{\gamma}_1}{((x_L^1, x_L^2), x_G) \xrightarrow{\gamma} (\top, y_G)} \gamma \in \mathbb{R}_{\geq 0}$$

$$\frac{(x_L^1, x_G) \xrightarrow{\gamma}_1 (y_L^1, y_G^1) \quad (x_L^2, x_G) \not\xrightarrow{\gamma}_2}{((x_L^1, x_L^2), x_G) \xrightarrow{\gamma} (\bot, y_G)} \gamma \in \{\tau\} \cup \mathbb{R}_{\geq 0}$$

$$\frac{(x_L^1, x_G) \not\xrightarrow{\tau}_1 \quad (x_L^2, x_G) \not\xrightarrow{\tau}_2}{((x_L^1, x_L^2), x_G) \xrightarrow{\tau} ((x_L^1, x_L^2), x_G)}$$

$$\frac{}{(\top, x_G) \xrightarrow{\gamma} (\top, y_G)} \gamma \in \{\tau\} \cup \mathbb{R}_{\geq 0}$$

Crucially, The dual of the structural product corresponds exactly to the quotient.

Theorem 6. *Let S and T be specifications. If $T\backslash\backslash S$ exists then for all implementations I we have $S \parallel I$ exists and $S \parallel I \sqsubseteq T$ iff $I \sqsubseteq T\backslash\backslash S$.*

On the syntactic level we can compute the quotient by the following RHA construction.

312   P. J. L. Cuijpers et al.

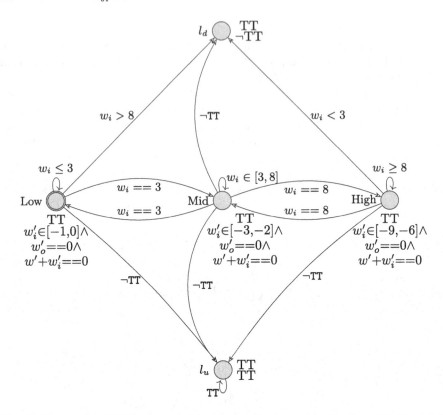

Fig. 8. The resulting RHA generated by the quotient construction by using the intake valve specification of Fig. 1a as its target and the simple consumer valve of Fig. 7b as its existing component. As expected, the intake valve specification of Fig. 7a indeed refines the quotient, the formal proof of which is omitted for the sake of brevity.

Definition 17 (Quotient composition).
Let $H^j = \langle L^j, l_0^j, \mathcal{V}^j, E^j, \mathrm{Inv}^j, \mathrm{rate}^j \rangle$ for $j \in \{1, 2\}$ be an RHA, where $\mathcal{V}_G^1 = \mathcal{V}_G^2$, such that $\mathcal{V}_L^1 \cap \mathcal{V}_L^2 = \emptyset$. We define the quotient composition of H^1 and H^2 as a new RHA $H^2 \backslash\backslash H^1 = \langle L, l_0, \mathcal{V}, E^j, \mathrm{Inv}, \mathrm{rate} \rangle$ where: $L = (L^1 \times L^2) \cup \{l_u, l_d\}$, $l_0 = (l_0^1, l_0^2)$, $\mathcal{V}_L = \mathcal{V}_L^1 \uplus \mathcal{V}_L^2$, $\mathcal{V}_G = \mathcal{V}_G^1$, $\mathrm{Inv}\left((l^1, l^2)\right) = \mathrm{Inv}(l_u) = \mathrm{Inv}(l_d) = TT$, $\mathrm{rate}\left((l^1, l^2)\right) = \mathrm{rate}^2(l_2) \oslash \mathrm{rate}^1(l_1)$, $\mathrm{rate}(l_u) = TT$, $\mathrm{rate}(l_d) = \neg TT$, and E is defined by the following rules:

- *If $(l^1, c^1, u^1, k^1) \in E^1$ and $(l^2, c^2, u^2, k^2) \in E^2$, then $\left((l^1, l^2), c, u, (k^1, k^2)\right) \in E$ where $u = u^2 \oslash u^1$ and $c = c^1 \wedge \mathrm{Inv}^1(l^1) \wedge u \triangleright \mathrm{Inv}^1(k^1) \wedge c^2 \wedge \mathrm{Inv}^2(l^2) \wedge u \triangleright \mathrm{Inv}^2(k^2)$;*
- *If $(l^2, c^2, u^2, k^2) \in E^2$ and $\forall k^1 \in L^1 : (l^1, c^1, u^1, k^1) \notin E^1$, then $\left((l^1, l^2), c, \alpha, u^2, (l^1, k^2)\right) \in E$ where $l^1 \in L^1$ and $c = \mathrm{Inv}^1(l^1) \wedge c^2 \wedge \mathrm{Inv}^2(l^2) \wedge u^2 \triangleright \mathrm{Inv}^2(k^2)$;*
- *If $l^1 \in L^1$ and $l^2 \in L^2$, then $\left((l^1, l^2), c, TT, l_u\right) \in E$ where $c = \left(\neg\mathrm{Inv}^1(l^1) \vee \mathrm{Inv}^2(l^2)\right) \wedge \bigwedge_{(l^1, c^1, u^1, k^1) \in E^1} (\neg c^1 \vee \neg u^1 \triangleright \mathrm{Inv}^1(k^1))$;*

- If $l^1 \in L^1$, $l^2 \in L^2$, then $\left((l^1, l^2), c, \epsilon, (l^1, l^2)\right) \in E$ where
  $c = c^1 \wedge = \mathrm{Inv}^1(l^1) \wedge \bigwedge_{(l^1, c^1, u^1, k^1) \in E^1}(\neg c^1 \vee \neg u^1 \triangleright \mathrm{Inv}^1(k^1)) \wedge$
  $\mathrm{Inv}^2(l^2) \wedge \bigwedge_{(l^2, c^2, u^2, k^2) \in E^2}(\neg c^2 \vee \neg u^2 \triangleright \mathrm{Inv}^2(k^2))$;
- If $(l^1, c^1, u^1, k^1) \in E^1$ and $l^2 \in L^2$, then $\left((l^1, l^2), c, TT, l_d\right) \in E$ where
  $c = c^1 \wedge \mathrm{Inv}^1(l^1) \wedge u^1 \triangleright \mathrm{Inv}^1(k^1) \bigwedge_{(l^2, c^2, u^2, k^2) \in E^2}(\neg c^2 \vee \neg u^2 \triangleright \mathrm{Inv}^2(k^2))$;
- $(l^u, TT, TT, l^u) \in E$.

An example quotient can be seen in Fig. 8.

The quotient product refines the underlying semantics defined by the quotient composition, and whenever the product is consistent then so is the composition.

Theorem 7. *Let H and H' be RHA then $[\![H]\!] \backslash\!\backslash [\![H']\!] \sqsubseteq [\![H \backslash\!\backslash H']\!]$.*

Theorem 8. *Let H and H' be RHA then $[\![H \backslash\!\backslash H']\!]$ is consistent iff $[\![H]\!] \backslash\!\backslash [\![H']\!]$ is consistent.*

Unfortunately, the syntactic construction and the semantic product do not fully coincide. In fact the syntactic construction is an abstraction of the semantic product. This is because the product insists that a state after some delay can act as a deadlock- or universal- state, which cannot be mimicked in the syntactic construction without introducing complex rate rules and appropriate mechanisms for handling universal and deadlock behaviour directly in the semantics of RHAs. For the sake of brevity and because it has no impact on practical applications (however still vital to a full characterization of the theory), this aspect is left as a topic for future research. Note also, that all three compositions always exists. This is because RHAs are defined over essentially internal discrete actions, as such, the signature of all RHA is the same. Indeed any RHA is defined over the set of all global resources. The notion of environment and component is solely dictated by the model. Intuitively, one can think of environments as components that provides a positive resource flow and vice versa for components. A more powerful extension of the theory with discrete inputs and outputs would complicate this aspect however. In such an extension, the notion of compatibility in terms of signature becomes relevant. We leave this aspect of compatibility as a topic for future research in the full discrete I/O characterization of the theory.

4   Assume-Guarantee Reasoning

With our specification theory of RHA, we have a robust and complete framework, suitable for component-wise design and refinement in the additive hybrid setting. We now show that our theory facilitates component-wise assume-guarantee reasoning. The main idea is to use the notion of pre- and post-conditions in order to characterize intended behaviour. Usually pre- and post-conditions define properties of sequential processes that must hold before respectively after some behaviour is encountered. Since we are dealing with systems that consists of real-time concurrent components the notion of 'before' and 'after' is better captured by structural compositional reasoning. As such a pre-condition defines an environment that affects our system, and a post-condition defines how a system should act whenever such an environment is within our sphere of influence. Mathematically, we are simply dealing with implications, i.e. for the pair (P, Q) consisting of a pre-condition and post-condition (as mentioned earlier, this is called a contract), a system upholds the pair if and only if whenever P holds then so does Q. We adopt the usual terminology used in the real-time setting, that is, pre- and post- conditions are referred to as assumptions and guarantees.

Let's first formally capture our notion of an assume-guarantee pair and satisfaction thereof. In our theory, assumptions and guarantees are defined by RHAs. We need to characterize an RHA that exactly describes the assume-guarantee implication. In the concurrent real-time setting this is known as a weakening and captured by a so-called weaken operation as defined in [12].

Definition 18 (Weaken). *Let A and G be RHAs. We define the weakening of G in A, as:* $G \gg A \sqsubseteq (A \parallel G) \backslash\backslash A$

Let's design a water pump based on a specification defined by a weakening. Our water pump's environment consists of two reservoirs; an input reservoir, for which the pump itself can only draw from, and an output reservoir, for which the pump can only provide to. We characterize the capacity of the input and output reservoirs by the global resources w_i and w_o. Our assumption on the environment and our guarantee on the water pump whenever that assumption holds is shown in Fig. 9.

We define our proposed water pump system S as the structural composition of the three RHAs shown in Fig. 1. We hypothesize that S refines $G \gg A$ thereby making it possible to use an implementation of S whenever we need an implementation of $G \gg A$. As such we retain the simple and intuitive model defined by the weakening when considering the water pump in a larger context while providing certainty that an actual system can be implemented using the more specialised but less intuitive model. We should note here that the reserve question is just as useful from a system design perspective. Looking at Fig. 1, clearly the composition results in a large RHA, in fact even the component-wise representation is large and cumbersome. If one finds that $G \gg A$ refines S then, from a design perspective, we can reason about the water pump specification simply by using the weakening instead.

A ⊙
TT
$w_i' \in [2,4]$
$w_o' \in [-5,-2]$

(a)

G ⊙
$w_i \in [1,8]$
$w_o \in [1,8]$
TT

(b)

Fig. 9. (a) An RHA modelling our assumption on the environment. We assume that the input reservoir gets filled by a rate in the interval $[2,4]$ and that the output reservoir gets saturated by rate in the interval $[-5,-2]$. Additionally, we assume that the environment never saturates the usage reservoir, thereby completely delegating that responsibility to the system from a modelling perspective. (b) Another RHA modelling our guarantee on the system if the assumption is fulfilled. We guarantee that the capacity of both the input and output reservoir stays in the interval $[1,8]$. Additionally, we guarantee that at any time, a discrete event can occur, as long as it performs no resets.

Now we have a system, a weakening and well defined set of operations on our language, all we need now is to ascertain whether the refinement holds.

5   Refinement

Unfortunately, checking refinement for general RHAs is undecidable. Indeed if it were, then that would imply that reachability for general LHA is decidable, which it is not [22]. Instead we explore how statistical model checking can be used to refute the existence of refinement. To that end, we utilize the verification engine of UPPAAL SMC [13] to conduct simulation based validation by translating the RHA models into Stochastic Hybrid Automata (SHA) [13]. Essentially, these are hybrid automata defined over a stochastic timed semantics, refining the non-deterministic mechanics of edge transitions and time delays into probabilistic occurrences based on some probability distribution. Much like RHAs, SHAs allows us to define linear differential equations on variable rates and also to consider such variables in guards and invariants. Hence can use resources of

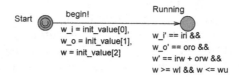

Fig. 10. The SHA agent responsible for computing the continuous rates of all resources in the composition. Here resources w_i, w_o and w are first initialized to their respective initial values; $\{1,1,10\}$ signified by the firing of action begin after which the mode Running in each time step sets the appropriate rate of each resource according to the real-valued variables iri, oro, irw and orw. Annotation ⌣ signifies that time cannot pass in a mode.

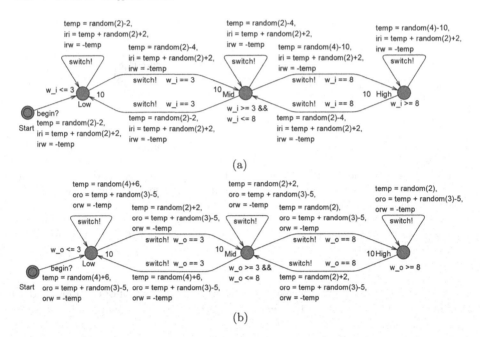

Fig. 11. The SHA interpretations of the intake valve (a) and the output valve (b) specifications of Fig. 1a and 1c. The discrete action switch is used to communicate that a transition has been fired. This aspect is crucial because we need to know when a possible refinement target must be able to do a transition. The red scalars next to each mode is a probability parameter and just an implementation detail, suffice it to say that larger numbers results in higher preference for taking a transition whenever one is enabled.

RHAs as is in SHAs. We can specify a convex interval of real numbers by using the function $random(max) = [0, max)$. SHAs are defined over a discrete action set of inputs (characterized by a question mark ?) and outputs (characterized by an exclamation point !). Sadly, SHAs are not natively additive, so this needs to be simulated. To do so is a simple matter of introducing a real-valued variable for each automata specific occurrence of a resource and define an additivity agent responsible for adding up the different rates into the actual rates. Our implementation of the agent model is shown in Fig. 10.

All that remains is to translate the capacity monitor, and the intake/output valve of Fig. 1 into SHAs. For convenience we have dedicated the responsibility of the capacity monitor to the additivity agent. Additionally, the rates defined by the assumption shown in Fig. 9 have been put directly on the intake and output valve. Their SHA interpretations are shown in Fig. 11

With that we have a stochastic realization of our water pump controller. To answer the question of whether the water pump refines the weakening $G \gg A$, we investigate whether the water pump controller in parallel with the assumption refines the composition of the assumption and the guarantee. One could also

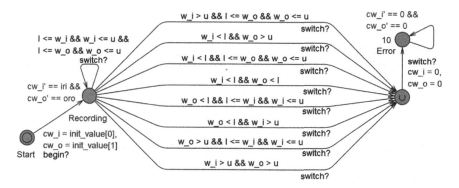

Fig. 12. The unfolded SHA interpretation of $A \parallel G$. Resources cw_i and cw_o are defined as clones of resources w_i and w_o. The mode Recording directly models the behaviour of $A \parallel G$. Whenever a transition is made, it is checked whether the invariants of $A \parallel G$ holds. Otherwise the invariant of Recording is unbounded, capturing values of w_i and w_o not admitted by the original composition. This is because we aim to explicitly capture illegal behaviour in order to direct it into the Error mode. The eight transitions leading to it simply captures the negation of the invariant defined by $A \parallel G$. Note that we need one for each case because stochastic semantics requires input-determinism.

$$G$$

$$w_i \in [1,10]$$
$$w_o \in [1,8)$$
$$\text{TT}$$

Fig. 13. An RHA modelling a slightly more strict guarantee.

just show the refinement to the quotient defined by $G \gg A$ directly, however the composition of A and G is arguable more intuitive.

The last step in our translation effort is to obtain a stochastic interpretation of our refinement target, namely the structural composition of A and G. This is shown in Fig. 12.

Using the SHA interpretation of the composition of our water pump controller and the assumption, we intend to drive the SHA model of $A \parallel G$. Our target property is supported by the following reasoning. If the error mode is ever entered and the clones of w_i and w_o get assigned the rate 0, then we know with absolute certainty that the original water pump controller cannot refine the weakening $G \gg A$. Since both SHAs are abstractions, this holds. We validate our property using the simulation capabilities of UPPAAL SMC.

We are now ready to conduct testing on our setup through simulations. Simulations shown in this paper all depict a number of sample runs as solid coloured lines. The metrics of interest are the evolution of the actual resources w_i and w_o together with the evolution of their clones cw_i and cw_o (y-axis) over time (x-axis).

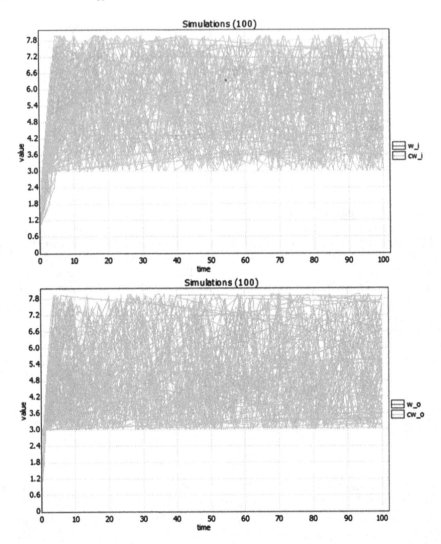

Fig. 14. Two sample simulation results obtained by queries $simulate[\Leftarrow 100]\{w_i, cw_i\}$ and $simulate[\Leftarrow 100]\{w_o, cw_o\}$ capturing the values of resource w_i and its clone respectively w_o and its clone. As may be expected, even with 100 simulations, the water pump controller seems to not be able to break the behaviour of $A \parallel G$. This is why we see only one variable in all traces, the clone perfectly matches the actual resource.

Let's start by simulating our water pump controller driving $A \parallel G$. The results of which are shown in Fig. 14. As can be seen, the controller seems to have difficulties breaking the invariant of $A \parallel G$. Of course we cannot conclude whether it is impossible, there might exist some execution that renders the invariant false, it just so happens that we have not found it.

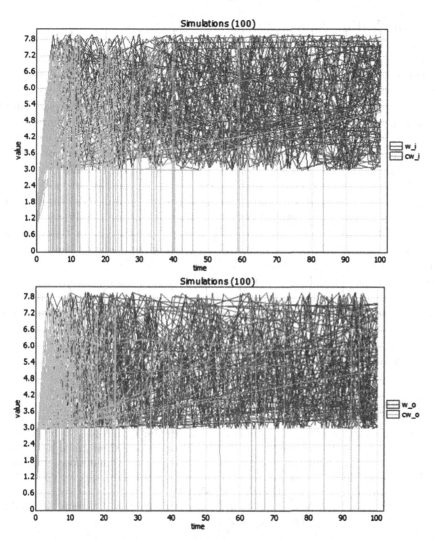

Fig. 15. Two sample simulation results obtained by queries $simulate[\Leftarrow 100]\{w_i, cw_i\}$ and $simulate[\Leftarrow 100]\{w_o, cw_o\}$ capturing the values of resource w_i and its clone respectively w_o and its clone. These results show that the water pump controller can force $A \parallel G$ into the Error mode, hence refuting the existence of a refinement into $G \gg A$.

Next we try to modify G slightly, maybe we can identify an interesting frontier for the upper limit of w_i and w_o. For that purpose, we use the slightly modified guarantee shown in Fig. 13. The simulation results are shown in Fig. 15. Now we clearly see that a capacity strictly below 8 cannot be guaranteed by our water pump controller under assumption A. Using the same reasoning as above, we can say with certainty that the composite of Fig. 1 under assumption A does not refine $G \gg A$.

6 Concluding Remarks

In this paper, we have proposed the complete specification theory of RHA, suitable for reasoning about step-wise refinement in the domain of additive resource-aware concurrent systems. As far as we know, this is the first such theory considering additive composition. We have shown how assume-guarantee reasoning is possible within the theory and exemplified a relevant sample case thereof. Furthermore, by translating RHAs into SHAs we have shown how one can refute the existence of refinement using a simulation based validation method.

In terms of further validation, a proper case study still remains to be conducted. Energy-aware systems, such as load-balancing and smart-grid analysis are prime candidates. Additionally, an intuitive and robust tool implementation through automated translation into SHA would significantly decrease the entry-level knowledge required to use the method presented. For that purpose, the discrete input/output extension of RHA would be required, including the complete characterization of the quotient construction in this setting. This full characterization of the theory could serve as a general meta theory in the additive hybrid domain, which would significantly push state-of-the-art in the real-time analysis setting if a useful and decidable instance of the theory is identified. Furthermore, showing how the weaken operation can be used to handle scalability issues is also desirable, i.e. lifting this result on Timed Input/Output Automata as shown in e.g. [12] to the additive hybrid setting.

References

1. de Alfaro, L., Henzinger, T.A.: Interface automata. In: Tjoa, A.M., Gruhn, V. (eds.) Proceedings of the 8th European Software Engineering Conference held jointly with 9th ACM SIGSOFT International Symposium on Foundations of Software Engineering 2001, Vienna, Austria, 10–14 September 2001, pp. 109–120. ACM (2001). https://doi.org/10.1145/503209.503226
2. Alur, R., Dill, D.L.: A theory of timed automata. Theoret. Comput. Sci. **126**(2), 183–235 (1994). https://doi.org/10.1016/0304-3975(94)90010-8
3. Bacci, G., Bouyer, P., Fahrenberg, U., Larsen, K.G., Markey, N., Reynier, P.-A.: Optimal and robust controller synthesis. In: Havelund, K., Peleska, J., Roscoe, B., de Vink, E. (eds.) FM 2018. LNCS, vol. 10951, pp. 203–221. Springer, Cham (2018). https://doi.org/10.1007/978-3-319-95582-7_12
4. Bauer, S.S., et al.: Moving from specifications to contracts in component-based design. In: de Lara, J., Zisman, A. (eds.) FASE 2012. LNCS, vol. 7212, pp. 43–58. Springer, Heidelberg (2012). https://doi.org/10.1007/978-3-642-28872-2_3
5. Benveniste, A., et al.: Contracts for system design. Found. Trends Electron. Des. Autom. **12**(2–3), 124–400 (2018). https://doi.org/10.1561/1000000053
6. Bergstra, J.A., Klop, J.W.: Algebra of communicating processes with abstraction. Theor. Comput. Sci. **37**, 77–121 (1985). https://doi.org/10.1016/0304-3975(85)90088-X
7. Boudol, G., Larsen, K.G.: Graphical versus logical specifications. In: Arnold, A. (ed.) CAAP 1990. LNCS, vol. 431, pp. 57–71. Springer, Heidelberg (1990). https://doi.org/10.1007/3-540-52590-4_40

8. Bouyer, P., Colange, M., Markey, N.: Symbolic optimal reachability in weighted timed automata. In: Chaudhuri, S., Farzan, A. (eds.) CAV 2016. LNCS, vol. 9779, pp. 513–530. Springer, Cham (2016). https://doi.org/10.1007/978-3-319-41528-4_28

9. Caillaud, B., Delahaye, B., Larsen, K.G., Legay, A., Pedersen, M.L., Wasowski, A.: Constraint Markov chains. Theor. Comput. Sci. **412**(34), 4373–4404 (2011). https://doi.org/10.1016/j.tcs.2011.05.010

10. Čerāns, K., Godskesen, J.C., Larsen, K.G.: Timed modal specification—theory and tools. In: Courcoubetis, C. (ed.) CAV 1993. LNCS, vol. 697, pp. 253–267. Springer, Heidelberg (1993). https://doi.org/10.1007/3-540-56922-7_21

11. Cuijpers, P.J.L., Reniers, M.A.: Lost in translation: hybrid-time flows vs. real-time transitions. In: Egerstedt, M., Mishra, B. (eds.) HSCC 2008. LNCS, vol. 4981, pp. 116–129. Springer, Heidelberg (2008). https://doi.org/10.1007/978-3-540-78929-1_9

12. David, A., et al.: Compositional verification of real-time systems using Ecdar. Int. J. Softw. Tools Technol. Transf. **14**(6), 703–720 (2012). https://doi.org/10.1007/s10009-012-0237-y

13. David, A., Larsen, K.G., Legay, A., Mikuăionis, M., Poulsen, D.B.: UPPAAL SMC tutorial. Int. J. Softw. Tools Technol. Transf. **17**(4), 397–415 (2015). https://doi.org/10.1007/s10009-014-0361-y

14. David, A., Larsen, K.G., Legay, A., Nyman, U., Wasowski, A.: Timed I/O automata: a complete specification theory for real-time systems. In: Johansson, K.H., Yi, W. (eds.) Proceedings of the 13th ACM International Conference on Hybrid Systems: Computation and Control, HSCC 2010, Stockholm, Sweden, 12–15 April 2010, pp. 91–100. ACM (2010). https://doi.org/10.1145/1755952.1755967

15. van Glabbeek, R.J.: The linear time - branching time spectrum I: the semantics of concrete, sequential processes. In: Bergstra, J.A., Ponse, A., Smolka, S.A. (eds.) Handbook of Process Algebra, chap. 1, pp. 3–99. Elsevier Science, Amsterdam (2001). https://doi.org/10.1016/B978-044482830-9/50019-9

16. Hansen, J., Larsen, K.G., Cuijpers, P.J.L.: Balancing flexible production and consumption of energy using resource timed automata. In: 2022 11th Mediterranean Conference on Embedded Computing (MECO), pp. 1–6 (2022). https://doi.org/10.1109/MECO55406.2022.9797191

17. He, J.: Process simulation and refinement. Formal Aspects Comput. **1**(3), 229–241 (1989). https://doi.org/10.1007/BF01887207

18. Jifeng, H.: Various simulations and refinements. In: de Bakker, J.W., de Roever, W.-P., Rozenberg, G. (eds.) REX 1989. LNCS, vol. 430, pp. 340–360. Springer, Heidelberg (1990). https://doi.org/10.1007/3-540-52559-9_70

19. He, J.: Service refinement. In: 15th Asia-Pacific Software Engineering Conference (APSEC 2008), 3–5 December 2008, Beijing, China, p. 5. IEEE Computer Society (2008). https://doi.org/10.1109/APSEC.2008.78

20. He, J., Hoare, C.A.R.: Unifying theories of programming. In: Orlowska, E., Szalas, A. (eds.) Participants Copies for Relational Methods in Logic, Algebra and Computer Science, 4th International Seminar RelMiCS, Warsaw, Poland, 14–20 September 1998, pp. 97–99 (1998)

21. He, J., Liu, Z., Li, X.: Towards a refinement calculus for object systems. In: Proceedings of the 1st IEEE International Conference on Cognitive Informatics (ICCI 2002), 19–20 August 2002, Calgary, Canada, pp. 69–76. IEEE Computer Society (2002). https://doi.org/10.1109/COGINF.2002.1039284

22. Henzinger, T.A., Kurshan, R.P.: The theory of hybrid automata. In: Inan, M.K., Kurshan, R.P. (eds.) Verification of Digital and Hybrid Systems. NATO ASI Series, vol. 170, pp. 265–292. Springer, Heidelberg (2000)

23. Hoare, C.A.R.: Communicating Sequential Processes. International Series in Computer Science. Prentice Hall (1985)

24. Hoare, C.A.R., He, J.: The weakest prespecification. Inf. Process. Lett. **24**(2), 127–132 (1987). https://doi.org/10.1016/0020-0190(87)90106-2

25. Hoare, T., He, J.: Unifying theories for parallel programming. In: Lengauer, C., Griebl, M., Gorlatch, S. (eds.) Euro-Par 1997. LNCS, vol. 1300, pp. 15–30. Springer, Heidelberg (1997). https://doi.org/10.1007/BFb0002714

26. Hoare, C.A.R., He, J., Sanders, J.W.: Prespecification in data refinement. Inf. Process. Lett. **25**(2), 71–76 (1987). https://doi.org/10.1016/0020-0190(87)90224-9

27. Jones, C.B.: Developing methods for computer programs including a notion of interference. Ph.D. thesis, University of Oxford, UK (1981). https://ethos.bl.uk/OrderDetails.do?uin=uk.bl.ethos.259064

28. Lamport, L.: Hybrid systems in TLA$^+$. In: Grossman, R.L., Nerode, A., Ravn, A.P., Rischel, H. (eds.) HS 1991-1992. LNCS, vol. 736, pp. 77–102. Springer, Heidelberg (1993). https://doi.org/10.1007/3-540-57318-6_25

29. Larsen, K., et al.: As cheap as possible: efficient cost-optimal reachability for priced timed automata. In: Berry, G., Comon, H., Finkel, A. (eds.) CAV 2001. LNCS, vol. 2102, pp. 493–505. Springer, Heidelberg (2001). https://doi.org/10.1007/3-540-44585-4_47

30. Larsen, K.G.: Modal specifications. In: Sifakis, J. (ed.) CAV 1989. LNCS, vol. 407, pp. 232–246. Springer, Heidelberg (1990). https://doi.org/10.1007/3-540-52148-8_19

31. Larsen, K.G., Rasmussen, J.I.: Optimal reachability for multi-priced timed automata. Theor. Comput. Sci. **390**(2), 197–213 (2008). https://doi.org/10.1016/j.tcs.2007.09.021. Foundations Software Science and Computational Structures

32. Larsen, K.G., Steffen, B., Weise, C.: The methodology of modal constraints. In: Broy, M., Merz, S., Spies, K. (eds.) Formal Systems Specification. LNCS, vol. 1169, pp. 405–435. Springer, Heidelberg (1996). https://doi.org/10.1007/BFb0024437

33. Larsen, K.G., Thomsen, B.: A modal process logic. In: Proceedings of the Third Annual Symposium on Logic in Computer Science (LICS 1988), Edinburgh, Scotland, UK, 5–8 July 1988, pp. 203–210. IEEE Computer Society (1988). https://doi.org/10.1109/LICS.1988.5119

34. Milner, R.: A Calculus of Communicating Systems. Lecture Notes in Computer Science, vol. 92. Springer, Cham (1980). https://doi.org/10.1007/3-540-10235-3

35. Owicki, S.S., Gries, D.: An axiomatic proof technique for parallel programs I. Acta Inform. **6**, 319–340 (1976). https://doi.org/10.1007/BF00268134

36. Pnueli, A.: The temporal logic of programs. In: 18th Annual Symposium on Foundations of Computer Science, pp. 46–57 (1977). https://doi.org/10.1109/SFCS.1977.32

37. Scholefield, D., Zedan, H., Jifeng, H.: Real-time refinement: semantics and application. In: Borzyszkowski, A.M., Sokołowski, S. (eds.) MFCS 1993. LNCS, vol. 711, pp. 693–702. Springer, Heidelberg (1993). https://doi.org/10.1007/3-540-57182-5_60

38. Xu, Q., de Roever, W.P., He, J.: The rely-guarantee method for verifying shared variable concurrent programs. Formal Aspects Comput. **9**(2), 149–174 (1997). https://doi.org/10.1007/BF01211617

Time: It is only Logical!

Frédéric Mallet[(✉)]

Université Côte d'Azur, CNRS, Inria, I3S, Nice, France
Frederic.Mallet@univ-cotedazur.fr

Abstract. Logical Clocks play an important role for the design and modelling of concurrent systems. The Clock Constraint Specification Language (CCSL) was built in 2009, as part of an annex of the UML Profile for MARTE, to give a proper syntax to handle logical clocks as first class citizens. The syntax gave rise to a series of different semantic interpretations along with various verification tools. Usecases are diverse and include languages to express timing requirements, temporal or spatio-temporal logics to capture expected safety properties, meta-languages to give an operational semantics to domain-specific languages. The application domains include avionics, safety-critical transportation systems, self-driving vehicles, systems engineering models, cyber-physical systems. This paper reviews the effort conducted since 2009 on CCSL. A large part of this effort was made possible by Professor He Jifeng and his will to build in Shanghai a research centre of excellence for trustworthy systems. Researchers there found inspiration in the heritage left by the different schools working around the world on concurrency theory, including the school of synchronous languages from which CCSL has emerged.

Keywords: Logical Time · Cyber-Physical Systems · Polychronous languages

1 Introduction

1.1 CCSL - Genesis

The Clock Constraint Specification Language (CCSL) was devised as an attempt to bring order into the galaxy of so-called standard notations and semantics that were emerging [37] following the adoption of the Unified Modelling Language 2.x [52]. Some complained that the official semantics was not precise enough [18], others that it was too constraining and not expressive enough. Each community working in the field of concurrency theory or formal languages was providing its contribution to give one interpretation, connected to its analysis or verification frameworks. The community of synchronous languages [7] was no exception and has provided its own contributions with Argos [40] and SyncCharts [2,4], as synchronous interpretations for the visual formalism of Harel's StateCharts [22] or also as a formal and sound alternative to UML State Machines.

The word *unified* was misleading as some people were trying to provide a unique, one size fits all, notation to do everything as the goal should have been to

J. P. Bowen et al. (Eds.): *Theories of Programming and Formal Methods*, LNCS 14080, pp. 323–347, 2023.
https://doi.org/10.1007/978-3-031-40436-8_12

provide a *unifying* framework to compare the legitimate different interpretations that are necessary to deal with the diversity of missions faced by software or system engineers. In his book on Unifying Theories of Programming [25] with C.A.R. Hoare, Professor He Jifeng gets us back on another path by stating *"A unifying theory is usually complementary to the theories that it links, and does not seek to replace them."*

CCSL was meant to give a complementary notation that would come as a companion of languages, whether visual or not, to clarify or make precise, if and when necessary, their interpretation and in particular, the subtle legitimate behavioural variations regarding temporal, timed or concurrent aspects of systems. Not a language to rule them all but rather a meta-language to allow different semantic interpretations to co-exist without ambiguities.

As UML semantic variation points were meant to be addressed in dedicated profiles, it was only natural to seek the definition of a profile for that purpose. Then what started as an attempt to build a synchronous reactive UML profile [49], soon became a participation of the Aoste I3S/Inria team to a Task Force within the Object Management Group. Our goal at that time, was to define something that would allow a synchronous reactive interpretation to co-exist with plenty other interpretations, including fully asynchronous ones. The UML Profile for Modelling and Analysis of Real-Time systems (MARTE) was adopted three years later in 2009 [53] and CCSL was described within annex C.3 of the specification.

1.2 Logical Time and Clocks

As the name suggests, logical clocks are the central and foundational element of CCSL. The word *clock* is also misleading as it has a deeply anchored popular meaning that turns out to characterize just a particular, although very important, kind of clock. A clock is *a device for measuring and showing time*. It usually works by comparing the duration of a phenomenon by counting the number of occurrences of ticks produced by a trustworthy source taken as a time reference. When the source is based on a regular physical phenomenon, for instance the resonant frequency of atoms in the case of atomics clocks, it is called a *physical clock*. However, the reference can also be an arbitrary recurrent event that is meaningful to the system for some reasons. In such cases, it is referred to as a *logical clock*.

Several digital systems react according to the speed of driving clocks that are not regular periodic physical events. A control system of a car engine reacts according to the rotation speed of the camshaft, this rotation speed changes continuously and can hardly refer to an absolute physical measure as 1) it would depend on too many external parameters; 2) it is neither necessary nor efficient to build the actual physical device.

In the origin of Communicating Sequential Processes (CSP [24]), we also find an interesting statement to support that position *"Another detail which we have deliberately chosen to ignore is the exact timing of occurrences of events. The advantage of this is that designs and reasoning about them are simplified, and furthermore can be applied to physical and computing systems of any speed and performance.".*

Leslie Lamport [30] has made popular logical clocks in the context of distributed systems by considering that *"the concept of time is derived from the more basic concept of the order in which events occur"*. Logical clocks were used, as a pragmatic solution, to reconstruct a total order of events and therefore provide a simple method for synchronizing spatially-separated processes or even physical clocks. Further away from those practical considerations, event structures [43] provide a theoretical framework to study the relation *happens before* at the heart of Lamport's logical clocks.

In the field of programming languages, and mainly for reactive systems, synchronous languages [7], like Esterel [8], Lustre [11] or Signal [32], have long promoted logical clocks as native programming artefacts. Clocks are used as activation conditions to decide when it makes sense to activate the different parts of a program so as to make sure that they operate correctly, for instance because all the necessary inputs are available. Synchronous (logical) clocks rely on the concept of instant, that denotes atomic actions, and allows for deciding whether some occurrences of events happen instantaneously, i.e., within the same instant. This leads to the notion of *happens together* or coincidence. Even though coincidence is a mental construct, it proved to be useful for the design of reactive and/or safety-critical systems [13].

Professor He has also proposed his own view of a clock model suitable for the construction of hybrid systems [23]. In his work, clocks are increasing sequences of non-negative reals. Those clocks refer directly to synchronous signals and the real values carried by clocks are the dates at which events occur. By considering sequences of reals, it implicitly assumes a global common time base. Other frameworks, like polychrony [33], do not assume the existence of a common global clock and rather push for solutions where clocks are not inherently related to each other. However, the potential existence of a common clock, may still become a good property that has to be proven or disproven by the compiler.

As an attempt to unify theories of time structures, tagged systems [34] and then tag machines [6] have become mainstream theoretical and practical (within the scope of Ptolemy [17] and variants like ForSyDe [47] and ModHel'X [21]) solutions to compare and combine models of computations (and communications).

While tag machines provide a nice mathematical framework, they do not provide any concrete syntax to build tag structures and define relations among them. CCSL intended to do that by focusing only on the underlying orderings among events, leaving out the tags themselves. It combines the two notions of *happens before* and *happens together*. An extension of CCSL, called TESL [55], brings back the tags and define some operators that build clocks depending on the tags or derives tags based on clock relations.

Finally, one must note that logical clocks of CCSL strongly differ from the (dense) clocks of timed automata [1]. Timed automata rely on a dense time model, meaning that clocks take values in a dense set. This is very useful and sometimes more natural for physical processes operating over continuous time. All these dense clocks increase at a uniform rate counting time with respect to a common global time frame. In certain conditions, the clocks can be stopped or reset. Timed automata, and their numerous derivatives, have given rise to a variety of powerful and very successful tools, like UPPAAL [31]. We show in Sect. 3 that we can combine such models with CCSL ones to benefit from both environments when one needs to access both logical and physical clocks.

The initial denotational semantics of CCSL [3] considered a model with dense-time but most CCSL-based tools [15] only work for discrete time and CCSL relies on timed automata [50] whenever it has to deal with dense-time relations.

1.3 Outline

This paper starts with a brief introduction to the syntax and semantics of CCSL in Sect. 2. Then, Sect. 3 describes two main use cases where CCSL is used not standalone, but as companion to other formalisms and notations. Section 4 describes some of the variants of CCSL. Then we briefly conclude.

2 Syntax and Semantics

A comprehensive theory of programming [25] treats a programming language under three styles of presentations: denotational, operational and algebraic. Here we do not go as far as proving consistency between the three definitions but we give a grasp of what it means in the context of CCSL.

We follow here the same path as Professor He. We start with the denotational semantics, then the operational one, and we end with a glimpse at the co-algebraic semantics.

2.1 Clocks, Schedules and History

Definition 1 (Logical clock). *A logical clock c is an infinite sequence (a stream) of ticks, $(c_n)_{n \in \mathbb{N}^+}$.*

While a logical clock can represent any kind of repetitive event, the ticks stand for their successive occurrences. All the events are assumed to be independent, so there is no relationship between the ticks of two clocks unless explicitly defined. Concretely, clocks can be used to observe the occurrence of events. In such cases, CCSL describes the expected observations. They can also be used as activation conditions to control the behaviour of a system.

CCSL constraints express some relationships between clocks, and their underlying ticks. One possible behaviour is captured as a synchronous schedule defined as an infinite sequence of steps. At each step, the schedule defines which clocks tick and which ones do not tick. A CCSL specification characterizes a set of valid schedules. Each constraint potentially reduces the number of valid schedules by forbidding some clocks to tick at some steps.

Definition 2 (Schedule). *Given a set C of clocks, a schedule of C is a total function $\delta : \mathbb{N} \to 2^C$ such that at each step n in $\mathbb{N}$, $\delta(n) \neq \emptyset$.*[1]

By the condition $\delta(n) \neq \emptyset$ in Definition 2 we exclude from schedules those *trivial*/stuttering steps where there is no clock ticking. As we deal with reactive systems, we expect the system not to stop, and therefore to have clocks that tick in infinitely many steps. As we show later, clocks that stop very often indicate a bad (or at least unexpected) behaviour of the system under consideration. Having this in mind, we thrive to build *good* schedules that have this property.

For a given schedule it may be useful to identify the step at which the ith tick occurred.

Definition 3 (Dates and time). *Given a schedule δ for a set of clocks C, $dates^\delta : C \to 2^{\mathbb{N}}$ is a map defined as $\forall c \in C, dates^\delta(c) = \{i \in \mathbb{N} | c \in \delta(i)\}$.*

Then, $time^\delta$ is a map $time^\delta : C \times \mathbb{N}^+ \to \mathbb{N}$ defined as $\forall c \in C, \forall i \in \mathbb{N}^+, time^\delta(c, i) = j$ such that $|\{k \in dates^\delta(c) | k \leq j\}| = i$.

$dates^\delta$ gives the set of steps where a clock ticks for a given schedule δ, while $time^\delta$ gives the step at which the ith tick of a given clock occurs, for a given schedule δ. If clocks tick infinitely many times, as they should, $dates^\delta$ is an infinite subset of natural numbers.

Purely synchronous constraints define when some clocks should tick together and when they cannot, i.e. synchronization conditions. Other more general constraints look at the past, the *history* (as far as they need) to decide what may happen at a given step.

Definition 4 (History). *The history of a schedule δ over a set C of clocks is a function $\chi^\delta : C \times \mathbb{N} \to \mathbb{N}$ such that for each clock $c \in C$ and $n \in \mathbb{N}$:*

$$\chi^\delta(c, n) = \begin{cases} 0 & \text{if } n = 0 \\ \chi^\delta(c, n-1) & \text{if } n > 0 \wedge c \notin \delta(n-1) \\ \chi^\delta(c, n-1) + 1 & \text{if } n > 0 \wedge c \in \delta(n-1) \end{cases}$$

Intuitively, $\chi^\delta(c, n)$ denotes the number of times that a clock c has ticked before reaching step n in the schedule δ. For simplicity, we write χ for χ^δ when the context is clear. The history computes the configuration for a given clock. This ability to look into the past as far as we need raises reachability problems unusual in traditional synchronous languages, which commonly look only at the preceding step.

The way history is built gives a natural carrier for the co-algebraic definition given in Sect. 2.5.

2.2 Syntax

The initial syntax of CCSL was defined in a research report [3]. It was defined under the form of a mathematical language. As CCSL became integrated into

---

[1] 2^C is the powerset of C.

programming environments, the syntax was modified to resemble more that of a programming language and be more tractable by standard text-based editors. TimeSquare [15] is the official tool to build and analyse CCSL specifications. The syntax in TimeSquare is meant to be integrated into modelling environments that stores artefacts as XML resources. A lighter syntax, called Light-CCSL[2], has then been defined to be more user-friendly. We use both the pure mathematical syntax and the light CCSL one here.

CCSL provides a set of binary or ternary **clock relations** that constrain the instants at which a clock can tick. When there is no constraint, all the schedules are possible. Each constraint reduces the set of possible schedules. For most specifications, an infinite number of schedules are valid. When only one schedule is possible, the system is fully determined. If no schedule is possible, the specification is inconsistent.

The two basic synchronous relations are *subclocking* ($c_1 \subseteq c_2$) and *exclusion* ($c_1 \# c_2$). *subclocking* is a relation that only allows c_1 to tick when c_2 ticks: $\forall s \in \mathbb{N}^+, c_1 \in \delta(s) \implies c_2 \in \delta(s)$. We get immediately that when $c_1 \subseteq c_2 \land c_2 \subseteq c_1$ then $dates(c_1) = dates(c_2)$, c_1 and c_2 are called synchronous ($c_1 \boxed{=} c_2$).[3]

Exclusion forbids c_1 and c_2 to tick at the same step: $\forall s \in \mathbb{N}^+, c_1 \notin \delta(s) \lor c_2 \notin \delta(s)$.

The Light-CCSL listing below defines two subclocking and one exclusion constraints, $c1 \subseteq c2 \land c2 \subseteq c3 \land c4 \# c3$.

```
Specification example1 {
    Clock c1 c2 c3 c4 [
        SubClocking c1  ←  c2  ←  c3
        Exclusion  c4 # c3
    ]
}
```

The two basic asynchronous relations are *causality* ($c_1 \preccurlyeq c_2$) and *precedence* ($c_1 \prec c_2$). *Causality* is the *happen before* relationship of event structures. It means that $\forall d \in \mathbb{N}^+, time(c_1, d) \leq time(c_2, d)$, the dth occurrence of c_1 cannot be after the dth occurrence of c_2. *Precedence* is a bit stricter, it means that $\forall d \in \mathbb{N}^+, time(c_1, d) < time(c_2, d)$.

The Light-CCSL listing below defines precedences and causalities, $c1 \prec c2 \land c2 \preccurlyeq c3 \land c3 \prec c4$.

```
Specification example2 {
    Clock c1 c2 c3 c4 [ Precedence c1 < c2 <= c3 < c4 ]
}
```

While CCSL relations reduce the set of valid schedules, CCSL expressions build new clocks that preserve some relations by construction. Some expressions build concrete subclocks, like *union* and *intersection*.

---

[2] https://github.com/frederic-mallet/ccsl-sts/tree/main/Examples/CCSL_Primitives.

[3] The boxed equality ($\boxed{=}$) is there not to confuse clocks that are equal from clocks that tick synchronously.

$u \triangleq c_1 + c_2$ (union of c_1 and c_2) builds a clock u such that $dates(u) = dates(c_1) \cup dates(c_2)$. We get immediately that $c_1 \subseteq c_1 + c_2$ and $c_2 \subseteq c_1 + c_2$.
$i \triangleq c_1 * c_2$ (intersection of c_1 and c_2) builds a clock i such that $dates(i) = dates(c_1) \cap dates(c_2)$. We get immediately that $c_1 * c_2 \subseteq c_1$ and $c_1 * c_2 \subseteq c_2$.

Another way to build a new clock is to use affine functions. $c_1 \triangleq c_2 \propto p$ makes c_1 tick every p^{th} tick of c_2. $c_3 \triangleq c_1 \$ d$ makes c_3 tick synchronously with c_1 after its dth tick. In Light-CCSL, on would write the following specification:

```
Specification Period {
    Clock c2 [
        repeat c1 every 3 c2
        Let c3 be c1 $ 2
    ]
}
```

From this listing we obtain the schedule shown in Fig. 1 as the only possible valid schedule since this specification is fully determined. In this schedule, $dates(c2) = \{0, 1, 2, 3, 4, 5, 6, 7, 8, 9\}$ as if $c2$ does not tick, none of the other clocks can tick. $dates(c1) = \{0, 3, 6, 9\}$ and $dates(c3) = \{6, 9\}$. Besides, $time(c2, 1) = 0$, $time(c1, 2) = 3$ and $time(c3, 1) = 6$.

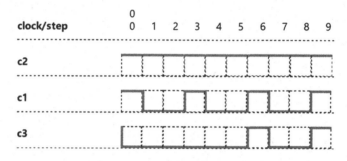

Fig. 1. A schedule with delays and periodic clocks.

Other expressions build new clocks that preserve causalities. $inf \triangleq c_1 \wedge c_2$ (infimum of c_1 and c_2) builds a clock inf such that $\forall d \in \mathbb{N}^+, time(inf, d) = min(time(c_1, d), time(c_2, d))$. We get immediately that $c_1 \preccurlyeq c_1 \wedge c_2$ and $c_2 \preccurlyeq c_1 \wedge c_2$.
$sup \triangleq c_1 \vee c_2$ (supremum of c_1 and c_2) builds a clock sup such that $\forall d \in \mathbb{N}^+, time(sup, d) = max(time(c_1, d), time(c_2, d))$. We get immediately that $c_1 \vee c_2 \preccurlyeq c_1$ and $c_1 \vee c_2 \preccurlyeq c_2$.

```
Specification Expressions {
    Clock a b c [
        Let i be inf(a,b,c)
        Let s be sup(a,b,c)
        Let union be a or b
        Let inter be a and b
```

]

}

2.3 Denotational Semantics

CCSL may serve different purposes. One main objective is to verify that a specification is consistent. This is for instance useful when using CCSL to build requirements. Informal or natural-language requirements are prone to errors. To check the consistency of requirements, we transform them into CCSL constraints and then we try to find at least one valid schedule for the derived specification [12]. TimeSquare [15] allows for making those transformations automatic by giving generic transformation rules from model elements and applying those transformation rules in a systematic way on a complete model (see Sect. 3.2). Checking the satisfaction of CCSL specifications has been done by many different methods [15,57,58] including through the use of an SMT-solver [58].

The semantics of CCSL given in Table 1 is interesting for that task as the encoding into an SMT solver is almost immediate. A schedule is defined as an undefined function[4], or rather as a set of undefined functions, one for each clock. Those undefined functions must satisfy all of the constraints in a specification. The SMT solver will then find a valid definition of those functions that satisfy all the constraints. If it manages to do so, that gives us immediately one valid schedule.

Table 1. Semantics of CCSL

1.	$\delta \vDash_{ccsl} a \subseteq b$	iff	$\forall i \in \mathbb{N}. a \in \delta(i) \rightarrow b \in \delta(i)$	(Subclock)
2.	$\delta \vDash_{ccsl} a \# b$	iff	$\forall i \in \mathbb{N}. a \notin \delta(i) \vee b \notin \delta(i)$	(Exclusion)
3.	$\delta \vDash_{ccsl} a \prec b$	iff	$\forall i \in \mathbb{N}. (\chi^\delta(a,i) > \chi^\delta(b,i) \vee (\chi^\delta(a,i) = \chi^\delta(b,i)) \rightarrow b \notin \delta(i))$	(Precedence)
4.	$\sigma \vDash_{ccsl} a \preccurlyeq b$	iff	$\forall i \in \mathbb{N}. \chi^\delta(a,i) \geq \chi^\delta(b,i)$	(Causality)
5.	$\delta \vDash_{ccsl} c \triangleq a + b$	iff	$\forall i \in \mathbb{N}. c \in \delta(i) \leftrightarrow (a \in \delta(i) \vee b \in \delta(i))$	(Union)
6.	$\delta \vDash_{ccsl} c \triangleq a * b$	iff	$\forall i \in \mathbb{N}. c \in \delta(i) \leftrightarrow (a \in \delta(i) \wedge b \in \delta(i))$	(Intersection)
7.	$\delta \vDash_{ccsl} c \triangleq c' \propto n$	iff	$\forall i \in \mathbb{N}. c \in \delta(i) \leftrightarrow (c' \in \delta(i) \wedge \exists m \in \mathbb{N}^+. \chi^\delta(c',i) = m \cdot (n+1))$	(Periodicity)
8.	$\delta \vDash_{ccsl} c \triangleq c' \$ n$	iff	$\forall i \in \mathbb{N}. \chi^\delta(c,i) = max(\chi^\delta(c',i) - n, 0)$	(Delay)
9.	$\delta \vDash_{ccsl} c \triangleq a \wedge b$	iff	$\forall i \in \mathbb{N}. \chi^\delta(c,i) = max(\chi^\delta(a,i), \chi^\delta(b,i))$	(Infimum)
10.	$\delta \vDash_{ccsl} c \triangleq a \vee b$	iff	$\forall i \in \mathbb{N}. \chi^\delta(c,i) = min(\chi^\delta(a,i), \chi^\delta(b,i))$	(Supremum)

Pure synchronous constraints (Table 1, rules 1, 2, 5, 6) do not involve the history. They are called stateless constraints and result in solving a pure Boolean satisfaction problem. Other constraints rely on the history (see Definition 4) that relies on integer arithmetic. Table 1-7 is the most difficult of them all at it uses an existential quantifier. Actually, we can remove this quantifier by unfolding the formula based on the length of p. This is easy, or at least systematic. However, when p is big, this results in a highly inefficient system. Overall, when you

---

[4] In SMT, we would rely on the theory called UF_LIA, Undefined functions, an extension with free sorts and function symbols, combined with Linear Integer Arithmetic. The signature of those functions matches the one given in Definition 2.

combine Boolean logics, with integer arithmetic and undefined functions, there is no guarantee of having a result as the theories that are used are undecidable. However, in most practical cases we have encountered so far, SMT solvers do reach a verdict. Nevertheless, there have been many attempts over the last decade to improve the performances of CCSL solvers but there is no definitive answer to this problem at the moment.

On a pure denotational way, we can consider that a *Clock* is a pair $\langle \mathcal{I}, \prec \rangle$ where $\mathcal{I}$ is a set of instants, $\prec$ is a quasi-order relation on $\mathcal{I}$, named *strict precedence*, it is a total, irreflexive, and transitive binary relation on $\mathcal{I}$.

A *discrete-time clock* is a clock with a discrete set of instants $\mathcal{I}$. Since $\mathcal{I}$ is discrete, it can be indexed by natural numbers in a fashion that respects the ordering on $\mathcal{I}$: $\mathrm{idx} : \mathcal{I} \to \mathbb{N}^+$, $\forall i \in \mathcal{I}$, $\mathrm{idx}(i) = k$ if and only if i is the kth instant in $\mathcal{I}$.

For any discrete time clock $c = \langle \mathcal{I}_c, \prec_c \rangle$, $c[k]$ denotes the kth instant in $\mathcal{I}_c$ (*i.e.*, $k = \mathrm{idx}_c(c[k])$). For any instant $i \in \mathcal{I}_c$ of a discrete time clock, $°i$ is the unique immediate predecessor of i in $\mathcal{I}_c$. For simplicity, we assume the existence of a virtual instant, which is the (virtual) immediate predecessor of the first instant.

A *Time Structure* is a pair $\langle C, \preccurlyeq \rangle$ where C is a set of clocks, $\preccurlyeq$ is a binary relation on $\bigcup_{c \in C} \mathcal{I}_c$, named *causality*. $\preccurlyeq$ is reflexive and transitive. From $\preccurlyeq$ we derive two new relations: *Coincidence* ($\equiv \stackrel{\Delta}{=} \preccurlyeq \cap \succcurlyeq$), *Precedence* ($\prec \stackrel{\Delta}{=} \preccurlyeq \setminus \equiv$).

Then, given two clocks a and b, we can define the basic clock relations as follows.

Definition 5 (Subclocking). *a is said to be a sub-clock of b, and b a super-clock of a, denoted as $a \subseteq b$.*

$$\langle C, \preccurlyeq \rangle \models a \subseteq b \Leftrightarrow \forall i_a \in \mathcal{I}_a, \ \exists i_b \in \mathcal{I}_b, \ i_a \preccurlyeq i_b$$

Figure 2 gives an example of valid schedule for $a \subseteq b$, but there are infinitely many valid schedules.

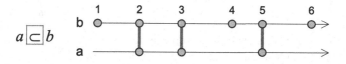

$a \boxed{\subseteq} b$

Fig. 2. Example of subclocking.

Note that this definition does not require the clocks to be discrete. Other CCSL relational operators are similar, see [3] for a comprehensive definition.

In a recent work [41], the semantics of CCSL has been mechanized in Agda. This dramatically improves the confidence we may have in reasoning with CCSL specifications. However, even though Agda gives some assistance to make proofs, it still needs some human interventions. One very interesting feature that was introduced with the help of Agda was the notion of refinement of CCSL ticks [42]. This refinement is akin to the notion of instantaneous causality that is well-known in synchronous languages [7].

2.4 Operational Semantics

In TimeSquare [15] the operational semantics gives a way to compute one possible valid schedule for a given CCSL specification. This works by iterating over two phases. The first phase consists in deciding what subset of clocks (called a configuration) is fireable instantaneously. In CCSL, this can be done by solving a pure SAT problem. The second phase consists in picking one fireable configuration, firing it and rewriting the system to update the history of each clock that has ticked.

If rather than a unique valid schedule, one wants to build a symbolic representation of all the valid schedules, this can be done by synchronous transition system where the (infinitely many) states represent the history of clocks and the transitions are labelled by a set of clocks, the ones that can fired depending on the history. This transition system captures all the fireable clocks, selecting one transition follows only one of the (possibly infinite number of) paths. In practice, we use one transition system for each constraint and we build the synchronous composition of all the transition systems needed for each constraint in a given specification. As we may have an infinite number of states, we sometimes try to fold the transition system to retain only so-called *periodic schedules* [57]. The folding consists in keeping a finite number of states, equivalent, up to a particular equivalence relation, to (infinitely many) other states.

Definition 6 (cLTS). *A* Clock-Labelled Transition System (cLTS) *is defined as a tuple* $\mathcal{A} = \langle S, T, s0, C \rangle$ *where*

- S *is a set of* states,
- $s0 \in S$ *is the* initial state,
- C *is a finite set of* clocks,
- $T \subseteq S \times 2^C \times S$ *is a set of* transitions, *with* $(s, Y, s') \in T$ *means that all the clocks in* $Y \subseteq C$ *tick when the transition from* s *to* s' *is fired.*

Pure synchronous constraints are represented by cLTS with only one state as the set of fireable clocks does not depend on the history. Figure 3(a) shows the cLTS for encoding $a \boxed{=} b$. Either a and b tick together, or neither of them can tick. Subclocking (see Fig. 3(b)) is weaker as b can also tick alone, but not a.

Other (stateful) constraints are represented with infinite-state transition systems. For instance, Fig. 4 gives the cLTS for the precedence $(a \prec b)$. The state records the difference in the number of ticks between a and b (see Table 1, rule 3.) In the state, as both a and b have ticked as many times, we have $\chi^\delta(a, i) = \chi^\delta(b, i)$, and therefore b cannot tick. In other states, a and b can tick alone, can tick jointly or neither of them can tick. The state is updated accordingly.

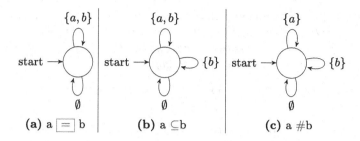

Fig. 3. CCSL synchronous relations as clock-Labelled Transition Systems

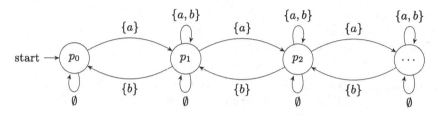

Fig. 4. CCSL precedence (infinite-state cLTS): $a \prec b$.

As there are an infinite number of states for some relations (like precedence), the set of potential execution is only intentional. *Safe* CCSL specifications [38] are the ones where only a finite number of states are actually reachable. We have established a sufficient condition for deciding whether or not a given CCSL specification is safe.

In a pure operational way, once the synchronous product of all the transition systems of all the CCSL constraints inside a specification has been computed (in intention or in extension), one can pick one path in this transition system to have a valid schedule. To get all the valid schedules, one must compute all the paths up to a given depth, depending on the length of the expected solution.

2.5 Coalgebraic Semantics

The theory of universal coalgebra [46] proposes a mathematical model, that differs from the approach of G. Plotkin for defining the operational semantics of software systems [45]. Indeed, considering transition systems as coalgebras gives useful insights for reactive systems and infinite data structures in general. Coalgebras appeared to be well fitted to capture the infinite-state transition systems underlying the semantics of some CCSL operators. We have used this style to define a notion of incompleteness for CCSL and then a possible generalized constraint model [39, 60].

Definition 7 (Transition system). *A transition system is a structure* $\langle \Gamma, \longrightarrow \rangle$ *where* Γ *is a set (of elements,* γ, *called configurations) and* $\longrightarrow \subset \Gamma \times \Gamma$ *is a binary relation (called the transition relation). Read* $\gamma \longrightarrow \gamma'$ *as saying that there is a transition from configuration* γ *to configuration* γ'.

Using the notion of coalgebra we obtain an alternative way to describe transition systems.

Definition 8 (Coalgebra). *A (powerset) coalgebra* [46] *is a structure* $\langle \Gamma, \alpha \rangle$ *where* α *is a map from* Γ *into the set of all subsets of* Γ, 2^{Γ}. *In this context* Γ *is called the carrier of the coalgebra.*

It is evident that any transition system $\langle \Gamma, \longrightarrow \rangle$ determines the coalgebra $\langle \Gamma, \alpha \rangle$, where $\gamma' \in \alpha(\gamma)$ if and only if $\gamma \longrightarrow \gamma'$, and conversely, any coalgebra $\langle \Gamma, \alpha \rangle$ determines the transition system $\langle \Gamma, \longrightarrow \rangle$, where $\gamma \longrightarrow \gamma'$ if and only if $\gamma' \in \alpha(\gamma)$.

Definition 9 (Subcoalgebra). *Let* $\langle \Gamma, \alpha \rangle$ *be a coalgebra,* B *be a subset of* Γ *then the structure* $\langle B, \alpha \rangle$ *is called a subcoalgebra of* $\langle \Gamma, \alpha \rangle$ *if the embedding* $\alpha(\gamma) \subset B$ *is true for each* $\gamma \in B$.

One can check that any coalgebra $\langle \Gamma, \alpha \rangle$ is a subcoalgebra of itself and the intersection of a family of subcoalgebras is a subcoalgebra too. Hence, for each subset $X \subset \Gamma$ there exists a least one subcoalgebra whose carrier contains X. In this case, the carrier of this subcoalgebra is denoted by $\langle X \rangle$.

To calculate $\langle X \rangle$ one can use Tarski's fixed point theorem [51] for the monotonic operator Ψ_X on the lattice $\mathcal{P}_X(\Gamma)$, where $\mathcal{P}_X(\Gamma)$ is the set of all Γ subsets that cover X. This operator is defined by the following formula

$$\Psi_X(V) = V \cup \{\gamma' \in \Gamma \mid (\exists \gamma \in V) \; \gamma' \in \alpha(\gamma)\}.$$

This ensures that an element $\gamma \in \Gamma$ belongs to $\langle X \rangle$ if and only if there exists a finite sequence $\gamma_0, \ldots, \gamma_{n-1}, \gamma_n$ formed by elements of Γ such that

$$\gamma_0 \in X \text{ and } \gamma_n = \gamma; \tag{1}$$
$$\gamma_k \in \alpha(\gamma_{k-1}) \text{ for } k = 1, \ldots, n. \tag{2}$$

Finite or infinite Γ-valued sequences satisfying (2) are used below, we give them the name "tracks".

Hence, conditions (1) and (2) mean that an element $\gamma \in \Gamma$ belongs to $\langle X \rangle$ if and only if there exists a track that links some element of X and γ.

We now assume that some finite set of clocks $\mathcal{C}$ has been given. Let us define the constraint-free coalgebra over a clock set $\mathcal{C}$ as the coalgebra with the carrier $\mathbb{N}^{\mathcal{C}}$ and the map $\alpha : \mathbb{N}^{\mathcal{C}} \to 2^{\mathbb{N}^{\mathcal{C}}}$ defined by the formula:

$$\chi' \in \alpha(\chi) \quad \text{if and only if} \quad 0 \le \chi'_a - \chi_a \le 1 \quad \text{for all} \quad a \in \mathcal{C}.$$

It is evident that for any $\chi \in \mathbb{N}^{\mathcal{C}}$ the map α is represented in the form

$$\alpha(\chi) = \chi + \{0, 1\}^{\mathcal{C}}.$$

This statement makes it obvious that a clock can only tick once at each instant and that all the evolutions are possible when no constraint is specified.

Proposition 1. *Let* $\langle \chi(t) \mid t \in \mathbb{N} \rangle$ *be a sequence of configurations then there exists a schedule* σ *such that* $\chi_a(t) = \chi_a^\sigma(t)$ *for all* $t \in \mathbb{N}$ *and* $a \in \mathcal{C}$ *if and only if this sequence is a track in the coalgebra* $\langle \mathbb{N}^{\mathcal{C}}, \alpha \rangle$ *such that* $\chi(0) = \mathbf{0}$.

A track $\langle \chi(t) \mid t \in \mathbb{N} \rangle$ is called *initial* if the condition $\chi(0) = \mathbf{0}$ holds.

One way to capture the notion of schedule, which are a sequence of steps where clocks tick simultaneously is to specify a map $\triangle : \mathbb{N}^{\mathcal{C}} \to 2^{\{0,1\}^{\mathcal{C}}}$ such that $\mathbf{0} \in \triangle(\chi)$ for any $\chi \in \mathbb{N}^{\mathcal{C}}$ and to define

$$\alpha_\triangle(\chi) = \chi + \triangle(\chi).$$

The map denotes at each step the set of clocks that tick.

A map $\triangle : \mathbb{N}^{\mathcal{C}} \to 2^{\{0,1\}^{\mathcal{C}}}$ that satisfies the condition $\mathbf{0} \in \triangle(\chi)$ for any $\chi \in \mathbb{N}^{\mathcal{C}}$ is called an *actuation distribution* on $\mathcal{C}$. The actuation distribution captures the set of sets of clocks that are allowed to tick simultaneously at one instant given a configuration.

Definition 10 (Actuation distribution). *Let* $\triangle : \mathbb{N}^{\mathcal{C}} \to 2^{\{0,1\}^{\mathcal{C}}}$ *be an actuation distribution and* $\langle \mathbb{N}^{\mathcal{C}}, \alpha_\triangle \rangle$ *be a coalgebra, where* $\alpha_\triangle(\chi) = \chi + \triangle(\chi)$, *then an element of* $\mathbb{N}^{\mathcal{C}}$ *is called* $\triangle$-*reachable configuration if it belongs to the carrier of the minimal subcoalgebra containing* $\mathbf{0}$.

Such a set of reachable configurations is denoted below by $R(\triangle)$.

Definition 11 (Clock coalgebra). *Let* $\triangle : \mathbb{N}^{\mathcal{C}} \to 2^{\{0,1\}^{\mathcal{C}}}$ *be an actuation distribution then the coalgebra* $\langle R(\triangle), \alpha_\triangle \rangle$ *is called the* clock *coalgebra associated with* $\triangle$.

Actuation distributions of some clock constraints do not depend on the current configuration, so we define stationary distribution to denote particular interesting kinds of constraints.

Definition 12 (Stationary distribution). *An actuation distribution* $\triangle :$ $\mathbb{N}^{\mathcal{C}} \to 2^{\{0,1\}^{\mathcal{C}}}$ *is called* stationary *if the map* $\triangle$ *is a constant map.*

Some primitive clock constraints, such as subclocking, exclusion, union and intersection, represent stationary actuation distributions. Therefore the question whether any stationary actuation distribution is represented by a set of stationary primitive clock constraints is interesting.

We have proven that this is true for 2-clock systems, but that this is not true in general [39]. Therefore, CCSL is incomplete as it should allow to build any actuation distribution. A very interesting construct that cannot be built is the n-m exclusion pattern, where n tasks share m resources. The 2–1 exclusion pattern is native ($c_1 \# c_2$), and the n-1 can be built by parallel composition of multiple 2–1 exclusions. The n-m would be useful to represent a concurrent access to m cores by n computing tasks.

For this observation, one can build a generalization of CCSL that is complete. This languages is called *GenCCSL* [60]. While the language is complete, there is no operational way at the moment to build a solution for GenCCSL.

3   CCSL - A Companion Language

CCSL was never meant to be a programming language but rather it was meant to be a specification language. So it is not meant to be used standalone but rather to allow for complementing other specification with expected (temporal and timed) properties of a system. Additionally, CCSL is a companion language so it is expected that the main (functional) part of the system under consideration is given by another language or notation (e.g., UML for instance, or a programming language).

3.1   A Companion to UML MARTE

As it was defined in an annex of UML MARTE, users are inclined to use UML first, as much as possible, to describe, for instance, components or behavioural models. Then, they should use MARTE stereotypes when the semantics of UML is ambiguous.[5] Finally, use CCSL as a last resort when necessary. The two main useful MARTE stereotypes for that purpose are « clock » and « NFPConstraint ». « clock » identifies a model artefact that must be interpreted as a clock. « NFP-Constraint » marks a constraint to be considered as a CCSL specification and potentially interpreted by adequate tools.

To give a simple example of what a companion language is, let us consider the BIP (Behaviour, Interaction, Priority) framework [5]. BIP is a framework for modelling heterogeneous real-time components with a correct-by-construction methodology. In BIP components, there are three layers. The lower layer describes the *behaviour* as transition systems. BIP uses a particular form of timed automaton. The intermediate layer includes a set of connectors describing the interactions between the transitions of the behaviour. The upper layer is a set of priority rules describing scheduling policies for interactions.

Figure 5 shows a small BIP example. Components have ports. Triangles denote so-called incomplete interactions while bullets identify complete ones. The upper connector with *tick1*, *tick2* and *tick3* implements a *rendez-vous*, i.e., the three ports are synchronized. The lower connector is a *broadcast*. CCSL provides no mechanism to build components or transition systems. It relies on other languages for that. One could use UML components and UML state machines for that purpose. However, UML state machines provide no built-in mechanism for describing rendez-vous. Using « clock » one would transform a UML event into a clock. Then using CCSL, one could enforce the semantics of BIP interactions (see the right-hand part of Fig. 5).

There are a bunch of papers [9,20,28,44,50,56] that show examples on how to use UML, MARTE and CCSL together, among those some prefer to use SysML instead of UML. There is a large contribution from the Software Engineering Institute in Shanghai. More importantly, each of these works provides a specific

---

[5] In UML wording, stereotypes are annotations of model elements that change the semantics of this element.

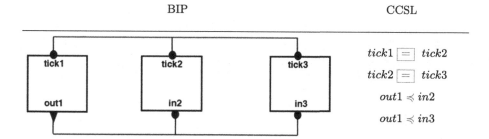

Fig. 5. Describing BIP interactions with CCSL

analysis tool to verify the temporal properties captured as a CCSL specification. These are either ad-hoc verification tools or transformations toward other mainstream verification languages (NuSMV, Timed Automata, VerilogHDL).

Figure 6 borrows an example of a temperature control system from [50] as an illustration. The temperature control system has two modes (*Diagnostic, Control*) depicted as a UML state machine. Moving from *Diagnostic* to *Control* is based on a time constraint. As UML does not have time units, we use MARTE to introduce them. In each mode, different constraints must hold to ensure the safety of the nuclear power plant. In *Diagnostic*, each diagnostic action (clock d) alternates with a reconfiguration action (clock c): $d \sim c$. A status update (clock s) is a particular kind of possible reconfiguration: $s \subseteq c$. Those constraints are captured in CCSL. To verify that the global model is consistent, a structural transformation based on the operational semantics (see Sect. 2.4) is performed to produce a timed automata (see right-hand side part of Fig. 6) that is fed into UPPAAL model-checker [31].

3.2 Semantic Adaptation of Domain-Specific Languages

While UML was the first language used as a support for CCSL specifications, it is not the only one. While UML has attempted a global union of lots of model elements, other approaches follow the *small is beautiful* mantra and advocate for the definition of small *Domain-Specification Languages* [19] just expressive enough for a given objective. Lots of dedicated modelling framework have emerged over the last two decades, the GeMoC studio [10] is one of them that was inspired by the international GeMoC initiative. Each language, or part of a language, is defined with its own abstract syntax and operational semantics. Then, to address large systems, several languages are composed to cover the different concerns (structure, states, data-flows, scenarios, properties). The languages are composed using a meta-language that derives from CCSL [29]. The approach is presented as a *unifying framework that reduces all structural composition operators to structural merging, and all composition operators acting on discrete behaviours to event scheduling.* This approach goes beyond what was discussed on UML as the *connectors* are defined between the two languages themselves and not on particular instances of those languages. Figure 7 shows an example

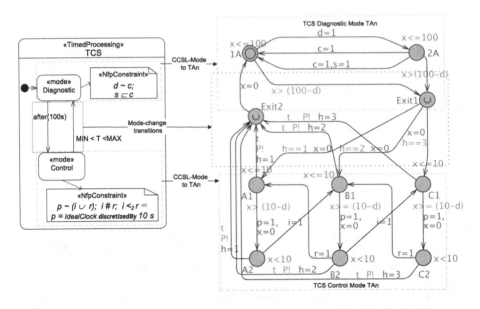

Fig. 6. A Temperature control system (TCS) with UML/MARTE/CCSL.

from that paper. We start with two languages (A and B). Language A involves some events a, b, c, while language B involves events 1, 2, 3, 4. The operational semantics of those two languages give execution rules. At the language level, we can build a constraint, say $a \preccurlyeq 1 \wedge b \preccurlyeq 4 \wedge 3 \preccurlyeq c$. Now, given two instances, one of A and one of B, we derive a set of possible traces for both models, a partial order, captured as event structures. Applying the composition rules (in black), we can reconstruct a global partial order that combines the traces from both languages (event structure es_c on the figure). Recently, this approach was applied to build a full-fledged simulator for Lingua Franca [14].

A similar exercise with a different tool/technology was done by another team [9] but still using CCSL to build a language for semantic adaptation.

4   CCSL Extensions and Derivatives

CCSL has led to several extensions or derivative languages that are briefly discussed in this section.

4.1   Valued Extensions

As CCSL was inspired by the Tagged Signal Model while removing the values of the tags and keeping only their orders, it was only natural to want to add the valued tags back into a language. In the Tagged-Event Specification Language (TESL) [54,55], clocks assign a time-stamp (aka a tag) to ticks with its own time scale. Tags represent the occurrence of the event at a specific

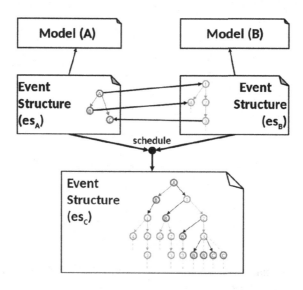

Fig. 7. DSL composition with clock relations.

time. Tag domains used for time must be totally ordered; typically, they are reals, rational numbers, integers, as well as the singleton Unit, which is used for purely logical clocks where (chronometric) time does not progress. TESL captures *event-triggered implications*, that are essentially CCSL-like clock constraints, time-triggered implications and *tag relations*. The time-triggered implication uses a chronometric delay (a reference to a physical time expression) to trigger an event. This delay is a duration (a difference between two tags) while in CCSL it would refer to a number of ticks or a difference between the number of ticks of two clocks. Tag relations link the different time scales. TESL allows for fairly general tag relations permitting acceleration and slow-down. Using affine tag relations makes the solving simpler as it amounts to handling linear equation systems. However, as the tags must be computed, TESL does not use any of the purely asynchronous constraints of CCSL (all the causality-based relations) as they do not allow for a constructive projection into the future and might lead to an infinity of possible futures.

Instead of schedules, TESL introduces so-called *runs*.

Definition 13 (Runs). *Given a set C of clocks, $\mathbb{B}$ the set of Booleans, $\mathbb{T}$ the ordered domain of timestamps. The set of runs is denoted Σ^{α} and defined by*

$$\Sigma^{\alpha} = \mathbb{N} \to C \to (\mathbb{B} \times \mathbb{T})$$

A (synchronous) run associates a pair to a step (a natural number) and a clock. The pair has a Boolean tag to identify whether the clock ticks or not and a timestamp that gives the current reading of the clock at this step. Compare to Definition 2.

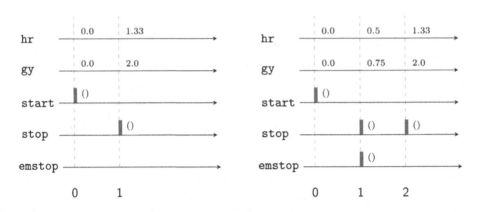

Fig. 8. Example of runs in TESL (Color figure online)

Figure 8 shows examples of runs taken from [55]. The black horizontal lines are temporal lines for clocks. The red rectangles denote ticks of clocks. The green annotations are timestamps, tags.

4.2 Other Extensions

There have been a variety of extensions, lots of them were proposed by teams at the Software Engineering Institute, following some work of Professor He.

In 2012, there was a first work [35] based on MARTE and CCSL to *"unify the logical time and the chronometric time variables, and extend the traditional events to CPS events"*. This work relied on Hybrid automata to introduce continuous evolutions of time and spatial constraints, as both constructs become necessary to model complex Cyber-Physical Systems (CPS).

This work was followed in two directions. On one side [48,59], trying to provide a spatio-temporal logics where both clocks and space are first-class citizens. On another side providing probabilistic extensions of CCSL.

For this second family of extensions, three alternative ways were studied. The first one used UML and profiling mechanisms as a support for extensions. This led to an hybrid form of MARTE state machines [36]. In that form, the systems was captured by combining UML, as much as possible, MARTE or stochastic stereotypes when needed and CCSL in the last resort. Verification was conducted by transforming the whole model into hybrid automata.

The two alternative solutions both considered extending CCSL with probabilistic parameters. This is necessary to capture the intrinsic uncertainty of complex environments for cyber-physical systems as for instance the temperature variation in a smart building, the likelihood of failure in an intelligent transport system.

Two such kinds of solutions were explored. The first solution called pCCSL [16], adds the notion of rate for the subclocking relation. When $a \subseteq b$, a may never tick, or always tick simultaneously with b. Both solutions, and all the intermediate solutions are valid. The rate guarantees a probabilistic ratio between the number of ticks of a and the number of ticks of b. The second solution, called PrCCSL [27], adds instead a probability that a given clock relation is not satisfied. We present here pCCSL.

cLTS from Definition 6 are extended with a probability parameter as follows:

Definition 14 (Probabilistic CLTS). *A Probabilistic Clock-Labelled Transition System (PCLTS) is a CLTS with an extended transition relation* $\longrightarrow \subseteq S \times 2^C \times P \times S$, *where* $P \subseteq \mathbb{Q}$ *is the set of rational numbers between 0 and 1 (i.e., a probability).*

For a given transition $t = (s, \Gamma, p, s') \in \longrightarrow$, $\pi(t) = p$ denotes the probability p that the transition t is fired. It is akin of a discrete-time Markov chain, where the probability to reach the next state depends on the current state.

For a PCLTS $\langle S, C, \longrightarrow \rangle$, we call $s^\bullet$ the set of all transitions whose source is s:

$$s^\bullet = \{(s, \Gamma, p, s') \in \longrightarrow\}$$

Note that $s^\bullet$ can never be empty since it is always possible to do nothing in CCSL, i.e., $(s, \emptyset, p, s)$ is always in $\longrightarrow$ for all $s \in S$ and for some value p.

Given a clock $c \in C$, let us call $s_c^\bullet$ the set of all transitions whose source is s and such that the clock c ticks:

$$s_c^\bullet = \{(s, \Gamma, p, s') \in \longrightarrow \mid c \in \Gamma\}$$

For a PCLTS to be well-formed, it must satisfy the two following conditions:

$$\forall s \in S, \sum_{t \in s^\bullet} \pi(t) = 1 \tag{3}$$

$$\forall s \in S, \forall c \in C, \sum_{t \in s_c^\bullet} \pi(t) = p_c \tag{4}$$

In Eq. 4, for each clock $c \in C$, the probability p_c is either manually assigned by the user with a declaration 'Clock c probability p', or derived using the rate in a subclocking relation or assigned to the default value $1/|s^\bullet|$ otherwise.

A 'normal' CLTS can be seen as a probabilistic CLTS where all the probabilities are assigned with default values $1/|s^\bullet|$ for all the states $s \in S$.

Let $a, b \in C$ be two clocks and $r \in \mathbb{Q}$ a rational number such that $0 \le r \le 1$. The *subclocking* relation (see Fig. 9(a)), $b \subseteq a$ rate r is defined as a PCLTS $\langle \{s_0\}, \{a, b\}, \longrightarrow_\subseteq \rangle$, such that $\longrightarrow_\subseteq = \{(s_0, \{\}, 1 - p_a, s_0), (s_0, \{a, b\}, p_a * r, s_0), (s_0, \{a\}, p_a * (1 - r), s_0)\}$, where $p_a \in \mathbb{Q}$ is the probability assigned to clock a. Let us note that Eq. 3 is satisfied since $\sum_{t \in s_0^\bullet} \pi(t) = (1 - p_a) + (p_a * r) + (p_a * (1 - r)) = 1$. Equation 4 is also satisfied since $\sum_{t \in s_{0b}^\bullet} \pi(t) = p_a * r = p_b$ and $\sum_{t \in s_{0a}^\bullet} \pi(t) = (p_a * r) + (p_a * (1 - r)) = p_a$.

If no probability is assigned then the default is $2/3$. If no rate is assigned, then r defaults to $1/2$. With default values, each one of the three transitions has a probability of $1/3$, i.e., each transition has the same probability to be fired.

Transition $\{b\}$ however has a probability of 0 since it would otherwise contradict the subclocking relation.

Note that if both the probability of a is given and the rate of b relative to a are given, then $p_b = p_a * r$. In any other cases, the specification is ill-formed.

The synchrony constraint is a special case of subclock defined as follows $a = b \equiv b \subseteq a$ rate 1, which implies $p_a = p_b$.

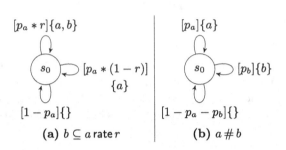

$$[p_a * r]\{a, b\} \qquad\qquad [p_a]\{a\}$$

(a) $b \subseteq a$ rate r (b) $a \# b$

Fig. 9. PCLTS for subclocking and exclusion

Compare Fig. 9(a) to Fig. 3(a).

4.3 (Machine) Learning CCSL

A very recent work observes that using CCSL may be difficult for capturing requirements. This is especially true early in the design process when requirements are unclear. Indeed, using a formal language forces semantic choices. Early requirements must be flexible. While logical clocks allow some form of flexibility deciding which CCSL operator must be used may be a tough choice. What is usually easier for the designer is to give examples of expected or unexpected scenarios. The recent work [26] was trying to deduce a full CCSL specification from a set of scenarios/traces and from a partial specification.

The goal, and difficulty, is to find a specification that is as precise as possible while still satisfying all the constraints. To explore alternative specifications, we use reinforcement learning. We have a reward function that rewards *tight* specifications. Making one constraint too tight may result in a suboptimal solution as relaxing this constraint might allow to make another tighter. Figure 10 gives an overview of the proposed framework. Each layer explores alternative solutions for each hole. In the example, we have four holes, hence four layers.

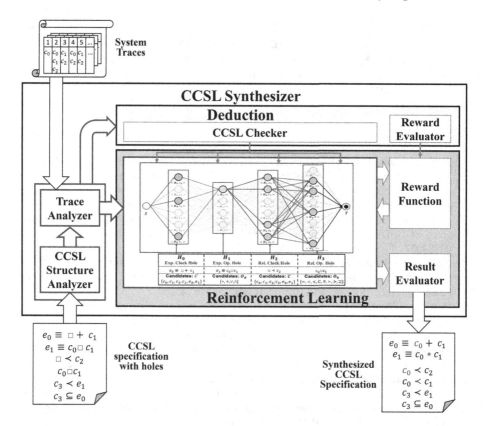

Fig. 10. Architecture and Workflow of a CCSL synthesizer accelerated by curiosity-driven exploration

5 Conclusion

The paper attempts to retrace part of the history of CCSL. A part of its evolution took place at the Software Engineering Institute in Shanghai. We also tried to retrieve the papers from Professor He Jifeng that impacted the most paths that were taken or ignored. Section 2 explores three semantics of CCSL. This is usually considered a good practice and this is recommended by the Unifying Theory of Programming. Hopefully, this section gives a good sense of why this could be useful to study languages under different perspectives. However, we did not go (yet) as far as showing the equivalence of the three semantics. This leaves some exciting perspectives for the future.

Acknowledgements. I would like to sincerely thank the reviewers for their very helpful and constructive comments. I would like to thank the Aoste team, in particular Charles André and Robert de Simone who were at the initiative of CCSL, and also Julien DeAntoni who joined soon after.

In SEI, under the leadership of He Jifeng, there also were academics from the beginning: 何积丰, 刘静, 陈仪香, 朱惠彪.. Then, a second generation: 张民 陈铭松, 陈小红, 杜德慧 and their students 尹玲, 张元瑞, 稿费, 胡铭.

This work was also made possible by Inria associated team Plot4IoT and by UCA DS4H (ANR-17-IDEX-0004).

References

1. Alur, R., Dill, D.L.: A theory of timed automata. Theor. Comput. Sci. **126**(2), 183–235 (1994). https://doi.org/10.1016/0304-3975(94)90010-8
2. André, C.: SyncCharts: a visual representation of reactive behaviors. Research report RR 95–52, rev. RR (96–56), I3S, Sophia-Antipolis, France (1996)
3. André, C.: Syntax and semantics of the clock constraint specification language (CCSL). Research report RR-6925, INRIA (2009). https://hal.inria.fr/inria-00384077
4. André, C., Peraldi-Frati, M.: Behavioral specification of a circuit using SyncCharts: a case study. In: EUROMICRO Conference, p. 1091. IEEE Computer Society (2000). https://doi.org/10.1109/EURMIC.2000.874620
5. Basu, A., Bozga, M., Sifakis, J.: Modeling heterogeneous real-time components in BIP. In: Software Engineering and Formal Methods (SEFM), pp. 3–12. IEEE Computer Society (2006). https://doi.org/10.1109/SEFM.2006.27
6. Benveniste, A., Caillaud, B., Carloni, L.P., Sangiovanni-Vincentelli, A.L.: Tag machines. In: Wolf, W.H. (ed.) Embedded Software (EMSOFT), pp. 255–263. ACM (2005). https://doi.org/10.1145/1086228.1086276
7. Benveniste, A., Caspi, P., Edwards, S.A., Halbwachs, N., Le Guernic, P., de Simone, R.: The synchronous languages 12 years later. Proc. IEEE **91**(1), 64–83 (2003). https://doi.org/10.1109/JPROC.2002.805826
8. Berry, G., Bouali, A., Fornari, X., Ledinot, E., Nassor, E., de Simone, R.: ESTEREL: a formal method applied to avionic software development. Sci. Comput. Program. **36**(1), 5–25 (2000). https://doi.org/10.1016/S0167-6423(99)00015-5
9. Boulanger, F., Dogui, A., Hardebolle, C., Jacquet, C., Marcadet, D., Prodan, I.: Semantic adaptation using CCSL clock constraints. Electron. Commun. Eur. Assoc. Softw. Sci. Technol. **50** (2011). https://doi.org/10.14279/tuj.eceasst.50.731
10. Bousse, E., Degueule, T., Vojtisek, D., Mayerhofer, T., Deantoni, J., Combemale, B.: Execution framework of the GEMOC studio (tool demo). In: van der Storm, T., Balland, E., Varró, D. (eds.) Software Language Engineering (SLE), pp. 84–89. ACM (2016)
11. Caspi, P., Pilaud, D., Halbwachs, N., Plaice, J.: LUSTRE: a declarative language for programming synchronous systems. In: Annual Symposium on Principles of Programming Languages, pp. 178–188. ACM Press (1987). https://doi.org/10.1145/41625.41641
12. Chen, X., Liu, Q., Mallet, F., Li, Q., Cai, S., Jin, Z.: Formally verifying consistency of sequence diagrams for safety critical systems. Sci. Comput. Program. **216**, 102777 (2022). https://doi.org/10.1016/j.scico.2022.102777
13. Colaço, J., Pagano, B., Pouzet, M.: SCADE 6: a formal language for embedded critical software development. In: Theoretical Aspects of Software Engineering (TASE), pp. 1–11. IEEE Computer Society (2017). https://doi.org/10.1109/TASE.2017.8285623

14. Deantoni, J., Cambeiro, J., Bateni, S., Lin, S., Lohstroh, M.: Debugging and verification tools for lingua franca in GEMOC studio. In: Forum on Specification & Design Languages (FDL), pp. 1–8. IEEE (2021). https://doi.org/10.1109/FDL53530.2021.9568383

15. DeAntoni, J., Mallet, F.: TimeSquare: treat your models with logical time. In: Furia, C.A., Nanz, S. (eds.) TOOLS 2012. LNCS, vol. 7304, pp. 34–41. Springer, Heidelberg (2012). https://doi.org/10.1007/978-3-642-30561-0_4

16. Du, D., Huang, P., Jiang, K., Mallet, F.: pCSSL: a stochastic extension to MARTE/CCSL for modeling uncertainty in cyber physical systems. Sci. Comput. Program. **166**, 71–88 (2018). https://doi.org/10.1016/j.scico.2018.05.005

17. Eker, J., et al.: Taming heterogeneity - the Ptolemy approach. Proc. IEEE **91**(1), 127–144 (2003). https://doi.org/10.1109/JPROC.2002.805829

18. Fecher, H., Schönborn, J., Kyas, M., de Roever, W.-P.: 29 new unclarities in the semantics of UML 2.0 state machines. In: Lau, K.-K., Banach, R. (eds.) ICFEM 2005. LNCS, vol. 3785, pp. 52–65. Springer, Heidelberg (2005). https://doi.org/10.1007/11576280_5

19. Fowler, M.: Domain-Specific Languages. Addison Wesley (2010)

20. Ge, N., Pantel, M.: Time properties verification framework for UML-MARTE safety critical real-time systems. In: Vallecillo, A., Tolvanen, J.-P., Kindler, E., Störrle, H., Kolovos, D. (eds.) ECMFA 2012. LNCS, vol. 7349, pp. 352–367. Springer, Heidelberg (2012). https://doi.org/10.1007/978-3-642-31491-9_27

21. Hardebolle, C., Boulanger, F.: ModHel'X: a component-oriented approach to multi-formalism modeling. In: Giese, H. (ed.) MODELS 2007. LNCS, vol. 5002, pp. 247–258. Springer, Heidelberg (2008). https://doi.org/10.1007/978-3-540-69073-3_26

22. Harel, D.: StateCharts: a visual formalism for complex systems. Sci. Comput. Program. **8**(3), 231–274 (1987). https://doi.org/10.1016/0167-6423(87)90035-9

23. Jifeng, H.: A clock-based framework for construction of hybrid systems. In: Liu, Z., Woodcock, J., Zhu, H. (eds.) ICTAC 2013. LNCS, vol. 8049, pp. 22–41. Springer, Heidelberg (2013). https://doi.org/10.1007/978-3-642-39718-9_2

24. Hoare, C.A.R.: Communicating Sequential Processes. Prentice-Hall (1985)

25. Hoare, C.A.R., He, J.: Unifying Theories of Programming. Prentice-Hall (1998)

26. Hu, M., Ding, J., Zhang, M., Mallet, F., Chen, M.: Enumeration and deduction driven co-synthesis of CCSL specifications using reinforcement learning. In: Real-Time Systems Symposium (RTSS), pp. 227–239. IEEE (2021). https://doi.org/10.1109/RTSS52674.2021.00030

27. Kang, E.-Y., Mu, D., Huang, L.: Probabilistic verification of timing constraints in automotive systems using UPPAAL-SMC. In: Furia, C.A., Winter, K. (eds.) IFM 2018. LNCS, vol. 11023, pp. 236–254. Springer, Cham (2018). https://doi.org/10.1007/978-3-319-98938-9_14

28. Khan, A.M., Rashid, M.: Generation of SystemVerilog observers from SysML and MARTE/CCSL. In: Real-Time Distributed Computing (ISORC), pp. 61–68. IEEE Computer Society (2016). https://doi.org/10.1109/ISORC.2016.18

29. Kienzle, J., Mussbacher, G., Combemale, B., Deantoni, J.: A unifying framework for homogeneous model composition. Softw. Syst. Model. **18**(5), 3005–3023 (2019). https://doi.org/10.1007/s10270-018-00707-8

30. Lamport, L.: Time, clocks, and the ordering of events in a distributed system. Commun. ACM **21**(7), 558–565 (1978). https://doi.org/10.1145/359545.359563

31. Larsen, K.G., Pettersson, P., Yi, W.: UPPAAL in a nutshell. Int. J. Softw. Tools Technol. Transf. **1**(1–2), 134–152 (1997). https://doi.org/10.1007/s100090050010

32. Le Guernic, P., Benveniste, A., Bournai, P., Gautier, T.: Signal - a data flow-oriented language for signal processing. IEEE Trans. Acoust. Speech Sig. Process. **34**(2), 362–374 (1986). https://doi.org/10.1109/TASSP.1986.1164809

33. Le Guernic, P., Talpin, J., Lann, J.L.: POLYCHRONY for system design. J. Circ. Syst. Comput. **12**(3), 261–304 (2003). https://doi.org/10.1142/S0218126603000763

34. Lee, E.A., Sangiovanni-Vincentelli, A.L.: A framework for comparing models of computation. IEEE Trans. Comput. Aided Des. Integr. Circ. Syst. **17**(12), 1217–1229 (1998). https://doi.org/10.1109/43.736561

35. Li, T., et al.: Runtime verification of spatio-temporal specification language. Mob. Netw. Appl. **26**(6), 2392–2406 (2021). https://doi.org/10.1007/s11036-021-01779-5

36. Liu, J., Liu, Z., He, J., Mallet, F., Ding, Z.: Hybrid MARTE statecharts. Front. Comput. Sci. **7**(1), 95–108 (2013). https://doi.org/10.1007/s11704-012-1301-1

37. Lund, M.S., Refsdal, A., Stølen, K.: 4 semantics of UML models for dynamic behavior. In: Giese, H., Karsai, G., Lee, E., Rumpe, B., Schätz, B. (eds.) MBEERTS 2007. LNCS, vol. 6100, pp. 77–103. Springer, Heidelberg (2010). https://doi.org/10.1007/978-3-642-16277-0_4

38. Mallet, F., Millo, J., de Simone, R.: Safe CCSL specifications and marked graphs. In: Formal Methods and Models for Codesign (MEMOCODE), pp. 157–166. IEEE (2013). https://ieeexplore.ieee.org/document/6670955/

39. Mallet, F., Zholtkevych, G.: Coalgebraic semantic model for the clock constraint specification language. In: Artho, C., Ölveczky, P.C. (eds.) FTSCS 2014. CCIS, vol. 476, pp. 174–188. Springer, Cham (2015). https://doi.org/10.1007/978-3-319-17581-2_12

40. Maraninchi, F., Rémond, Y.: Argos: an automaton-based synchronous language. Comput. Lang. **27**(1/3), 61–92 (2001). https://doi.org/10.1016/S0096-0551(01)00016-9

41. Montin, M., Pantel, M.: Mechanizing the denotational semantics of the clock constraint specification language. In: Abdelwahed, E.H., Bellatreche, L., Golfarelli, M., Méry, D., Ordonez, C. (eds.) MEDI 2018. LNCS, vol. 11163, pp. 385–400. Springer, Cham (2018). https://doi.org/10.1007/978-3-030-00856-7_26

42. Montin, M., Pantel, M.: Towards multi-layered temporal models: a proposal to integrate instant refinement in CCSL. In: Peters, K., Willemse, T.A.C. (eds.) FORTE 2021. LNCS, vol. 12719, pp. 120–137. Springer, Cham (2021). https://doi.org/10.1007/978-3-030-78089-0_7

43. Nielsen, M., Plotkin, G.D., Winskel, G.: Petri nets, event structures and domains, part I. Theor. Comput. Sci. **13**, 85–108 (1981). https://doi.org/10.1016/0304-3975(81)90112-2

44. Peters, J., Przigoda, N., Wille, R., Drechsler, R.: Clocks vs. instants relations: verifying CCSL time constraints in UML/MARTE models. In: Formal Methods and Models for System Design (MEMOCODE), pp. 78–84. IEEE (2016). https://doi.org/10.1109/MEMCOD.2016.7797750

45. Plotkin, G.D.: A structural approach to operational semantics. J. Log. Algebraic Program. **60–61**, 17–139 (2004)

46. Rutten, J.J.M.M.: Universal coalgebra: a theory of systems. Theor. Comput. Sci. **249**(1), 3–80 (2000). https://doi.org/10.1016/S0304-3975(00)00056-6

47. Sander, I., Jantsch, A.: System modeling and transformational design refinement in ForSyDe [formal system design]. IEEE Trans. Comput. Aided Des. Integr. Circ. Syst. **23**(1), 17–32 (2004). https://doi.org/10.1109/TCAD.2003.819898

48. Shao, Z., Liu, J., Ding, Z., Chen, M., Jiang, N.: Spatio-temporal properties analysis for cyber-physical systems, pp. 101–110 (2013)
49. de Simone, R., André, C.: Towards a "synchronous reactive" UML profile? Int. J. Softw. Tools Technol. Transf. 8(2), 146–155 (2006). https://doi.org/10.1007/s10009-005-0206-9
50. Suryadevara, J., Seceleanu, C., Mallet, F., Pettersson, P.: Verifying MARTE/CCSL mode behaviors using UPPAAL. In: Hierons, R.M., Merayo, M.G., Bravetti, M. (eds.) SEFM 2013. LNCS, vol. 8137, pp. 1–15. Springer, Heidelberg (2013). https://doi.org/10.1007/978-3-642-40561-7_1
51. Tarski, A.: A lattice-theoretical fixpoint theorem and its applications. Pac. J. Math. 5(2), 285–309 (1955)
52. The Object Management Group: Unified Modeling Language, Version 2.0 (2005). https://www.omg.org/spec/UML/2.0
53. The Object Management Group: A UML Profile for MARTE, v. 1.0 (2009). https://www.omg.org/spec/MARTE/
54. Nguyen Van, H., Balabonski, T., Boulanger, F., Keller, C., Valiron, B., Wolff, B.: A symbolic operational semantics for TESL. In: Abate, A., Geeraerts, G. (eds.) FORMATS 2017. LNCS, vol. 10419, pp. 318–334. Springer, Cham (2017). https://doi.org/10.1007/978-3-319-65765-3_18
55. Van, H.N., Boulanger, F., Wolff, B.: TESL: a model with metric time for modeling and simulation. In: Muñoz-Velasco, E., Ozaki, A., Theobald, M. (eds.) Temporal Representation and Reasoning (TIME). LIPIcs, vol. 178, pp. 15:1–15:15. Schloss Dagstuhl (2020). https://doi.org/10.4230/LIPIcs.TIME.2020.15
56. Yang, J., Chen, X., Yin, L.: Eliciting timing requirements for cyber-physical systems: a multiform time based approach. In: Theoretical Aspects of Software Engineering (TASE), pp. 199–206 (2021). https://doi.org/10.1109/TASE52547.2021.00024
57. Zhang, M., Dai, F., Mallet, F.: Periodic scheduling for MARTE/CCSL: theory and practice. Sci. Comput. Program. 154, 42–60 (2018). https://doi.org/10.1016/j.scico.2017.08.015
58. Zhang, M., Song, F., Mallet, F., Chen, X.: SMT-based bounded schedulability analysis of the clock constraint specification language. In: Hähnle, R., van der Aalst, W. (eds.) FASE 2019. LNCS, vol. 11424, pp. 61–78. Springer, Cham (2019). https://doi.org/10.1007/978-3-030-16722-6_4
59. Zhang, Y., Mallet, F., Chen, Y.: A verification framework for spatio-temporal consistency language with CCSL as a specification language. Front. Comp. Sci. 14(1), 105–129 (2018). https://doi.org/10.1007/s11704-018-7054-8
60. Zholtkevych, G., Labzhaniia, M.: Understanding safety constraints coalgebraically. In: Computational Linguistics and Intelligent Systems (COLINS), vol. 2604, pp. 1–19 (2020). http://ceur-ws.org/Vol-2604/paper1.pdf

Applying Formal Verification to an Open-Source Real-Time Operating System

Andrew Butterfield[1]([⊠]) and Frédéric Tuong[2]

[1] Trinity College Dublin, Dublin, Ireland
butrfeld@tcd.ie
[2] Simon Fraser University, Burnaby, BC, Canada
ftuong@sfu.ca

Abstract. This paper describes work done using formal methods to verify parts of the RTEMS real-time operating system, as part of an activity sponsored by the European Space Agency to qualify multi-core processors for spaceflight. A variety of formalisms were investigated, keeping in mind the need to be a good fit with the RTEMS community in general. The technique that was deployed used Promela to model aspects of the operating system behavior, and the SPIN model-checker to do test generation. This involved developing Promela models, which are formal artifacts, and then developing a simple machine-readable observation language that made it easy to connect model behavior to the generation of C test code. The observation language was then refined to code using a dictionary mapping observable elements to test code snippets. Neither the observable language of the dictionary mapping are formal, so this paper also explores how these might be given UTP semantics, and linked together, in which the research of He Jifeng plays a key role. It finishes defining a future research agenda that uses this work with a real-world application to drive the research.

Keywords: Unifying theories of programming · Model checking · Promela/SPIN · Test Generation · Real-Time Operating Systems · RTEMS

1 Introduction

The first author's first academic interaction with He Jifeng was his 2002 paper with Adnan Sherif on Circus Time [42]. This was a key starting point for early work on Slotted Circus [16]. One earliest memory of meeting He Jifeng in person was at UTP2008 which was hosted in Trinity College Dublin, at which he gave the keynote talk [29] (among others!). This paper explores how Unifying Theories of Programming (UTP [33]) might be used to give an overarching description of work we did using formal methods to verify parts of RTEMS [11]. In particular, we look at how the work of He Jifeng provided, and continues to provide, key material towards fulfilling this aim.

Supported by ESA Contract No. 4000125572/18NL/GLC/as, and assistance from Lero and the RTEMS community.

J. P. Bowen et al. (Eds.): *Theories of Programming and Formal Methods*, LNCS 14080, pp. 348–366, 2023.
https://doi.org/10.1007/978-3-031-40436-8_13

This paper describes work we did to introduce formal methods into an activity sponsored by the European Space Agency (ESA) to qualify a new version of the RTEMS[1] open-source real-time operating system [5], tailored for multicore processors. It also looks at how Unifying Theories of Programming (UTP) [33] could be used to fill the formal semantic gaps that arose as a result of our approach.

The ESA activity, *Qualification of RTEMS Symmetric Multiprocessing (SMP)*, was led by Thales Edisoft, involving also Embedded Brains, the CISTER Research Centre at U. Porto, Jena Optronik, and ourselves. A single-core version of RTEMS had previously been qualified by Edisoft, and this new activity looked at upgrading that to cover multi-core, and to also provide tooling to ease the cost of the testing, reporting, and document generation involved. Edisoft, Embedded Brains and CISTER worked on these aspects, and they had to meet the standards expected, as defined by the relevant standards for software assurance [24]. All the artifacts that they would produce were to be made available, open-source, in the RTEMS git repositories [2], in a manner that adhered to the RTEMS community guidelines [46, §1.3]. Jena Optronik used a proprietary real-world application of theirs to assess the methodology developed by the other partners.

Our role was to explore how best to use formal methods to support qualification, in a way that would also fit with RTEMS community guidelines. After an initial survey and review of suitable formalisms, we elected to use the model-checker Promela/SPIN[35] to do test generation. This focussed on parts of the RTEMS API that dealt with task synchronization facilities, including signalling events, synchronization barrier, message-passing, and semaphores. The emphasis was on the functional correctness of the relevant API calls, when invoked by concurrent tasks. Also, the success criteria for the qualification effort as a whole was not tied to our efforts, in that the other partners had to meet the relevant standards, including those regarding test coverage, independently of what we achieved.

In the Background section (Sect. 2) we give an overview of the RTEMS qualification project, and introduce the Promela language and SPIN model-checker. In the Formal Models section (Sect. 3) we give more details of the formal approach and give an overview of one the models we constructed. In the Refinement section (Sect. 4) we explain how we map the counter-examples generated from SPIN into RTEMS C test code. In all of the above we explore how UTP might be applied to formally connect all the pieces. We then discuss Related Work (Sect. 5) and finish with Conclusions and future work (Sect. 6).

2 Background

2.1 RTEMS

RTEMS[5,11] is a real-time operating system aimed mainly at embedded systems. It is open-source and freely available [2], mainly under a BSD-2 license.

---

[1] Real-Time Executive for Multiprocessor Systems.

It is an operating system of choice for ESA, who have funded a number of past initiatives [3,4] to bring RTEMS up to the quality standards they require These are European-based standards for critical space software [23,24], involving a lot of testing, traceability and documentation, but no formal methods. The *qualification* so obtained covered versions of RTEMS aimed at single-core processors.

However, the widespread availability of multi-core processors, including those that are space-hardened, has led to increased demand for their approval for space missions. In addition, two recent new multi-core adaptations of existing scheduler algorithms were implemented for RTEMS. These were the $O(m)$ Independence-Preserving Protocol (OMIP) [12], and the Multiprocessor Resource Sharing Protocol (MrsP) [13]. Both were merged and added to RTEMS [18] and have been updated and enhanced several times since [28]. The move to multi-core support caused a large increase in the complexity of the code, especially as far as scheduling was concerned. This ranges from the implementation of synchronisation primitives such as semaphores, barriers, events, messaging, and a key component underlying these: *thread queues.*

This led to the establishment in 2018 of an activity called "Qualification of RTEMS Symmetric Multiprocessing (SMP)" to perform a pre-qualification[2] of two- and four-core processors for spaceflight. This activity had a number of key goals beyond just producing a pre-qualified version of multi-core RTEMS. These included:

- Developing tools to automate the generation and reporting of the evidence needed to demonstrate that the qualification standards had been achieved.
- Providing all the tooling, and code improvements in a form that could be fed back into the RTEMS open-source repositories.

The second goal is key. The purpose of this work went beyond just the needs ESA had for qualifying software, but also included the desire by the RTEMS community to gain expertise themselves in the ability to perform safety critical certification and qualification. The idea is that the techniques could be reused by RTEMS users in other safety critical application areas.

This second goal meant that all qualification materials should fit in with RTEMS community guidelines [46, §1.3],[45, §2]. One key consequence of this is to consider the needs of all users, from hobbyist to safety-critical system developers. This means that large complex software entities with many dependencies should be avoided where possible. Another principle is that licensing must have a BSD-2 flavour, rather than something like GPL—this is because it is expected that companies will link RTEMS with proprietary applications.

Formal Methods for ESA for RTEMS. The investigation into the use of formal methods had three phases: an initial exploration of available and suitable formal techniques; apply the chosen techniques to selected parts of

---

[2] ESA uses qualification to refer to an entire mission. RTEMS is a sub-component of a mission, so such partial treatments are called pre-qualifications.

```
stmt ::= skip                    // do nothing
       | v = e                   // assignment
       | e                       // expression-statement
       | assert(e)               // assertion
       | run procName(e,..,e)    // start a process
```

Fig. 1. Simplified syntax for atomic Promela statements.

```
stmt +:= stmt ; stmt      // sequencing
       | stmt -> stmt      // sequencing (alt.)
       | if                // conditional
         :: stmts1
            ...
         :: stmtsN
         fi
       | do                // iteration
         :: stmts1
            ...
         :: stmtsN
         od
       | atomic{stmts}
```

Fig. 2. Simplified syntax for composite Promela statements. Here stmts denotes one or more sequenced stmts.

RTEMS; and producing a final report. The initial investigation explored a range of techniques, including, among others, Isabelle/HOL [39], Frama-C [36], and Promela/SPIN[35]. The outcome was a decision to focus on using Promela/SPIN to perform test generation, as this technology is a good fit with the RTEMS guidelines, and the 2009 survey paper by Hierons et al. [32] makes a very good case for using model-checkers like SPIN in this way.

2.2 Promela/SPIN

Promela/SPIN is easy to install (spinroot.com), requiring little more than a C compiler along with the lex and yacc utilities. This made it a good fit for RTEMS users in terms of its size and installation. Promela is the modelling language, while SPIN is the model-checker. The Promela language, based loosely on C, is imperative in character, with a notion of state defined by variables, and notation that allows concurrent process behavior to be defined. Behavior is defined by statements which can be atomic (Fig. 1), such as assignment, or composite (Fig. 2), like conditionals or iteration. Communication between processes can be via shared global variables, or using CSP-like channel-based message passing. The semantics is based on arbitrary interleaving of the sequence of atomic actions performed by each process. Each process has a "program counter" that identifies the next statement to be executed. The state of a Promela model is defined by the values of all the variables and the program counters of the live processes.

The above description could be of a concurrent programming language, but Promela is for modelling, and so its semantics differs in crucial ways. The first key difference is the notion of "executability". Some language constructs are always ready to run, while others may only run in certain model states. The skip, assignment and assertions are always executable. While assert(e) is always executable, if e evaluates to false, then the model run/analysis aborts, reporting a violation. A "bare" expression can occur where a statement is expected. It is blocked in any state in which it evaluates to zero. If not blocked, it can proceed, and behaves like skip. In effect it waits for itself to become true, which means there is no need in many cases to model waiting with some kind of busy-waiting loop. The run statement is blocked if the current number of processes equals the maximum allowed. If this is not the case, then it is an atomic action that starts an instance of the named process.

For composite statements, executability depends on that of the atomic statements that are first in line to execute. For sequential composition, the whole is executable if the first statement is. The conditional and iteration notation is very similar to that in Dijkstra's Guarded Command Language[22]. The only difference here is that the first (guard) component can be a general statement, and need not be an expression. Both the if and do statement are executable if at least one of their statement sequences is executable. If more than once choice is executable, then a non-deterministic choice is made between them. The if-statement terminates when its chosen branch does, while the do will repeat the whole choice process. There is a special atomic statement break, only valid in loops, that terminates the loop. The atomic keyword makes its enclosed statements execute atomically (no other process can run). The exception is if a sub-statement is not executable, in which case the atomicity breaks to allow other processes run. When that statement once more becomes executable, then it resumes running atomically.

Promela has datatypes similar to those found in C, with some variants where it is possible to specify the number of bits. It also allows one-dimensional arrays, and a record notation very similar to defining C "structs".

The scope for procedural abstraction is quite limited. Process types are defined using the proctype keyword, take named parameters, and can define local variables. However these define complete processes, and can't be used to abstract a part of the process behaviour. The Promela language uses the C preprocessor, and also the inline construct, which has named parameters, but performs syntactic substitution.

The SPIN model-checker takes a Promela file and compiles it into a C model-checking program tailored to the model defined in that file. It then can perform a wide range of exhaustive analyses of that model, looking for deadlock, livelock, starvation, unfairness, and failing assert statements. In addition, it can take temporal properties described using Linear Temporal Logic (LTL) and check those for possible violations. The models used by SPIN are extended Büchi automata [35, Chp. 6,7]. These are finite-state machines to which a criterion for accepting infinite sequences has been added, namely that every cycle in the model involves visiting a designated accepting state. It is interesting to note that He Jifeng has been involved in explorations of the relationship between LTL and Büchi automata [37].

3   Formal Models Of RTEMS

We being with an overview of the formal approach adopted, followed by using one of our models as an example of what is actually involved. We present a high level overview, and then use one model/test scenario to discuss some of the complexity that arises, and finish describing other processes used to model OS behavior.

3.1   Formal Approach

Our overall approach was to start with the RTEMS documentation, most notably that contained in the Classic API Guide[44]. This has sections that cover key concepts, as well as specific sections describing services in terms of *Managers*. These sections typically define an Application Interface (API) by specifying the relevant C prototypes, describing how to call these, what their effects are, and what kinds of error or success indicators get returned.

The Chains API [44, §34] was used initially to figure out the end-to-end methodology, from a Promela model to running passing tests on both simulators and real hardware. The Promela model would describe correct behavior, and also specify desirable properties using assertions and LTL. We would use SPIN to check it in the usual way to ensure correctness of our model (deadlock freedom, assertion checks, etc.) We then used the fairly obvious idea[17] of taking each property, negating it, and re-running the model-checker. It would then report a violation and issue a counterexample. However, this counterexample is an example of a correct run of the system, and hence can be used as a scenario for test generation.

Normally SPIN stops once any error is found and returns the relevant counterexample, but, it can also be asked to continue checking the entire model to find *all* errors. This can be exploited to get a collection of scenarios that give a range of correct behaviours. If we have models that are guaranteed to terminate, then they can be used to generate *all* possible correct behaviours by adding `assert(false)` at the end.

All of the models completed to date are ones that terminate. This is because, in addition to the Chains API, we have focussed on modelling Managers associated with task synchronisation of some form: events, barriers, messages, semaphores. None of these require models that run forever, because the requirements focus on the outcomes of making the various API calls, in terms of side-effects and return codes. What is important is the interaction between such calls performed by concurrent tasks. The key metric being used to gauge test quality is code coverage. This does not require models to be non-terminating.

In addition, we need to ensure that the scenarios we produce from our models do terminate, because a test is not helpful if it fails to terminate (in practice test frameworks put timeouts in place to abort looping tests).

We now describe how we modelled parts of RTEMS using Promela, in a manner that would support test generation, using the Events Manager [44, §15] as a running example. The Chains API got the basics going, but only involved one RTEMS task, while this Manager involves at least two tasks in general, and also has requirements regarding priority and preemption for these tasks.

3.2   The RTEMS Event Manager

The Events Manager [44, §15] allows RTEMS tasks to send and receive event-sets, where an event is a number between 0 and 31 inclusive. The meanings of these numbers are application-specific, so the Events Manager is only concerned with their transmission, and does not care what they might mean. There are two API calls in this Manager (Send,Receive):

- (Send) `rc = rtems_event_send(id,events)` sends the event-set `events` to the task with identifier `id`.
- (Receive) `rc = rtems_event_receive(wanted,options,ticks,rcvptr)` is called by a task looking to receive events in event-set `wanted`, and if successful, will find the obtained events at the location pointed to by `rcvptr`. The parameters `options` and `ticks` are used to specify waiting criteria and a timeout interval.

Both calls return an RTEMS status code, shown above as `rc`.

We modelled all behavior of these API calls, including the situations that resulted in error status codes. These include invalid values for parameters such as task identifiers `id` or the receive pointer `rcvptr`. The Receive operation has various waiting options (none,timeout,forever) so can report being unsatisfied or having timed out. These can all be checked with a test that just calls one or other API appropriately.

The gist of correct behavior is as follows: every RTEMS task has an associated pending event-set variable, initially empty. The effect of sending an event-set is to add those events into the pending set. When, or if, the receiver is satisfied, the satisfying events only are removed from the pending set and are written to the location pointed to by `rcvptr`. The tests need to verify that these pending event-sets are modified correctly. This can be done using the Receive call, specifying an empty set for `wanted` which simply returns the current value of the pending set without modifying it.

In our Promela model, we only needed at most four events, to get all relevant test combinations, that exercise all paths through the code. For a given call of Receive, one model event models all unwanted events, then we have two model events to capture that it may take more than one send to satisfy the receive.

Any combination of 32-bit wanted and sent event sets can be refined down to 4-bit sets that capture the same pattern of behavior.

3.3   High Level Model Overview

It is clear that our Promela model needs to capture the correct behavior of the two API calls, based on a careful reading of the documentation. We determined how these could then be orchestrated to produce useful tests by looking at existing RTEMS test code for the Events Manager. The basic structure of a test was that an initial runner task would be started which would initialise the test state and also start a number of worker tasks, as needed to participate in the test. The runner task would then call parts of the API, while the worker tasks would typically do something complementary. For the Events Manager, the runner played the role of a task doing Receive, while one worker did one or two Sends. When the test was done, the runner task would perform the appropriate teardown procedure.

We use Promela processes to model RTEMS runner and worker tasks. So we chose to model a situation that had two RTEMS tasks, one that would perform between zero and two event sends (**Send**), while the other performed at most one receive operation (**Receiver**). We wanted to support a range of scenarios, from those that checked error-reporting for individual API calls, to those that mixed a receive call with up to two send calls. We defined general scenario types using Promela's only enumeration type:

```
mtype = {Send,Receive,SndRcv,SndRcvSnd,...};
mtype scenario;
```

The idea is to specify that the scenario choice is nondeterministic. We do this using a conditional statement where each guard is an always executable assignment:

```
if
::    scenario = Send;
::    scenario = Receive;
::    scenario = SndRcv;
::    scenario = SndRcvSnd;
::    ....
fi
```

The value of **scenario** would then be used by deterministic conditionals to initialize variables that determined detailed flow of control.

3.4   Modelling Send;Receive;Send

We will now look at a single scenario where the worker performs a Send first, and then the runner does a Receive, where it opts to wait either for a timeout or indefinitely, and finally the worker does a second Send. We assume that the first Send does not satisfy the Receive, but that the second Send adds in what was missing. The description of Send and Receive given earlier focussed on the receiver's wanted and pending event sets, but this is not the full picture. We have two tasks synchronizing over these event sets, when the receiver, when called, is not satisfied. So it blocks, either indefinitely or for a specified timeout interval. These are different blocking circumstances that can lead to different return code outcomes, so we need to model this distinction in our Receive API model.

While the behavior of the Send seems simple, just being an update of the pending set, we do in fact also need to model that this may unblock a waiting receiver. In effect, we need to have a variable state associated with each Promela process that models the corresponding tasks RTEMS scheduler state (executing, ready, blocked, dormant, and non-existent [44, §5.2.5]). In practice we need to model Ready, and three variants of being blocked (EventWait,TimeWait, OtherWait). The first two model Receive waiting indefinitely or for a timeout. The third models a case where the Send can be forced to wait, due the following requirement for rtems_event_send:

"The calling task will be preempted if it has preemption enabled and a higher priority task is unblocked as the result of this directive."[44, §15.4.1, Notes]

Clearly we needed to model priorities as well but we don't discuss this here.

```
inline event_send(self,tid,evts,rc) {
atomic{
    if
    ::  tid >= BAD_ID -> rc = RC_InvId
    ::  tid < BAD_ID ->
        tasks[tid].pending = tasks[tid].pending | evts
        unsigned got : NO_OF_EVENTS;
        bool sat;
        satisfied(tasks[tid],got,sat);
        if
        ::  sat ->
            tasks[tid].state = Ready;
            preemptIfRequired(self,tid) ;
            waitUntilReady(self);
        ::  else -> skip
        fi
        rc = RC_OK;
    fi }}
```

Fig. 3. Promela specification of rtems_event_send

The resulting behavior for Send is modelled by the Promela inline definition in Fig. 3. There are three other inlines called by event_send:

- `satisfied` encodes when a receiver is satisfied.
- `preemptIfRequired` checks if the sender is required to be preempted, and if so sets its state to `OtherWait`.
- `waitUntilReady` blocks internally on the expression statement `state == Ready`, waiting for something else to make it so.

In the Receiver, we use `satisfied`, can set state to `TimeWait` or `EventWait`, and call `waitUntilReady`.

Given that both Send and Receive can block, we need some other mechanism to unblock them. A satisfying Send can unblock a waiting Receiver, but so can a timeout. We also need to model a preempted Send being eventually free to run again, once the higher priority Receive is done. This achieved by adding two Promela processes called `Clock` and `System`. The `Clock` process emits regular clock ticks and decrements timeout data associated with processes in state `TimeWait`, setting their state to `Ready` when the timeout reaches zero. The `System` process models relevant parts of the RTEMS scheduler, mainly the fact that processes in state `OtherWait` eventually become `Ready`. The Send and Receive processes terminate and set their state to `Zombie`, and the system process watches for this and then ends the model run when all processes are done. The last line in the model used for test generation is:

```
assert(false);
```

3.5 Towards a UTP Semantics for Promela

We can summarise the subset of Promela that we use with the following abstract syntax. We assume appropriate types t, expression syntax e, and process names p. We then start with statements:

$$s ::= II \mid e \mid x := e \mid \textbf{assert } e \mid s_1; s_2$$
$$\mid \textbf{ if } s_1, \ldots, s_n \textbf{ fi} \mid \textbf{do } s_1, \ldots, s_n \textbf{ od}$$
$$\mid \textbf{ atm } s \mid \textbf{run } p(e_1, \ldots, e_n)$$

The language here is very reminiscent of *stateful-failure reactive designs* in Foster et al. [25], with some laws like the following:

$$\textbf{if} i \in I \bullet b(i) \rightarrow P(i)\textbf{fi} = \left(\bigsqcap_i b(i) \rightarrow P(i) \right) \sqcap \left((\neg \bigvee_i b(i)) \rightarrow \textbf{chaos} \right)$$

However, guards b above can be general statements s here, with the Promela notion of executability. In particular, an **if** with all branches blocked is simply blocked itself, and does not behave like **chaos**, and their $b \rightarrow P$ becomes $b; P$ in our language.

He Jifeng and his colleagues have been exploring semantics for Verilog for two decades [31, 41, 50] A common feature of this work is using UTP to help link the different semantic forms: algebraic, denotational, and operational. In recent work on MDESL, a Verilog-like language, they address shared variable concurrency using *pre-emption points* [40, Defn. 2.1]. These occur at specific points related to timing and parallel constructs, and are the only places where the scheduler can allow the environment to run. A discrete time model is presented as time-stamped sequences of sequences of snapshots. A chop operator $(P \frown Q)$ defines sequential composition on this model, and then auxiliary design variables (e.g. ok) are added, and MDESL sequential composition is defined using chop. The final result is a healthy process

$$\mathbf{H}(\neg div(P) \vdash wait(P) \lhd wait' \rhd ter(P))$$

which also has the form of Foster et al.'s *reactive contract* [26].

In Promela, every basic action is a pre-emption point, with the exception of inside an `atomic`, which corresponds closely to the notion of *atomic action* in the MDESL semantics. In a sense Promela is very close to maximally interfering shared-variable concurrency, as modelled in our work on UTCP[15]. However this is very low-level, and needs to have abstractions built on top in order to be useable. Perhaps MDESL could be such an abstraction?

Finally, we note that the concept of model-checking and associated temporal logics has been given a UTP formulation by Anderson et al. [8].

4   Refining Promela to C

4.1   Observing SPIN Counterexamples

Once satisfied that the Promela model is correct by using SPIN to verify properties, we then negated those properties in order to obtain test scenarios. The counter-example output produced by SPIN is designed to be read by the model authors, and reports state values using Promela syntax, as well as line-numbers in the model text. However, we wanted to automate the process of converting a counterexample into a test, so we needed to have a more generic way to see what was happening in the model, using a notation that was easy to parse.

Promela has a `printf` statement that supports a simple subset of the one available in C. It has no effect when SPIN performs a verification run, but does produce output when SPIN is run in simulation mode, or when counterexamples are being displayed. We defined a simple observation language that we used to generate an appropriate textual *abstraction* of Promela state.

As an example, consider invoking `event_send` in the model. We want to know that we have called it, what its inputs were, and what its return code was when it returned. So we bracket its invocation with two `printf` statements:

```
printf("@@@ %d CALL event_send %d %d %d sendrc\n",
        _pid,taskid,sendTarget,sendEvents);
event_send(taskid,sendTarget,sendEvents,sendrc);
printf("@@@ %d SCALAR sendrc %d\n",_pid,sendrc);
```

Note here that the parameter `taskid` is the index into a task array, and is
not the corresponding Promela process id. We start every such output with a
marker string `@@@`, which is used to filter these statements out of SPIN's own
reporting material. We then output the Promela process number, denoted by
special Promela variable `_pid`. This is very important as we need to know when
the running process changes if we are to generate test code that reproduces this
scenario.

The next component is a keyword indicating what kind of observation is
being presented. We use `CALL` to denote a function call, and `SCALAR` to denote
a simple value. The function call then displays the arguments for the `inline`
call (including the *name* of the `sendrc` placeholder). The scalar value will be
the value of the return code. There is a wide range of other keywords that cover
declarations, initialisation, atomic and structured values, task management, and
logging.

An example output might be:

```
@@@ 3 CALL event_send 1 2 10 sendrc
@@@ 3 SCALAR sendrc 0
```

Here we see that Promela process 3 performed a call to `event_send` in which it
identifies itself as being RTEMS task 1, with RTEMS task 2 as target, passing
the event set $\{3, 1\}$, and storing its return code in variable `sendrc`. We then see
that `sendrc` is a scalar variables whose current value is zero.

4.2   Refining `printf` Observations

In order to get test code we need to define a *refinement relation* we use to get
from model output to C test code. We use a Python dictionary that maps names
with arguments to a text item into which those arguments can be substituted.
The keywords like `CALL`, `SCALAR`, and others, determine precisely how both the
dictionary lookup and the resulting substitution is done. The dictionary is itself
stored as a YAML file.

The process for refining both these observations is to lookup the name that
immediately follows the keyword, substitute the arguments into the retrieved
text, and add it to the code being generated. The refinement entries for
`event_send` (simplified) and `sendrc` are:

```
event_send: |
  {3} = rtems_event_send( {1}, {2} );
sendrc:
  T_rsc( sendrc, {0} );
```

The `CALL` observation is refined by substituting in 2, 10, and `sendrc` into the
`event_send` entry, while the `SCALAR` observation involves looking up `sendrc` and
substituting in 0. This results in the following C test code snippet:

```
  sendrc = rtems_event_send( 2, 10 );
  T_rsc( sendrc, 0 );
```

Here, `T_rsc` is a test function that checks that a return code has the specified value.

The YAML refinement dictionary is not the whole story. In addition to including the test framework, where `T_rsc` is defined, we also have to define some C functions that support the refinement. The actual test program will consist of a preamble in which such functions are defined, followed by the test code generated by the YAML refinement, and finishing off with a postamble that does proper test teardown.

4.3   Refining Task Switches

So far we have not discussed the use of the `_pid` number that follows the `@@@` marker. Consider the following (very) simplified extract from one of the Event scenarios, with added line numbers. This is the `SndRcvSnd` scenario, where the sender process sends some events to the receiver, then the receiver asks to receive some of those events plus others not just sent, and finally the sender sends more events that satisfy the receiver.

```
1.  @@@ 3 CALL event_send 1 2 2 sendrc
2.  @@@ 4 CALL event_receive 10 1 1 0 2 recrc
3.  @@@ 4 STATE 2 EventWait
4.  @@@ 3 CALL event_send 1 2 8 sendrc
5.  @@@ 4 SCALAR recrc 0
```

Line 1 shows the sender sending event set {1} to the receiver. Lines 2–3 shows the receiver request to receive all events in {3}, but then blocks because it is not satisfied and hence enters the state `EventWait`. Line 4 shows the sender running again and sending event-set {3}. This satisfies the receiver. Line 5 shows the receiver with a success return code.

The first use of `_pid` is to partition the refined C code into distinct segments, one for each value of `_pid` that occurs. In the above example, the refinement of lines 1 and 4 will be added to segment 3 (Worker), while those in lines 2, 3, and 5 will be added to segment 4 (Runner).

The temporal sequencing of the three Event API calls here is important. These means that the corresponding C test code needs to suspend and waken the two RTEMS Tasks at appropriate points. In particular, the RTEMS test code needs to be *reproducible* in that it always interleaves concurrent code execution the same way every time. Effectively *all* the non-determinism has to be refined away.

The standard way of doing this is to used a so-called *simple binary semaphore*, that has two API calls, one to obtain such a semaphore, another to release it. Only one task can obtain it at a time, but any task can release it. Simple binary semaphores are suitable for task synchronisation, and the Promela model includes models of binary semaphores which are used appropriately, reported using `CALL`, and refined to calls to the RTEMS equivalent.

4.4   Towards a UTP Semantics of Promela-to-C Refinement

There are two stages to the refinement from the Promela model to C test code. The first stage links the semantics of the model that of the observation language used in the `printf` statements (e.g. `CALL`, `SCALAR`, etc.). The second stage links the observation semantics to that of the C code itself. In each case we need UTP semantics for the two parts along with a linking Galois connection [33, Chp. 4].

UTP Semantics of Model Observables. The observation semantics is fairly straightforward as it is really just a simple way of reporting basic Promela events, such as calling an inline definition, or reporting the observed value of a model variable. The definition of the linking predicates will need to make use of the contents of the refinement YAML file, and this observation semantics.

UTP Semantics of C. The first step in this stage is to have a UTP semantics for C. We don't need to work with the whole C language, but can restrict ourselves to the subset that is actually used in safety critical systems, for example, the widely used MISRA-C Standard [9]. These forbid the use of C constructions that are semantically problematic, such as an expression in an assignment that calls functions that update global variables. ESA mandates the use of coding standards [24], while RTEMS has its own [45, §6.3], which also result in safe C code.

This means we can treat the sequential parts of C as being essentially UTP Designs [33, Chp. 3], with the addition of separation logic, to deal with C pointers. We already have UTP material on separation logic in Woodcock et al. [49], which treated it as a sub-theory in a setting of heterogenous theories.

Concurrency semantics is also needed to cover both concurrent RTEMS Tasks, and hardware-level concurrency with a software impact, most notably interrupts. Again, it looks like our work on UTCP [15], and the work by He Jifeng and colleagues on MDESL [41] may help here also. Another key area to explore is the linkages between denotational and operational semantics, that have been explored by extensively by He Jifeng and colleagues down the years [30,33,40, Chp. 10].

5   Related Work

Promela Semantics. Most of the formal semantics material for Promela/SPIN is operational in nature. An early example was the notion of a *symbolic labeled transition system* [38]. This then inspired work using ACL2 for abstract syntax which defined the semantics as a functional program [10]. Another approach used SOS notation to build a three-layered operational semantics [48]. In the SPIN book [35], there are sections on its semantics, based on extended Büchi automata, with states defined with representations of variables, messages, processes and other system attributes. It then defines a *semantic engine*, which is basically a program in pseudo-code over this state space.

Formal Methods and Testing. In 1995 Gaudel wrote a seminal paper relating formal methods and testing [27]. This established a formal framework for talking about the relationship between formal specifications and test code. Here we shall discuss the key concepts in the context of our work with RTEMS. Key points made in that paper include the fact that a specification generally can not serve as a test oracle, and some form of refinement needs to be established between it and test code. For our work we need to construct a refinement from Promela via observations to C code. This provides what Gaudel terms the *conformance relation*. It is possible to formally define an exhaustive test set, which has all valid behaviours and is usually infinite in nature. but techniques need to be found to shrink this to a finite test set that is adequate. In our case, model-checking requires us to produce a finite model, and test generation requires limiting it to finite behaviours, so we address this during Promela model design. Papers about formal methods and testing in UTP include works by Cavalcanti and Gaudel [19,20] and Aichernig et al. [6,47]. These all explore the conformance relation concept. Also related is work by Aichernig and Jifeng on mutation testing [7].

Formalising Pointers. There have been a number of treatments of pointers in UTP, most looking at them in an object oriented context. Hoare and He did [34] early work on a trace model. Cavalcanti et al. [21] looked at pointers where storage is an equivalence class of variables that share the same memory location. Smith and Gibbons [43] present a similar notion based on sharable and containable locations.

6   Conclusions

We have described some of the work we did applying formal methods to an ESA-sponsored qualification activity for multi-core RTEMS. We focused on our use of Promela to model synchronisation facilities in RTEMS, and on using SPIN to generate tests. This involved defining a simple but novel observation language to output information about key model events that could be interpreted as a test specification. We then mapped these observations to actual C test code snippets.

During the above, we also explored how we could extend the formality of the work beyond just that of the operational semantics of Promela. This involved identifying what pre-existing UTP theories could be used to model both Promela itself, and the refinement chain that involves the observation language and a suitable subset of the C programming language.

The current state of play is that models and test generation software for the Chains API, and the Event, Barrier and Message Managers, are now available from the RTEMS Central git repository [1], in the `formal` sub-directory. A new draft section on Formal Verification for the RTEMS Software Engineering manual [45] is under review by the community. More work has since be done mainly involving student projects, that has yet to be submitted to RTEMS for review and inclusion. This ongoing work in this area is hosted on Github [14].

6.1   Future Work

There is much work still to be done, with RTEMS. We plan to model far more of RTEMS than done so far, as well as revisiting and re-factoring the existing models. In particular, there is a need to formalise the new SMP-aware scheduler thread queue algorithms, that are considerably more complex than the single core versions, involving, for instance, task migration between cores.

In addition, the work done by Edisoft, Embedded Brains and CISTER has resulted in a new concept for requirements capture called *specification items* [45, §5], that encode enough information about RTEMS code artifacts to allow tools to build test code, run tests, collect data, and generate reports. None of this material is formal in any sense, but it does included descriptions that map abstract pre/post-conditions to test code snippets. This opens the possibility, given an appropriate UTP semantics, of being able to extract material to contribute to a formal specification in UTP.

The real plan for future work here is to use RTEMS, with the Promela models, the observation language, and the explicit use of C code, as a case study for using UTP to develop a unified semantic model of all these components, and their linkages. As has been pointed out, the work of He Jifeng has a great amount to contribute to this endeavour.

References

1. RTEMS Central GIT repository. https://git.rtems.org/rtems-central
2. RTEMS GIT repositories. https://git.rtems.org/
3. RTEMS Improvement by Edisoft. https://www.esa.int/Enabling_Support/ Space_Engineering_Technology/Software_Systems_Engineering/RTEMS_ EDISOFT
4. RTEMS Improvement by Embedded Brains. https://www.esa.int/Enabling_ Support/Space_Engineering_Technology/Software_Systems_Engineering/ RTEMS-SMP_Improvement_for_LEON_multi-core
5. RTEMS website. https://www.rtems.org/
6. Aichernig, B.K.: A testing perspective on algebraic, denotational, and operational semantics. In: Ribeiro, P., Sampaio, A. (eds.) UTP 2019. LNCS, vol. 11885, pp. 22–38. Springer, Cham (2019). https://doi.org/10.1007/978-3-030-31038-7_2
7. Aichernig, B.K., He, J.: Mutation testing in UTP. Form. Asp. Comput. **21**(1–2), 33–64 (2009). https://doi.org/10.1007/s00165-008-0083-6
8. Anderson, H., Ciobanu, G., Freitas, L.: UTP and temporal logic model checking. In: Butterfield, A. (ed.) UTP 2008. LNCS, vol. 5713, pp. 22–41. Springer, Heidelberg (2010). https://doi.org/10.1007/978-3-642-14521-6_3
9. Banham, D., et al.: MISRA C:2012 Guidelines for the Use of the C Language in Critical Systems. MISRA Limited, March 2013
10. Bevier, W.R.: Toward an operational semantics of PROMELA in ACL2. In: SPIN'97. Twente University, Enshede, Netherlands, pp. 1–20 (1997). https:// spinroot.com/spin/symposia/ws97/bevier.pdf
11. Bloom, G., Sherrill, J., Hu, T., Bertolotti, I.C.: Real-Time Systems Development with RTEMS and Multicore Processors, 1st edn. CRC Press, Boca Raton, November 2020

12. Brandenburg, B.B.: A fully preemptive multiprocessor semaphore protocol for latency-sensitive real-time applications. In: Proceedings of the 25th Euromicro Conference on Real-Time Systems (ECRTS 2013), pp. 292–302 (2013). http://www.mpi-sws.org/~bbb/papers/pdf/ecrts13b.pdf

13. Burns, A., Wellings, A.J.: A schedulability compatible multiprocessor resource sharing protocol - MrsP. In: Proceedings of the 25th Euromicro Conference on Real-Time Systems (ECRTS 2013) (2013). http://www-users.cs.york.ac.uk/~burns/MRSPpaper.pdf

14. Butterfield, A.: Formal RTEMS-SMP repository. https://github.com/andrewbutterfield/RTEMS-SMP-Formal

15. Butterfield, A.: UTCP: compositional semantics for shared-variable concurrency. In: Cavalheiro, S., Fiadeiro, J. (eds.) SBMF 2017. LNCS, vol. 10623, pp. 253–270. Springer, Cham (2017). https://doi.org/10.1007/978-3-319-70848-5_16

16. Butterfield, A., Sherif, A., Woodcock, J.: Slotted-circus. In: Davies, J., Gibbons, J. (eds.) IFM 2007. LNCS, vol. 4591, pp. 75–97. Springer, Heidelberg (2007). https://doi.org/10.1007/978-3-540-73210-5_5

17. Callahan, J., Schneider, F., Easterbrook, S.: Automated software testing using model-checking, pp. 118–127 (1996)

18. Catellani, S., Bonato, L., Huber, S., Mezzetti, E.: Challenges in the implementation of MrsP. In: Reliable Software Technologies - Ada-Europe 2015, pp. 179–195 (2015)

19. Cavalcanti, A., Gaudel, M.-C.: A note on traces refinement and the conf relation in the unifying theories of programming. In: Butterfield, A. (ed.) UTP 2008. LNCS, vol. 5713, pp. 42–61. Springer, Heidelberg (2010). https://doi.org/10.1007/978-3-642-14521-6_4

20. Cavalcanti, A., Gaudel, M.-C.: Specification coverage for testing in circus. In: Qin, S. (ed.) UTP 2010. LNCS, vol. 6445, pp. 1–45. Springer, Heidelberg (2010). https://doi.org/10.1007/978-3-642-16690-7_1

21. Cavalcanti, A., Harwood, W., Woodcock, J.: Pointers and records in the unifying theories of programming. In: Dunne, S., Stoddart, B. (eds.) UTP 2006. LNCS, vol. 4010, pp. 200–216. Springer, Heidelberg (2006). https://doi.org/10.1007/11768173_12

22. Dijkstra, E.W.: Guarded commands, nondeterminacy and formal derivation of programs. Commun. ACM **18**(8), 453–457 (1975). https://doi.org/10.1145/360933.360975

23. ECSS: ECSS-E-ST-40C - Software general requirements. European Cooperation for Space Standardization (2009). https://ecss.nl/standard/ecss-e-st-40c-software-general-requirements/

24. ECSS: ECSS-Q-ST-80C Rev. 1 - Software product assurance. European Cooperation for Space Standardization (2017). https://ecss.nl/standard/ecss-q-st-80c-rev-1-software-product-assurance-15-february-2017/

25. Foster, S., Baxter, J., Cavalcanti, A., Miyazawa, A., Woodcock, J.: Automating verification of state machines with reactive designs and Isabelle/UTP. In: Bae, K., Ölveczky, P.C. (eds.) FACS 2018. LNCS, vol. 11222, pp. 137–155. Springer, Cham (2018). https://doi.org/10.1007/978-3-030-02146-7_7

26. Foster, S., Cavalcanti, A., Canham, S., Woodcock, J., Zeyda, F.: Unifying theories of reactive design contracts. Theor. Comput. Sci. **802**, 105–140 (2020). https://doi.org/10.1016/j.tcs.2019.09.017

27. Gaudel, M.-C.: Testing can be formal, too. In: Mosses, P.D., Nielsen, M., Schwartzbach, M.I. (eds.) CAAP 1995. LNCS, vol. 915, pp. 82–96. Springer, Heidelberg (1995). https://doi.org/10.1007/3-540-59293-8_188

28. Gomes, R.: Analysis of MrsP Protocol in RTEMS Operating System. Master's thesis, CISTER, Departmento de Engenharia Informática, Instituto Superior de Engenharia do Porto (ISEP), Portugal (2019)

29. Jifeng, H.: Transaction calculus. In: Butterfield, A. (ed.) UTP 2008. LNCS, vol. 5713, pp. 2–21. Springer, Heidelberg (2010). https://doi.org/10.1007/978-3-642-14521-6_2

30. He, J., Li, Q.: A new roadmap for linking theories of programming and its applications on GCL and CSP. Sci. Comput. Program. **162**, 3–34 (2018). https://doi.org/10.1016/j.scico.2017.10.009

31. He, J., Xu, Q.: An operational semantics of a simulator algorithm. In: Arabnia, H.R. (ed.) Proceedings of the International Conference on Parallel and Distributed Processing Techniques and Applications, PDPTA 2000, 24–29 June 2000, Las Vegas, Nevada, USA. CSREA Press (2000)

32. Hierons, R.M., et al.: Using formal specifications to support testing. ACM Comput. Surv. **41**(2), 9:1–9:76 (2009). https://doi.org/10.1145/1459352.1459354

33. Hoare, C.A.R., He, J.: Unifying Theories of Programming. Prentice-Hall, Hoboken (1998). http://unifyingtheories.org

34. Hoare, C.A.R., Jifeng, H.: A trace model for pointers and objects. In: Guerraoui, R. (ed.) ECOOP 1999. LNCS, vol. 1628, pp. 1–18. Springer, Heidelberg (1999). https://doi.org/10.1007/3-540-48743-3_1

35. Holzmann, G.J.: The SPIN Model Checker - Primer and Reference Manual. Addison-Wesley, Boston (2004)

36. Kirchner, F., Kosmatov, N., Prevosto, V., Signoles, J., Yakobowski, B.: Frama-c: a software analysis perspective. Form. Asp. Comput. **27**(3), 573–609 (2015). https://doi.org/10.1007/s00165-014-0326-7

37. Li, J., Pu, G., Zhang, L., Wang, Z., He, J., Guldstrand Larsen, K.: On the relationship between LTL normal forms and Büchi automata. In: Liu, Z., Woodcock, J., Zhu, H. (eds.) Theories of Programming and Formal Methods. LNCS, vol. 8051, pp. 256–270. Springer, Heidelberg (2013). https://doi.org/10.1007/978-3-642-39698-4_16

38. Natajaran, V., Holzmann, G.J.: Outline for an operational semantics of PROMELA. In: SPIN'96. Rutgers University, NJ, USA, pp. 1–17 (1996). https://spinroot.com/spin/symposia/ws96/Na.pdf

39. Paulson, L.C., Nipkow, T., Wenzel, M.: From LCF to Isabelle/HOL. Form. Asp. Comput. **31**(6), 675–698 (2019). https://doi.org/10.1007/s00165-019-00492-1

40. Sheng, F., Zhu, H., He, J., Yang, Z., Bowen, J.P.: Theoretical and practical aspects of linking operational and algebraic semantics for MDESL. ACM Trans. Softw. Eng. Methodol. **28**(3), 14:1–14:46 (2019). https://doi.org/10.1145/3295699

41. Sheng, F., Zhu, H., He, J., Yang, Z., Bowen, J.P.: Theoretical and practical approaches to the denotational semantics for MDESL based on UTP. Form. Asp. Comput. **32**(2–3), 275–314 (2020). https://doi.org/10.1007/s00165-020-00513-4

42. Sherif, A., Jifeng, H.: Towards a time model for circus. In: George, C., Miao, H. (eds.) ICFEM 2002. LNCS, vol. 2495, pp. 613–624. Springer, Heidelberg (2002). https://doi.org/10.1007/3-540-36103-0_62

43. Smith, M.A., Gibbons, J.: Unifying theories of locations. In: Butterfield, A. (ed.) UTP 2008. LNCS, vol. 5713, pp. 161–180. Springer, Heidelberg (2010). https://doi.org/10.1007/978-3-642-14521-6_10

44. The RTEMS Project contributors: RTEMS Classic API Guide (2021). https://docs.rtems.org/branches/master/c-user/index.html

45. The RTEMS Project contributors: RTEMS Software Engineering (2021). https://docs.rtems.org/branches/master/eng/

46. The RTEMS Project contributors: RTEMS User Manual (2021). https://docs. rtems.org/branches/master/user/

47. Weiglhofer, M., Aichernig, B.K.: Unifying input output conformance. In: Butterfield, A. (ed.) UTP 2008. LNCS, vol. 5713, pp. 181–201. Springer, Heidelberg (2010). https://doi.org/10.1007/978-3-642-14521-6_11

48. Weise, C.: An incremental formal semantics for PROMELA. In: SPIN'97. Twente University, Enshede, Netherlands, pp. 1–20 (1997). https://spinroot.com/spin/ symposia/ws97/weise.pdf

49. Woodcock, J., Foster, S., Butterfield, A.: Heterogeneous semantics and unifying theories. In: Margaria, T., Steffen, B. (eds.) ISoLA 2016. LNCS, vol. 9952, pp. 374–394. Springer, Cham (2016). https://doi.org/10.1007/978-3-319-47166-2_26

50. Huibiao, Z., Bowen, J.P., Jifeng, H.: From operational semantics to denotational semantics for Verilog. In: Margaria, T., Melham, T. (eds.) CHARME 2001. LNCS, vol. 2144, pp. 449–464. Springer, Heidelberg (2001). https://doi.org/10.1007/3-540-44798-9_34

KnowLang – A Formal Specification Model for Self-adaptive Systems

Mike Hinchey and Emil Vassev[✉]

Lero–The Science Foundation Ireland Research Centre for Software,
University of Limerick, Limerick, Ireland
`mike.hinchey@lero.ie`, `emil.i.vassev@ul.ie`

Abstract. KnowLang is a framework for knowledge representation and reasoning (KR&R) that aims at efficient and comprehensive knowledge structuring and awareness based on logical and statistical reasoning. It tackles both explicit representation of domain concepts and relationships and explicit representation of particular and general factual knowledge, in terms of predicates, names, connectives, quantifiers and identity. Moreover, it handles uncertain knowledge in which additive probabilities are used to represent degrees of belief. Other remarkable features are related to knowledge cleaning and knowledge representation for autonomic self-adaptive behaviour. Knowledge specified with KnowLang takes the form of a Knowledge Base (KB) that outlines a KR context. A special KnowLang Reasoner operates in this context to allow for knowledge querying and update. In addition, the reasoner can infer special self-adaptive behaviour.

At its very core, KnowLang is a formal specification language providing a comprehensive specification model aiming at addressing the knowledge representation problem of self-adaptive systems. The complexity of the problem necessitated the use of a specification model where knowledge can be presented at different levels of abstraction and grouped by following both hierarchical and functional patterns. In this paper, we outline the formal semantics of the KnowLang multi-tier specification model. The model is outlined in terms of layers dedicated to knowledge corpuses, KB operators, and inference primitives.

Keywords: KnowLang · self-adaptive systems · formal specification

1 Introduction

Contemporary computerized systems like autonomous robots may boast intrinsic intelligence that helps them reason about situations where autonomous decision making is required. Robotic intelligence mainly excels at formal logic, which allows it, for example, to find the right move from hundreds of previous moves or by applying probability algorithms. The basic compound in this reasoning process is appropriately structured knowledge used by embedded inference engines. The knowledge is integrated in a system via knowledge representation techniques

© The Author(s), under exclusive license to Springer Nature Switzerland AG 2023
J. P. Bowen et al. (Eds.): *Theories of Programming and Formal Methods*, LNCS 14080, pp. 367–392, 2023.
https://doi.org/10.1007/978-3-031-40436-8_14

to build a computational model of the operational domain in which symbols serve as knowledge surrogates for real world artefacts, such as system's components and functions, task details, environment objects, etc. The domain of interest can cover any part of the real world or any hypothetical system about which one desires to represent knowledge for computational purposes. Knowledge representation primitives such as rules, frames, semantic networks, concept maps, ontologies, and logic expressions might be used to represent distinct pieces of knowledge that are worth being differently represented. Moreover, these primitives might be combined into more complex knowledge elements. Whatever elements they use, engineers must structure the knowledge so that the system can effectively process it and eventually derive its own behaviour.

KnowLang [14,15,17–20] is a framework for KR&R that aims at efficient and comprehensive knowledge structuring and awareness based on *logical* and *statistical reasoning*. It helps us to tackle 1) explicit representation of domain concepts and relationships; 2) explicit representation of particular and general factual knowledge, in terms of predicates, names, connectives, quantifiers and identity; and 3) uncertain knowledge in which additive probabilities are used to represent degrees of belief. Other remarkable features are related to knowledge cleaning (allowing for efficient reasoning) and knowledge representation for autonomic self-adaptive behaviour. Knowledge specified with KnowLang takes the form of a Knowledge Base (KB) that outlines a KR context. A special KnowLang Reasoner operates in this context to allow for knowledge querying and update. In addition, the reasoner can infer special self-adaptive behaviour.

The rest of this paper is organized as follows. Section 2 presents the KnowLang formal specification model including the constructs for specifying self-adaptive behaviour. Section 3 provides a discussion on how KnowLang copes with challenging problems such as encoded versus represented knowledge, the specification of states, situations, goals and policies, and how sensory data is converted to KR symbols. Section 4 outlines the KnowLang syntax. Section 5 provides and example of KR for Self-adaptive Behaviour with KnowLang and Sect. 6 describes a case study where KnowLang has been used to specify and formalize an eMobility autonomous system. Finally, Sect. 7 provides brief concluding remarks and a summary of our future goals.

2   Specification Model

At its very core, KnowLang is a formal specification language providing a comprehensive specification model aiming at addressing the knowledge representation problem for self-adaptive systems. The complexity of the problem necessitated the use of a *specification model* (inspired by the ASSL's specification model [11]) where knowledge can be presented at different levels of abstraction and grouped by following both hierarchical and functional patterns. KnowLang imposes a multi-tier specification model (see Fig. 1), where we specify a KB composed of layers dedicated to *knowledge corpuses*, *KB (knowledge base) operators* and *inference primitives*.

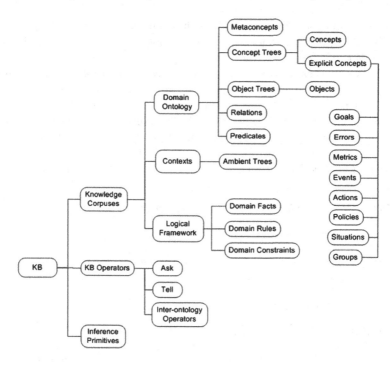

Fig. 1. KnowLang Specification Model

Definitions 1 through 58 outline a BNF-like [6] formal representation of the KnowLang Specification Model. As shown in Definition 1, a Knowledge Base is a tuple of three main knowledge components – *knowledge corpus* (Kc), *KB operators* (Op) and *inference primitives* (Ip). A Kc is a tuple of three knowledge components – *ontologies* (O), *contexts* (Cx) and *logical framework* (Lf) (see Definition 2). Further, a domain ontology is composed of hierarchically organized sets of *meta-concepts* (Cm), *concept trees* (Ct), *object trees* (Ot), *relations* (R) and *predicates* (V) (see Definition 4). Note that the trees in our model (e.g., concept trees, object trees, etc.) can be direct acyclic graphs. Moreover, note that in the definitions below we denote a finite set of elements El with $\{el_1, el_2, \ldots, el_n\}, n \geq 0$ where by omitting el_0 we allow an empty set, e.g., see the definition of meta-concepts (Cm) 5.

Meta-concepts (Cm) provide a *context-oriented interpretation* (i) (see Definition 6) of concepts and might be optionally associated with specific contexts (the square brackets "[]" mean "optional"). Meta-concepts help ontologies to be viewed from different context perspectives by establishing different meanings for some of the key concepts. This is a powerful construct providing for interpretations of a concept and its derived concept tree depending on the current context. Concept trees (Ct) consist of semantically related concepts (C) and/or explicit concepts (Ce). Every concept tree (ct) has a root concept (tr) because the architecture ultimately must reference a single concept that is the connection point to concepts that are outside the concept tree. A root concept may optionally inherit a meta-concept, which is denoted $[tr \succ cm]$ (see Definition 8) where "$\succ$" is the inherits relation. Every concept has a set of *properties* (P) and optional sets of *functionalities* (F), *parent concepts* (Pr) and *children concepts* (Ch) (see Definition 10). Explicit concepts are concepts that *must be presented* in the KB of the system. Explicit concepts are mainly intended to support 1) the autonomic behaviour of the SCs; and 2) distributed reasoning and knowledge sharing among the SC of a SCE systems. These concepts might be *goals* (G), *errors* (Er), *metrics* (M), *policies* (Π), *events* (E), *actions* (A), *situations* (Si) and *groups* (Gr) (see Definition 13), i.e., they allow for quantification over such concepts.

FORMAL REPRESENTATION OF KNOWLANG

Definition 1. $Kb := <Kc, Op, Ip>$ *(Knowledge Base)*

Definition 2. $Kc := <O, Cx, Lf>$ *(Knowledge Corpus)*

DOMAIN ONTOLOGIES

Definition 3. $O := \{o_{sc}, o_{sce}, o_{env}, o_{si}\}$ *(Domain Ontologies)*

Definition 4. $o := <Cm, Ct, Ot, R, D>, o \in O$ *(Domain Ontology)*

Definition 5. $Cm := \{cm_1, cm_2, \ldots, cm_n\}, n \geq 0$ *(Meta-concepts)*

Definition 6. $cm := <[cx], i>, i \in Icx$ *(Meta-concept, cx – Context, i – Interpretation)*

Definition 7. $Ct := \{ct_1, ct_2, \ldots, ct_n\}, n \geq 0$ *(Concept Trees)*

Definition 8. $ct := <tr, C, [Ce]>$ *(Concept Tree)*
        $tr \in (C \cup Ce), [tr \succ cm]$ *(tr – Tree Root)*

Definition 9. $C := \{c_1, c_2, \ldots, c_n\}, n \geq 0$ *(Concepts)*

Definition 10. $c := <P, [F], [S], [Pr], [Ch]>$ *(Concept)*
        $Pr \subset (C \cup Ce), c \succ Pr$ *(Pr – Parents)*
        $Ch \subset (C \cup Ce), Ch \succ c$ *(Ch – Children)*

Definition 11. $P := \{p_1, p_2, \ldots, p_n\}, n \geq 0$ *(Properties)*

Definition 12. $F := \{f_1, f_2, \ldots, f_n\}, n \geq 0$ *(Functionalities)*

Definition 13. $Ce := G \bigcup Er \bigcup M \bigcup \Pi \bigcup E \bigcup A \bigcup Si \bigcup Gr$ *(Explicit Concepts)*

Errors (Er) are explicit concepts representing the *space of errors* that can occur in the system. An error (er) is specified with *error information* (i_{er}) and an optional set of *erroneous actions* (A_{er}) that could be considered as eventual sources of error (see Definition 15). Error occurrence can cause a state transition (see Definition 22). Metrics (M) are explicit concepts providing a *prognostic space* of valuable information that can be gathered from the environment or from the system itself. A metric (m) is specified with a metric source (sr_m) and data (d_m)(see Definition 17). The metric source may eventually represent a system sensor used to monitor the environment.

Definition 14. $Er := \{er_1, er_2, \ldots, er_n\}, n \geq 0$ *(Errors)*

Definition 15. $er := <i_{er}, [A_{er}]>$ *(Error)*
$\quad A_{er} \subset A$ *(A_{er} – Erroneous Actions)*

Definition 16. $M := \{m_1, m_2, \ldots, m_n\}, n \geq 0$ *(Metrics)*

Definition 17. $m := <sr_m, d_m>$ *(Metric)(sr_m – Metric Source, d_m – Metric Data)*

The KnowLang policies (Π) drive the autonomic behaviour of the system. A policy π has a *goal* (g), *policy situations* (Si_π), *policy-situation relations* (R_π), and *policy conditions* (N_π) mapped to *policy actions* (A_π) where the evaluation of N_π may eventually (with some degree of probability) imply the evaluation of actions (denoted with $N_\pi \overset{[Z]}{\rightarrow} A_\pi$) (see Definition 19).

A condition is a Boolean expression over ontology (see Definition 21), e.g., the occurrence of a certain event. *Policy situations* Si_π are situations (see Definition 25) that may trigger (or imply) a policy π, in compliance with the policy-situations relations R_π(denoted with $Si_\pi \overset{[R_\pi]}{\rightarrow} \pi$), thus implying the evaluation of the policy conditions N_π(denoted with $\pi \rightarrow N_\pi$)(see Definition 19). A policy may comprise optional policy-situation relations (R_π) justifying the relationships between a policy and the associated situations. The presence of probabilistic beliefs in both *mappings* and *policy relations* justifies the probability of policy execution, which may vary with time. Note that Sect. 5 discusses in detail how the KR of policies, situations and relations provides for self-adaptive behaviour.

A goal g is a desirable transition ($\Rightarrow$) to a state or a transition from a specific state to another state (denoted with $s \Rightarrow s'$) (see Definition 22). The system may transit ($\Rightarrow$) to a state (s) when the properties (P) of an object (ob) are updated (denoted $TELL \rhd ob.P$), the properties of a set of objects are updated, or some errors or events have occurred or actions have been realized in the system or in the environment (denoted with $TELL \rhd Er_s$, $TELL \rhd E_s$ and $TELL \rhd A_s$) (see Definition 22). Note that $TELL$ is a KB Operator involving knowledge inference. In KnowLang, a state s is a Boolean expression over ontology ($be(O)$)(see Definition 23), e.g., "a specific property of an object must hold a specific value".

A situation is expressed with a state (s), a history of actions ($A \overset{\leftarrow}{si}$) (actions executed to get to state s), actions A_{si} that can be performed from state s and an optional history of events $E\overset{\leftarrow}{si}$ that eventually occurred to get to state s (see Definition 25).

Definition 18. $\Pi := \{\pi_1, \pi_2, \ldots, \pi_n\}, n \geq 0$ *(Policies)*

Definition 19. $\pi := <g, Si_\pi, [R_\pi], N_\pi, A_\pi, map(N_\pi, A_\pi, [Z])>$ *(Policy)*

$\quad A_\pi \subset A, N_\pi \overset{[Z]}{\rightarrow} A_\pi$ *(A_π – Policy Actions)*

$\quad Si_\pi \subset Si, Si_\pi := \{si_{\pi_1}, si_{\pi_2}, \ldots, si_{\pi_n}\}, n \geq 0$ *(Si_π – Policy Situations)*

$\quad R_\pi \subset R, R_\pi := \{r_{\pi_1}, r_{\pi_2}, \ldots, r_{\pi_n}\}, n \geq 0$ *(R_π-Policy-Situation Relations)*

$\quad \forall r_\pi \in R_\pi \bullet (r_\pi := <si_\pi, [rn], [Z], \pi>), si_\pi \in Si_\pi$

$\quad Si_\pi \overset{[R_\pi]}{\rightarrow} \pi \rightarrow N_\pi$ *(Policy situations may imply the policy they are related to)*

Definition 20. $N_\pi := \{n_1, n_2, \ldots, n_k\}, k \geq 0$ *(Policy Conditions)*

Definition 21. $n := be(O)$ *(Condition – Boolean Expression over Ontology)*

Definition 22. $g := \langle \Rightarrow s' \rangle | \langle s \Rightarrow s' \rangle$ *(Goal)*

$\quad \Rightarrow s := \langle TELL \rhd ob.P \rangle | \langle TELL \rhd \{ob_0.P, ob_1.P, \ldots, ob_n.P\} \rangle | \langle TELL \rhd Er_s \rangle |$

$\quad\quad\quad \langle TELL \rhd E_s \rangle | \langle TELL \rhd A_s \rangle$ *(State Transition)*

$\quad Er_s \subset Er, E_s \subset E, A_s \subset A$ *(Er_s – State Errors, E_s – State Events, A_s – State Actions)*

Definition 23. $s := be(O)$ *(State – Boolean Expression over Ontology)*

Definition 24. $Si := \{si_1, si_2, \ldots, si_n\}, n \geq 0$ *(Situations)*

Definition 25. $si := <s, A\overset{\leftarrow}{si}, [E\overset{\leftarrow}{si}], A_{si}>$ *(Situation)*

$\quad A\overset{\leftarrow}{si} \subset A$ *($A\overset{\leftarrow}{si}$ – Executed Actions)*

$\quad A_{si} \subset A$ *(A_{si} – Possible Actions)*

$\quad E\overset{\leftarrow}{si} \subset E$ *($E\overset{\leftarrow}{si}$ – Situation Events)*

KnowLang events (E) are a means of high-priority monitoring and messaging. In general, an event (see Definition 27) can be activated (raised) by a variety of factors such as time (t_e), goals (G_e), metrics (M_e), errors (Er_e), actions (A_e) and even other events (E_e). A special *guard* (gd_e), represented as a Boolean expression over ontology (see Definition 28), may restrict the event activation. Events may participate in Boolean expressions or be used to specify event-driven policies, goals, situations, etc.

In KnowLang, actions are activities (routines) that can be performed by the system. Actions must be implemented by the system and with KR we represent an abstraction (counterparts) of the routines and classes used to implement these actions. Therefore, an action concept must refer to real implementation. From KR perspective, an action a is a tuple of optional pre- (rc_a), and post-conditions (pc_a), a set of parameters (Pm_a), output (rn_a) and errors (Er_a) that can be raised by the action (see Definition 30).

Definition 26. $E := \{e_1, e_2, \ldots, e_n\}, n \geq 0$ *(Events)*

Definition 27. $e := <[gd_e], activ>$ *(Event)*
$\qquad activ := t_e|G_e|M_e|Er_e|A_e|E_e$ *(Activation Factor)*
$\qquad G_e \subset G, M_e \subset M, Er_e \subset Er, A_e \subset A, E_e \subset E$

Definition 28. $gd_e := be(O)$ *(Event Guard)*

Definition 29. $A := \{a_1, a_2, \ldots, a_n\}, n \geq 0$ *(Actions)*

Definition 30. $a := <[rc_a], [pc_a], [Pm_a], [rn_a], [Er_a]>$ *(Action)*

A group (gr) involves objects (Ob_{gr}) related to each other through a distinct set of relations (R_{gr})(see Definition 32). Note that groups (G) are explicit concepts intended to (but not restricted to) represent knowledge about the structure of the system.

Object trees (Ot) are conceptualization of how objects existing in the world of interest are related to each other. The relationships are based on the principle that objects have properties, where sometimes the value of a property is another object, which in turn also has properties. Such properties are termed object properties (Pb). An object tree (ot) consists of a root object (ob) and an optional set of object properties (Pb) – sub-trees of objects (see Definitions 34 and 36). An object (ob) is an instance of a concept (denoted as $instof(c)$ – see Definition 35) and inherits that concept's properties.

Definition 31. $Gr := \{gr_1, gr_2, \ldots, gr_n\}, n \geq 0$ *(Groups)*

Definition 32. $gr := <Ob_{gr}, R_{gr}>$ *(Group)*
$\qquad Ob_{gr} \subset Ob, R_{gr} \subset R$ *(Ob$_{gr}$-Group Objects, Ob – Objects, R$_{gr}$-Group Relations)*

Definition 33. $Ot := \{ot_1, ot_2, \ldots, ot_n\}, n \geq 0$ *(Object Trees)*

Definition 34. $ot := <ob, [Pb]>$ *(Object Tree)*

Definition 35. $ob := instof(c), ob \in Ob, c \in C$ *(Object)*

Definition 36. $Pb := \{ot_1, ot_2, \ldots, ot_n\}, n \geq 0$ *(Object Properties – sub-trees of objects)*

Relations (R) connect two concepts (including predicates V), two objects, or an object with a concept and may have *probability distribution* Z (e.g., over time, over situations, over concepts' properties, etc.) (see Definition 38). A relation has an optional name, i.e., when the name is missing we have the implication relation. Probability distribution is provided to support *probabilistic reasoning*. By specifying relations with probability distributions we actually specify Bayesian Networks [7] connecting the concepts and objects of an ontology. Note that KnowLang considers binary relations only, but there could be multiple relations relating the same concepts/objects.

Definition 37. $R := \{r_1, r_2, \ldots, r_n\}, n \geq 0$ *(Relations)*

Definition 38. $r := <re_k, [rn], [Z], re_n>$ *(Relation, re – Relation Entity, Z – Probability Distribution)*
$$re \in C \bigcup Ob \bigcup V \quad (C - Concepts, \; Ob - Objects, \; V - Predicates)$$

Definition 39. $V := \{v_1, v_2, \ldots, v_n\}, n \geq 0$ *(Predicates)*

Definition 40. $v := <C_v, S_v, be(O)>$ *(Predicate)*
$$C_v \subset C, S_v \subset S \quad (C_v - Predicate's \; Concepts, \; S_v - Predicate's \; States)$$

Predicates (V) are special KR structures that specify distinct inter-state relations or schemes for evaluation of complex states. For example, we can specify a predicate that verifies if the Motion System of a robot is operational. A predicate might be used by the KnowLang Reasoner to check whether an object (or the entire system) is in a specific state. Thus, a predicate (v) formally can be presented as tuple of predicate concepts (C_v), predicate states (S_v) and a Boolean expression over ontology ($be(O)$) that determines what conditions must hold to conclude that the predicate states are "active" (occupied) (see Definition 40.

KNOWLANG CONTEXTS

Definition 41. $Cx := \{cx_1, cx_2, \ldots, cx_n\}, n \geq 0$ *(Contexts)*

Definition 42. $cx := <At, [Icx]>$ *(Context)*

Definition 43. $At := \{at_1, at_2, \ldots, at_n\}, n \geq 0$ *(Ambient Trees)*

Definition 44. $at := <ct, Ca, [i]>$ *(Ambient Tree)*
$$ct \in Ct \quad (Concept \; Tree \; hosted \; by \; an \; ontology)$$
$$Ca \subset C \quad (Ca - Ambient \; Concepts)$$
$$i \subset Icx \quad (i\text{-}Ambient \; Tree \; Interpretation)$$

Definition 45. $Icx := \{i_1, i_2, \ldots, i_n\}, n \geq 0$ *(Context Interpretations)*

Contexts Cx are intended to extract the relevant knowledge from an ontology. Moreover, contexts carry interpretation for some of the meta-concepts (see Definition 42), which may lead to new interpretation of the descendant concepts (derived from a meta-concept – see Definition 8). We consider a very broad notion of context, e.g., the environment in a fraction of time or a generic situation such as currently-ongoing system action (e.g., observing or listening). Thus, a context must emphasize the key concepts in an ontology, which helps the inference mechanism narrow the domain knowledge (domain ontology) by exploring the concept trees down only to the emphasized key concepts.

Depending on the context, some low-level concepts might be subsumed by their upper-level parent concepts, just because the former are not relevant for that very context. For example, a robot wheel can be considered as a thing or as an important part of the robot's motion system. As a result, the context interpretation of knowledge will help the system deal with "clean" knowledge and the reasoning will be more efficient. A context (cx) consists of ambient trees (At) and optional context interpretations (Icx) (see Definition 42). An ambient tree (at) refers to a concept tree (ct) described by an ontology (o) and carries ambient concepts (Ca), part of the concept tree, and optional context interpretation (i).

The *ambient concepts* (see Definition 44) explicitly determine new level of deepness for their original concept tree, i.e., ambient concepts subsume all of their child concepts (if any). As result, when the system reasons about a particular context (expressed with ambient trees), the reasoning process does not consider those child concepts, but their ambient parents, which are far more generic, and thus less detailed. This technique reduces the size of the relevant knowledge, by temporarily removing from the concept trees all the ambient concepts' children (descendant concepts). We may think about ambient trees as filters the system applies at runtime to reduce the visibility of concepts of a concept tree. Note that this technique has been further developed in [16].

KNOWLANG LOGICAL FRAMEWORK

Definition 46. $Lf := <Fa, Rl, Ct>$ *(Logical Framework)*

Definition 47. $Fa := \{fa_1, fa_2, \ldots, fa_n\}, n \geq 0$ *(Facts)*

Definition 48. $fa := be(O) \rightarrow \boldsymbol{T}$ *(Fact – True statement over ontology)*

Definition 49. $Rl := \{rl_1, rl_2, \ldots, rl_n\}, n \geq 0$ *(Rules)*

Definition 50. $rl := <be(O), do(A_{rl})> | <be(O), do(V_{rl})>$ *(Rule)*
$A_{rl} \subset A, V_{rl} \subset V$ *(A_{rl} – Rule's Actions, V_{rl} – Rule's Predicates)*

Definition 51. $Ct := \{ct_1, ct_2, \ldots, ct_n\}, n \geq 0$ *(Constraints)*

Definition 52. $ct := be(O)$ *(Constraint)*

The KnowLang Logical Framework helps developers realize the explicit representation of particular and general factual knowledge, in terms of additional rule-based predicates, names, connectives, quantifiers and identity. The Logical Framework (Lf) is composed of *facts* (Fa), *rules* (Rl) and *constraints* (Ct) (see Definition 46). Note that Lf's KR structures must be specified with ontology terms, i.e., predefined concepts, objects, predicates and relations. Facts define true statements in the ontologies (O) by applying Boolean expressions over ontology (see Definition 48). Rules relate hypotheses to conclusions where the former are expressed as Boolean expressions over ontology and the latter decide what actions to be performed or predicates to be enforced (see Definitions 50). A constraint is a Boolean expressions over ontology (see Definitions 52), e.g., constraints might negate the execution of particular actions or forbid the application of particular predicates. Constraints might be used to enforce knowledge consistency.

KNOWLEDGE BASE OPERATORS

Definition 53. $Op := <Ask, Tell, Oop>$ *(Knowledge Base Operators)*

Definition 54. $Ask := retrieve(Kc) \rightarrow Ip \lhd Kc$ *(query knowledge base)*

Definition 55. $Tell := update(Kc) \rightarrow Ip \rhd Kc$ *(update knowledge base)*

Definition 56. $Oop := fo(Oi) \rightarrow Ip \rhd Kc, Oi \subset O$ *(Inter-ontology Operators)*

INFERENCE PRIMITIVES

Definition 57. $Ip := \{ip_1, ip_2, \ldots, ip_n\}, n \geq 0$ *(Inference Primitives)*

Definition 58. $ip := impl(FOL)|impl(FOPL)|impl(DL)$ *(Inference Primitive)*

The Knowledge Base Operators (Op) can be grouped into three groups: *ASK Operators* (retrieve knowledge from KBs), *TELL Operators* (update KB) and *Inter-Ontology Operators* (Oop) are intended to work on one or more ontologies (specified as a function $fo(Oi)$ over ontologies (Oi)) (see Definitions 53 through 56). The Inter-Ontology Operators are still under development, but overall they can be related to operations like *merging, mapping, alignment*, etc. Note that all the Knowledge Base Operators (Op) may imply the use of inference primitives (Ip).

The Inference Primitives (Ip) (see Definition 58) are algorithms for reasoning and knowledge inference needed by the KnowLang Reasoner. These primitives are implementation (denoted with *impl* in Definition 58) of reasoning algorithms based on First Order Logic (FOL) [2] (and its extensions), First Order Probabilistic Logic (FOPL) [4] and Description Logics (DL) [1]. FOPL increases the power of FOL by allowing us to assert in a natural way "likely" features of objects and concepts via a probability distribution over the possibilities that we envision. Having logics with semantics gives us a notion of deductive entailment. Note that these algorithms together with the appropriate reasoning engines shall help the KnowLang Reasoner to query and update KB.

3   Meeting the Challenges

Both the KnowLang Specification Model and KnowLang Reasoner have been developed by taking into consideration some explicit challenges comprehensively described in our publications [17,20,21].

3.1   Encoded Versus Represented Knowledge

Developers may encode a large part of the "a priori" knowledge (knowledge given to the system before the latter actually runs) in the implemented classes and routines. In such a case, the knowledge-represented pieces of knowledge (e.g., concepts, relations, rules, etc.) may complement the knowledge codified into implemented program classes and routines. For example, KnowLang actions could be based on classes and methods and a substantial concern about the KR of such actions is how to relate the knowledge expressed with actions to implemented methods and functions. A possible solution is to map KR concepts and objects to program classes and objects respectively.

To properly represent the program implementation (classes, methods, etc.) in the KB, all the concepts and objects have an *IMPL Property* that relates a KnowLang structure to its program counterpart, if any. For example, a KnowLang concept might be specified with an IMPL property to link the concept to a program class or method. The following is the grammar definition supporting that [12].

```
Concept-Impl := IMPL { Impl-Reference }
```

3.2   States, Situations, Goals and Policies

A big challenge is *"how to express situations and reason about the same"*. Situations trigger self-adaptive behaviour (see Sect. 5) and it is very important to allow the reasoner to recognize them. To support this approach, KnowLang has introduced the *STATE explicit concepts* (see Definition 23 in Sect. 2). This helps each KnowLang concept to be specified with a set of important states the concept instances can be in. Thus, we explicitly specify a variety of states for important concepts (e.g., states "operational" and "non-operational" for the robot's Motion System). A KnowLang state is specified as a Boolean expression over ontology where we can use activation of events, execution of actions or changes in properties to build a state's Boolean expression [12]. Further, to facilitate the evaluation of complex states, we specify *PREDICATES* (see Definition 40 in Sect. 2). Complex states (e.g., system states) are the product of other states (e.g., the states of the system's components). States (usually system states) are also used to specify *GOALS*, another class of KnowLang explicit concepts (see Definition 22 in Sect. 2). Goals participate in the specification of KnowLang policies. A goal can be specified as a transition from a state to another. Recall that policies and situations participate in KnowLang relations (see Definition 19 in Sect. 2) that drive the *self-adaptive behaviour* (see Sect. 5). Therefore, because every situation is explicitly related to a state (a situation is determined by a state), it is relatively easy to check for the feasibility of a policy triggered by a specific situation, i.e., the policy's goal must have the same departing state as the situation's state.

3.3   Converting Sensory Data to KR Symbols

One of the biggest challenges is *"how to map sensory raw data to KR symbols"*. Our approach to this problem is to specify special explicit concepts called *METRICS* (see Definition 17 in Sect. 2). In general, a SCE system has sensors that connect it to the world and eventually help it to listen to its internal components.

These sensors generate raw data that represent the physical characteristics of the world. The problem is that these low-level data streams must be: 1) converted to programming variables or more complex data structures that represent collections of sensory data; 2) those programing data structures must be labeled with KR Symbols. Hence, it is required to relate encoded data structures with KR concepts and objects used for reasoning purposes. In our approach, we assume that each sensor is controlled by a software driver (e.g., specified in SCEL and implemented in Java) where appropriate methods are used to control the sensor and read data from it. Both the *sensory data* and *sensors* should be represented in the KB by using *METRIC* explicit concepts and instantiate objects of these concepts. By specifying a METRIC concept we introduce a *class of sensors* to the KB and by specifying objects, instances of that class, we give the actual KR of a real sensor. KnowLang allows the specification of four different types of metrics [12]:

- RESOURCE – measure SC resources like capacity;
- QUALITY – measure SC qualities like performance, response time, etc.;
- ENVIRONMENT – measure environment qualities and resources;
- ENSEMBLE – measure SCE qualities and resource; might be a function of multiple SC metrics both of RESOURCE and QUALITY type.

4   KnowLang Syntax

We used the Backus-Naur Form (BNF) notation [6] to describe the syntax of the language and formally specify the KnowLang Grammar [12]. This helps the KnowLang framework to process sentences written in the KnowLang language. BNF [6] is a powerful meta-language that allows a context-free grammar specification. A partial presentation of the KnowLang Grammar in BNF is the following [12]:

```
KL-Spec := bof Knowledge-Spec eof
Knowledge-Spec := Spec-References KL-Spec-Units
Knowledge-Spec := KL-Spec-Units
KL-Spec-Units := KL-Corpuses KL-Operators Inference-Primitives
...
KL-Spec-Units := KL-Corpuses
KL-Spec-Units := KL-Operators
KL-Spec-Units := Inference-Primitives
```

As shown, the full KnowLang context-free grammar specification is obtained by the reduction of the (*KL-Spec -> bof Knowledge-Spec eof*) rule, which determines that a KB specified with KnowLang consists of *specification units*, each formed by a combination of *knowledge corpuses*, *KB operators* and *inference primitives*. Due to the complex structure of the KnowLang specification model (see Sect. 2) where each tier has its own structure, the complete KnowLang Grammar's specification cannot be presented here (please refer to [12] for the full KnowLang Grammar in BNF). Instead, we present an abstraction of the KnowLang Grammar, i.e., a meta-grammar. The following is a generic meta-grammar in Extended BNF [6] presenting the syntax rules for specifying KnowLang tiers.

```
GroupTier := FINAL? GroupTierId { Tier+ }
Tier := FINAL? TierId TierName? { TierClause+ }
TierClause := FINAL? ClauseId ClauseName? { Data* }
Data := PredefType | ConceptNames | BlnExpr | Reference | Number
ConceptNames := ConceptName [,ConceptName]*
```

As shown, in general a KnowLang tier is syntactically specified with a *tier identifier* (predefined KnowLang name), an optional *name* and a *content block* bordered by curly braces. Moreover, we distinguish two syntactical tier types: *single tiers* (*Tier*) and *group tiers* (*GroupTier*) where the latter comprise a set of single tiers. Each single tier has an optional *name* (*TierName*) and comprises a set of *tier clauses* (*TierClause*), which are composed of a *clause identifier*, an optional *clause name* and optional *data* (*Data*). The latter presents a predefined KnowLang type (e.g., $METRIC$ type), a collection of names (e.g., concept names or objects names), a Boolean expression over ontology, an implementation reference (e.g., $IMPL\{Sensors.LightSensor.getSourceAngle()\}$) or a number. Note that identifiers participating in KnowLang expressions are either simple, consisting of a single identifier, or qualified, consisting of a sequence of identifiers separated by "." tokens. Identifiers could be concept names, object names, relation names, predicate names, property names or function names, and it is important to specify them with their qualified name, e.g., pointing where a concept resides in a concept tree. When we use ".." token, we let the KnowLang Reasoner find the specified identifier presuming it is unique in the current tree.

5   KR for Self-adaptive Behaviour with KnowLang

KnowLang has intrinsic features supporting KR for autonomic systems. An *autonomic system* [5,13] is considered to be a self-adaptive system that changes its behaviour in response to stimuli from its execution and operational environment. Such behaviour is considered *autonomic* and *self-adaptive* [13] and is intended to drive a system in situations requiring adaptation. Any long-running system is subject to uncertainty in its execution environment due to potential changes in requirements, business conditions, available technology, etc. Thus, it is important to capture and cater for uncertainty as part of the development process. Failure to do so may result in systems that are too rigid to be fit for purpose, which is of particular concern for the domains that typically make use of self-adaptive technology. We hypothesize that modeling uncertainty and developing mechanisms for managing it as part of KR&R will lead to systems that are:

- more expressive of the real world;
- fault tolerant due to fluctuations in requirements and conditions being anticipated;
- flexible and able to manage dynamic changes.

The ability to represent knowledge providing for *self-adaptive behaviour* is an important factor in dealing with uncertainty. In our approach, the autonomic self-adaptive behaviour is provided by *policies, events, actions, situations*, and *relations* between policies and situations (see Definitions 18 through 25 in Sect. 2).

Ideally, policies are specified to handle specific situations, which may trigger the application of policies. A policy exhibits a behaviour via actions generated in the environment or in the system itself. Specific conditions determine, which specific actions (among the actions associated with that policy – see Definition 19 in Sect. 2) shall be executed. These conditions are often generic and may differ from the situations triggering the policy. Thus, the behaviour not only depends on the specific situations a policy is specified to handle, but also depends on additional conditions. Such conditions might be organized in a way allowing for synchronization of different situations on the same policy. When a policy is applied, it checks what particular conditions are met and performs the associated actions via special mappings (see $map(N_\pi, A_\pi, [Z])$) in Definition 19 in Sect. 2). An optional probability distribution (Z) may additionally restrict the action execution. Although initially specified, the probability distribution at the mappings is recomputed after the execution of any involved action. The recomputation is based on the consequences of the action execution, which allows for reinforcement leaning.

The cardinality of the *policy-situation relationship* is many-to-many, i.e., a situation might be associated with many policies and vice versa. The set of *policy situations* (situations triggering a policy) is open-ended, i.e., new situations might be added or old might be removed from there by the system itself. Moreover, with a set of *policy-situation relations* we may grant the system with an initial *probabilistic belief* (see Definition 19) that certain situations require specific policies to be applied. Runtime factors may change this probabilistic belief with time, so the most likely situations a policy is associated with can be changed. For example, the successful rate of actions execution associated with a specific situation and a policy may change such a probabilistic belief and place a specific policy higher in the "list" of associated policies, which will change the behaviour of the system when a specific situation is to be handled. Note that situations are associated with a state (see Definition 25) and a policy has a goal (see Definition 19), which is considered as a transition from one state to another (see Definition 2). Hence, the *policy-situation relations* and the employed *probabilistic beliefs* may help a cognitive system what desired state to choose, based on past experience.

As a proof of concept, we applied the approach to a case study on Ensemble of Robots. To illustrate autonomous behaviour based on this approach, let us suppose that we have a marXbot robot that carries items from point A to point B by using two possible routes – route one and route two (see Fig. 2).

A situation si_1: *"robot is in point A and loaded with items"* will trigger a policy π_1: *"go to point B via route one"* if the relation $r(si_1, \pi_1)$ has the higher probabilistic belief rate (let's assume that such a rate has been initially given to this relation because *route one* is shorter – see Fig. 2a). Any time when the robot gets into situation si_1 it will continue applying the π_1 policy until it gets into a situation si_2: *"route one is blocked"* while applying that policy. The si_2 situation will trigger a policy π_2: *"go back to si_1 and then apply policy π_3"* (see Fig. 2.b). Policy π_3 is defined as π_3: *"go to point B via route two"*. The

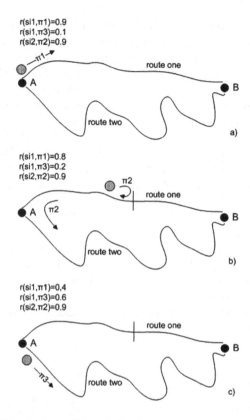

r(si1,π1)=0.9
r(si1,π3)=0.1
r(si2,π2)=0.9

route one

A

B

route two

a)

r(si1,π1)=0.8
r(si1,π3)=0.2
r(si2,π2)=0.9

π2

route one

A π2

B

route two

b)

r(si1,π1)=0,4
r(si1,π3)=0.6
r(si2,π2)=0.9

route one

A

B

π3

route two

c)

Fig. 2. A marXbot Self-adaptation Case Study

unsuccessful application of policy π_1 will decrease the probabilistic belief rate of relation $r(si_1, \pi_1)$ and the eventual successful application of policy π_3 will increase the probabilistic belief rate of relation $r(si_1, \pi_3)$ (see Fig. 2b). Thus, if route one continues to be blocked in the future, the relation $r(si_1, \pi_3)$ will get to have a higher probabilistic belief rate than the relation $r(si_1, \pi_1)$ and the robot will change its behaviour by choosing route two as a primary route (see Fig. 2c). Similarly, this situation can change in response to external stimuli, e.g., *route two* got blocked or a *"route one is obstacle-free"* message is received by the robot.

6 Formalizing eMobility with KnowLang

In eMobility, vehicles move according to a schedule defined by a driver [9,10]. Every e-vehicle component is responsible for driving along the optimal route, meeting time constraints imposed by the driver's schedule and reserving spaces at a particular Point of Interest (POI). Vehicles are competing for infrastructure resources of the traffic environment and a set of locally optimal solutions should be computed for each individual driver. Each e-vehicle is equipped with a Vehicle Planning Utility (Route Planner) that plans travels including a set of alternative routes. Traffic routes are composed of multiple driving locations, e.g., POIs. A set of locally optimal solutions is computed for each individual user. This set is negotiated on a global level in order to satisfy the global perspective. The set of locally optimal solutions guarantees a minimum quality for each individual driver. The global optimization scheme guarantees optimal resource distribution within the local constraints. The size of the set of locally optimal solutions determines the cooperative nature of the individual driver. The smaller the set, the more competitive the driver is. The larger the set the more cooperative the driver is. The process of Route Selection (RouteSAM) advises on a route choice, which is made from a set of alternative routes generated by the route planner. The RouteSAM considers road capacity and traffic levels. It optimizes overall throughput of the roads by balancing the route assignments of the vehicles. From a local vehicle perspective the journey time is minimized, from a global perspective, the congestion levels are minimized. The route selection process strives to satisfy global optimality criteria of road capacity. Once a vehicle is in the close vicinity of a destination, it computes a set of locally optimal parking lots. Again, the selection process of parking lots satisfies global optimality criteria of parking capacity.

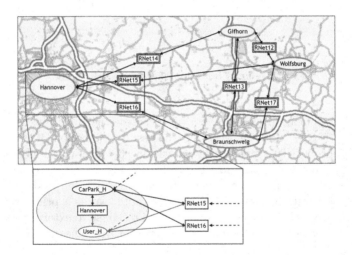

Fig. 3. eMobility Example [10]

Figure 3 shows a formal petri net representation of a real example scenario that considers four destinations (Wolfsburg, Gifhorn, Braunschweig, and Hannover), the road network between the destinations and the processes which are taking place at the destination locations [10]. The road network is described by several transition framed sub nets (e.g. RNet15). It is assumed that the journeys between destinations contain a limited set of variants. Typically three alternative routes and three alternative driving styles are considered, generating a set of maximally 9 variants. Each destination is represented by a transition framed subnet (e.g. Hannover), which models both the vehicle charging process (e.g. CarPark H) and user specific processes (e.g. User H) such as appointments. The charging stations that are connected to the car parks support three different charging modes (normal, fast and ultra-fast charging).

In this constraint environment, self-adaption is required by situations that occur when the availability of infrastructure resources does not match the demand – not enough capacity, or environment constraints (e.g., speed limit, or delay due to high traffic) hinder the e-vehicle goals. eMobility considers five different levels of self-adaptation [8]:

- *Level-1*: A vehicle computes a set of alternative routes for its current destination. This operation is performed locally by the use of the vehicle's planning utility.
- *Level-2*: A vehicle chooses the best option from those alternatives that are computed in the previous level. The vehicle observes the situation and adapts by triggering a new adaptation cycle, starting at Level-1 to the changes in the environment. This operation may require central planning and reasoning at group (ensemble) level.
- *Level-3*: A vehicle computes a set of parking lots nearby the current destination. This operation is local and is performed by the vehicle's planning utility.
- *Level-4*: A central parking lot planner (PLCSSAM) chooses the best option from those alternatives that are provided by the vehicle in the previous level. As a result vehicles are assigned an optimal or near-optimal parking lot reservation. At the same time, a "near-optimal parking lot" load balancing is established.
- *Level-5*: A vehicle issues a reservation request to the selected parking lot. As a result the parking space at that parking lot is booked. Both the vehicle and the parking lot monitor the situation. If required, a new adaptation cycle is triggered.

Based on the rationale above, we derived the eMobility goals along with the self-* objectives assisting these goals when self-adaptation is required. Note that the required analysis and process of building the goals model for eMobility along with the process of deriving the adaptation-supporting self-* objectives is beyond the scope of this paper. Figure 4 depicts a goals model for eMobility where goals are organized hierarchically at four different levels. As shown, the goals from the first two levels (e.g., "Take Journey", "Arive on Time", "Provide Route", "Provide Parking Lot", and "Sufficient Battery") are *main system goals* captured at different levels of abstraction. The 3rd level is resided by *self-* objectives* (e.g., "Optimize Speed", "Avoid Low Speed Zones", "Reduce Parking Time", and "Ensure Sufficient Battery") and *supportive goals* (e.g., "Low Route Traffic") associated with and assisting the 2nd-level goals. Finally, the goals from the 4th level are self-* objectives (e.g., "Reduce Route Traffic") assisting the supportive

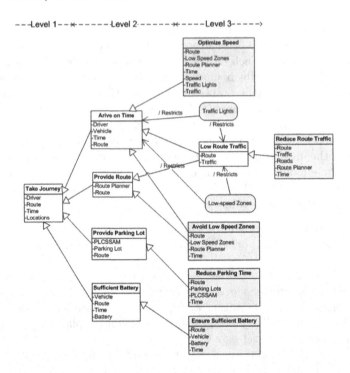

Fig. 4. eMobility Goals Model with Self-* Objectives for System Goals from Level 3

goals from the 3rd level. Basically, all the self-* objectives inherit the system goals they assist by providing behaviour alternatives with respect to these system goals. The eMobility system switches to one of the assisting self-* objectives when alternative autonomous behaviour is required (e.g., a vehicle needs to avoid low-speed zones). In addition, Fig. 4 depicts some of the environment constraints (e.g., "Traffic Lights" and "Low-speed Zones"), which may cause self-adaptation.

6.1 Specifying eMobility Ontology

In order to specify eMobility, the first step is to specify a knowledge base (KB) representing the eMobility system in question, i.e., e-vehicles, parking lots, routes, traffic lights, etc. To do so, we need to specify ontology structuring the knowledge domains of eMobility. Note that these domains are described via domain-relevant concepts and objects (concept instances) related through relations. To handle explicit concepts like situations, goals, and policies, we grant some of the domain concepts with explicit state expressions where a state expression is a Boolean expression over the ontology.

Figure 5, depicts a graphical representation of the eMobility ontology relating most of the domain concepts within an eMobility system. Note that the relationships within a concept tree are "is-a" (inheritance), e.g., the RoadElement

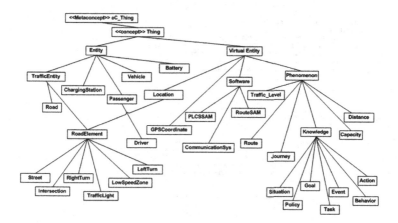

Fig. 5. eMobility Ontology Specified with KnowLang

concept is a TraficEntity and the Action concept is a Knowledge and consecutively Phenomenon, etc. Most of the concepts presented in Fig. 5 were derived from the eMobility Goals Model (see Fig. 4). Other concepts are considered as explicit and were derived from the KnowLang's specification model [22].

The following is a sample of the KnowLang specification representing three important concepts: *Vehicle*, *Journey*, and *Route*. As specified, the concepts in a concept tree might have properties of other concepts, functionalities (actions associated with that concept), states (Boolean expressions validating a specific state), etc. For example, the Vehicle's *IsMoving* state holds when the vehicle speed (the VehicleSpeed property) is greater than 0.

```
// e-Vehicle
CONCEPT Vehicle {
  PARENTS {eMobility.eCars.CONCEPT_TREES.Entity}
  CHILDREN {      }
  PROPS {
    PROP carDriver {
      TYPE {eMobility.eCars.CONCEPT_TREES.Driver} CARDINALITY {1} }
    PROP carPassengers {
      TYPE {eMobility.eCars.CONCEPT_TREES.Passenger} CARDINALITY {*} }
    PROP carBattery {
      TYPE {eMobility.eCars.CONCEPT_TREES.Battery} CARDINALITY {1} }
  }
  FUNCS {
    FUNC startEngine {TYPE {eMobility.eCars.CONCEPT_TREES.StartEngine}}
    FUNC stopEngine {TYPE {eMobility.eCars.CONCEPT_TREES.StopEngine}}
    FUNC accelerate {TYPE {eMobility.eCars.CONCEPT_TREES.Accelerate}}
    FUNC slowDown {TYPE {eMobility.eCars.CONCEPT_TREES.SlowDown}}
    FUNC startDriving {TYPE {eMobility.eCars.CONCEPT_TREES.StartDriving}}
    FUNC stopDriving {TYPE {eMobility.eCars.CONCEPT_TREES.StopDriving}}
  }
  STATES {
    STATE IsOperational{
NOT eMobility.eCars.CONCEPT_TREES.Vehicle.PROPS.carBattery.STATES.batteryLow }
    STATE IsMoving{ eMobility.eCars.CONCEPT_TREES.VehicleSpeed > 0 }
  }
}

CONCEPT Journey {
  PARENTS {eMobility.eCars.CONCEPT_TREES.Phenomenon}
  CHILDREN {}
  PROPS {
    PROP journeyRoute {TYPE {eMobility.eCars.CONCEPT_TREES.Route} CARDINALITY {1}}
    PROP journeyTime {TYPE {DATETIME} CARDINALITY {1}}
    PROP journeyCars {TYPE {eMobility.eCars.CONCEPT_TREES.Vehicle} CARDINALITY {*}}
  }
  STATES
  {
```

```
STATE InSufficientBattery {/* to specify */}
STATE InNotSufficientBattery {
    NOT eMobility.eCars.CONCEPT_TREES.Journey.STATES.InSufficientBattery}
STATE Arrived {eMobility.eCars.CONCEPT_TREES.Journey.PROPS.journeyRoute.STATES.AtEnd}
STATE ArrivedOnTime { eMobility.eCars.CONCEPT_TREES.Journey.STATES.Arrived AND
                    (eMobility.eCars.CONCEPT_TREES.JourneyTime <=
                        eMobility.eCars.CONCEPT_TREES.Journey.PROPS.journeyTime)
                    }
    }
}

CONCEPT Route {
  PARENTS {eMobility.eCars.CONCEPT_TREES.Phenomenon}
  CHILDREN {}
  PROPS {
    PROP locationA {TYPE {eMobility.eCars.CONCEPT_TREES.Location} CARDINALITY {1}}
    PROP locationB {TYPE {eMobility.eCars.CONCEPT_TREES.Location} CARDINALITY {1}}
    PROP intermediateStops {TYPE {eMobility.eCars.CONCEPT_TREES.Location} CARDINALITY {*}}
    PROP currentRoad {TYPE {eMobility.eCars.CONCEPT_TREES.Road} CARDINALITY {1}}
    PROP alternativeRoads {TYPE {eMobility.eCars.CONCEPT_TREES.Road} CARDINALITY {*}}
  }
  FUNCS {
    FUNC getCurrentLocation {TYPE {eMobility.eCars.CONCEPT_TREES.GetCurrentLocation}}
    FUNC takeAlternativeRoad {TYPE {eMobility.eCars.CONCEPT_TREES.TakeAlternativeRoad}}
    FUNC recomputeRoads {TYPE {eMobility.eCars.CONCEPT_TREES.RecomputeRoads}}
  }
  STATES {
    STATE AtBeginning {eMobility.eCars.CONCEPT_TREES.Route.FUNCS.getCurrentLocation =
                        eMobility.eCars.CONCEPT_TREES.Route.PROPS.locationA}
    STATE AtEnd {eMobility.eCars.CONCEPT_TREES.Route.FUNCS.getCurrentLocation =
                    eMobility.eCars.CONCEPT_TREES.Route.PROPS.locationB}
    STATE OnRoute { NOT eMobility.eCars.CONCEPT_TREES.Route.STATES.AtBeginning AND
                    NOT eMobility.eCars.CONCEPT_TREES.Route.STATES.AtEnd}
    STATE InHighTraffic {
        eMobility.eCars.CONCEPT_TREES.Route.PROPS.currentRoad.STATES.InHighTraffic}
    STATE InLowTraffic {
        eMobility.eCars.CONCEPT_TREES.Route.PROPS.currentRoad.STATES.InFluentTraffic}
  }
}
```

As mentioned above, the states are specified as Boolean expressions. For example, the state *Route*'s *OnRoute* holds (is true) while the *Route* is neither *AtBeginning* nor at *AtEnd* states. A concept realization is an object instantiated from that concept. As shown, a complex state might be expressed as a Boolean function over other states. For example, the *Journey*'s state *Arrived OnTime* is expressed as a Bollean expression involving the *Journey*'s *Arrived* state and *Journey*'s properties.

Note that *states* are extremely important to the specification of *goals* (objectives), *situations*, and *policies*. For example, states help the KnowLang Reasoner determine at runtime whether the system is in a particular situation or a particular goal (objective) has been achieved.

6.2   Specifying Self-Adaptive Behaviour

To specify self-* objectives with KnowLang, we use *goals*, *policies*, and *situations*. These are defined as explicit concepts in KnowLang, and for the eMobility Ontology we specified them under the concepts *Virtual_entity→Phenomenon→ Knowledge* (see Fig. 5). Figure 6, depicts a concept tree representing the specified eMobility goals. Note that most of these goals were directly interpolated from the goals model (see Fig. 4).

Recall that KnowLang specifies goals as functions of states where any combination of states can be involved. A goal has an arriving state (Boolean function of states) and an optional departing state (another Boolean function of states). A goal with departing state is more restrictive, i.e., it can be achieved only if the system departs from the specific goal's departing state.

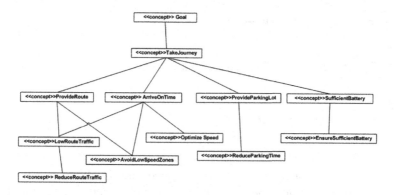

Fig. 6. eMobility Ontology: eMobility Goal Concept Tree

The following code samples present the specification of two simple goals. Usually, goals' arriving and departing states can be either single states or sequences of states. Note that the states used to specify the goals below are specified as part of both *Journey* and *Route* concepts.

```
//
//==== eMobility Goals ===========================================
//
CONCEPT_GOAL ArriveOnTime {
  CHILDREN {eMobility.eCars.CONCEPT_TREES.Goal}
  PARENTS {}
  SPEC {
    DEPART { eMobility.eCars.CONCEPT_TREES.Journey.PROPS.journeyRoute.STATES.AtEnd }
    ARRIVE { eMobility.eCars.CONCEPT_TREES.Journey.STATES.ArrivedOnTime }
  }
}
CONCEPT_GOAL LowRouteTraffic {
  CHILDREN {eMobility.eCars.CONCEPT_TREES.Goal}
  PARENTS {}
  SPEC {
    DEPART { eMobility.eCars.CONCEPT_TREES.Route.STATES.InHighTraffic }
    ARRIVE { eMobility.eCars.CONCEPT_TREES.Route.STATES.InLowTraffic }
  }
}
```

The following is a specification sample showing an eMobility policy called *Reduce RouteTraffic* – as the name says, this policy is intended to reduce the route traffic. As shown, the policy is specified to handle the goal *LowRouteTraffic* and is triggered by the situation *RouteTrafficIncreased*. Further, the policy triggers via its *MAPPING* sections conditionally (e.g., there is a *CONDITONS* directive that requires the *Route*'s state *OnRoute* to be hold) the execution of a sequence of actions. When the conditions are the same, we specify a probability distribution among the *MAPPING* sections involving same conditions (e.g., *PROBABILITY*0.7), which represents our initial belief in action choice.

```
CONCEPT_POLICY ReduceRouteTraffic {
  CHILDREN {}
  PARENTS {eMobility.eCars.CONCEPT_TREES.Policy}
  SPEC {
    POLICY_GOAL {eMobility.eCars.CONCEPT_TREES.LowRouteTraffic}
    POLICY_SITUATIONS {eMobility.eCars.CONCEPT_TREES.RouteTrafficIncreased}
    POLICY_RELATIONS {eMobility.eCars.RELATIONS.Situation_Policy_1}
    POLICY_ACTIONS {eMobility.eCars.CONCEPT_TREES.TakeAlternativeRoad,
                    eMobility.eCars.CONCEPT_TREES.RecomputeRoads}
    POLICY_MAPPINGS {
      MAPPING {
        CONDITIONS {eMobility.eCars.CONCEPT_TREES.Route.STATES.OnRoute}
```

```
        DO_ACTIONS {eMobility.eCars.CONCEPT_TREES.Route.FUNCS.takeAlternativeRoad}
        PROBABILITY {0.7}
      }
      MAPPING {
        CONDITIONS { eMobility.eCars.CONCEPT_TREES.Route.STATES.OnRoute}
        DO_ACTIONS { eMobility.eCars.CONCEPT_TREES.Route.FUNCS.recomputeRoads,
                     eMobility.eCars.CONCEPT_TREES.Route.FUNCS.takeAlternativeRoad}
        PROBABILITY {0.3}
      }
      MAPPING {
        CONDITIONS { eMobility.eCars.CONCEPT_TREES.Route.STATES.AtBeginning}
        DO_ACTIONS { eMobility.eCars.CONCEPT_TREES.Route.FUNCS.recomputeRoads,
                     eMobility.eCars.CONCEPT_TREES.Route.FUNCS.takeAlternativeRoad}
      }
    }
  }
}
```

As specified, the probability distribution gives initial designer's preference about what actions should be executed if the system ends up in running the *ReduceRouteTraffic* policy. Note that at runtime, the KnowLang Reasoner maintains a record of all the action executions and re-computes the probability rates every time when a policy has been applied and consecutively, actions have been executed. Thus, although initially the system will execute the function *takeAlternativeRoad* (it has the higher probability rate of 0.7), if that policy cannot achieve its goal with this action, then the probability distribution will be shifted in favor of the function sequence *recomputeRoads, takeAlternativeRoad*, which might be executed the next time when the system will try to apply the same policy. Therefore, probabilities are recomputed after every action execution, and thus the behaviour change accordingly.

Moreover, to increase the goal-oriented autonomicity, in policy specification, we may use a special operator implemented in KnowLang called *GENERATE _NEXT_ACTIONS*. This operator will automatically generate the most appropriate actions to be undertaken by eMobility. The action generation is based on the computations performed by a special *reward function* implemented by the KnowLang Reasoner. The *KnowLang Reward Function* (KLRF) observes the outcome of the actions to compute the possible successor states of every possible action execution and grants the actions with special reward number considering the current system state (or states, if the current state is a composite state) and goals. KLRF is based on past experience and uses Discrete Time Markov Chains [3] for probability assessment after action executions [22].

Note that when generating actions, the *GENERATE_NEXT_ACTIONS* operator follows a sequential decision-making algorithm where actions are selected to maximize the total reward. This means that the immediate reward of the execution of the first action, of the generated list of actions, might not be the highest one, but the overall reward of executing all the generated actions will be the highest possible one. Moreover, note that, the generated actions are selected from the predefined set of actions (e.g., the implemented eMobility actions). The principle of the decision-making algorithm used to select actions is as follows:

1. The average cumulative reward of the reinforcement learning system is calculated.
2. For each policy-action mapping, the KnowLang Reasoner learns the value function, which is relative to the sum of average reward.

3. According to the value function and *Bellman optimality principle*[1], is generated the optimal sequence of actions.

As mentioned above, policies are triggered by situations. Therefore, while specifying policies handling eMobility objectives, we need to think of important situations that may trigger those policies. These situations shall be eventually outlined by scenarios. A single policy requires to be associated with (related to) at least one situation, but for polices handling self-* objectives we eventually need more situations. Actually, because the policy-situation relation is bidirectional, it is maybe more accurate to say that a single situation may need more policies, those providing alternative behaviours or execution paths out of that situation. The following code represents the specification of the situation *RouteTrafficIncreased*, used for the specification of the *ReduceRouteTraffic* policy.

```
CONCEPT_SITUATION RouteTrafficIncreased {
  CHILDREN {}
  PARENTS {eMobility.eCars.CONCEPT_TREES.Situation}
  SPEC {
    SITUATION_STATES {eMobility.eCars.CONCEPT_TREES.Route.STATES.InHighTraffic}
    SITUATION_ACTIONS {eMobility.eCars.CONCEPT_TREES.TakeAlternativeRoad}
  }
}
}
```

As shown, the situation is specified with $SITATION\_STATES$ (e.g., *InHigh Traffic*) and $SITUATION\_ACTIONS$ (e.g., *TakeAlterna-tiveRoad*). To consider a situation effective (i.e., the system is currently in that situation), the situation states must be respectively effective (evaluated as true). For example, the situation *RouteTraf-ficIncreased* is effective if the *Route*'s state *InHighTraffic* is effective (is hold). The possible actions define what actions can be undertaken once the system falls in a particular situation. For example, the *RouteTrafficIncreased* situation has one possible action: *TakeAlternative Road*.

Recall that situations are related to policies via relations. The following code demonstrates how we related the situation *RouteTrafficIncreased* to the policy *Reduce-RouteTraffic*.

```
RELATION Situation_Policy_1{
  RELATION_PAIR {
    eMobility.eCars.CONCEPT_TREES.RouteTrafficIncreased,
    eMobility.eCars.CONCEPT_TREES.ReduceRouteTraffic}
  }
}
```

In general, a self-adaptive system has sensors that connect it to the world and eventually help it listen to its internal components. These sensors generate raw data that represent the physical characteristics of the world. The representation of monitoring sensors in KnowLang is handled via the explicit *Metric concept* [22]. In our approach, we assume that eMobility sensors are controlled by software drivers (e.g., implemented in C++) where appropriate methods are

---

[1] The Bellman optimality principle: If a given state-action sequence is optimal, and we were to remove the first state and action, the remaining sequence is also optimal (with the second state of the original sequence now acting as initial state).

used to control a sensor and read data from it. By specifying a *Metric* concept we introduce a class of sensors to the KB and by specifying objects, instances of that class, we represent the real sensor. KnowLang allows the specification of four different types of metrics [22]:

- *RESOURCE* – measure resources like capacity;
- *QUALITY* – measure qualities like performance, response ti-me, etc.;
- *ENVIRONMENT* – measure environment qualities and resources;
- *ENSEMBLE* – measure complex qualities and resources where the metric might be a function of multiple metrics both of *RESOURCE* and *QUALITY* type.

The following is a specification of metrics mainly used to assist the specification of states in the specification of the eMobility concept (see Sect. 6.1).

```
// metrics
CONCEPT_METRIC RoadTrafficLevel {
   CHILDREN {}
   PARENTS {eMobility.eCars.CONCEPT_TREES.Metric}
   SPEC {
      METRIC_TYPE { ENVIRONMENT }
      METRIC_SOURCE {        "ECarClass.GetRoadTrafficLevel" }
      DATA_TYPE { NUMBER }
   }
}
CONCEPT_METRIC BatteryEnergyLevel {
   CHILDREN {}
   PARENTS {eMobility.eCars.CONCEPT_TREES.Metric}
   SPEC {
      METRIC_TYPE { RESOURCE }
      METRIC_SOURCE {        "ECarClass.GetBatteryEnergyLevel" }
      DATA_TYPE { NUMBER }
   }
}
CONCEPT_METRIC VehicleSpeed {
   CHILDREN {}
   PARENTS {eMobility.eCars.CONCEPT_TREES.Metric}
   SPEC {
      METRIC_TYPE { RESOURCE }
      METRIC_SOURCE {        "ECarClass.GetVehicleSpeed" }
      DATA_TYPE { NUMBER }
   }
}
CONCEPT_METRIC JourneyTime {
   CHILDREN {}
   PARENTS {eMobility.eCars.CONCEPT_TREES.Metric}
   SPEC {
      METRIC_TYPE { RESOURCE }
      METRIC_SOURCE {        "ECarClass.GetJourneyTime" }
      DATA_TYPE { DATETIME }
   }
}
```

7 Conclusion and Future Work

In the course of this R&D process, we shaped our research activities towards focusing on the KnowLang Framework where our ultimate goal is to structure computerized knowledge so that a computerized system can effectively process it and gain awareness capabilities and eventually derive its own behaviour. To provide comprehensive and powerful specification formalism, we developed a powerful multi-tier specification model where ontologies are integrated with rules and Bayesian networks. The approach allows for efficient and comprehensive knowledge structuring and awareness based on logical and statistical reasoning. We used the KnowLang notation to specify some knowledge models for different case studies. This exercise demonstrated the ability of KnowLang to handle KR for systems from different application domains. A very important feature is the KnowLang mechanism for self-adaptive behaviour where knowledge representation and reasoning help to establish the vital connection between knowledge, perception, and actions realizing self-adaptive behaviour. The knowledge is used against the perception of the world to generate appropriate actions in compliance to some goals and beliefs.

Future work is mainly concerned with further development of the KnowLang Reasoner as part of the full implementation of the KnowLang Framework, involving tools and a test bed for verification and validation of KnowLang models.

Acknowledgements. This work was supported, in part, by Science Foundation Ireland grant 13/RC/ 2094_P2 and co-funded under the European Regional Development Fund through the Southern & Eastern Regional Operational Programme to Lero–the Science Foundation Ireland Research Centre for Software (www.lero.ie) and by University of Limerick, Limerick, Ireland.

References

1. Baader, F., Nutt, W.: Basic description logics. In: Baader, F., Calvanese, D., McGuinness, D.L., Nardi, D., Patel-Schneider, P.F. (eds.) The Description Logic Handbook, pp. 43–95. Cambridge University Press, Cambridge (2003)
2. Brachman, R., Levesque, H.: Knowledge Representation and Reasoning. Elsevier, New York (2004)
3. Ewens, W., Grant, G.: Stochastic Processes (i): Poison Processes and Markov Chains. Statistical Methods in Bioinformatics, 2nd edn. (2005)
4. Halpern, J.Y.: An analysis of first-order logics of probability. Artif. Intell. **46**, 311–350 (1990)
5. Kephart, J.O., Chess, D.M.: The vision of autonomic computing. IEEE Comput. **36**(1), 41–50 (2003)
6. Knuth, D.E.: Backus normal form vs. backus naur form. Commun. ACM **7**(12), 735–736 (1964)
7. Neapolitan, R.: Learning Bayesian Networks. Prentice Hall, Hoboken (2003)
8. Serbedzija, N., et al.: D7.3: Third Report on WP7 Integration and Simulation Report for the ASCENS Case Studies (2013). ASCENS Deliverable
9. Serbedzija, N., et al.: D7.2: Second Report on WP7 Ensemble Model Syntheses with Robot, Cloud Computing and e-Mobility (2012). ASCENS Deliverable
10. Serbedzija, N., et al.: D7.1: First Report on WP7 Requirement Specification and Scenario Description of the ASCENS Case Studies (2011). ASCENS Deliverable
11. Vassev, E.: ASSL: Autonomic System Specification Language - A Framework for Specification and Code Generation of Autonomic Systems. LAP Lambert Academic Publishing (2009)
12. Vassev, E.: KnowLang grammar in BNF. Technical report. Lero-TR-2012-04, Lero, University of Limerick, Ireland (2012)
13. Vassev, E., Hinchey, M.: The challenge of developing autonomic systems. IEEE Comput. **43**(12), 93–96 (2010)

14. Vassev, E., Hinchey, M.: Towards a formal language for knowledge representation in autonomic service-component ensembles. In: Proceedings of the 3rd International Conference on Data Mining and Intelligent Information Technology Applications (ICMIA 2011), pp. 228–235. AICIT, IEEE Xplore (2011)

15. Vassev, E., Hinchey, M.: Awareness in software-intensive systems. IEEE Comput. **45**(12), 84–87 (2012)

16. Vassev, E., Hinchey, M.: Efficient reasoning with ambient trees for space exploration. In: Vinh, P.C., Hung, N.M., Tung, N.T., Suzuki, J. (eds.) ICCASA 2012. LNICST, vol. 109, pp. 176–182. Springer, Heidelberg (2013). https://doi.org/10.1007/978-3-642-36642-0_18

17. Vassev, E., Hinchey, M.: Knowledge representation for cognitive robotic systems. In: Proceedings of the 15th IEEE International Symposium on Object/Component/Service-oriented Real-time Distributed Computing Workshops (ISCORCW 2012), pp. 156–163. IEEE Computer Society (2012)

18. Vassev, E., Hinchey, M.: Knowledge representation with KnowLang - the marXbot case study. In: Proceedings of the 11th IEEE International Conference on Cybernetic Intelligent Systems (CIS 2012). IEEE Computer Society (2012)

19. Vassev, E., Hinchey, M.: Knowledge representation and reasoning for self-adaptive behavior and awareness. TCCI - Special Issue on ICECCS 2012 (2013, pending)

20. Vassev, E., Hinchey, M., Gaudin, B.: Knowledge representation for self-adaptive behavior. In: Proceedings of C* Conference on Computer Science & Software Engineering (C3S2E 2012), pp. 113–117. ACM (2012)

21. Vassev, E., Hinchey, M., Gaudin, B., Nixon, P., Bicocchi, N., Zambonelli, F.: D3.1: First Report on WP3. Software requirements, knowledge modeling and knowledge representation for self-awareness - report and survey with experimental results for intelligent multi-agent systems (2011). ASCENS Deliverable

22. Vassev, E., Hinchey, M., Montanari, U., Bicocchi, N., Zambonelli, F., Wirsing, M.: D3.2: Second Report on WP3: The KnowLang Framework for Knowledge Modeling for SCE Systems (2012). ASCENS Deliverable

The Future Roadmap

A Coq Implementation of the Program Algebra in Jifeng He's New Roadmap for Linking Theories of Programming

Rundong Mu and Qin Li[✉]

Shanghai Key Laboratory of Trustworthy Computing, East China Normal University,
Shanghai, China
qli@sei.ecnu.edu.cn

Abstract. Jifeng He has proposed a roadmap for linking theories of programming and presents an algebra of programs capable of generating both denotational and operational representations from the refinement relation. In this paper, we implement this algebra of programs and its refinement relation using the interactive theorem prover Coq. Encoding the algebra into CIC (Calculus of Inductive Constructions), the main formalism in Coq, facilitates machine-aided interactive proving for the properties of programs using predefined algebraic laws. The implementation of the algebra for finite programs enables us to prove that every finite program can be reduced to the normal form and to check the refinement between two finite programs. The implementation of the algebra for infinite programs supports formalizing recursive programs with one variable and checking the refinement between one finite and one infinite program. Then, we present examples of proving the refinement relationship between two finite programs and a finite program and an infinite program.

Keywords: Unifying theories of programming · Coq · Program algebra · Refinement

1 Introduction

Formal semantics for programs are usually constructed using one of two approaches, as described in [7]. The first approach is a top-down approach that starts with a denotational model and links the algebraic properties with it by establishing the soundness and completeness between them. This approach is used in works such as [2,4,14]. The second approach is a bottom-up approach that begins with an operational representation and defines a rich variety of bisimulations to identify the equivalences among programs. This approach is used in works such as [1,15]. Algebraic laws are then generated from the study of the equivalence relations like [16].

In Jifeng He's paper [7], he explores a new roadmap for linking theories of programming other than the top-down and bottom-up approaches. It begins

J. P. Bowen et al. (Eds.): *Theories of Programming and Formal Methods*, LNCS 14080, pp. 395–412, 2023.
https://doi.org/10.1007/978-3-031-40436-8_15

from an algebra of programs and generates both denotational and operational representations from the algebraic refinement relation. For the initial step of this approach, a program algebra $(\mathcal{P}, \sqsubseteq_A)$ consisting of a set of laws is presented to express the algebraic properties of programs. This program algebra is the basis of this approach, and the main criterion of the algebra is whether it is sufficient to convert every program in the domain $\mathcal{P}$ to a normal form. This criterion is stated in Theorem 2.1 in [7]. The refinement order $\sqsubseteq_A$ is defined on normal forms to support comparing the behaviors of two programs.

This paper aims to implement the program algebra in [7] with the interactive theorem prover Coq and prove the corresponding theorems relating the algebra with the aid of it. We chose Coq because of its strong type system, which can support the binding and value model required by He's model. Although efforts have been made to develop more suitable value models, such as the one proposed in [5], we opted for a deep embedding approach to gain greater control over the proof process during refinement steps. Specifically, we restrict ourselves to a monomorphic value type with a fixed representation, similar to what was done in [11]. Different from shallow embedding like [3], deep embedding allows for more accurate operations on values and enable more effective use of corresponding libraries of certain types. However, it can be less convenient for proving. By encoding in an algebraic way, we can separate the value and abstract algebra parts. For the latter, we can still leverage proof facilities to simplify the proving process. For the former, we can make assertions on values rather than providing concrete values. Additionally, deep embedding allows us to manipulate the data at a more granular level using Coq's library.

- We translated the finite operators over algebra into CIC (Calculus of Inductive Constructions) that can be accepted in Coq.
- We encoded the algebraic laws as rules that can be used for deduction between finite algebras. In doing so, we proved Theorem 2.1 in [7], which states that all finite algebras can be transformed into some normal form by giving the concrete transformation program. We proved that such transformation converts all programs to some normal form, and such transformation is only a composition of the laws outlined in He's paper.
- We provided a method to check the refinement relationship between two finite programs in mechanical proof.
- Furthermore, our work extends He's paper by providing a solution for comparing certain infinite programs and finite programs within finite steps.

The paper is organized as follows:

Section 2 briefly introduces the algebra of programs and refinement relation intended to be implemented.

Section 3 encodes the operators of the algebra into CIC and implements the algebraic laws for finite programs. The theorem that every finite program can be reduced to normal form is proved based on the implementation. Additionally, we implemented the refinement relation between finite programs and present an example of checking refinement between two finite programs.

Section 4 present our in-progress work on the infinite cases of the algebra together with an example of checking the refinement between an infinite program and a finite program.

Section 5 discusses the limitations and alternative solutions.

Section 6 concludes this article and talks about future works.

2   Preliminary

In Jifeng He's paper [7], he presents a program algebra $(\mathcal{P}, \sqsubseteq_A)$ for the following syntax of sequential programs. This algebra is built upon the foundation established by [8].

$$P, Q ::= \bot \mid var := exp \mid P \lhd bexp \rhd Q \mid P; Q \mid P \sqcap Q \mid X \mid \mu\, X \bullet P(X) \quad (1)$$

where

- $\bot$ stands for a chaotic program that does not terminate and can yield any behaviour unpredictably.
- $var := exp$ stands for the assignment statement assigning the values of a list of expressions to a list of variables.
- $P \lhd bexp \rhd Q$ stands for the conditional choice where $bexp$ is the boolean condition. It executes P when $bexp$ holds and executes Q otherwise.
- $P; Q$ stands for sequential composition.
- $P \sqcap Q$ stands for non-deterministic choice. In the following, we extend this operator to compose more than two operands. For example, $\sqcap\{P_1, P_2, ..., P_n\}$ means $P_1 \sqcap P_2 \sqcap ... \sqcap P_n$.
- X stands for a syntactic program that can be only used in the scope of a recursive program that binds it.
- $\mu X \bullet P(X)$ stands for the recursive program with X as the bounded recursive identifier.

Jifeng He developed an approach to construct algebraic equivalence classes between algebras based on some predefined algebraic laws, as detailed in Appendix A of [7]. These laws employ the $=_A$ notation to represent algebraic equivalence, which is distinct from the syntactical equality $(=)$ used in Coq. Algebraic equivalence $(=_A)$ satisfies transitivity, reflexivity, and commutativity. Additionally, it adheres to a composition law that allows any subterm within an algebra to be replaced with its corresponding subterm within the same algebraic equivalence class. We ensure that the resulting term remains within the same algebraic equivalence class as the original term.

With the algebraic equivalence defined above, we can define the normal form of programs. The normal form is defined in two ways: the finite normal form (FNF) and the infinite normal form (INF).

Definition 1 (Finite Normal Form). *Let $bexp$ be a boolean condition, $v := e_i$ be a total assignment. The finite normal form is defined as follows.*

$$\bot \lhd bexp \rhd \sqcap_i(v := e_i) \quad (2)$$

The algebraic refinement relation on the finite normal forms is defined with the following two rules.

Definition 2 (Algebraic Refinement for Finite Program). *Let P and Q be programs. The refinement order $\sqsubseteq_A$ for finite programs is defined as follows.*

1. *If $P =_A \sqcap \{v := e_i \mid i \in I\}$, $Q =_A \sqcap \{v := f_j \mid j \in J\}$, then*
   $P \sqsubseteq_A Q$ *iff for any $f \in \{f_j \mid j \in J\}$, we have $\forall x \bullet f(x) \in \{e_i(x) \mid i \in I\}$.*
2. *If $P =_A \perp \lhd b \rhd R$, $Q =_A \perp \lhd c \rhd S$, then*
   $P \sqsubseteq_A Q$ *iff $[c \Rightarrow b]$ and $[b] \vee (R \sqsubseteq_A S)$*
   The notation $[bexp]$ means $\forall v \bullet bexp(v)$ where v is the list of all free variables in bexp.

The infinite normal form is defined as the infinite sequence of finite normal forms.

Definition 3 (Infinite Normal Form). *Let S_i be programs of finite normal form $\perp \lhd b_i \rhd Q_i$, S_i, S_{i+1} form an ascending chain $S_i \sqsubseteq_A S_{i+1}$, and for any i, j with $b_i = b_j$, $\perp \lhd b_i \rhd Q_i =_A \perp \lhd b_j \rhd Q_j$. The infinite normal form is defined as follows.*

$$\sqcup \{S_i \mid i \in N\} \tag{3}$$

where $\sqcup S$ stands for the least upper bound of the set S.

The algebraic refinement relation on the infinite normal forms is defined as following two rules.

Definition 4 (Algebraic Refinement for Infinite Program). *Let P and Q be programs. The refinement order $\sqsubseteq_A$ is defined as follows.*

1. *If $S =_A \perp \lhd b \rhd R$, $T =_A \{\perp \lhd c_i \rhd U_i \mid i \in N\}$, then*
   $S \sqsubseteq_A (\sqcup T)$ *iff $[(\bigwedge c_i) \Rightarrow b]$ and $\forall i \in N \bullet R \sqsubseteq_A U_i$.*
2. *If $P =_A \sqcup \{S_i \mid i \in N\}$, $Q =_A \sqcup \{T_i \mid i \in N\}$, then*
   $P \sqsubseteq_A Q$ *iff $\forall i \in N \bullet S_i \sqsubseteq_A Q$.*

As mentioned above, the infinite program relies on finite programs and their refinement relation. Therefore, it is advisable to prioritize encoding the finite programs first.

3   Encoding Algebra for Finite Programs

Jifeng He uses algebraic laws to represent the deduction of program algebra and refinement relations. In this section, we will discuss how to encode the laws related to finite algebra into Coq code. Coq employs the formalism called Calculus of Inductive Constructions [12]. This formalism replaces property verification with the check of type signatures of expression captured by Coq's special sort, `Prop`. Moreover, inductive definitions will automatically generate induction hypotheses, which assist us in our proofs.

3.1   Translating Syntax of Finite Algebra

In this section, an inductive type `Alg` is constructed to represent all finite programs that do not include recursion. The `Alg` type is composed of two types, `Atomic` and `Comp`, which correspond to different kinds of valid program syntax.

```
Section alg.
    Inductive Atomic : Type :=
    | Chaos : Atomic
    | Assn : Assign → Atomic
    | Empty : Atomic.
    Inductive Comp : Type :=
    | Seq : Comp
    | NDC : Comp
    | CDC : Boolexp → Comp.
    Inductive Alg : Type :=
    | Lift : Atomic → Alg
    | Comb : Comp → Alg → Alg → Alg.
    Definition NDCList (l : list Alg) : Alg :=
        match l with
        | []  ⇒ Lift Empty
        | h :: tl ⇒ fold_left (fun a b ⇒ (Comb NDC a b)) tl h
        end.
End alg.
```

The finite operators in program algebra correspond to the `Comp` type. These operators include sequential composition (`Seq`), non-deterministic choice (`NDC`), and conditional choice (`CDC`). On the other hand, the chaotic program (`Chaos`) and assignment statement (`Assn`) correspond to `Atomic` type.

The symbol $\sqcap l_{n \in N}$ represents the non-deterministic choice of a set l, where N is the set of natural numbers. In our implementation, we represent sets using lists and encode the non-deterministic choice of the list as `NDCList` This encoding is straightforward, except for the empty set, which we represent using a special algebraic structure called `Empty`.

For the sake of readability, we will use the following notations to denote the syntax, the notations are similar to the original symbol in Jifeng He's paper.

The algebra of a single assignment statement can be represented using the following notation:

```
Notation "·{ e }" := (Lift (Assn e)) (at level 10).
```

The assignment statement e can be divided into two parts: the variable part and the expression part. The variable part is a user-defined type, which is injected through a type class. The expression part is simply a function, where the domain and range are both a list of variables.

```
Definition Exp := (list Var) → (list Var).
Record Assign := makeAssign {
    ids: (list Var); values : Exp;
}.
```

It can be represented using the following notation:

Notation "var :== exp" := (makeAssign var exp)(at level 51).

The chaotic program is represented using a notation similar to ⊥.

Notation "_|_" := (Lift Chaos)(at level 10).

The conditional choice of program p and q is represented using the notation below.

Notation "p <| b |> q" := (Comb (CDC b) p q) (at level 15).

The boolean condition b in the branching expression is defined as a function that takes a list of variables as its input and outputs a boolean value.

Definition Boolexp : Type := (list Var) → bool.

The notation below is used to represent the sequential composition of program p and q.

Notation "p ;; q" := (Comb Seq p q)(at level 14, left associativity).

To represent the non-deterministic choice of program p and q, we use the notation below.

Notation "p /-\ q" := (Comb NDC p q)(at level 13, left associativity).

The non-deterministic choice of a set can use the following notation.

Notation "|-| l" := (NDCList l)(at level 10).

Specifically, the representation of non-deterministic choice for the empty set is denoted using the following notation.

Notation "-o-" := (Lift Empty)(at level 10).

3.2   Representing Algebraic Equivalence Relationship

The algebraic equivalence relation ($=_A$) is a property defined on two algebras. It is denoted as rwtrel in the following Coq code.

```
Section rwtrel.
    Parameter rwtrel : Alg → Alg → Prop.
    Axiom rwt_refl : forall (a: Alg), rwtrel a a.
    Axiom rwt_trans : forall (a b c : Alg), rwtrel a b →
        rwtrel b c → rwtrel a c.
    Axiom rwt_comm : forall (a b : Alg), rwtrel a b → rwtrel b a.
    Axiom rwt_comb : forall (a b c d : Alg) (e : Comp), rwtrel a b →
        rwtrel c d → rwtrel (Comb e a c) (Comb e b d).
End rwtrel.
Notation "a ←→ b" := (rwtrel a b) (at level 20, left associativity).
```

The relation satisfies the properties of reflexivity, transitivity, commutativity, and the composition law. These properties correspond to the following axioms: rwt_refl, rwt_trans, rwt_comm, and rwt_comb.

The notation ($\longleftrightarrow$) is used to represent algebraic equivalence ($=_A$). In the code that follows, all algebraic laws for the program algebras described in [7] are expressed using rwtrel.

3.3   Encoding the Algebraic Laws

All algebraic laws can be categorized into three layers. The first layer concerns operations on assignments, while the second layer involves the combination of non-deterministic choices over different assignments. The third layer deals with operations on the finite normal form (without recursion). With the help of these predefined algebraic laws, we intend to establish a theorem saying that all finite programs can be reduced to their normal forms.

Due to space limitations, we refer the readers to the Appendix A of Jifeng He's paper [7] to see all the corresponding algebraic laws.

Assignment. Regarding the first layer, most laws simply require a straight-forward translation into code. For example, Law A.2.(2) can be translated into code as follows:

```
Axiom Assign_Seq : forall (v : list Var) (g h : Exp),
   ·{v := g} ;; ·{v := h} ← → ·{v := (fun x ⇒ h (g x))}.
```

Law A.2.(1) states that any assignment can be extended into its correspond-ing total assignment.

```
Axiom Assign_extends : forall (v : Assign), ·{v} ← → ·{extends_assign v}.
```

we interpret extending an assignment to its corresponding total assignment as an extension of the variable part to include all possible variables in the GLOBVARS. We then proceed to extend the expression function accordingly.

```
Definition extends_assign (v : Assign) :=
   makeAssign GLOBVARS (extends_mapping v.(ids) v.(values)).
```

The function extends_mapping maps the variable in the domain of the orig-inal assignment to its original range while leaving all other variables unchanged. This can be achieved with the help of extends_mapping_help function.

```
Definition extends_mapping (us : list Var) (m : (list Var) → (list Var)) :=
   fun k ⇒ (extends_mapping_help us (m us) k).
```

The function extends_mapping_help allows for the extension of a target expression mapping's domain. Specifically, it maps elements in the range of us to their corresponding values in $m(us)$. Any element that is not in the range of us but is within the range of k remains unchanged. The function utilizes the lookup_help function to determine whether a target variable exists within an assignment's domain.

```
Fixpoint extends_mapping_help (us rs k : (list Var)) : (list Var) :=
    match k with
    | [] ⇒ []
    | v:: vl ⇒
        lookup_help v us rs :: extends_mapping_help us rs vl
    end.
```

If the variable a is within the domain vs, lookup_help will return its corresponding value within the range us. Otherwise, the variable a remains unchanged.

```
Fixpoint lookup_help (a: Var) (vs rs: (list Var)) : Var :=
    match vs, rs with
    | _, [] ⇒ a
    | [], _ ⇒ a
    | v:: vl, r:: rl ⇒
        if (eqb a v) then r else lookup_help a vl rl
    end.
```

Non-deterministic Choice. Law A.3 in [7] states the absorption properties of non-deterministic choice of total assignments. It relies on syntax checking whether a program is in the form of non-deterministic choices over total assignments, which we denote as CH. We define the following function CH to achieve that.

```
Definition CH (p : list Alg) : Prop :=
    forall (x : Alg), In x p → exists y, x = ·{y} ∧ Total_Assign y.
```

where the function Total_Assign checks whether a target assigning is total.

```
Definition Total_Assign (a : Assign) :=
    forall v:Var, In v GLOBVARS → In v a.(ids).
```

Therefore, the law of the conditional operation over CHs (Law A.3.(2)) is defined as follows.

```
Axiom Cond_over_Choice : forall (a b : list Alg) (bexp : Boolexp),
    CH a → CH b → (|−| a) <| bexp |> (|−| b) ← →
    |−| (map (fun g ⇒ (fst g) <| bexp |> (snd g)) (list_prod a b)).
```

Finite Normal Form. The laws on the absorption properties of finite normal forms (Law A.4) can be similarly defined. For instance, the law of the non-deterministic operation over finite normal forms (Law A.4.(1)) is defined as follows.

```
Axiom NF_over_Choice : forall (a b : list Alg) (c d : Boolexp),
    CH a → CH b → (((_|_) <| c |> (|−| a)) /−\ ((_|_) <| d |> (|−| b))) ← →
    ((_|_) <| (fun g ⇒ orb (c g) (d g)) |> ((|−|a) /−\ (|−| b))).
```

The proof of the following theorem relies on the laws defined above.

3.4   Proof of Finite Normal Form Reduction

In this part, we would use the implications given above to prove the key Theorem 2.1 in [7], which states that every finite program can be reduced to FNF. The corresponding theorem is presented in Coq as follows.

> Theorem FNF_closure : forall (P : Alg),
>   exists Q, P ←→ Q ∧ **FNF** Q.

where the function FNF (Definition 1) is defined to check whether a program is in the finite normal form.

> Definition FNF (P : Alg): Prop :=
>   exists bexp R, P = (_|_) <| bexp |> (|−| R) ∧ CH R.

We proved this theorem through the implementation of a program that converts any input program to its normal form, referred to as Normal. In order to prove the above, we imposed two crucial rules.

The first law states that the resulting program must conform to the normal form condition, which can be expressed as follows:

> Theorem NormalisNF : forall x, FNF (Normal x).

Listing 1.1. Normal is in normal form

The second law, which states that all finite programs subjected to the transformation should still yield algebraic equivalent outcomes, can be formalized as the following theorem:

> Theorem NormalRWT : forall x, x ←→ Normal x.

Listing 1.2. Normal is algebraic equivalent

The transformation function Normal that satisfies the above conditions is implemented as follows:

```
Fixpoint Normal (a : Alg) : Alg :=
    match a with
    | Lift e ⇒
       match e with
       | Assn a ⇒ (_|_) <| false_stat |> |−|[·{extends_assign a}]
       | Empty ⇒ (_|_) <| false_stat |> |−|[]
       | Chaos ⇒ (_|_) <| true_stat |> |−|[·{empty_assn}]
       end
    | Comb s p q ⇒
       match s with
       | Seq ⇒ Normal_comb_Seq (Normal p) (Normal q)
       | CDC b ⇒ Normal_comb_CDC (Normal p) (Normal q) b
       | NDC ⇒ Normal_comb_NDC (Normal p) (Normal q)
       end
    end.
```

When a program belongs to Atomic, it can be translated into its corresponding normal form directly. However, if it contains any operators belonging to the

Comp, it must then be divided into two sub-programs for translation. The sub-programs are subsequently translated individually and then combined to form a new program that is also in its normal form.

In the above definition, the function Normal_comb_Seq transforms two sub-programs combined in normal form with 'Seq' into a new program in its normal form. Firstly, it combines the subprograms as Law A.4.(5) dictates. However, the right part of the resulting program is not assignment sequences, so we need to transform it accordingly.

```
Definition Normal_comb_Seq (p q : Alg) :=
    match p, q with
    | Comb x _ a, Comb y _ b ⇒
        match x, y with
        | CDC c, CDC d ⇒ (_|_) <| (fun g ⇒ orb (c g)
          (CH_over_Boolexp (Alg_to_CH a) d)) |>
        |−| (CH_comb_Seq (Alg_to_CH a) (Alg_to_CH b))
        | _, _ ⇒ −o−
        end
    | _, _ ⇒ −o−
    end.
```

The function Alg_to_CH converts the algebra that consists of assignments linked by non-deterministic choices into a list format.

```
Fixpoint Alg_to_CH (a : Alg) : list Alg :=
    match a with
    | Lift e ⇒ match e with
                | Assn a ⇒ [·{a}]
                | _ ⇒ []
                end
    | Comb s p q ⇒ match s with
                    | NDC ⇒ (Alg_to_CH p) ++ (Alg_to_CH q) % list
                    | _ ⇒ []
                    end
    end.
```

The function Alg_to_CH must meet the following condition to ensure its correctness.

Lemma Alg_to_CH_id : forall l, CH l → Alg_to_CH (|−| l) = l.

The function CH_comb_Seq combines two lists of assignments together in the manner described by Law A.3.(3).

```
Definition CH_comb_Seq (a b : list Alg) :=
    (map (fun g ⇒ Assign_comb_Seq (fst g) (snd g)) (list_prod a b)).
```

The function Assign_comb_Seq applies Law A.2.(2) to transform a program consisting of two assignments combined with Seq into a single assignment statement.

```
Definition Assign_comb_Seq_help (a b : Assign) :=
    a.( ids) :== fun x ⇒ b.(values) (a.(values) x).
```

```
Definition Assign_comb_Seq (a b : Alg) :=
    match a, b with
    | Lift x, Lift y ⇒
        match x, y with
        | Assn s, Assn t ⇒ ·{(Assign_comb_Seq_help
            (extends_assign s) (extends_assign t))}
        | _, _ ⇒ −o−
        end
    | _, _ ⇒ −o−
    end.
```

The function `Normal_comb_CDC` and the function `Normal_comb_UDC` is defined similarly. Upon completion of the definition of the function `Normal`, we need to ensure that it satisfies the conditions outlined in Listing 1.1 and Listing 1.2.

Listing 1.1 states that the program after transformation should be in normal form. The process of proving can be divided into two types of sub-goals. The first type involves only operators in the Atomic group, which we can prove directly.

The proof of Listing 1.2 requires the use of induction hypotheses. The process of proving is similar to that of the previous theorem. For subgoals involving only operators in the Atomic group, we prove them directly by applying laws. For subgoals involving induction hypotheses, we first ensure that the condition part is correctly constructed before moving on to the assignment part. Since list operations are involved, we cannot apply the reducing law directly. Instead, we must define a new lemma that connects the reducing equivalence relation between individual elements with the reducing equivalence relation across the entire list.

```
Lemma rwt_ext_Forall : forall A (f g : A → Alg) (l : list A),
    Forall (fun x ⇒ f x ←→ g x) l → |−|(map f l) ←→ |−|(map g l).
```

The complete proof can be found at the following link on GitHub[1]. In addition, the techniques for proving the above theorem can help us to convert any program to its normal form.

3.5 Definition of Refinement on Finite Programs

The refinement relation defined in Definition 2 can be implemented in Coq for finite programs by comparing two assignment expressions for equality, and checking if one non-deterministic choice of total assignments is a subset of another.

```
Definition Refine (P Q : Alg) :=
    exists bexp cexp U V,
        (P = (_|_) <| bexp |> (|−| U) ∧ CH U)
        ∧ (Q = (_|_) <| cexp |> (|−| V) ∧ CH V)
        ∧ (Constraints → ((cexp GLOBVARS = false ∧ (RefineCH U V))
        ∨ (bexp GLOBVARS = true))).
```

---

[1] https://github.com/DonnotPanic/Program-Algebra-in-Jifeng/blob/main/ProgramAlgebra.v.

The function **Refine** corresponds to the second case of Definition 2 where two programs are in FNF. With the introduction of **Constraints**, we can specify certain limitations on the variables in GLOBVARS, which determines the possible range of variables.

```
Definition RefineCH (A : list Alg) (B : list Alg) :=
    forall x, In x B → exists y , In y A ∧ subAssn x y.
```

The function **RefineCH** encodes the first case of Definition 2 where two programs are both non-deterministic choices of total assignments.

```
Definition subAssn (x : Alg) (y : Alg) :=
    match x, y with
    | Lift e, Lift f ⇒
        match e, f with
        | Assn m, Assn n ⇒ subEval (extends_assign m) (extends_assign n)
        | _,_ ⇒ False
        end
    | _, _ ⇒ False
    end.
```

The function **subAssn** is defined to find whether two assignments form a subset relation, i.e., $x \subseteq y$.

```
Definition subEval (x y : Assign) :=
    forall a, In a (x.( values) x.(ids)) → In a (y.(values) y.(ids)).
```

The **subEval** function is designed to determine whether a given set of variables x, represented as a list, is a subset of another set y.

3.6 Example of Refinement on Finite Programs

In this part, we will use Coq to prove the refinement on two finite programs T_1 and T_2 presented as follows.

$$T_1 =_{def} (\{a, b, c := a + 1, b + 1, c + 1\};$$
$$(\{a, b, c := a, b, c\} \lhd (a \geq 20) \rhd \{a, b, c := a - 1, b - 1, c - 1\})) \quad (4)$$
$$\lhd (a \leq 10) \rhd \bot$$

$$T_2 =_{def} \bot \lhd (a > 10) \rhd \{a, b, c := a + 1, b + 1, c + 1\};$$
$$((\{a, b, c := a + 1, b + 1, c + 1\} \sqcap \{a, b, c := a - 1, b - 1, c - 1\})) \quad (5)$$

Since the refinement relation is defined on normal forms. The proof is conducted by first reducing the two programs T_1, T_2 to their corresponding normal forms N_1, N_2 and then show that $N_2 \sqsubseteq_A N_1$.

In order to encode the two programs with our Coq implementation, we need to first instantiate the parameters of our formalism.

```
Instance myParams : UserParams :=
    Build_UserParams MyVar GLOBVARS eqbVar Constraints.
```

The instantiation involves providing the concrete type of each variable, and a function that decides whether two variables are equal.

We set the type of variables to be a tuple consisting of a string and a natural number with `MyVar`.

```
Record MyVar := mkVar {
    id: string;
    val : nat;
}.
```

The function `eqbVar` determines whether two variables have the same name and value of natural numbers.

`GLOBVARS` is a user-defined parameter that keeps track of all variables used in the relevant programs. It functions as a dictionary that enables us to convert arbitrary assignments into total assignments. Initializing `GLOBVARS` with concrete values is not strictly necessary. Instead, we use `Constraints` to specify the properties that `GLOBVARS` must satisfy. Typically, this means including all possible variables that could appear. In our case, we instantiate `GLOBVARS` as $\{a, b, c\}$ where a, b, and c are different variables.

The programs T_1 and T_2 are encoded as Coq instances `testAlg` and `testAlg2` respectively.

```
Definition testAlg := ((·{ascassn}) ;;
    (((·{empty_assn}) <| hdge2 |> (·{dscassn}))) <| hdle1 |> (_|_).
Definition testAlg2 := (_|_) <| (fun x ⇒ negb (hdle1 x)) |>
    (·{ascassn}) ;; (((|−|[ ·{ascassn};·{dscassn}])).
```

In the code above, `hdge2` represents the condition $a \geq 20$, while `hdle1` represents $a \leq 10$. The program `empty_assn` is the assignment statement that keeps all variables' values unchanged. On the other hand, `ascassn` is the assignment statement that increases all variables' values by 1, while `dscassn` decreases all variables' values by 1.

After completing the pre-work, the only work that remains to be done is to prove the following property.

```
Example testrefine : Refine (Normal testnf2) (Normal testnf).
```

The proof consists of three steps. Firstly, we pattern match `Normal testnf` and `Normal testnf2`. Let us denote the boolean expression of `Normal testnf` as b_1, and its assignment list as l_1. Similarly, let the boolean expression and assignment list of `Normal testnf2` be denoted by b_2 and l_2, respectively.

In the second step, we categorize the possible values of variables. We ensure that there is no condition where b_2 is false and b_1 is true; in other words, either b_2 is true or b_1 is false.

For the third step, we simplify l_1 and l_2 based on the condition that b_1 is false. `lia`, a tactic for linear integer arithmetic, is used to simplify conditional functions in expressions. Then, by substituting the variables in expressions, we check if all possible values in l_1 exist in l_2. This process involves rewriting by substituting the variables in the hypothesis into the goals.

The full process of this proof can be found in GitHub[2].

4   Encoding Algebra for Infinite Programs

In this section, we will delve into the intricacies of handling infinite programs and draw comparisons with their finite counterparts. Specifically, our focus will be on analyzing the infinite program generated by recursive functions with a single variable. This particular structure allows for comparisons between finite and infinite programs, without the added complexity of navigating through the expanding order of the recursive function.

4.1   Representing Infinite Programs

Throughout our discussion, we will focus specifically on recursive functions that take only a single variable. To generate infinite series for analysis, we will use a function that maps from one finite algebra to another. Specifically, we will be working with a datatype called `Stream`, which is an infinitely long list composed of two parts: the current element which is its head, and the rest of the infinite list.

Using the `CoFixpoint`, we can define an infinite list called `Recur` in such a way that every element in the list is the result of applying the function f to the previous element and the first element of the list is a.

```
Variable f : Alg → Alg.
Definition AlgStr := Stream Alg.
CoFixpoint Recur (a : Alg) : AlgStr := Cons a (Recur (f a)).
```

We can define the normal form for a given algebra stream $\{S_i\}$ by verifying that $\forall i \in \mathbb{N} \bullet S_i \sqsubseteq S_{i+1}$ as defined in Definition 3, A stream satisfying this property is said to be in its normal form using the following Coq code, where h and m are the first two elements of the stream s. The use of `Forall` ensures that the property holds for all suffixes of the given stream.

```
Definition FNFPres(P Q : Alg) :=
    exists R S, (P ← → R ∧ FNF R) ∧ (Q ← → S ∧ FNF S) ∧ Refine R S.
Definition AlgPresStep (s : AlgStr) :=
    let h := Streams.hd s in
    let m := Streams.hd (Streams.tl s) in
    FNFPres h m.
Definition AlgPres := Streams.ForAll AlgPresStep.
```

Coq's automatic tactic for infinite structures has a limitation in generating proper induction laws automatically. Therefore, we need to define the induction law ourselves.

```
Lemma AlgPresInd : forall y, FNFPres y (f y) →
    (forall x, FNFPres (f x) (f (f x))) → AlgPres (Recur y).
Proof.
    intros. unfold AlgPres. intros. apply HereAndFurther.
    unfold AlgPresStep. auto. simpl. generalize y. cofix Pres.
    intros. apply HereAndFurther.
    − unfold AlgPresStep. simpl. apply HO.
    − simpl. apply Pres.
Qed.
```

4.2   Refinement Between Finite and Infinite Program

According to the first case of Definition 4, to find out whether an infinite program refines a finite program is to find if there exists some item in the infinite program normal form series that is strong enough to refine the given finite algebra. To find such an item, we can either use the Str_nth function defined in Stream library to trace the nth item, or we can define a SthExists function to find whether the given algebra exists (or in the same deducing-closed class with the item) in the series.

```
Definition SthStep (a : Alg) (s : AlgStr) :=
    let h := Streams.hd s in a ← → h.
Definition SthExists (a : Alg) := Streams.Exists (SthStep a).
```

With the definition given above, we can prove $F \sqsubseteq G$.

$$F =_{def} (\{a, b := a, b\} \sqcap \{a, b := b \bmod a, a\} \lhd (a = 0) \rhd \bot \qquad (6)$$

$$G =_{def} \lambda X \bullet (\{a, b := a, b\} \lhd (a = 0) \rhd (\{a, b := b \bmod a, a\}; X)) \qquad (7)$$

F is a finite program that can be encoded as follows:

```
Definition falg := |−| [skip;GCDAssn] <| hdeqz |>(_|_).
```

G is a program that uses the Euclidean algorithm to solve for the greatest common divisor. The Coq encoding of G (GCDStr) is shown below:

```
Definition GCDStep (a : Alg) : Alg :=
    skip <| hdeqz |> (GCDAssn ;; a).
Definition GCDStr := Recur GCDStep (_|_).
```

In the above definition, hdeqz is used to determine whether a is equal to zero. The program skip denotes an assignment that does not change anything. Finally, GCDAssn updates the value of a and b according to the Euclidean algorithm: $a, b := b \bmod a, a$.

```
Definition empty_assn := makeAssign GLOBVARS refl_exp.
Definition skip := ·{ empty_assn }.
Definition GCDAssn := ·{ makeAssign GLOBVARS GCDFunc }.
```

In this case we will initialize GLOBVARS as $\{a;b\}$. First of all, we would like to know if such a sequence is in its normal form.

Lemma GcdStrPres : AlgPres GCDStr.

After that, we want to find some item in the series that can be deduced to GCDRes.

Definition GCDRes := (_|_) <| (fun x ⇒ negb (orb (hdeqz x)
        (Assign_over_Boolexp hdeqz GCDAssn))) |>
    ·{ GLOBVARS :== exp_Cond refl_exp GCDFunc hdeqz}.
Lemma GcdReachRes : SthExists GCDRes GCDStr.

GCDRes is picked up to represent GCDStr. Our goal now is to demonstrate that GCDRes refines finite program falg.

Lemma refinegcd : exists r s, (r ← → falg ∧ FNF r) ∧
    (s ← → GCDRes ∧ FNF s) ∧ Refine r s.

Since both GCDStr and falg are finite programs, we can perform a finite comparison between them. We can use the proving techniques introduced in Sect. 3.6.

The full process of this proof can be found in GitHub[3].

5 Discussion

In this paper, we implemented Jifeng He's approach to establishing program equivalence and refinement relations using axioms, and encoded it in Coq. Our approach is based on axiomatic semantics, which distinguishes it from the [6] project that utilizes the denotational model and builds alphabetized predicates. To facilitate program comparison, we transform each program into a normal form, separating the abstract program part from the concrete evaluation part. This approach accommodates diverse computational models. In this paper, we utilize a simple model that applies abstract variables to functions directly, making comparisons between functions challenging.

We have also made progress in automating the proving process by utilizing Coq's mechanics. We have successfully automated the transformation of the abstract algebra part to its normal form. However, there remain challenges in the refinement process. The proof can be verbose, as issues may arise with unifying the type of variables in our library and the type of user-defined variables when importing our library.

This paper focuses on a special case of recursive programs with one variable, which serves as the foundation for more general recursive programs that can eventually be transformed to some recursive program with a composite variable. We are currently working on extending our work to this area.

When dealing with infinite cases, we encountered limitations due to the difficulty of representing any proposition that is a finite and terminating structure of

---

[3] https://github.com/DonnotPanic/Program-Algebra-in-Jifeng/blob/main/
testGCD.v.

an infinitely recursive program series because it is impossible to compute infinite loops. We found two approaches to address this issue. The first involves simplifying the problem into some finite cases, where we found that comparing infinite programs to finite ones can be simplified by unrolling the infinite series a finite number of times. This results in a computable process. The second approach involves translating the problem of infinite computing to a continuity problem that we can symbolically reason about. We are still working on finding a general method for this.

6 Conclusion and Future Work

In this paper, we present our implementation of the program algebra introduced by Jifeng He in Coq. We have translated the formalism of the algebra into Coq syntax and implemented the algebraic laws and refinement relation defined by He. Using our framework, we provide machine-aided proofs for key theorems that demonstrate every finite program can be reduced to its normal form, and we give a concrete transformation program. Additionally, we provide examples to illustrate how our implementation can be used to check refinement relationships between two finite programs or a finite program and an infinite program in a theorem-proving manner.

In the future, we intend to improve our work in the following aspects.

- Determining the most appropriate way to express infinite programs still require further exploration. We will try to develop a suitable model to represent the algebra between infinite structures.
- The value model in this paper needs further improvement to meet the need of actual use.
- The refinement proof process can be verbose, but there may be techniques available to simplify it such as developing automatic tactics to extract variables hypotheses and substitute them into goals, rewrapping the expression type to simplify the comparisons between functions, changing the lazy evaluation of the expression to eager one and so on.

Furthermore, our framework can serve as a foundation for several works based on process algebra, such as probability programs [10], parallel programs [13], quantum programs [9], and more. These works can potentially be extended using our framework.

Acknowledgment. We would like to express our sincere gratitude to Simon Foster for his exceptional contribution to this paper. His valuable insights and expert guidance have greatly enhanced the quality of our work, and we are truly appreciative of his dedication and commitment to this project. Without his suggestions and feedback, the paper would not have been as comprehensive and insightful as it is now.

References

1. Ngondi, G.E., Koutavas, V., Butterfield, A.: Translation of CCS into CSP, correct up to strong bisimulation. In: Calinescu, R., Păsăreanu, C.S. (eds.) SEFM 2021.

LNCS, vol. 13085, pp. 243–261. Springer, Cham (2021). https://doi.org/10.1007/978-3-030-92124-8_14

2. Ekembe Ngondi, G.: Denotational semantics of channel mobility in UTP-CSP. Formal Aspects Comput. **33**(4), 803–826 (2021)

3. Feliachi, A., Gaudel, M.-C., Wolff, B.: Unifying theories in Isabelle/HOL. In: Qin, S. (ed.) UTP 2010. LNCS, vol. 6445, pp. 188–206. Springer, Heidelberg (2010). https://doi.org/10.1007/978-3-642-16690-7_9

4. Foster, S.: Hybrid relations in Isabelle/UTP. In: Ribeiro, P., Sampaio, A. (eds.) UTP 2019. LNCS, vol. 11885, pp. 130–153. Springer, Cham (2019). https://doi.org/10.1007/978-3-030-31038-7_7

5. Foster, S., Baxter, J., Cavalcanti, A., Woodcock, J., Zeyda, F.: Unifying semantic foundations for automated verification tools in Isabelle/UTP. Sci. Comput. Program. **197**, 102510 (2020)

6. Foster, S., Zeyda, F., Woodcock, J.: Isabelle/UTP: a mechanised theory engineering framework. In: Naumann, D. (ed.) UTP 2014. LNCS, vol. 8963, pp. 21–41. Springer, Cham (2015). https://doi.org/10.1007/978-3-319-14806-9_2

7. He, J., Li, Q.: A new roadmap for linking theories of programming and its applications on GCL and CSP. Sci. Comput. Program. **162**, 3–34 (2018)

8. Hoare, C.A.R., et al.: Laws of programming. Commun. ACM **30**(8), 672–686 (1987)

9. Jorrand, P., Lalire, M.: Toward a quantum process algebra. In: Proceedings of the 1st Conference on Computing Frontiers, pp. 111–119 (2004)

10. Morgan, C., McIver, A., Seidel, K., Sanders, J.W.: Refinement-oriented probability for CSP. Formal Aspects Comput. **8**(6), 617–647 (1996). https://doi.org/10.1007/BF01213492

11. Oliveira, M., Cavalcanti, A., Woodcock, J.: Unifying theories in ProofPower-Z. In: Dunne, S., Stoddart, B. (eds.) UTP 2006. LNCS, vol. 4010, pp. 123–140. Springer, Heidelberg (2006). https://doi.org/10.1007/11768173_8

12. Paulin-Mohring, C.: Introduction to the calculus of inductive constructions (2014)

13. Woodcock, J., Hughes, A.: Unifying theories of parallel programming. In: George, C., Miao, H. (eds.) ICFEM 2002. LNCS, vol. 2495, pp. 24–37. Springer, Heidelberg (2002). https://doi.org/10.1007/3-540-36103-0_5

14. Xu, X., Zhan, B., Wang, S., Talpin, J.P., Zhan, N.: A denotational semantics of simulink with higher-order UTP. J. Logical Algebraic Methods Program. **130**, 100809 (2023)

15. Yan, G., Jiao, L., Li, Y., Wang, S., Zhan, N.: Approximate bisimulation and discretization of hybrid CSP. In: Fitzgerald, J., Heitmeyer, C., Gnesi, S., Philippou, A. (eds.) FM 2016. LNCS, vol. 9995, pp. 702–720. Springer, Cham (2016). https://doi.org/10.1007/978-3-319-48989-6_43

16. Zhu, H., He, J., Qin, S., Brooke, P.J.: Denotational semantics and its algebraic derivation for an event-driven system-level language. Formal Aspects Comput. **27**, 133–166 (2015)

Author Index

J. P. Bowen et al. (Eds.): *Theories of Programming and Formal Methods*, LNCS 14080, p. 413, 2023.
https://doi.org/10.1007/978-3-031-40436-8